Y0-BEA-482

THE PIANO-FORTE

Da Capo Press Music Reprint Series

GENERAL EDITOR

FREDERICK FREEDMAN

VASSAR COLLEGE

THE
PIANO-FORTE

Its History Traced to the Great Exhibition of 1851

By ROSAMOND E. M. HARDING

DA CAPO PRESS • NEW YORK • 1973

Library of Congress Cataloging in Publication Data

Harding, Rosamond Evelyn Mary, 1898-
 The piano-forte.

 (Da Capo Press music reprint series)
 Reprint of the 1933 ed.
 Bibliography: p.
 1. Piano—History. 2. Piano—Construction.
I. Title.
ML652.H26   1973   786.2'1'09   69-15634
ISBN 0-306-71084-6

Published by Da Capo Press, Inc.
A Subsidiary of Plenum Publishing Corporation
227 West 17th Street, New York, New York 10011

THE PIANO-FORTE

Cristofori Pianoforte, 1726, Leipzig, No. 170. By permission of the Musikwissenschaftliches Institut, Leipzig.

THE PIANO-FORTE

ITS HISTORY TRACED TO

The Great Exhibition of 1851

BY

ROSAMOND E. M. HARDING
Ph.D. Cantab.

CAMBRIDGE
AT THE UNIVERSITY PRESS
1933

PRINTED IN GREAT BRITAIN

To

MY FATHER & MOTHER

IN GRATITUDE

for having made the publication of
this Volume possible, and to

I. M.

for her unfailing sympathy
and encouragement

CONTENTS

PART ONE

THE PIANOFORTE IN THE EIGHTEENTH CENTURY

Chap. I. The invention of the Pianoforte in Italy   *page* 3

A musical instrument is usually the outcome of some musical need—the importance of discovering the motives for its invention—so-called precursors of the pianoforte not discussed but it is to be shown how the pianoforte was invented in response to new artistic ideals—the preference of one inventor for the using of the harpsichord and another the clavichord as the working basis for experiments is of secondary importance compared with artistic need that suggested the experiments—keyboard musical instruments in use at the close of the seventeenth century—the organ and the harpsichord as members of the orchestra—the organ, harpsichord and clavichord in the home—the organ and the harpsichord inexpressive compared with the clavichord—dissatisfaction with the organ and the harpsichord—speculations at Florence relating to the revival of classical drama on the lines adopted by the ancient Greek tragedians—invention of the cantata—attention drawn to the value of accentuation—the emotional significance of a musical phrase could be intensified as could that of a line of poetry by the use of inflections—the harpsichord and the organ incapable of inflections—Hans Haydn of Nuremberg attempts in 1600 to make the harpsichord expressive by means of a ring-bow mechanism—Galilei states that such an instrument had been invented before—two instruments called *Piano e forte* referred to by Paliarino in 1598—perfection of the violin family in Italy and consequent rise of the Italian school of violin-playing draws attention afresh to expression—experiments in dynamic expression on the string orchestra—the "swelling and singing of the notes" desired for the harpsichord—Cristofori about 1709 makes the harpsichord expressive by using hammers instead of jacks—Maffei discovers Cristofori—he describes Cristofori's *Gravicembalo col piano e forte*—and indicates the causes that led to its invention—effects of dynamic expression popular at the concerts of stringed instruments held at Rome—these effects are found in Giustini's pianoforte music of 1732—quotation from Burney's History relating to the concerts at Rome—the action of the *Gravicembalo col piano e forte*—the harpsichord seen to be the working basis of the invention—the escapement—the invention of the *Gravicembalo col piano e forte* not favourably received in Italy—the new musical possibilities—interpretation of music—the performer to be the prophet of the composer.

Chap. II. The invention of the Pianoforte in France   *page* 11

Cuisinié's clavecin of 1708—Cuisinié's hammers probably suggested those used by Marius—Marius' four clavecins of 1716—the first clavecin with action similar to the clavichord—the second clavecin with down-striking or up-striking action—the third clavecin; an upright instrument—the fourth clavecin with actions for both jacks and hammers—the stringing and compass of the four clavecins.

Pantaleon Hebenstreit is the first to discover 'pianistic effects' and to design an instrument
for their production—Hebenstreit's improved dulcimer or *Hackbrett*—Hebenstreit's
dulcimer named the 'Pantaleon' by Louis XIV—the Pantaleon becomes a fashionable instrument at the courts of German princes—but soon goes into disfavour owing to the difficulty of execution and the expense of maintenance—Binder shows Dr Burney the remains of
the Pantaleon—two important results follow the invention of the Pantaleon—(1) amateurs
invent keyed Pantaleons; (2) mechanism for raising the dampers from the strings to imitate
Pantaleon effects (i.e. the forte pedal) invented—Schröter—his dissatisfaction with the
harpsichord—Schröter hears Hebenstreit play the Pantaleon—determines to make the
harpsichord expressive by means of a hammer action—and invents two hammer actions in
1717—submits a model embodying both actions to the Saxon Court in 1721—unfortunate
episode at the Court—Schröter is unable to regain his model actions—seeks employment
away from Dresden.

                                § II

Schröter supposed to have made the first pianoforte action in Germany—the writer's dis-
agreement with this view—Pantaleons and Pianofortes—Pantaleons too expensive and
difficult to make—further attempts to make the harpsichord expressive—the clavichord is
taken as the working basis for these experiments—development of the *Prellmechanik*—the
German Action developed from the *Prellmechanik*.

                                § III

Cristofori's influence on pianoforte construction in Germany—his pianoforte of 1720—his
pianoforte of 1726—his action copied and modified in Germany—essential differences
between the Cristofori and the German actions—Cristofori's action of 1726 adapted to the
upright pianoforte—the same action adapted to the square pianoforte—and to the 'grand'
pianoforte—the Anglo-German Action developed out of the Cristofori and the German
actions.

                                § IV

The sound-board and strings of old German pianofortes—German pianoforte stops.

Further attempts to make the harpsichord expressive—the pianoforte is added as a characteristic stop to the harpsichord—Merlin, in 1774, combines the pianoforte, clavichord and
spinet in one instrument—the invention of the Tangent Action—the Cembalo stop—its two
forms.

Father Wood builds the first English pianoforte in 1711—Plenius, the harpsichord maker,
copies Father Wood's pianoforte—Mason's Action—the arrival in London of J. C. Bach in
1759 gives a stimulus to pianoforte building—Zumpe and eleven other German pianoforte
makers arrive in London about 1760—Zumpe attaches himself to the harpsichord maker
Shudi—the pianoforte business now begins in real earnest—John Broadwood joins Shudi in
1761—the pianofortes of Zumpe and Pohlmann become the rage—the English Single
Action (i.e. Zumpe's First Action)—'Zumpe's Second Action'—various types of dampers
used with the Single Action—the English Double Action patented by John Geib in 1786—
English Grand Action first made about 1777—uncertainty as to the inventor—first made by
John Broadwood—Pether's down-striking Action—devices for regulating the touch, 1787,
1790—Crang Hancock's action with 'spring-key touch', 1782—Landreth's action for
Upright pianoforte, 1787—Stodart's Upright Grand pianoforte, 1795—copied by Söderberg

PART TWO
THE PIANOFORTE IN THE NINETEENTH CENTURY

SECTION I

THE PIANOFORTE AS A CHAMBER ORCHESTRA

PREFACE

In compiling the present work musical considerations have concerned me more than mechanical. I have, therefore, divided the material into two parts; the first dealing with the origin of the instrument in an attempt to make the harpsichord expressive, the second tracing its subsequent development from being merely an altered harpsichord to a pianoforte recognised as such by Beethoven and the great pianists.

But the desire to make the harpsichord expressive had more than this one development, for certain makers thought its attractiveness could be increased by converting it into a kind of mechanical orchestra.

On this account it seemed desirable to interrupt the history of the normal pianoforte by a section on the "Pianoforte as a Chamber Orchestra" (Part II, Section I). An illustrated summary of this section appeared in the *Proceedings of the Musical Association*, fifty-seventh session, 1930–31. An attempt has been made in Part II, Section II, to show the influence of the Bravura pianists on the one hand, and of Beethoven and his followers on the other, on the concert grand pianoforte, resulting in a repetition action and numerous improvements relating both to its power and quality of tone. In Part II, Section III, the various types of household instruments are dealt with and particularly the upright pianoforte.

An explanation of the system of staveless notation used in this work will be found under the list of abbreviations. The gauge beneath each diagram is a decimetre unless otherwise stated.

In conclusion I desire to express my grateful thanks to Prof. Edward J. Dent for the kind interest he has taken in this work and for his useful criticism and advice.

I am greatly indebted to Prof. Curt Sachs; Prof. G. E. Pazaurek and Dr H. Josten of Stuttgart; Dr H. Neupert of Nuremberg; the Authorities of the Neues Grassi Museum, Leipzig; the Director of the Victoria and Albert Museum; Prof. Schmidt of the Stadt Schloss Museum, Berlin; Messrs John Broadwood and Sons, for most kindly permitting me to publish drawings of actions and illustrations of pianofortes in their care; and to Monsieur A. Blondel of Maison Érard for allowing me to reproduce the picture of Sébastien Érard by David.

To Messrs John Broadwood and Sons I am also under special obligation for permitting me to draw upon many valuable documents in their possession.

I have to thank the Cambridge University Librarian for the illustrations of French Patents and the example of Bertini's music reproduced from works in the University Library.

My sincere thanks are due to Dr I. Manton for much useful criticism.

I have also received valuable services from Mrs R. T. Barnes, Mademoiselle M. L. Pereyra and Monsieur Paul Brunold of Paris, Maison Pleyel et Cie, Dr Alexander Wood of Cambridge, Dr Walter Pfeiffer of Stuttgart, and also from Mr W. J. Moore, Messrs Miller and Son and Messrs Stockbridge and Sons of Cambridge.

The Photographs by Mr W. Tams, Messrs Palmer Clarke, and Fräulein Steudel have added value to the work.

Finally I must thank the compositors and proof-readers of the University Press for their great care, and for much patience.

R. E. M. H.

1933

LIST OF PLATES

PART I

PART II. SECTION I

LIST OF ABBREVIATIONS

CAPITAL LETTERS denote the Appendices, which are lettered from A to H; thus A means Appendix A; B, Appendix B, and so on.

Am.	= America	Belg.	= Belgium
Aust.	= Austria	Eng.	= England
Bav.	= Bavaria	Fr.	= France

Berlin = Sammlung Alter Musikinstrumente bei der Staatlichen Hochschule für Musik.

Brussels = Musée Instrumental du Conservatoire Royal de Musique.

Leipzig = Heyer Coll. Mus. Insts. Neues Grassi Museum.

Paris = Musée du Conservatoire National de Musique.

Stuttgart = Landesgewerbemuseum.

PART I

THE PIANOFORTE IN THE EIGHTEENTH CENTURY

Le Clavecin est parfait quant à son etendue, et brillant par luy même; mais comme on ne peut enfler, ny diminuer ses sons, je sçauray toûjours gré à ceux qui par un art infini, soutenu par le goût, pourons ariver à rendre cet instrument susceptible d'expression.

COUPERIN

CHAPTER I

THE INVENTION OF THE PIANOFORTE
IN ITALY

A MUSICAL instrument is usually the outcome of some musical need; therefore, when tracing the history of any instrument, it is of the first importance to discover the underlying motives for its invention. On this account, it is not proposed to discuss how the pianoforte *evolved* from those instruments which are usually called its 'precursors', but to show how it was invented in response to new artistic ideals.

The fact that certain musical instrument-makers preferred the harpsichord as the working basis for experiments, whilst others preferred the clavichord, is of secondary importance compared with the artistic need that suggested these experiments—the problem that all alike were attempting to solve.

At the close of the seventeenth century there were three keyboard instruments in ordinary use; the organ, the harpsichord and the clavichord.

The organ and the harpsichord shared the duty of filling in the 'continuo' in orchestral and concerted music both in public and in the chamber, in fact the harpsichord formed an integral part of the orchestra. There were usually two harpsichords at the opera; at one the *Maestro di Cembalo* stood to conduct, whilst it was the duty of his subordinate to accompany the solo portions and recitatives upon the other.

Every house would possess its chamber organ, in the same way as at one time every house possessed its harmonium when this was a new and fashionable instrument. And in addition to the organ there would probably be a light harpsichord, fulfilling the same function as our modern pianoforte, and also a clavichord.

The clavichord was particularly fitted for the performance of contrapuntal music where musical effect frequently depended on the emphasis of one particular note more than others in the clashing parts. The harpsichord and the organ were deficient in this power of emphasis, but dissatisfaction with these instruments had been slowly gathering on another account.

The speculations made by a party of amateurs meeting at the Palazzo Bardi at Florence shortly before the close of the sixteenth century, as to the possibility of reviving classical drama on the principles adopted by the ancient Greek tragedians, led to experiments resulting, as is well known, in the invention of the Cantata—a secular song set in declamatory recitative and accompanied by a single instrument—thus abruptly changing the whole musical outlook.

Attention was directed to the value and importance of accentuation. It was clearly perceived that the emotional significance of a musical phrase could be intensified, as could that of a line of poetry, by an appropriate use of inflexions.

The harpsichord and organ were totally incapable of these inflexions, and this defect was felt not only in Italy but in other countries. Hans Haydn of Nuremberg, as early as 1600, devised a mechanism for bowing the harpsichord strings, in the hope of making it capable of inflexions. Vincenzo Galilei, who had taken an active part in the discussions already referred to at the Palazzo Bardi, stated that such an instrument had been considered at an even earlier date.[1] Two instruments called *Piano e forte* are indeed referred to, but not described, in two letters addressed by Paliarino to Alfonso II, Duke of Modena in 1598;[2] but Galilei cannot have known about these instruments, since he died in 1591.

The perfection of the violin family in Italy, and the consequent rise of the great Italian school of violin playing, directed attention afresh to the possibilities of expression. Some musicians seem to have been a little dismayed by the modern developments, for the great violinist Francesco Veracini[3] was looked upon as eccentric owing to the life and power he threw into his playing. Despite dissatisfaction in certain quarters, the older and graver type of contrapuntal music was being discarded in favour of a style more lively and dramatic in character. "Everything which is serious is call'd in derision 'the old cow path' and represented as dull and heavy."[4]

The fact that dynamic expression could be used as an important factor in musical design was now fully grasped.

[1] Vincenzo Galilei (b. Florence about 1533; d. there 1591) was the father of the astronomer Galileo Galilei.

[2] B 49 (*f*), p. 150.

[3] A contemporary of Sebastian Bach, born at Florence about 1685, died at Pisa about 1750.

[4] B 25, p. 209.

As Discords in Music are like Shades in Painting, so is the *Piano* like the fainter Parts or Figures in a Picture; both of which do greatly assist in constituting and supporting an agreeable variety.[1]

It was inevitable that musicians should use the string orchestra for their experiments in this respect. In fact, the interest in the string orchestra and its music was such that the fashionable classes insisted that instrumental *ritornelli* should be introduced even into their Church services.

'The swelling and singing of the notes' so easily obtained by means of the bow on stringed instruments was desired for the harpsichord. But all hope of making this instrument expressive appears to have been abandoned when, at the beginning of the eighteenth century, about 1709, the problem was as unexpectedly as simply solved by the harpsichord maker Bartolommeo Cristofori,[2] formerly of Padua, now removed to Florence and in the service of Prince Ferdinand dei Medici as keeper of the Prince's musical instruments.

Cristofori substituted hammers in place of the harpsichord jacks and by this simple means made the harpsichord capable of producing gradations of tone.

Scipione Maffei discovered Cristofori when he visited Prince Ferdinand in 1709 to seek his patronage for the *Giornale dei Letterati d'Italia*. Not only does Maffei give us a description of this new invention—the *Gravicembalo col piano e forte* as Cristofori named it[3]—but also of the causes that led to its invention. His paper is of great significance, as it shows how the effects of graded dynamic expression that were being tried at Rome upon the string orchestra evidently inspired Cristofori to invent a harpsichord capable of reproducing these gradations. Maffei writes thus:

It is known to everyone who delights in music, that one of the principal means by which the skilful in that art derive the secret of especially delighting those who listen, is the piano and forte in the theme and its response, or in the gradual diminution of tone little by little, and then returning suddenly to the full power of the instrument; which artifice is frequently used and with marvellous effect, in the great concerts of Rome....

Now, of this diversity and alteration of tone, in which instruments played with the bow especially excel, the harpsichord is entirely deprived, and it would have been thought a vain endeavour to propose to make it so that it should participate in this power. Nevertheless, so bold an invention has been no less happily conceived than executed in Florence, by Signor Bar-

[1] B 24, p. 143.   [2] Born 1665, died 1731.
[3] B 84, pp. 95–100. See also B 64.

tolommeo Cristofali [*sic*], of Padua, harpsichord-player, in the service of the
most serene Prince of Tuscany.

He has already made three, of the usual size of other harpsichords, and
they have all succeeded to perfection. The production of greater or less sound
depends on the degree of power with which the player presses on the keys, by
regulating which, not only the piano and forte are heard, but also the gradations and diversity of power, as in a violoncello. . . . This is properly a chamber
instrument, and it is not intended for church music, nor for a great orchestra.
. . . It is certain, that to accompany a singer, and to play with one other instrument, or even for a moderate concert, it succeeds perfectly; although this is
not its principal intention, but rather to be played alone, like the lute, harp,
viols of six strings, and other most sweet instruments. But really the great
cause of the opposition which this new instrument has encountered, is, in
general, the want of knowledge how, at first to play it; because it is not sufficient to know how to play perfectly upon instruments with the ordinary
finger board, but being a new instrument, it requires a person who, understanding its capabilities, shall have made a particular study of its effects, so as
to regulate the measure of force required on the keys and the effects of de-
creasing it, also to choose pieces suited to it for delicacy, and especially for the
movement of the parts, that the subject may be heard distinctly in each. . . .

This invention has also been effected in another form, the inventor having
made another harpsichord, with the piano and forte, in a different and somewhat more simple shape.[1] [There is no further description of this instrument.]
(*Rimbault's translation.*)

[1] Egli è noto a chiunque gode della musica, che uno de' principali fonti, da' quali
traggano i periti di quest' arte il segreto di singolarmente dilettar chi ascolta, è il piano,
e 'l fortezzo, sia nelle proposte e risposte, o sia quando con artifiziosa degradazione
lasciandosi a poco a poco mancar la voce, si ripiglia poi ad un tratto strepitosamente:
il quale artifizio è usato frequentemente, ed a maraviglia ne' gran concerti di Roma.
. . . Ora di questa diversità ed alterazione di voce, nella quale eccellenti sono, fra gli
altri, gli strumenti da arco, affatto privo è il gravecembalo; e sarebbe, da chi che sia,
stata riputata una vanissima immaginazione il proporre di fabbricarlo in modo, che
avesse questa dote. Con tutto ciò, una sì ardita invenzione è stata non meno felice-
mente pensata, che eseguita in Firenze dal Sig. Bartolommeo Cristofali [*sic*], Pada-
vano, Cembalista stipendiato dal Serenissimo Principe di Toscana. Egli ne ha finora
fatti tre della grandezza ordinaria degli altri gravecembali, e son tutti riusciti perfettamente. Il cavare da questi maggiore o minore suono dipende dalla diversa forza, con
cui dal sonatore vengono premuti i tasti, regolando la quale, si viene a sentire non soli
il piano, e il forte, ma la degradazione, e diversità della voce, qual sarebbe in un violoncello. . . . Questo è propriamente strumento da camera, e non è pero adattabile a una
musica di chiesa, o ad una grand' orchestra. . . . Egli è certo, che per accompagnare un
cantante, e per secondare uno strumento, ed anche per un moderato concerto riesce
perfettamente; benchè non sia però questa l' intenzion sua principale, ma si quella
d' esser sonato a solo, come il liuto, l' arpa, le viole di sei corde, ed altri strumenti
de' più soavi. Ma veramente la maggior opposizione, che abbia patito questo nuovo
strumento, si è il non sapersi universalmente a primo incontro sonare, perchè non basta
il sonar perfettamente gli ordinari strumenti da tasto, ma essendo strumento nuovo,
ricerca persona, che intendene la forza vi abbia fatto sopra alquanto di studio partico-
lare, così per regolare la misura del diverso impulso, che dee darsi a' tasti, e la graziosa
degradazione, e tempo e luogo, come per iscegliere cose a proposito, e delicate, e

Plate I. Gavotta from Sonata No. 9. Lodovico Giustini di Pistoia, 1732.

This illustrates the effect of graded dynamic expression referred to by Scipione Maffei (see p. 7).

Furthermore, in a volume of twelve sonatas for the *Cimbalo di piano, e forte* composed by Lodovico Giustini, and published at Florence in 1732, are found both the effects of expression referred to by Maffei; the gradations of tone from *forte* to *piano* being indicated by the three terms *forte, piano, più piano* used in succession (Plate I). This music was almost certainly composed to be played upon one of Cristofori's 'pianofortes'.[1]

The "great concerts at Rome" were doubtless the "splendid and majestic *accademie*" held at "Cardinal Ottoboni's every Monday evening" under the leadership of Arcangelo Corelli; the orchestra seems to have been chiefly composed of bowed stringed instruments. Burney informs[2] us that in 1686 when "King James II piously sent an ambassador to Pope Innocent XI to make tender of his duty as a faithful son of the Romish church, at a grand accademia which Christina Queen of Sweden, then a proselyte, and resident in the *Alma Città di Roma*, gave on the occasion, the Music was composed by *Bernardo Pasquini,*[3] and the band, amounting to one hundred and fifty performers on bowed instruments, *instrumenti d'arco* (was) led by Arcangelo Corelli".

Maffei made a diagram of the action of the *Gravicembalo col piano e forte*, and, although this is crude and evidently drawn from memory, it enables us to understand the principles of the invention (Fig. 1).

When the key is depressed the block at its further extremity knocks up the pivoted lever *E*, causing the upright jointed piece *G* which we have called the escapement to jerk up the hammer to strike the string. The escapement *G* is controlled by a spring and bends under the blow, 'escaping' to its original position, thus leaving the hammer free to return immediately after striking.

massimamente spezzando, e facendo camminar le parti, e sentire i soggetti in più luoghi....Quest' invenzione è stata dall' artefice ridotta ad effetto anche in altra forma, avendo fatto un altro gravecembalo più col piano e forte, con differente, e alquanto più facile struttura."

[1] This work was discovered and recognised as being the earliest music written for the pianoforte, by the late A. J. Hipkins, who refers to it in his *History of the Pianoforte* (London, 1896, Novello Primer, No. 52), Part III, p. 99, but he does not describe it nor has anyone either described or edited it to the present writer's knowledge.

[2] B 31, p. 551.

[3] An interesting statement is made by Fétis in his *Biographie universelle des Musiciens* (2ème éd., Tome VI, p. 462) as follows: "En 1679, Pasquini écrivit la musique de l'opéra intitulé: *Dov' è amore e pietà;* pour l'ouverture du théâtre Capranica, où il était accompagnateur au piano, tandis que Corelli dirigeait la partie de premier violon".

Whilst this has been happening the further extremity of the lever *G* was lowered, bringing the damper away from the string. Upon releasing the key, the lever regains its position and the end *Q* rises and presses the damper against the string.

It will be seen at once that Cristofori used the harpsichord as the working basis of his invention. He took from it shape, keys and strings and transformed one register of jacks into dampers.

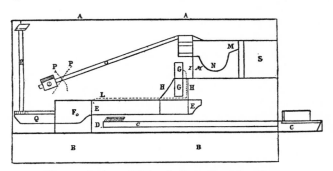

Fig. 1. Action of Cristofori's earliest Pianoforte.

A, string; *B*, key frame; *C*, key; *D*, block; *E*, lever; *F*, pivot; *G*, escapement; *H, H*, jaw-bone-shaped pieces between which the escapement is pivoted; *I*, wire regulating the play of the escapement; *L*, escapement spring; *M*, hammer rail in which the hammer butts are pivoted; *N*, the circular hammer butt pivoted within the rail; *O*, hammer with head clothed with leather; *P*, silken strings which receive the hammer when at rest; *Q*, end of the lever; *R*, damper; *S*, part of the frame.

Possibly the clavichord action suggested to Cristofori the use of hammers, but it is still more probable that he saw a keyed dulcimer,[1] or perhaps one of the instruments called *Piano e forte* referred to by Paliarino in 1598, or such an instrument as that described and illustrated by Father Mersenne in 1637, in which tubes of wood are struck by hammers from below—a primitive keyed xylophone (Fig. 2).[2]

Dr Heinrich Herrmann[3] suggests that the escapement was developed out of the clavichord tangent: this is very probable. But the conception may have been derived from the primitive escapement controlled by a bristle or spring on the jack which enables the tongue to escape from the string after plucking it.

The importance of Cristofori's invention was not realised

---

[1] There is a fifteenth-century drawing of a keyed dulcimer in the National Library at Paris, No. 1295.

[2] B 68, Tome II, Bk. 3, p. 175 and B 68 (*a*), p. 360.

[3] B 48.

by his countrymen. No doubt composers were at a loss to know how to write for the new instrument in order to make the part writing clear and we know from Maffei's statement that they found the touch difficult to acquire.

The 'Professors' objected that its tone was "softer and less distinct" than the ordinary cembalo. Maffei replied that the ear soon adapted itself and became charmed with it; that it never tired and that the common harpsichord no longer pleased.

The truth is that the harpsichord tone is exotic and the more colourless timbre of the *piano e forte* could be heard longer without exhausting the ear. The pianoforte was bound eventually to succeed the harpsichord, but for a long time the two instruments shared the same popularity—hence the quantity of music written for *Harpsichord or Piano Forte*.

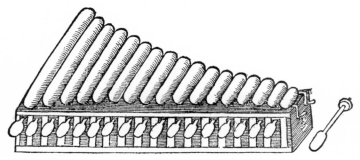

Fig. 2. Primitive Xylophone. Fr. Mersenne.

It took ninety years for men to realise that the pianoforte was not a "New kind of harpsichord with Hammers", but a keyed dulcimer on a grand scale, and it was long before they appreciated the value of personal interpretation which Cristofori's invention now made possible.

Veracini was considered eccentric because he played with expression. The delight in mechanical perfection of execution is strikingly illustrated by the quantities of musical automata,[1] barrel-organs and musical clocks constructed at this period.

No doubt these were of great value with their perfect execution and exquisite phrasing in stimulating performers towards the acquisition of these qualities and harpsichord makers to perfect their instruments. But the dawn of personal interpretation was

[1] A fine collection in the Deutsches Museum, Munich.

destined to carry the progress of music further.[1] The clavichord could be played with expression, but the clavichord was a delicate instrument too feeble in tone for large audiences and only used *in camera*. Cristofori's pianoforte opened up a new era in which the cembalist was no longer to be the automaton of the composer but his prophet.

[1] There is a marked tendency to return to mechanical perfection in music and to do away with the personal touch. The following extract will make this clear: "*Reproducing Pianos of the Future*. Reproducing pianos are to-day able to present interpretations which the recording artists themselves recognise as superior to the renditions from which the records are made. One of the greatest pianists of the present age, after listening to a record made from his own playing, despairingly exclaimed: 'Why can't I play that way!' The reason he could not 'play that way' is that human muscles do not always follow the prompting of the brain directing them, and the result is inaccurate as compared with the intention.... But all such inaccuracies can be corrected and smoothed out in detail in the record in accordance with the intention as clearly shown in its broad outline but not faithfully executed by the player's muscles. ... It is not at all impossible that great pianistic artists will soon be taking 'retouched' records of their own playing as models to be studied", etc. (B 83, p. 253).

CHAPTER II

THE INVENTION OF THE PIANOFORTE
IN FRANCE

A DISCOVERY or invention made by several persons simultaneously in different lands is a phenomenon of which history can give us many examples. We say that such a thing is "in the air". Certainly the idea of the pianoforte was in the air during the early years of the century, for besides Cristofori's pianoforte there were independent inventions in France and in Germany.

Whilst Cristofori was inventing his *Gravicembalo col piano e forte* at Florence, Cuisinié, at Paris, was repeating the experiment made over one hundred years previously by Hans Haydn of Nuremberg, an experiment to make the harpsichord expressive.

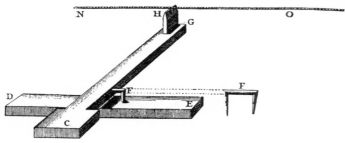

Fig. 3.

"La touche *C* est supportée sur la pièce *DE* par un petit étrier *F*, autour duquel la touche peut se mouvoir. A l'extrémité *G* de cette touche est un *maillet H* posé verticalement, et fait en couteau; de sorte que quand on appuie sur l'extrémité *C* le maillet *H* frappe la corde *N, O* et en tire le son."[1]

Cuisinié exhibited his clavecin in 1708 to l'Académie Royale des Sciences de Paris. The basis of this instrument is a *vielle* or *hurdy-gurdy* improved by the addition of a treadle and crank to revolve the resined wheel that bowed the strings, thus freeing both the performer's hands for playing. In the official description of this instrument the tangent that stopped the string is called a *maillet*, and it is probable that these *maillets* may have suggested to Marius, who doubtless saw this instrument, the hammers he used for his own *Clavecin à maillets* of 1716; the similarity between the

[1] B 4, Tome II, pp. 155, 156, Pl. 127.

two will be observed (Figs. 3, 4). Cuisinié's *maillets* were, no doubt, suggested by the clavichord tangent.

Marius submitted models for four *Clavecins à Maillets* to l'Académie Royale des Sciences de Paris, in 1716. In the first (No. 172) the shape of the hammers seems to have been suggested by those used by Cuisinié in his improved Vielle (Fig. 3). Marius' hammers were, however, of varying thicknesses and in this he was clearly thinking on the right lines, as the hammers as well as the strings must be graded. There is no attempt at an escapement or damper action and the hammer acts directly against the string

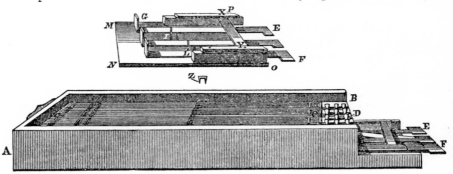

Fig. 4. Marius' Clavecin, No. 172 (1716).

A, B, case; *C*, hitch pins; *D*, screw wrest pins; *M, N, O, P*, key frame; *O, L, P*, blocks with grooves into which the ends of a strip of wood *X, Y,* are fitted, the key pivots lie underneath *X, Y*; *E, F*, keys; *G*, square hammer heads; *I, L*, guide pins; *Z*, strip of iron under which the key works; *E* (in lower drawing), a key in action.

like the tangent of a clavichord. Rimbault states that the hammers were clothed with leather to soften the sound, but there is no mention of this in the official description contained in *Recueil des Instruments et Machines Approuvés par l'Académie Royale des Sciences.*[1]

At the end of the description of the first clavecin there occurs the following statement:

L'on croit que par des clavecins de cette construction, l'on pourra tirer des sons plus ou moins aigus en employant des forces connuës sur les touches suivant les différens tons et les différentes mesures indiquées par les pièces que l'on voudra exécuter.

Mean tone temperament was the custom in France at this time. The scale is obtained by rising or falling repeatedly by two or more

[1] B 4, Tome III, p. 83, Pl. I.

flattened fifths and returning by a true octave. Only keys nearly
related to C are possible for ordinary use, as in extreme keys the
necessary notes do not exist and even in the nearly related keys the
fifths and minor thirds are a quarter of a comma flat. If the engraving is correct it would seem that in Marius' first instrument
these imperfections of intonation could be corrected by a little
extra pressure on the key.[1] Extreme keys were not used unless "an
imperfect sound was suited to the expression of the words or
harshness was to be expressed by the voice".[2]

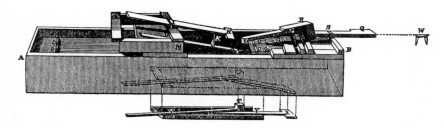

Fig. 5. *The upper diagram:* Marius' Clavecin, No. 173 (1716).

A, B, case; *C, D* and *E, F,* two sets of strings; *G,* hammer striking down on to the
strings; *H,* key; *I,* band under which the key *H* works; *K,* jack; *L,* hammer pivot;
M, N, keyboard; *O,* hammer which strikes the strings *D, C*: this hammer *O* is
attached at *P* by *W,* an iron band; *Q,* key which works the hammer *O*; *S,* iron band
under which the key *Q* works. The hammer is returned by the weight of its butt from
off the strings.

The lower diagram.

T, hammer movable at *V*; *X,* key movable at *Y.* The hammer is made heavier than
the butt.

In his second *Clavecin à Maillets* (No. 173) (Fig. 5)[3] Marius
experiments with different forms of actions. He gives two examples
of a hammer striking down upon the strings and an example of a
hammer striking from below. The hammer butts are to serve as
counter weights for removing the hammers from the strings. No
damper or escapement is used. The downstriking action was
probably suggested by Pantaleon Hebenstreit's performance on
the dulcimer. This famous player visited Paris in 1705 and Marius
may have heard him.[4]

[1] As they could be on the clavichord.
[2] Maffei quoted by Rimbault, B 84.
[3] B 4, Tome III, p. 85, Pl. 2.
[4] See Chap. III.

The third *Clavecin à Maillets* (No. 174) (Fig. 6)[1] is an upright instrument and differs from its predecessors, inasmuch as the jack has a peg which strikes the strings underneath[2] and has at a "particular spot" a piece of cloth to damp the sound. Marius states that the advantage of an instrument with this action consists in the fact that the jacks will not require requilling.

Fig. 6. Marius' Clavecin, No. 174 (1716).

A, B, jack which is attached to the back end of *G,* the key, at the point *E*; *C,* peg projecting from the jack: this peg strikes *D,* the strings, from below; at a "particular spot" round the peg there is a piece of cloth to damp the strings; *F,* key pivot.

His fourth *Clavecin* (No. 175) (Fig. 7)[3] is a combination of hammers and jacks. Both can be used simultaneously or they can be used separately. The hammers are disconnected by pushing in a wedge on the side of the keyboard which causes them to be lowered out of striking distance of the strings.

An examination of the engravings of Marius' *Clavecins* shows that the first, second and third are trichord and the fourth bichord.

[1] B 4, Tome III, p. 87, Pl. 3.
[2] Could this have suggested the Tangent Mechanik?
[3] B 4, Tome III, p. 89, Pl. 4. See also B 84, pp. 104–108.

As the keyboards are not marked out correctly it is impossible to say what compass Marius chose for his clavecins, but it was probably between four and five octaves in accordance with the usual custom at that time. His invention does not appear to have been received with interest and there is no further mention of a *Clavecin à Maillets* in the Official Reports of Inventions submitted to l'Académie des Sciences for forty-three years.

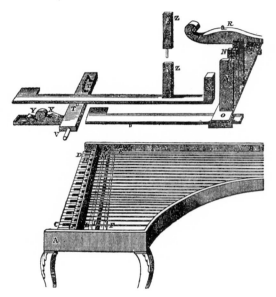

Fig. 7. Marius' fourth Clavecin, No. 175 (1716).
Combined pianoforte and harpsichord.

A, B, body of the harpsichord; *C, D*, lower keyboard serving to operate *E, F*, a set of jacks; *G, H*, upper keyboard serving to operate *I, K*, a set of hammers; *L, M*, dampers, clothed with cloth; *N, N*, jacks passing along *P, O*, a plank placed upon brackets with grooves within which the plank can move in a horizontal direction; *P, O*, a piece movable at *K* (see lower drawing): by moving this piece *P, O* away from him, by its extremity ℐ, the performer advances the jacks into the position for action, whilst, by a contrary motion, he disconnects them; *S*, hammer; *T*, pivot; *V*, bar of wood: to this bar is attached *X*, a piece which extends to either extremity of the keyboard; *Y*, wedge acting under *X*: to lower the hammers out of striking distance of the strings the player pushes the wedge *Y* under the piece *X*; *Z*, dampers.

CHAPTER III

THE INVENTION AND DEVELOPMENT OF THE PIANOFORTE IN GERMANY

§ I

PANTALEON HEBENSTREIT is not honoured as the inventor of the pianoforte, yet he first discovered 'pianistic effects' and designed an instrument for their production.[1] Hebenstreit, Cristofori and Marius saw the same vision. But the virtuoso dulcimerist troubled only to improve the 'corps de résonnance' of his instrument, his skill as a performer making a hammer action unnecessary. Hebenstreit's improved dulcimer was the first realisation of the 'pianoforte idea' in Germany and had such far-reaching effects that a description of it is necessary.

The dulcimer, or Hackbrett, was the peasants' harpsichord; and served the purpose of filling in the harmonies in their music. It is trapeze-shaped, and hollow with two rose-shaped sound-holes. The strings, secured to wrest pins on the right side of the instrument, are stretched over two bridges which determine their vibrating length and are hitched over pins embedded on the opposite side. There are sometimes as many as five unison strings to a note. The size of the instrument varies but the usual measurement is about 1·22 cm. for the longest side. The player used wooden hammers, which could be wound with wool to soften the sound.

Hebenstreit constructed a Hackbrett twice the size of those in general use and put a sound-board on both sides of the instrument, stringing the upper one with steel and the under with overspun 'fiddle' strings. All the major and minor scales were available as he adopted equal temperament tuning. Instead of the usual single-headed beaters, he used two-faced *hammers*. Both these faces were of leather but one side was hard and the other soft for the purpose of playing *forte* or *piano*.

As early as 1697 Hebenstreit had attained great proficiency as a performer on this instrument and in 1705 he played it before Louis XIV, who named it the *Pantaleon* in honour of the inventor. On his return to Germany he was attached to the Court at Eisenach,

[1] B 57, p. 28.

but in 1708 became attached to the Court at Dresden. And he began, about this time, to train pupils to play upon the Pantaleon.

Hebenstreit became famous and news of the instrument spread far and wide. Despite this enormous popularity the Pantaleon soon fell into disrepute, owing no doubt to its excessive difficulty[1] and the great expense of keeping it in order.[2]

During Dr Burney's visit to Dresden, whilst collecting material for his history, Binder, the Court Organist, and a former pupil of Hebenstreit, took him to his house to show him the ruins of the famous Pantaleon.

"It is more than nine feet long", writes Burney, "and had, when in order, 186 strings of catgut...the strings were now almost all broken, the present Elector will not be at the charge of furnishing new ones, though it had ever been thought a court instrument in former reigns, and was kept in order at the expense of the prince. M. Binder lamented that he could not possibly afford to string it himself, as it was an instrument upon which he had formerly employed so much time."[3]

The invention of the Pantaleon had two important results: (1) Amateurs and instrument-makers were stimulated to invent a hammer action which should make Pantaleon playing within the reach of the amateur. (2) The artistic effect of the blended harmonies arising from concordant arpeggios when the strings were undamped, together with the good effect of passages played over a bass note, which sounded, as Kuhnau relates, like a sustained key on the organ, added to the fact that overtones up to the 6th were plainly audible, and this effect was much admired, led to the invention of the damper-lifting device known as the *forte pedal* and accounts for the fact that some of the early pianofortes have no dampers at all.

Amongst those persons who attempted to invent a hammer action, the only *name* that comes down to us is that of Christoph Gottlieb Schröter. For many years it was firmly believed that he had actually invented the Pianoforte.

Schröter was distinguished both as a theoretical and practical musician. He was born at Hohenstein in Saxony in 1699 and as early as 1715 Schröter, who was now residing at Dresden, was entrusted with the musical education of pupils of high rank. Training these pupils, as was customary, upon the clavichord, he

---

[1] Hebenstreit practised not only during the day but also far into the night.
[2] Hebenstreit received 200 Thaler a year for the stringing alone.
[3] B 30, Vol. II, pp. 57, 58.

was frequently worried by their complaints that they could not play their pieces upon the harpsichord with expression. His friend and patron, Kapellmeister Schmied, advised him to try a *Nürnbergisches Geigenwerk*.[1] Although Schröter preferred it to the harpsichord he was unable to overcome his dislike to the treadles, which he was obliged to work like a 'linen-weaver'.

During the year 1717 Schröter heard Hebenstreit play on the Pantaleon and became convinced that the harpsichord could only be made expressive by the addition of hammers.

Before the end of the year 1717 he invented two actions with hammers: one down-striking and the other up-striking. He consulted his cousin, a carpenter, and succeeded, eventually, in constructing a double model embodying both designs. Schröter was unable to bear the cost of having instruments made and decided in 1721 to take his 'double model' to the Saxon Court.

The King promised that a full-size pianoforte should be made according to the up-striking model. But an unfortunate incident, which occurred on a subsequent visit to the Court, determined Schröter to seek work away from Dresden. From this moment his fortune changed. The promised instrument was never made and the 'double model' was permanently retained.

In 1738 when the hammer action had been universally accepted and every fashionable musical-instrument-maker pretended to its invention, Schröter published his claims to the invention in a letter to Mizler inserted in the *Neu-eröffnete Musikalische Bibliothek* (Leipzig, 1736–54, Band III, S. 474–6) and repeated them in *Marpurg's Kritische Briefe* (Berlin, 1764, Band III, S. 85).

He expresses the view in this Proclamation that many persons including an "ingenious man at Dresden" (a reference to Silbermann), and even Cristofori himself, had tried to imitate his models and he accounts for the difference between their actions and his by their having misunderstood the principle of his invention.

Probably a few persons really saw his double model and tried to imitate the two actions. A statement to this effect was sent to him in a letter from an instrument-maker in 1742. The writer states that two drawings, one of a down-striking and one of an up-striking action were given to him by a brother formerly in the service of Count Vitzthum, a Chamberlain at the Saxon Court. But the worthy man declares that if he ever sells other instruments

[1] Unfortunately we are not told whether this instrument had been made by Hans Haydn or merely by an imitator.

of the same sort he will say they were invented by Herr Schröter, the organist at Nordhausen.

Schröter refers to his down-striking action in his Proclamation but gives neither drawing nor description. He states that he considers it unsatisfactory, as the springs necessary to occasion the return of the hammer are liable to get out of order. The down-striking action illustrated below (Fig. 8) was taken from a model

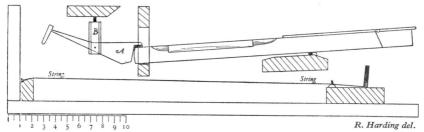

Fig. 8. Down-striking action[1] attributed to Schröter by Welcker (Stuttgart, No. B 35). *A*, hammer; *B*, Kapsel or fork in which the hammer is pivoted.

R. Harding del.

by Dr Pfeiffer based on a diagram by Welcker,[2] who supposed it to have formed part of the 'double model' of 1721; but it cannot

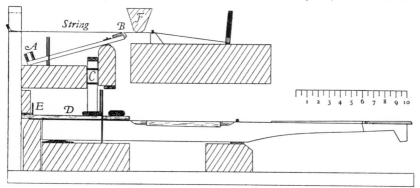

Fig. 9. Schröter's pianoforte (Stuttgart, No. B 25). R. Harding del.

A, the hammer of very light wood no thicker than a harpsichord jack having a head clothed with leather; *B*, the damper padded with satin or plush; *C*, the jack, made of light wood and no thicker than those used in a harpsichord, is kept in position between two rows of pins: this jack is purposely unattached to the hammer in order to prevent what is technically known as blocking, *i.e.* the jamming of the hammer against the string; *D*, a lever pivoted at *E* serving to transmit motion from the key to the jack; *F*, an iron bar pressing on the strings for the purpose of giving brightness to the tone: this foreshadows the Capo Tasto bar of later days.

---

[1] Note the gauge under each diagram represents one decimetre.
[2] B 94, S. 26, Fig. 17.

have been Schröter's *original* down-striking model, as there is no spring and the hammer is returned by the weight of its butt. The up-striking action which actually formed a part of the double model of 1721 is illustrated on page 19 (Fig. 9).[1]

Schröter states that if changes of tone colour are desired Lute and Harp and other stops may be added.

A pianoforte was actually made according to this model under Schröter's supervision,[2] for a "Foreign Patron of high rank" in 1739. When this patron had seen Telemann's description of the "eye organ" invented by Father Castel,[3] which Schröter had sent to him, he asked whether such an "optical amusement" could be arranged on a pianoforte. Schröter considered the matter for several days and then produced his third design, a Tangent Action (Fig. 10).

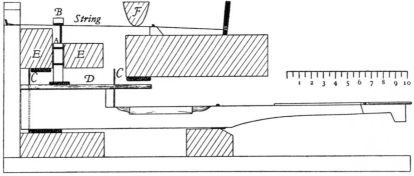

R. Harding del.

Fig. 10. Schröter's Tangent Action (Stuttgart, No. B 20).

A, the hammer, made of light wood and no thicker than a harpsichord jack, and tipped with leather at *A*, is suspended between *E*, *E*, in such a way that it does not rest directly on the lever *D*; *B*, the damper, fixed by a wire to the hammer, is clothed with satin or plush. The upper side of the damper is covered with parchment on which "all kinds of colours are painted". When not in use these painted upper parts are concealed within a perforated rack lying above them. When in play they pop in and out of the rack and provide the optical amusement. (Schröter states that he has omitted to draw the rack in order to save confusion.) *C*, *C* are two pins which guide the lever *D*, transmitting motion from the key to the jack; *E*, *E*, two blocks between which the jack is suspended; *F*, an iron bar used for the same purpose as in the previous design. It will be observed that there can be no possibility of leaving the strings undamped, as the dampers are fixed to the hammers.

---

[1] For convenience Schröter's lettering has been altered, as his lengthy description is unnecessary for the present purpose.

[2] For Schröter's scheme of stringing the instrument, see D 2, pp. 361, 362.

[3] Le père Castel, auteur du clavecin oculaire, avait supposé que les sept couleurs produites par l'effet du prisme sur les rayons de la lumière se rapportaient exactement

A fourth action remains to be described.

It is illustrated by Welcker, who thought it was one of the two original designs. Dr Oscar Paul, an authority on Schröter, dismisses Welcker's drawings of the Schröter actions as incorrect. The down-striking action is at least referred to by Schröter but the action described below (Fig. 11) is not mentioned. If it is his he must have designed it after 1738, otherwise it would have been referred to in the Proclamation.

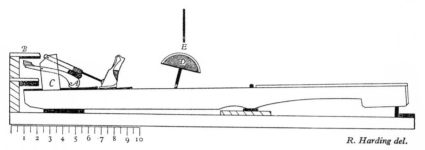

R. Harding del.

Fig. 11. Square pianoforte by H. Chr. Heyne, 1777 (Berlin, No. 337). Welcker von Gontershausen shows a diagram of an action similar to this and attributes it to Schröter.[1]

A, lever pivoted below the hammer in a sheath known technically as the Kapsel: when the key is depressed the back end of the lever knocks against a projection *B,* in the back of the case—technically known as the *Prelleiste*: the blow on the back of the lever causes it to throw up the hammer to the string; *D* is the damper lifter; *E,* a portion of the damper stick.

§ II

It is often stated that Schröter was the first to invent a pianoforte in Germany and that his designs at first formed the working basis of the pianofortes constructed by other persons. There is so little

aux sept sons de la musique, et intercalant, entre ces sept couleurs principales, des demi-couleurs ou demi-teintes, il composa sa gamme chromatique visuelle de la manière suivante:

L'*ut* répondait au bleu, l'*ut-dièse* au céladon, le *ré* au vert gai, le *ré-dièse* au vert olive, le *mi* au jaune, le *fa* à l'aurore, le *fa-dièse* à l'orangé, le *sol* au rouge, le *sol-dièse* au cramoisi, le *la* au violet, le *la-dièse* au violet bleu, le *si* au bleu d'iris.

Et l'octave recommençait ensuite de même; seulement les teintes des couleurs devenaient de plus en plus légères. Le père Castel, en faisant paraître ou disparaître, au moyen du clavier, les couleurs correspondantes aux sons d'une mélodie agréable, prétendait par-là dédommager ceux à qui la nature a refusé ou émoussé le sens de l'ouïe, en procurant à l'œil une sensation agréable analogue à celle que la musique fait éprouver à l'oreille. (B 70 (*a*), p. 206.)

[1] B 94, S. 26, Fig. 18.

evidence that it may be permissible to advance a theory which is not exactly in accordance with this view.

Probably experimenters first attempted to invent a down-striking hammer action in imitation of the Pantaleon player's downward stroke upon the strings. Owing to the technical difficulties of constructing this type of action, it would soon be given up and attempts would be made to solve the difficulty in a more simple way.

An up-striking action would be the obvious alternative. Schröter[1] states that instruments with a down-striking action were called *Pantaleons*, whilst those with an up-striking action were called *pianofortes*. Thus all attempts to construct Pantaleons would soon be given up in favour of the more easily constructed pianoforte.

Some authorities think that the instrument-makers were content to follow Friederici (who is supposed to have invented the 'square' pianoforte) in perfecting the clavichord. The writer ventures to differ from them since, if Schröter's actions really inspired men to invent pianoforte actions of their own, they would also wish to follow his example of trying to make the *harpsichord* expressive. In any case the early pianoforte action can hardly be called an improvement on the clavichord, since so much of the characteristic expressiveness is lost. It seems more probable that they endeavoured to perfect the harpsichord, and as few persons would be able to afford to experiment upon a full-sized instrument the natural expedient would be to use the clavichord as a working basis. Dr Josten points out that from this simple experimenting upon the clavichord, for whatever purpose, the German action was eventually developed.[2]

The development of the Prellmechanik. The first step would consist in adapting another bridge to the clavichord for the purpose of determining the vibrating length of the strings in accordance with the musical scale. The second step would consist in substituting a hammer in the place of the tangent.

A hammer with its shank is laid upon the key with its head pointing upwards at the place formerly occupied by the tangent. The hammer is so placed that its shank projects a little beyond the end of the key. It is hinged to the key by a strip of leather. A projection is contrived in the back of the case for the purpose of catching the projecting shank when the key is depressed. By this simple means the hammer shank is converted into a lever which when jerked up against the projection at the back of the case lifts the hammer to the string. This projection at the back of the case is known as the *Prelleiste*: a technical term that will be adhered to throughout. Pianofortes after this and similar patterns could be constructed cheaply and sold for a purely nominal sum. Fig. 12 (see Plate V(*a*)) represents the action described[1] and Fig. 13,[2] a variation of it from a late example at Berlin. A diagram of the clavichord action (Fig. 14) is given for comparison.

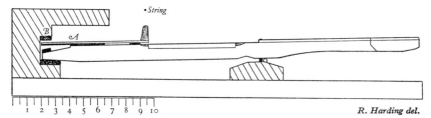

Fig. 12. Primitive *Prellmechanik* (Stuttgart, No. C 5).
A, the hammer shank attached to the key by a leather hinge; *B*, the Prelleiste.

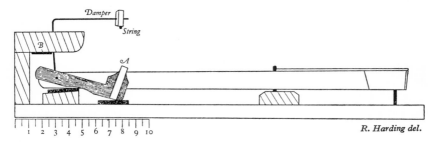

Fig. 13. Primitive *Prellmechanik* (Berlin, No. 2172); second half of the eighteenth century.
A is the hammer around which is glued a strip of soft leather; *B* is the Prelleiste.

The invention of the *Prellmechanik*, of which the two preceding actions are very primitive examples, is attributed to Silbermann.

[1] Other examples occur: (*a*) Deutsches Museum, Munich. (*b*) Historisches Museum, Basle.

[2] Other examples occur: (*a*) Deutsches Museum, Munich. (*b*) Musée Instrumental du Conservatoire Royal de Musique, Brussels, No. 2951. (*c*) Neues Grassi Museum (Heyer Coll.), Leipzig, No. 114, with the dampers acting *under* the string. See B 49 (*f*), p. 156, footnote illustration. (*d*) Musée du Conservatoire National de Musique, Paris, No. 336. Similar to the Leipzig example.

On that account the example at Stuttgart (Fig. 12) is supposed to have come from his workshop but it is difficult to believe that such crude mechanisms as any of these could have originated in the workshop of so able a master.

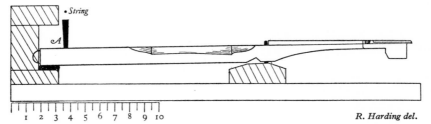

Fig. 14. Clavichord action (Stuttgart, No. A 1).

It seems more probable that he saw these tentative experiments, realised their value, grasped instantaneously those alterations necessary to their success and proceeded to construct an action alike in principle but with a hammer pivoted within a sheath or *Kapsel*[1] fixed to the key, having its butt produced into a beak or *Hammerschnabel* for the purpose of engaging the *Prelleiste*. This is the developed *Prellmechanik;* it is found both in grand and

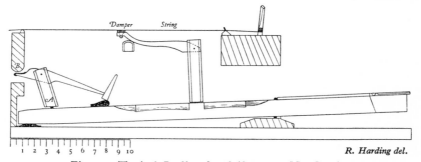

Fig. 15. Typical *Prellmechanik* (Stuttgart, No. C 20).
A, the wooden Kapsel within which the hammer is pivoted through its butt;
B, the Prelleiste.

square pianofortes. Fig. 15 shows a typical example of the developed *Prellmechanik,* and Fig. 16 a variation by J. G. Mahr. There are, in fact, many variations of the *Prellmechanik,* some having dampers acting from above.

---

[1] German technical term for the sheath within which the hammer in a pianoforte with German Action is pivoted. The term *Kapsel* will be adhered to throughout. (See A.)

The German action. The final stage is reached when Andreas Stein, a pupil of Silbermann, contrived an escapement. He cut through the *Prelleiste*, pivoted it to the bottom of the case and controlled its movement by a spring. It serves precisely the same

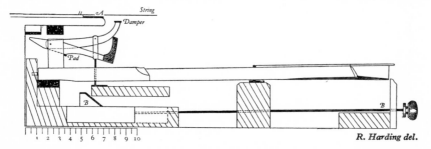

Fig. 16. Square pianoforte action by Johann Gottfried Mahr, 1774 (Berlin, No. 818). Drawing of the action for F₁ (compass F₁ to f‴).

A, piano stop; *B, B*, the block and iron rod which form part of the apparatus for working the forte stop. The hammer is made of pear wood. (See Plate X for a general view of the keyboard with its clavichord-like keys.)

purpose as the escapement invented by Cristofori. After giving the hammer its impetus towards the strings it escapes, in this case from the hammer beak, and leaves the hammer free to fall back from the strings (Fig. 17).

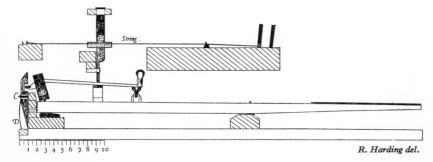

Fig. 17. German Action by Stein for grand pianoforte, 1773 (Stuttgart, No. C 25). *A*, the wooden Kapsel; *B*, the escapement—a transformed Prelleiste; *C*, one of two guide wires to keep the escapement steady; *D*, the escapement spring; *E*, the damper. This type of damper, the *Kastendämpfer*, is typical of the German Action.

This mechanism is known by the name of the German action and its principle may be summarised as follows:

The *hammer* is pivoted within a sheath technically called a Kapsel and *fixed to the key* in such a way that *its head points towards the front of the instrument. The butt is produced into a beak* known technically as the *Hammerschnabel, for the purpose of engaging* the Escapement, *Auslöser*.[1]

This form of action is used for both square and grand piano-fortes, and it is found in the popular portable pianoforte called the Orphica.[2]

Mozart, who admired Stein's instruments, gives the following account of one of them in a letter written from Augsburg to his father on October 17th, 1777:

I must now tell you about Stein's pianos. Before seeing these, Späth's pianos were my favourites; but I must own that I give preference to those of Stein, for they damp much better than those in Ratisbon. If I strike hard, whether I let my fingers rest on the notes or lift them, the tone dies away at the same instant that it is heard. Strike the keys as I choose, the tone always remains even, never either jarring or failing to sound. It is true that a piano of this kind is not to be had for less than three hundred florins, but the pains and skill which Stein bestows on them cannot be sufficiently repaid. His instruments have a feature of their own; they are supplied with a peculiar *escapement*. Not one in a hundred makers attends to this; but without it, it is impossible that a piano should not buzz and jar. His hammers fall as soon as they touch the strings, whether the keys be held down by the fingers or not.... He warrants the sounding board neither breaking or cracking; when he has finished one, he exposes it in the air to rain, snow, sun, and every kind of devilry, that it may give way, and then inserts slips of wood which he glues in, making it quite strong and solid.... The pedals, pressed by the knees, are also better made by him than by anyone else; you scarcely require to touch them to make them act, and as soon as the pressure is removed not the slightest vibration is perceptible. (*Lady Wallace's translation.*)

A consideration of the preceding diagrams will show that Schröter's fame is not due to any direct influence which he exercised upon the construction of the pianoforte. Of the four actions attributed to him the down-striking action (Fig. 8) may have suggested to Stein the use of the Kapsel, but it is doubtful whether this action (attributed to him by Welcker) is really by Schröter, as Dr Paul does not recognise it. On the other hand the up-striking action (of 1717, Fig. 9) and that with the 'optical amusement' (of 1739, Fig. 10) may have suggested the form of action known as the 'Tangent' Action. This is in fact the opinion held by Dr Herrmann.[3] The other up-striking action (Fig. 11) is not

[1] See A for list of technical terms relating to the pianoforte.
[2] Invented by Rolling in 1795. It is slung round the player by a strap and is re-markable in that it has an iron frame.
[3] B 48. This action will be described later.

mentioned by Schröter, but it is merely attributed to him by Welcker and is not recognised by Dr Paul.

It is probable that by the time Schröter published his claims with the drawings of the two actions indisputably his, pianoforte building had advanced too far to profit by these experiments.

§ III

Cristofori's influence in Germany. Besides those instruments with the German action either in its primitive[1] or developed state, pianofortes with a different type of action were being constructed. The two forms seem often to have been made side by side in the same workshop.

In order to account for the origin of this second type, some historical details must be given.

Bartolommeo Cristofori was not discouraged by the adverse criticism that his first pianofortes received from the musical amateurs and teachers. He continued his experiments, and by the year 1720 had already brought the pianoforte to a high state of perfection. The clumsy intermediate lever (marked *F* in Maffei's diagram, Fig. 1) is modified into an elegant strip which is hinged to a block and works directly under the hammer butt. There is also a check piece to catch and hold the hammer until the key is released. Motion is transmitted from the key to the intermediate lever by an escapement as in the first example. The dampers rest upon the back end of the key instead of on the end of the intermediate lever (*Ջ* in Maffei's drawing). The strings are placed above the sound-board and there are two strings to each note.

By the year 1726 Cristofori had reached the zenith of his power as an inventor. A pianoforte of that date, the second and latest of the only two which have been preserved, is interesting in showing us the type of hammer that he used for his later work. (This instrument is in its original state with the exception of some of the strings and the key for C and the dampers for b'''.)

The hammer shank is made of Italian cedar, a wood suitable for this purpose on account of its elasticity. The head consists of a small block of wood curved at the top to receive a small cylinder composed of strips of parchment. This cylinder is glued to the block and a pad of leather is glued to its upper side. The purpose of the cylinder is probably to give elasticity. There are two strings

[1] The stage known as *Prellmechanik*, see Figs. 12, 13, 15 and 16.

to each note and they are secured underneath the wrest block. The arches which connect the sound-board to the wrest block are not of iron or steel but carved out of wood, owing no doubt to the prejudice against using metal in stringed musical instruments[1] (Fig. 18; see Frontispiece).

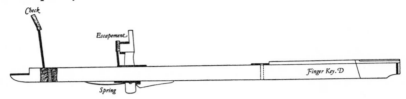

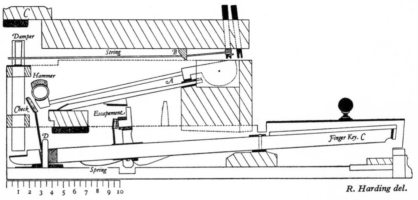

R. Harding del.

Fig. 18. Pianoforte by Cristofori, 1726 (Leipzig, No. 170). The drawing represents the action for C and the key for D (compass C to c'''). Inscription printed in Roman lettering: BARTHOLOMAEVS DE' CHRISTOPHORIS PATAVINVS INVENTOR FACIEBAT FLORENTIAE M. DCCXXVI.

A, intermediate lever; B, wrest-block bridge; C, 'Ruler', a strip of wood to prevent the dampers jumping out; D, one of two wood guide posts to keep the key steady. The natural keys are faced with box.

There is no stop for forte but only 'Verschiebung' (i.e. Una Corda), a mechanism for sliding the keyboard and action laterally so that the hammers strike one only out of each pair of strings. This stop is worked by wrought iron levers placed underneath the keyboard, one on the left and one on the right.[2] The number XX

[1] Besides this makers thought that a pianoforte or harpsichord improved with age like a violin and on this account would construct their instruments out of old boxes or other ancient wood.

[2] It is thought a few further details may be of interest. In the Neues Grassi Museum

is stamped upon the action frame and it may be concluded that he only made twenty pianofortes between the years 1709 and 1726.

Cristofori died in 1731 and no doubt his pupils[1] either set up workshops on their own account or sought work in the shops of other masters. Intercourse between Northern Italy and Dresden was firmly established at that time and many Italian workmen were employed at Dresden. Probably some of Cristofori's workmen made their way to Dresden and to other parts of Germany.

In addition to this a translation by König of Maffei's description of Cristofori's *Gravicembali* had appeared in Mattheson's *Musikalische Kritik* (Band III, Hamburg, 1725, S. 340).

Cristofori's actions were susceptible of modification and it seems clear from the evidence before us in the great German museums that pianofortes both with this action in its perfect form and others, either modifications or crude imitations of it, were constructed in Germany.

But before proceeding further it is desirable to summarise the essential differences between the Cristofori and the German actions.

at Leipzig where this pianoforte is preserved (No. 170), there is a harpsichord (No. 85) of the same date by Cristofori which was probably made as a companion instrument. The outer cases of both instruments are almost identical. The keyboard of both instruments is the same: four octaves C_1 to c'''. The following are the case measurements: the harpsichord, length 2·57 m., breadth 94 cm., height 1·08 m.; the pianoforte length 2·50 m., breadth 91½ cm., height 97½ cm.

Comparison of the 1720 and 1726 Cristofori Pianofortes

Earlier			Later		
Length...	232·4 cm.		Length...		2·50 m.
Breadth	99·1 cm.		Breadth		91·5 cm.
Vibrating length of the longest string ...	188·0 cm.		Vibrating length of the longest string (approx.)		195·5 cm.
Vibrating length of the shortest string ...	11·5 cm.		Vibrating length of the shortest string (approx.)		14·4 cm.
Compass: 4 octaves and a 4th (C to f''')			Compass: 4 octaves (C to c''')		
Stops: none			Stops: one, *Verschiebung* (*i.e.* Una Corda)		

[1] The chief of whom were: Giovanni Ferrini, Geronimo of Florence, and Gherardi of Padua.

THE ESSENTIAL DIFFERENCES BETWEEN THE CRISTOFORI ACTION AND THE GERMAN ACTION SUMMARISED

THE CRISTOFORI ACTION

Developed form. Stosszungenmechanik or *Englische Mechanik* (English Action).
(1) The hammer is pivoted to a rail forming a part of the action frame.
(2) The hammer head points towards the back of the instrument.
(3) Motion is transmitted to the hammer by means of an escapement fixed to the key.
(4) A check piece is usually added.

Simplified form. The Stossmechanik.
(1) The hammer is pivoted or hinged by leather or parchment to a rail forming part of the action frame.
(2) The hammer head points towards the back of the instrument.
(3) Motion is transmitted to the hammer by a fixed piece or jack attached to the key.
(4) There is no check piece.

THE GERMAN ACTION

Developed form or *Deutsche Mechanik* (German Action).
(1) The hammer is pivoted within a Kapsel fixed to the key.
(2) The hammer head points towards the front of the instrument.
(3) Motion is transmitted to the hammer by an escapement behind the key.
(4) A check piece is usually added.

Simple or undeveloped form. The Prellmechanik.
(1) The hammer is pivoted within a Kapsel fixed to the key or is sometimes hinged directly to the key itself.
(2) The hammer head points towards the front of the instrument.
(3) Motion is transmitted to the hammer by a projection at the back of the case called a Prelleiste.
(4) There is no check piece.

Cristofori's actions were, as has been pointed out, susceptible of modification in various ways.

The earliest example of this occurs in an upright pianoforte by an unknown maker in the Neues Grassi Museum (Heyer Collection) at Leipzig (No. 106). On the topmost key f''' the date 1735 is inscribed[1] (Fig. 19). The escapement has been modified into a fixed piece or 'jack' which acts *directly* under the hammer butt. The hammer is fixed to a metal shaft. A square block of lead is placed directly behind the head to facilitate its return and no doubt to give a greater impetus to the blow. The hammer head is made of wood covered with soft leather. The damper is fixed to a metal

---

[1] Dr Georg Kinsky objects to this date and states that it should be read as 1765 or

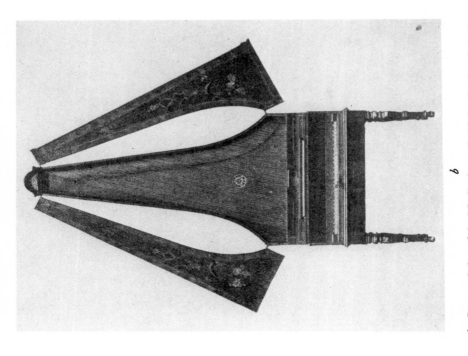

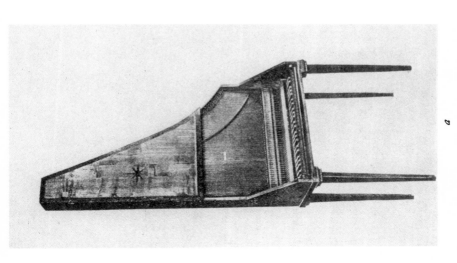

a

b

Plate II (a). Upright Pianoforte, 1735. Leipzig, No. 106. By permission of the Musikwissenschaftliches Institut, Leipzig. (b). Pianoforte by Friederici, 1745. Brussels, Musée du Conservatoire Royal de Musique, No. 1631.

shaft embedded in the lever *D*. It is raised by a jack attached to the key. This pianoforte has one stop: a contrivance for raising the dampers known as 'fortezug' or simply 'forte'. The player takes hold of the leather strap attached to the lever *A* and loops it over the hook *B*, this causes the piece *C* which is fixed to *A* to raise the damper lever *D* and thus lift the dampers away from the strings.

possibly as 1785, as this type of damping ('Einzel' damping) did not come into use until the year 1765. But as Dr Kinsky points out on the preceding page the 'Einzel' damping was introduced by Cristofori as early as 1726. There is insufficient evidence for the later date, while the crudeness of the action strongly supports the earlier inscription on the key. (B 59, Band 1, S. 127, footnote, 126.)

Even if the date of this is not accepted, Cesare Ponsicchi gives a diagram of one in his book *Il Primo Pianoforte Verticale* (Firenze, 1898) which he informs us was constructed by Don Domenico del Mela di Gagliano in 1739. Dr Pfeiffer, referring to it in a work entitled *Die Verlängerung im Hammerwerk des Klaviers* (Berlin Schöneberg, 1924), states that the drawing as shown by Ponsicchi is unworkable. The adjoining figure was drawn from Dr Pfeiffer's model. This action is clearly an adaptation of the Cristofori action of 1726 to an upright instrument. (I am indebted to Dr Josten of Stuttgart for the information relating to Don Domenico.)

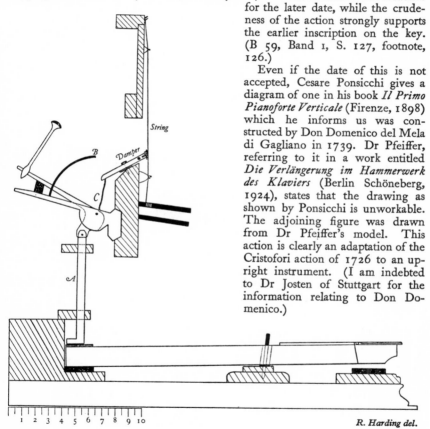

R. Harding del.

Upright Pianoforte Action by Don Domenico del Mela di Gagliano, 1739 (Stuttgart, No. E 10).

A, sticker; *B*, one of two guide wires; *C*, cord. The great length of the hammer head should be noted.

The action of an upright pianoforte made by Silbermann's famous pupil, Christian Ernst Friederici of Gera, in 1745 (in the *Musée du Conservatoire Royal de Musique*, Brussels (No. 1631)), shows another modification of Cristofori's Action of 1726. Here, again, the escapement has been modified into a jack and the intermediate lever is omitted (Fig. 20). Another upright pianoforte attributed to him and remarkable for its elegant appearance is in

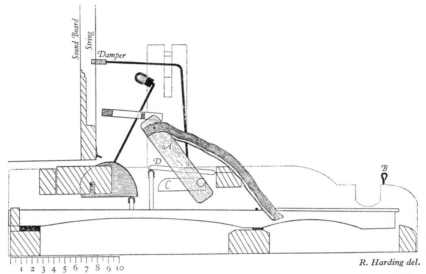

Fig. 19. Upright pianoforte dated 1735 at Leipzig (No. 106). The drawing represents the action for C (compass C to f'''). Plate II (*a*) (*description*, pp. 30, 31).

the Schloss Museum at Berlin (Fig. 21; Plate III). The action is another crude adaptation of Cristofori's Action in which the intermediate lever is omitted and the escapement is modified into a fixed piece or jack. This instrument is in a pyramidal case with carved openwork doors upon a stand with four curved legs. Friederici was an organ builder as well as a pianoforte maker and the influence of the organ on this instrument can be seen in the iron trackers attached to the keys by wooden pivots. This clumsy arrangement is made necessary owing to the fact that the strings are arranged symmetrically, the longest being in the centre of the instrument. Thus it follows that the key for a bass note must be connected by a tracker to the action for its proper length of string.

It is of some interest to compare this instrument *attributed* to Friederici with that *known* to be his work at Brussels. In the

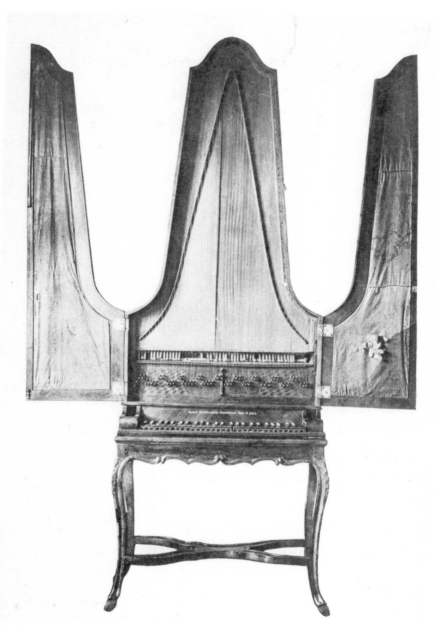

Plate III. An Upright Pianoforte in a case of Walnut, attributed to Friederici.
Schloss Museum, Berlin.

Brussels example, previously mentioned, the strings are not arranged symmetrically but lie over the sound-board in a diagonal position. They are hitched to a block following the curve of the

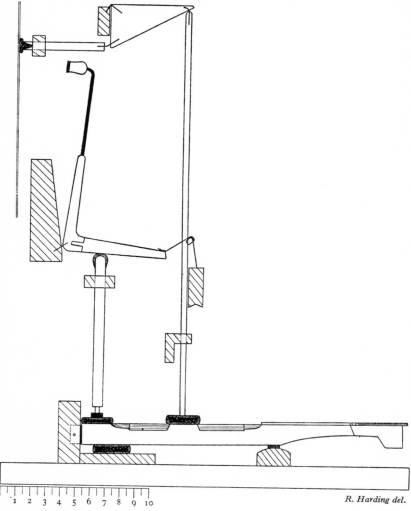

R. Harding del.

Fig. 20. Friederici, 1745 (Stuttgart, No. E 15). Plate II (*b*).
The hammer is fixed to a metal rod. The head is of wood to which is glued a pad of leather.

right-hand side of the instrument and there is a rose-shaped sound-hole. There are two stops: Lute and forte, whereas in the Berlin example there are none, nor are there any dampers. The case, though handsome, lacks the elegance of that in the Schloss Museum at Berlin. If, indeed, the two pianofortes are from the hand of Friederici there can be no doubt that the Berlin pianoforte is the older of the two instruments. Friederici called his upright piano-

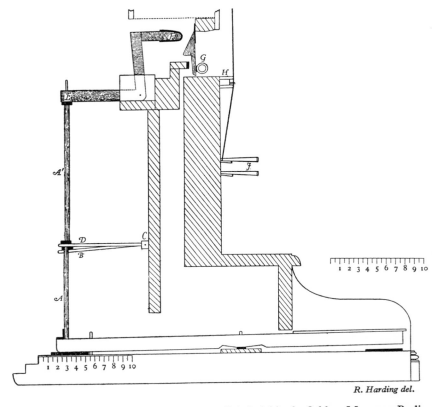

R. Harding del.

Fig. 21. Upright pianoforte attributed to Friederici in the Schloss Museum, Berlin. The drawing represents the action for F (compass F to f''').

To the back end of the key there is fixed a wooden upright *A*, which is connected by an iron lever *D* to an iron tracker (seen edgeways in the diagram) *C*. At the end of the tracker *C* is another iron lever *B* to which is attached a further wooden upright *A'*. The upright *A'* works the S-shaped piece or jack *E, F*. *E, F* is tipped with leather at *F* and strikes the hammer shank from behind. The hammer *G* is pivoted at the upper extremity of the shank by a piece of parchment glued to a block behind the sound-board. The hammer head consists of a cylinder composed of several layers of parchment. The leather pad which was originally glued to it has disappeared. There are no dampers. *H* is a bridge. *J* are the wrest pins. The strings are arranged symmetrically and are hitched to the hitch-pin block which follows the curve of the sides. The longest strings are in the centre and the shortest ones at the sides.

fortes 'Bienfort'. Mahillon says that this was a pun on the word Pianoforte, signifying that it was necessary to play *bien fort* to make them sound at all.

As in the upright pianoforte, so also in the square, the two principal modifications of Cristofori's Action consist in the omission of the intermediate lever and the substitution of a fixed upright or jack in place of the escapement. Sometimes Cristofori's Action was adapted in its complete form to the square pianoforte, as in the example by J. H. Silbermann (Fig. 22). Wagner, on the

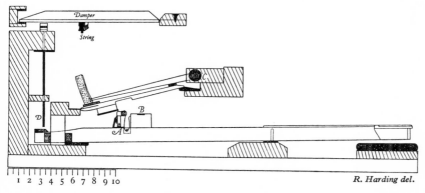

R. Harding del.

Fig. 22. Square pianoforte action by J. H. Silbermann (Stuttgart, No. C 75).

A, the escapement; *B*, a lead weight countersunk into a wooden block, for the purpose of giving a correct balance to the key; *C*, a patch of paper pasted on the hammer pivot; *D*, the damper stick ending in a button for the purpose of raising the damper lever, *i.e.* the wooden strip to which the damper is attached. This arrangement is called an 'over damper'.

other hand, has modified the dampers and omitted the intermediate lever (Fig. 23). Owing to the use of wooden hammers (*i.e.* unclothed hammers) the normal tone is that of the cembalo, but by coupling the Lute stop the clavichord tone is imitated. This pianoforte has the following stops: Lute,[1] forte, piano and swell worked by knee pedals. In order to work these pedals the player raises his heel, thus lifting his knee to the pedal and pushing it flat to the under side of the case. Wagner invented this type of instrument in 1775, calling it the *Clavecin Royal*[2] (Plate IV (*b*)).

Cristofori's influence is again found in a square pianoforte by

[1] 'Harfe' in Cat. B 87 (*a*), S. 83.
[2] Wagner's charges were as follows: Pianofortes in Rose or Yew, 36 Ducats, Pianofortes in Oak, 28 Ducats.

Senft in the same collection as the previous instrument. Unfortunately the pianoforte itself cannot be seen. One key is preserved as a specimen and from that the diagram was made. It will be seen that it is a mixture of the Cristofori and German principles (Fig. 24). The hammer is pivoted within a brass fork fixed to the

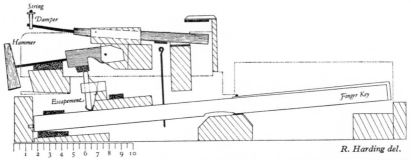

Fig. 23. Square pianoforte by Johann Gottlob Wagner, Dresden, 1788 (Berlin, No. 1174). The drawing represents the action for the note F_I (compass F_I to g''').

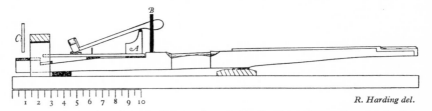

Fig. 24. Square pianoforte by Ignace Joseph Senft of Augsburg (last third of the eighteenth century) (Berlin, No. 1280).[1]

A, jack; *B*, brass fork or Kapsel; *C*, portion of the damper stick.

key, but it is pointing *away* from the front of the instrument. It is knocked up by the block *A*, which is a modified jack. This jack is set in motion by a lever which is jerked up against a Prelleiste. If the hammer is removed there remains an action similar to that represented in Fig. 12 (Chap. III, § II, p. 23).

The final stage in the simplification of Cristofori's action is reached when Silbermann or Zumpe, his pupil, substituted for the wooden jack a wire with a wooden button covered with leather at its upper extremity.[2] Over dampers are used with a spring of whalebone to keep them pressed on to the strings (Plate V (*b*);

[1] Another example in the Deutsches Museum, Munich, and in the Museum of the Bachhaus at Eisenach, No. 75.

[2] Zumpe modified this action in later years. See p. 55, Fig. 39.

a

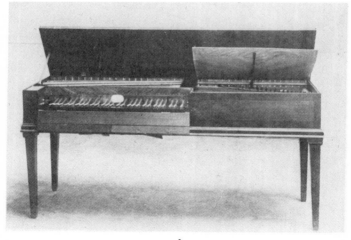

b

Plate IV (*a*). Pianoforte by Silbermann, 1776.
Berlin, Hochschule für Musik, No. 12.

(*b*). Wagner's Clavecin Royal. Berlin, No. 1174.

Fig. 25). Square pianofortes with this action became extremely popular, as they were economical to construct and could be sold cheaply. In fact, they constituted the normal type of cheap instrument sold in England, France and Italy in the latter half of the eighteenth century.

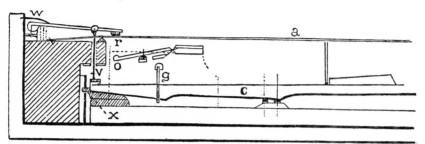

Fig. 25. Zumpe's First action, 1760. By courtesy of the Metropolitan Museum of Art, New York. From the *Handbook of Keyboard Instruments*.

a, string; *C*, key; g, jack; *O*, hammer; r, damper (Hebeldämpfer); *V*, damper stick; *W*, whalebone spring to facilitate the return of the damper and keep it pressed against the string; *X*, whalebone piece working in a groove serving to keep the key steady.

We shall now pass on to consider Cristofori's influence on the 'grand' pianoforte.

Silbermann had made an early attempt to build grand pianofortes but the adverse criticism these instruments received from Sebastian Bach discouraged him from building them for some years. About the year 1745 he made another attempt. On this occasion his fifteen grand pianofortes not only won the approbation of Bach but also that of Frederick the Great who is said to have bought them all and placed them about his Palaces at Potsdam.

Of these fifteen pianofortes only three remain. A drawing by Bechstein of that in Frederick's music room at the Neues Schloss and a drawing of the one in the Stadt Schloss[1] at Potsdam reveal the Cristofori action of 1726.

In the case of the Silbermann pianoforte in the Stadt Schloss, stops for forte and cembalo (*i.e.* a stop for imitating the harpsichord tone), divided into bass and treble, are placed in addition to that for piano.

About 1776, or possibly before this, he devised a method of constructing the action more economically. Instead of the semi-

[1] The drawing was presented by a friend at Berlin.

circular hammer butt pivoted within a rack by a wire running through the set, he attached each hammer separately by a strip of leather to a rail. The time saved in construction would be considerable and also it would be more easy to detach and repair any hammer (Fig. 26; Plate IV (*a*)). The principal modifications of Cristofori's Action already referred to in connection with the upright and the square pianofortes are also found in this action when applied to the grand pianoforte and it is superfluous to give further examples. Harpsichords were sometimes converted into pianofortes[1] and there is more than one pianoforte of about this date in

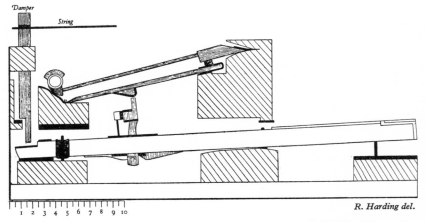

Fig. 26. 'Grand' pianoforte by J. H. Silbermann, 1776 (Berlin, No. 12). The drawing represents the action for E (compass F to f''').

an ancient cembalo case, in the museum of musical instruments attached to the Hochschule für Musik in Berlin.

The 'Anglo-German' Action. Attention has already been drawn to the fact that pianofortes with the Cristofori Action in its perfect and modified states, together with instruments with German Action in a primitive or developed form, were often constructed in the same workshops. The reason is that there is a difference in the 'touch' between the two forms. The Cristofori Action gave a powerful tone but had a heavier touch than the German form. The German Action had a light and agreeable touch but gave a much weaker tone, and consequently both types had to be made to suit the taste of various clients.

[1] According to Thon (B 91, Chap. 1, § 4), Späth of Ratisbon "converted many claviers into Forte Pianos".

A desire to procure the good qualities of both types in one action seems to have led to an attempt to combine the two. At first this combination was in a primitive form without the escapement, but later the escapement was added and thus the developed form evolved. The house of Nannette Streicher and Son obtained a patent for this developed form as late as 1831. Their action included a check (see p. 152, Fig. 1). As there is more resemblance to a modification of Cristofori's Action, known as the English Grand Action (see Fig. 43, p. 58), than to the German in this combination it is called *die englische Mechanik*. The primitive form does not seem to have been recognised and is called *die Stossmechanik*.

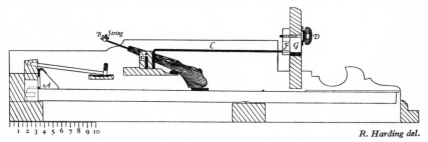

R. Harding del.

Fig. 27. Primitive Anglo-German Action in a square pianoforte by "Joh. Söcher im Obern Sonthofen, Allgäu 1742"[1] (see Plate VI), at the Musikhistorisches Museum Neupert, Nuremberg. Drawing of the action for the key C (compass C to f‴).

A, jack which transmits motion to the hammer; *B*, damper pressed against the string by its heavy counterweight resembling the butt of a rifle; *C*, length of iron wire embedded in a block supporting the damper on the left, and into a lever *F* on the right; *D*, handle of the forte stop which moves the lever *F*: to use this stop push down *D* through the space *G*; *E*, iron pivot (fixed to the frame) upon which the block supporting the damper swings.

In order to distinguish *die englische Mechanik* from that usually constructed by the London makers, we shall call it the *Anglo-German* Action. As a matter of fact the two types of action (the Cristofori and the German) seem to have been combined almost from the beginning of pianoforte construction in Germany. The principle can be summarised thus: the hammer is *hinged* to a rail behind the key with its *head pointing towards the front* of the instrument as in the German Action. A jack or *escapement on the key* sets the hammer in motion as in the Cristofori Action.

An example of the primitive Anglo-German Action, *i.e.* without the escapement, occurs in a pianoforte by Söcher dated 1742 (Fig. 27) and in a still more primitive type, made by Schmahl of

[1] B 76, p. 147, Fig. 94.

Ulm in his little portable pianofortes intended to be carried on coach journeys (Fig. 28), whilst another type, differing from the others in that the hammer is pivoted above and not behind the 'back end' of the key, is illustrated in Fig. 29. The three examples mentioned above may be taken as typical of the primitive Anglo-German Action, though variations of them occur. (See also Fig. 32.)

The characteristic of the developed Anglo-German Action consists of a hammer pivoted to a block behind the key and pointing

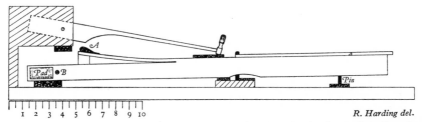

R. Harding del.

Fig. 28. Primitive Anglo-German Action in a pianoforte in the form of an Ottavina or lying harp by Johannes Matthäus Schmahl of Ulm, about 1770 (Berlin, No. 8). The drawing represents the action for the key C (compass C to f′′′).

A, modified jack consisting of a strip cut in the key bent up and wedged in position by a block beneath; B, lead weight.

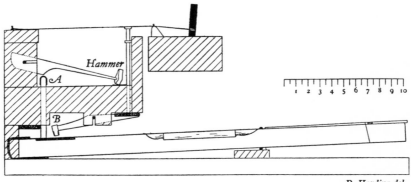

R. Harding del.

Fig. 29. Primitive Anglo-German Action by J. M. Schmahl, about 1770[1] (Stuttgart, No. C 45).

A, jack which differs from the others in that it is not fixed to the key: this may have been suggested to Schmahl by Schröter's first up-striking model (Fig. 9); B, leaden counterweight of the damper lever or 'crank'.

---

[1] Other examples similar to Fig. 29 occur in (i) the Museum of the Bachhaus at Eisenach, (ii) Deutsches Museum, Munich.

towards the front of the instrument, whilst it is set in motion by an escapement fixed to the key.

A typical example of this principle applied to the grand pianoforte is found in an instrument at Berlin, dated 1796, by Siemens Andrew (Fig. 30), whilst an example by Philipp Johann Warth

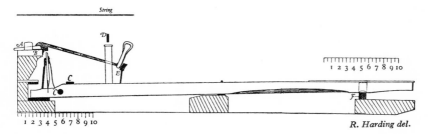

Fig. 30. Anglo-German Action (developed form) in a grand pianoforte by Siemens Andrew of London, dated 1795 (Berlin, No. 342). The drawing represents the action for the key F_I (compass F_I to f''').

A, the larger of two wedges which may be drawn out for the purpose of releasing the hammer; *B*, thin strip of leather lying over the hammer pivot and kept in place by the wedges: to remove the hammer draw out the wedges and lift up the flap of leather; *C*, lead weight; *D*, a portion of the damper stick; *E*, a piece resembling a check[1] and interesting in showing that not every maker understood the function of the check: this sham check frequently occurs; *F*, a 'bat pin' carved in wood. (The bat pin of a modern grand pianoforte is a small metal piece shaped like a cricket bat. It is placed with the 'handle' downwards into the block, whilst the 'blade' works in a slot on the under side of the key.)

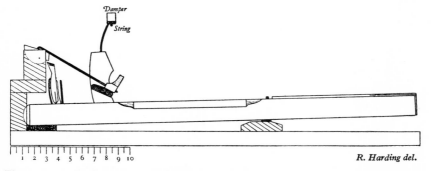

Fig. 31. Anglo-German Action (developed form) in a square pianoforte by Philipp Johann Warth, 1790 (Stuttgart, No. C 80).

---

[1] The function of a check is to catch and hold the hammer after it has fallen from the strings to prevent it from rebounding against them—a defect technically known as 'blocking'. The check acts only as long as the key is pressed down.

may be taken as typical of this action as used in the square pianoforte (Fig. 31). It will be noticed that in the action by Warth the
dampers are fixed to the key in such a way that they cannot be
raised independently.

The table at the conclusion of this chapter will, it is hoped,
make clear these developments.

§ IV

Before concluding the survey of the two main schools of pianoforte building in Germany a few words about the stringing, stops
and appearance of these instruments may be found useful.

The Strings. The sound-board and strings were the last part of the
pianoforte to receive attention. It is the more remarkable as it is this
part which contains its soul. To the end of the eighteenth century
and even later the mass and length of the strings used for the clavichord and the harpsichord still suggested to pianoforte makers the
type of strings they used for their instruments. Pianoforte strings
were naturally thicker than those used upon a harpsichord, but, at
least at first, they were kept as thin as possible to preserve the
harpsichord tone. Brass or steel wire was used for the bass strings,
whilst German iron or British steel wire was used for the treble.
The English steel wire was preferred owing to its greater durability
and better tone. Overspun bass strings do not seem to have been
used until the last quarter of the century.

No metal bars strengthen the frame as the light stringing made
an iron or steel frame unnecessary.

In some square pianofortes the upper half of the bass register
tended to be too weak to support the harmonies. The treble also
was frequently feeble in tone. This defect is overcome in a square
pianoforte in the Neues Grassi Museum at Leipzig (with a compass
of five octaves, F_1 to f''') by an additional set of hammers from F_1
to the top of the treble, for the purpose of coupling the octave
(Fig. 32).

Pianoforte Stops. Hammers of unclothed pear wood or covered
with soft deer leather seem to have been used according to the fancy
of the client for brilliant or subdued cembalo tone. The thin strings
account for their miniature size. On the whole the wooden
hammers seem to have been sparingly used. The sound produced
by the leathered ones was recognised as the typical pianoforte
tone.

Changes of tone colour were provided as a matter of course. The sostenuto in the harpsichord, as Kraus points out,[1] was obtained in the first half of the eighteenth century by keeping down the key; as the damper acted only when the jack fell down, the string continued to vibrate whilst the jack was kept raised. But in some later instruments independent dampers were sometimes added. The clavichord had cloth threaded in and out of the strings to damp the after sounds. Schröter's two authentic models were

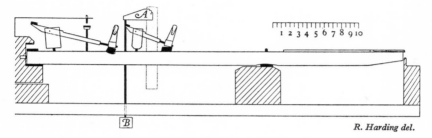

R. Harding del.

Fig. 32. Square pianoforte by Wilhelm Constantin Schiffer of Cologne, 1793 (Leipzig, No. 120). The drawing represents the action for the key F (compass F_1 to f''').

These additional hammers may be uncoupled by raising the Prelleiste *A* by a pedal attached to the lever *B*.

fitted with dampers but with no means to raise them. But many of the early German pianofortes were either without dampers or were provided with a means for raising them. Marius of Paris departed from the inevitable rule of dampers in his first two *Clavecins à Maillets*.

Hebenstreit, it will be remembered, visited Paris in 1705, where his pantaleon playing was no doubt heard by Marius. On his return, news of the wonderful effects that he obtained from his instrument spread throughout the Empire. We know from the evidence of Kuhnau that the blended harmonies mingling as it were in the air, when the strings were left *undamped*, were much admired.

Thus it may be concluded that the absence of dampers in a pianoforte or the presence of a damper-lifting device is due to the influence of Hebenstreit and his pantaleon; that the forte pedal was added to the pianoforte to enable the performer to obtain 'Pantaleon' effects.

[1] B 60.

The following are the most usual stops applied to the German pianofortes through the century:

Fortezug:	A mechanism for raising the dampers. Often divided in order that the treble and bass could be affected separately or together.
Pianozug: *Pianissi-* *mozug:*	A mechanism consisting of a strip of wood to which are glued tongues of leather about 2·50 cm. in length which are interposed between the hammers and the strings to the extent of half their length for piano and produced to their full extent to muffle a further length of string for pianissimo.
Piano[1] (alone): *Jeu Céleste;* *Jeu de buffle.*	A mechanism having the same principle as the above but with shorter strips of leather. Often divided in the same way as the forte.
Harfenzug: *Harp.*	A mechanism consisting of a strip of wood to which is attached a fringe of wool or silk which mingles with the strings and dries the tone.
Verschiebung: *Harmonica* *Keyboard* *Glide;* *Una Corda.*	A mechanism for sliding the keyboard laterally so that one only out of a pair of unison strings is struck or two out of three strings. It was most probably suggested by the Buff stop (known as *Lautenzug* on German harpsichords). Its value for facilitating tuning was soon discovered.
Schweller: *Swell.*	A mechanism for raising the plate of wood which lies over the strings in some square pianofortes, technically known as the dust plate or *Zwischendeckel*. It may also apply to a device for opening the lid or working a Venetian swell.
Lautenzug: *Lute.*	A mechanism consisting of a strip of wood covered with leather or cloth which is made to press upon the whole

extent of the strings either from above, or from below at a position immediate-ly in front of the hitch-pin bridge. It is sometimes made to act in two halves like the forte. (Fig.

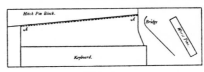

Fig. 33.

A, A indicates the position of the Lute stop.

33 shows the position of this stop in a square pianoforte.)

The 'Verschiebung' is introduced by Cristofori in his piano-forte of 1726.[2] Another well-known instance of its use occurs in Stein's pianoforte, the *String Harmonica*, where, in order to make the pianissimo fade away to nothing, he added another string to every pair of unisons. In ordinary playing all three strings were struck, but by means of a mechanism that moved the action

---

[1] Sometimes called *pianissimo*.
[2] See Chapter III, p. 28.

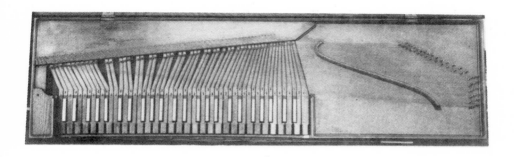

a

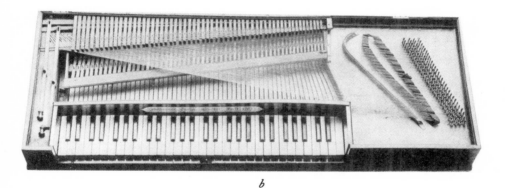

b

Plate V (*a*). Square 'Clavichord' Pianoforte at Stuttgart: Würtembergisches Landesgewerbemuseum.

The action is built within an oak case. Length 128·5 cm., breadth 34·7 cm., depth
9·9 cm. Height from the ground with the lid open 71 cm. The instrument is single
chord throughout. Compass: four octaves and a fourth C to f3. There are *no dampers*.
Vibrating length of the longest string 114 cm. Vibrating length of the shortest string
10·8 cm.

(*b*). Square Pianoforte bearing the inscription: Johannes Zumpe Londini Fecit
1767 (By courtesy of the Victoria and Albert Museum, London).

The two hand stops are for the purpose of raising the dampers in the bass and treble
respectively—'Forte stop'.

laterally—the 'Verschiebung', the hammers played upon the third string or 'Spinett' whilst the other strings vibrated sympathetically.

The sound faded gradually away and the tone acquired a new and brilliant character. In 1789 Stein sold this instrument for 100 louis d'or and received in addition a barrel of Rhine wine.

The Lute stop when used in connection with a set of pear wood hammers produces the illustration of the clavichord tone. Thus we sometimes see an instrument resembling a clavichord but with cembalo tone—a pianoforte which by a movement of the player's hand, knee or foot is instantaneously transformed into a clavichord. The economical value of such pianofortes will be recognised at once.

Directions for the use of stops in eighteenth-century printed music only occur as a rule in the case of the Forte, Piano, Pianissimo, and Una Corda (Verschiebung).[1]

The fact that there was a stop for Pianissimo leads us to conclude that although there were many pianofortes there were as yet few pianists.

The Casework of the German Pianofortes. On the whole the casework is remarkable for its elegance in the better class of instrument and particularly in the square pianofortes and pyramidal upright instruments.

An effort seems to have been made not only to construct pianofortes with an efficient action but to clothe these instruments in a case which should be a work of art. They are sometimes richly carved and ornamented in the Rococo style. Occasionally the whole case of a grand pianoforte is ornamented with marquetry, while the inner side of the lid in a square pianoforte is sometimes decorated with a pictorial scene, after the manner of the old clavichords and harpsichords (Plate VI).

The favourite woods used for the casework are walnut, mahogany, oak and cherry wood, whilst alder, pear, spruce and maple are also employed.

More than one wood is used in the more elaborate and costly instruments. A favourite combination seems to have been mahogany, walnut and cherry wood.

The keyboard is often remarkable for its beauty and the hand

---

[1] It is necessary to warn those who consult old German works about the construction of stops that they are frequently described under a wrong name. Thus Lautenzug is often found under the name of Harfenzug owing to a superficial likeness to the harp stop on the harpsichord.

of the artist craftsman is discernible in the cut of the keys. The rich ebony naturals sometimes have the forepart, which sinks out of sight when the key is down, decorated with a Gothic design and not infrequently painted or gilded, whilst the back of the keys is often shaped with the carver's knife to present a pleasing design. A typical set of keys for a square pianoforte is illustrated on Plate VII (b).

The length of the keys from front to back is shorter, both in German and other old pianofortes, than that of present time, owing to the custom of holding the hand in such a position that the thumb was placed a little in front of the naturals rather than over them, the fingers attacking them nearer to the front edge.

THE CRISTOFORI ACTION (1726)

(1)	(2)	(3)
*Cristofori (1726)	*Without intermediate lever. With or without check. (Stosszungenmechanik)	With jack in place of the escapement. (Stossmechanik)

THE GERMAN ACTION

(4)	(5)
Prellmechanik (primitive)	*Deutsche Mechanik (developed)

ANGLO-GERMAN ACTION

(6)	(7)
Primitive 'Anglo-German', *i.e. without* escapement. Called Stossmechanik	Developed 'Anglo-German', *i.e. with* escapement and usually thought to have originated by a union of (2) with (5) but actually developed from (6) under the influence of (2) and of (5), and is known in Germany as 'Die englische Mechanik'

* = With escapement.

N.B. The Cristofori types (2) and (3) became known as the English Action owing to the preference of the English for these forms. As there was more 'English' than 'German' in (7) it also became known as the 'englische Mechanik', but it is *not the same* as the English Grand Action.

Cristofori's Action was modified in two ways:

(1) By the omission of the intermediate lever.

(2) By the substitution of a jack in place of the escapement.

A desire to combine the lightness of touch of the German Action with the powerful tone obtained with the Cristofori (later called the English Action) led to a combination of these actions. This is the Anglo-German Action, the principle of which may be summarised as follows: the hammer is pivoted to a rail behind the back end of the key. Its head points in German fashion towards the front of the instrument. Motion is transmitted from the key to the hammer in one of two ways:

(1) *By a jack* in the oldest instruments. (This does not seem to have been recognised as a primitive type of the 'englische Mechanik' and it is still called 'Stossmechanik'.)

(2) *By an escapement* in the later instruments. (This developed combination is called the 'englische Mechanik' because it embodied all the principles of the English Grand Action, a modified form of the Cristofori Action; the only difference being in the position of the hammer.)

CHAPTER IV

THE TANGENT ACTION AND THE CEMBALO STOP

EVERY device that mechanical genius could contrive was applied to the harpsichord in order to render its tone more expressive.

Pascal Taskin reintroduced a register of jacks quilled with soft leather to soften the tone.[1]

A pedal was arranged to enable the player to swell or diminish the sound by gradually raising or lowering a portion of the lid. The same effect was improved by an invention made in Germany and later patented under the name of 'Venetian swell' by Shudi in England,[2] by means of which variation in tone was obtained by opening or closing a mechanism resembling a Venetian blind in the same way as upon the swell organ.

The harpsichord makers carried the war even farther into the enemy's country by taking the pianoforte and adding it to their instruments as one of many changes of the tone colour. Marius of Paris was the first to combine the two instruments;[3] in his fourth *Clavecin à Maillets* (1716), there was a set of hammers in addition to the jacks.

Weltman,[4] in 1759, invented a harpsichord with *a kind of jack, which instead of plucking the strings strikes these from below* in addition to the ordinary action. He also provided a new and *singular* effect by using the dampers belonging to the hammer action upon the strings plucked by the jacks. Two knee pedals which could be used together or separately to work the 'sourdines' were arranged chiefly for the purpose of diminishing the volume of sound at the cadences.

Joseph Merlin, a mathematical instrument maker, residing in London, patented a harpsichord in 1774 to which he had added a set of sixty hammers clothed with leather and cloth,[5] and in 1792 John Geib invented *A New Musical Instrument, the End and invention of which is to play the Pianoforte, Clavichord, or Spinnett,*

---

[1] In 1768.
[2] C 804.
[3] See Chapter II, p. 14, Fig. 7.
[4] B 5, volume for 1766, p. 161.
[5] C 846.

with two Sets of Keys, to which either of these Three Instruments may be joined together, etc.[1]

A compromise was effected when Humphrey Walton, an English musical-instrument-maker, invented in 1787 a grand pianoforte in which little jacks capped with leather or cloth were thrown up against the strings, striking them from below instead of plucking them from the side. The tone could be varied according to the impetus given to the jacks, or "perpendicular hammers" as he calls them, by pressure on the key. His invention consists in using the ordinary square pianoforte action and employing the hammers as levers to throw up the jacks (Fig. 34).

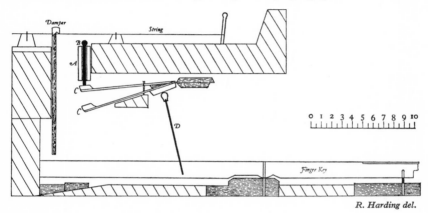

Fig. 34. Tangent Action for grand pianoforte. Humphrey Walton, 1787. (Drawn from the patent.)

A, section of the frame through which the "perpendicular hammer", *B,* works. "This hammer projects from the top and bottom of the frame about one quarter of an inch." "(The top of this hammer must be covered with leather or cloth.)" *C C* are "hammers made the same as hammers in the common or square pianofortes only made flat on the top where they hit the perpendicular hammers". *D* is the jack.

Walton's invention seems, however, to have been anticipated by the founder of the well-known firm of Späth and Schmahl of Ratisbon, Franz Jacob Späth. But Dr Heinrich Herrmann states, in his interesting monograph on Späth and Schmahl, that he has not discovered any tangent-pianoforte by Späth, all those instruments by the firm of Späth and Schmahl being by Späth's son-in-law and former partner, Christoph Friedrich Schmahl, and made between 1790 and 1800[2] (Fig. 34 *a*).

[1] C 842.   [2] B 48, S.24.

Welcker von Gontershausen mentions a similar type of instrument being made by Hopkinson of Paris as early as 1780.[1]

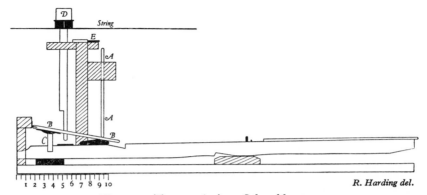

Fig. 34*a*. Tangent Action. Schmahl, 1795.

A, tangent; *B*, intermediate lever; *C*, jack; *D*, damper; *E*, piano stop.

An independent discovery of a similar tangent action seems to have been made in Sicily some time between the years 1767 and 1773:

> A Catane, en Sicile, un prêtre napolitain a inventé plusieurs clavecins singuliers. Dans l'un, les sautereaux viennent *marteler* la corde avec tant de vivacité, qu'ils lui sont rendu un son aussi fort, aussi brillant que le pincement de la plume, sans en avoir le glapissement, et laissent au musicien la facilité du forte-piano, par le plus ou moins de force à battre sur la touche... il a encore l'avantage en fatiguant moins la corde, de ne lui faire presque jamais perdre son accord.[2]

Weltman of Paris seems to have made a still earlier use of the Tangent Action. In the description of his clavecin submitted to l'Académie Royale des Sciences de Paris in 1759 we find that, in addition to the ordinary jacks, there are "marteaux; espèce de sautereaux qui, au lieu de pincer les cordes, les frappent en dessous".[3] But the invention of the Tangent Action rests with Schröter, whose action of 1739 with the 'optical amusement' is undoubtedly the earliest example.[4]

It has been suggested that the tangent was an adaptation of the clavichord tangent, but it seems more probable that the harpsichord

[1] B 94, S. 115.   [2] B 92, p. 283.

[3] B 5, Année 1759, *Mécanique: Machines approu. en* 1759, pp. 241, 242.

[4] See Chapter III, Sect. I, pp. 19 and 20, Figs. 9 and 10 (see also B 48).

jack suggested this arrangement; and the quotations cited above seem to confirm this idea. Although these instruments resemble the harpsichord in tone they are usually called pianofortes, owing to their power of dynamic expression.

Two other ways of imitating the harpsichord on the pianoforte remain to be described.

The first consists in providing two hammers for every note. One hammer is of wood, that is to say unclothed, whilst the other hammer is capped with a pad of leather. The wooden hammer gives the cembalo (*i.e.* the harpsichord) tone, whilst the leather hammer gives the usual pianoforte tone. The hammers are pivoted

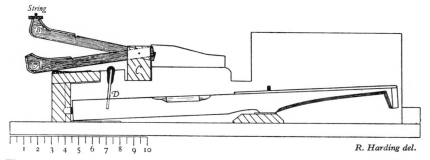

R. *Harding del.*

Fig. 35. Square pianoforte in the Musikhistorisches Museum Neupert in Nuremberg, with two hammers for every note. The drawing represents the action for the key C (compass C to f‴).

A, hammer of wood, *i.e.* unclothed; *B*, hammer clothed with a pad of leather; *C*, sliding rail, to which the hammers are pivoted; *D*, the jack.

to a sliding rail to enable the performer to use either set at will. This principle is exemplified in a very old square pianoforte in the Musikhistorisches Museum Neupert in Nuremberg (Fig. 35).

According to Thon[1] this is one of the ways of producing the forte and piano, but other pianofortes of this type have come to our notice. Two out of three are provided with a stop for subduing the sound. Dr Neupert's instrument has the Lute stop and No. 3194 in the Musée Instrumental du Conservatoire Royal de Musique at Brussels is provided with a stop for both the forte and the piano. No. 2040 in the same collection has no stops. Nevertheless this is sufficient indication that the hammers were not intended primarily for the purpose of obtaining the forte and piano.

Another method of producing the cembalo tone consisted in adding to the pianoforte a device known as the Cembalo stop. The

[1] B 91, S. 67.

earliest instance of it occurs in the Silbermann pianoforte in the Stadt Schloss at Potsdam.

This stop consists of five single parts which are arranged in a frame. The lower side of the three parts lying over the bass is edged with a strip of ivory whilst the lower sides of the two parts lying over the treble are edged with a strip of brass. The thickness of these strips is graded from 6 mm. in the bass to $\frac{1}{2}$ mm. in the treble.[1]

The cembalo tone is produced by lowering the strips upon the strings in front of the dampers. The pressure is regulated by springs and screws. Another form of this stop was patented by Samuel Bury of London in 1788[2] and consisted in interposing 'strips of cloth, leather or parchment' on the upper sides of which were fixed 'small pieces of whalebone, or any hard substance' between the hammers and the strings in such a way that the hammers struck the strips against the strings. The strips were attached to a sliding board and could be drawn off at will.

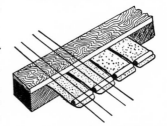

Fig. 36. The Cembalo Stop (second type).

A fine example of this stop, with strips of leather to which are glued pieces of ivory, occurs in a grand pianoforte presented by Fräulein A. von Ebel in Hoheneck to the Musical Instrument Department of the Württembergisches Landesgewerbemuseum at Stuttgart.[3] According to family tradition it was used by Queen Louise at the house of von Auerswald, at that time 'Oberpräsident' in Königsberg. Probably it was introduced into this instrument as a humorous effect calculated to raise a titter amongst those accustomed to regard the harpsichord as old-fashioned.

[1] This information, together with drawings of the action and stop and photographs of the instrument, was communicated by a friend at Berlin. I personally inspected the instrument but was unable to see or hear the stop, as no mechanic was available.

[2] C 772.   [3] B 57, S. 48.

Plate VI. The oldest known example of a Square Pianoforte. Johann Söcher, 1742.
Musikhistorisches Museum Neupert in Nuremberg.

CHAPTER V

THE PIANOFORTE IN ENGLAND

§ I

ALTHOUGH England was to take a distinguished part in the development of the pianoforte she did not begin to construct this type of instrument to any great extent until about the year 1760.

According to tradition Father Wood, an English monk at Rome, built a pianoforte in 1711 which he sold to Samuel Crisp, a friend of Dr Johnson.

Crisp eventually sold it to Fulke Greville for one hundred guineas and it became famous as the only one of its kind in London, being evidently regarded as a great curiosity. Plenius, the harpsichord maker, obtained permission to copy it and seems to have attempted to found a pianoforte business, but the preference for the harpsichord obliged him to give up this project. There can be little doubt that the action of Father Wood's pianoforte, copied

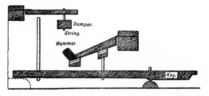

Fig. 37. Mason's Action. From Rimbault: slightly modified for the sake of clarity.

by Plenius, was a reproduction of Cristofori's earlier experiment, and it is interesting to note that there were two attempts to copy this action and that both were unsuccessful.[1]

The Rev. William Mason, poet and composer, returned to England in 1755 from a tour in Germany with a little pianoforte he had bought at Hamburg. Hitherto only pianofortes in the form of a horizontal harpsichord had been built and it is probable that Mason now attempted to introduce the square. The type of action that he suggested to the English makers was the simplified form of the Cristofori action invented by Zumpe or by Silbermann (Fig. 37). For some years it was thought in England that Mason

[1] Silbermann's first two pianofortes were probably copies of the earliest Cristofori Action; he was a friend of König and no doubt saw his translation of Maffei's description of Cristofori's Gravicembali in Mattheson's *Musikalische Kritik* (Band III, S. 340, Hamburg, 1725). It will be recalled that these early instruments were severely criticised by J. S. Bach.

himself was the inventor, and the action illustrated in Fig. 37 was known as 'Mason's' action. The arrival of Johann Christian Bach in London in 1759 gave a great stimulus to pianoforte building, as it was well known that he preferred this instrument to the harpsichord or clavichord.

A German named Viator and the Dutchman, Americus Backers, attempted to improve the action, preparing the way for a party of professional pianoforte makers who arrived from Germany during the following year.

The Seven Years' War had put an end to pianoforte building in Saxony. The workshops were disbanded and the men were forced to seek employment elsewhere. A party of twelve, several of whom came from Silbermann's workshop, arrived in England in

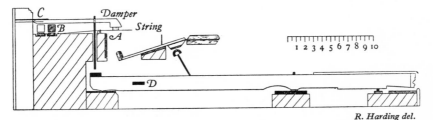

R. Harding del.

Fig. 38. Single action by Pohlmann, 1784. (From a pianoforte in the possession of Mr W. J. Moore, Cambridge.)

A, lute stop; B, one of the levers for raising the dampers; C, spring of whalebone serving to expedite the return of the damper; D, lead weight.

the year 1760, bringing with them the Cristofori tradition. Johannes Zumpe, a pupil of Silbermann, was one of the company. His arrival in England was an event of national importance, for the art of pianoforte building commenced soon after he entered the service of the harpsichord maker, Burkat Shudi.

The following year John Broadwood came from the north of England to London, where he became attached to Shudi as a harpsichord maker. Eight years later he married Barbara Shudi and in 1770 he became Shudi's partner. In this way the distinguished house of John Broadwood and Sons was founded.

As a description of Zumpe's action has already been given, it is unnecessary to describe it further. His square pianofortes, for he made no other kind, became the rage. Everyone who considered himself to be a person of fashion had a pianoforte as a matter of course. The square instruments of Johannes Pohlmann became nearly as celebrated as those of Zumpe (Fig. 38). He fixed the usual combination of from two to three hand stops, placing them on the left-hand side within the case. These were to raise the dampers in the bass and treble respectively and to secure the action of the Lute. Occasionally he used also a pedal to raise a portion of the lid to obtain a swell. Pohlmann made a pianoforte for Glück in 1772 and Crotch, when a child, played upon one of his instruments at a concert given at Leicester in 1782.

Owing to the preference of the English for this type of action it was called the 'English Single Action' in spite of the fact that it was invented by Silbermann, or Zumpe his pupil, in Germany.

A modification of the English Single Action is found in square pianofortes by Schoene and Co., who were successors to Zumpe at the premises in Hanover Square (Fig. 39). In this action the

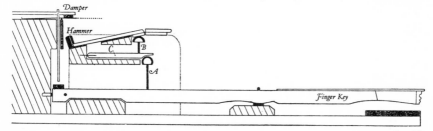

R. Harding del.

Fig. 39. Square pianoforte by Schoene and Co. 1793, showing *Zumpe's second action*. *A*, first jack; *B*, second jack; *C*, intermediate lever.

jack does not act directly against the hammer, for a lever carrying a second jack is interposed between them. The purpose seems to be to facilitate repetition and to prevent blocking, as the intermediate lever with its jack falls back *before* the hammer actually touches the string just as the hopper escapes before the hammer has made its blow. Whether Schoene invented this action is uncertain, but we have observed it in a pianoforte by Zumpe dated 1788 in the Museum of the Conservatoire of Music[1] in Paris (No. 377) and this evidence, together with the fact that Schoene and Co. advertised themselves as 'Successors to Johannes Zumpe', seems to indicate that this action was invented by Zumpe himself. It is called therefore *Zumpe's second action* to distinguish it from his first—the 'Single Action'.

[1] Other examples: Paris, No. 342, Freudenthaler of Paris; M. Paul Brunold, Organist of St Gervaise, Paris; Schoene and Co. 1788. Brussels, No. 1622, Ermel of Brussels, 1818. Victoria and Albert Museum, London, unsigned example.

The Single Action is susceptible of variation with regard to the method of damping. The type of damper used by Zumpe and Pohlmann and in the earliest Broadwood pianofortes is called the 'over damper' (Hebeldämpfung), whereas the type of damping shown in the following diagram (Fig. 40) is known as the 'crank damper'.

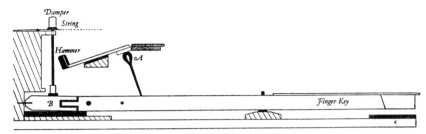

R. Harding del.

Fig. 40. Single Action with *crank* damper by Longman and Broderip, about 1780 (in the possession of Mr W. J. Moore, Cambridge).

A, jack; *B*, damper *crank* hinged to the back of the case and fitting on to the key· The damper stick is fastened to the crank by a strip of leather and the whole apparatus can be slightly raised in order to clear the string when 'forte' is required. The two black spots on the key represent lead weights.

Another type of damping used in the Single Action was patented by Southwell of Dublin in 1794 and is known as the 'Irish damper'. The damper stick is hinged directly to the key itself. Thus when the key is depressed the 'back end' is raised and lifts the damper up and away from the string. When the key is released the damper falls with it and is pressed by the weight of the key upon the string. The 'forte' stop could only be fitted with the greatest difficulty if at all.

The under damper is also found in connection with the Single Action. Broadwood obtained a patent for it in 1783 (Fig. 41).

No patent was taken out for the Single Action, but one was obtained for the 'English Double Action' in 1786 by John Geib, a workman employed by Longman and Broderip. Geib was probably a German. His Double Action is a modified form of the '1726' Cristofori Action. He gives two drawings in his patent. The second one shows hammers with heads similar to those of Marius' first clavecin. The Double Action was used for the better class of square pianofortes, but the two forms were offered by good makers for some little time after the beginning of the nineteenth century. Both the Single and Double Actions were copied by makers in France and in Italy. But eventually the Double Action superseded the Single Action in England.

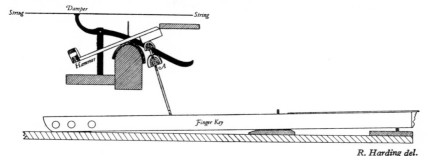

R. Harding del.

Fig. 41. Broadwood's Single Action with under-damper action, 1783 (in the possession of Messrs John Broadwood and Sons, London).

The damper is made of brass. Its counterweight rests upon *A*, a block of wood covered with leather. When the key is depressed the block *A* lifts the damper away from the string.

A typical example of the Double Action from a square piano-forte by Broadwood is illustrated below (Fig. 42).

The English Grand Action is, again, another modification of Cristofori's Action. The intermediate lever is omitted and the

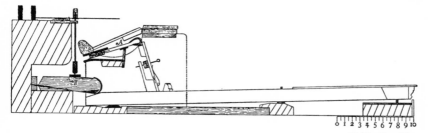

R. Harding del.

Fig. 42. English Double Action by John Broadwood and Sons, about 1815.

There is an escapement which was known as the hopper, a shortened form of 'grass-hopper', the name under which it was patented by Geib. The escapement (hopper) works under an intermediate lever *A*, called the 'under hammer'; *B* is the damper crank which lies over the key: its weight keeps the damper pressed down upon the strings, and by this means there is no difficulty in raising the dampers.

escapement (hopper)[1] acts directly against the hammer butt. Either a crank damper or an over damper is used.

The earliest drawing of this action appears in a patent for a

---

[1] Geib patented his improved escapement under the name of 'Jack' but it has been classified as an escapement in Appendix C, since it is an escapement and not a jack.

combined pianoforte and harpsichord by Robert Stodart, dated
1777. James Shudi Broadwood, writing to the *Gentleman's
Magazine* in 1812, attributed it to Backers and places the date of
the invention as early as 1772, but in his MS. notes printed for
private circulation he gives the date as 1776. Henry Fowler Broadwood, in some footnotes to his father's statement in the MS. notes,
declares that his grandfather, John Broadwood, with his apprentice
Robert Stodart, assisted Backers to perfect this action.[1] Pierre
Érard states that the authorship of the invention is uncertain and
that even the London makers themselves were in doubt about the

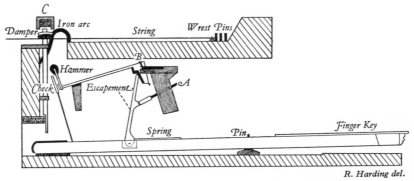

R. Harding del.

Fig. 43. English Grand Action by John Broadwood and Sons, dated 1795 (formerly
in the possession of Messrs Miller and Son, Cambridge).

A, screw to regulate the play of the escapement or hopper; *B*, screw binding the
hammer to a wire pivot: by unscrewing it the hammer can be removed; *C*, ruler or
rail to regulate the action of the dampers (a relic of the harpsichord ruler to prevent
the jacks from jumping out). The check catches and holds the hammer after it has
fallen from the strings, to prevent it from rebounding against them. The check acts
only so long as the key is pressed down.

matter. It is certain at least that the English Grand Action was
first made by Messrs Broadwood. Beethoven preferred it to the
German (or Viennese Action) and made no secret of the fact when
he received the gift of a grand pianoforte from them in 1807
(Fig. 43).

Some makers thought that a pianoforte with a down-striking
action remained in tune longer than one with the ordinary action;
for the up-striking action tended to force the string up and away
from the bridge and in this way to put it out of tune. The down-
striking action, on the other hand, struck the string towards the

[1] B 49 (*f*), p. 156.

bridge and did away with this disadvantage. Makers began to experiment once more with the down-striking action, and amongst them George Pether, of London.

But it is doubtful whether Pether was concerned with the problem of keeping his instrument in tune or whether he was attempting to solve a mechanical problem as yet unsolved. Whatever his aim, Pether has designed a beautiful action, very light to the touch and with a good tone (Fig. 44). He has simply inverted the *Prellmechanik* and poised his hammer by means of a lead weight in such a position that the hammer is lifted up by it without the necessity of using a spring. The damper is fixed to the key and mutes the vibrations of the strings as the key returns to its position of rest.

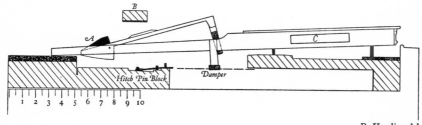

R. Harding del.

Fig. 44. Pether's Down-striking Action (Leipzig, No. 142). The drawing represents the action for the key C (compass C to f''').

A, lead weight; *B*, Prelleiste; *C*, hollow space to lighten the key.

The English pianoforte makers were beginning to discover that the mysterious thing called 'touch' was a matter of considerable importance.

The touch of the harpsichord differed from that of the clavichord, whilst both differed considerably from the touch of the pianoforte. The touch on the German pianoforte was lighter than that of the English instruments, where the key 'fall' was deeper.

The touch of the same pianoforte would appear to be heavy or light according to whether the player possessed a strong or weak hand. Walton seems to have been the first to take this matter into consideration. In 1787 he arranged a screw to regulate the touch[1] and he was followed by Ball in 1790.[2] Crang Hancock patented an action with 'spring key touch' in the same year[3] and built it in

[1] C 1234.   [2] C 1235.   [3] C 13.

grand and smaller instruments, though he had been using it since 1782 (Fig. 45 and Plate VII (*a*)).

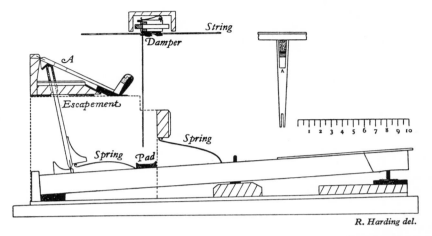

R. *Harding del.*

Fig. 45. Hancock's action with 'Spring Key Touch', 1782, from a pianoforte in the Collection of Messrs John Broadwood and Sons.

This is a modified form of the Anglo-German Action. The hopper escapes through a hole in the hammer shank at *A*. The damper is fitted with a spring which keeps it pressed tightly to the strings. The spring touch is effected by a brass spring fixed to the key in front of the balance pin and fitting under a rail on the key frame.

This action is built within a spinet-shaped case and Hancock, who evidently had the historic sense, makes his keyboard with the traditional short octave in imitation of these instruments. The compass is five octaves, F to f‴ with the lowest F sharp omitted.

Hitherto mention has been made only of horizontal pianofortes, but three patents were granted for upright instruments. They must briefly be discussed.

In the year 1787 Landreth patented an action with escapement and check for an upright pianoforte showing Cristofori's influence (Fig. 46).[1] Unfortunately, there is no drawing of the case and as there is, as far as we know, no upright pianoforte by this maker in existence, it is impossible to form any opinion as to its appearance.

Stodart brought out his upright grand pianoforte "in the form of a bookcase" in 1795. Haydn called at his shop in Lad Lane

[1] C 10.

a

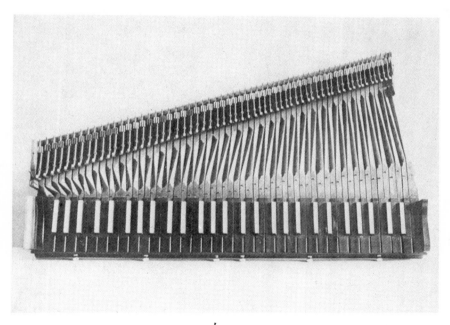

b

Plate VII (*a*). Crang Hancock Pianoforte dated 1782 (in the possession of Messrs John Broadwood and Sons). The pedal is for the purpose of raising the dampers, *e.g.* 'forte'. The case is in walnut with brass hinges. Compass five octaves less F sharp; F to f3. Length of the long side 182·1 cm. Depth with cover open 22·1 cm. There is no number. A modification of this type of instrument, known as the *Querflügel*, was made extensively in Germany.

(*b*). Keyboard of a Pianoforte by J. G. Mahr, 1774, showing the black natural keys typical of German instruments. No. 818. Tafelklavier, Hochschule für Musik, Berlin.

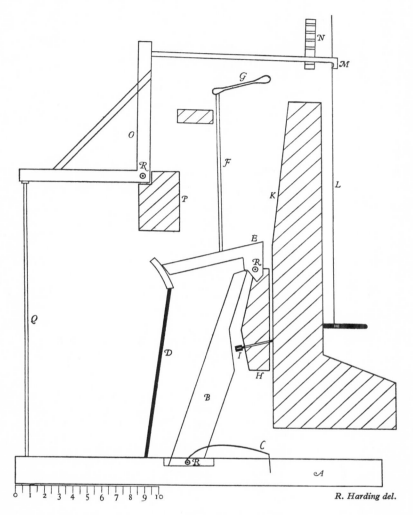

Fig. 46. Upright pianoforte action. John Landreth, 1787. (Drawn from the patent.)

A, key; *B*, jack or lever (escapement); *C*, spring; *D*, check; *E*, hammer tail; *F*, hammer shank; *G*, hammer head; *H*, hammer rail; *I*, button to regulate the jack (escapement); *K*, wrest-pin block; *L*, string; *M*, damper; *N*, socket in which the damper moves; *O*, crank; *P*, crank rail; *Q*, 'sticker which moves the crank and lifts the damper from the string'; *R*, *R*, *R*, centres in which 'cork is introduced or woolly substance manufactured after the manner of a hat' (to prevent the pieces from rattling).

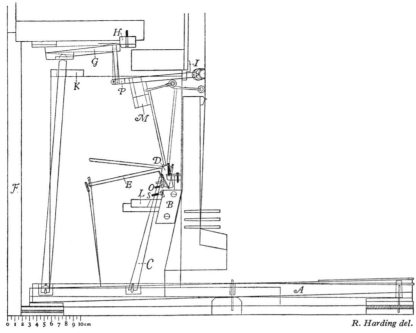

Fig. 47. Upright Grand pianoforte action by Stodart, 1795.
(The gauge gives the *approximate* size.)

Here follows description as on the patent.

A is a Key precisely upon the usual Principle. *B* a Rail upon which the Hammers
are centred. *C* a Lever the means of raising the Hammer *D* to its acting Elevation
from whence it is again relieved by the Button *O* (which Button is regulated by a Screw
or by a similar Button represented by the Letter *S* the Hammer being thus relieved
returns to its inactive Position by virtue of the Weight *E*; the Weight is formed of
Wood, Metal or any other Substance the Inventor may prefer; its Form that described
by *E* or any other that Experience may point out as most convenient.

F a Lever commanding the Damper *G* which Damper is annexed to the Rail *H*
by means of a Hinge of Vellum, Leather, Parchment or any other similar Material
or Substance or by a Centre.

P a Joint of the Damper covered with Leather to prevent noise and acting upon
a centre or Hinge of Leather, Vellum &c.ª similar to that described by the Letter H
The Damper after acting is returned by the Weight of that part marked *G* and
like the Weight *E* is both in Form and Substance under the Control of the Inventor;
thus the grand Principle of Action is that both the Hammers and Dampers after
performing are returned by Weight.

L a Socket the means of regulating the Lever *C*.

K a Ditto for the Lever *F*.

I a Ditto for the Damper *C*.

M a Rail upon which the Hammer *D* rests.   (*William Stodart.*)

to see it and expressed himself delighted with the new possibilities it foreshadowed in case-making and with the quality of the tone.

In appearance the instrument was simply a grand pianoforte vertically encased in a rectangular cupboard and placed upon a stand with four legs. Two pedals, one for 'piano' (Verschiebung; Una Corda) and the other for 'forte', were fixed in the centre of the stand. The doors opened, and in the unoccupied space

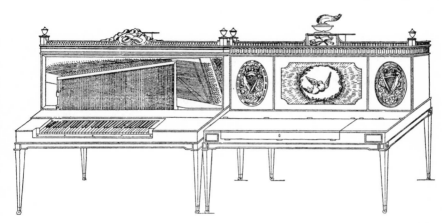

Fig. 48. Upright pianoforte by William Southwell of Dublin, 1798. From the patent. The arms of Ireland should be noted.

within shelves were placed, on which music could be stored[1] (Plate VIII).

These pianofortes were often very elaborate, with glass doors and panelling. They began to go out of fashion at about the end of the first quarter of the nineteenth century. How much they influenced pianoforte building in other countries is uncertain. There are examples of the rectangular case amongst the French patents and at least one copy of an upright grand pianoforte was made by Johann Söderberg of Stockholm in 1808.[2]

In 1798 Southwell, the inventor of the Irish Damper, brought out a patent for "certain new improvements in the action and

[1] See F, p. 378–9, for a detailed account of the cost of an upright grand pianoforte built by Broadwood in 1828.

[2] It is exhibited in the music department of the Landesgewerbemuseum at Stuttgart.

construction of pianofortes and other musical instruments".[1] He placed a square pianoforte on its side upon a stand. The front, as shown in his drawing, is covered in, and decorative panels are introduced (Fig. 48). As the striking point of the hammers is at the top of the instrument these had to be connected to the keys by wooden rods or 'stickers' worked by a jack. Each damper works through a hole in the sound-board immediately behind the strings, and is connected by a sticker to the back end of the key. The uppermost treble notes have no dampers as is usual. This is the primitive form of an action afterwards to become well known as the 'Sticker Action'. The hammers can be moved to one string without the necessity of shifting the keyboard, and a pedal to raise the dampers is added (Fig. 48a).

In the meantime experiments were being made to improve the tone of the pianoforte; in the first place by improving the covering for the hammer heads and striking place, also by improvements to the sound-board. The old habit of using leather alone was being superseded by the practice of using leather as the foundation, whilst the surface was covered with cloth. Bury in 1788 patented hammers in which "felt, cloth, wool, or anything elastic" should be used "under the leather upon the hammer".[2]

In order to equalise the tension on the bridges of the square pianoforte, John Broadwood in 1783[3] transferred the wrest pins from off the sound-board to the left side of the back of the case and added a second sound-board beneath the original one and connected to it by a sound post for the purpose of enhancing the tone, whilst in the grand pianoforte he divided the bridge, giving the bass strings a bridge to themselves. Garcka, anxious to make his sound-board as large as possible, placed his wrest plank and pins immediately in front of the name board. By this means he was able to extend the sound-board from end to end of the instrument.[4]

The striking place affects the tone since "the hammer abolishes the node at the striking place, and with it the particle belonging to it throughout the string". In this way the tone can be brightened or made hollow according to the taste of the maker. Hipkins states that

Harpsichords and spinets. . .had no fixed point for plucking the strings. It was generally from about one-half to one-seventh of the vibrating length, and although it had been observed by Huyghens and the Antwerp harpsi-

[1] C 20.   [2] C 544.
[3] C 1286.   [4] C 1287.

Plate VIII. Stodart's Upright Grand Pianoforte. Berlin, Hochschule für Musik, No. 15.

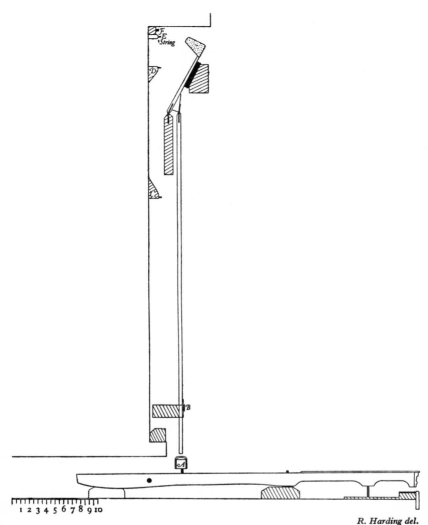

Fig. 48*a*. Primitive 'Sticker' Action, probably by Southwell of Dublin, about 1798 (Paris, 1081).[1] The drawing represents the action for one of the upper treble keys (compass F_1 to c'''').

A, jack; *B*, pin which can be turned to release the sticker; *C*, *D*, the two ends of the curved bridge seen edgeways; *E*, wrest-plank bridge pin; *F*, hitch pin.

---

[1] In the Catalogue of the Museum of the Conservatoire de Musique in Paris, this instrument is attributed to John Barclay, owing to the fact that his name is inscribed upon it in various places. This is, however, of no consequence, since the merchant frequently inscribes or stamps his name on an instrument. The arms of Ireland appear in the fretwork of the upper right-hand corner of the resonance body and although the action is not exactly as in Southwell's patent there is a strong resemblance to Southwell's pianoforte of 1798.

chord maker, Jan Couchet, that a difference of quality of tone could be obtained by varying the plucking place on the same string, which led to the so-called lute stop of the eighteenth century, no attempt appears to have been made to gain a uniform striking place throughout the scale. Thus in the latest improved spinet, a Hitchcock, of early eighteenth-century, in my possession, the striking place of the c's varies from one-half to one-seventh, and in the latest improved harpsichord, a Kirkman of 1773, also in my possession, the striking distances vary from one-half to one-tenth and for the lute stop from one-ninth to one-twenty-ninth of the string, the longest distances in the bass of course, but all without apparent rule or proportion. Nor was any attempt to gain a uniform striking place made in the first pianofortes. Stein of Augsburg (the favourite pianoforte maker of Mozart, and of Beethoven in his virtuoso time) knew nothing of it, at least in his early instruments. The great length of the bass strings as carried out on the single belly-bridge copied from the harpsichord, made a reasonable striking place for that part of the scale impossible.

John Broadwood, about the year 1788, was the first to try to equalise the scale in tension and striking place. He called in scientific aid, and assisted by Signor Cavallo and the then Dr Gray of the British Museum, he produced a divided belly-bridge, which shortening the too great length of the bass strings, permitted the establishment of a striking place, which, in intention, should be proportionate to the length of the string throughout. He practically adopted a ninth of the vibrating length of the string for his striking place, allowing some latitude in the treble. This division of the belly-bridge became universally adopted, and with it an approximately rational striking place.[1]

Experimental Keyboards. In England in the eighteenth century, undoubtedly mean tone temperament seems to have been the usual custom.

No doubt Zumpe, finding that unequal temperament tuning was customary in England, was at first obliged to conform to it, but in one of his instruments he provides the necessary additional notes without which modulation to any but nearly related keys would be intolerable. This pianoforte is dated 1766 and is in the possession of Messrs John Broadwood and Sons. In order to introduce the additional notes Zumpe divides some of the black keys. This practice was, of course, well known and had been used in Italy in the seventeenth century. The instrument is bichord with a compass extending from G_1 to f''' with the lowest G sharp omitted. Although *all* the black keys *appear* to be divided the divisions actually begin from E flat and extend to a sharp (Plate IX).

Clagget in 1788[2] invented a pianoforte which he called the

[1] B 46, footnote, p. 77.
[2] C 932. Dr K. Chr. Fr. Krause of Dresden had an instrument made for him by Rosenkranz of Dresden, in which all the keys were on the same level and of the same breadth and colour.

'Telio-chordon'. Every octave could be divided into thirty-nine gradations of sound and any key could be made to sound one of these degrees of intonation. In order to produce these variations he added two extra bridges placed nearer to the hammers, "but in a just proportion to the musical division of the string suited to the tone" needed. Movable bars of wood or metal were arranged directly over the bridges, within proper guides so that they would descend exactly parallel. These bars were pressed upon the strings by means of pedals. In this way the original bridge lost its power which was transferred to the secondary bridges or bars. "By this means", he states, "the temperature of the thirds and fifths can be highly improved and what is called the 'wolfe' is entirely done away." Clagget is, of course, thinking of the mean tone system where the fifths and thirds are a quarter of a comma flat.

In order to facilitate the playing of shakes and trills in which the music of this period abounds Clagget arranged a keyboard in which all the keys were the same length and breadth and level. They were rounded at the top like a fan and were to be one-sixth of an inch in distance from each other and to have the same distinguishing colours as usual. By means of this arrangement he states that one mode of fingering could be used for all the keys, that the shake was always even and much easier whilst there was not any danger of touching one key for another.

The inventions described above constitute the most important improvements in pianoforte building in England during the eighteenth century. They were made in response to the increasing demand for improved pianofortes; for that instrument was rapidly superseding the harpsichord in the popular estimation for solo performances; but the harpsichord was still preferred as an accompaniment to the voice and was retained in the theatres on that account, but even then it was soon destined to be deposed by the new instrument.

§ II

The pianoforte was first brought to the notice of the English public at a benefit concert for Miss Brickler on May 16th, 1767, when Dibdin accompanied songs upon it,[1] but it was first introduced as a *solo* instrument in 1768 by Johann Christian Bach at a concert "for the benefit of Mr Fischer". On this occasion Bach used a Zumpe square pianoforte for which he had paid £50.[2]

[1] B 84, p. 133.   [2] B 90, p. 113.

Michael Arne presided at the pianoforte during the performances of 'Lionel and Clarissa' in 1779.[1]

Drury Lane had an official pianist[2] in 1770 and a few years
later Griffith Jones was appointed to this office at Covent Garden.
By 1795 a pianoforte was introduced into the King's Band.

A large amount of music was written for "Harpsichord or
Piano Forte" but as we approach the year 1800 the heading is
frequently reversed and we read "for Piano Forte" often printed
in large letters whilst "or Harpsichord" if not omitted is often
printed in smaller type. Dr Burney published the first pianoforte
duets in 1777. These duets were to be performed by two persons
at *one* pianoforte not upon different instruments as hitherto. This
was an invention of considerable importance and had far-reaching
effects on the development of the keyboard and also on pianoforte
technique.

The widespread interest in the orchestra stimulated by the
works of Haydn and Mozart and numerous imitators led to two-
and four-hand pianoforte reductions being made of their works.
The craze for these appears to have come in about the year 1800
though reductions with additional accompaniment were made even
earlier. The pianoforte was thus turned into a substitute for the
orchestra. The keyboard of the instrument had to be extended
in order to keep pace with the compass of the orchestra, thus the
compass of the horizontal grand pianoforte is always five and a half
to six octaves at the end of the century. Square pianofortes were
constructed with 'additional keys' to meet this demand for a wider
range. The words "For pianoforte with additional keys" are
frequently printed upon the title-page of the music of this period
and there is sometimes an alternative version of the music itself
for the pianoforte with the additional keys.

William Southwell of Dublin first thought of adding these extra
notes to the square pianoforte in 1794.[3] These keys run underneath the sound-board and are partly separated from the others by
a partition. A hole is made in the sound-board for the hammers to
pass through to the strings which are differently arranged. Those
strings which belong to the additional keys are often hitched over
pins embedded in a cavity cut out in the back of the case in order
not to encroach upon the sound-board, while the keys themselves
are attached to a separate frame (Plate X).

[1] Composed by Dibdin and performed in London about the year 1768.
[2] Mr Burney, a nephew of Dr Burney.   [3] C 645.

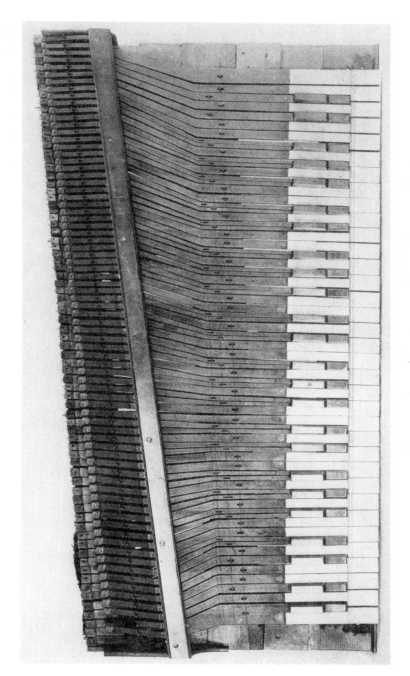

Plate IX. Pianoforte by Zumpe, 1766 (in the possession of Messrs John Broadwood and Sons).

In 1797 Harrison began to publish his *Pianoforte Magazine*. It was to be complete in 250 weekly numbers at a cost of 2*s*. 6*d*. each and to contain 100 guineas' worth of music. Each number was to contain a note of hand signed by Harrison and these 250 notes could be handed in to the publishers for a "Brilliant toned and elegant Piano Forte, far superior to many instruments sold for twenty-five guineas each". A specimen pianoforte was kept in the shop for inspection.

The public was kept well supplied with music, for Pleyel, Corri and Dussek's *Musical Journal* began to be published in the same year.

The passion for the pianoforte is further illustrated by the fact that, whenever possible, keys were fitted to other instruments after the manner of a pianoforte. The English (keyed) guitar came into fashion about the year 1770. Its vogue was so great as almost to ruin the harpsichord and spinet makers. Kirkman is said to have saved the situation by purchasing cheap examples and presenting them to the milliner girls and street singers. Christian Claus[1] obtained a patent in 1783 for a keyed guitar to make it "the more capable of being played upon in the manner of a pianoforte".

In the following year William Jackson patented 'The British Lyre'.[2] It is a lyre with a keyboard and action for working hammers with two heads. One head is of wood and the other is of wood covered with leather. Either could be used at will. This miniature action was also fitted with dampers.

§ III

English Pianoforte Stops. The usual stops on a grand pianoforte were Forte and Una Corda (Verschiebung), (later called 'Piano' in England); whilst on a square pianoforte there were usually two hand stops to raise the dampers in the bass and treble respectively, and not infrequently in the better class of instruments a Lute stop was added.

The following is a list of stops used on English pianofortes during the eighteenth century.

Forte.　　A mechanism for raising the dampers:
          (1) By hand stops.
          (2) By a foot pedal patented by John Broadwood in 178.
          (No. 1379).

[1] I suggest this was the same Claus as the Clement Claus of Stuttgart who saile from London to America to set up as a pianoforte builder in that country.
[2] Eng. Pat. No. 1449.

(3) By a sliding board that throws up the dampers "whereby the tone becomes exactly similar to a DULCIMER and when drawn off...the instrument is then a perfect pianoforte"; patented by Bury in 1788 (No. 1637). What was said about Hebenstreit's dulcimer and how it probably suggested the forte or damper-lifting stop for the purpose of obtaining dulcimer effects on the pianoforte will be recalled.

Piano. A mechanism for interposing strips of "cloth, leather, or anything that will produce a sweet and mellow tone" between the hammers and the strings. Patented, but unnamed by Bury in 1788 (No. 1637). This is the same as the German 'Pianozug'.

A variation of this suggesting the 'Pianissimozug' was patented by Isaac Hawkins in 1800 (Eng. Pat. No. 2446): he describes the invention thus: "In all instruments when the tone is produced by hammers striking strings or bells there are to be introduced between the hammer and the sounding bodies generally, at the pleasure of the performer, by a pedal or otherwise, pieces of leather or other substances, the parts of which are of different degrees of density, thickness, or hardness, so as gradually to vary the tone from loud to soft, or vice versa, by the hammers striking through the medium of the hard, soft, thick or thin parts of the said pieces".

Una Corda. A mechanism whereby the hammers can be made to strike one, two, or three strings by the movement of a pedal. Merlin patented this effect in order to obtain the "swell of an organ" in 1774 for his combined harpsichord and pianoforte (No. 1081). Walton patented it in 1787 (No. 1607). Érard patented it in 1794 (No. 2016). This is the same as the 'Verschiebung'.

Harp. A mechanism for interposing a strip of leather between the hammer and one string of each pair of unisons. The hammer being moved so as to be opposite to the string under which is placed the leather. When drawn off the strips of leather lie *between* the strings (No. 1743). Hancock, 1790. This is a combination of the 'Verschiebung' and the 'Pianozug' and is not the same thing as the 'Harfenzug'.

Buff Stop. A mechanism similar to that on a harpsichord (see Part II, Sect. III, p. 229, n. 1). John Geib patented it in 1786 (No. 1571). He does not place it along the full extent of the pianoforte but merely along the treble to facilitate tuning. This is the same as the harpsichord 'Lautenzug', 'harp' or 'buff' stop.

Sordin or Mute. A piece of wood curved to lie along the sound-board bridge and lined with "soft leather, hair or silk shagg". It is hinged to the case and is lifted off or on to the strings by means of a pedal. Patented by Broadwood in 1783 (No. 1379). This is the same as the 'Lautenzug' (Pianoforte stop) if soft leather is used but if hair or silk shagg is used it then *resembles the 'Harfenzug'*.

Cembalo or Harpsichord Stop.	A mechanism for interposing tongues of leather tipped with a hard substance, such as bone or ivory, between the hammers and the strings in such a way that the hard substance is struck against the strings. This stop was used in Germany. Patented in 1788 by Bury (No. 1637).
Swell.	A mechanism for raising: (1) a portion of the lid, (2) the dust plate. Also a mechanism resembling a Venetian blind lying over the strings by which the sound could gradually be augmented or diminished as in the swell organ. It was invented in Germany and patented in England by Shudi in 1769 (No. 947).
Drum.	A mechanism whereby a hammer is made to strike the sound-board and produce the sound of a drum. An escapement action is fitted and the hammer is worked by a foot pedal. Patented by William Rolfe and Samuel Davis in 1797 (No. 2160). This is the earliest specification for 'Turkish Music' in relation to a pianoforte.
Celestina.	"Consists in winding upon a reel of a proper size the fine silken threads of the cocoon of the silk worm, or other fine silken threads, so that these threads, when transferred to the pulleys of the Celestina, may have the form of a narrow tape or endless fillet, which, rub'd with resin dissolved in spirits of wine, produces the tone" (Clagget, No. 1644 (1788)).

A note on the Sordino Stop. The terms *Sordino* and *Sordini* refer to different damping agencies. The term *Sordini* when used in pianoforte music relates to the dampers, 'con sordini' signifying with the dampers down and 'Senza sordini' signifying with the dampers up. Hence the direction in the original edition of Beethoven's 'Moonlight' Sonata (Op. 27, No. 2); 'Senza sordini' placed at the beginning of the first movement means that the dampers are to remain lifted throughout the movement. But the term *Sordino* does not relate to the dampers but to a special extra mechanism for muting the tone. The *Sordino* is merely another name for the lute stop.

It seems to have been a long time before musicians acquired the pianoforte touch. This is not surprising as most of them would also play the harpsichord, organ and clavichord. In short they were clavecinistes who also played the pianoforte. Thus artificial aids were provided for the production of the piano and the pianissimo which a modern pianist obtained by his touch alone. (Our piano pedal is used chiefly as a change of tone colour.) In the eighteenth century there were, besides the ordinary piano stop, various substitutes for it. 'Verschiebung' or 'una corda', harp and lute subdued the sound and no doubt the client chose whichever he preferred. It was customary to fit at least one of these stops for muting the tone to any good pianoforte whether square or grand.

In France according to both Adam and Steibelt the large square pianofortes and the grand pianofortes were fitted with four pedals. For the grand piano these were the jeu de luth or jeu de harpe, forte, céleste (pianozug) and una corda (Verschiebung) and for the large square pianoforte the same were fitted except the una corda, the place of which was taken by the swell.

The English square pianofortes had often the lute and divided forte, though the grand pianofortes had merely una corda and forte. This may be summarised by saying that the Continental pianofortes usually had either the lute or the piano pedals or both and that even the English square pianoforte often had the lute stop. The lute stop or pedal became known eventually as the sordino. It was patented under the name of 'Sordin' by Broadwood in 1783. (Weltman's harpsichord pianoforte of 1759 had *besides* the dampers a Sordino consisting of tongues of leather, but this is clearly the *piano* stop.)[1]

[1] C 845.

CHAPTER VI

LATER DEVELOPMENTS IN FRANCE

WELTMAN submitted in 1759 a *Clavecin à Maillets* to l'Académie des Sciences de Paris. Forty-three years had elapsed since a harpsichord with hammer action had been submitted for the approval of that learned body. Marius' fourth *Clavecin à Maillets* had been the last. This instrument has been referred to before, and, as there is no accompanying drawing with the description, a lengthy description is unnecessary. It is a combined harpsichord and pianoforte. Sourdines worked by knee pedals are fitted to enable the performer to diminish the volume of sound more gradually. There is also a carillon struck by hammers and worked from the keyboard, the compass of both carillon and harpsichord being the same. A set of dampers is added for the purpose of damping the after sounds of the bells.

In 1772 L'Epine, organ builder to the King of France, submitted a 'Forte Piano' to l'Académie des Sciences which he suggested could be built in the form of a secrétaire in order to form a light and agreeable piece of furniture. To this instrument he attached an organ.[1] A second manual "combined the speech of an eight-foot bass, a treble flute, a bassoon and oboe stop".[2] The sound could be augmented or diminished at will by a foot pedal. The pianoforte was so arranged that it could be lifted out and carried away without affecting the organ.

Pianofortes with an organ attachment were very common at the end of the eighteenth century. In Germany the makers offered instruments with or without the organ as a matter of course.

Piano-organs were still made in the nineteenth century, but they do not always seem to have met with the approval of musicians. Spohr heard a concerto played upon one when he visited St Petersburg in 1802 and remarks that the "tone . . . of the strings and of the organ had together a very bad effect".[3]

---

[1] C 851.
[2] B 85, p. 144 (part in inverted commas).
[3] B 89, p. 44. 'Flute' should have been translated as 'organ'.

The German instrument by Kühlewind dated 1791, illustrated below, may be taken as a typical example (Fig. 49).[1]

Pascal Taskin, the inventor of the famous harpsichord with 'peau de Bouffle' was also a pianoforte maker of note. In 1787 he

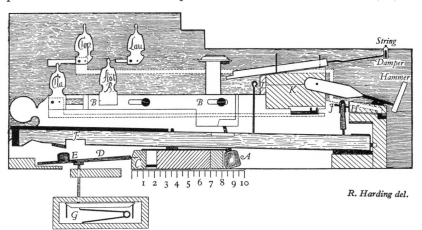

R. Harding del.

Fig. 49. Pianoforte with organ attachment by Samuel Kühlewind, 1791 (Berlin, No. 14).

The block A is connected to $B, B,$ by an iron rod. A is also connected to C by a wire. To C is attached a lever D carrying a projection E. When the block E is in the position as seen in the drawing, the organ is coupled, for D lies over a rod connected with the pallet. When the key is depressed the projection E of the lever D pushes the rod down and opens the pallet G. To uncouple the organ, B, B must be pushed back by means of its ivory handle 'Flöt', thus pushing A back and drawing C, to which is attached D, into such a position that its projection E lies under the hollow F of the key. Thus it is untouched when the key is depressed, *i.e.* '*Flöt*' *to the right = organ off*. For the rest: '*Cop*' lifts H, which is attached to the frame by a wire and pivot at J, thus raising the hammer out of action, *i.e.* '*Cop*' *right = pianoforte off*. '*Cla*' pushed to the right raises the piece L by means of a mechanism under K and thus removes the dampers from the strings, *i.e.* '*Cla*' *right = forte*. '*Lau*' was formerly Lautenzug but has been converted into Piano: '*Lau*' *left = piano*.

built a pianoforte,[2] which not only shows the influence of the Cristofori, the German and the 'Tangent' Actions, but is remarkable on account of the mechanical wrest pin (Fig. 50).

Sébastien Érard, one of the greatest of the French pianoforte makers, was born at Strasburg, Alsace, in 1752. On the death of his father he determined to seek employment in Paris, and

[1] Crang Hancock patented a pianoforte with an organ attachment in 1790, calling the organ the 'German Flute'. Its compass only extended down to violin G (C 852).

[2] See B 87 (*a*), p. 92 and B 52, pp. 8, 9.

arrived there in 1768. He obtained employment with a harpsi-chord maker, but soon wearied his master by repeated questions respecting the principles upon which instruments were constructed and was dismissed.

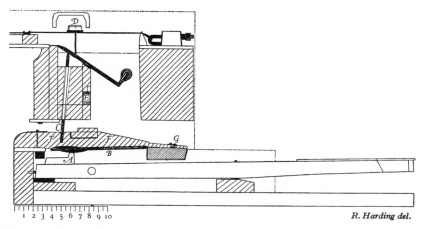

R. Harding del.

Fig. 50. Grand pianoforte action; Pascal Taskin, 1787 (from a model by Herr Adolf Hartmann, Berlin, No. 917).

A, jack; *B*, intermediate lever; *C*, another jack attached to the hammer; *D*, damper attached to the hammer. In order to raise the damper the strip *E*, in which there is a tooth (seen edgeways in the drawing), is moved by a stop so that it lifts the piece above it and thus raises the hammer into such a position that when it falls the damper does not touch the string. The following diagram will illustrate the principle. It will be re-membered that in the modern upright pianoforte *piano* is often produced by a *shortening* of the radius of the blow. Here, on the contrary, when *forte* is required the

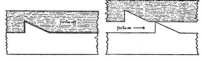

blow is shortened. The entire block through which the second jack *C* passes takes down and also the key may be removed by unhooking *G* and lifting up the piece *F, F*. This pianoforte is remarkable in that it has a mechanical wrest pin, the two strings being stretched by the same tension.

Another harpsichord maker then took Érard into his service and seems to have recognised his great ability from the first. When he decided to construct a harpsichord with a sensitive touch and tone hitherto unattained he asked Érard to undertake this work. This harpsichord made Érard's reputation. The Duchesse de Villeroi allotted him a suite of apartments and a workshop in her Château and it was there in 1777 that he constructed his first pianoforte. But these premises became too small and he removed to Rue de Bourbon, where he began business in partnership with his brother Jean-Baptiste.

Érard's increasing reputation excited the jealousy of the 'Luthiers' of Paris who caused his premises to be raided on the pretext that he had not obeyed the laws of the Company of Fanmakers to which the 'Luthiers' belonged. But Louis XVI conferred a patent upon Érard which permitted him to construct pianofortes without molestation.

At first the Parisians preferred the square pianoforte made by Zumpe, but the Érards soon won over their countrymen by the excellence of their instruments. They began by copying the Zumpe pianofortes and used his Single or 'First action' in their bichord instruments with five octaves, of the year 1780 (Fig. 51).

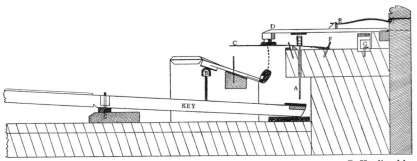

R. Harding del.

Fig. 51. Érard's action for bichord pianofortes, 1780 (No. B 39. Plate II reversed).

A, damper stick; *B*, jack with its head covered with leather; *C*, string; *D*, damper; *E*, damper spring; *F*, hitch pin; *G*, portion of the mechanism for raising the damper.

In 1790 they modified the action by the addition of an intermediate lever to which they added another jack (Fig. 52). This is most probably a modification of Zumpe's 'Second action' and its purpose may have been to facilitate repetition and to prevent blocking. There is, unfortunately, no explanation attached to their drawing. They used this action for their trichord pianofortes with five and a half octaves.

Sébastien Érard came to London in 1792 and opened a manufactory in Great Marlborough Street whilst his brother managed the business in Paris. In 1794 he obtained an English patent (No. 2016) for an action in which the hammers could be made to strike one, two or three strings. He also invented a mechanism

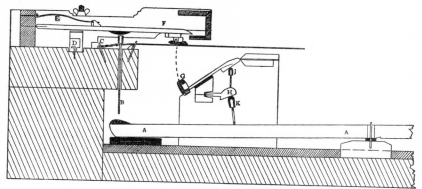

Fig. 52. Érard's action 'à double pilotes', 1790 (No. B 39. Plate III reversed).

A, key; *B*, the damper stick; *C*, hitch pin; *D*, portion of the mechanism for raising the damper; *E*, damper spring; *F*, damper; *G*, the hammer; *H*, the "false hammer" or intermediate lever; *J*, *K*, the jacks.

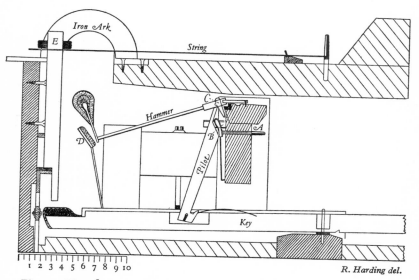

Fig. 53. The Érard grand action, 1796 (No. B 39. Plate IV reversed).

A, regulating screw working upon a spring; *B*, spring; *C*, set of buttons; *D*, check; *E*, damper.

for producing an effect called 'Harmonic Sounds' in the mysterious language so often used by patentees. It is simply an action for producing the harmonic octave by causing a copper upright, tipped with cloth, to press the strings from below at their middle point. There are also various other improvements both to the pianoforte and to the harp.

The Érards made their first grand pianoforte about the year 1796. They appear to have taken the English Grand Action as a working basis (Fig. 53). For a short time they made pianofortes with German Action and check but as these proved unsuccessful they were soon given up.

CHAPTER VII

THE PIANOFORTE IN AMERICA

VERY little is known about the early history of the piano-forte in America.

The earliest notice of the instrument is found in the *New York Herald* of 1774, where, amongst the list of goods sold by auction from the wrecked ship *Pedro*, there is mentioned "a set of hammer harpsichords, slightly damaged".

John Brent of Philadelphia made the first American pianoforte in 1774. The privateering frigate *Boston* sailed by Captain Tucker brought in a merchant ship as a prize to Boston in 1779. Amongst the booty was a 'London made Pianoforte'.

The Marquis de Chastellux states that he saw pianofortes in Boston drawing-rooms as early as 1780.

Very little effort seems to have been made to build these instruments. When they were required they were imported from London.

John Jacob Astor, a German by birth, came to America and settled as a fur merchant in 1783. When exporting fur he occasionally imported a few pianofortes.

Charles Jarvis, a Scotsman, settled in Philadelphia in 1785, where he began to build pianofortes, and in the same year John Adams advertised himself in the *Independent Journal*, and George Ulscheefer exhibited instruments of his own at New York.

In 1788 Clement Claus, a native of Stuttgart, came from London to New York, and in the following year began to make pianofortes in Philadelphia which were for the most part copies of those made in London.

Boston could now boast of a harpsichord and pianoforte teacher. Three years later, according to a newspaper report, there were twenty-seven pianofortes in the city and all were of 'London make'. In this year Brissot de Warville wrote that in Boston "one sometimes hears the Forte Piano, though the art is in its infancy —God grant that the Bostonian Women may never, like those of France, acquire the malady of perfection in this art. It is never attained except at the expense of the domestic virtues".[1]

1 B 71.

The first patent was granted in 1796 to James Sylvanus McLean for "Improvements in pianofortes" but, unfortunately, it is not recorded what these improvements were.

Some time between the years 1798 and 1800 Benjamin Crehore, destined to become a famous maker of pianofortes in Boston, settled at Milton, Mass. The date of his earliest pianoforte is not known, but by 1791 he had already acquired a reputation in Boston, New York, and Philadelphia, as a maker of violins and other instruments.

It will be seen by the foregoing account, which is adapted from Spillaine's History,[1] that America received her stimulus to build pianofortes from the instruments imported from London. By 1795 pianoforte making had begun in real earnest in Philadelphia and Boston.

[1] B 88.

Additional Keys

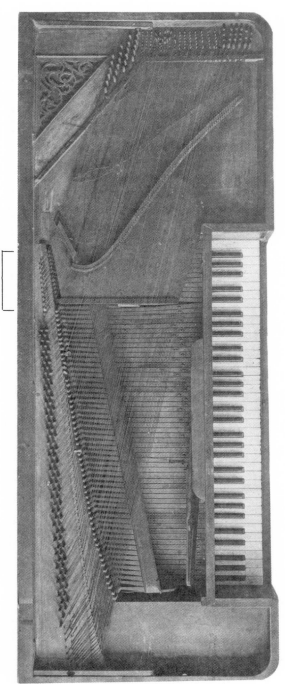

Plate X. Square Pianoforte with 'additional keys' by Goulding, Dalmaine, Potter and Co. (in the possession of Mr W. J. Moore, Cambridge).

Chapter VIII

THE MUSICAL SIGNIFICANCE OF THE NEW INSTRUMENT

HITHERTO it has been necessary to describe the pianoforte as a machine rather than as a musical instrument, in order to trace its origin and development in different countries. But the history of its action is not the whole history of the pianoforte any more than a detailed account of the mechanics or science of music could be a complete history of music. A few remarks as to the musical significance of the new instrument must now be made.

The pianoforte as a musical instrument was long considered as of doubtful value. It began by being a new kind of harpsichord upon which it was possible to obtain dynamic expression. Its inferiority at first to the harpsichord, and the fact that it was less suited to the performance of music in parts, made instrument-makers chary of constructing large instruments in any quantity, and we may surmise that at first they were supplied to the less wealthy customers as a substitute for the harpsichord—as instruments which were less costly to keep in order owing to the fact that there was no need to requill. Small pianofortes, with the tone of the harpsichord and fitted with a means for simulating the tone of the clavichord, were constructed and may have been sold as compromise instruments to those who could not afford to possess both. Thus for many years there were no pianists. Those who could afford to keep the new instrument in addition to their harpsichord and clavichord were really *clavecinistes* who played the pianoforte.

The genius of the pianoforte clearly was misunderstood. Scarcely any attention was paid to the *corps de résonnance*, whilst the variety of changes of registration placed at the performers' disposal shows us that musicians were long in separating it off in their minds as a species distinct from the harpsichord. The 'forte pedal', as it used to be called, was at first added to the pianoforte for the purpose of obtaining the Pantaleon effect so much admired at the beginning of the century.

The pianoforte, at first a substitute for the harpsichord, began to be recognised as an independent instrument towards the last quarter of the century. But it was not until Stein invented an escapement action in 1773, and the English Grand Action was evolved from that of Cristofori a few years later, that composers considered it worthy of their serious attention. The harpsichord then began to go into disfavour and there arose a host of virtuoso pianists, of whom Mozart was the first.

The pianists often advised the makers and showed their instruments to customers. John Field, as a young man, was employed in this capacity by Clementi both in London and St Petersburg. Spohr, who visited St Petersburg in 1802, states that he sometimes used to accompany Clementi in the evening to his large pianoforte warehouse, where Field was often obliged to play for hours to display the instruments to the best advantage to the purchasers.

"I have still in recollection", wrote Spohr, "the figure of the pale overgrown youth whom I have never seen since. When Field, who had outgrown his clothes, placed himself at the piano, stretched out his arms over the keyboard so that the sleeves shrunk up nearly to his elbows, his whole figure appeared awkward and stiff to the highest degree; but as soon as his touching instrumentation began, everything else was forgotten, and one became all ear."[1]

The heads of great pianoforte houses ranked as musicians and gathered round themselves a brilliant circle of composers and pianists. Thus we find Stein on terms of friendship with Mozart, and Beethoven intimate with the Streichers.

From about 1760 a white-hot enthusiasm was concentrated on the pianoforte and on pianoforte music. Giustini's early attempt to write for this new instrument had long been forgotten and it was Emanuel Bach who had laid the foundation of pianoforte technique by writing for the clavier and playing upon it in a 'cantabile' style. And this style was adopted by all the composers and players of this time; Beethoven himself carried on the tradition in his early works for the instrument. In 1773 Clementi wrote his famous Sonata Op. 2, a work considered to have been the first piece of music composed in a style entirely suited to the pianoforte as an instrument distinct from the harpsichord. Four years later (1777) Dr Burney wrote the first duets for two performers on one pianoforte. Jacob Kirkman tried the experiment of writing a duet for pianoforte and harpsichord (Opus 2). It was published by Longman and Broderip about 1785. Most

[1] B 89, Vol. 1, p. 39.

significant of all was the use of the pianoforte in place of the harpsichord as the solo instrument in the concerto. This innovation seems to have been largely due to the influence of Mozart, whose twenty-six pianoforte concertos are amongst his finest and most interesting works and are, generally speaking, on a grander scale than his symphonies. In fact the concerto in Mozart's day was of more importance than the symphony, because it had all the advantages of the symphony with the addition of Mozart's inimitable powers as a performer and as an improviser.

Other fine players would naturally choose the concerto form and the pianoforte rather than the harpsichord as their solo instrument on account of its greater expressiveness. Beethoven wrote his first pianoforte concerto about 1795.

In spite of the fact that so much was written for the pianoforte some of the composers were still a little doubtful which of the two instruments the public preferred. Thus Beethoven's first eight sonatas are written for 'Clavecin or Piano Forte'.

But a change of style may be detected. The melodic line tends to become clearer as those ornaments necessary to mark important notes on the harpsichord lose their point on the pianoforte. Harmonic figures in the bass are used to support themes in sustained notes placed in the treble, and long notes held in the left hand sustain florid passages played with the right.

The treatment of dynamic expression is also changed. During the first half of the century 'diminuendo poco a poco' followed by a sudden return to forte was the admired effect and it seems to have been the first attempt to treat dynamic expression as a part of musical pattern. When Beethoven comes all is changed. The gradual working up to forte followed by a sudden drop to pianissimo and the frequent use of the sforzando are the characteristics of a change of style moving away from the impersonality of the older masters towards the personal and dramatic.

In 1799, according to the title of the original edition, announced in the *Vienna Journal* of December 22nd of that year, Beethoven published his first work for the pianoforte as distinct from the clavecin. This work was the two sonatas Op. 14, Nos. 1 and 2, dedicated to "Madame la Baronne de Braun".

PART II

THE PIANOFORTE IN THE NINETEENTH CENTURY

This picture, by Sir William Orchardson, R.A., shows a Pianoforte by Van der Hoef of Amsterdam, with Turkish music. (Formerly in the possession of Wm Orchardson, R.A., now in the Bethnal Green Museum, London, No. 461.)

SECTION I

THE PIANOFORTE AS A CHAMBER ORCHESTRA

The pianoforte...may be considered in a double point of view: as an orchestral instrument, or as forming a complete small orchestra in itself.
H. BERLIOZ, Treatise on Instrumentation

CHAPTER I

THE PIANOFORTE AS A CHAMBER ORCHESTRA

DURING the earlier years of the nineteenth century, a pianoforte recital without an orchestral accompaniment to at least one of the works was a rarity, and the concerto form was almost always used in the greater performances.

The typical 'celebrity' concert of the eighteen-twenties consisted of orchestral and vocal items interspersed between the solo performances. If the celebrity was a pianist he usually played at least one of his own works, and sometimes extemporised freely upon a well-known theme or upon a subject given him by a member of the audience. The following account of a concert given by Moscheles at the Argyll Rooms on Monday, June 16th, 1823, will make this clear.

Mr F. Cramer led the band, and Mr Cramer sat at the pianoforte as conductor. A strong vocal phalanx assisted on this occasion, amongst whom were Mesdames Camporese, and Ronzi de Begnis; Mademoiselles Caradori, Paton and Goodall, Signori Begrez, De Begnis, Mr Welsh etc.... M. Moscheles played a new concerto in which deep musical knowledge and fancy were happily blended. In his finale he introduced the well known English tune, the Grenadier March, and put every head and almost as many hearts into motion. In the second part he performed a fantasia *extempore*,[1] and excited as much astonishment by the readiness of his invention, as by the indescribable rapidity of his execution and power of hand.[2]

[1] Owing to the fashion for extempore playing and the desire on the part of those who heard it to preserve a record of the music, stenographical apparatus was invented to be applied to pianofortes. Three patents were granted for stenographical pianofortes, viz. French patents to Eisenmenger (1836) and Guérin (1844) for his *Piano-Graphe* and a Bavarian patent to Flamm in 1849 (C 255, 256, 257). An example in working order of a stenographical harpsichord is exhibited at the Deutsches Museum, Munich.
[2] One of the themes was the Romance from *La Donna del Lago*.

From about 1830 there were occasional important concerts where the orchestra was not included, but they were rare; in fact it was not until February 1837 that Moscheles ventured to introduce pianoforte evenings without the addition of an orchestra. And even then he felt obliged to include vocal items and introduced the harpsichord. The following is the programme of this concert:

Part I. Grande Sonate brillante (C major, in four movements), Pianoforte, Mr Moscheles; Weber.—Cantata, Miss Birch, 'Mad Bess'; Purcell.—Three preludes and Fugues (C sharp major, C sharp minor, and D major), Pianoforte, Mr Moscheles; S. Bach.—German Song, Miss Masson, 'Das erste Veilchen' (The first violet); Mendelssohn.—Sonate dramatique (D minor, Op. 29, in three movements), Pianoforte, Mr Moscheles; Beethoven. Part II. A selection from the Suites and Lessons (including the celebrated Cat's Fugue), as originally written for the harpsichord, and, by desire, performed on that instrument by Mr Moscheles; D. Scarlatti.—'The Harmonious Blacksmith', with Handel's Variations, Mr Moscheles; Handel.—Duet, Miss Birch and Miss Masson, 'Così fan Tutte'; Mozart.—Les Adieux, l'Absence, et le Retour, sonate caractéristique, Pianoforte, Mr Moscheles; Beethoven.—Glee, Miss Birch, Miss Masson, Messrs Vaughan and Bradbury, 'Go, feeble tyrant'; Jackson.—A selection of new manuscript studies, Pianoforte, Mr Moscheles; Moscheles. Conductor of the Vocal Music, Sir George Smart.

There was evidently considerable diversity of opinion whether the concert would prove successful, for a writer in the *Musical World* informs his readers that "it was thought that a whole evening of pianoforte composition would be found wearying". The success seems to have resulted from admiration at Moscheles' power of adapting himself to music of so many different styles. This is clearly seen by some further remarks upon the concert by the same writer:

The performance of Scarlatti's celebrated Cat Fugue...was received with considerable interest by the audience, on account of the introduction of the old harpsichord.[1] In playing this fugue, the cautious manner in which this fine player indicated the subject, was like a piece of good acting, and, indeed, it excited no small amusement among the company. It was encored. One circumstance at the conclusion of the entertainment particularly struck us, and that was the manner in which Mr Moscheles threw himself into the various character [*sic*] of the music he was playing. The style in which he

---

[1] The harpsichord that Moscheles used for this concert was made by Shudi in 1771 and is now in the possession of Messrs J. Broadwood and Sons. It has 4½ octaves, C_1 to f''', "Venetian Swell and five stops, comprising the two unisons and octave of the Ruckers, with a slide of jacks striking the strings much nearer to the bridge (also a Ruckers contrivance), and producing a more twanging quality of tone, the so-called 'lute' stop and a 'buff' stop".

executed a fugue of Bach, and a florid finale of Weber or Beethoven, was as perfectly according with the genius, and we should suppose the intention of each composer, as if he had studied in his school alone.[1]

In March of this year Moscheles gave another concert on the same lines and again introduced the harpsichord, playing upon it selections from the Suites and Lessons of Scarlatti.

But in spite of these innovations, nearly all the great pianists wrote concertos or divertissements for their instruments in order that these works could be performed by the amateur in his home, where there could be no orchestra; all the 'tuttis' were printed in short score and with the appropriate dynamic marks. Thus a pianist often found himself playing music originally designed for strings, brass or wood wind. In consequence of this and the insatiable desire on the part of these amateurs for two- and four-hand reductions of operatic and symphonic works, numerous devices were added to the pianoforte for the purpose of giving the illusion of an orchestra. These may be grouped under the following headings:

(1) Devices for sustaining the sounds after the note had been struck.

(2) Octave couplers.

(3) Characteristic stops such as (a) Wornum's 'Pizzicato pedal', (b) bassoon stop, (c) Janissary music.

(4) Special pianoforte actions to make it possible to imitate the *tremolando* of the violinist.[2]

Curious pseudo-orchestral music was sometimes written for pianofortes with these attachments.

There is no doubt that the pianoforte owes its invention to the deep interest taken by 'Amateurs' and 'Professors' in the orchestra, particularly in the string band when experiments in the use of dynamic expression as a part of the musical design were being tried for the first time.[3] It will be remembered that Cristofori's invention of a *Gravicembalo col piano e forte* was the outcome of a desire to make the harpsichord expressive by the touch alone and unaided by machinery, as was the case with the string players.

But the composers of keyboard music were not only interested in the possibilities of dynamic expression but also in the tone,

[1] B 75 (b), pp. 155, 156.
[2] These actions will be dealt with in Sect. II.
[3] See Part I, Chap. I.

colour and characteristics of the orchestral instruments themselves. This is illustrated by an occasional conscious imitation, in the music of the sixteenth, seventeenth and eighteenth centuries, of a Horn, Trumpet, Drum and certain wood wind instruments, whilst typical string passages occur more and more frequently as time flows on.

Both the harpsichord and the newly invented pianoforte suffered from a grave defect when compared to the bowed string or wind instruments, since the tone faded rapidly away after the note had been struck. This defect may partially account for the fact that so many harpsichords and pianofortes were fitted with an organ attachment.

Bedford[1] informs us that in London at his time (1700) the young ladies used to attend divine service expressly for the purpose of hearing their harpsichord pieces played upon the organ "where the *Concords* may be more fully heard, and the *sound* will hold on as long as the *Artist* pleases, without the repeating of the *Stroke*".

In order to overcome this deficiency many attempts were made not only to devise a mechanism to bow the harpsichord or pianoforte strings, but also to incorporate an orchestra within the case —a chamber orchestra in which all the instruments would be perfectly together since a single performer controlled their action— a keyboard instrument with the power of dynamic expression and the capabilities of a full band.

The earliest attempt to construct this type of harpsichord where the strings were bowed in imitation of the viols was made by Hans Haydn of Nuremberg in the year 1600. He was followed by a numerous band of imitators. Since a list of them will be found in Dr Curt Sachs' *Real-Lexicon der Musik-Instrumente* (Berlin, 1913, Art. *Streichklavier*) it is unnecessary to enumerate them all. A few of the more curious will be described.

In 1742 le Voir[2] constructed a clavecin in which he incorporated a violoncello and a viola. Both of these instruments were provided with several bridges over which the strings were passed to be secured to their tuning pegs. These strings were divided into two portions, each giving out a note appropriate to its vibrating length. By this means there were only twenty-five strings, although there were fifty notes. A mechanism for bowing the strings was arranged so that it could be worked by treadles. It consisted of bundles of

[1] B 25, p. 208. [2] B 4, Tome VII, p. 183.

horse-hair which were passed around rollers. The action of the performer's feet on the treadles kept the rollers and consequently the bow continuously revolving, whilst the keys, when depressed by his fingers, cut off the vibrating length of string proportional to the note. Within the body of another clavecin of the year 1749 by the same maker there were two violins, a drum, a viola and a large violoncello; whilst in le Gay's[1] clavecin, built about the year 1764, the performer had a choice of tone colour ranging from a theorbo or guitar to a consort of viols.

The reader will have observed that these instruments are intended to imitate the expressiveness of the *string band*. In the instruments about to be mentioned the object seems to have been to imitate an *orchestra*.

In 1730 a preacher at Znain in Moravia, named Procopius Diviss or Divisch,[2] constructed a keyboard instrument in which there were 790 strings, and 130 changes of registration. He also added a means for giving the performer an electric shock. No doubt he thought that some stimulus was necessary to enable the player to control this 'Denis D'or', as he names it! Milchmeyer of Mainz[3] built a harpsichord with 250 stops. In the year 1795 Dr Vincenz von Blaha caused an organised pianoforte to be built under his supervision with a complete band of Janissary music and many other novelties.

Another instrument of this type was built by Thomas Kunz of Prague[4] between 1796 and 1798. It was in the form of what is now called a 'grand pianoforte' and had an organ attachment consisting of 360 pipes. There were 230 strings and 150 changes of registration. In the year 1800 Zink,[5] an official at Hesse-Homburg, caused a piano-harmonica to be constructed which is said to have comprised fourteen instruments.[6] There were three manuals: the upper one sounded a 'Franklin' glass harmonica, the middle one a pianoforte and organ, whilst the lowest manual secured the imitation of several wind instruments.

Johann Heinrich Völler of Angersbach, Hesse-Darmstadt,[7] built a grand pianoforte with an organ attachment and with an automaton in the form of an eight-year-old boy who blew the flute.

[1] B 5, volume for 1762, p. 191.
[2] B 94.   [3] *Ibid.*
[4] *Ibid.* (Prof. Sachs gives the date as 1799. See B 87, Art. 'Streichklavier'.)
[5] *Ibid.*   [6] *Ibid.*
[7] *Ibid.* The reader should also consult Gerber's *Neues historischbiographisches Lexikon der Tonkünstler*, Leipzig, 1812–14.

This automaton is even said to have removed the flute from its mouth during the pauses. No doubt Völler intended his 'Apollonion', as he called it, to represent a flute concerto accompanied by an orchestra, but in this case the *soloist* was imitated mechanically instead of the *orchestra*. The parallel instance of the organ, 'Voix céleste' accompanied by orchestral stops, will be recalled.

Yet another strange instrument remains to be described. Schnell and Tschenky brought out their 'Animo-Corde' or 'Wind-clavier' in 1790. They hoped to imitate the tones of the æolian harp by subjecting the strings to currents of air, but the slowness with which some of the strings responded to this stimulus obliged them to add a ring bow mechanism to initiate their vibrations. Schnell was appointed to the post of Court Instrument Maker to the Duchess of Artois, and Marie Antoinette herself is said to have listened enraptured to his playing on this instrument. She even endeavoured to purchase it, and offered Schnell a gratuity of 50,000 livres in addition to the sum of 100,000 livres for the Animo-Corde itself. Unhappily her coffers were so depleted owing to her enormous expenditure that she was unable to fulfil her promise. An Englishman then came forward and offered to take Schnell to London and to exhibit the Animo-Corde for a month, at the same time guaranteeing him the sum of " 10,000 guineas a week [*sic*]" and a further sum of 1800 pounds for the instrument when the month had expired. Schnell refused this offer on account of his faithfulness to the Queen.

On the outbreak of the revolution he narrowly escaped the guillotine. At the last moment, when the rebels had come to capture him, he was rescued by his wife and enabled to make his escape in safety to Ludwigsburg.[1]

It will have been observed that the instruments enumerated above fall into three distinct classes:

(1) Stringed keyboard instruments with a ring bow mechanism.

(2) Harpsichords and pianofortes with a multiplicity of stops.

(3) An instrument where the sounds are prolonged by the action of currents of air directed against the strings.

In the first the intention is to imitate the tone and expressiveness

[1] B 94. See also B 2 (1842, Heft VIII und IX, S. 584) and B 33 (Erster Jahrg., No. 3, S. 39–44, Tafel 1).

of the stringed band. In the second the desire is to produce a complete chamber orchestra, whilst in the third the orchestral effect of a sustained tone is produced. All three types had a distinct and important influence on the construction of the pianoforte in the nineteenth century, and it will be seen how the Animo-Corde suggested a series of inventions for prolonging the sound by the use of currents of air and how the *Streichklaviere* suggested another series of experiments on the same lines, whilst the strange instruments with their multiplicity of stops for the purpose of imitating the sounds of an orchestra were a continual source of inspiration to inventors.

CHAPTER II

DEVICES FOR THE PURPOSE OF SUSTAINING
THE TONE

THE language of the orchestra plays an important part in the clavier works of Mozart, whilst when we come to the age of Beethoven it had become an essential part of the pianoforte composer's technique. Westerby points out a good example of the orchestral style in Beethoven's Sonata Op. 28 where it is illustrated by the frequent use of "broken octaves as a substitute for the tremolando of strings, in the sustained bass notes with superadded wavy and violin accompaniment figuration, in the short melodic figures in octaves in the bass ('cello and double bass), and in the inversion of themes in what is called double counterpoint —a device constantly used by Beethoven". Again in the Andante he calls attention to the "pizzicato-like bass" and "flute-like triplets".[1] Dr Hans von Bülow even went so far as to draw the pianist's attention to certain orchestral effects in his edition of the Master's pianoforte works. We quote a passage from Sonata Op. 53.[2]

Ex. 1. Beethoven Sonata Op. 53.

Again in Sonata Op. 57 in the 'Andante con moto', at (a) fifteen bars from the end, he directs the pianist to play the left-hand passage 'mezzo forte' and to concentrate on the tone colour of violoncello as if he were playing a free fantasia upon that instrument.[3]

Ex. 2. Beethoven Sonata, Op. 57, *Andante con moto*.

[1] B 95, pp. 83, 84.　　　[2] B 98, Vol. IV, p. 8.　　　[3] B 98, Vol. IV, p. 77.

The instrument-makers endeavoured to meet the needs of composers for a pianoforte in which the sounds could be sustained after the manner of bowed strings. Some of them partially succeeded and the enthusiasm this caused amongst musicians will be seen by a passage in Berlioz' *Treatise on Instrumentation*.

Alexandre invented a mechanism which could be applied to the organ or pianoforte to enable the player to sustain any note or chord whilst he could accompany them with melodic figures either above or below. It is of this invention that Berlioz writes:

> The prolongation of sound is the most important recent musical invention that has been brought into keyboard instruments. This invention...gives the player the power of sustaining for an indefinite time...a note, a chord, or an arpeggio, in all the compass of the keyboard.... The player, having his hands at liberty, can not only strike and make other notes speak which form no part of the prolonged chord, but also the prolonged notes themselves. It will be at once perceived to what a multitude of various and charming combinations this invention affords scope on the melodian organ and piano. They are absolute orchestral effects, of the nature of those which are produced when the stringed instruments execute four or five parts diversely designed amidst a sustained harmony of the wind instruments (flutes, hautboys, and clarinets); or, better still, like those which result from a piece in several parts played by wind instruments, during a harmonious holding-on of *divided violins*; or when the harmony and the melody are moving above or below a pedal point.

One means of overcoming the lack of sustaining power in the pianoforte consisted, as we have already stated, in adding an organ to it. In later years, not only were organs coupled to pianofortes, but also the harmonium and æolian attachment.[1] In the æolian attachment the pianoforte was provided with free reeds acted on by wind and sounded by the ordinary pianoforte keys. This mechanism could, of course, be uncoupled, and seems to have been popular.

The three other devices for sustaining the tone, about to be enumerated, follow on naturally from those mentioned in the previous chapter. In many cases the inventors are aiming at the production of a sustained note which should also have the timbre of a bowed stringed instrument.

(1) *A device for sustaining the tone and for producing the illusion of a string band by means of the* RING BOW MECHANISM. Many

---

[1] For corroboration of my statement that organ and harmonium attachments were used to give the illusion of a sustained sound upon the pianoforte see Fr. Pat. No. 2744 (1846) for Jaulin's 'Panorgue-piano' (C 820).

of the *Sostenente* instruments about to be mentioned can scarcely be termed *pianofortes* since there are no hammers, but they are useful in showing the connection of thought between the older inventions listed in the previous chapter and those to be described in the following sections.

John Conrad Becker devised a means of vibrating his pianoforte strings by means of a wheel or wheels above or below them, in 1801.[1]

In 1802 John Isaac Hawkins of Philadelphia, U.S.A., brought out the 'Claviol', a tall instrument vertically encased and fitted with a ring bow mechanism, which he exhibited in London in 1813.[2] Schmidt of Paris patented a unichord pianoforte in 1803 with the compass of five and a half octaves and brass strings. For the ordinary square instrument he arranged a single band composed of some flexible material to bow the strings. This band was passed around pulleys some distance apart. Pressure on a treadle revolved the pulleys and consequently circulated the band. In the case of a grand pianoforte there were two bands, a broad one for the bass strings and a narrow one to bow the treble. Pressure on the key lifted the string to meet the band and the tone could be varied by *pressing the string* lightly or heavily against it. Thus expression was obtained in the opposite way to that of the string player, who varies his tone by *pressing his bow against the strings*. At first the tone seemed somewhat strange, but when the ear became accustomed to it the listener imagined himself in the midst of an orchestra. Perhaps the most famous of these instruments was brought out in 1817 in England by Isaac Henry Robert Mott[3] of Brighton, a teacher and composer of music. It was most probably based on an invention by Adam Walker—'the Celestina' patented by him in 1772 (Eng. No. 1020). (Fig. 1 shows Mott's application of his invention to the pianoforte.)

In 1822 Abbé Grégoire Trentin invented his 'Violicembalo', an instrument in the form of a grand pianoforte with the compass of six octaves. It was mounted with catgut strings which could be raised either singly or together by the action of the keys to meet a cylindrical bow composed of horse-hair and revolved by a treadle.[4] Thomas Todd patented a similar piece of machinery in 1823. He describes his invention thus:

A flat endless band consisting of woollen cloth, hair or silk, or any other

[1] C 1201.   [2] B 49, p. 97.
[3] C 925.   [4] B 45 (*b*), p. 37.

substance that will receive and retain rosin upon it is made to pass near to each string, over and around two cylinders or rollers. . . about six inches apart. . . . These rollers turn upon centres so that when one of them is put in motion, either by means of a pedal or otherwise, the band continues to run without touching the string unless it is brought in contact therewith.[1]

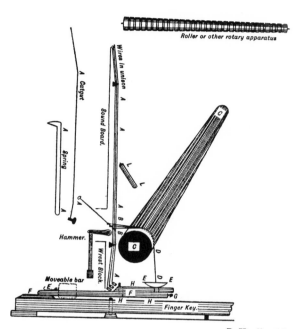

R. Harding del.

Fig. 1. Action of Mott's Sostenente apparatus as seen applied to an upright pianoforte. From the specification reversed.

A, A, vibrating bodies; *B, B*, connectors or communicators; *C, C,* roller or other rotary apparatus (wound round with silk or other suitable material and sprinkled with powdered rosin); *D, D,* conductor; *E, E, E,* bow and other springs; *F, F,* levers in a movable frame; *G,* screw and other regulators; *H, H, H,* silken or other chord attachment to the regulator and conductor; *L, L,* an intersecting bridge for producing harmonic sounds.

Abbé Grégoire Trentin came forward with yet another device for prolonging the tones in 1824; this was the *Metagofano*, a two-octave attachment to be fitted to the upper part of the case of a pianoforte for the purpose of doubling the strength and *duration* of the sounds. This mechanism was operated by means of a pedal.[2] Gama of

[1] C 1204.

[2] C 1205.

Nismes brought forward the Plectroeuphon (πλῆκτρον εὔφωνον or *Harmonious bow*) in 1828. It was played as an ordinary pianoforte and could supply the place of four stringed instruments. It could also imitate the timbre of the violoncello and the deeper notes of the double bass so as to render the illusion complete. The writer who describes this instrument suggests that "to the musician desirous to obtain orchestral effects in order to try a dramatic composition, it will prove an invaluable companion". He continues to say that, though he is unable to speak of the internal structure, yet in his opinion "considered merely as a piece of furniture for the decoration of the drawing-room it is of the most handsome and finished kind".[1] Two other inventions on a similar principle were patented, but unfortunately with no description: these were (1) Wheatstone and Green's[2] pianoforte with "Continuous sounds produced from strings, wires or springs" (1837) and (2) Lichtenthal of Brussels,[3] *Piano-Viole* (1830). Roeder of Paris invented in 1849 a mechanism which, although it produced the same effect as those previously mentioned, consisted in a different principle. Instead of a band composed of horse-hair he used a revolving cylinder covered with loose layers of material such as rags or leather whose action of flapping the strings continued their vibrations and suggested a stringed instrument played with a bow.[4]

(2) *A device for sustaining the tone in imitation of* BEBUNG *by means of a* REPEATING HAMMER. The second type of 'Sostenente' pianoforte consisted in keeping the hammer perpetually striking the strings so long as the key was depressed. This type of instrument is of interest since it recalls the 'tremolo' used on the clavichord for the purpose of giving the illusion of a sustained tone. This tremolo, it will be remembered, consisted in the rapid reiteration of the note without the finger leaving the key or the necessity of the key returning to its level. It was sometimes called 'Bebung'. In one of the pianofortes this effect of 'Bebung', or 'Italian Tremendo' as the patentee called it, is consciously imitated, whereas in other cases the hammers were made to strike the strings with sufficient rapidity to cause the repeated strokes to blend into a continuous stream of sound.

Once again the list will begin with the name of Hawkins, but on this occasion it was Isaac Hawkins the father, who took out a patent in England in 1800 for his son, John Isaac Hawkins of

---

[1] B 45 (♭), pp. 37, 38.   [2] C 1207.
[3] C 1206.   [4] C 1215.

Plate I. Viennese Pianoforte about 1800 in the Empire style. Stuttgart,
Würtembergisches Landesgewerbemuseum.
This instrument was frequently played upon by Beethoven when he visited the house
of its former owner, Dr Kanka of Prague.

Philadelphia. A section of this patent is devoted to a new invention called the 'Poiatorise Stop'.[1] A cylinder with projecting teeth is made to revolve with considerable velocity. The teeth engage either the tail of the hammer itself or a lever connected with the hammer and keep it continually striking the strings so long as the key is depressed. The firm of Érard Frères of Paris patented a similar invention in 1812.[2] In their pianoforte continuous sounds were produced by a toothed cylinder acting against a lever which communicated motion to the hammer. It is a matter of some interest to observe that this invention is shown applied to their action 'à double pilotes', originally brought out about the year 1790.[3] Henri Pape of Paris paid considerable attention to the perfection of pianofortes of this kind. One of his most original inventions consisted in an instrument in which he had substituted springs of steel, copper, brass or any metal according to the quality of tone desired, in place of the usual strings, whilst a toothed barrel kept the hammers continually striking them[4]. This was not his first attempt, for he patented a similar though less interesting version of it as early as 1825.[5] Fig. 3 shows his later development of this action as applied to a square pianoforte.

An interesting 'Sostenente' device of this type was patented by Christian Then,[6] a pianoforte maker at Augsburg, in 1841 (Fig. 2).

"A pianoforte fitted with a device whereby the sound could be prolonged at the same degree of intensity, whilst the key [was] kept down and an 'Italian tremendo' [sic] produced", was patented in 1841 by Madame Girard-Romagnac[7] of Paris. The invention is particularly interesting, as she evidently intended to produce the

---

[1] C 1216. [2] C 1217. [3] See Part I, Chap. VI, Fig. 51.
[4] C 1219. [5] C 1218. [6] C 1221.
[7] C 1222. This action ought to have been a welcome addition to the Home pianoforte owing to the prevalence of repeated note melodies in the drawing-room pianoforte music of this period (and much later) such as the *Maiden's Prayer* by Thekla Badarczewska, b. 1838, d. 1862. As early as 1797 Milchmeyer of Dresden gave instructions for imitating the mandolin on the pianoforte in his book on pianoforte playing. We quote a section of his example below (B 103).

Um die Mandoline nachzuahmen, muß man das Pianoforte ohne Pedal mit dem zugemachten Deckel auf folgende Art spielen.

effect of 'Bebung' in order to add to the expressiveness of her
instruments. The mechanism, which bears a striking resemblance
to that patented by Christian Then (in 1841), follows the usual
principle: a cylinder with several teeth engaged the tail of the
hammer and kept it continually striking the strings so long as the
key was depressed. The latest patent for an instrument of this
kind that occurs within our period was taken out in England in
1844 by Charles Maurice Elizee Sautter.[1] His pianoforte was to
be fitted with a cylinder acting upon the hammers in the usual

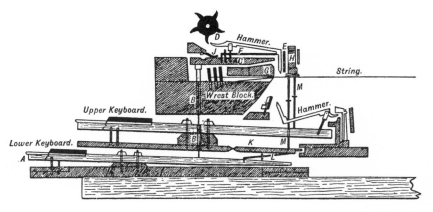

R. Harding del.

Fig. 2. Then's pianoforte with device for producing continuous sounds (1841).
Pressure on the key *A* causes the wire *B* to lift the lever *C* to a position in which the tail
of the hammer *E* engages the teeth of the cylinder *D*. This cylinder is connected with
a wheel which is revolved by a large fly-wheel. This fly-wheel is revolved by means
of a pedal placed opposite to the player's left foot. Pressure on this pedal causes the
hammer to strike the strings twenty-five blows in sufficiently rapid succession to cause
them to blend into a continuous stream of sound. *F*, spring giving elasticity to the
hammer; *G*, support to the lever *C*; *H*, damper; *J*, spring; *K*, lever serving to work
the damper lifter; *L*, spring; *M*, damper lifter. The upper keyboard plays in the
usual way.

way. The intensity of the tone could be varied by altering the
pressure on the key. Sautter's action is similar to Madame
Girard-Romagnac's and Christian Then's.

(3) *A device for sustaining the tone in imitation of the 'Animo-Corde'
by subjecting the strings to* CURRENTS OF AIR. The third and last
type of Sostenente pianoforte consists in an attempt to prolong
the sounds by subjecting the strings to a current of air. The reader
will, no doubt, recall what was said concerning the 'Animo-Corde'

[1] C 1223.

invented by Schnell and Tschenky in 1790 and how the strings, after they had been set in motion by a ring bow mechanism, were subjected to the influence of currents of air in order to prolong and augment their vibrations. In the instruments about to be mentioned the principle is the same, except that a hammer action is used in place of the ring bow.

About the year 1828 Eschenbach invented the *Eolodicon*[1] in which the sound was produced by the action of currents of air directed against metal springs. No doubt these springs had previously been struck by a hammer. Five years later Alphonse-Jean Grus[2] of Paris designed a pianoforte with an opening in the back of the case to allow a current of air to act against the strings in order to increase their vibrations after they had been struck by the hammers. In 1836 Wheatstone and Green[3] patented an invention whereby continuous sounds were produced by causing a current of air to act on the strings "after or at the same time as" they had been set in motion by a striking agent. Henri Pape of Paris mentions a device for sustaining the vibrations of strings and of springs in his patent of 1839,[4] and in a 'Brevet d'Addition' dated July 31st, 1840,[5] he has designed another means for sustaining the vibrations of metal springs by a current of air. Yet another application of this invention is seen in his French patent of 1850,[6] whilst in his English patent[7] of the same year he has devised a means whereby a stream of air can be poured on to strings and springs attached to each other by a silken cord in order that they may vibrate sympathetically.

A departure from the strict chronological order has purposely been made with a view to describing Pape's inventions together, as they are concerned, for the most part, with pianofortes with metal springs instead of strings. A brief description will now be given of an instrument with the usual strings invented by Isoard in 1842.[8] Underneath the strings there was a small movable box which contained as many compartments as there were strings to be vibrated. Each of these compartments was connected to a wind box by means of a valve. A special container took up compressed air from a double bellows. The keys controlled the passage of air

---

[1] B 45 (*b*), p. 37.   [2] C 1208.
[3] C 1210.   [4] C 1211.
[5] To the Fr. Pat. of 1834 (C 1219).
[6] C 1213.   [7] C 1212.
[8] B 2 (1842, Hefte VIII und IX, S. 584).

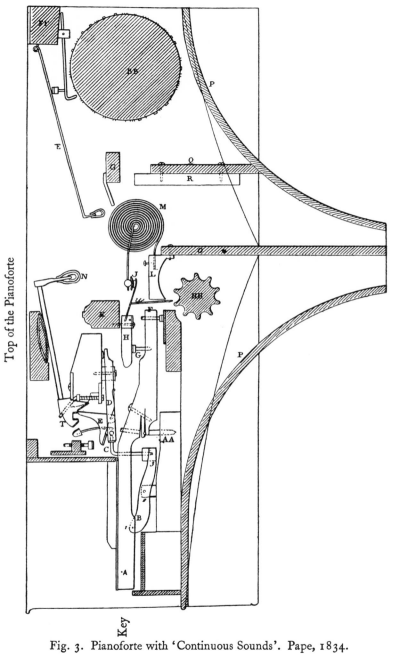

Top of the Pianoforte

Key

Fig. 3. Pianoforte with 'Continuous Sounds'. Pape, 1834.

into the bellows and its subsequent outpouring on to the strings. In the case of the 'Animo-Corde' invented by Schnell and Tschenky, it was necessary to stimulate the strings into motion before subjecting them to the currents of air, and they used a ring bow mechanism for the purpose. Isoard, also, was obliged to follow their example, but preferred the use of an ordinary hammer action.

For the purpose of obtaining dynamic expression Isoard fitted a pedal which enabled the player to move the wind box near or

---

DESCRIPTION OF FIG. 3 (*opposite*).

A, touche du clavier. *A*, *A*, nouvelle pointe en cuivre étamé. *B*, bascule portant trois centres 1, 2, 3, et, à son extrémité, un crochet *C* qui prend sous la bascule *D* portant l'échappement *E*, qui soulève la noix du marteau *T* et fonctionne comme à l'ordinaire. La touche *A* porte à son extrémité, une vis à bouton en cuivre *F*, servant à régler le clavier de hauteur. Tout à côté est un autre bouton à vis *G*, qui en soulevant la bascule, la fait pivoter sur le centre *I*, et baisse le bout opposé, portant l'étouffoir *J*. Cette bascule est vissée sous la pièce de bois mobile *K*. À chaque extrémité de cette pièce de bois est percé un trou dans lequel passe une broche de fer avec écrou en haut, et portant un ressort à boudin qui tient constamment la pièce de bois élevée contre cet écrou, ainsi qu'il est indiqué en dehors du plan. En faisant baisser la pièce de bois par la tringle *U*, qui communique aux pédales, on opère le *forte* sans que la bascule *H* quitte le bouton; avantage qui n'existe pas dans les pianos ordinaires, où l'étouffoir sert en partie à relever le clavier, qui se trouvant déchargé de son contrepieds, pendant que l'étouffoir est tenu en l'air, fait que la touche ne remonte plus avec la même vivacité. *L*, sommier en fer après lequel sont fixés les ressorts *M* faits de divers métaux. Une branche, réservée au centre, se présente sous le coup du marteau *N*. Cette branche est taraudée et porte un écrou en plomb, en forme de balle. L'étouffoir *J* sert à éteindre le son, comme dans les autres pianos. Au sommier de fer *L* est adaptée la table horizontale *O*, qui pose sur une autre table concave *P*, formée de quatre morceaux qui, se réunissant au bas en seul point, forment un entonnoir. *Q*, autre table horizontale adaptée sur le deuxième sommier de fer *R*. A ce sommier, qui porte 4 pouces de haut, sont adaptés les divers ressorts.

J'ai adapté aussi à cet instrument un mécanisme pour exécuter seul.

Le cylindre *BB* est mis en action par un mouvement à ressort placé sur la droite de l'instrument; en tournant, il lève le clavier *D*,[1] qui porte un pilote servant à relever le marteau *E*, qui, étant à ressort, frappe, en retombant, sur la lame, qui produit le son. Ce marteau est attaché à la pièce de bois *FF*, qui est mobile. *G*, pédale pour adoucir le son. *HH*, cylindre denté mis en mouvement par la même machine et servant à prolonger le son par le moyen d'une pédale: il avance contre la branche *ii*, fixée à celle de l'étouffoir en baleine. La touche, en faisant basculer l'étouffoir *H*, baisse la branche *ii* contre le cylindre, qui, en opérant sa rotation de gauche à droite, lui imprime un mouvement continu, qui fait soutenir le son tant que la touche reste baissée. (*Abridged.*)

[1] Letters *D*, *I* and *U* are missing in the original diagram (C 1219).

far from the strings according to his desire for a loud or soft tone. A still greater variation could be obtained if each octave was provided with a wind box and pedal to itself. The current of air could be withdrawn if the normal pianoforte tone was preferred.[1]

The reader may perhaps feel that he has attended a psychological lecture on the 'nightmares of musical instrument makers', but the familiar organ itself is no less astonishing than some of the inventions enumerated, for it is a wind instrument to which has been added stops for gaining the illusion of strings and even the human voice—a sham orchestra in which even Janissary music has been added from time to time.

[1] This instrument was inspected by the following personages: Messrs Cherubini, Berton, Halevy, Carafa and Spontini; Argo, Puissant, Becquerel, Dutrochet; Poncelet and Pouillet, whilst M. Séguier acted in the capacity of reporter. The result of the examination was satisfactory to M. Isoard.

CHAPTER III

OCTAVE COUPLERS AND 'DUOCLAVE'
PIANOFORTES

DURING a period covering the lives of symphony writers
such as Beethoven, Schubert, and Mendelssohn and such
popular composers of operas as Rossini, Bellini, Donizetti,
Meyerbeer and Weber, it is not surprising to find a concentration
of interest on the orchestra, accompanied by an increasing demand
for pianoforte reductions of orchestral and operatic scores.

The duet has always been of value to the amateur, since it enables him to become widely read in music which would otherwise
be inaccessible to him. The difficulties of execution are divided
between the two performers, whilst a fuller tone and consequently
a more realistic impression of the original may be gained.

But the duet was not only used as a translation of orchestral
music into the terms of the pianoforte, but also as a distinct art
form. Mozart wrote nine duets, two of which were originally
intended for a mechanical organ or clock, whilst Schubert's numerous compositions in this form comprise some of his finest music.

The widespread use of the duet led to the invention of special
pianofortes fitted with two separate keyboards and actions placed
opposite to each other within a single case. The advantages of such
instruments are obvious, for the players were the less incommoded,
and thus enabled to play with greater precision.

As a second performer was not always available, the amateur
had often to content himself with a two-hand arrangement of his
favourite duet, symphony or operatic air, resulting in a considerable loss of effect.

Some ingenious pianoforte makers, observing the use of octave
couplers on the harpsichord, hit upon the idea of applying this
mechanism to the pianoforte. By this means the second performer
was supplied mechanically, though the musical instrument makers
had no idea of the benefit they were conferring. The octave passages were always perfectly together without the necessity of continual practice. The technical difficulties of execution were halved,
and the fullness of an orchestra admirably counterfeited.

Pianofortes with Octave Couplers. PATENTS. It was the firm of Érard Frères who first experimented in this direction. In 1812 they brought out a pianoforte in the form of a 'Secrétaire',[1] in which there were two sound-boards, one above the other, each with its separate set of strings and action. The strings of the upper sound-board were tuned an octave above those of the lower and the usual system of three unisons to a note was adopted. If the performer preferred all the strings to be in unison he could alter the bridge on the upper sound-board to a position corresponding to that on the lower. Both sets of strings could be coupled by the action of a pedal. Thus the performer had at his command a tremendous 'fortissimo' suggesting the return of the 'tutti' including the full brass band, whilst he could also drop to as sudden a 'pianissimo'. A mechanical decrescendo or a crescendo rising from one or two strings to three and from three to four or five strings and culminating in a fortissimo in which all the six strings were used together was also placed at the player's disposal. Another effect of considerable emotional value would result if the same range of strings was passed through whilst keeping effect 'piano'. Beethoven may have had such a pianoforte in view when he wrote in the *Adagio ma non troppo* of his Sonata Op. 101 the following directions, first "eine Saite", then towards the end of the Cadenza leading to 'Tempo del Primo' "nach und nach mehrere Saiten", followed by the direction "tutto il Cembalo *ma piano*".[2]

Johann Streicher designed an instrument in 1824[3] in which the octave of the note struck could be sounded in order to strengthen the tone. About the year 1827 Charles Lemoine brought out a pianoforte in which strings a "double octave to the bass" were sounded when coupled by a pedal. J.J.D., who writes of this invention in a letter to the editor of *The Harmonicon*, dated November 20th, 1827, describes the effect in the following words: "The tone is superb and will render it most useful in a theatre; it may almost compete with a small orchestra".[4] In a Giraffe pianoforte with six pedals patented in 1831 by Julius Kisselstein of Nuremberg[5] pedals 2 and 3 are octave couplers. Pedal 2 couples the octave above from F_1 to e', whilst pedal 3 couples the octave

---

[1] C 352.

[2] N.B. Beethoven had a range of three strings at his disposal, as the early Una Corda (Verschiebung) enabled the performer to use one, two or three strings.

[3] C 353.   [4] B 54, Vol. vi, p. 6.

[5] C 354.

Plate II. Giraffenflügel. By Joseph Wachtl of Vienna. No. 2186, Hochschule für Musik, Berlin. The case is mahogany with bronze caryatides and bronze ornaments. The most striking feature is the large black carved wooden figure of Apollo. [Height 255 cm., breadth 120 cm., thickness 58 cm.] There are five pedals as follows: (1) Forte, (2) Piano, (3) Piano (cop.), (4) Una Corda, (5) Bassoon. A pianoforte of this type appears to have cost about eighty-one pounds. We quote an advertisement dated March 1st, 1817 [1]: "An upright pianoforte, with six and a half octaves, white ivory keys and five pedals: (1) Forte, (2) Piano, (3) Bassoon, (4) Una Corda, (5) Turkish Music. The case in beautiful maple pattern. There hangs above a wreathed oak garland, and at the end [sic] a figure with an Apollo lyre as a symbol of music, all most artistically carved and very richly gilded. Price 80 Carolins [2]".

[1] B 2 (1817), No. 9, March 1st, p. 144.   [2] One Carolin = £1. 0s. 4d.

above from e' to f'''. Madame Girard-Romagnac patented a means for coupling either the octave or the octave below in 1842.[1] Boisselot et fils of Marseilles patented a pianoforte in 1843 with two strings in unison tuned an octave above the three unisons which formed the usual scale. A pedal and mechanism for sliding the keyboard and action laterally enabled the player to couple the five strings. The hammer beam was divided so that the octave strings could be used either in the bass or in the treble or for the complete range as desired.[2] A slightly different arrangement was invented by Charles Maurice Elizee Sautter in 1844.[3] It consisted in a lever one end of which acted on the key touched whilst the other end communicated motion to the hammer for the octave above. A somewhat similar action was brought out by Pleyel during this year to enable the pianist to obtain orchestral effects ordinarily impossible upon the pianoforte.

Yet another action for the same purpose consisted in the addition of one or more supplementary strings struck by the ordinary hammers and so arranged that they could be muted through the agency of a special damper when they were not required. This new arrangement was invented by Oliver and Jackson of Utica, U.S.A., in 1845.[4] In the same year their countryman, Simon W. Draper,[5] of Boston, invented an action for striking the octave below. This was effected by fixing an additional string to every note of the instrument. It was also in 1845 that Samuel Warren,[6] a native of Montreal, Canada, designed a mechanism in which "any number of keys or hammers were connected together by coupling levers, so that the striking of any one key should by means of the coupling lever strike the note of its octave". This coupling was so arranged that the parts striking the octave could be thrown out of action at pleasure by means of a pedal. Warren states that he does not limit the application of his invention to the production of octaves, but is prepared to adapt it to any other series of notes. Yet another invention belonging to this year is that of Benjamin Nichels,[7] who devised a plan for combining a horizontal with an upright pianoforte. In this instrument there were to be two sound-boards with their separate sets of strings and action and a manual to act upon each. The lower manual worked the action for the horizontal portion of this monster, whilst the upper

[1] C 355. [2] C 356. [3] C 357.
[4] C 359. [5] C 360. [6] C 361.
[7] C 362.

manual coupled the upright with the horizontal. The upper manual could be disconnected by means of a pedal from the lower one if the performer wished to play upon the upright portion alone. Nor was this all, for a pedalier was also designed to be attached. Soudet of Havre[1] invented a 'Pédale de Mélodie' in 1847 which enabled the player to reduplicate a theme, and Zeiger of Lyons[2] arranged a coupling device worked by oblique levers which could be disconnected by means of a pedal.

The drawback to all the inventions enumerated above consists in the additional weight they add to the touch, and this accounts for the fact that they did not become popular. Attempts have been made down to the present day to invent an action without this defect, but the difficulties have not as yet been surmounted.

An example of a pianoforte with octave couplers may be seen in the collection of musical instruments attached to the Hochschule für Musik in Berlin. It is No. 813 and was built by J. C. Schönemann of Berlin about the second quarter of the nineteenth century. There are four pedals: octave couplers for the bass, for the whole range of the notes and for the treble alone, and forte.

Duoclave Pianofortes. Hitherto only the inventions for coupling the octave have been enumerated. But pianofortes in which the inventor suggests the possible addition of a second keyboard opposite to the first, and other instruments expressly designed for two performers—'Duoclave' pianofortes on which both types of duets could be played—were also made.

In 1800 Matthias Müller of Vienna invented a duoclave 'pianino', or small upright pianoforte, which he named *Ditanaklasis*. An idea of its appearance may be gained from Plates I, II, Part II, § 3, if a second keyboard is imagined on the other side of the instrument opposite to the one shown. The double *Ditanaklasis* was considered a useful invention, since it occupied no more space than a tea-table and would fit into a small room.[3]

The firm of Érard Frères were the first to patent a 'Duoclave' pianoforte; this was their 'Piano-Secrétaire', already mentioned, where an additional keyboard could be fitted if the owner desired. In the same year they brought out a tall upright instrument[4] with

---

[1] C 363. [2] C 364.

[3] (*a*) A double *Ditanaklasis* may be seen in the Crosby Brown Collection of Musical Instruments in the Metropolitan Museum of Art, New York. (*b*) For an engraving of the *Ditanaklasis* see B 22.

[4] C 865.

a sound-board in the form of a cylindrical column to which a second keyboard could be added if desired (Part II, § 3, Fig. 30, p. 287).

Yet another instrument of theirs, patented in 1821,[1] was intended from the first to be a 'Duoclave' and was in the form of a square pianoforte of five feet eight inches long and twenty-nine inches[2] broad. The stringing was to be trichord over a range of seven octaves and there were to be four or five pedals (Fig. 5). Another instrument in the form of a 'Duoclave' was brought out by Jean-Baptiste Charreyre[3] of Paris in 1825. It had three pedals: Bassoon, Forte and Célestine ('Célestine' is Charreyre's name for 'Una Corda'). The hammers in this pianoforte are arranged on stickers for three octaves whilst their striking points vary from a

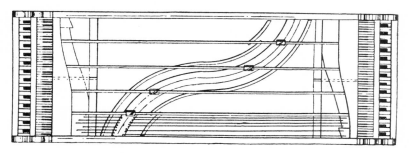

Fig. 4. Pirsson's 'Double-grand' pianoforte, 1850. From the patent.

position near to the top of the instrument to a position opposite to the performer's hand. Edward Dodd[4] states in a patent dated 1840 that he sometimes makes 'double-pianofortes'. An instrument with two keyboards was patented in 1850 by Van der Cruyssen[5] of Ghent. There is no description and consequently it is impossible to say whether this is a 'Duoclave' or simply a two-manual pianoforte. N. Hainaught[6] of Binche in Belgium invented a double pianoforte in 1851, but it has unfortunately not been possible to secure a description of this instrument.

Two 'Duoclave' pianofortes were exhibited in the Great Exhibition of 1851: Messrs Jones and Co., an English firm, sent a 'double pianoforte' consisting of two piccolo uprights placed back to back and in such a way that one frame did duty for both

---

[1] C 866.
[2] N.B. Parisian inches [Parisian foot or *pied de roi* = 325 mm.].
[3] C 867.   [4] C 868.
[5] C 870.   [6] C 871.

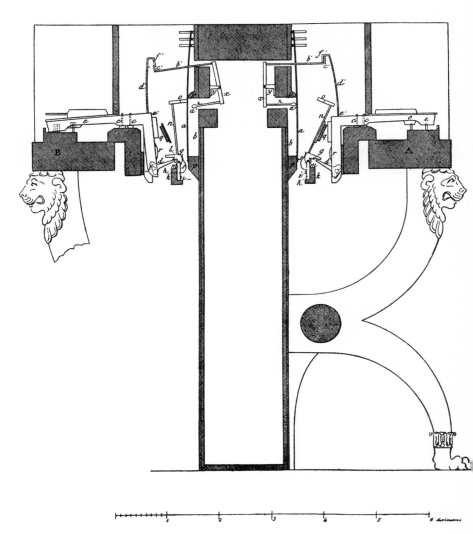

Fig. 5. Duoclave Pianoforte. Érard, 1821.

instruments. Pirsson, of New York, sent a "double-grand piano, which may be described as consisting of two grands, enclosed in one large oblong rectangular case (Fig. 4)—the players sitting at the two opposite ends facing one another. One string plate serves for both instruments, the short strings of one came in a line with the long strings of the other".[1] He patented this in 1850.[2]

[1] B 82, pp. 30, 41.   [2] C 869.

DESCRIPTION OF FIG. 5 (*opposite*).

a, Corde.
b, Table d'harmonie.
c, Centre du mouvement.
d, Languette d'échappement posée dans la partie basse de la touche.
e, Touche.
f, Goupille sur laquelle tourne la languette *d.*
g, Base du marteau.
h, Tasseau en bois de buis.
i, Vis de cuivre.
l, Deux petites platines en cuivre.
m, Petite tringle en acier.
n, Tige du marteau.
o, Tête du marteau.
p, Chevalets sur lesquels repose la corde *a.*
q, Barre où repose la tige *n* du marteau.
r, Ressort agissant sur la languette *d,* pour replacer son extrémité dans la position qu'elle a quittée et est indiquée dans le clavier A.
s, Autre ressort pour faciliter le retour du marteau lorsqu'il a frappé la corde.
x, tringle en bois tenue par...
y, une fourchette à deux platines en cuivre.
z, Fil de laiton garni de ses extrémités
a', pour étouffer la corde *a.*
b', Fil de laiton vissé dans la partie supérieure de la tringle *x*; il forme un crochet à
c', l'extrémité opposée.
d', Montant du même fil de laiton vissé dans la touche au pointe
e', et formant un crochet
f' qui saisit le crochet *c',* de manière qu'on appuyant sur la touche *e,* le fil de laiton montant *d'* tire en avant le crochet *c'*; la tringle *x* devient mouvante et imprime le mouvement à la fourchette *y,* et la tringle *z* qui est garni à l'extrémité, quitte la corde *a* au moment où le marteau frappe cette corde, et retombe aussitôt que le doigt a quitté la touche *e.*

CHAPTER IV

THE INFLUENCE OF PROGRAMME MUSIC ON THE CONSTRUCTION OF THE PIANOFORTE

AFTER the invention of the escapement action in its various forms already described, there arose a host of virtuoso pianists who devoted much attention to discovering the possibilities of the instrument and to embodying their researches in a form which should be of use to future students of the art. Thus the first instruction-books dealing exclusively with pianoforte technique came to be written, beginning with Clementi's famous *Gradus ad Parnassum* and followed by those of Hummel, Czerny, Herz and others.

The pupil is thoroughly taught, in these works, to obtain expression by his touch upon the keys alone, whilst he is warned against the excessive use of the pedals (as they were called when the stops were arranged to be worked by the feet). The general consensus of opinion amongst the great pianists seems to have been that only the 'forte', now known as the 'Damper Pedal', Una Corda, and 'piano' pedals, were legitimate, whilst all the others were useless additions. Hummel writes:

Though a truly great Artist has no occasion for Pedals to work upon his audience by expression and power, yet the use of the damper-pedal, combined occasionally with the piano-pedal. . . has an agreeable effect in many passages. . . . *All other Pedals are useless, and of no value either to the performer or to the instrument.* [1]

The nature of the pianoforte was now thoroughly understood and consequently it might be expected that all the stops would disappear with the exception of those for forte, piano and Una Corda (Verschiebung). But, as a matter of fact, this was not the case, the stops did not disappear, but on the contrary others were added to those already in existence. We have seen that they would find no favour with Hummel, and Czerny was no less severe in his criticism. There is a passage in the famous *Pianoforte School* where he informs his pupil that there are three necessary pedals:

(1) The damper pedal (Forte).
(2) Una Corda (Verschiebung).
(3) Piano (Piano).

[1] B 102 (Part III, Sect. II, Chap. III, p. 62).

He then remarks that the 'Piano' is rarely used, even in Germany, whilst "all other pedals, as the Fagotto and Harp pedals, or the Drum and Bells, or Triangle, etc., are childish toys of which a solid player will disdain to avail himself".[1] Moscheles also is said rarely to have used the pedals. In spite of these severe remarks the 'childish toys' continued to be built into pianofortes well into the 'forties', if not later. Who, then, used these pianofortes, and what kind of music was played upon them?

During the early years of the nineteenth century a quantity of descriptive pianoforte music was written, such as Battles, Pastoral Scenes, Storms, descriptive pieces of all kinds, ranging from a tiger hunt to a thanksgiving service at St Paul's or a public christening on the Neva at St Petersburg. In this quasi-romantic programme music, crude realism plays a prominent part. In the battle scenes the Trumpet calls, sounding of alarm bells and cannons firing and Drums beating are imitated as realistically as possible.[2] A certain young lady owned a pianoforte by Astor with two pedals: one for sustaining the sound and the other for opening the short side of the lid for the purpose of obtaining a pleasing 'swell'. When playing a battle piece she illustrated the explosion of cannon by suddenly releasing her foot from the swell pedal and allowing the lid to fall with a crash.[3] In some of the older music the 'Wolf' keys of the organ or the harpsichord had even been employed where "harshness was to be expressed by the voice",[4] whilst Leopold Mozart actually ordered whistling through the fingers inserted into the mouth in a pastoral representing a rural wedding.

The rise of the programme symphony in the eighteenth century exercised an important influence on pianoforte composers, who were inspired to write similar works for their instrument. The Comte de Lacépède, in his book entitled *Poétique de la Musique* (1785), writes that "A Symphony consists usually of three pieces of music.... The Composer ought to consider them as three grand acts of a theatrical piece, and imagine himself to be working at a tragedy, a comedy, or a pastoral".[5]

An interesting example of an attempt to write a descriptive

---

[1] B 99 (Part III, Chap. VI, pp. 57, 65).
[2] So well known was the drum rhythm in England that the word *Drum* was used as a technical term signifying 'measure without melody' (B 56, Pl. 26, Ex. CXVII).
[3] B 71, pp. 261, 262.   [4] Maffei's paper quoted in B 84.
[5] B 78, p. 102.

H P

symphony for the pianoforte is to be seen in Auguste Bertini's *Fantasia* (No. 9) written for six hands on *one pianoforte* (Fig. 6). Bertini was a pupil of Clementi and the musical instructor of his younger and more famous brother Henri.

The warlike period from 1789 to 1815 called forth many warlike pieces, the most famous of which is Beethoven's *Battle Symphony* which he arranged himself as a pianoforte solo, and *The Battle of Prague* by Kotzwara, originally written about 1788 for pianoforte, with accompaniments for a Violin, Violoncello and Drum *ad libitum*, but early arranged both as a pianoforte solo and as a duet. The battle pieces of Daniel Steibelt also attained considerable popularity.

There was a certain convention about these 'plays in music'. The 'Commemorative' pieces or 'Comedies' usually depict a thanksgiving ceremony[1] and include a section representing

[1] In order to give some idea of this type of music we quote the programme to Steibelt's "Overture in Commemoration of His Britannic Majesty's Solemn Procession to the Cathedral of St Paul's" to return thanks for Admiral Duncan's Victory.

Allegro Moderato. (*a*) The crowing of the cock.
(*b*) The dawn of day.
(*c*) The chirping of birds.

Ex. (*a*).

Ex. (*c*).

Ex. (*d*).

'Divine Service' and 'military music'. The Battle pieces include Trumpets, Drums, cannons firing, cries of the wounded, marches, and a section representing the joy of the victorious, whilst the

Moderato.   (*e*) The Clock strikes ten.

Ex. (*e*).

Allegro Moderato.   (*f*) The King's departure and the sound of trumpets.
                 (*g*) Cannons (represented by octaves in the bass).
Maestoso   (*h*) God Save the King. Change of Time.
Andante   (*i*) The French Colours.
Allegro.   (*k*) Rule Britannia.
Andante.   (*l*) The Spanish Colours.
Allegro.   (*m*) Rule Britannia.
Andante.   (*n*) The Dutch Colours.
Allegro.   (*o*) Rule Britannia.
                 (*p*) Huzza, Huzza.
Maestoso.   (*q*) Triumphant March.
Adagio Maestoso. (*r*) The King enters St Paul's.
Adagio.   (*s*) Divine Service begins.

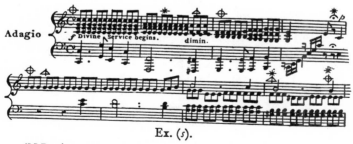

Ex. (*s*).

(N.B. ⊕ = forte pedal; △ = piano pedal; * = release pedal.)

Moderato   (*t*) And all the people rejoiced and said.
Moderato.   (*u*) Long Live the King (etc.).
Presto   (*v*) Finale.
                 (*w*) Huzza.
                 (*x*) Drums beat.
                 (*y*) Huzza.
                 (*z*) Cannons.

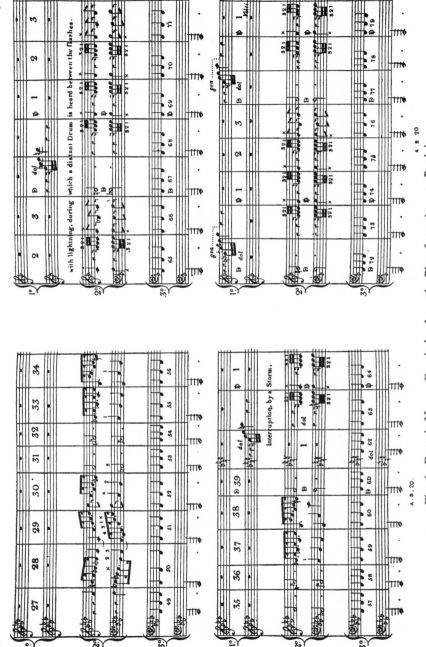

Fig. 6. Fantasia No. 9. For six hands on the Pianoforte. Auguste Bertini.

This is a Waltz "which is meant to represent the Rustic style of music (N.B. the Pastoral) in the French Province of Auvergne; the bass note being in imitation of the tabor Drum".

Pastorals must include a storm which interrupts the merry-making of peasants (Fig. 6). They suggest some of the old landscape and genre pictures painted in the studio according to a more or less set formula. These works are distinctly theatrical in character and their method of representation had also to be theatrical. It was the pianist's business to orchestrate them on the pianoforte, and the pianoforte maker's duty to make it possible for him to do so.

In order to understand the musical instrument makers and what it was they were trying to do with their characteristic stops and novel effects, it is necessary to imagine the old pianofortes against their historical background. The audience appear to have looked upon their concerts almost in the light of another form of theatrical entertainment and it was not considered improper to applaud the artist *during* his performance, whilst a display of excessive emotion does not seem to have been uncommon. William Gardiner, who was present at a concert given by Paganini at the Opera House, London, in 1831, informs us that Paganini's celebrated performance on a single string was interrupted with the "loudest bursts of laughter". At a concert given by Chopin at Rouen in 1838 "the room was as if electrified, and resounded with bursts of admiration". An audience was even reduced to tears by an automaton violinist: Bruyère, who was present, writes that the automaton "played a most beautiful fantasia in E natural, with accompaniments, including a movement 'allegro molto' on the fourth string solo, which was perfectly indescribable. The tones produced were like anything but a violin; and expressive beyond conception. "I felt", he said, "as if lifted from my seat, and burst into tears, in which predicament I saw most persons in the room."[1] Scenes of this type seem to have been of only too frequent occurrence. In fact, it is said that before a performance of Bellini's opera, *I Montecchi e Capuleti*, was to take place at Bucharest the following notice was placed at the foot of the playbill: "To avoid the lamentable effect at the end of the fourth act, Romeo and Juliet will *not* die".

[1] B 75 (c). At the conclusion of the performance the conductor "showed the company the interior of the figure, which was completely filled with small cranks"!

CHAPTER V

THE INFLUENCE OF TURKISH MUSIC UPON
THE PIANOFORTE

THE addition of the Turkish musical instruments to the
military band had a far-reaching effect upon music. The
Bass Drum, Triangle and Cymbals became permanently
associated not only with military music but also with dance music.
This important fact led to their introduction into the pianoforte
and into other keyboard instruments. It is proposed briefly to
trace the circumstance that led to this development.

Towards the end of the eighteenth century the Russian General,
Marshal Kirilowitsch, is said to have formed the first Horn band.
Each of the musicians was provided with a hunting Horn capable of
emitting but one single note. To perform music with such a troupe
required the highest precision and skill on the part of the musicians,
who had often to wait for some considerable time before it was
their turn to play. In fact, this Horn music was a prodigy after
the hearts of the eighteenth-century nobles and gentry of Russia.
It was introduced into the army and became so widely dispersed
and popular as to be regarded as a kind of national music. But
many of the musical amateurs who had served in the Turkish wars
were not satisfied with their Horn music, and desired to have in
addition a Turkish band.

On the occasion of the grand *fête* to celebrate her conclusive
treaty with the Turks, the Empress Catherine of Russia decided to
provide a band of Janissary music to entertain her guests at the
feast. After an unsatisfactory attempt to form such a band, it was
recalled that the Empress Elizabeth had a certain chamber musician
named Schmirpfeil in her service, who had been to Constantinople.
Schmirpfeil's Turkish troupe was composed of twelve to fifteen
musicians and was considered to be an exact imitation of the
Janissary band. It consisted as follows:

2, 3 or 4 Turkish Hautboys ⎫ very piercing in tone.
    2 Large Turkish Hautboys ⎭
    1 Transverse Flute (very shrill).
    2 Small Kettle-drums.
    1 Bass Drum.

a

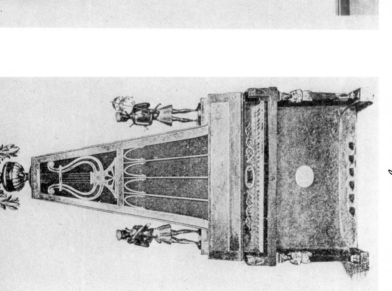

b

Plate III (*a*). Pyramidenflügel. C. Schlimbach of Koenigshofen. By permission of the Musikwissenschaftliches Institut, Leipzig. [Heger Coll. No. 192.] The case is in walnut. [Height 2·74 m., breadth 1·15 m., thickness 62 cm.] There are six pedals as follows: (1) Forte, (2) Piano, (3) Pianissimo (i.e. Lute), (4) Una Corda, (5) Bassoon, (6) Janissary Music. Pedal No. 6 not only sounds the drum and bells but causes the automata to play their instruments.

(*b*). Giraffenflügel, by F. Seiffert of Vienna. Berlin, Hochschule für Musik, No. 1275. The case is mahogany with bronzed caryatides. [Height 231 cm., breadth 127 cm., thickness 50 cm.] There are five pedals as follows: (1) Forte, (2) —, (3) Bassoon, (4) Una Corda, (5) Turkish Music.

2 Pairs Cymbals.
1 Pair very large Cymbals.
2 Triangles.
(All the music was played either in unison or in octaves.)

After this, the band of expert hautboyists attached to the Imperial Guard practised upon the Turkish instruments with a view to entertaining their officers during mess.[1] According to some authorities Turkish music had become rampant in certain parts of Germany at an even earlier date.

The 'Cymbalstern' or 'Étoile Sonore' or 'Vox Stellarum', a pseudo-Turkish instrument representing the Magi's star (consisting of a star-shaped metal case to the points of which were attached little bells which jingled when the star was moved), was built into the organ of the monastic church at Weingarten as early as 1750. It is also to be found in the church of Waltershausen, and at Hamburg in the churches of St Michael, St Catherine, St James and St Nicholas. The Cymbal Pauke (Cymbals and Drums) was also occasionally introduced into organs: an example still exists in the church of St Catherine at Dantzig.[2]

On the occasion of the visit of the Turkish Ambassador, Achmet Effendi, to Berlin,[3] a band of Turkish music was provided for his entertainment. When some courtiers ventured to inquire how His Excellency enjoyed the music, he exclaimed: "ceci n'est point turc", accompanied with a significant shrug of the shoulders. When this was reported to the King of Prussia, he hesitated no longer and took Turkish musicians into his service. The Prussians were not satisfied with the Turkish music alone, but preferred to add ordinary instruments to it, particularly the Bassoon and Trumpet.

The Emperor of Austria was not to be outdone by the King of Prussia; he too formed a Turkish band, which was used by Gluck at the theatre.[4] It will be recalled how he avails himself of it in *Iphigénie en Tauride*, where it accompanies the terrible dance of the Scythians.

By the end of the eighteenth century the bands of most of the famous European regiments included the Turkish instruments: Bass Drum, Side Drum, Cymbals, Triangle and Pavillon Chinois or Turkish Crescent.

[1] B 58, pp. 128–130.   [2] B 93, p. 35.
[3] Date not cited by Kastner. See reference below.
[4] See B 58, pp. 130–131.

The 'Tambour de Basque', or Tambourine, was also included in certain French regiments.[1]

Turkish music became the rage and it was the custom to attire the musicians in fantastic costumes. When Turks themselves were not available negroes were hired instead. An excellent idea of the appearance of these musicians may be gained from the Collection of Christmas Cribs at the Bavarian National Museum at Munich, where a Neapolitan artist of the eighteenth century has introduced Turkish bands composed of negroes and Turks into some of the groups.[2]

The introduction of the Turkish instruments into the English military bands was somewhat retarded by the dislike of King George III to this type of music. Mrs Papendiek states that "one circumstance (which) greatly disturbed the King, and it is feared brought forward his direful malady to a more violent crisis, was the return of the Duke of York from Hanover, without permission, and the unceasing endeavours of His Royal Highness to persuade the King to allow him to introduce into the Guards' band the Turkish musical instruments, with ornamental tails, crescents, etc."[3]

Eventually, in fact, these instruments were introduced, and negroes fantastically attired as Turkish musicians were employed not only to play the Janissary instruments, but also to play upon some of the others.

---

[1] B 58, p. 171.

[2] Bav. Nat. Mus. 1st floor, rooms 82 to 90. See the following:

(a) *Italienischer Palasthof mit Gefolge der heiligen drei Könige.* Band consisting of: 4 Recorders, 1 Bassoon, 1 Zinke, 1 Serpent, 2 Trumpets, 3 Horns, one of which is a Russian Horn, 1 Chapeau Chinois, 2 pairs Cymbals.

(b) *Zelt mit Gefolge der heiligen drei Könige.* Band consisting of the following: 3 Recorders, one bass, 2 Double Recorders, 1 Double Bassoon, 2 Horns, one larger than the other, 2 Trumpets, 1 Chapeau Chinois, 1 pair Cymbals, 1 pair large Clappers, 1 pair Kettle-Drums, 1 Side Drum, 1 Bass Drum.

(c) *Massen, Messer, Stöcke, Pfeifen, Instrumente für die heiligen drei Könige.* The following instruments: 1 small Trumpet, 4 Horns (natural), 1 pair Kettle-Drums, 1 Tambourine with bells, 1 circular set of Bells, 1 Chapeau Chinois.

(d) *Group* (unnamed) *representing the three holy Kings riding accompanied by retainers.* The following instruments carried by retainers: 2 Trumpets, one of which is a Valve Trumpet, 3 Horns, two natural and one Russian Horn, 1 pair Cymbals, 1 Triangle.

(e) *Miscellaneous group of figures* carrying the following instruments: 7 Recorders, one double, 3 Bassoons, 1 Serpent, 2 Trumpets, 1 large Russian Horn.

N.B. An illustrated catalogue is in course of preparation.

[3] B 40, p. 73.

There had been some attempt to introduce Turkish music before this: the Drum pedal was inserted into the organ at St Nicholas' Church at Deptford by Father Smith, and Renatus Harris had introduced it into the organ at Salisbury Cathedral in 1710.[1] But Kettle-Drums seem to have been used somewhat as a novelty by Handel in his Dettingen Te Deum in 1743. It is said that a pair of brass Drums was taken at the battle and was used at the first performance of this work at Leicester, when they were played by the Earl of Sandwich. William Gardiner informs us that Lord Sandwich "...was so enamoured with the thunder of the Drums, that he had one side of his music-room strained with parchment, upon which being suddenly struck, so alarmed the company, as to throw many into fits, which his Lordship maintained was a certain proof of the boldness of the effect".[2]

We can see a remnant of the Turkish music rage on our oldest 'Merry-go-rounds' where soldierly automata are often to be seen beating upon Drums and clashing Cymbals.

In fact the 'Turkish Taste' put its mark upon everything from playing-cards to children's toy soldiers and ladies' head-dresses, whilst its influence is also to be seen in the literature of this period.

Turkish music was only used by composers as a particular effect, for instance in a barbarian scene, as in Gluck's *Iphigénie en Tauride* in the chorus of the Scythians, or as a humorous effect, as in the chorus of Janissaries in Mozart's opera *Die Entführung aus dem Serail*, and again in Schubert's opera *Des Teufels Lustschloss* in the scene when "Ein Chor geschmückter Jungfrauen erscheint paarweise auf türkischen Instrumenten spielend", and in military movements.

Besides the use of Turkish music in military movements and barbarian scenes, characteristic Turkish pieces were written, such as Leopold Mozart's *A Turkish Piece* and Wolfgang's *Sonata* in A major (K. 331) composed in 1778, where the Rondo is marked *alla Turca*. In fact Turkish Marches were a great favourite with composers.

Turkish music was naturally introduced into dance orchestras, and was a useful addition to the Waltz. In the smaller orchestras the Drum was sometimes replaced by the Tambourine.

Daniel Steibelt's marriage with a young English woman who was an excellent player upon this instrument led him to write a

[1] B 93, p. 62.
[2] B 43, pp. 355, 356.

Fig. 7. Waltz No. xxiii for Pianoforte and Tambourine. Daniel Steibelt.

part of it in his 'Bacchanales' or Waltzes. It is said to have been due to him that the Tambourine and Drum pedals became a popular addition to the pianoforte. Marmontel writes: "Sa musique colorée, pittoresque exigeait l'emploi des différentes pédales, y compris celle qui faisait mouvoir un tambourin nécessaire à l'accompagnement de ces 'bacchanales'"[1] (Fig. 7).

It will readily be seen from the foregoing remarks that the Bassoon pedal and Janissary music were an almost necessary addition to the pianoforte at this time.

[1] B 67, p. 171.

CHAPTER VI

TURKISH MUSIC AND OTHER PEDALS

SOMETHING more than the player's unaided touch was needed for the purpose of giving expression to the programme or theatrical descriptive music, whilst Janissary music was essential in military marches and in the dance orchestra.

Consequently the old stops were retained, but their purpose was changed. No longer did the Piano stop enable the performer to play softly, nor was the Forte stop used any more for the purpose of giving the illusion of a loud sound. The Harp and Lute, Swell, Una Corda and 'Harmonic sounds' were retained for the purpose of orchestrating programme music upon the pianoforte. Moreover Janissary music and Bassoon, as well as devices for obtaining a sudden fortissimo and pizzicato, were also added. It is necessary to ask the reader to glance through the list of patents for pedals and stops at the end of this chapter before attempting to explain their use.

The Piano Pedal. The reader will have noticed that a new stop for obtaining 'piano' has been added to the pianoforte. The effect was produced by shortening the radius of the blow of the hammer upon the strings—the 'Piano pedal' upon the modern upright pianoforte.[1] It seems to have originated in a dislike of the change of tone which resulted when the Una Corda pedal was used. Czerny says: "It is only in a few passages very rich in melody that it is desirable to use this pedal (Una Corda) in order to produce *another species of tone*". But there was another reason for the invention of a new Piano pedal. This was the difficulty in fitting the Una Corda mechanism to an obliquely strung pianino. Though there was but one patent for the (old) *piano pedal* ('Pianozug', 'Jeu Céleste'), that it was retained is evident from the old pianofortes themselves and from the pianoforte instruction-books by great pianists, where instructions are given for its proper use. Czerny informs the pupil that "it is advantageously applicable only in a very soft *Tremando*

---

[1] Kraus states that "in the beginning of 1700, Pietro Prosperi, spinet-maker of Siena, invented the spinet sourdine-pedal, which acted upon the keyboard, raising it on the back side by means of a simple wire, and thus modifying the blow of the jacks". B 60.

on the lower octaves of the instrument, in conjunction with the 'Damper pedal', when it produces the imitation of distant thunder".[1] (We quote his musical example.)

Ex. 3. Adagio. *Col Pedale del Piano*. Czerny. 'Distant Thunder.'

The thunderstorm, it will be remembered, formed an integral part of the programme of a 'Pastoral'. But there was another use for the Piano or 'Muffle Pedal' as it was sometimes called, and this was for the purpose of producing the illusion of muffled Drums. (We quote from Auguste Bertini's *Marshal's Funeral in a Cathedral*, where the muffled Drum effect is obtained by means of this pedal.)

Ex. 4. Auguste Bertini. Grand Fantasia Militaire. 'Muffled drum.'
(N.B. Đ = Piano and Forte pedals, S = used together.)

Jean-Louis Adam considered that the 'Céleste', as he calls the Piano pedal, was useful when coupled with the Forte pedal in tremolando passages. In fact, he did not consider this pedal to be really 'celestial' unless it was used with the Forte pedal. By means of the two together it was possible to imitate the Harmonica.[2]

Steibelt states definitely that this pedal must not be used without the Forte pedal and its use requires foresight and judgment. He draws attention to the fact that when it is released the tone of the pianoforte appears to have become sharper, and says that the Forte pedal must be released first[1] (Fig. 8).

The Pianissimo. This stop is retained and Schubert has indicated its use in his song 'Morgenlied' (Op. 4, No. 2), composed in 1820, in which, at the beginning, occurs the following direction: *durchaus mit dem Pianissimo.*

Air Suisse nommé le rans des vaches imitant les échos.

Fig. 8. A Pastoral by L. Adam, written for the Pianoforte with four pedals. From his *Méthode de Piano du Conservatoire*, An XII.
Ped. 1 = Lute. Ped. 2 = Forte. Ped. 3 = Céleste.

The Una Corda. Adam says that this pedal must not be used except for *piano, crescendo* or *diminuendo* passages, and that it is possible very nearly to obtain the same effect with the Una Corda and the Forte pedals used together on a grand pianoforte, as that

[1] B 104, pp. 52–54.

obtained with the Céleste ('Jeu Céleste', 'Piano') used with the Forte pedal on a square pianoforte.

Steibelt, in his *Méthode de Piano*, has accidentally given it the wrong name, and called it 'Céleste'; but by his description of the stop it is clear that he means the Una Corda. He says that its proper name should be 'pianissimo', and that it is possible to produce an agreeable effect in 'harmonious' music in a slow tempo by the combined use of the Forte and Piano,[1] and the Una Corda pedals.

The Una Corda pedal was patented by some American makers and is interestingly mentioned by Julius Kisselstein of Nuremberg in his description of his Giraffe pianoforte of 1831, where he states that pedal No. 6 is for 'Verschiebung' [*i.e.* Una Corda] producing sounds "which are very similar to those of a glass harmonica".

The Lute Pedal or Sordino. The Lute stop is often alluded to in French patents under the name of 'Sourdine', but Adam calls it "jeu de Luth ou de Harpe".

He states that this stop should only be used in rapid passages, such as staccato passages, or arpeggio variations, and in chromatic scales and music that requires playing with clarity; for, owing to the dryness of tone that results from its use, clarity and brilliance are greatly enhanced. The pupil is warned that, owing to these qualities, a misplaced note is distinctly heard.

Adam also says that when the right hand is playing arpeggios and the left sustained notes, the Forte pedal may be added to take away the dryness of tone by leaving the strings longer to vibrate. The Lute stop is also, in his opinion, useful as an accompaniment to the voice and when imitating pizzicato or the staccato of stringed instruments.

Steibelt also speaks of it, but says it should never be used without the Forte pedal, and that when so used the tone is that of the Lute or the Harp. But Thalberg uses it, under the name of Sourdine, both with and without the Forte pedal in the harp effects so much admired by Moscheles[2] (see Fig. 9), and Schubert has used it in his song 'Der Tod und das Mädchen (Op. 7, No. 3), composed in 1817, in which, at the beginning, we find *pp* (*sempre con Pedale e Sordino*).

Milchmeyer says that this stop, which he erroneously calls *Harfen- oder Lederzug*, may be used to imitate the Harp. It may also be used with the pianoforte lid closed to imitate the Side Drum

[1] He calls this "Jeu de Buffle".   [2] Part I, pp. 70, 71.

Fig. 9. Grand Fantasia. Sigismund Thalberg, Op. 42.
This illustrates the use of the Sordino pedal in combination with the Forte pedal.

(*kleine Trommel*). When 'Spanish Music' is to be imitated the stop must be used with the pianoforte lid closed. The music must be in the key of G major and both hands must play Mezzo Forte.[1]

The Pedal for 'Harmonic Sounds'. The pedal for *Harmonic Sounds*, which consisted in touching the strings lightly at their centre by means either of a set of hammers or a bar, seems clearly to have been invented for the purpose of producing the illusion of an echo—another favourite effect found in the 'Pastorals'. Fig. 11 shows the action as applied to an upright pianoforte by Cromwell. In this case the harmonic octave is produced, but the patentee suggests that the strings may be stopped at one-third or two-thirds of their vibrating distances.

The Forte Pedal. The *Forte Pedal* is, of course, retained, and may be used in a new way for giving the illusion of the Æolian Harp or of distant music. The directions for the production of this new effect originate with Czerny:

> In passages which are to be played with extreme softness and delicacy, the pedal (*i.e.* forte) may occasionally be held down during several dissonant chords. It produces in this case the soft undulating effect of the Æolian Harp, or of very distant music. In such cases the shifting (*i.e.* Una Corda) pedal may be added with advantage.[2]

The Dolce Compana. The *Dolce Compana* is an invention which consists in applying weight or pressure on to the sound-board of a pianoforte either directly or through the bridge. The effect of this pressure lowers the pitch of the instrument, and if the apparatus is put on and off rapidly a kind of vibrato would ensue (Fig. 10).

The Swell. The use of the *Swell* is not, of course, for the purpose of dynamic expression in the two later patents of Lepère and Badlain, but was most probably intended for that purpose by the two earlier patentees, Bemetzrieder and Pommer.

The *Harmonic Swell* is really a new kind of forte. The pianoforte was provided with two bridges. The performer by lifting a 'valve' allowed the lengths of the strings between the bridges to vibrate in sympathy with the ordinary vibrating lengths of the strings in use. This did not produce confusion, since every note was regularly damped as the performer lifted his finger. By the use of this stop a threefold augmentation of power became possible.

---

[1] B 103, pp. 59, 64.   [2] B 99 (Part III, Chap. VI, p. 61).

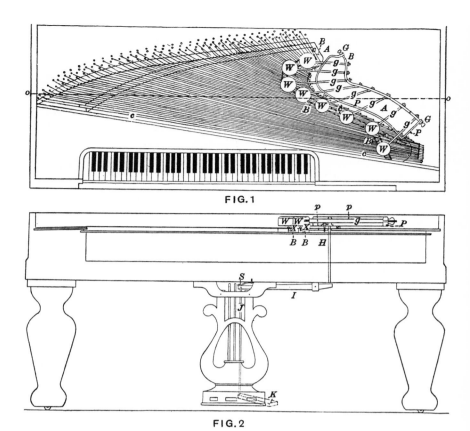

Fig. 10. Dolce Compana Attachment. Parker, 1849. From the patent.

The first was obtained by lifting the Harmonic Swell, the second by dropping the Harmonic Swell and raising the dampers (*i.e.* using the Forte pedal), the third by raising the Harmonic Swell and the dampers together. In this way the performer added all the overtones which were sympathetically elicited from the strings between the original bridge and the second one, which the patentee named the "bridge of Reverberation". An effect of extraordinary richness and power is said to have resulted from this arrangement.[1]

[1] B 74.

DESCRIPTION OF FIG. 10 (*opposite*).

Figure 1 is a plan of the Invention, Figure 2 a sectional elevation of the same, and Figure 3 the weights and frame drawn to a large scale. The parts marked *W* are a series of weights made of any ponderous substance, and of any convenient shape (they are made by me of the form shown in the Drawings, and of lead cased ornamentally in brass). These weights are arranged directly above the crooked bridge *B, B,* which is attached to and forms part of the sounding board of the instrument, and to each weight there is attached an arm or lever marked *g,* which projects horizontally from them. And one method of constructing and working this apparatus is as follows: the ends of the arms or levers *g* are secured to a cross bar *e, e,* forming part of the frame *P, P,* the cross bar being pivoted at its extremities upon upright supports *G, G,* these supports *G, G* being secured to the metallic plate or frame (so called) of the piano. The cross bar *e, e,* and the curved bar *P, P,* form one frame, *P, P, R, e, e,* the arms of the weights passing through the front bar *P, P,* and being secured into the rear bar *e, e,* the object of this frame being merely to support and steady the movement of the weights. The weights are moved to and from the crooked bridge *B* (upon which they are intended to operate by pressure) by a pedal under the piano through the means of the rod *H,* Figure 2, which passes from beneath to any part of the front bar *P, P,* through the instrument, and by means of lever *I* and a rod *J* is connected with the pedal *K,* it being necessary, in the ordinary use of the piano, to keep the weights from touching the bridge *B.* This is effected by a spring *S,* which keeps the long arm of the lever *I* depressed, and holds the other end of it with rod *H,* and the superincumbent frame *P, P, R, e, e* raised until the pedal is brought into action. To enable the weights to operate on the bridge to the best advantage, and to regulate conveniently each one's independent action, I fix into the bridge directly under the centre of each weight a screw *X,* Figure 2, which can be raised or lowered in adjustment of the weight over it.

Now whereas in the above arrangement it will be seen that the pressure required is produced by the use of weights, but whereas weights are not absolutely necessary, as substitutes for them may be made of wood and other material, and pressure effected by a spring below, or by the pressure of the foot with greater or less force upon the pedal, the rod *H* in that case being attached to the frame *P, P, R, e, e.* But to secure equal and uniform pressure, and a correspondent effect upon the tones of the instrument, weights arranged according to the plan above specified I consider best. Nevertheless I do not limit myself to the number of weights shown in the drawing; neither do I limit myself to the application of weights to the crooked bridge. But I propose, if more convenient, to apply the weights direct to the sounding board near the place occupied by the bridge. (*William Phillips Parker, abridged.*)

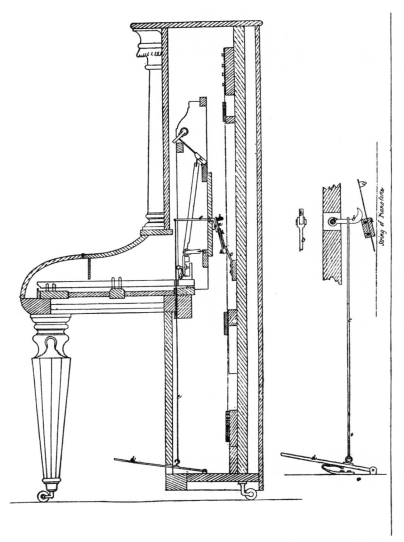

Fig. 11. Cromwell Pianoforte with harmonic sounds. Eng. Pat. No. 10,937 (1845).
From the patent.

Cross section of a Cottage Pianoforte.

A, A, bar which carries the harmonic stops. "This bar is composed of two flat pieces of metal, attached together in such a manner as to leave a space or slot between them (of nearly their whole length), in which space or slot metallic springs *a, a, a* are placed vertically parallel to each other, at such distances apart that each shall stand in front of the strings of the note it is intended to command or act upon"..."*b* is a piece of metal which stands out at right angles with the spring" *a,* "and has a slot cut in its outer edge to receive a piece of leather—the pressure of which upon the strings will lessen the vibration and produce the new effect"..."*c, c,* springs attached to the

The Pizzicato Pedal. The exact form of Wornum's *Pizzicato Pedal* is far from clear. It may have been a kind of Lute stop used in connection with raised dampers.[1]

The Buff and Polychorda stops require no further explanation.

The Pedals for Turkish Music. By far the most curious pedals that were added to the pianoforte are those for Bassoon ('Basson', 'Fagott') and the Drum ('Schlagzug', 'Bodenschlag', 'Tambour Guerrier') to which is frequently coupled the Triangle and Cymbals. The Triangle usually consists of three small semicircular bells differently toned, or in one larger bell unpleasantly reminiscent of that used on a modern telephone, and struck with a metal beater. Occasionally there is a pedal for 'Triangle' (or Bells) alone. In a horizontal grand pianoforte by Jeorg Taschta of Vienna (*a*) and a giraffe pianoforte by Van Der Hoef of Amsterdam (*b*) in the Bethnal Green Museum, London, there is a pedal for triangle (lit. bells) alone (see Fig. 12).

Sir William Orchardson, R.A., to whom these pianofortes formerly belonged, painted them in his pictures 'A tender chord' and 'Music when soft voices die'—the Taschta in the former and the Van Der Hoef in the latter.

<table>
<tr><td colspan="2" align="center">(a)</td><td colspan="2" align="center">(b)</td></tr>
<tr><td>(1)</td><td>Bassoon.</td><td>(1)</td><td>Bassoon.</td></tr>
<tr><td>(2)</td><td>Una Corda.</td><td>(2)</td><td>Drum.</td></tr>
<tr><td>(3)</td><td>Bassoon (lighter).</td><td>(3)</td><td>Piano.</td></tr>
<tr><td>(4)</td><td>Piano.</td><td>(4)</td><td>Triangle (lit. bells).</td></tr>
<tr><td>(5)</td><td>Forte.</td><td>(5)</td><td>Una Corda.</td></tr>
<tr><td>(6)</td><td>Piano.</td><td>(6)</td><td>Forte.</td></tr>
<tr><td>(7)</td><td>Drum and Triangle.</td><td></td><td></td></tr>
<tr><td>(8)</td><td>Triangle alone.</td><td></td><td></td></tr>
</table>

[1] C 796.

---

frame of the pianoforte and intended to act upon the bar *A* and keep the stops of that bar clear from the strings." *d*, pedal; *e*, rod; *f*, lever. "It will now be seen that if the foot of the performer is placed on the pedal *d* the long end of the lever *f* will be depressed and the bent end *g* being consequently raised will drive forward the bar *A* and bring the stops *b* in contact with the strings."

Enlarged detail. "*a* is a fixed centre pin on the frame of the 'action', and on this pin a peculiarly formed arm *b* works freely. The end of this arm is formed into a cam or tappet, and it is worked up and down by a rod *c* attached to a pedal *d* at its lower end; on the upper end of this rod *c* an eye or slot is formed, which embraces the arm *b*, and draws it down when the pedal is depressed by the foot of the performer. When thus depressed the largest diameter of the cam or tappet end of the arm *b* will come in contact with the vibrating bar *A* (which carries the stops), and press the stops forward on to the strings." (*Cromwell.*)

Fig. 12. Left-handed Waltz *without the Note B*. Auguste Bertini.

An example of a pianoforte piece where the right-hand part
may be played on a triangle (or bells) if desired.

The Cymbals consist of from two to three thin strips of brass which are knocked against the bass strings. The Drum itself usually consists of a large padded hammer which strikes against the under side of the sound-board in a horizontal pianoforte and against the back of the sound-board in an upright instrument. Another arrangement is to be seen in Nannette Streicher's pianoforte of the year 1826 at Windsor Castle. Here a parchment Drum-head is let into the bottom of the instrument and sounded by means of two leaden beaters. The earliest patents that have reference to the

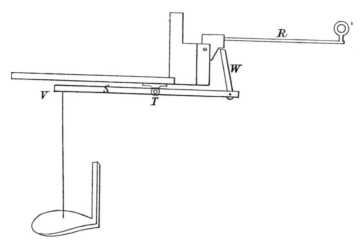

Fig. 13. Drum Pedal for horizontal pianoforte. Rolfe and Davis, 1797. Eng. Pat. No. 2160.

R, hammer; *S*, beam; *T*, centre or balance which "beam being pulled at *V*, by means of a wire affixed to the pedal, raises the lever *W*, which conducts the hammer against the vibrating body".

introduction of Turkish music into the pianoforte are English. The first, dated 1797, was granted to William Rolfe and Samuel Davis (Fig. 13); the second was granted to Smith in 1799 for "bracings and extenders to the case" of pianofortes to permit the introduction of a "drum, tabor or tambourine and triangle, with sticks and beaters".

Rolfe and Davis' Drum mechanism is a modification of the English 'Single Action', but the German example illustrated below (Fig. 14) shows the 'Prellmechanik'.

The Bassoon stop consists of a strip of wood covered with parchment or specially stiffened paper. When pressed against the strings a nasal Bassoon-like tone ensues. This stop only affects the bass portion of the instrument, that is to say from the lowest note up to middle C, but occasionally it extends as far as e' (see Fig. 17 (Bassoon) and Figs. 18 to 20 (Drum)).

Curious though these pianofortes seem to us now, it is of importance to remember that they were made in great numbers and their presence in the home of an Austrian, German, Netherlander

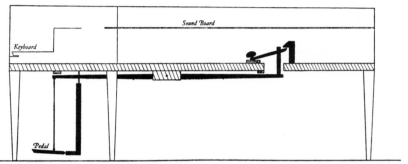

R. Harding del.

Fig. 14. Drum pedal for horizontal grand pianoforte. From an unnamed specimen in the Historisches Museum Neupert, Nuremberg.

The hammer head is padded with wash-leather. The lever which receives motion from the pedal and transmits it to the hammer is Y-shaped. The end which operates the drum is shown in the drawing, the other end works three small bells, differently toned—the Triangle, and flaps three strips of brass 18·6 cm. long by 2·1 cm. broad, and 1·5 mm. thick, suspended one above the other, against the bass strings—the Cymbals.

or Frenchman would have occasioned no astonishment during the earlier half of the nineteenth century.

There is a grand pianoforte of this type in the Landesgewerbemuseum in Stuttgart[1] which was formerly in the possession of Dr Johann Kanka of Prague, an advocate. According to his statement this instrument was frequently played upon by his client, Beethoven.

It is in a walnut case with rounded corners and decorated by a frieze of gilt hanging tendrils and is supported by three dark green caryatides which stand upon square plinths. They wear scale armour and military vestments (Plate I).

[1] B 57, S. 46, 47.

There are six pedals as follows:

(1) Bassoon up to d″.
(2) 'Stummzug', *i.e.* Lautenzug.
(3) Forte.
(4) Piano.
(5) Former purpose no longer recognisable but now coupled with Piano.
(6) Turkish music.

In a drawing of Rossini by Louis Dupré,[1] the composer is seen standing against a square pianoforte with at least six pedals. Only half of the instrument is shown in the drawing and yet three pedals are visible. Weber possessed a pianoforte by Brodmann of Vienna which had four pedals:

(1) Verschiebung (Una Corda).
(2) Laute (?).
(3) Piano.
(4) Forte.

It is also of some interest to note that Napoleon owned a pianoforte by Érard Frères, made in 1801,[2] with five pedals:

(1) Una Corda.
(2) Bassoon.
(3) Forte.
(4) Piano.
(5) Drum and Triangle.

Patents for Pianofortes with Several Pedals. Pianofortes with several pedals are to be found amongst the patents belonging to the first half of the nineteenth century.

In 1806 Pfeiffer et Cie[3] of Paris brought out a tall upright instrument, *The Harmomelo*, with four stops:

(1) Harp.
(2) Bassoon.
(3) Una Corda.
(4) Forte.

Thory[4] of Paris patented an instrument in 1815 which was to have five pedals (unspecified) and 'Tambour guerrier'. Érard

[1] Plate XLIX, Grove's *Dict. Mus.* (3rd ed. London, 1927), Vol. III.
[2] B 49, p. 109.   [3] C 883.
[4] C 927.

Frères[1] of Paris brought out a Duoclave Pianoforte in 1821 which was to have four or five pedals (unspecified in their patent).

Étienne Eulriot[2] of Paris designed an instrument in 1825 which was to be fitted with three pedals:

(1) Sourdine.
(2) Jeu Céleste (Piano).
(3) Bassoon.

And in the same year Jean-Baptiste Charreyre patented his upright pianoforte with three pedals as follows:[3]

(1) Bassoon.
(2) Forte.
(3) Célestine (Una Corda).

Pape mentions the following pedals in connection with a square pianoforte in his French patent of 1826:[4]

(1) Forte.
(2) Sourdine (which imitates the harp).
(3) Bassoon.
(4) Jeu Céleste.

Charles Côte[5] of Lyons produced a design for an instrument in 1827 with four pedals:

(1) Bassoon.
(2) Grand Jeu (Forte)
(3) Jeu Céleste (Piano).
(4) Sourdine.

The Sourdine seems in this case to be a kind of Buff stop, as it damps one string out of every pair in order to facilitate the tuning.

Mathieu Frost[6] (père) et fils (Jean-Jacques) of Strasburg patented a pianoforte with three pedals in 1828:

(1) Forte.
(2) Piano.
(3) Una Corda.

Joseph Baumgartner[7] of Munich designed a pianoforte in 1831 which was to have three pedals (unspecified), and in the same year

---

[1] C 866.   [2] C 872.
[3] C 867.   [4] C 50.
[5] C 877.   [6] C 937.
[7] C 879.

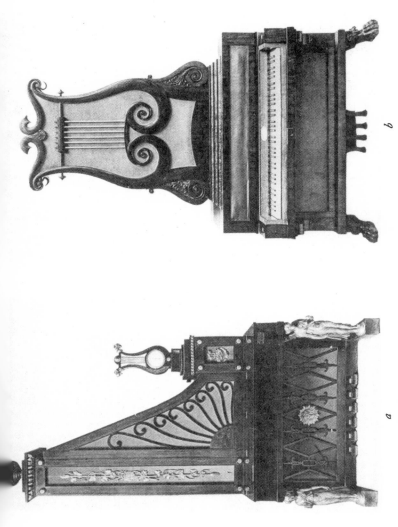

a

b

Plate IV (*a*). Giraffenflügel, by Christopher Erlich of Bamberg. In the Würtembergisches Landes-gewerbemuseum, Stuttgart. For the prices charged by Erlich for his pianofortes see F, p. 376. This pianoforte is dated 1820. It has six pedals as follows: (1) Forte, (2) Una Corda, (3) Piano, (4) Piano, (5) Drum, (6) Bassoon.

(*b*). Lyraflügel, by J. A. Westerman of Berlin. Berlin, Hochschule für Musik, No. 1383. The date is about 1830. [Height 215 cm., breadth 127 cm., thickness 59 cm.] There is another example in Dr Neupert's Collection at Nuremberg.

Julius Kisselstein[1] of Nuremberg specified his 'Giraffen-Flügel' with six:

(1) Forte.
(2) Octave coupler contra F to e'.
(3) Octave coupler e' to f'''.
(4) Piano.
(5) Pianissimo.
(6) Una Corda (which produces sounds similar to those of a glass harmonica).

The reader is referred to a series of upright pianofortes of the 'chamber-orchestra' type, Plates II to IV, and also to Appendix H, containing a list of signs used for pianoforte pedals and stops.

One of the most curious developments that occurred in pianoforte building at this time was an attempt to introduce Tambourines or Kettle-Drums tuned to a chromatic scale into the body of the instrument.

Paul-Joseph Sormani of Paris invented the 'Piano Basque' in 1841. It was a pianoforte which appears to have consisted entirely of tambourines whose beaters were worked from a keyboard. This instrument is so peculiar that we quote his description in full (Fig. 15 shows the diagram).

Ce piano peut se composer d'un nombre indéterminé de tambours de basque; cependant, pour obtenir la gamme chromatique, il en faut treize comme dans le dessin.

Chaque tambour de basque séparément est composé de deux cercles; sur l'un l'on tend la peau, et l'autre sert à obtenir la tension voulue de la peau comme dans les timbales ordinaires.

Ces deux cercles sont rapprochés entre eux par des boulons ou vis de rappel.

Chaque cercle porte, en outre, deux oreilles parallèles percées d'outre en outre, dans lesquelles on passe un boulon à écrou. Elles servent à porter les baguettes destinées à frapper sur la peau du tambour.

Les baguettes sont de deux matières, l'une de bois, l'autre métallique, qui se tiennent solidement; la partie en bois sert à frapper, l'autre partie est placée entre les deux oreilles, où elle est affermie par un boulon à écrou; la partie de la baguette qui est opposée à celle qui frappe est prolongée d'une partie déterminée soit en ligne droite, soit en ligne oblique, selon que la position exigée par le tambour de basque qui les porte sera déterminée.

L'extrémité de ces baguettes sera couverte en peau ou laissée nue à volonté.

La partie opposée à celle qui frappe, que j'appelle bras de levier, est attachée à une petite corde en soie qui va s'attacher directement à la touche du

---

[1] C 822.

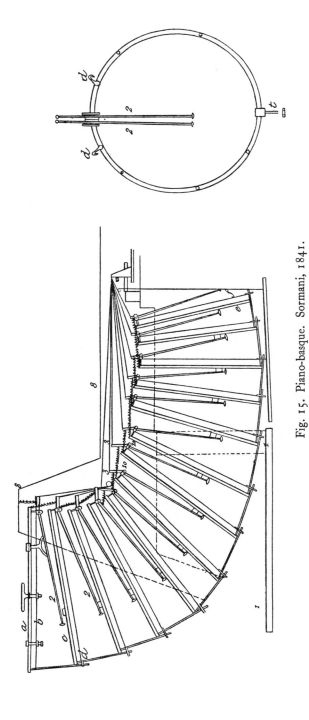

Fig. 15. Piano-basque. Sormani, 1841.

a, c, e, indiquent les cercles sur lesquels les peaux sont tendues; *b, d, f,* cercles sur lesquels on place le cercle à peau pour être tendu comme dans les timbales ordinaires: No. 1, châssis en bois qui soutient les cercles dans leur position semicirculaire et qui sert aussi à les renfermer; 8, 8, couvercles mobiles pour régler le mécanisme; 2, 2, baguettes de percussion; 10, charnière ou porte-baguette; 3, 3, bras de levier; *d, d,* écrous qui suspendent les tambours de basque; *t,* queue taraudée pour entrer dans les tringles.

clavier ou indirectement, soit par des poulies, bascules ou autre qui serviraient à faire parvenir le cordon en soie verticalement sur la direction de la touche.

La touche est une espèce d'équerre. Le bras de levier des baguettes est attaché, du côté opposé à la touche, à un ressort fait en spirale destiné à rappeler la baguette.

Chaque cercle porte, du côté opposé des baguettes, une tringle sur laquelle est placé du velours pour empêcher que les baguettes du cercle voisin frappent sur la peau de l'autre.

Chaque tambour ayant deux baguettes, le clavier est composé d'un nombre double de touches qu'il y a de tambours de basque.

Derrière les touches se trouve une tringle qui, au moyen d'une pédale, peut diminuer la course du bout de levier en cas de forte-piano.

Toute la partie du piano-basque où se trouve le mouvement est renfermée tant sur les côtés qu'à la partie supérieure.

Les deux châssis en bois sont unis entre eux par des tringles horizontales et parallèles destinées à recevoir la partie du tambour de basque qui porte les baguettes.

Les tambours de basque sont fixés auxdites tringles au moyen de deux écrous qui se trouvent l'un en deçà des oreilles et l'autre au delà, assez écartés entre eux pour déterminer la solidité de l'instrument.

Vis-à-vis les oreilles se trouve une queue taraudée et fixée à l'un des cercles qui servent à maintenir les tambours éloignés entre eux au moyen de tringles numérotées sur le plan 777, etc.; au moyen d'écrous où consolide lesdites tringles pour empêcher tout mouvement.

A pianoforte with chromatic Kettle-Drums was patented by Nunns and Fischer of New York, U.S.A., in 1847. This instrument, which had been called the 'Melodicon with drums', consisted in combining a series of Kettle-Drums with an ordinary pianoforte, so that the strings and Drums should sound simultaneously.

The finger keys were connected with a series of rods which either passed through a longitudinal opening in the back of the case or through a series of holes specially bored to receive them, and worked another hammer action underneath the pianoforte. This second set of hammers played upon the Drums which were in tune with the pianoforte strings. A damping arrangement was provided to stop the vibrations of the Drums after the finger left the key. (Fig. 16 represents one application of this invention.)

A possible solution of the problem of why chromatic Tambourines and Kettle-Drums were introduced into the pianoforte may be found in the fact that many persons still looked upon the pianoforte as a makeshift orchestra upon which reductions of orchestral works could be played.

Berlioz had been experimenting with Kettle-Drums, and had

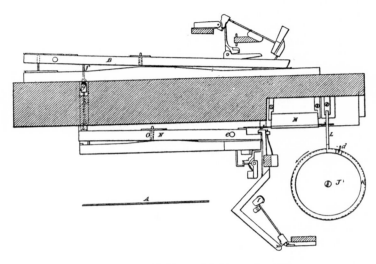

Fig. 16. 'Melodicon with Drums', 1847.

A représente une corde du piano; B, une touche. N est un levier placé sous la planche de fond du piano; il a son point d'appui en O, et est chargé, à son extrémité *e*, pour assurer sa descente. De la touche *B* descend une tringle métallique *f* qui porte sur une pièce cylindrique *g*, dont le sommet est couvert de peau; à ce cylindre est liée une autre tringle *h* qui passe par un trou pratiqué dans la planche du fond du piano. *i* est une pièce cylindrique semblable, liée à l'extrémité inférieure de la tige ou tringle en fil de fer *h*, dont le bout inférieur est recouvert de peau et porté sur le levier *N*, dont le bout antérieur sera amené à descendre par la descente de la touche. (This sets in motion the hammer *I* which strikes the drum *J*.)...La plaque *M*, par laquelle est soulevé l'étouffoir du timbre, est représenté élevée par un fil de métal *j* qui y est lié et qui repose sur l'extrémité interne du levier *N*. *K représente un étouffoir annulaire, qui est amené en contact avec le bord du timbre,....l'étouffoir...doit être recouvert en peau ou autre substance molle; il est représenté fixé à un petit bras L. En enfonçant la touche, on élève ce bras de manière à affranchir l'étouffoir du timbre quand celui-ci est frappé par le marteau.... d est un arrêt pour limiter le mouvement de l'étouffoir.* Nous avons représenté qu'un seul timbre, mais il doit y avoir un timbre adapté à chaque note; tous ces timbres pourront être montés sur une barre ou sur des barres de longueur suffisante et à une distance convenable pour qu'ils puissent recevoir le coup de leurs marteaux respectifs. Les timbres, placés sous la planche du piano, peuvent, si on le désire, être environnés d'une boîte que l'on ouvrirait et qu'on fermerait au moyen d'une pédale; on obtiendrait ainsi un effet semblable à celui de la pédale de forté.[1]

[1] C 901. Three different methods of applying the Drums are shown. The illustration above is fig. 24. For the description of certain parts the reader is referred to fig. 22. This is set in italics.

Fig. 17. Ferdinand Päer. "Primo Pot-Pourri Con Variazioni per il Forte-Piano."

[Note ② = forte pedal on; ⊗ = forte pedal off; ② ④ = bassoon pedal on in conjunction with the forte pedal.]

210

Fig. 18. Marcia. Auguste Bertini. For six hands on one Pianoforte or five hands and an Octave Flute. ⊕ = double-drum pedal.

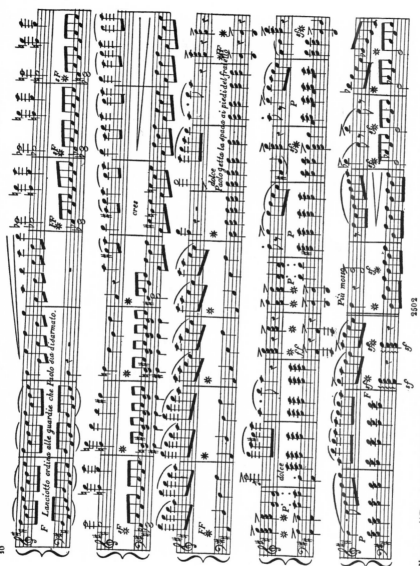

Fig. 19. "Pezzi Scelti Nel Ballo Francesca da Rimini." Music by Vincenzo Schira. Pianoforte reduction by Luigi Truzzi.

✳ = "Il pedale della banda."

Fig. 20. Luigi Truzzi. "Atto III° del Ballo Antigone." Music by Schira. Pianoforte reduction by Luigi Truzzi.
⊕ = "Il colpo di banda."

used as many as eight pairs—sixteen drums—in his *Requiem*, which was first performed in 1837. He writes thus:

> In order thus to obtain a certain number of chords in three, four and five parts, more or less doubled, and moreover a striking effect of very close rolls, I have employed in my grand requiem mass eight pairs of drums, tuned in different ways, and ten drum players.

It is a little difficult to understand how Messrs Nunns and Fischer succeeded in fitting Drums to all the bass notes in their instrument since, as Berlioz remarks, "the difficulty of getting a parchment sufficiently large to cover a vessel bigger than the great bass Kettle-Drum is perhaps the reason which prevents our obtaining sounds lower than F".[1]

A list of Patents for Pianoforte Stops granted to makers in Europe, America, and Canada from the year 1801 to 1851 inclusive.

Dolce Compana.

1849 Gray, of Albany, New York [Am. Pat. No. 6223].
Weight or pressure applied upon the sound-board either directly or upon a crooked bridge.

1849 Parker, of London [Eng. Pat. No. 12,609].
Probably a communication from the above.

Harmonic Sounds.

1821 Wagner, Jean-Baptiste, of Arras, Dept. du Pas-de-Calais [Brevet d'Addition January 18th, 1821, to Fr. Pat. No. 1380 (1820)].
A rod of iron covered with buckskin falls across the middle of the strings. This is worked by pedal No. 6.

1839 Stumpff, Andres, of London [Eng. Pat. No. 7971].
A series of stops fixed to the end of rods are arranged in a frame such that through the agency of a pedal and spring they press upon the strings exactly at the middle of their striking length.

1845 Walker, E. L., of Carlisle, Pa., assignee of Cherry, C. W., of Alexandria, Md. [Am. Pat. No. 3888].
Hammers or weights arranged in a frame are brought down on to the strings at the centre of their length by a pedal or analogous device.

1845 Warren, Samuel R., of Montreal, Canada [Canadian Pat. No. 78].
A rail carrying a projection of leather or felt, etc., is brought into contact with the strings by means of a pedal.

1845 Cromwell, Samuel Thomas [Eng. Pat. No. 10,937; Fr. Pat. No. 2129 (1846)].
(1) Pressure on the strings at their middle point.

[1] B 26, pp. 199, 214.

(2) Stops placed at other "harmonic distances on the strings such as one-third or two-thirds the length of the vibrating portion of the strings".

Piano.

> 1808 Érard, Sébastien [Eng. Pat. No. 3170].
> The usual 'Pianozug'.

Piano by means of altering the radius of the hammer stroke.

> 1836 Lidel, Joseph [Eng. Pat. No. 7006].
> Pedal to work a mechanism for the purpose of obtaining the 'piano' and 'crescendo' without alteration to the character of the tone.

> 1837 Greiner, Georges-Frederic, of Würtemberg [Certificat d'Add. May 3rd, 1837, to Fr. Pat. No. 10,989 (1836)].
> "Pedal to work a mechanism to lessen the course of the hammers for the purpose of producing loud or soft effects without changing the nature of the sound."

> 1841 Newhall, Daniel B., of Boston, Mass. [Am. Pat. No. 2330].
> Pedal to work a mechanism for varying the "points at which the force is applied to the hammer so as to produce at pleasure piano or a pianissimo".

Pizzicato Pedal.

> 1826 Wornum, Robert [Eng. Pat. No. 5384] (an addition to his 'Professional Pianoforte').
> "It is a third pedal introduced between the two common pedals, communicates in the usual way by cranks and moves a block or artificial slide at the bass end of the damper rail by which the dampers are cleared from the wires, and in play a most pleasing effect of pizzicato results."

Polychorda. Additional strings brought into play (unnamed in the patents).

> 1812 Érard Frères, of Paris [Fr. Pat. No. 1332].
> A second sound-board carries three additional strings to a note, together with a separate action. A total of six unisons can be sounded simultaneously if desired or three unisons an octave higher (already referred to in Chap. III).
> Pape, Jean-Henri, of Paris [Brevet d'Add. 1826 to Fr. Pat. No. 4198 (1826)].
> Two sets of unisons for every note with a separate hammer for each. One hammer strikes a pair from above whilst the other strikes a pair from below. A pedal is arranged to alter the position of the hammers.

> 1840 Ziegler, Albrecht, of Ratisbon [Bav. Pat. No. —].
> A pianoforte with two manuals acting on two actions, one up-striking, the other down-striking. The manuals could be used together or separately.

> 1846 Soudet, of Havre [Fr. Pat. No. 2311].
> An upright pianoforte is fitted with strings double the length of those in ordinary use and divided so that each part gave out a corresponding note. Both parts could be brought into play by means of a pedal.

> 1851 Robertson, Joseph Clinton [Eng. Pat. No. 13,601].
> A combined horizontal and upright pianoforte. By means of a pedal the two actions could be combined.

Sordino.

1827 Érard, Sébastien [Fr. Pat. No. 5086].

Sordino ('Sourdine') pressed against the under side of the strings by means of a spring. No further description is given. An illustration shows the Sordino in section. It appears to consist of a strip of wood or metal covered with cloth or some other suitable material.

Swell.

1801 Bemetzreider, R. Scott, J. Scott and A. Scott [Eng. Pat. No. 2552].

The top of the instrument (a square pianoforte) opens at the back by means of a pedal.

1819 Pommer, of Philadelphia (no description).

1844 Lepère, of Paris [3ème Brevet d'Add. to Fr. Pat. No. 10,599 (1836)].

A door is placed in the upper half of the back of an upright pianoforte, which can be opened and closed by means of a pedal.

1845 Badlain, Edward, of Potsdam, New York [Am. Pat. No. 4241].

Shutters covering over the strings, which can be opened or closed by means of a foot pedal. (This is the same as the 'Venetian Swell'.)

1847 Spear, John [Eng. Pat. No. 11,681].

Harmonic Swell.

1821 Collard, F. W., of London [Eng. Pat. No. 4542].

In a pianoforte with an additional bridge to enable the after-lengths of the strings to vibrate sympathetically with the striking lengths; a piece of wood about one inch square and clothed on its under side with soft material is placed nearly parallel to the additional bridge. Its purpose is to damp the vibration of the after-lengths, upon which it can be lowered by means of a pedal.

Una Corda.

1831 Currier, Ebenezer R., of Boston, Mass. [Am. Pat. No. —].

The keyboard and action of a square pianoforte to be moved laterally so that the hammers may strike ONE, TWO or THREE STRINGS.

1831 Greiner und Schmidt [Bav. Pat. No. —].

In a pianoforte with four unison strings to a note, lateral movement of the keyboard permits the use of one, two, three or four strings at a time.

1842 Loud, Thomas, of Philadelphia, Pa. [Am. Pat. No. 2523].

Pedal to move the action laterally so that the hammers strike either ONE or TWO of the STRINGS.

Pédale d'expression.

1851 Montal, Claude [3ème Brevet d'Add. to Fr. No. 3711 (1848)].

A foot pedal worked a mechanism for shortening the radius of the hammer stroke, at the same time modifying the touch in proportion to the shortened (or increased) radius of the stroke. It was thus possible to increase or decrease the sound by varying the pressure on the pedal.

The effect of Una Corda produced.

1838 Brown, Edwin, of Boston, Mass. [Am. Pat. No. 1014].
A mechanism worked by a pedal clamps one of the two unisons to prevent it from vibrating.

1839 Cumston, William, of Boston, Mass. [Am. Pat. No. 1375].
Wedges arranged on a beam mute one out of each pair of unisons. This is worked by a pedal and is for the purpose of avoiding the necessity for moving the action.

Buff Stop.

1811 Wornum, Robert [Eng. Pat. No. 3419].
Damps one out of every pair of unisons. (Usual buff stop.)

1832 Fischer, Pierre Frederic [Eng. Pat. No. 6304].
(Unnamed in the patent.) To facilitate tuning.

Harp.

1808 Érard, Sébastien [Eng. Pat. No. 3170].

Varying and increasing the sound by regulating the column of air.

1845, Pape, Jean-Henri [Eng. Pat. No. 10,668 and 1st add. Pat. to Fr. Pat. No. 313 (1844)].

Sébastien Érard, by David (1811). By courtesy of Maison Érard.

SECTION II

THE PIANOFORTE AS A SOLO INSTRUMENT IN THE EARLY NINETEENTH CENTURY

*Die weitere Entwickelung des modernen Pianofortebaues
ging mit dem Streben nach glänzenderer Virtuosität
und nach grösserem Tonreichthume Hand in Hand.*
OSCAR PAUL

CHAPTER I

§ I

THE CONCERT GRAND PIANOFORTE

AFTER the pianoforte had been improved by the addition of the escapement it attracted the attention of eminent musicians, who scientifically explored its possibilities.

At first the ideal style of pianoforte playing seemed to be that of a perfectly even tone combined with velocity, and it was, in fact, in some measure the combination of the clavichord technique with that of the harpsichord. Emanuel Bach endeavoured to play upon the clavier and to write for it in a cantabile manner, and this ideal was transmitted directly to his pupil Dussek who became renowned for his beautiful legato, and indirectly to Mozart and to other musicians of his day. The distinguished Italian composer Muzio Clementi appears to have adopted this ideal owing to the deep impression made upon him by Mozart's singing touch and exquisite taste. Clementi afterwards became known as the 'Father of the pianoforte'. His Sonata Op. 2 is considered to have been the first piece of keyboard music entirely suitable to that instrument, whilst his technical work, the *Gradus ad Parnassum*, is the first pianoforte instruction-book. In this work stress is laid on equality of touch and velocity with the power of bringing out the melody. Cramer, Field, and Hummel became Clementi's pupils, but Cramer and Hummel had received previous instruction from Mozart. Clementi's greatest pupil, John Field, an Irishman, is remembered now for his nocturnes, where, by the skilful use of the sustaining pedal, he obtained new effects with widespread chords. He is, in fact, the spiritual ancestor of Chopin, and is said, like that master, to have preferred to play upon the square or the upright pianoforte rather than upon the grand.

Cramer, as would be expected from one who had received instruction from Clementi, was noted for his expressive touch and occupies, technically, the position between Clementi and Hummel, aiming at the cultivation of music in general rather than the discovery of new effects. In Hummel, the Viennese, or Mozart's school culminates; but Hummel added new technical discoveries of his own, and his 'Pianoforte Method' forms in some degree the basis of that written by his pupil Czerny.

There can be no doubt that the style of these musicians was very greatly influenced by the type of pianoforte that they used.

At this time (1824) only two types of pianofortes were recognised, those with the English Action giving a powerful tone, but unsuitable for rapid execution owing to a somewhat heavy touch, and those with the Viennese or German Action giving a comparatively poor tone, but with a light touch suitable for very rapid playing. (All other types, including the Anglo-German, were regarded merely as variations of these.) It was upon the Viennese pianofortes that the musicians mentioned above played during their[1] earlier years. Hummel states clearly the advantages of both the types of pianoforte in his 'Pianoforte Method'.

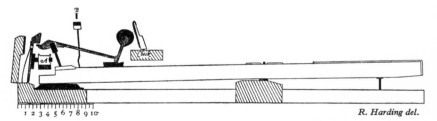

1 2 3 4 5 6 7 8 9 10   *R. Harding del.*

Fig. 1. Nannette Streicher, 1829 (Berlin, No. 3265).
A, screw to regulate the touch; *B*, portion of the damper stick. It will be observed that there is a check fixed to a separate block behind the hammer. This check serves the same purpose as that in the English Action, namely, to prevent the hammer from rebounding against the strings.

---

[1] Fig. 1 represents the improved Viennese (or German) Action. The German Action began to be called the Viennese Action after Stein's son Andreas and his daughter Nannette commenced business in Vienna, where they had removed upon Nannette's marriage with Johann Streicher. In 1802 the partnership between the brother and sister was dissolved. The two houses, known respectively as 'Matthäus Andreas Stein' and 'Nannette Streicher, geborene Stein', became famous. In 1823 the Streichers took their son Johann Baptist into partnership and on Streicher's death he managed the business for his mother.

The German piano may be played upon with ease by the weakest hand. It allows the performer to impart to his execution every possible degree of light and shade, speaks clearly and promptly, has a round fluty tone, which in a large room contrasts well with the accompanying orchestra, and does not impede rapidity of execution by requiring too great an effort. These instruments are likewise durable, and cost about half the price of the English pianoforte.

To the English construction, however, we must not refuse the praises due on the score of its durability and fullness of tone. Nevertheless this instrument does not admit of the same facility of execution as the German; the touch is heavier, the key sinks much deeper, and, consequently, the return of the hammer upon the repetition of a note cannot take place so quickly . . . this mechanism is not capable of such numerous modifications as to degree of tone as ours. . . .

In the first moment [*i.e.* when first using an English pianoforte] we are sensible of something unpleasant, because, in forte passages in particular, on our German instruments we press the keys quite down, while here, they must be only touched superficially, as otherwise we could not succeed in executing such runs without excessive effort and double difficulty. As a counterpoise to this, however, through the fullness of tone of the English pianoforte, the melody receives a peculiar charm and harmonious sweetness.

In the meantime, I have observed that, powerfully as these instruments sound in a chamber, they change the nature of their tone in spacious localities; and that they are less distinguishable than ours, when associated with complicated orchestral accompaniments; this, in my opinion, is to be attributed to the thickness and fullness of their tone.[1]

Hummel instructed both Czerny and Thalberg. Thalberg had also imbibed the Clementi tradition through Kalkbrenner, under whom he had also studied. Thus the two great schools were united in him, and he was undoubtedly one of the greatest pianists of his day. In fact, his only serious rival was Liszt, and the opinion seems to have been that Liszt was slightly superior; it was said that Liszt "out-Thalberged Thalberg". In Thalberg, Liszt and Czerny and the two pianoforte-maker pianists Herz and Kalkbrenner, we find combined with the power of cantabile playing a new element— the bravura. These pianists are, in fact, the leaders of the new school where purely musical interest tends to count less than new technical discoveries. They embodied these discoveries in their own works; they tended to play nothing but their own compositions, and a writer to the *Musical World* in 1838 commented upon this in the following words:

Few musicians of the present day are capable of performing the music of Scarlatti, and above all John Sebastian Bach; because the modes of fingering

[1] B 102, Part III, Sect. II, Chap. IV, pp. 64, 65.

necessary for the execution of this music are almost incompatible with the habits acquired in the practice of the present style. The sustained legato playing of the logical harmonies of the old masters resembles in nothing that brilliant execution which marks the performances of such pianists as Liszt and Kalkbrenner.[1]

Moscheles, one of the greatest technicians of his day, cannot be classed merely as a bravura player, though he wrote and played bravura music: educated at the Prague conservatorium under Dionys Weber who brought him up on Mozart and Clementi, Moscheles retained a love of the older masters and, as has already been shown, he made a speciality of the performance of their music. The programme of a concert given by him in 1837 has already been quoted where, besides playing works of Sebastian Bach, Weber and Beethoven, he even played Scarlatti's *Cat Fugue* on the harpsichord. But the public, at least in London, seem to have been more interested in the technical skill of the performer than in the music. In order to understand this it may be helpful to imagine ourselves at a concert about the year 1840 where a famous pianist is about to appear.

He is seated at his instrument in the midst of a fashionable assembly of amateurs and professors. A searching glance at this audience is the signal for the commencement of a performance which is amazing to the verge of the miraculous.

The room is crammed to suffocation and the audience stands up whilst he plays. The first piece is a capriccioso in E flat instinct with novelty of passage and fine modulation. At one time we have a sweet cantabile manner and then a whole flood of chords and arpeggios sweeping over the keys. His rushes over the keyboard are like the combined powers of many great players; in fact he is not "forty playing like one" but "one playing like forty". In the Grand Military Divertimento, surrounded by his orchestral troops, he appears to do battle with his instrument, striking wide intervals, playing octave passages with both hands and astonishing all by the amazing rapidity of his reiterated notes in imitation of the violin tremolando.

"His fantasia on themes from *La donna del Lago* is less surprising but replete with *tours* of grace and beauty." "The great man is greater than ever and intreats the piano with his two hands as if half a dozen pairs were soliciting it to speak. And this is done as quietly, and with as little apparent effort as if, instead of listening

[1] B 75 (*d*), p. 103.

to wonders, we were hearing commonplaces." "But the most astonishing of his novelties is his new Andante in which he plays a cantabile in octaves with the bass, and a full accompaniment; myriads of notes sounding from one extremity of the instrument to the other without disturbing the subject in which the three distinct features of this combination are clearly brought out by his exquisite touch."[1] He rises—"the orchestra crowds round him, so great, so intense is the interest he excites"—"the enthusiasm is tremendous". At the conclusion of his variations on the theme of *God Save the King*, the audience is unable to restrain itself further and pours forth a storm of bravos with the waving of hats and handkerchiefs and other marked signs of approbation. But sitting in one of the anterooms, glum, and by no means joining in the uproar, are several venerable persons. To these gentlemen he is one of the 'new pianists'—a bravura player whose exploits are in their eyes "a degradation and an insult to music". One critic complains that his feeling when listening to it is much the same as that produced by witnessing the wondrous performances of Van Amburg and his lions. Another angrily asserts that the object seems to be to play the greatest number of notes in a given time and that piano playing has fallen to the level of opera dancing; the one as well as the other being meant only to make one stare.[2]

But it is not the pianist or the music which is primarily of interest to us now, but the pianoforte upon which he performs. This pianoforte had to be brilliant and powerful for the bravura player, and it was power that the Viennese pianofortes lacked, and sweet and voice-like in quality for the cantabile player, sombre and resonant for the expressive performance of works such as the symphonic *Études* of Schumann. In neither of these two types of pianofortes, the Viennese nor the English, were all these qualities to be found. Moscheles considered that the strong metal plates used by Broadwood to strengthen his instrument gave a "heaviness to the touch" but a fullness and vocal resonance to the tone well adapted

---

[1] This was Thalberg's *Fantasia*, Op. 1. The new technical device of dividing a melody between the two hands in order that a bass could be played with the left and an accompaniment with the right, giving the effect of three independent hands, seems to have been adopted by Mendelssohn in his E minor prelude after hearing Thalberg play. The priority of publication, however, rests with Thalberg in whose fantasia on 'Moïse' it appears. (See B 53 (*a*), p. 311.)

[2] Compiled from reviews of Thalberg's concerts. B 75 (*h*), p. 135 and B 75 (*k*), p. 153.

to Cramer's *Legato*, whilst Moscheles himself preferred Clementi's instruments; he said: "I use Clementi's more subtle mechanism for my repeating notes, skips and full chords".

It was clear that the pianoforte makers had to improve their instruments and it occurred to them to endeavour to unite once more the good qualities of the Viennese and the English Actions. This had already been attempted before and produced the Anglo-German Action. But the new pianofortes had not only to unite the powerful English tone with the light Viennese touch, giving the power of speed; but also a third element—that of facile repetition. Our imaginary pianist has astonished us by his reiterated notes in imitation of the violin tremolando and Moscheles stated that he preferred Clementi's flexible action for his *repeated* notes. What were the pianists writing that required an action giving a quick repeat?

Owing to the increasing interest in the orchestra and in the opera that began during the last quarter of the eighteenth century, and the demand for reductions of orchestral and operatic scores, musicians were frequently playing purely orchestral music on the pianoforte, and its influence is to be seen in a marked degree in the works of the advanced or bravura school where imitations of violin-like cadenzas are frequently introduced. (We quote the cadenza from the first movement of a concerted work by Herz, but it will clearly be seen that the orchestra is merely an addition to give the work importance at a concert, and that Herz is content that it should be played without this addition in the privacy of the home (Fig. 2).)

The music of this period is full of figures with repeated notes in imitation of the violin tremolando, and sometimes of vocal recitative. Many of the old pianofortes were capable of giving a very rapid repeat. A difficulty occurred when a complicated rhythm was introduced or the rhythm was suddenly changed; for the key had to return to its level to give emphasis to the blow. In order to give music of this kind its true rhythmical phrasing it was necessary to have an action where the note could sound at two different levels of the key; that is where the key itself need not rise to its full height in order to restrike.

It was Sébastien Érard who set himself the difficult task of inventing an action which should fulfil these requirements, an action combining a powerful stroke with a light flexible touch giving the power to restrike a note with extreme rapidity.[1] This problem had

[1] Eng. Pat. No. 3170 (1808).

Fig. 2.

Herz, *Fantasie et Variations pour le Piano sur la Marche d'Otello de Rossini*, Op. 67.

"In the absence of the orchestra the small notes are to be played" [Herz].

been engaging Érard's attention for many years and he had already, in 1808, brought out his first 'repetition action',[1] which he called the 'mécanisme à étrier' because the upper part of the escapement lever was shaped like a stirrup.

It was upon the first pianoforte built with this new action that Dussek made a profound impression at the Concert at the Odéon given that year (1808) by Rode, Baillot and Lamare on their return from Russia. But unfortunately the action was not durable; after it had been used for some time it became noisy and the touch faulty (Fig. 11).

Thirteen years later Sébastien Érard completed the repetition action for which he subsequently became famous, and then he was too old to work it. His nephew, Pierre Érard, patented it in England in 1821. This great invention forms the working basis of nearly all modern double escapement actions[2] of the present day; that is, of nearly all the grand pianofortes that are now made. At first there was a feeling that it was too complicated to be durable, but after Henri Herz[3] had simplified it into the form known as the Herz-Érard Action its usefulness was recognised by Broadwood, Collard, Steinway, Bechstein, Pleyel and others.[4]

Without this action the art of pianoforte playing could not have attained the state of perfection to which it has now risen; in fact we may say that modern pianoforte technique was built upon it.[5]

There is no doubt that many variations of this mechanism were tried by the Érards, and Moscheles called from time to time to see how the work progressed. He visited the firm just after Pierre Érard had patented the action in England in 1821, and wrote in his diary:

Young Érard took me to-day to his pianoforte factory, to try the new invention of his Uncle Sébastien. This quicker action of the hammer seems to me so important that I prophesy a new era in the manufacture of pianofortes. I still complain of some heaviness in the touch and therefore prefer to play upon Pape's and Petzold's instruments: I admired the Érards, but am not thoroughly satisfied, and urged him to make a new improvement.[6] [Fig. 12.]

Moscheles still preferred Pape's and Petzold's instruments;

---

[1] B 70 (a), p. 217.   [2] C 209.
[3] The pianist, who also became a well-known pianoforte maker.
[4] B 49, pp. 34–35.
[5] An explanation of the term 'double escapement' cannot be attempted without a diagram; the reader should see Figs. 4, 11 and 12.
[6] B 72, Chap. IV, p. 59.

'L'échappement de Petzold', as it was called, had a long, powerful hammer fitted with a special fork, with a screw by which the play of the hammer could be adjusted. The action was also fitted with a means for regulating the play of the escapement. In the later examples there was a pilot fixed below the hammer ruler by which the escapement could be adjusted with even greater precision, and a check piece completed this action. The one defect consisted in the escapement spring which was liable to break, but this was eventually rectified. The illustration below shows an early version, about 1810 (Fig. 3). At the time Moscheles wrote (1821) Pape was making good pianofortes similar to Petzold's.[1]

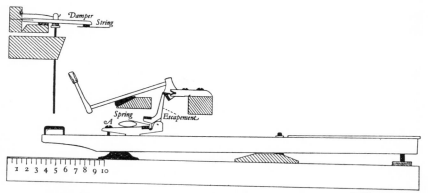

R. Harding del.

Fig. 3. L'échappement de Petzold (Paris, No. 1090).
A, screw to regulate the play of the escapement.

Returning once more to the evolution of the repetition action: Moscheles wrote in his diary under the date June 1st, 1825: "Pierre Érard showed and explained to me on a dumb keyboard his Uncle Sébastien's now completed invention, for which the firm has just taken out a patent.... It consists in the key, when only sunk half way, again rising and repeating the note. I was the first to play upon one of the newly completed instruments and found it of priceless value for the repetition of notes. In matter of fullness and softness of tone, there is something yet to be desired, and I had a long conversation on the subject with Érard".[2]

The firm had recently obtained a patent for a compensation frame, and it is strange that Moscheles makes no mention of this, since it probably affected the tone.

[1] B 70 (a), p. 220.   [2] B 72, pp. 106, 107.

In 1828 Érard presented Moscheles with a 'grand concert piano' valued at 160 guineas.[1] Of this magnificent gift Moscheles wrote that "externally the instrument is all that could be wished for but the tone of the higher notes is somewhat dry and I find the touch still too heavy. My Clementi, therefore, still remains my favourite instrument although Érard's instruments have begun steadily to make their way".[2] Two years later (1830) he evidently

[Fig. 4 shows an example of the Érard Action about this date (1832). The same lettering has been used as that in a later example, about 1890, Fig. 17 in *Grove's Dictionary of Music and Musicians* (Art. 'Piano').]

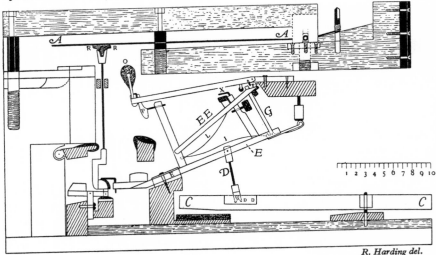

R. Harding del.

Fig. 4. Érard's 3rd repetition action (not later than 1833). (B 39.)

A, A, string; *C, C,* key; *D,* pilot, centred at *D, D,* to give the blow, by means of a carrier *E,* holding the escapement (hopper) *G* which delivers the blow to the hammer *O,* by the thrust of the escapement (hopper), which escapes by a forward movement after contact with a projection from the hammer, covered with leather, answering to the notch in the hammer butt of the English Action. This escapement is controlled at *X;* a double spring *I, L* pushes up a hinged lever, *E, E,* (the repetition lever), the rise of which is checked at *P, P,* and causes the second or double escapement; a little stirrup at the shoulder of the hammer, known as the repetition, pressing down *E, E* at the point, and by this depression permitting *G* to spring back to its place, and be ready for a second blow, before the key has been materially raised. The check *P* is attached by an adjustable screw into an upright fixed to the carrier (intermediate lever) *E, E.* This lever *E, E,* when the key is put down, brings down the under damper *R, R.*

---

[1] For comparison of the prices of pianofortes, the reader is referred to F, pp. 376–384.

[2] B 72, p. 219. Érards had patented another version of the repetition action both in France and in England in 1827 for horizontal pianofortes, but it was intended

tried some more of these pianofortes, for he wrote: "the touch in particular is vastly improved, I begin to revel in these instruments".[1] In the following year he used an Érard for the first time in preference to his Clementi and seems to have done so ever afterwards. Madame Moscheles notes that "his progress although mainly originating with Moscheles himself, was greatly favoured by the improvements made in Érard's pianos; their organ-like tone and full resonant sounds gave Moscheles such pleasure that no doubt he had every incentive to bring into relief these great excellences, and display them in his adagios. 'A very violoncello', he used to say, praising the tone, which he could prolong without the use of pedals; to the excessive use of which he had a rooted aversion".[2]

Thalberg began, about this period, to identify his wonderful playing with these instruments, and his power of "singing on the pianoforte" may have been partly due to the violoncello-like tone that Moscheles so much admired. This power of "singing on the pianoforte" is said to have inspired Mendelssohn, who also possessed an Érard, to write the E minor *Prelude*, which contains a favourite device of Thalberg's, and possibly also many of the "Songs without Words".[3]

The Érard pianofortes were rapidly gaining ground on the continent; Hummel, Thalberg, Steibelt, Moscheles, Herz, Pixis, Madame Dulcken, Verdi and Mendelssohn, and Liszt possessed an Érard at one time or another.

Steibelt originally preferred the English pianofortes, but, as Marmontel points out, it was necessary for him to have a pianoforte with a flexible action to produce his tremolo in imitation of the bowed stringed instruments and also his famous storm effects.[4]

Successful though the Érards were on the continent, in England, on the other hand, it was long before they were known, as "certain unfounded notions were circulated to their disadvantage". In order to set this right a court of inquiry was held and persons were examined on oath before the Judicial Committee of the Privy Council on the petition of Pierre Érard on December 15th, 1835. "Mr Peel, Mr Cresswell, Lord Lyndhurst, Lord Brougham, and Baron Parke" examined witnesses representing the trade, the

---

primarily for the square and it is not likely that it was used for this 'Grand Concert' instrument.

[1] B 72, p. 245. [2] *Ibid.* pp. 246, 247.
[3] B 53 (*a*), p. 311. [4] B 67, pp. 170, 171.

"Amateurs and Professors". From their replies certain points of interest emerge: Monsieur Latour, Director of the Philharmonic Concerts in 1827, 1828, stated that Érard pianofortes were generally used at these concerts. Signor Scappa, leader of the Opera, remarked that Érard's pianofortes had "a great deal more strength and power than any other instrument and greater effect in accompanying the voice". Madame Dulcken[1] stated that they had the same advantages as the German pianofortes with a greater brilliancy of tone, and that when visiting Russia she had observed that they stood the climate, whilst other instruments did not. They also remained in tune better than ordinary pianofortes; her own needed tuning only three or four times a year.[2]

As a result of this satisfactory inquiry Érard obtained an extension of his patent of 1821 on the ground of the loss sustained in working it.

Many of the more important firms of pianoforte makers now proceeded to invent repetition actions of their own, but these had little ultimate effect on pianoforte construction. Broadwoods had, of course, their own repetition action and it was upon one of these instruments that Döhler played at a concert at Manchester on Wednesday, June 19th, 1839. We quote part of a press notice:

Mr Döhler[3] played in the first part (of the performance) his fantasia on "Vivi tu" and brought tones from the piano equal to any we have heard. He played on one of Broadwood's repetition grand pianos; and we know not whether it was his extraordinary touch or not, but we thought we had never heard so fine a tone produced.[4]

Jean-Georges Kriegelstein, a pupil of Pape, invented in 1844 a repetition action which was considered a 'chef-d'œuvre' of simplicity and precision and was used by many other makers.[5] He states that Sébastien Érard's repetition action was too complicated to be durable and that after a time it began to clatter. Receiving encouragement from Savart, he succeeded after many attempts in inventing a simple, durable and noiseless repetition action in which the key was pivoted or hinged instead of moving over the usual key pivot and with the screw for regulating the play of the escapement provided with a little roller to prevent friction (Fig. 13).

Two years later (1846) Antoine-Jean-Denis Bord invented the

[1] Afterwards pianist to H.M. Queen Victoria.
[2] B 38.   [3] A pupil of Czerny.
[4] B 75 (j), p. 136.   [5] B 80, p. 193.

repetition action illustrated below.[1] Born at Toulouse in 1814 he learned his art at Marseilles, then at Lyons, and when nineteen years old he settled at Paris (1843). The pianoforte action that Bord invented in 1846, when he had been established only three years as a pianoforte maker, is interesting on account of the spiral spring at [*i*] in the diagram, Fig. 5; as, although this is not used now in grand pianofortes, it is to be found in almost every upright instrument of the present day.

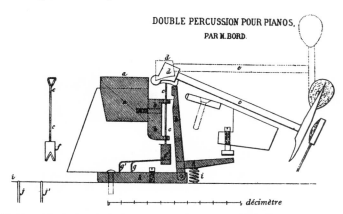

Fig. 5. Bord's Double Escapement Action, 1846. From the patent.

Contre la barre à des marteaux, s'adapte à vis un support *b*, servant de guide à une tige *c*, à laquelle je donne le nom de pilote; cette tige, dessinée à part, est recourbée en forme de fourche en contre-haut pour s'appuyer, au besoin, sous le nez de la noix *d* du marteau *e*. La même tige *c* s'implante en contre-bas dans un tasseau en bois *f*, suspendu à cette tige par le ressort *g*.

Pour conserver la même force à toutes les tiges *c*, je rends les ressorts *g* progressifs, c'est-à-dire que ceux *g*, qui sont pour la basse, sont plus court que ceux *g'* des dessus.

Le marteau est indiqué dans deux positions distinctes. L'échappement *h* est disposé comme d'ordinaire, ainsi que la touche *i* avec ses deux centres de mouvement *j*, *j'*.

Ce mécanisme produit l'effet suivant: Lorsque la touche *i* remonte et qu'elle arrive à mi-course, le ressort *g* repousse de bas en haut le pilote *c* qui fait relever le marteau *e*, et le maintient pour forcer l'échappement à rentrer sous le nez de la noix du marteau. Le résultat de ce mouvement est de faire instantanément réagir le marteau, sans être obligé de laisser relever la touche jusqu'à son point ordinaire, ce qui est un avantage immense pour la répétition des notes dans les morceaux difficiles. (*A.-J.-D. Bord.*)

A curious action was invented in 1851 by Hopkinson,[2] the founder of the now well-known house of that name, with a repetition so rapid that it was possible by manipulating the key to produce a tremolo similar to that used by singers. One of these

[1] C 236.   [2] C 247.

instruments was exhibited in the Great Exhibition of 1851. Their prospectus contains the following statement:

HOPKINSON'S NEW PATENT AND TREMOLO, CHECK ACTION GRAND PIANOFORTE

...a valuable improvement, which also shows the accurate and sensitive character of the mechanism, is that the 'Tremolo' (similar in effect to that produced by the violinist or the voice of a finished singer) may be produced by this action upon the pianoforte.

The tone of the Instrument is rich, powerful and of a *liquid voice-like quality*.[1] [Fig. 6.]

But these inventions were not of great importance and it is to Érard that the honour of inventing the modern grand pianoforte must be assigned, for his action forms the working basis of nearly all the modern double escapement actions.

§ II

Another type of pianoforte action must now be considered. This is the down-striking action which was invented to overcome two defects in the up-striking type, namely that the hammer striking upwards tended to unseat the string from the bridges and thus modify the tone, and secondly, that the sound-board had to be cut through to allow the hammers to pass up to the string; thus weakening the wooden frame.

These down-striking actions may be divided into two groups; those in which the hammer was lifted from the string by a counterweight and those in which it was raised by a spring. Again, this last class may be divided into repetition and non-repetition actions.

Many nineteenth-century makers experimented with the down-striking action, amongst whom may be mentioned Nannette and Johann Streicher, Matthias Müller and Wilhelm Leschen, of Vienna; Kollmann, Lidel, Greiner (originally from Würtemberg), Wornum and Burkinyoung of London; of American makers mention must be made of Thomas Loud, Charles Saltonstall Seabury, John Pethick and Ebenezer Currier; and of French makers, Henri Pape, Paulinus Meideck, Grus, Kriegelstein and Arnaud, Bernhardt, Wolfel and Wirth.

It is interesting to note that Hummel owned a pianoforte made by Nannette Streicher in 1825 with a down-striking action (illus-

[1] For the price of these instruments see F, p. 383.

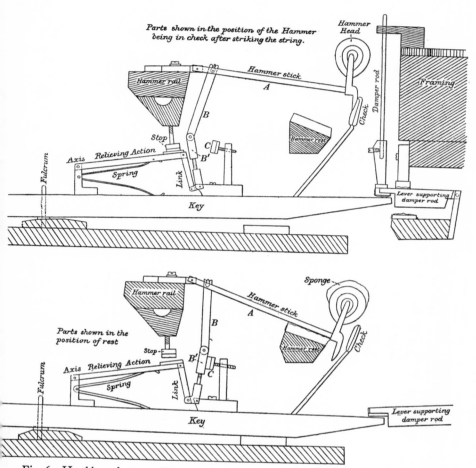

Fig. 6. Hopkinson's patent 'Tremolo check action' of 1851. (A simplified version.)
From the patent.

A, hammer, "clothed with sponge, is put in motion by the instrument *B*, which it will be seen is composed of two parts, and these parts are jointed at *B'*, so as to allow of movement in the length; *C* is a stop (faced with cloth or other suitable material, to prevent noise) which does not permit the arm or instrument bending but in one direction." (*Hopkinson*.)

trated below, Fig. 7). He used it at a concert at Weimar and Ferdinand Hiller, Willmers and Adolf von Henselt played upon it when they were his pupils.

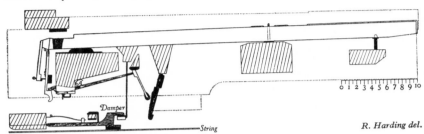

R. Harding del.

Fig. 7. Down-striking action (in which the hammer is returned by spring) by Nannette Streicher, 1825 (Leipzig, No. 199).

A, spring.

The present writer has been informed that it was the down-striking action by Streicher that inspired Henri Pape to experiment in that direction. A German by birth, Pape learnt his art under Pleyel at Paris and about 1818 commenced business on his own in that city. About 1827 he began to construct pianofortes with the down-striking actions of the second type, that is, where the hammer is returned by a spring. A man of genius, Pape was certainly one of the greatest of the French makers; his pianoforte actions are characterised by their elegance of design, the various parts being bent and curved in graceful lines to economise space. Sometimes, when particularly pressed for space, he turned the hammer towards the player, thus gaining an additional length of string. In one down-striking action, patented in 1848, the hammer, with its head pointing towards the pianist, passed *through* the key (which was specially strengthened with metal) to the string. It was Pape who invented the down-striking French Grand Action, and there is no doubt that the interest in this type of action that spread through Europe and America was largely due to his influence (Fig. 8).

Mr Pape's Soirée. A very delightful musical evening was passed at this gentleman's establishment in Frith Street, on Saturday last, where many eminent professors assembled. Among them were Messrs Moscheles, Thalberg, Servais, Lipinski, and Sedlatzek. Miss Clara Novello, and Herr Kroff, also assisted in the entertainment. The principal object in giving the soirée was, that Mr Pape might exhibit the new construction of his piano-fortes; and which present so many advantages, that in the course of a few years, they have become generally adopted in France. Mr Pape, in short, is the Broadwood of the French capital. He is by birth a Hanoverian, and formerly worked in London. He now carries on in Paris one of the largest manufactories for this class of musical instruments....

The advantages which these newly-invented pianos offer, are the following:—they unite more richness as well as sweetness of tone and power, to a greater solidity and less external size. One of the greatest defects in the old system, against which the manufacturers have struggled in vain for the last twenty years, arose from the mechanism being placed beneath the sounding-board; whence it became necessary, in order that the hammers might strike the strings, to form an opening in the sounding-board, by which the solidity of the instrument was more or less compromised. Endeavours had been made to remedy this defect by double bracing, so as to prevent the resistance of the strings; but complete success had never attended these attempts: and as to the opening in the sounding-board, and the injurious influence it had in diminishing the tone of the instrument, it was impossible under such a system to obviate it. With such difficulties, therefore, it became necessary to change the whole plan.

In the new invention of Mr Pape, the mechanism of the instrument being placed above the sounding-board, the two blocks now form but one; since they are, as well as the sounding-board, directly united, and without any opening whatever; by which arrangement such a solidity is obtained, that it is next to impossible for the sounding-board or block to give way—a circum-

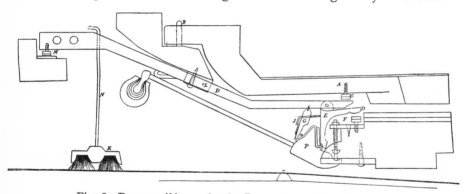

Fig. 8. Down-striking action by Pape, 1839. From the patent.

"Mechanism applicable to different forms of pianos, horizontal, grand, table, oval and square. This action is very simple and requires very little room. The height of the cases may be reduced to five and a half inches. The key of these instruments is reduced to a length of seven and a half inches. *A*, key; *B*, lever; *L*, centre; *C*, pilot which presses on the lever *D*, containing the hopper *E*; *F*, screw to regulate the escapement; *G*, movable check which has the double advantage of keeping the hammer by the notch, and facilitates the hopper to take the hammer up again by the nut *P* without being obliged to take the fingers off, as is the case in the common actions. At the same time this check retains the hammer and the hook *J* presses *G* against the nut. The lever *D* serves likewise for the dampers, by which the height of the hoppers is regulated; also by the screw *M*. The keys are regulated by the screw buttons *C*."

stance of very frequent occurrence in pianos constructed upon the old system. Besides, the keys communicating more immediately with the mechanism of the instrument; and the hammers striking the strings from above, against the bridge and the sounding-board, there results a much greater power and clearness of sound, as well as a greater facility in execution. The strings likewise being pressed by every stroke of the hammer upon the bridge, retain the instruments in tune a greater length of time than in the old pianos, in which the strings were continually being lifted up. A fortunate circumstance in the present invention is, that it requires much less solid wood; and the iron bars which they were compelled to make use of under the old plan, have been entirely laid aside.[1]

Two well-known down-striking actions by American makers must now be mentioned.

In 1827, just about the time that Pape was beginning to use the down-striking action, Thomas Loud patented a down-striking

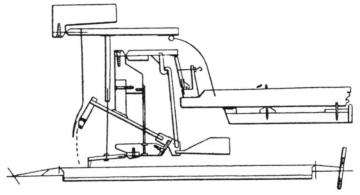

Fig. 9. Thomas Loud's down-striking action, 1827. From the patent.

action (illustrated above, Fig. 9).[2] The check piece and also the damping are controlled by a spring on the key in front of the characteristic 'hopper' or escapement of the English action.

The example by Ebenezer Currier[3] (Fig. 10), four years later, shows a certain 'family likeness', but it will be noticed that there is no check and that the damper is placed behind the hammer butt instead of immediately behind the hammer, as in Loud's example. In both of these actions the hammer is returned by a spring.

The type of down-striking action in which the hammer is returned by weight is rare. An eighteenth-century example of it applied to a square pianoforte has already been illustrated.[4]

[1] B 75 (a), pp. 39, 40.   [2] C 52.
[3] C 71.   [4] Part I, Chap. v, p. 56, Fig. 44.

In 1825 George Augustus Kollmann obtained a patent[1] for a down-striking action with 'counter balancing' hammers and on the favourable decision of the Judicial Council of the Privy Council

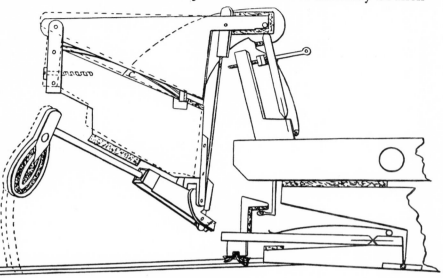

Fig. 10. Down-striking action by Ebenezer Currier, 1831. From the patent.

a renewal of his patent in 1839. The action is intended for grand or square pianoforte and the principle is the same for both instruments.

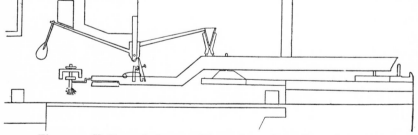

Fig. 10*a*. Kollmann's down-striking action, 1825. From the patent.

The hammer is provided with a lever at the end of which is a weight which is sufficiently heavy to lift it up from the strings. Kollmann gave two concerts to display this instrument. He seems

[1] C 43.

to have been a fine pianist and also something of a composer, for at the first of these concerts he played a sonata of his own composition.[1] The following is an extract from a press notice which occurred in the *Musical World* of his concert in July 1838.

On Thursday, this gentleman gave a second concert, for the purpose of exhibiting his recently invented piano. He performed a quintet, assisted by Messrs Blagrove, Sedlatzek, Fleischer, and Hausman; the sonata in F, for pianoforte and violin (with Blagrove); the concerto in C major, the compositions of Beethoven; and a duet for violin and piano, by Mayseder. These were played in a musician-like style, and well calculated to display the qualities of the instrument. The tone is powerful, and reached every part of the room; and, from the freedom of the touch, appeared to be capable of great variation.

[Mr Kollmann had engaged the services of Mrs Bishop, Miss Birch, Miss F. Woodman, Mr Bennett, Mr Balfe, and Mr Parry, junior.]

Occasionally an attempt was made to construct a repetition down-striking action. Amongst those who experimented in this direction must be mentioned Pape, Wirth and Wolfel, whose pianoforte action designs may almost be said to possess aesthetic charm. But the extreme mechanical difficulties associated with this action, apart from any added complications such as the repetition, prevented it from ever becoming popular with the manufacturers.

Another means of overcoming these supposed defects of the up-striking action consisted in placing the sound-board above the strings. In this way, though the hammers struck upwards in the usual way, they struck the strings towards the bridge on the sound-board instead of away from it and the sound-board itself was stronger, since there was no need to cut it through to allow for the hammers to pass through it to strike the strings.

Johann Jacob Goll patented this arrangement in 1822[2] and his name has become associated with it. Other persons who tried it were Henri Herz[3] the pianist pianoforte maker (Fig. 13), Robert Wornum[4] (Plate I) and Claude Montal.[5] The disadvantages of this arrangement consisted in the fact that the top of the pianoforte had to be lifted off each time a broken string was replaced, and strings were often broken;[6] Liszt sometimes had two pianofortes on the platform at once, so that one could be moved up whilst the strings of the other which he had broken were re-

[1] B 75 (*f*), p. 137 and 75 (*g*), p. 178.
[2] C 986.   [3] C 990.
[4] Not patented.   [5] C 991.
[6] For the mass of old pianoforte strings and schemes of scaling see D (1), (2).

placed—"And off flew the hammer from its joint, and crash went some half dozen strings—with such fury did I dash my hand upon the keys of the pianoforte", as Weber says in his *Arabeske*. Montal partially overcame this difficulty of replacing broken strings by making the resonance body of his pianoforte independent of the case and movable upon a pivot, so that it could be swung up and propped in a position for the string to be replaced. But the clumsiness of this type of pianoforte was a serious bar to usefulness and there was never any great demand for it.

DESCRIPTION OF FIG. 11.

Fig. 11. Mécanisme à étrier. (Explanation of diagram.)

A, C, No. 9, represents the key of a pianoforte, movable upon the fulcrum or pin *B,* and acting upon a second lever *C, I,* which last hath its point or fulcrum at *D* attached to the fixed piece *E,* and on the same fixed piece is situated the supports for the motion of the hammer *N, O, P,* which by its rise strikes the wire or spring *R, S. M, F, G* is a lever standing upon the extremity of *C, I.* Its sides *F, F,* are thin plates, as shown in No. 2, by the same letters of the alphabet to the same parts, so that the tail *N* of the hammer passes through its upper parts, and is subject to the action of the small round connecting bars *M* and *L* at the termination of the fork-shaped ends of the side bars *F, F.* The centre *G* is duly placed, and adjusted by the small screw *I,* which carries the socket piece in which the pin thereof turns, and the spring *H* gives a gentle tendency in the lever *F, G,* to move or press towards *D.* The piece *K* is an adjusting screw with a bearing part, which serves to produce a small motion in the contrary direction in *F, G,* when *I* is depressed by the action of the finger at *A.* And lastly, the face of the hammer tail, upon which the part *L* is made to act, is sloped from the place of action outwards from the fulcrum of the hammer, so that by virtue of that slope and of the altered position of the hammer tail when depressed, the hold at *L* is very nearly destroyed, and the hammer left at liberty to recoil after the stroke; and the action or effect of the said apparatus is as follows: When (as described in the figure) the key *A* is up, and also *I* and *L,* and *L* is kept forward towards *O* by the fender spring *II,* the hold upon the hammer tail is direct and upon pressing *A* the point *I* descends and the hammer flies up: but at the instant the string has received the blow the hammer being thrown back by the recoil causes *L* to recede, and this effect is rendered extremely easy by the very oblique action of *L* at that instant upon the hammer tail, and the further assistance afforded by the lift at *K.* But again, when the point *A* is suffered to rise (even through a very small space), the piece *L* will advance and recover its hold, and by that means afford the power of giving repeated strokes without missing or failure, by very small angular motions of the key itself, which is an advantage of such magnitude and singularity as will not require to be further explained or pointed out to the artists and performers of or upon the said instrument.

In No. 3 is exhibited a different construction of the lever *M, F, G,* in which the same letters denote the same things, and consequently no further explanation is needful for understanding the same. This last construction is in some respects more convenient for the workman. No. 4 shows an improved damper particularly advantageous on its application to the lower strings, of which the vibration is strong and powerful. *A* represents the common damper, which in its descent falls or rests upon the tail *B* of a lever movable on the joint or fulcrum *D,* and by that means raising (with the assistance, if need be, of the small spring beneath) the second damper *C,* and by that means effectually stops all sound from the spring against which the said dampers are to be applied. The upper delineations represent the plan and the lower with the same letters represent the vertical sections of the same parts and things. No. 5 represents an apparatus for producing a tone in the strings of the instrument which is very pleasing and resembles that of the harp. The strings *G* are kept in their situation by passing beneath the inverted or reversed bridge *A*, and near that bridge is placed a face of leather *B*, movable at the extremity of a lever or wire curled into a spring of a few turns at *C*. The letter *D* represents a small loop of leather fastened to the instrument at *D*, but capable of rising and falling at the looped extremity thereof along with the wire which passes through the same. *E, F* represents a piece or stop consisting of a number of inclined faces or wedges, which, being connected in a line, may be slided all at once under the levers or wires *B, C*, belonging to the whole series of strings throughout the instrument, and when so slided will raise all the pieces *B*, and give the strings the property of affording the harp tone so long as the said pieces shall be kept in the said situation. No. 6 represents an apparatus by which the tone of the instrument is rendered particularly soft. *A* is a piece of wood or other fit material extending across the instrument, and *B* are certain small pieces of leather glued above and beneath a thin slip or projecting arm, so as to project beyond the same, and to remain in part in the air with a very small space between the said leathers: and when *A* is moved in the direction from *A* towards *B*, the insulated or projecting parts of the leathers become opposite the parts where the stroke of the hammer is given, and the said leathers receive the stroke, which is transmitted through them to the string under that kind of modification which produces the effect on the tone last mentioned, and this effect continues as long as the said position is suffered to remain and continue. No. 7 indicates an improvement effected by placing the lowest or additional wires or strings *C, C, C* (when required) beneath the bottom of the instrument which serves as the sound board, where the same are acted upon by the hammers *A, B*, by the touch from the keys, as shown in the drawing. The advantage of this disposition is, that the instrument itself is considerably shorter, and the stroke may be given by a hammer of greater power and effect than usual. No. 9, upon the key or first lever of the instrument, is placed to indicate that the said levers or keys, with the supports and connections thereunto belonging, may be slided inwards and the instrument completely closed up, while the other levers and apparatus supporting and more immediately acting on the hammers will be left undisturbed, and the said levers or keys with their supports and connections may be again and immediately brought into effect by drawing out the same to the first position or situation thereof. No. 8 shows a very convenient method of closing the instrument by a falling leaf or lid, which is raised to the position *A, C*, when the instrument is in use. At No. 10 is shown a method of more immovably fastening or fixing the pins on which the extremities of the strings are looped, which is effected by indenting or cutting into the solid plank or board which constitutes the end of the case itself, instead of glueing or otherwise fastening a separate piece as usual to receive the said pins. No. 11 shows an improvement in the arch of connection or support of the instrument by making the faces by which the same is screwed or fixed thereto in the middle of the same, and giving by that means a much greater breadth and consequently stiffness to the piece itself than usual. And I do also improve the curved bridge of the said instrument by making the same of two straight pieces, having the fair grain lengthways throughout, and the flexure given to the compound piece by bending and keeping the same bended while the glueing is done, and until the glue is quite dry, after which the figure remains constant, and the bridge thus formed is less liable to change or to occasion damage to the other parts in the course of time than bridges made in the common manner.

(*Sébastien Érard, abridged.*)

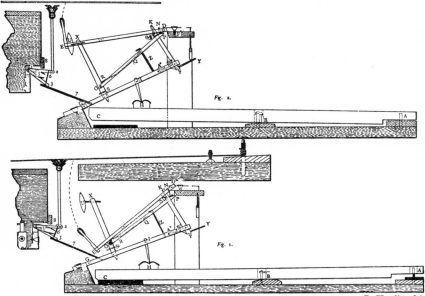

R. *Harding del.*

Fig. 12. Sébastien Érard's Double Escapement Action for grand pianoforte, 1821.
Drawn from the patent.

Fig. 1 exhibits the new mechanism as it stands when the key is up and at rest; Fig. 2
represents the same when the key is pressed quite down. (The same letters of reference
are used to denote the same parts whenever they occur in the two figures.) *A, B, C,*
Fig.1, is the key; its centre of action being at *B*; *D, E* is the hammer, with its centre of
motion at *D*; *F, G*, intermediate lever between the key and the hammer, having its
centre of motion in *G*; the motion of the key is communicated to the intermediate
lever *F, G* by the piece *H, I* which turns on its centre at *I* and rests in a notch on the
key at *H*. This motion is communicated from the intermediate lever to the hammer by
the piece *F, K*, the escapement (sticker), by means of the metal or other staple *M*, fixed
under the tail of the hammer, from which it escapes: *the 1st escapement.* But the
hammer is supported also by a spring *Q, R, S* which is mounted on the auxiliary
lever *P, O* and keeps it apart from the intermediate lever *G, F* by pressing against
the piece at *Q*. The opening of the spring and of its lever *P, O* is regulated by the
wire hook *Z*, the lower end of which is a screw tapped into the intermediate lever *F,
G*. The hammer tail rests at the same time on the escapement (sticker) *F, K* and on the
spring or auxiliary lever *P, O* by means of the staple *M*. The hammer is carried to the
string by the several parts as will be seen at Fig. 2, which shows the different positions
which each of them takes. The key in this figure has been entirely depressed by the
finger, and it clearly exhibits the advantages of this new mechanism; the dotted line
indicates that the hammer has described that line to strike the string; but whilst this
operation is performing, the extremity *P* of the auxiliary lever *P, O*, Figs. 1 and 2,
comes into contact with the tail of the hammer very near to its centre of motion
at *N*, see Fig. 2 (which causes the *2nd end escapement*), and the hammer *D, E*
having now more power to descend on account of the point of bearing *N* being nearer
its centre, such hammer by its own weight forces the lever *O, P* to go down, in

opposition to its spring Q, R, S. In that situation the spring Q, R, S has no power or effect on the hammer, which is then supported upon a notch by the escapement (sticker) F, K alone, by means of the staple M resting on such notch, see Fig. 2, until the projecting arm or tail F, Y of the escapement (sticker), which turns on its centre at F, comes into contact with the adjustable stop; and by pressing upon which the notch of the escapement (sticker) F, K is made to escape from under the staple M, see Fig. 2, at the same moment the hammer falls past the wedge-formed point of the adjustable piece U (*i.e.* the check), see Fig. 2, which prevents its flying up to the string again, and is there kept secure as long as the key is kept entirely down. A^*, B^* is a slight spring, acting in any convenient form and manner upon the escapement (sticker) F, K, so as to elevate the end Y of its tail, and keep it in a proper position for engaging with the staple M, the point of contact N, between the hammer and auxiliary lever P, O, may be contrived and adjusted in several different ways, such as by a swell in the shape of the hammer, or in that of the lever P, O or with one or several thicknesses of leather, or with a screw for better regulating the pressure, as shown at N, Figs. 1, 2, which latter method is preferable. The wedge-formed piece U (*i.e.* the check), which stops the hammer in its fall, is mounted with a long screw for its adjustment, as shown in Fig. 1, upon the branch or arm V, X, which is immovably fixed at V upon the intermediate lever F, G, and by turning the piece U with its screw, more or less, the hammer may be stopped with the greatest precision; a screw S, which presses on the spring Q, R, S at one of its extremities, is indispensable to regulate its strength or tightness for supporting the lever P, O, upon which all the weight of the hammer rests, when by the escapement it no longer bears on the notch or step L of the sticker (Fig. 1), which, together with the lever, had put it in action. 1, 2, 3, Figures 1 and 2, represent new contrivances for a damper, which possess considerable advantages over those now in use, namely, that of stopping the vibration of the wire short, by means of the pressure of a spring, besides the weight of the key; 1, 2 and 1, 3, are two little pieces or levers mounted and moving upon the same centre 1, and kept apart from each other by a spring 5, mounted upon the same centre; they are maintained at their proper distance apart by a little hook or wire pin 6, at the extremity of the upper lever. 1, 2, is attached by a moving centre; the rod 2, 4, which carries the damper up to the string 3, 7, is a long pin or wire screwed into or otherwise affixed to the intermediate lever F, G, as before mentioned, and moving with it upon their common centre G; this rod or wire of course partakes of the motion of the lever when the key is depressed and the several pieces which compose the damper come down with it, and allow the string to vibrate freely, as is shown at Figure 2. To produce the forte with the pedal, or to take off the dampers from the strings, an appropriate piece of wood or metal (8) is introduced, and this, by the well-known ordinary contrivances of levers, pedals, or a pedal, comes down upon the upper piece or lever 1, 2, which carries the damper, 2, 4, and makes it quit the string and allows it to vibrate freely; the little spring 5, admits of this depression without disturbing at all the other parts of the mechanism. (*Sébastien Érard, abridged and with additions by R. H.*)

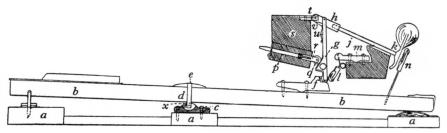

Fig. 13. Repetition Action. Kriegelstein, 1844.

Profil du mécanisme à double échappement avec la touche montée sur une pointe mobile de mon nouveau système.

a, châssis du clavier.

b, touche.

c, chevalet dans lequel la pointe *d* marche sur le pivot *x*.

e, vis sans tête qui est placée dans le haut de la touche traversant un petit taquet collé sur elle. La vis *e* repose sur la pointe *d*; elle est séparée par une petite mouche en cuir, pour que le contact des deux métaux de la vis et de la pointe ne fasse point de bruit. La touche reste fixe sur la pointe, et ces deux pièces marchent ensemble sur le pivot *x*. La vis *e* sert à régler la touche de hauteur.

f, chevalet à double talon vissé sur la touche pour recevoir l'échappement.

g, échappement.

h, noix du marteau.

j, manche du marteau.

k, tête du marteau.

l, pièce destinée à attraper l'échappement et à le renvoyer sur le second talon du chevalet *f*: cette pièce est fixée, par un fil de ressort, en anneau sur le chevalet *m*, vissé sur le pont *o*.[1] Au moyen de cette pièce, on peut régler l'attrape *l*, par les deux vis qui la traversent, en l'approchant ou l'éloignant de l'échappement *g*, afin de produire l'effet du double échappement.

n, attrape-marteau servant à tenir la tête du marteau pour qu'il ne tremble pas, et ne retombe sur le pont que quand la touche est en repos.

p, vis à régler la distance de la corde à laquelle le marteau doit échapper. Cette vis fait avancer ou reculer la fourche *r*, dans laquelle est monté le galet *q*, sur lequel vient toucher la pente de l'échappement *g* quand le marteau *k* a touché la corde. Ce galet le fait retomber sans aucun frottement.

s, pont sur lequel sont montés les pivots des marteaux dans le cuivre ou les fourches *t*.

u, ressort de l'échappement qui est accroché dans un cordonnet en soie *v*, tenant à la noix du marteau *h*. Ce ressort est destiné à rappeler l'échappement et à le maintenir contre les talons du chevalet *f*. En outre, il a l'avantage, par sa combinaison, d'alléger le marteau, au lieu de le rendre plus lourd, comme cela arrive avec les ressorts des mécaniques ordinaires. Je ferai observer que le double talon au chevalet *f* n'est pas obligatoire, et qu'on peut le faire à un seul talon.

[1] Letter *o* is missing in the original diagram.

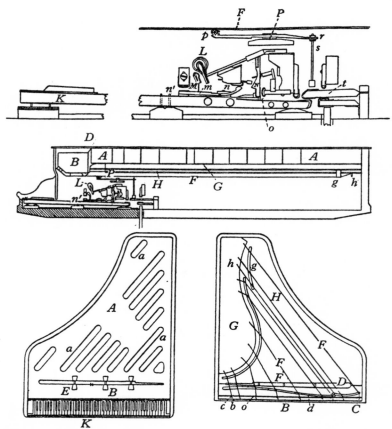

Fig. 14. Pianoforte with the sound-board above the strings. Herz, 1843.

Les mêmes lettres indiquent les mêmes pièces dans les diverses figures.

A, châssis en bois; les entailles *a* qu'on y a pratiquées servent au passage du son rendu par la table d'harmonie qui se trouve immédiatement dessous; *B,* sommier de cheville formant la prolongation du châssis *A,* dont il n'est séparé que par l'ouverture destinée à faciliter l'opération de l'accord, et se trouvant immédiatement après [*sic*] le clavier. *C,* plan incliné formant chanfrein ou biseau pratiqué au sommier, à l'arête ou angle qui se trouve au-dessus du clavier, et destiné à recevoir les chevilles. *D,* intervalle laissé entre le châssis *A* et le sommier des chevilles, et se continuant en contrebas ce sommier et la table d'harmonie, lequel intervalle forme une ouverture destinée à faciliter l'opération de l'accord, en même temps qu'en laissant voir le dessus des marteaux et des étouffoirs elle permet de les régler. *E,* arcs-boutants en fer destinés à maintenir au droit de l'intervalle *D* l'écartement du châssis du sommier contre lequel le châssis *A* vient butter. *F,* cordes placées obliquement ou plutôt diagonalement par rapport au carré de l'instrument. *G,* sommier. *H,* table d'harmonie placée au-dessus des cordes. *J,* fourche en fer placée dans le sens du tirage des cordes et destinée à consolider l'instrument. *K,* touche pouvant s'enlever sans démonter la mécanique: elle porte en *i,* l'angle rentrant formant l'arête d'échappement du marteau. *L,* marteau. *M,* attrape-marteau monté sur la bascule *m,* dont le pivot *n* porté par la touche, détermine, en suite du mouvement de cette dernière, le mouvement et l'action de l'attrape-marteau, concurremment avec les points extrêmes *n′* de buttée de la bascule. *N,* échappement du marteau, dont la base *o* échappe sur la saillie angulaire *i* de la touche. Le système d'échappement sur la touche même donne la plus grande facilité à l'exécutant pour les trilles et les cadences. *P,* branche à bascule portant, à une de ses extrémités, l'étouffoir *p* et dont l'autre reçoit en *r* le pilote *s,* porté par le bras à bascule *t* que lève l'extrémité de la touche.[1]

[1] N.B. letters *J* and *i* are missing in the original.

Plate I. Wornum's Imperial Grand Pianoforte (1838). [The upper half is on
the right, the lower half is on the left] (in the possession of the writer).

Inscription: "Imperial Grand Horizontal Piano, Invented and Patented by Robert
Wornum. Music Hall, Store St., Bedford Square, London. [1838]".

Note. Wornum moved to Store Street in 1832.

No. 5135. Vibrating length of longest string 180 cm., vibrating length of shortest
string 5·5 cm. Two pedals acting in the usual way. The dampers act under the
strings. The last thirty are double. Case: Rosewood on three carved legs (with box-
wood castors). Dimensions of case: length 237 cm., breadth across keyboard 120 cm.

CHAPTER II

SOME IMPROVEMENTS IN THE CONSTRUCTION OF THE PIANOFORTE RELATING TO THE PRODUCTION OF A LOUD AND SONOROUS TONE

ONE of the chief defects of the early pianofortes was their lack of sustaining power, but this defect was often turned to artistic account by composers who sustained the tone by using a modified 'Bebung' (Exs. 2, 3). These rapidly repeated notes are a familiar feature from the time of Domenico Scarlatti to Beethoven.

Ex. 2. Beethoven, Op. 110.

Ex. 3. Clementi, *Sonata* in C Major.

Besides the 'Bebung', various devices for giving the illusion of a full tone were employed. The examples in Ex. 4 are of frequent occurrence in the music of this period but tended to disappear as the pianoforte gained sonority.

Owing to the thin strings still in use the bass of the early nineteenth-century pianofortes was often too weak to support the harmonies if both hands played with the same force, and it seems to have been necessary in some cases to strike more boldly with the left hand than with the right. In order to do this Dussek is said to have taken his seat a little to the left of the middle of the pianoforte; in fact the phrase "Il basso ben marcato" occurs frequently in the music of this period.

This thinness of tone was not a serious defect in Mozart's day but by the close of Beethoven's life it began to be seriously felt by all musicians, but most of all by those who sought to interpret Beethoven and to compose in his style.

Ex. 4.

These circumstances led to strenuous efforts on the part of the makers to improve their instruments both in respect to loudness and to the richness of the tone. As Helmholtz remarks, "the peculiar quality of tone commonly termed *poverty*, as opposed to *richness*, arises from the upper partials being comparatively too strong for the prime tone", and he says that force of these upper partial tones in a struck string depends in general on:

(1) *The nature of the stroke.*
(2) *The place struck.*
(3) *The density, rigidity and elasticity of the string.*

(1) *The nature of the stroke.* If the string is struck with hard material, the tone is piercing and tinkling and a multitude of high partial tones are audible; if, on the other hand, the string is struck with a soft hammer the tone becomes less bright, but more soft and harmonious, for the higher partial tones have disappeared. Helmholtz accounts for this in the following way:

If the string is struck by a sharp-edged metallic hammer which rebounds instantly, only the one single point struck is directly set in motion. Immediately after the blow the remainder of the string is at rest. It does not move until a wave of deflection rises, and runs backwards and forwards over the string. This limitation of the original motion to a single point produces the most abrupt discontinuities, and a corresponding long series of upper partial tones, having intensities, in most cases equalling or even surpassing that of the prime. When the hammer is soft and elastic, the motion has time to spread before the hammer rebounds. When thus struck the point of the string in contact with such a hammer is not set in motion by a jerk, but increases gradually and continuously in velocity during the contact. The discontinuity of the motion is consequently much less, diminishing as the softness of the hammer increases, and the force of the higher upper partial tones is correspondingly decreased.

"This is the reason why", he says, "it has been found advantageous to cover pianoforte hammers with thick layers (or a thick layer) of felt, rendered elastic by much compression." The hammers for the lower octaves are heavier and consequently take longer to rebound from the string than the hammers used for the treble, which are lighter and harder. The reason for the use of hard hammers with a narrow striking surface for the treble is that the stiffness of these strings tends to hinder the formation of the higher partial tones and that consequently a hammer favourable for their formation is required to equalise the quality of tone.[1]

Pianoforte hammers. The use of felt as a substitute for the old method of covering the hammer with leather[2] does not seem to have been finally and universally accepted until after the first half of the century. Welcker[3] states that formerly sheepskin was generally used for covering the hammer heads and was supplied of the best quality by Kaindel, a tanner of Linz, but eventually the deer leather prepared by Trümpfer of Vienna was considered to be the best. Welcker writes that at his time (1856) deer leather was still tanned according to Trümpfer's method and was considered to be the most durable material for covering the hammer head; it would satisfy everyone if the skins were always of the best quality, of even thickness all over, and of even elasticity, which unfortunately was never the case. This is interesting as it shows that leather as an outer covering for the hammers was still much in use in Germany, if not elsewhere, as late as 1856. Welcker states that formerly experiments were tried in England with molton[4] and that satisfactory results were obtained with it so far as the tone was concerned, but the material was not durable and was but rarely used in consequence. Pape of Paris then began to experiment with hat felt, which gave a good tone but was even less durable than leather. Welcker says that this felt had two layers and appeared to be made of fine sheep's wool and mixed with rabbit's hair. It was prepared in sheets the length and breadth of a keyboard and graded from about $\frac{28}{100}$ inch to $\frac{9}{100}$ inch. Fortunately Pape's own description of how he prepared the felt is preserved in his French patent of 1826[5] and is as follows:

Je prends une partie de poil de lapin et un sixième de bourre de soie que je fais carder ensemble: ce mélange sert à former une première couche; je prends ensuite une partie de poil de lièvre que je mêle avec un tiers d'édredon, et je fais également carder ensemble ces deux matières dont je forme une seconde

[1] B 46, pp. 74–80.
[2] For a detailed account of the method of tanning the leather coverings for hammers, see E (3).
[3] B 94, S. 47, 48.
[4] A kind of coarse woollen cloth.
[5] C 538.

12-2

couche: ces matières ainsi disposées, je les fais fortement feutrer par les procédés connus, jusqu'à ce que l'étoffe ait une consistance convenable et la souplesse nécessaire.

He was followed in 1827 by Côte who obtained a patent for "Hammers covered with very thick felt in which the covering was made out of a single piece of felt, and took the place of the seven or eight pieces of leather which usually formed the hammer head".[1] This type of hammer is called a 'single coated hammer' and it is supposed to promote an evenness of tone throughout the set greater than that obtained with hammers formed of several layers. In the meantime a great many experiments had been tried with other materials. In England various makers had used cloth as an outer covering for the hammer, which had as usual a basis of several layers of leather. Joseph Merlin refers to this type of hammer in his patent of 1774[2] and an example may be seen in Hawkins' 'portable grand pianoforte' in the collection of Messrs John Broadwood and Sons. Samuel Bury in 1788, it will be remembered, suggested that felt could be used as an *under* covering to the hammer, which should have an *outer* covering of leather as usual.[3] John Antes in 1806[4] states that he tried both sponge and tinder as a substitute for leather; he considered that the sponge gave the most brilliant tone, but it was difficult to obtain a sufficient quantity of the right texture. He then tried common tinder, which when properly prepared he found to be equally good, but here again the difficulty arose of obtaining a sufficient quantity, as the softer parts were considered the best for striking fire. He states that both the tinder and the sponge had lasted unchanged for several years and suggested that if beech tinder of fine quality was used and carefully prepared it might be brought to great perfection for this purpose.[5]

In 1827 Edward Dodd of London invented a hammer[6] in which the outer layer of leather could be tightened and loosened according to the quality of tone required (Fig. 15). It will be realised

---

[1] C 539.   [2] C 846.

[3] C 544.

[4] For John Antes' account of his experiments with tinder as a covering for hammer heads see E (2).

[5] German tinder (Amadou) prepared from species of *Polyporus* and *Fomes*— fungi that grow on trees; formerly much used as a match and a styptic, etc.
"Some give to the Amadou the name of pyrotechnical sponge." (*Encycl. Brit.* 1815. Vol. I, p. 761.)

[6] C 532.

from what has already been said that the tone could be brightened by tightening the hammer or made less bright and more sonorous by unscrewing it, as the hardness of the hammer could then be varied.

In the following year John Mackay of Boston, U.S.A., patented a new form of hammer[1] with the head weighted by a piece of lead, pewter, solder, zinc, tin, iron, etc., being let into the top of the head to produce a firmer and bolder tone. Alpheus Babcock of Philadelphia made hammers in which the wooden portion of the head was made concave "to receive a small roll, or pad, or woollen

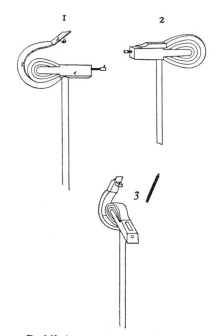

Fig. 15. Dodd's hammers, 1827. From the patent.

"No. 1 exhibits the hammer with the outer leather unbraced. No. 2 exhibits the hammer complete and ready to strike the strings. No. 3 exhibits the same hammer in another position, which shows the mortise which receives the brass nut. The first three or four coverings of leather are glued or otherwise fastened on block 1 of the hammer at both ends, in the usual way, but the outer leather 2 which is exhibited unbraced, I glue to block 1 only at one end, the other to a detached piece of wood 3, in the centre of which is a brass nut 4 which receives the screw 5 at the extremity of block 1, by means of which the quality of tone is regulated with the greatest accuracy."

[1] C 546.

cloth, or other suitable" material, over which the covering of leather was to be placed as usual. The use of cloth in place of leather is also claimed.[1] In 1835 Pierre Fischer patented covering hammers with felt of varying thicknesses.[2] Timothy Gilbert, another American maker, invented a hammer head with a groundwork of cork covered with soft buff leather and patented this in 1841,[3] but the use of cork had already been advocated by Clagget in England as early as 1788.

Meanwhile some more improvements in felt making were in progress and Pape came forward with an unprimed felt in 1844.[4] Four years later another experiment was tried which consisted in the use of india-rubber as an outer covering for the hammer. This was the invention of Van Gils of Paris.[5]

Nickels, in 1845, patented a new invention relating to clothing hammers,[6] which consisted in employing short lengths of felted cord inserted into a socket in the hammer head and retained in position by means of a screw. As the hammer struck the strings with the ends of the fibres of which the felted cord was formed it gained a 'peculiar elasticity'.

Woolley of Nottingham in 1846 patented a form of hammer head which could be unscrewed and removed. The purpose of this was to enable the performer to substitute another set of hammers to "produce a different quality of tone to that previously obtained"; for this purpose Woolley observes: "I clothe the hammer heads with various materials, such as woollen or other yarns, or strips of felt or other material, which instead of being glued on, as is now commonly the case, I wrap round and round till the required quantity is applied, when the end may be secured by gluing or otherwise".[7]

Browne of Boston tried (1851) a piece of gutta-percha on the top of the hammer head,[8] in lieu of some of the layers of leather. Mata of London obtained a French patent[9] and Hopkinson of London[10] an English one in 1851 for clothing hammers with sponge.

Interest in felt making was steadily increasing and it is evident that felt was used by most makers, though the number of experiments in other directions indicate that all the makers were not yet satisfied. (For methods of preparing the felt see E (1).)

[1] C 547. [2] C 540.
[3] C 548. [4] C 542.
[5] C 550. [6] C 543.
[7] C 536. [8] C 551.
[9] C 553. [10] C 552.

b

a

Plate II (*a*). An example of the old method of stringing pianofortes. The separate strings have their further ends twisted into an eye for the purpose of being looped or 'hitched' over the hitch pins. From a Cabinet Pianoforte by George Wilkinson, not later than 1829. (In the possession of Mrs R. T. Barnes.)

(*b*). Section of stringing illustrating Stewart's patent for improved stringing. Pat. No. 5475, March 22nd, 1827. Instead of two strings each looped over its own hitch pin, one string double the length is passed round a single hitch pin. The loose ends are fastened to two wrest pins. From a Cabinet Pianoforte by Clementi not later than 1832. (In the possession of Mr W. J. Moore, Cambridge.)

(2) *The striking place*. The striking distance in pianofortes varies from one-seventh to one-ninth, for the middle part of the instrument, though occasionally experiments were tried with a striking place nearer to the centre of the string. The first maker of any keyboard-stringed musical instrument who attempted to fix a definite striking place was John Broadwood who, according to Hipkins, about the year 1788, practically adopted one-ninth of the vibrating length for his striking place, allowing some latitude in the treble. Kützing, writing in 1844, considered that one-eighth of the distance produced the best quality of tone.

The impact of the hammer theoretically abolishes the node of the striking place, and with it the partial belonging to it throughout the string and it is said that the striking distance of one-seventh was adopted in order to eliminate the seventh partial tone. As the striking point approaches the end of the string a prominence is given to the upper partial tones at expense of the lower ones, and it is owing to this that the treble hammers are sometimes made to strike almost against the bridge to obtain greater brilliancy of tone.[1]

(3) *The strings*.[2] It is a mistake to imagine that the strings used for early nineteenth-century pianofortes were thick like those of our modern instruments. In the few late grand pianofortes that we have had the opportunity to examine (for so few exist) the thickness of the extreme bass strings corresponds approximately to the first bass strings on a modern upright instrument.

Little comparatively is known about nineteenth-century pianoforte strings. At the beginning of the century, according to Otto Paul, strings manufactured by Fuchs of Nuremberg were considered the best, but about 1820 the Berlin wire was preferred.[3] Pleyel of Paris obtained a patent for the mode of tempering both brass and steel pianoforte wire in 1810.[4] But in spite of these experiments, tempered steel wire does not appear to have been extensively used until a later period; Pape was probably the first to make a practice of using it, for we find the following statement in a French patent granted to him in 1826:

Jusqu'à ce moment on a toujours employé des cordes en fil de fer ou en fil de laiton; je me propose de faire usage de cordes en acier détrempé; l'ex-

[1] See B 46, pp. 77–78 and footnote on pp. 77, 78.
[2] For further details relating to strings see D and Sect. III, p. 261.
[3] B 79, S. 152.
[4] C 1224. For Pleyel's method of tempering wires see D (5).

périence m'a démontré qu'elles étaient plus solides et qu'elles produisaient un son plus doux et en même temps plus sonore.

John Broadwood and Sons were using both English and German steel wire in 1815. By another entry in their books it is certain that Webster of Birmingham, the manufacturer of the celebrated cast steel wire, was working in 1831, for a "set of covered strings on Webster's steel wire" for a square pianoforte cost 3s. 6d. and for a grand 4s.[1]

Giorgio di Roma, the author of a little book on tuning the pianoforte (dedicated to Rossini), writing in 1834, states that there were only three kinds of pianoforte wire, "cordes anglaises, cordes de Berlin, et cordes de Nuremberg. Les premières sont en acier, les secondes en fer, et les troisièmes en cuivre".[2] He states that the Berlin and Nuremberg wires had the same gauge numbers and were sold on bobbins with the numbers inscribed on them. The English steel wire, on the other hand, had a different set of numbers and was sold in envelopes with the numbers inscribed on the outside. Considerable difficulty arises in correlating the mass indicated by the gauge numbers between the English and the German wire and even between the two types of German wires themselves. When half numbers were introduced, the task becomes almost impossible owing to the irregularity with which these wires were manufactured. The English steel wire was considered to be the best for the treble notes on account of its durability and more brilliant quality of tone.

John Hawley, a watch maker in London, was making steel wire in 1840 and obtained a patent for a method of tempering it in this year. He did not always make these wires with an even diameter, for he says:

I make the strings for the bass or deeper toned notes much thicker in the central parts than at the ends, and in forms either cylindrical, conical or angular, and I so arrange them on the piano as that the hammer shall strike them on the thickest part.[3]

The firm of Sanguinède et Capt of Paris also obtained a patent for tempering steel wires in 1840 and they made the wires for the lower octaves of varying thicknesses.[4]

About 1843 the best brass strings were made at Birmingham and the next best at Vienna.

[1] For the prices of pianoforte wire see D (4).
[2] B 86, p. 36.   [3] C 1226.
[4] C 1227. The methods of tempering wire used by Hawley, and Sanguinède et Capt of Paris, will be found in D (5), p. 372.

With regard to the covered strings, there is practically no information forthcoming. The core wire seems undoubtedly to have been steel and the covering wire copper. These strings were evidently used early in the century, for their flexibility was more favourable to the tone than a thick string of the requisite weight, for this tended to be stiff and inelastic.

The desire to obtain increased elasticity, and consequently a louder tone owing to the possibility of increased amplitude, seems to have led William Bundy to use platinum instead of silver for his covering wire. What he evidently did was to *plate* his copper covering wire with platinum instead of with silver, for it was usual at this time to give the covering wire a protective coating of silver.

"For this purpose", Bundy writes, "gold will apply well, but I use platina (being of the greatest specific gravity). In the use of the heavy metal platina, I find purity and power of tone is increased with the quality used, and that the strength of the string covered, whether brass, steel, iron or any other metal or material, must determine the quality, for if too much platina be added the string will not stand drawing up to its proper tension.... I make the covered wire [*i.e.* the core] rough by drawing a sharp bastard cut file along the wire several times, which prepares the string to receive the covering platina wire, whose ductile nature admits of being forced by pressure (whilst spinning or covering) into the indents made by the file, and renders it perfectly secure, tho' the ends terminate with the pins."[1]

Nickels in 1845 endeavoured to avoid the metallic sound peculiar to pianoforte strings by wrapping them with a thread of india-rubber, gutta-percha or cat-gut. If india-rubber was used, Nickels states that it should be vulcanised or otherwise "proofed against different atmospheres". For the deep bass notes of a pedallier (which forms a part of this patent) he combined "two, three or more wires previously covered or not" (but he preferred them covered) "to be bound round or plaited, so as to form one string with either of the above-mentioned materials".[2]

Improvements in fixing the strings. Before the makers could do much about increasing the tone of their instruments, they were obliged to reconsider the method of fixing their strings. The old

[1] C 1232. The relation between the mass of a string and its pitch is shown by the following formula:

$$n = \frac{1}{2l}\sqrt{\frac{P}{m}},$$

where l = length in cms.,
   P = stretching force in dynes,
   m = mass per unit length in grams per cm. (Dr Alexander Wood).
[2] C 1180.

way of forming a note on the pianoforte consisted of fixing *separate* strings; from one to three for every note. These strings were attached to wrest pins at one end, whilst the other end was looped or 'hitched' over a pin by means of an eye made in the string (Plate II *a*).[1] This was a most unscientific procedure, since the eye was liable to break, and the strings, when there were two or three to a note, were not stretched by the same tension, nor were they exactly of the same length. Consequently changes in temperature affected them differently. It is for this reason that many old pianofortes when played upon suggest the 'voix célestes' stop on the organ. The trembling, voice-like quality of the upper notes has a certain charm when heard occasionally, but after a little time the dissimilarity of pitch becomes highly disagreeable. Pascal Taskin was the first, so far as it has been possible to discover, in 1787, to use a single string in the place of the two unison strings and to stretch them by the same tension. He effected this by the use of a screw wrest pin in the form of a metal loop through which the strings were passed. One end of the loop passed through a block of wood in such a way that it could be moved backwards or forwards by means of a nut (see Part 1, Fig. 50).

But mechanical wrest pins were expensive and some more simple and less costly means for overcoming the difficulty was required.

In 1827 James Stewart invented what is now the basis of modern stringing by doing away with the eye and using one continuous wire of double the length to serve for the two unison strings. It was passed round a single hitch pin made of stout wire,[2] the two loose ends were then secured by two wrest pins. Stewart states that "The friction on the hitch pin is quite sufficient when the string is drawn to a certain degree of tension to prevent the portion of the strings which is on one side of the hitch pin from being affected by raising or lowering the tone of that portion of the string which is on the other side of the hitch pin, so that the note may be tuned with the same accuracy as if the two unisons were formed by two wires attached to two separate hitch pins". If three unisons were used, he says, "the wire which forms the third unison must be continued to the first tuning pin of the succeeding note, and will thus form the first unison of that note" (Plate II *b*).

---

[1] A machine for making these eyes is illustrated in Montal's *L'Art d'accorder* (B 70 (*a*)), Pl. VI, Fig. 25.   [2] C 1170.

Spillane states that Stewart was "well known as the first partner of Jonas Chickering" and that "The idea of stringing formulated in this patent by Stewart was carried over from Boston, where it was commonly known as early as 1820".[1] The idea was next tried by Babcock[2] in 1830. But in this case the strings are crossed round either a hook at the end of a metal rod projecting from the hitch-pin block, or round a stout hitch pin. An alternative method of attaching the strings is shown where, although the strings are twisted round the hitch pin as in the former case, they are kept apart by a pin inserted between them. Wise, of Baltimore, also proposed in 1833[3] to draw up two strings at once by allowing one continuous wire to form two unisons.

Although Stewart's method of stringing is the only one that survived, some other experiments intended to solve the same problem of making the unisons of the same length and strained to the same tension are worthy to be recorded. Boisselot et fils of Marseilles passed a single wire round a pulley and secured the two loose ends to a nut fixed into the hitch-pin block. The pulley was fixed to a short bar which could be wound forwards or backwards by the action of an endless screw. By this means both the strings were of equal length and tension, and both were tuned together. This they patented in 1839.[4] John Godwin patented a system of carrying the strings round pulleys to the wrest pins in 1841. He was followed by Jean-Édouard Daniel in 1844;[5] in this case the two strings were attached to a single wrest pin drilled with two holes to admit of the introduction of the two ends of the string and the two strings were drawn up together.

The invention of the Agraffe, Harmonic and Capo Tasto bar. In the meantime some other very important improvements in relation to fixing the strings were made. The first of these consisted in the invention in 1808[6] of the agraffe by Sébastien Érard. The agraffe is a metal stud pierced with as many holes as there are unison strings to a note, and both the agraffe and the harmonic bar, a metal bridge through which the upper treble notes were passed, invented by Pierre Érard in 1838, were useful in exactly fixing the down-bearing and thus preventing the tendency of the hammers to strike the strings up and away from the bridges. In the upright instrument this does not of course apply, since the

[1] B 88.   [2] C 1142.
[3] C 1247.   [4] C 603.
[5] C 604 and C 607.   [6] C 249.

hammer strikes the strings in the direction of the bridges; but the agraffe and bar are useful in permitting the deflection of the strings to any convenient angle.

Both the agraffe and the bar were taken up and modified by many makers and became in fact common property (Fig. 16).

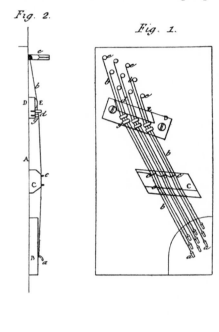

Fig. 2.

Fig. 1.

Fig. 16. Agraffe by Jelmini,[1] 1842. From the patent.

The 'Capo Tasto bar', the second of the three well-known inventions of Antoine Bord, invented by him in 1843, is a form of wrest-plank bridge, consisting of a metal bar—a pressure bar—worked to a blunt edge which presses on the strings collectively on the line of bearing[2] and thus performs the same function as the agraffe and harmonic bar. These inventions added

---

[1] For convenience of illustration an agraffe by Jelmini has been chosen to illustrate this invention.

Fig. 1re et 2e, partie de la table d'harmonie d'un piano droit. *A,* table d'harmonie; *B,* sommier des pointes; *C,* chevalet ordinaire; *D,* sillet et sommier des chevilles.

Les cordes *b, b,* fixées aux pointes *a, a,* contournent les pointes *c, c* du chevalet ordinaire *C,* passent sur les chevalets *g, g,* puis s'introduisent dans les agrafes *d, d,* et sont dirigées, par le pont rond *E,* vers les chevilles *e, e.*

[2] See also C, Wrest-Pin Block, *with harmonic or pressure bar.* See B 49, pp. 26–27.

greatly to the rigidity of the instrument and consequently added to its sonority and power of tone, and they are still used at the present day in one form or another.

Certain attempts were made to obtain a loud and powerful tone by the use of from four to six unison strings to a note acted upon by one hammer. Graf of Vienna made a pianoforte with four strings to a note for Beethoven on account of his deafness; it may be seen at the Beethoven Museum at Bonn. A patent was obtained by Joseph Baumgartner of Munich in 1831 for a horizontal grand pianoforte, of six octaves with five strings to every note even in the bass, but he states that as an alternative four or three strings might be used instead. This instrument was to have a sound-board slightly broader than usual and was to be tuned a quarter of a tone above concert pitch.[1] In the same year, Greiner and Schmidt patented a pianoforte with four unison strings to a note.[2] Henri Pape proposed to draw up from two, three, four or six at the same time by means of a single mechanical wrest pin.[3] If these strings were all drawn up at once so that they could easily be tuned at the same time by a single wrest pin, the fourfold or even sixfold stringing presented no great convenience either to tune or to keep in tune. But such wrest pins would necessarily add greatly to the cost of an instrument.

Whether Baumgartner ever made his instrument with five strings to a note or Pape his instrument with six, history does not relate, but pianofortes with fourfold stringing were undoubtedly made; the extreme difficulty in tuning them was the principal cause, according to Montal, why this type of stringing was given up.[4]

The four or five strings were all grouped together, but another system was tried in which the strings were halved into two sets. This arrangement seems to have been invented by Nicolas Sulot of Dijon who obtained French patents for it in 1841 (with additional patent in 1843) and 1847[5] respectively. Besides the two sets of strings struck by a single double hammer, he even suggests the use of four sets of strings struck simultaneously by two double hammers. The ordinary key not only worked its own double

---

[1] C 1190. [2] C 814.
[3] C 1278. [4] B 70 (a), pp. 105, 106.
[5] C 1229, 1231. N.B. Various improvements relating to the method of placing the bridges on the sound-board and to the sound-board itself and to the wrest pins resulting from the new arrangement of double hammers are included in the patent C 1229.

hammer but also, through the agency of a spring, communicated motion to a lever or dummy key below it which worked a second action with double hammer similar to the first. If a still louder

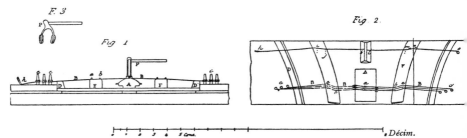

Fig. 17. Bader's double stringing with two-faced hammers striking both sets of strings at once, 1844.

A, sillet central ou commun aux deux systèmes de cordes. L'un des jeux de cordes *B* existe sur la gauche de ce sillet central, et l'autre jeu *B'* sur la droite...les jeux de cordes formant le double système sont complètement indépendants l'un de l'autre, et se raccordent à part, quoique pour produire les mêmes sons.

Ainsi les deux cordes *B* du système de gauche ont une de leurs extrémités fixée à la droite du sillet central *A,* puis se dirigent vers les chevilles *c,* en s'appuyant sur l'arrière des goupilles *a,* sur le devant des goupilles *b* du chevalet de gauche *F,* sur l'arrière des goupilles *e* du même chevalet, et en prenant appui sur le sillet latéral *D.* Ce qui distingue cette disposition de tout ce qui a été fait jusqu'à présent, c'est que les jeux de cordes formant le double système sont complètement indépendants l'un de l'autre, et se raccordent à part, quoique pour produire les mêmes sons. Ainsi les jeux de cordes correspondants aux mêmes goupilles du sillet central *A* appartiennent à deux systèmes distincts frappés simultanément par le même marteau à deux battants, pour produire un son bien semblable, bien égale, mais nécessairement beaucoup plus puissant, à conditions égales, que le son produit dans les pianos ordinaires.

L'avantage caractéristique de cette disposition perfectionnée est, si l'un des jeux vient à manquer par la rupture des cordes, que l'autre jeu fonctionne, il ne produit alors que le son des pianos ordinaires à simple système; mais le son n'est pas muet, comme cela résulterait de la disposition Fig. 2e où c'est la même corde qui appartient aux deux systèmes. Ainsi la corde, fixée à une goupille inclinée *h* se trouve dirigée par les goupilles *i, j, k, l, m, n* pour venir à se rompre, les deux systèmes sont muets, et de plus, l'accord est très-difficile.

Le marteau *P,* commun à chaque double système, a ses deux battants disposés à l'instar d'une fourche. La distance des battants varie selon les notes ou sons, c'est ce qui motive les marteaux Fig. 1re et 3e.

Les jeux de cordes à deux systèmes sont surtout indispensables pour les sons aigus, dont ils augmentent la puissance.

Il est facultatif alors de n'adopter le double système que pour les notes aiguës et de conserver les jeux simples pour les autres notes.

sound was required, the patentee suggests the use of four strings instead of two to be struck by each of the two double hammers. François-Xavier Bader[1] obtained a French patent in 1844 for a

[1] C 1230.

somewhat similar invention. Two sets of strings were to be struck simultaneously by a single row of double-headed hammers in such a way that, if one set of strings forming a note broke, the other was uninjured and playable (Fig. 17). The use of additional strings was not likely to become popular owing to the difficulty of tuning and the added strain to the instrument necessitating a heavier frame to support it. Even trichord stringing was disliked by some. In 1803 Tobias Schmidt submitted some pianofortes with bichord and trichord stringing to the Académie Royale des Sciences at Paris.

The committee who examined them, consisting of Lacépède, Hauy, Charles, Grétry, Gossec and Méhul, decided in favour of the bichord pianofortes. Their objections to trichord stringing are clearly given in their Report and are briefly stated as follows:

The strings were necessarily fixed too close together, which was injurious to the tone. If the hammer was at all uneven it tended to strike one string with greater force than the others and to put that string out of tune with the remaining strings. Or the hammer tended to strike the strings one after the other, which produced a heterogeneous quality of tone. Tuning and keeping a trichord pianoforte in tune was also a matter of considerable difficulty. But above all they considered the enormous strain on all the parts of the instrument, owing to the increased tension of the strings, to be the worst fault.

An ingenious means for doing away with the third unison string without losing the volume of tone was patented by Matthias Müller of Vienna in 1827.[1] Instead of the usual bridge pins (no doubt he is referring to the pins on the wrest-pin block bridge), tuning forks of steel or brass were fixed by means of tuning pins. These forks were tuned to the note of their particular strings and were set in vibration by them. By this means the third string was rendered superfluous and the tone was said to become stronger, fuller and more bell-like. This seems to have been suggested by the nail violin (*Nagelgeige*; *Violon de fer*), an instrument which consists of a sound-box, circular or semicircular, around which are inserted 'nails'. These nails vary in height and thickness according to the sound they are intended to produce and are vibrated by means of a bow. In order to increase their sound, in some later examples, a set of strings is provided to vibrate sympathetically with the nails. These are not, however, attached to the nails themselves but to wrest pins and hitch pins. Here the strings vibrate to enhance the

[1] C 1141.

tone of the nails but in Müller's pianoforte the forks vibrate in sympathy with the strings. No doubt the idea of the forks themselves may have been suggested by the nails and the strings passing across them may have suggested the new arrangement of the strings.[1]

Some means for counteracting the effects of the 'atmosphere' on the strings. The pianofortes which were kept in a building such as a concert hall, or in fact any room that was not often occupied, were liable to be injured by damp. Broadwood supplied covers for his pianofortes, in roan leather of different colours according to the client's choice and also covers of double baize. But some other ways of counteracting the effect of the atmosphere were also tried. Aury, in 1846, did away with the after-lengths of the strings by using a rod fixed into the hitch pin by its bent end and extending to 0·02 m. of the bridge. To the end of this rod the three unison strings were attached—one directly to the rod itself, the other two to a metal attachment fixed to the rod. The purpose of this invention consisted in making the strings shorter and less liable to be affected by the atmosphere.[2] Another method of reducing the after-lengths consisted in enlarging the metal hitch-pin plate and suspending it over the sound-board to within a short distance of the bridge. (The plate followed the curve of the bridge.) Pleyel appears to have invented this in 1828. Not only were the lengths of the strings altered by the changes of temperature and thus put out of tune, but they became rusty and liable to break. The rusty strings also damaged the surface of the hammer heads. In 1800 Isaac Hawkins[3] patented "gut, silk, or other strings, rendered waterproof by being impregnated with drying oils or gums, or other drying substances dissolved in oils or menstrua, designed to resist the action of the atmosphere by which strings are frequently put out of tune". This invention, though it does not seem to refer to pianoforte strings, at least indicates the situation. A proposal was made in a Leipzig paper, about 1825, to use platinum instead of steel, copper or brass for pianoforte strings, as this metal was more elastic and did not rust. It was affirmed that platinum could be alloyed with iron. In 1845 Pape claimed coating the strings with German silver in his patent of that year.[4] Isaac Mott, in the following year, patented "strings electroplated with gold, silver, platina, zinc, or other metals, to prevent the hammers from in-

[1] See B 65, Vol. I, p. 207. [2] C 609.
[3] C 1194. [4] C 1191.

crustation arising from contact with ordinary strings"[1] which, he should have added, had become rusty. In 1851 H. J. Newton of New York patented "coating the smaller strings of pianofortes with silver or an alloy, for the purpose of improving the tone and to prevent the rusting of the strings".[2]

Pape in 1845 invented a means for overcoming this difficulty by the use of hammers with reversible heads (Fig. 18). When a surface became worn, the head could be turned so as to present a fresh surface.[3]

No. 1   *movable hammer heads*   No. 2

Fig. 18. Pape's hammers with reversible heads, 1845. From the patent.
No. 1. *A*, hammer head. *B*, centre, through which is introduced a piece of wire *C*, the end of which is square, and which is fixed to the claws *D* of the hammer by screws *E*. To turn the head, the screws must be undone and the wire drawn out, when the hammer may easily be turned. No. 2. Here the hammer head is held by metal plates *F*, containing teeth *G*. It is necessary to remove one of these pieces in order to change the position of the head.

The Sound-board. Without the sound-board the strings would be practically inaudible. It acts as a resonator to them, and receives and amplifies their vibrations, as does the box upon which a tuning fork is fixed. The sound-board is therefore important and must be carefully prepared and the wood fully seasoned, if it is to be effective.

The early method of preparing the pine wood for sound-boards was a laborious process. Mozart describes how Stein prepared the wood by exposing it to the action of rain and sun and gluing up the cracks as they occurred. This was a lengthy procedure. When the demand for pianofortes increased, as it did at the beginning of the nineteenth century, a more speedy method had to be discovered. In May 1808 Wachtl and Bleyer of Vienna began to

[1] C 1192.
[2] C 1193. I am informed by Dr Alexander Wood that the protective coatings mentioned above, unless they added appreciably to the weight of the wire, would not affect the tone.
[3] C 535.

season their boards as Herr Mundinger, a master joiner and citizen of Vienna, had done for the last twelve years.

This procedure consisted in exposing the pine to steam from salt water for forty-eight hours, which brought the resin up to the surface, where it could be seen in large brown drops. After this it was dried in a heated drying chamber.

Bleyer states that if it had been exposed to the atmosphere for fifty years a better result could not have been obtained.

Another method was tried in 1817 by a Viennese maker who remains anonymous. The wood was packed tightly into a box through which 'water vapour was disseminated'.[1] Holes were bored in the bottom of the box to enable the water to escape. This process cleansed the wood from all mucilaginous and resinous deposit, in fact it lost three-twenty-fifths of its weight and was said to become less susceptible to damp.[2]

At a later date the selection and preparation of the wood used for the sound-boards seems to have become a business to itself. In 1832 Franz Bienert, a merchant in Ober Krebitz in Bavaria, obtained a patent for the preparation of this wood.[3] He selected fir trees from the Duke of Schwarzenberg's plantations in Stubenbach and Langendorf. The trunks were passed through a saw mill and cut up into planks one-quarter of an inch thick and carefully planed. After this they were numbered so that they could be used in the same order as they occurred in the trunk. (It was generally believed that the boards would vibrate with greater regularity if their grain coincided.) From a patent which he obtained ten years later, it seems that he seasoned the wood by soaking it or exposing it to the rain and then drying it in a heated chamber.[4]

In the district of Hohenau, Wolfstein, in Bavaria it was customary to fell the tree and then to split up the trunk into strips of such a size that they could be planed down to the requisite thickness. This was a wasteful method, since the split did not always occur evenly and the wood was frequently not thick enough for a hollow to be planed out. Johann Segl, a sawyer at Hohenau, noticed the waste of wood and loss of time occasioned by this splitting, and invented a saw for cutting up the trunks into planks. In his patent for the new saw, which he obtained in 1836,[5] he gives an account of his method of preparing the wood. A sound-board to be good must be

---

[1] "Durch die [*i.e.* the box] ein wasseriger Dunst sich verbreitet."
[2] B 2 (1817), S. 344.   [3] C 1036.
[4] C 1038.   [5] C 1037.

made of straight fine grained fir wood. Segl was obliged to go to the deepest part of the forest for his wood; to a place where the sun did not penetrate, for the action of the sun on the tree coarsened the grain and made it unsuitable for his purpose. He states that he found suitable wood in the district of the Royal Forestry of Wolfstein, and especially at Schönberg, in the district between the mountains Rachel and Lusen, "where", he says, "there is annually a deep fall of snow". He then chose old and very straight trees and felled them in the winter before the sap had risen. The lower part of the trunk, which was the only part that was useful, was split up into four pieces and sawn into planks about six to seven feet long and varying from five to fifteen inches in breadth and a third of an inch thick.[1] He then numbered the planks as Franz Bienert had done, and exposed them to air and sunshine and finally dried them in a heated drying chamber. After this the planks were packed up into boxes to be kept dry.

The thickness of the sound-board affects the tone.

The old makers seem often to have made it thicker in the treble than in the bass; this is clearly shown by a statement made by Gunther in a patent dated 1828 for a pianoforte with two sound-boards; speaking of the upper board he says: "when hard wood is used, five-eights of an inch will be sufficient thickness in the treble and middle parts of the instrument, but it should be made rather thinner in the bass part, *as is usual in the sounding boards of other pianofortes as generally constructed*".[2]

Kützing, writing in 1844,[3] gives the following table of thickness for sound-boards for pianofortes without agraffes:

Thickness of resonance boards in millimetres:

4·0 4·5	perceptibly weaker in sound with less pleasant tone.
5·0 5·5 6·0 6·5	almost equal strength of sound, whilst the tone changes with the increasing thickness and becomes more powerful.
7·0 7·5 8·0 8·5 9·0 9·5 10·0	decrease in strength of sound with more pleasant tone.

---

[1] Bavarian inches (Bavarian foot = 292 mm.).
[2] C 1084.   [3] B 63, S. 65.

He states that the thickness between 5·0 to 6·5 mm. is the best in every case, and also that the thickness of the sound-board must always stand in a 'certain relationship' to the stringing. In the table $a°$ has a tension of 98 kgs.; but if the tension is greater the board must be made proportionally thicker.[1] In the modern pianoforte, Nalder states that the thickness of the sound-board varies with the caprice of the maker and may be anything from 7 mm. to 10 mm.[2]

It is the general practice to place the grain of the sound-board parallel to a line drawn through the sound-board bridge (the long bridge in modern terminology) with the bars running at right angles to the bridge. The low rate of travel across the grain is thus counteracted by the action of the bars.[3]

Some of the early makers were uncertain about the position of the grain of the wood and tried placing it in all positions from that mentioned above to a position almost at right angles to the bridge; one or two makers were also a little uncertain about the bars and

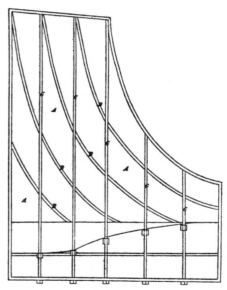

Fig. 19. Pape's sound-board (1845). From the patent.
A, sound-board; *B*, bars on which are glued the fixed rods *C*.

---

[1] He does not state what the proportion between the thickness of the sound-board and the tension of the strings should be—it was probably arrived at by guesswork.
[2] B 76, p. 166.   [3] B 76, Chap. XI.

tended to think that these impeded the vibrations, for Gunther, speaking of his two sound-boards which were to be united by a rim, says, "it will not be necessary to glue the usual slips or bars upon its lower side (*i.e.* of the upper board) to increase its strength, as these *impede its vibration*".[1] But Henri Pape was fully aware that the bars were useful in aiding the propagation of the tone, for, in 1845,[2] he invented a new arrangement of the sound-board, which "consists (he states) in using for every note a rod of the same length as the string, to which rod is adapted the system of drawing the strings".

These rods were glued to the bracing bars of the sound-boards and were the width of the key and varied in height from one inch for the treble to two inches for the bass. Pape concludes by stating that "this arrangement is very favourable for the tone by reason that the vibration of the string is communicated by the rods to a greater part of the belly. It also renders the construction of the case more simple, and reduces considerably its weight" (Fig. 19).

Exactly when the practice of giving these sound-boards a protective covering of varnish came into general use is uncertain. The early nineteenth-century square pianofortes usually have the upper surface varnished. In 1826 Hora and Kinderfreund patented a sound-board in which *both* sides were to be varnished,[3] and Dr Otto Paul states that Freundenthaler of Paris (b. 1761) varnished his sounding boards.

[1] C 1084.   [2] C 1104.   [3] C 1061.

CHAPTER III

THE METAL FRAME

IT was but grudgingly that the pianoforte makers resorted to the use of iron to brace their instruments against the increased strain of the heavier strings; for the old idea that iron was deleterious to the tone still prevailed. At first they strengthened the pianoforte with wooden braces and struts but these added greatly to the weight and made the instrument clumsy and 'unportable'. One of the reasons for Pape's preference for the downstriking action was that the strings being placed along the floor of the instrument, at that part which was best able to bear the strain, the iron framing and heavy wooden braces were not necessary.

Another means for avoiding the use of iron consisted, in the upright pianoforte, of dividing the strings by fixing them on both sides of the sound-board to equalise the strain, but this often necessitated the use of two hammers at once for every note, and added greatly to the weight of the touch; though Henri Pape in 1839 overcame the difficulty by using strings of double the length.[1] But the metal frame had eventually to be used because the higher octaves that were added to the treble increased the tension on the case and sound-board. Herz, the composer and pianoforte maker, sometimes wrote an alternative part in his music, for a pianoforte of seven octaves, and Martin of Toulouse, another French maker, stated in his patent of 1840 that composers and pianists were far too restricted on a pianoforte with six and a half octaves and that makers were obliged to build them with seven.[2] Pape went even further, for in his patent of 1845 for a pianoforte of the console type he shows a drawing of the front elevation of a pianoforte of the size required for eight and a half octaves.[3]

These additional octaves added greatly to the strain. Both this and the ever-rising pitch to which pianofortes had to be tuned in order to keep in tune with the wind instruments, which were being made sharper to increase their brilliancy, made the use of a metal frame a necessity, for the wooden braces were far too cumbersome.

[1] C 826.   [2] C 1047.   [3] C 827, Fig. 1.

The complete iron frame was not used at first; the initial stage consisted in the use of metallic braces. These braces were of two kinds: metallic bars or compensating tubes. In the days before the use of central heating, variation of temperature, which is usually alluded to as the 'atmosphere', was a matter of serious consideration to the pianoforte maker. But when still heavier strings were used and the higher octaves were added, the problem of resistance became more pressing than that of compensation.

Stronger frames composed of solid bars and plates to withstand the ever-increasing tension of the strings occupied the attention of the pianoforte makers. The final stage in the perfection of the metal frame consisted in uniting the various segments into a solid casting.

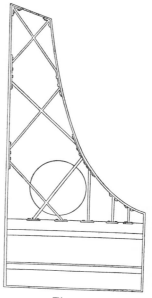

The enormous tension on the strings tended to make the wrest pins sag in their sockets and various attempts were made to overcome this difficulty by using a solid metal wrest-pin block. Roller, Schwieso and Pierre Érard, amongst others, patented various forms of this in 1823, 1831 and 1850[1] respectively but the invention was not found to be practicable and was superseded by a block composed of wood and metal.

Composite iron resistance frames. No history of the development of the iron frame would be complete without a passing reference at least to Rollings' metallic frame which he used for the Orphica, a

Fig. 20.

portable pianoforte invented by him in 1795; and to Joseph Smith whose iron frame was clearly based on the inner frame of the harpsichord (Fig. 20); nor must we omit to mention Hawkins, who suspended the sound-board within a metal frame and braced it behind with metal rods in his portable grand pianoforte of 1800. But these inventions were but tentative experiments and had no direct bearing on the development of the metal frame.

An article in *The Times* of May 7th, 1851, about the pianofortes in the Great Exhibition of that year provoked a controversy

[1] C 1337, 1340, 1341.

between the Editor and Messrs Broadwood concerning the use of metal bracing bars and by whom they were first applied.

From Messrs Broadwood's first letter, dated May 10th, 1851, it is certain that they applied tension bars to the treble of grand pianofortes as early as 1808; that they used from three to five bars in grand pianofortes in 1821; that their employee, Samuel Hervé, applied the first metal hitch-pin plate to a square pianoforte of their make in the same year and that such plates were frequently used for square pianofortes by them from 1822.

The Editor printed a reply below Broadwood's letter stating that "steel bracing bars extended longitudinally over the strings" were "first introduced into general use by Érard's house in 1824" and "that they were not adopted as a principle of manufacture by Messrs Broadwood until 1827" (Fig. 21). He also asked the question: "If Messrs Broadwood manufactured pianos in 1821 with from three to five metal bracing bars, how was it that they obtained a patent six years later for four such bars?" As a matter of fact Pierre Érard in 1825 obtained a patent in England for a method of fixing iron bars to the wooden braces of the pianoforte by means of bolts passing through apertures cut to receive them in the sound-board. The application of sheet iron placed between the two sides of the case for the purpose of uniting the "wrest-pin block with the key-bottom so as to form almost an entire block was also included in this patent".[1] But Broadwood, in his reply dated May 12th, 1851, makes the following conclusive statement: "We have in our house a piano, constructed in 1823, with steel tension bars above the strings. It is true that we took out a patent for a combination of solid bars in combination with a fixed metal string plate. This does not disprove the fact that metal tension bars had been many years in use".

It seems clear from the above evidence that Broadwood was the first to introduce the bars into general use.

In 1825 Pleyel used an iron frame and copper string plate for his 'Unichord Pianoforte'.[2] Two years later Broadwood obtained the patent for four bars in connection with a fixed metal string plate.[3] (Plate III shows a square pianoforte by Broadwood with metal string plate and suspension bar.)

---

[1] Note this patent did not include a metal string plate which Broadwood had been using since 1821. Broadwood's patent of 1827 was for a combination of the string plate and bars.

[2] C 933.   [3] C 464.

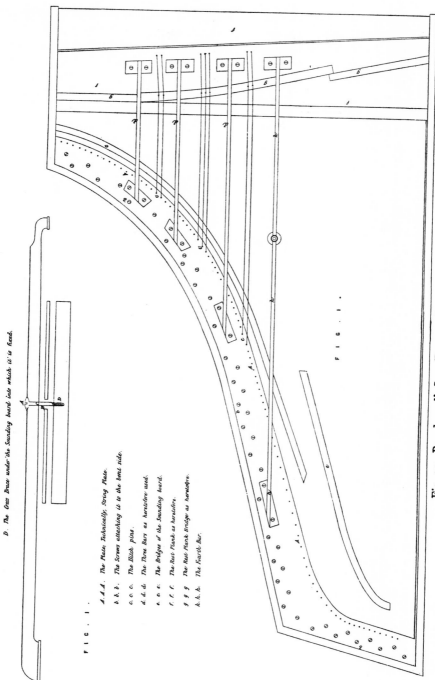

F I G . 2 .

A. The Centre hole of Iron bar or Stretcher.

B. The Aperture in the Sounding board.

C. The Screw six inches long & ⅜ diameter.

D. The Cross Brace under the Sounding board into which it is fixed.

F I G . 1 .

A A A. The Plate Technically, String Plate.

b b b. The Screws attaching it to the bent side.

c c c. The Hitch pins.

d d d. The Three Bars as heretofore used.

e e e. The Bridges of the Sounding board.

f f f. The Bass Plank as heretofore.

g g g. The Bass Plank Bridge as heretofore.

h h h. The Fourth Bar.

F I G . 1 .

Fig. 21. Broadwood's Iron Frame, 1827. From the patent.

Matthias Müller of Vienna patented in 1829 an iron frame connected with the wrest-pin block with a suspension bar of iron.[1] Becker of Frankenthal obtained a patent in 1839 for horizontal grand and square pianofortes with iron frames.[2]

The first Canadian patent (1840) that was granted in connection with pianofortes concerned an iron frame. John Thomas Morgan and Alexander Smith of Toronto obtained it for their invention of "A *new* improvement in the construction of pianofortes".[3] It consisted in a metal plate screwed upon the wrest-pin block. This plate was attached to the common metal hitch-pin plate. A metal bar, which ran parallel to the lowest string, completed this frame which was clearly intended for a square pianoforte. In 1847 Messrs Broadwood invented their special concert grand iron framing with diagonal tension bar and transverse suspension bar. This type of frame was used by them until 1895.[4]

Compensation frames. The compensation frame was invented for the purpose of preventing the fluctuations in the pitch of the strings which arose from changes in atmospheric temperature.

It was invented by Thom and Allen, two workmen employed by William Stodart, and patented in 1820,[5] but Stodart immediately purchased their interest in it.

From a contemporary magazine article[6] we learn that within the frame were fixed parallel tubes about three-quarters of an inch in diameter, of a metal similar to the string beneath, *i.e.* brass above the brass strings and steel above the steel ones.

The effect contemplated was that, as the temperature affected the strings either by expansion or contraction, so also it would affect the tubes, which extending or relaxing 'consentaneously' with the strings would compensate the difference by allowing the whole frame to coincide with their action. A grand pianoforte on this plan was "removed from a low to a high temperature, and back again, without undergoing any perceptible difference in the pitch, or going out of tune in the smallest degree".

The same writer states that the invention afforded other benefits such as facility in tuning, superior excellence in the tone, which was improved in volume and quality.

"This circumstance", he writes, "may be traced either to four separate causes or to a combination of them all:

1. From the whole tension of the strings being taken off the sounding

[1] C 465.   [2] C 475.   [3] C 478.
[4] B 49 (*f*), Fig. 14.   [5] C 275.   [6] B 74 (*a*).

Plate III. Square Pianoforte by Broadwood. The metal hitch-pin plate is perforated to allow the free escape of the sound and strengthened with a suspension bar bolted to the wrest-pin block. No date. No. 2001 (?). (In the possession of Mr W. J. Moore, Cambridge.)

board, which is thus left to a free and natural vibration. The proof is to be perceived in the longer duration of the vibration in an instrument of this construction, when the strings are struck and the dampers taken off. This duration exceeds, by almost one-third, the length of time which pianofortes upon the old plan continue their sound. In slow movements, the tones therefore *syncopate* or connect themselves much more beautifully.

2. No braces are required to strengthen the instrument. A great weight of wood is therefore removed, and the body of the pianoforte remains hollow, which certainly improves the tone.

3. The tubes themselves may, by their cylindrical form, add to the augmentation of the tone.

4. As there will be no strain upon the belly of the instrument, it will be more likely to continue to preserve its original level shape, and retain undiminished its power of vibration—a circumstance which cannot fail to add to the durability of the instrument, for in a six-octave grand pianoforte the pull upon the strings is at least equal to the prodigious weight of six tons and a half." [Fig. 22.]

In 1822 Pierre Érard obtained a patent in France for a compensation frame which seems to be an exact copy of that designed by Thom and Allen (Fig. 23).

A comparison of the two diagrams and descriptions (Figs. 22 and 23) will convince the reader on this point.[1] Érard describes the object of his invention thus:

Cette invention a pour objet de mieux faire tenir le piano d'accord, en modifiant l'effet du chaud et du froid sur les cordes métalliques, ou en diminuant l'influence qu'ont sur ces mêmes cordes le gonflement et le renflement des bois dont l'instrument est composé, variations occasionées par l'humidité et la sécheresse de l'atmosphère ou par tout autre cause. Les moyens employés pour atteindre ce but consistent, en principe, à dégager la charpente de la caisse de l'instrument du tirage des cordes métalliques; elles n'y sont plus attachées que par un bout, elles sont tendues à l'autre par des barres, plaques ou *tubes de cuivre et de fer* convenablement adaptés, de manière que les cordes n'éprouvent plus qu'une très légère variation dans leur tension dans le passage du froid au chaud, de l'humide au sec, *et vice versâ*.

Three years later (1825) Francis Melville applied two tubular bars to a square pianoforte.[2] The ends of these tubes were inserted in cup-shaped brackets similar to those seen in Plate IV. Although

[1] C 276. Hipkins does not seem to have recognised this as a compensation frame. He writes thus: "In 1822 Sébastien and Pierre Érard patented in Paris a complete system of nine iron bars from treble to bass, with fastenings piercing the bars, and through apertures in the belly to the wooden bracings beneath". But it will be observed that there are *thirteen tubular bars* in this patent, as there were in Thom and Allen's design, and that no reference is made to apertures through the sound-board for the admission of bolts to secure these bars (B 49, p. 16).

[2] C 280.

he states that the 'apparatus' is for the purpose of "more effectually resisting the tension of the strings" we think that the real
purpose of this invention was 'compensation'.

Thomas Loud of Philadelphia in 1837 patented metallic tubes
or bars to strengthen the frame.[1] Spillane states that his "compensating tubes were generally adopted in New York in 1838".

It will have been seen that there were two types of composite
frames, the one composed of *solid* bars and plates and the other
of *tubular* bars and plates. The first was intended for resistance,
whilst the second type was intended for compensation. But the
problem of resistance became the most pressing as still heavier
strings were required, and thus compensation became of secondary
importance.

This led to the important step of uniting the various segments
of a resistance frame into a single casting.

The cast-iron frame. The cast-iron frame is certainly one of the
most far-reaching improvements that have ever been applied to
the pianoforte. It is due to Alpheus Babcock of Boston who
patented a complete metal frame with the hitch-pin block in
one casting for the square pianoforte, on December 17th, 1825.
Hipkins states that it was a failure, but Spillane stoutly denies this[2]
and the evidence quoted by Hipkins himself seems to indicate that
it was not a failure but on the contrary a success. He quotes
Spillane's extract from the records of the Franklin Institute of
Philadelphia relating to the Fourth Annual Exhibition of 1827.
In this record "Especial mention is made of a horizontal piano by
A. Babcock, of Boston, of an *improved construction*, the frame which
supports the strings being of *solid cast-iron* and strong enough to
resist their enormous tension".

Hipkins states that Babcock appears also to have taken out a
patent at Philadelphia for an "almost identical iron framing for a
square piano, except that there were three bars for resistance instead of one. That in the treble part of the scale was in both patents
and two were added lower down in the latter". He states that this
latter patent was dated May 24th, 1830, and was obtained for
cross-stringing pianofortes[3] (Fig. 24).

There is consequently no doubt as to the patent Hipkins refers
to. We are unable to discover the three bars alluded to. Perhaps
he refers to the "metallic rod or stout metal wire" fixed to the

[1] C 293.   [2] C 460, see B 88, p. 116.
[3] B 49, pp. 18–19.

string-plate over which the string was to be looped, or could he have been misled by the strings themselves?

In 1826 Pape[1] of Paris patented a new hitch-pin block of cast iron, a cast-iron bridge placed on the sound-board and a frame of cast iron. Petzold followed in 1829 with a cast-iron frame, open at the sides and at the base, with the sound-board independent of this structure[2] (Fig. 25).

The next invention of importance is Allen's cast-iron grooved frame (1831).[3] It will be remembered that he had invented the compensating frame in connection with Thom in 1820. This new invention consisted of a cast-iron frame with a wrest-pin block formed of several pieces of wood firmly dovetailed together inserted between grooves formed to receive it. There was also a single cast-iron brace to afford additional strength to resist the strain of the strings (Fig. 26). This seems to have been an excellent invention but nevertheless it did not meet with favour.

Two years later Louis Fissore, a French pianoforte maker formerly in the employ of Pleyel in Paris, arrived in Baltimore and in July obtained a patent[4] for a cast-iron frame in which the "Tuning pins (wrest pins) were passed through a cast-iron plate, and were fixed so that their tightness did not depend upon their being driven in, but upon a washer passing over a square shank at the back of the plate, the pin being drawn up to a shoulder by means of a screw nut".

Hipkins states that Conrad Meyer of Philadelphia claimed to have invented the metal frame in a single casting in 1832 and that he saw and tried an instrument by Meyer with such a frame made in 1833.[5] In 1836 Isaac Clark of Cincinnati patented an entire frame made of cast or wrought iron.[6] In this year Wheatley Kirk, an English maker, patented the first complete iron frame for an upright pianoforte and a little later in the same year Debain of Paris, and Seuffert of Vienna, patented pianofortes in which there was this new improvement.

In 1840 Chickering of Boston invented an improvement in the construction of the iron frame which "consists", he says, "in combining the bridge over which the strings pass to the straining pins (wrest pins), and the socket through which the damper wires pass to the iron frame, by casting them thereon or by casting the

[1] C 463.   [2] C 466.
[3] C 468.   [4] C 469.
[5] B 49 (f), p. 162.   [6] C 470.

whole together in one piece" (Fig. 27). In 1843 he patented a frame for the grand pianoforte in one casting.

Passing notice must be made to some later patents. Bonifas obtained in 1851 a patent for a pianoforte with "wide surfaces of iron, opposed to longitudinal bars, the whole forming a case and framework of iron".[1] Herding's *Piano en Fer* of 1848[2] attracted considerable attention. Bachman's pianoforte patented in 1850 was to have a sound-board in iron.[3] And finally Bacon and Raver[4] of New York patented a cast-iron frame for a square pianoforte in 1851.

No attempt has been made even to mention all the frames or braces of steel or iron that were patented up to the close of the year 1851. The intention has been merely to indicate the order of invention of the various types of frames and the first use of metallic braces.

[1] C 499.   [2] C 491.   [3] C 1032.   [4] C 496.

DESCRIPTION OF FIG. 22 (*opposite*).

Fig. 22. Thom and Allen's Compensation Frame, 1820.

Fig. 1 is a plan of a horizontal grand pianoforte with the cover taken off, and without the keys and other movements which need not there be shown: Fig. 2 is a section and side view of the same, with the side of the instrument removed, in order to exhibit the different parts. (The same letters refer to the same parts in both figs.) B, B is the block to which the strings are affixed at one of their ends by the wrest pins, C, C, as usual: D, D is an iron bar resting at each end in gaps made in the two iron plates E, E, which are firmly secured to the sides of the frame of the instrument, and supported besides in other gaps made in the iron arches or brackets F, F, etc., which are firmly secured to the block B, B. One side or edge of the bar D, D is made angular to fit into gaps or notches made in one end of each of the brass tubes G, G, etc., and of the iron tubes H, H, etc., in order to steady and support those tubes resting or abutting against the said bar. These tubes G, G, etc., and H, H, etc., pass through holes made in the wooden bars or stays I, I, etc., which are firmly secured at each end to the sides of the frame of the instrument, and thereby support the tubes, and prevent them from being bent from the strain of the strings upon them. The other ends of the tubes lodge or rest upon short iron cylindrical studs entering into them, and which studs are firmly united to the iron brackets or arms J, J, etc., which are likewise securely fixed upon the iron or other fit and proper metal plates or bars K and L, which plates or bars are movable, according to the expansion or contraction of the tubes, they merely resting or lying upon the belly or sounding board, etc., of the instrument. The iron or metal plate K has the other ends of all the brass wires or strings affixed to it by means of the studs N, N; and the other plate L receives those of the iron wires or strings by means of similar studs O, O upon it, and thus the brass strings are kept stretched or extended by the brass tubes G, G, etc., and the iron ones by the iron tubes H, H, etc., each wire by a tube of similar metal to itself, and thereby are nearly equally affected with the tubes by any change of temperature from hot to cold, or the contrary, and are little liable to be affected by moisture or dryness, as they are only connected with the sounding board......by means of the bridges P, P, and Q, Q, and the studs and pins which are fixed into or upon them, as usual. (*Thom and Allen, abridged.*)

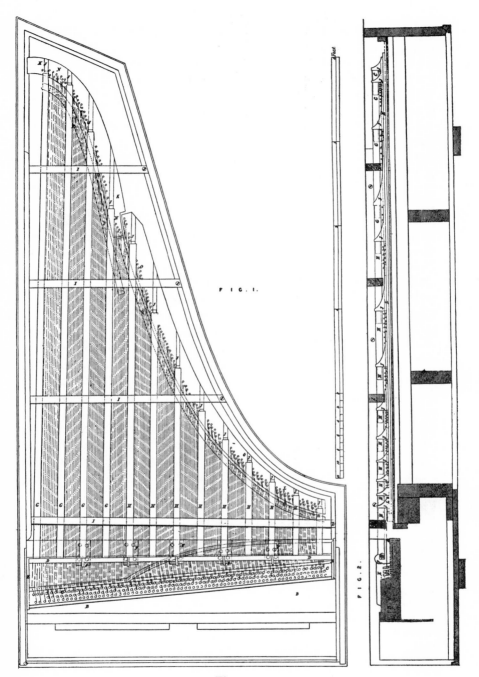

F I G . I.

F I G . 2.

Fig. 22.

England was the first to adopt metallic bracing bars as a general principle of construction. The first compensation frame was also due to Englishmen. The cast-iron frame was an American invention that found favour with the French and Danish pianoforte makers, but apparently not with the English, Germans or Austrians, who seem to have preferred the composite frame.

Hipkins states that Broadwood's iron grand model of 1851 was the first pianoforte to be made with a complete metal frame in England.[1]

The records of the Great Exhibition of 1851 show clearly the feeling of the various countries concerning the metal frame. Chickering exhibited a grand with "the whole framing consisting of string-plate, longitudinal bars, wrest block and drilled bridge (for upward bearing) of iron cast in one piece and a grand-square pianoforte also with a cast-iron frame". Pape used a "strong open frame of cast iron or wood strengthened by iron". Érard exhibited a full-sized grand with a metallic string-plate and longitudinal tension bars and wrest-pin block of metal. This wrest-pin block was formed of a framework of brass in which was fixed a strip of beech to receive the pins. The whole combination formed an entire metallic frame. Messrs Broadwood and Sons contributed four full-sized grands, 7 octaves, with repetition action, but differing with regard to external decoration and in the construction of the metallic bracing. Two of them had three bars parallel with the strings; one had one parallel bar and one placed diagonally; whilst the other had one parallel and two diagonal bars, the latter lying at different angles. They all had the long transverse bar over the wrest-pin block. Hornung of Copenhagen exhibited a grand and a square "with wrest block, longitudinal stretchers and string-plate, cast in one piece of iron *on the American plan*". Hoxa of Vienna used metallic bars for his seven-octave grand.[2]

There was but one compensation frame: it was in a grand pianoforte by Messrs Stodart.

Thus it will be seen that with the exception of Denmark the composite frames either for resistance or compensation were in the usual European custom, whilst the cast-iron frame was 'American'.

As Nalder points out, "it was not until Steinway and Sons in 1855 demonstrated at New York that overstrung scaling with a solid iron frame could yield the desired volume and quality of tone" that the battle for the iron frame was won.[3]

[1] B 49, p. 18. [2] B 81, pp. 25, 35, 40, 41. [3] B 76, p. 50.

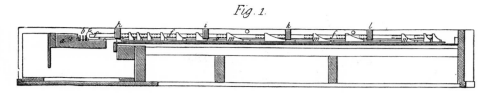

Fig. 1.

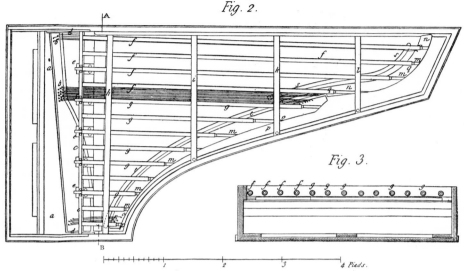

Fig. 2.

Fig. 3.

Fig. 23. Érard's Compensation frame, 1822.

Fig. 1re. Coupe verticale et longitudinale d'un grand piano ou piano à queue sans couvercle.

Fig. 2e. Plan ou vue par-dessus.

Fig. 3e. Coupe transversale faite suivant la ligne ponctuée (*A*, *B*, Fig. 2e). Les touches et le mécanisme ne sont point indiqués dans ces figures, parce que ces parties de l'instrument n'offrent rien de particulier sur les moyens de les établir ordinairement.

a, sommier auquel les cordes sont attachées, par un bout, aux chevilles *b*, comme de coutume.

c, barre de fer dont les deux extrémités sont ajustées dans les entailles pratiquées dans deux plaques de fer *d*, qui sont solidement attachées aux côtés de la caisse de l'instrument; elle est en outre maintenue dans d'autres entailles faites dans les consoles *e* solidement fixées sur le sommier. Un des bords de la barre de fer *c* est taillé en angle, pour recevoir les crans ou entailles pratiqués à l'une des extrémités des tubes de cuivre *f* et des tubes de fer *g*, qui reposent sur cette même barre contre laquelle ils forment arcs-boutants.

Les tubes *f*, *g* passent par des trous au travers de barres de bois ou supports *h*, *i*, *k*, *l* solidement fixés, à chaque bout, contre la caisse de l'instrument; ces barres servent à soutenir les tubes et à les empêcher de se courber par le tirage des cordes: l'autre bout de ces tubes s'emboîte ou repose sur des supports en forme de cylindres qui entrent dans les tubes; ces supports sont fortement attachés aux consoles ou bras *m*, qui sont eux-mêmes solidement fixés sur les plaques de fer ou d'autre métal convenable *n*, *o*; ces plaques ou barres sont mobiles, de manière à céder ou à suivre l'expansion et le raccourcissement des tubes; elles reposent simplement sur la table *p* de l'instrument. La plaque de métal *n* reçoit toutes les cordes de cuivre qui y sont attachées par les points *q*, et les cordes de fer sont attachées aux points *r*, sur l'autre plaque; de cette manière, les cordes de cuivre se trouvent tendues par les tubes de même métal *f*, et celles de fer le sont par les tubes de fer *g*; chaque espèce de corde est tendue par des tubes du même métal.

Le passage du froid au chaud ou du chaud au froid agit donc à peu près également sur les cordes et sur les tubes, et l'humidité ou la sécheresse a peu d'effet sur eux, puisqu'ils ne sont en contact avec la table *p* qu'au moyen des chevalets *s*, *t* et des pointes qui les y fixent comme d'habitude. Etc., etc.

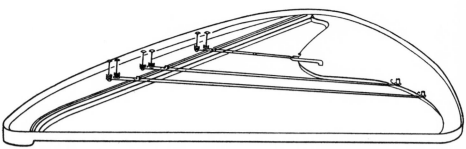

Fig. 24. Babcock's iron frame for a square pianoforte, 1830. From the patent for cross-stringing the pianoforte.

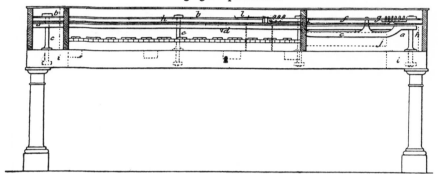

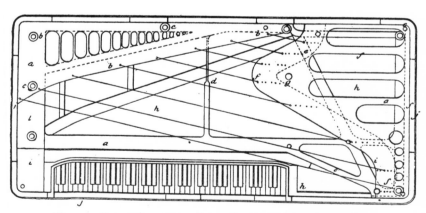

Fig. 25. Petzold's cast-iron frame for square pianoforte, 1829.

a, grand châssis en fer fondu; *b*, sommier des pointes [hitch-pin block]; *c*, têtes de boulons à écrous; *d*, traverse qui joint la barre de devant avec le sommier des pointes; *e*, barres en biais qui se croisent et se lient; *f*, sommier de chevilles [wrest-pin block] en fer fondu d'une seule pièce, avec des ouvertures ovales et rondes laissant voir la table [the sound-board] à travers; *g*, tenons soutenant le sommier de chevilles et passant à travers la table; *h*, la table d'harmonie; *i*, châssis de bois figurant le fond avec quatre traverses; *j*, ouvertures dans la caisse où l'on peut adapter des soupapes et des ornements découpés; *l*, cordes de piano.

Fig. 2

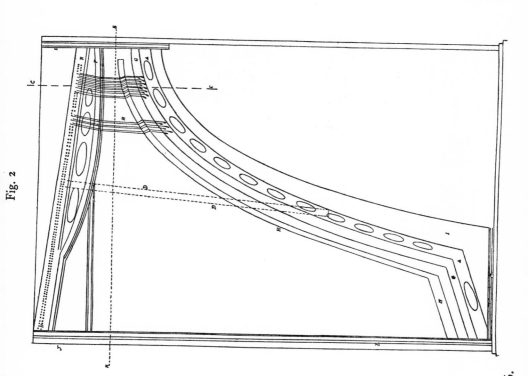

Fig. 26.

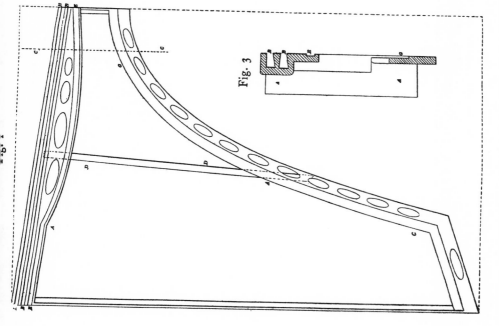

Fig. 3

14-2

DESCRIPTION OF FIG. 26 (*previous page*).

Fig. 26. Allen's cast-iron frame, 1831.

The drawings in the specification show a cast-iron grooved frame applied to a cabinet pianoforte, but Allen claims that his invention can be adapted to suit any kind of pianoforte.

Fig. 1 is a front view of a cast-iron frame *A*, *A*, with two dovetailed grooves *B*, *B* formed in it. (See Fig. 3, which is taken at the dotted lines *C*, *C*, Figs. 1.)

Into the grooves *B*, *B* dovetailed bars of wood are driven tightly and secured by means of glue or other proper cement. These wooden bars are for the purpose of receiving the wrest pins which are driven tightly into the holes drilled to receive them. These pins, Allen claims, are less liable to slip owing to the compression of the wood in the grooves, and consequently the pianofortes to which they are applied will be kept more properly in tune.

D, *D*, in Fig. 1, is a cast-iron brace (shown by dotted lines in Fig. 2) for the purpose of affording additional strength to resist the pull of the strings; *E* (Figs. 1 and 3) is a groove to receive the bridge *F* (Fig. 2) into it. *G*, *G* (Figs. 1 and 2) is a recess formed in the face of the frame *A*, *A* to receive the hitch pins. *H*, *H* (Fig. 2) is the bridge fixed to the sound-board *I*, *I*. The sound-board *I*, *I* is secured to the iron frame *A*, *A* and to the external case *J*, *J* (Fig. 2) of the pianoforte. (*Allen, modified by R. H.*)

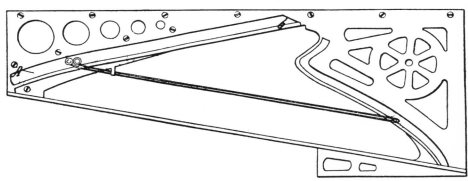

Fig. 27. Chickering's cast-iron frame for a square pianoforte, 1840.
From the patent.

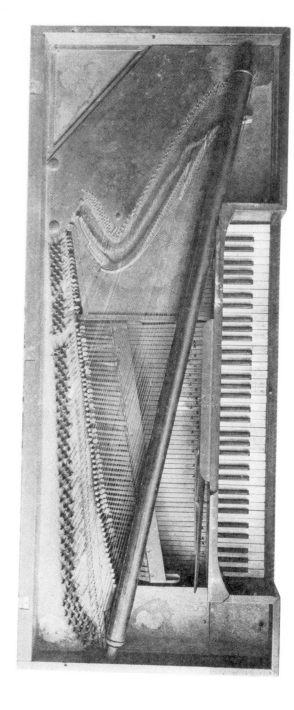

Plate IV. Square Pianoforte by William Stodart and Sons. Showing an application of Thom and Allen's patent to a square pianoforte. The iron tubular brace is 154 cm. in length and has a diameter of 16·5 cm. No date. No. 9287. (In the possession of Mr W. J. Moore, Cambridge.)

CHAPTER IV

PITCH AND TEMPERAMENT

T HE *pitch to which pianofortes were tuned*. It is not possible to say definitely to what pitch pianofortes were tuned. During the eighteenth century they were probably tuned to the Mean Continental Pitch from a' 415 to a' 427.7.[1]

Blaikley states that undoubtedly the works of Handel and Mozart, and the other classical musicians, were written with this pitch in view. Sir George Smart decided to adopt a' 423.3 for the Philharmonic when that Society was founded in 1813.

Ellis states that the general rise in pitch which took place all over Europe at varying rates seems to have originated in 1814 when, at the Congress of Vienna, the Emperor of Russia presented new and sharper wind instruments to an Austrian regiment of which he was Colonel. This regiment became renowned for the brilliant tones of its band. In 1820 another Austrian regiment received even sharper instruments. As the theatres were, for the most part, dependent on regimental bands, they were obliged to adopt this pitch. In this way the Vienna pitch gradually rose from a' 421.6 (Mozart's pitch) to a' 456.1, a rise of nearly three-quarters of a tone.[2]

Down to about 1827 there appears to have been little variation. The pitch of c" varied from 520 to 515, but in England during the next thirty years its frequency had risen to 538. Sir George Smart had fixed the pitch of a' in 1813 at 423.3, but in about the year 1828 he fixed the pitch of c" at 518. This gave a mean tone temperament a' 433 and an equal temperament a' 435.4 exactly French pitch. Another refixing of the pitch took place under Sir Michael Costa; the mean pitch of the Philharmonic band between 1846 and 1854 was a' 452.5.[3]

In France according to Montal's statement there used to be three pitches in use about 1829: the Grand Opera a' 434, the Italian Opera a' 435, and the Opéra Comique at the Théâtre

---

[1] The most universal pitch used now (1932) is Continental Pitch a' 435, over a quarter of a tone above Mozart's or 'Classical Pitch', giving an equal temperament c" 517.4.

[2] B 37, p. 512.

[3] B 28, pp. 242, 243.

Feydeau a′ 438.[1] When writing in 1836, he states that, at the
present time, "there are really only two pitches in use; that of the
Italian Opera a′ 437, and that used at the Grand Opera and the
Opéra Comique which are the same (namely) a′ 441", and that
the pitch of the Grand Opera was that used at public concerts.[2]
According to Roma's *Manuel de l'Accordeur* of 1834, the pitch used
at the Théâtre Feydeau was nearly always used for pianofortes.[3]
This statement is again repeated by Armellino in 1855.[4]

With regard to the pitch used in Germany it is extremely difficult
to say much. Joseph Baumgartner of Munich patented a horizontal
grand pianoforte in 1831, which was to be tuned to a quarter of a
tone above concert pitch. There appear to have been several pitches
to which pianofortes were tuned as occasion demanded. Hummel
protested against this lack of uniformity of pitch in a footnote
to the chapter on tuning the pianoforte, in his *Pianoforte School*:

"It is much to be wished", he wrote, "that a uniform mode of tuning
were universally introduced. To what disagreeables are we not exposed, particularly with regard to wind instruments. Sometimes they are not in tune
with the piano forte, at other times in the orchestra not with one another.
One is constructed according to the mode of tuning in use at Dresden, another
to that of Vienna, a third to that of Berlin. One gives the pitch more usual in
the chamber, another that in the theatre, and another again that in the
Church. How is it possible, among all this diversity, to obtain a pure and
equal mode of tuning? At all times Singers have been the greatest impediment
to this arrangement.[5] Would that in all countries they would agree upon some
uniform system of tuning and upon a pitch neither too high nor too low to
employ it alike in the theatre, as *alla camera*, and, when possible, also in the
Church. By this means they would everywhere meet with their accustomed
pitch, and would sing with less exertion, without being compelled to have
recourse to transposition."[6] [See Tables I and II.]

With regard to vagaries of these singers, someone at the time
bitterly remarked: "why not supply their place with musical
automata, and then if anything went wrong the clockmakers could

---

[1] Claude Montal was, according to his statement: "Ancien répétiteur à l'Institu-
tion Royale des Jeunes Aveugles, professeur d'accord, accordeur des professeurs de
piano les plus célèbres du Conservatoire et de divers grands établissements publics".

[2] Montal adds a footnote giving the sources of his information as follows: "Les
trois anciens diapasons...m'ont été communiqués par M. Kopp, comme ayant été
accordés sur l'orchestre de l'Opéra, sur celui des Italiens, et sur celui de Feydeau vers
1829. Les trois nouveaux viennent d'être accordés par moi-même avec beaucoup
de soin aux mêmes théâtres". See B 70 (a), pp. 25–27.

[3] B 86, p. 33.　　　　　　　　　　　　[4] B 23, p. 28.

[5] In 1824 the pitch of the Paris Opera had been suddenly lowered for Mme
Branchu, whose voice was failing (B 37, p. 497).

[6] B 102, Part III (Sect. II, Chap. VI, footnote on p. 69).

set all to rights". The singers on the other hand blamed the orchestras and even the "whims and intrigues of pianoforte makers (who) raise the pitch of their instruments, some a half tone to give brilliancy and richness of tone, and some a whole tone above what is denominated *chamber pitch*; caring not, nor thinking what havoc they make among singers, as long as it answers the purpose of creating a demand for their instruments".[1]

Uniformity of pitch is not yet established, though the action of the French Government in 1859 in fixing a standard pitch for France went a long way towards it; for their pitch a' 435 is now widely adopted. In 1899 England, which had hitherto adhered

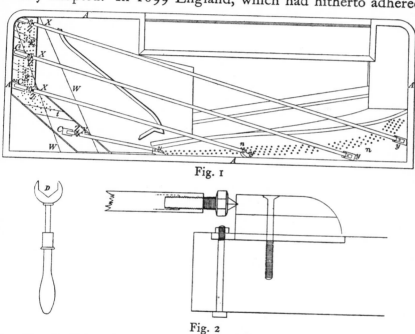

Fig. 1

Fig. 2

Fig. 28. Dettmer's apparatus for altering the pitch of pianofortes, 1827.
Fig. 1. *A, A, A, A* is a plan of the case of the instrument, which, with the wrest-pin block *n, n,* is on the usual construction. The hitch-pin block is shown at *u, t,* being in modern instruments usually bent into an angular form at *u,* but whether in this form or in the straight form running obliquely across the instrument, as formerly used, and as shown by the lines *W, W,* or with an iron plate to carry the hitch pins, my principles of construction equally apply. The hitch-pin block as usually constructed is supported upon a timber bed, similar in form to itself, and extending to the bottom of the instrument. In my construction I make the hitch-pin block about two inches thick, and detached from the bed underneath it, so that it is free to move. The top of

[1] B 75 (*l*), p. 246.

the bed and the bottom of the hitch-pin block are, however, made smooth, and to coincide in a truly horizontal position, and I unite them together by metal dovetail sliding joints. Dovetail plates are let into and screwed upon the under side of the hitch-pin block at the three places marked *t, t, t,* and the corresponding plates *E, E* to form the sliders are also let into and screwed upon the wooden bed under the block. These sliding joints are not placed parallel to the back and front of the instrument, but in the direction of the metal braces, *X, X, X,* etc., to be afterwards described, and as may be seen at *t, t, t,* where they are shown by dotted lines. These sliding joints so fixed and prepared not only serve to hold the hitch-pin block down in its place, but also allow of its moving backwards and forwards in a sufficient degree to alter the pitch of the instrument, as aforesaid. In order to allow of this motion, care must be taken to allow sufficient space between the back end of the hitch-pin block and the back of the instrument, because if this is not done it will bend against the back as it advances, on account of the direction of its motion. The tension of the wires will always draw the hitch-pin block forwards, consequently the only thing to be provided for is a sufficient power to drive or move it backwards, and this I obtain by the metal braces *X, X, X, X,* which are placed as short a distance as possible (so as to be out of the way) above the wires. One end of each of these braces fits by a tongue or tenon of metal into one of the metal brackets or buttresses *y, y, y, y,* which are firmly bolted down to the wrest-pin block *n,* and the other end of each brace is equipped with a screw, as at *Z, Z, Z, Z,* having a four, six, or eight canted head for turning it, and a conical steel point projecting beyond its head to press against other metal brackets or buttresses *C, C, C, C,* which are let in and firmly bolted down to the hitch-pin block for the purpose of receiving such pressure. One of these screws, together with the brackets or buttresses and the end of a metal brace, is shown in Fig. 2, and *D* is a key or wrench made to fit on to the heads of all the screws in common for the purpose of turning them. The operation of this machinery will be evident on inspection of the drawing, for since the hitch-pin block is separate and detached, not only from the belly of the instrument but from its case, also so upon turning the screws *Z, Z, Z, Z,* the said hitch-pin block can be moved nearer or further from the wrest-pin block, and the pitch of the instrument be varied accordingly. The several screws will not require to be turned in an equal degree, because a much smaller quantity of motion will suffice for the treble than for the bass wires, but by trying the notes while turning the screws there will be no difficulty in keeping the instrument in tune, or restoring it to the tune, if deranged by the operation, provided it was in tune in the first instance. It may be necessary to observe that in first stringing the instrument the hitch-pin block must be set nearly as far as it will go from the wrest-pin block, because the tension of the strings will draw it up a little, and if this precaution was not attended to the tension of the strings might break or strain the belly, and would likewise prevent the pitch of the instrument being lowered, although it would not interfere with its being raised. In fixing the aforesaid brackets or buttresses, I generally use screw bolts made on purpose, or such bolts in combination with the best finished carpenter's wood screws, but whenever they occur I always place the heads or the nuts uppermost, so as to admit of the brackets or buttresses being taken off with facility in case of derangement or accident; and as the two longest braces cover a portion of the wrest-pin block in which tuning pins should be placed, but which could not be got at without great inconvenience, so I find it better to place eight hitch pins in two rows under each of such longest braces in the wrest-pin block, and to put a corresponding number of wrest pins in the hitch-pin block, as at *E, E,* by which all inconvenience in tuning the instrument is avoided. I likewise find it necessary to shorten the heads of those dampers that work under the said braces, in order to prevent their striking against the same and producing a noise. (*William Dettmer, abridged.*)

to the high pitch, decided to adopt a' 439 (c" 522)[1] or New Philharmonic Pitch as a standard. This pitch is now almost as universal in this country as upon the continent, though pianofortes are occasionally tuned to the old Philharmonic pitch, a' 454 (c" 540).

Altering the Pitch of Pianofortes when in Tune. After what has been said about the various pitches to which pianofortes often had to be tuned, it will readily be understood why an attempt was made by pianoforte manufacturers to devise a means for altering the pitch of an instrument quickly and with as little exertion as possible. In order to effect this, William Dettmer of London patented in 1827 a means of constructing pianofortes so as to allow the pitch, to which they might have been tuned, to be altered and made higher or lower, both in the grand and square pianofortes at pleasure "by a short and simple process, instead of the long and tedious one formerly resorted to, of altering the pitch of each individual wire in succession". This was effected by making either one or both of the pin blocks movable in the direction of the tension of the strings and by this means altering the tension of these strings by means of screws (Fig. 28).[2] Pape adopted the idea, and in 1842 patented an arrangement which allowed the whole of the piano to be raised or lowered by means of screws.[3]

Table I. *Pitches to which Pianofortes were probably tuned*

ENGLAND

Date		Pitch a'
1800	Broadwood's c" (505·7) fork from which the following was calculated	422·7
1813	Pianoforte at the Philharmonic Society	423·3
1820	Broadwood's lowest pitch	433
1828	Philharmonic Society	435·4
1846–1854	Philharmonic Society	452·5
1849–1854	Broadwood's original medium pitch	445·9

FRANCE

1811	Paris, Grand Opera [Pitch of the Opera Pianoforte]	427·1
1824	„ „	425·8
1826	„ „	431·7
1829	„ „	434
1836	„ „	441
1823	Paris, Italian Opera	424·2
1829	„ „	425
1836	„ „	441

[1] B 76 and other sources.   [2] C 692.   [3] C 694.

		Pitch a'
Date		
1820	Paris, Théâtre Feydeau	423
1823	" "	427·6
1829	" "	438
1836	" "	441
1836	Wolfel's pianofortes	443·3

Table II
GERMANY

		Pitch a'
Date		
1834	Berlin, Opera	441·8
1815–1821	Dresden, Band of the Opera under Weber	423·2
1826	" " " Reissiger	
	[This is considered to have been the pitch	
	used at Dresden from 1825 to 1830]	435

AUSTRIA

		Pitch a'
Date		421·6
1780	Stein for Mozart	
1834	Vienna, Opera, Scheibler fork 1	433·9
1834	" " " 2	436·5
1834	" " " 3	439·4
1834	" " " 4	440·3
1834	" " " 5	441·1
1834	" " " 6	445·1
1834	Vienna, old sharp pitch	456·1

[The tables are compiled from Helmholtz and Montal.]

Equal temperament. It is not possible to state with certainty when equal temperament tuning was adopted as a general rule for the pianoforte. Early attempts to introduce it into Germany were made by Hebenstreit and Sebastian Bach; pianofortes probably were tuned in equal temperament earlier in Germany than elsewhere. In France, Montal[1] advocated its use in 1836 and gave rules for tuning the pianoforte in equal temperament in his *L'Art d'Accorder* published in that year. In England the matter came to a crisis early in the nineteenth century, which may be seen from Lord Stanhope's correspondence with the Duke of Cumberland, Dr Callcott's replies and John Farey's *Scientific Essays*. Lord Stanhope questioned his friends who numbered some of the most learned musicians of his day and found their opinion divided on the matter. In 1806 he published his treatise on the art of tuning in equal temperament entitled *Principles of the Science of Tuning Instruments with Fixed Tones*. The advantage of tuning in equal

[1] B 70 (*a*), pp. 40–48.

temperament was thus brought before many of the English 'amateurs and professors'. But in spite of this, equal temperament tuning does not seem to have become general for the pianoforte in England until midway through the century. Broadwood did not adopt it until 1846.

The Pedal Mechanism of the Harp indicated a means for avoiding the disadvantages of temperament. There were still theorists who persisted in a vain attempt to construct pianofortes with just intonation and there were others who, though they accepted mean tone temperament, were dissatisfied with it and sought some means for overcoming its defects. The pedal harp, owing to the excellent improvements which had been lately made in it, by Cousineau, Érard, and others, had become a widely popular instrument. This pedal mechanism seems undoubtedly to have suggested a means for avoiding the difficulties of temperament.

Mention has already been made of Clagget's 'Telio-chordon' patented in 1788.[1] In this instrument the octave could be divided into thirty-nine gradations of tone by means of pedals which worked movable bridges for altering the pitch of the strings. Any key would produce "three different degrees of intonation" and by this means the "temperature of all 'thirds' and 'fifths' (could) be highly improved and what (was) called the 'wolfe' (was) entirely done away". William Hawkes, in 1808, endeavoured to obtain a complete enharmonic scale in both the pianoforte and the organ.[2]

"My improvement in the pianoforte", he writes, "is effected by adding seven diatonic and five flat tones to our present scale of twelve fixed tones, which form two chromatic scales, the one termed a flat scale and the other a sharp scale, and is done by adding two sets of strings of two unisons to each set, which are acted upon without the addition of a key to the keyboard by a pedal, by which the keyboard is made to move forward and backward about one-fourth of an inch, the same hammers striking each set of strings both in the flat and sharp scale, by depressing the pedal with the foot when the sharp scale is wanted, and elevating the pedal when the flat scale is wanted."

Loeschman followed in 1809. In this case the pedal mechanism of the harp is still more clearly seen to have suggested the invention. The following description is from the patent in Loeschman's own words:

The scale of the pianoforte or organ, on the common principle, having 12 sounds within the octaves, I have by my Invention extended to 24 distinct

[1] C 932.   [2] C 955.

sounds, which enables the performer to play in 33 perfect keys, 18 major and 15 minor thirds; and this I have effected by means of *six pedals*, that cause the hammers to act upon 24 distinct sets of strings or unisons. *Three pedals bring the flats on to the treble, and the like number bring on the sharps to the bass.* By reversing my mechanism I produce also the same effect, in which case by three of the pedals the flats are brought on to the bass, and by the other three the sharps are brought on to the treble. Every pedal has a separate movement and spring which acts independently of the keys. On each movement are fastened two of the twelve hammers belonging to each octave throughout the compass, so that a pedal for the flats brings on two additional flats in each octave, and in like manner a pedal for the sharps brings on in each octave two additional sharps. . . . The mechanism for the flats and sharps is so constructed, that if more sharps or flats are wanted than one pedal will produce, a second without the first will be sufficient to bring on two of each in addition. So also, if more sharps or flats than the second pedal will produce are wanted, the third, without the first or the second, is sufficient to bring on two of each in like manner. *Each pedal is made to fasten if it should be wanted.*[1] (*Loeschman, abridged.*)

[1] C 956.

The name plate from Hawkins' Portable Grand Pianoforte
(in the possession of Messrs John Broadwood and Sons).

SECTION III

THE PIANOFORTE AS A DOMESTIC INSTRUMENT IN THE EARLY NINETEENTH CENTURY

If the piano cannot show itself to advantage in a large room, amidst a crowd of instruments, it plays its part well in private, where it forms a literal concert. It is the treasure of the harmonist and the singer. How many evenings does it remove from ennui and dullness, and enliven with all the charms of melody!

CASTILE BLAZE, quoted by W. Gardiner, 1849

CHAPTER I

THE UPRIGHT PIANOFORTE

THE wonders that the celebrated artist achieved in public the amateur attempted in the privacy of his study and thus pianoforte makers were stimulated to invent new improvements and new forms of pianofortes of every size and shape that would be suitable for the home.

At the present day the word 'piano' calls up the forms of an upright or of a grand, but a hundred years ago we should have thought of at least half-a-dozen different kinds of pianofortes. But the most important historically are the various forms of upright pianofortes, since it is the upright which, owing to its cheapness, is found in the average home of to-day.

It will no doubt be remembered that Stodart invented a new type of upright grand pianoforte in 1795 and that Southwell of Dublin had invented a smaller upright in 1798 consisting of a square pianoforte placed on its side on a stand; but this idea as has been pointed out was not new. It was not until the year 1800 that it occurred to two pianoforte makers simultaneously that the instrument would be greatly improved by dispensing with the stand and allowing the pianoforte itself to rest upon the floor, thus considerably lowering its height. Matthias Müller of Vienna and Isaac Hawkins of Philadelphia share the honour of this invention.

The compass of the Berlin example of Müller's 'Ditanaklasis', as he named his instrument, is five octaves, F_1 to f''', the strings are bichord and perpendicular; the striking point, which is much nearer to the middle of the vibrating length of the strings, was supposed to be the cause of its mellow tone, which was said to resemble the voice, or the tone of the best wind instruments, more closely than even the finest horizontal grand pianoforte.[1]

The most conspicuous feature of the action in the earlier example (Fig. 1 *a*) of Müller's 'Ditanaklasis' is the ingenious arrangement of the check. It will be seen that it works against a thin strip of wood attached at its upper extremity to the back of the hammer head and its lower extremity to a projecting strip of wood fixed to the hammer shank immediately above the butt. But in the later example (Fig. 1 *b*) this peculiarity is dispensed with in favour of an overhead check. A point of especial interest in this later action is the 'tape', a little leather strap attached to the hammer butt at the side of the round black spot—a lead weight— into which one end of the spring is inserted, whilst the other end is fixed into the key. This helps to return the hammer from the string and is in fact a primitive 'tape-check action'.[2]

The 'Portable Grand Pianoforte' of Isaac Hawkins is remarkable for several important innovations. The sound-board is suspended within a metal frame and is braced from behind with metal rods. The strings are attached to mechanical wrest pins working in a metal wrest-pin block. The hammers and dampers are pivoted within a light brass frame. The hammers themselves consist of a groundwork of layers of leather with an outer covering of cloth. The keyboard closes up and it is thought that the instrument was intended for a ship's cabin. The height including the ornamental brass rail (Plate III) is 138 cm., the compass five octaves (F_1 to c'''). Hipkins stated that the Portable Grand Pianoforte was played at a concert at the Franklin Institute of Philadelphia

---

[1] If a string be struck in the middle, the second partial tone disappears, because it has a node at that point. But the third partial tone comes out forcibly, because its nodes lie at $\frac{1}{3}$ and $\frac{2}{3}$ the length of the string from its extremities, the string is struck half way between these two nodes. The fourth partial has its nodes at $\frac{1}{4}$, $\frac{2}{4}$ ($= \frac{1}{2}$), and $\frac{3}{4}$ the length of the string from its extremity. It is not heard, because the point of excitement corresponds to its second node. The sixth, eighth, and generally the partials with even numbers disappear in the same way, but the fifth, seventh, ninth, and other partials with odd numbers are heard. By this disappearance of the evenly numbered partial tones when a string is struck at its middle, the quality of its tone becomes peculiar.... It sounds somewhat hollow or nasal.... If a string is struck at $\frac{1}{3}$ its length, the third, sixth, ninth, etc. partials vanish. This also gives a certain amount of hollowness, but less than when the string is struck at its middle. B 46, pp. 76, 77.

[2] See p. 247, Figs. 15, 16.

Plate I. Müller's 'Ditanaklasis', 1800.
Musikhistorisches Museum Neupert in Nuremberg.
This instrument has two knee pedals: piano and forte. Height in the middle 1·54 m.,
at the sides 1·84 m.; breadth 1·06 m.

No. 1.

No. 2.

Plate II. Müller's 'Ditanaklasis' (Berlin, Hochschule für Musik, No. 2278). Height 153·4 cm.

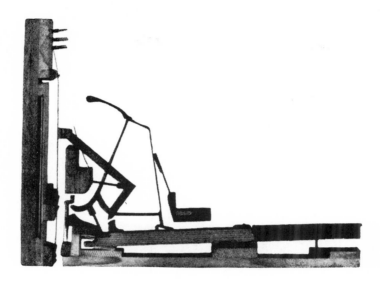

Fig. 1 (*a*). Müller's 'Ditanaklasis' (1800). The earliest example [Plate I].
Musikhistorisches Museum, Neupert in Nuremberg.

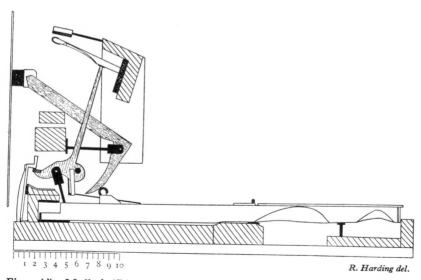

1 2 3 4 5 6 7 8 9 10

R. Harding del.

Fig. 1 (*b*). Müller's 'Ditanaklasis'. A later example [Plate II]. Berlin, No. 3378.

in 1802. There is at present only one example of this pianoforte known and this is in the possession of Messrs John Broadwood and Sons (Fig. 2).

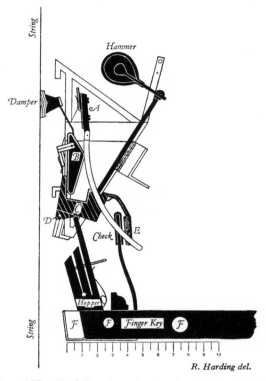

R. *Harding del.*

Fig. 2. The action of Hawkins' Portable Grand Pianoforte, about 1800. From the Portable Grand Pianoforte by I. Hawkins (in the possession of Messrs John Broadwood and Sons).

A, part of the 'forte' apparatus. *B*, a wooden block edged with lead serving as a counter weight to swing the damper away from the string when it is relaxed by the projection of the hammer butt against which it is seen to be resting. *C*, hammer butt. *D*, pivot upon which the hammer butt swings. *E*, check. *F*, *F*, *F*, lead weights. The forward movement of the hammer towards the string causes also a forward movement of the projection of its butt against which the damper counter weight *B* is pressing. This counter weight is so balanced that it follows this projection in its forward movement, thus lifting the damper away from the strings.

It was in England that the next attempt to improve the upright pianoforte was made. Thomas Loud of London patented, in 1802, a pianoforte which was to be only six feet three inches in height (190·5 cm.); this was simply an attempt to make a more portable

No. 2.

No. 1.

Plate III. Hawkins' 'Portable Grand Pianoforte' (in the possession of Messrs John Broadwood and Sons). Height, including the brass rail, 138 cm.

upright grand pianoforte by removing the stand, and making the vertical strings reach down to the ground. If greater portability was required, Loud suggested "fixing the bass strings from the *left*-hand upper corner to near the *right*-hand lower corner, and the rest of the strings in a parallel direction". By this means, he writes, "an instrument standing only five feet high and four feet wide in front will admit of the bass strings their full length which is five feet two inches [157·5 cm.]".[1] But this was not the first time that oblique stringing had been used, for Friederici had strung the pyramid he made in 1745 obliquely, in order to obtain the exceptional long and thin bass strings so dear to the early piano-forte makers.

This valuable invention of placing the strings obliquely does not seem to have been recognised at once, for small upright piano-fortes with vertical strings and a proportionately poor tone were made for many years. The writer has one by Clementi which measures 135·6 cm.; the vibrating length of the longest string is only 110·5 cm. instead of the 157·5 cm. (five feet two inches) that Loud considered necessary. By the simple expedient of placing the strings obliquely Clementi could have obtained the long bass strings and a better tone (Plate IV).

This pianoforte and others of the same type were made with the English Sticker Action, similar to the action used by Southwell in his upright pianoforte of 1798 with the exception that an escape-ment (hopper) is used in place of Southwell's jack and the dampers act upon the strings in front of the sound-board and not through an aperture in it. A wire fixed to a projection on the sticker works these dampers.

Pfeiffer et Cie, a French firm of pianoforte makers, brought out their 'Harmomelo', a tall upright instrument in which the strings reached to the ground, in 1806; it was vertically strung with three unisons to a note, and it had a compass of six octaves (unspecified). The height also is unspecified but it seems to have been about 2 m. or possibly a little less. The case was highly ornamented, and was decorated in front with two panels filled with taffeta. The keyboard cover turned back and formed a book-rest; and also a part of the pedestal upon which the instrument stood could be turned down to form a foot-rest. Four ornamental iron pedals, each formed like a leaf, operated the Harp, Bassoon, Una Corda and Sourdine[2] (Fig. 17). The action is a form of sticker action with a check, based

[1] C 935.   [2] C 883. At this time Pfeiffer was in partnership with Petzold.

upon the German (or Viennese) Action.[1] It will be convenient to call it the German Sticker Action.

In the following year William Southwell invented the 'cabinet pianoforte' and completed his invention of the English Sticker Action by adding the escapement and improving the position of the dampers in the way already mentioned. This action is important, for some pianoforte makers used it until within the last fifty years, as it was adaptable for both tall and short instruments (Fig. 3; see also Plate V).

Southwell added a check to this action working over the hammer head in 1821, but this does not seem to have come into general use. The cabinet pianoforte was probably suggested by Loud's tallest instrument as the strings reach down to the ground and are vertical and the pianoforte must have been about the same height though Southwell does not specify this. The leading motive of the invention was to make an upright pianoforte with the action outside the sound-board so that the sound-board had not to be cut through to allow either the hammers or the dampers to strike the strings, as in the ordinary upright pianoforte. This old arrangement weakened the structure and caused the pianofortes to go out of tune. It was clearly based on the grand action and it has been shown how certain grand pianoforte makers endeavoured to overcome it by placing the sound-board above the strings or the action striking down on to the strings from above.

Southwell's new arrangement prevented this weakness and made the instrument remain in tune for a longer time.[2] He was no doubt unaware that the experiment had been tried as early as 1735. The cabinet pianoforte had an open panel in front which was 'silked' and had a carved cornice sometimes supported upon carved pillars (Plate VI).

These tall upright pianofortes had three defects; they were cumbersome articles of furniture in a small room; the performer had to sit with her back to the audience, and, if she was a singer, she sang into the instrument instead of out into the room.

These defects led to determined efforts to overcome them by making a small upright pianoforte. In 1811 there were three attempts to construct such an instrument. In the first it will be seen

---

[1] If the action is looked at from the side this will become clear, for P is nothing but the 'Auslöser' (escapement) acting as usual over the 'Hammerschnabel' (hammer beak).

[2] C 839.

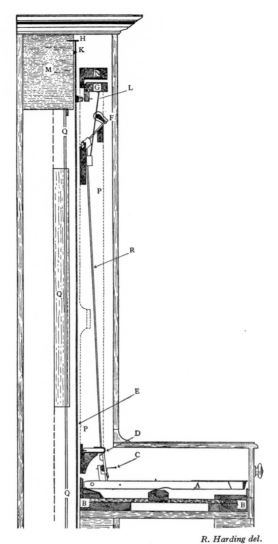

R. Harding del.

Fig. 3. Sticker Action of a Cabinet Pianoforte by George Wilkinson (in the possession of Mrs R. T. Barnes). Length of the sticker [R] is 68·5 cm.

Sticker Action, bass aspect, by George Wilkinson, between 1816 and 1829.

When the key *A* is depressed the hopper *C*, engaging in the crank *D*, causes the hammer *F* to strike the string *E* by means of the sticker *R* which connects the crank with the hammer butt. A stout wire *L* raises the damper *G* which is hinged to the damper rail *N* with parchment. (All other joints are of leather.) *H*, wrest pin. *K*, bridge from which project bridge pins. *M*, wrest-pin block. *Q, Q*, sound-board. *P, P*, action frame. *B, B*, levers and blocks under the keys which form part of the mechanism for shifting the action. Two iron bars strengthen the action frame, otherwise there is no metallic bracing.

that it was the difficulty about the singer that Southwell was attempting to overcome; but the other two inventors Wornum and Collard were trying to make a small pianoforte which would be an agreeable article of furniture for the small drawing-room.

Southwell's upright pianoforte of this year (March 4th) was a square placed on its side on a stand but the shape differed from his earlier one of 1798 in that the strings and sound-board sloped away from the performer in a backward direction. He called it the 'Piano

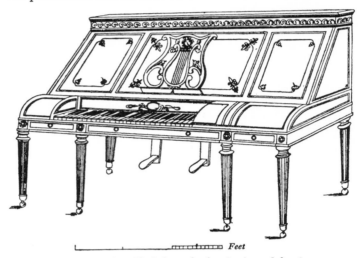

Feet

Fig. 4. Southwell's 'piano sloping backwards', 1811.

sloping backwards'; the height from the ground to the top was 4 ft. 6 in. (137·2 cm.), the breadth about 5 ft. 5 in. (165·1 cm.); the depth of the instrument at the key level was 1 ft. 7 in. (48·3 cm.) but at the top it was only about 4 in. (10·2 cm.). Southwell draws attention to the fact that "from its oblique shape the advantages to the performer must be evident, the front of the instrument being [*sic*] so much away from the face". The music desk of this pianoforte was fitted with a 'Volto Subito' (*i.e.* a device for turning over the leaves of music), which was worked by a foot-pedal (Fig. 4).

In the same year (March 26th) Robert Wornum patented a small upright pianoforte with strings reaching to the ground.[1] The action is an adaptation of the 'English Double Action' to the upright pianoforte; the dampers are worked by a projection on the fixed part of the escapement (hopper) known as the jack. When

[1] C 29. An example in the London Museum (St James' Place).

Plate IV. Pianino by Clementi, first quarter of the nineteenth century, with two pedals: Una Corda and Forte. Height about 137 cm. (in the possession of the writer).

the key is depressed the projection works against the damper wire or 'lifter' and moves it away from the strings. This pianoforte had two pedals: buff[1] and forte (Figs. 5 and 5 (*a*)).

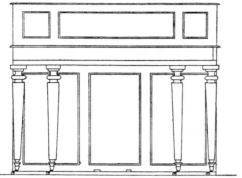

Fig. 5. Wornum's 'Cottage piano', 1811.

About six months later Frederick William Collard patented an upright pianoforte which consisted once more in placing a "square pianoforte turned upwards on its side" on a stand.[2] The dimensions of Collard's instrument were as follows: the length was about 5 ft. (52·5 cm. approx.), the height above the legs about 2 ft. 6 in. (76·2 cm. approx.); the depth from back to front of the upper part about 8 in. (20·4 cm. approx.) and the depth at the key level about 18 in. (45·7 cm. approx.). The instrument was provided with a check action somewhat similar to Stodart's upright grand, but, with the important difference that the hammers strike the strings towards the sound-board whilst it is the dampers and not the hammers that pass up through the sound-board to the strings. In 1813 Wornum made another small upright pianoforte, but this time with vertical stringing. At first it was called the 'harmonic' but afterwards it became known as the 'cottage', the small upright instrument that has been popular for so many years. His piano-fortes were now attracting the attention of Ignace Pleyel of Paris who was in partnership with the pianist Kalkbrenner. The house of Pleyel et Cie was founded by the well-known composer Ignace Pleyel, a pupil of Haydn, who at the age of fifty began a piano-forte business at Paris in 1807. In 1815 Pleyel et Cie obtained

[1] The drawing illustrates the usual form of the Buff stop, but occasionally the leather presses one of each pair of unisons from *below* as in the case of that patented by John Geib in 1786 (C 768).

[2] C 30.

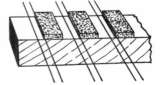

the assistance of Henri Pape to organise the construction of cottage pianofortes of the Wornum pattern.[1]

The interest that was aroused by Sébastien Érard's repetition action of 1821 seems to have inspired Henry Smart, a London

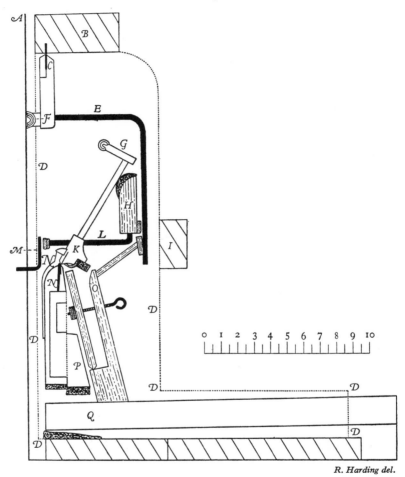

R. *Harding del.*

Fig. 5 (*a*). Cottage pianoforte action, Wornum, 1811. From the patent (reversed). *A*, line of the strings; *B*, damper rail; *C*, hinge part of the damper; *D*, right cheek of the action frame; *E*, damper wire; *F*, damper head; *G*, hammer shank and head; *H*, hammer ruler, also the damper lifter; *I*, damper ruler lined with baize; *K*, hammer butt; *L*, wire employed to push off dampers; *M*, wire communicating with the above; *N̖*, hammer beam, dotted lines a mortise; *N̖*, spring; *O*, grasshopper (*i.e.* escapement); *P*, back touch rail; *Q*, key. (*Robert Wornum.*)

[1] B 80 and 49 (*f*).

Plate V. Vertical stringing in a Cabinet Pianoforte by George Wilkinson, *circa* 1829 (in the possession of Mrs R. T. Barnes).

The vibrating length of the longest string is 180·5 cm. The vibrating length of the shortest string is 7·7 cm. There is no metallic support in the frame.

pianoforte maker and the father of the conductor Sir George Smart, to attempt something of the kind for the upright pianoforte.

Like many others he evidently thought that the springs used by Érard were liable to get out of order, for in his own repetition action of 1823 there are no springs at all.

By an ingenious arrangement of levers and weights the note could be repeated without the necessity of raising the key to more than half its level and the hammer could be held in check close up to the string in a position ready to restrike[1] (Fig. 18).

Three years later, in 1826, Wornum brought out another small pianoforte under the name of the 'professional pianoforte'.[2] He designed for this instrument a 'single' and a 'double' action. "The novelties of the double action" consisted in the use of "a double hammer rail, to which were fixed both hammers and hoppers" (escapement) and also in a check acting against the hammer head. In the single action there was but a single hammer rail and overhead checking (Fig. 6). The 'professional pianoforte' possessed also another 'novelty' which consisted in the 'pizzicato pedal' already referred to. A further improvement in 1828 completed Wornum's 'cottage piano';[3] in this the overhead checking was given up in favour of that illustrated in Fig. 7 where "The novelty is applied to the lever and the key, and effects a check to the hammer when in action. The lever is longer than usual"; its tail projects over a wooden-headed upright fixed to the key. "Its use is to press against the back or tail of the lever after every blow given to the front by the hopper (escapement), thereby effecting a

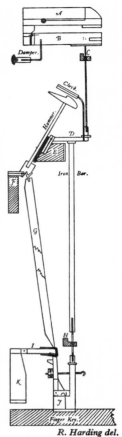

R. *Harding del.*

Fig. 6. Wornum's Single Action for upright pianoforte, 1826. Drawn from the patent (drawing No. 2 with dampers added from drawing No. 1).

A, 'damper hammer'; *B*, damper; *C*, socket for damper wire; *D*, check lever; *E*, hammer ruler; *F*, hammer rail; *G*, 'strikers'; *H*, socket; *I*, lever; *J*, hopper (escapement) with centre and mortise for the pin to work in, both brushed with cloth; *K*, lever rail and back touch.

[1] C 210. Another action entirely without springs was patented by Wetzels in 1833. It was adapted both to upright and to horizontal pianofortes. C 84.

[2] C 910.   [3] C 61.

most simple and perfect check against unnecessary motion in the hammer", etc.

These pianofortes were, according to the dimensions found on one of Wornum's price lists (1838), 3 ft. 10 in. in height (117 cm. approx.). They were vertically strung and owing to their diminutive size Pleyel called them 'pianino'; after this until about

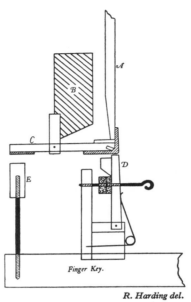

R. Harding del.

Fig. 7. Wornum's improved check for upright pianoforte, 1828.
Drawn from the patent.

A, sticker; *B*, lever rail; *C*, lever; *D*, hopper (escapement);
E, "wooden-headed upright".

1836 all very small vertically strung pianofortes were known, on the continent, as 'pianino' to distinguish them from the obliquely strung 'piano droit' and the 'piano vertical' or cabinet pianoforte with vertical strings. The pianino was soon copied by Pleyel et Cie and others in France and it was France that was eventually to stimulate Germany and Austria to copy their instruments and to design 'pianinos' and 'piano droit' of their own. Meanwhile the German and Austrian makers were at this time (the first quarter of the nineteenth century) designing tall upright pianofortes in a remarkable series of ornamental shapes.

The well-known giraffe was invented at Vienna by an unknown

Plate VI. Cabinet Pianoforte by Clementi. (From an instrument in the
possession of Mr W. J. Moore, Cambridge.)
Height 188 cm. Inscription: "Clementi & Co., London", No. 482.

maker about the same time as the upright grand pianoforte (1798) and continued to be made until the end of the first half of the nineteenth century. It consisted in placing a grand piano-forte with the broad end upon the ground and the tail uppermost. This tail is usually curved over into a scroll and sometimes the short side is formed into a shelf to take a vase or clock or even a wooden figure of Apollo as a symbol of music.

The action of the large giraffe usually is an adaptation of the German or Viennese Action, known as the 'hängende' German Action (Fig. 8), in which the hammer is suspended

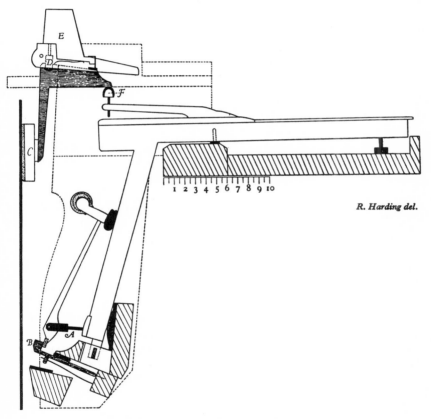

R. Harding del.

Fig. 8. 'Hängende' German Action. From a giraffe
by C. Erlich of Bamberg (Berlin, No. 1274)

A, Kapsel; B, escapement; C, damper; D, Kapsel within which the damper C is pivoted: this Kapsel is fixed to the block of wood E; F, pilot on the key which raises the damper from off the string when the key is depressed.

below the key in such a way that it readily responds to the lightest touch.

A small giraffe pianoforte placed on a stand was also made about 1830. The strings are placed obliquely in order to reduce the height. An instrument of this type by Bowitz of Breslau is to be seen at Berlin (Plate VII). The action is an adaptation of the German or Viennese Action to the upright pianoforte (Fig. 9). In this

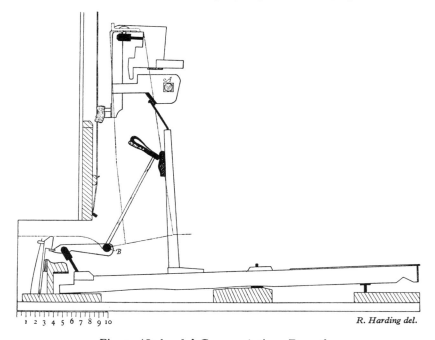

1 2 3 4 5 6 7 8 9 10   *R. Harding del.*

Fig. 9. 'Stehende' German Action. From the
pianoforte by Bowitz (Berlin, No. 991).

A and *B* are lead weights. The dotted lines represent a part of the action frame.

case the hammer stands in a Kapsel on the key and the action is called the 'stehende' German Action to distinguish it from the 'hängende' Action where the hammer is below the key level, as it were suspended below it or 'hanging' from it.

Dr Neupert's interesting collection of pianofortes at Nuremberg contains some experimental upright instruments belonging to this period. The makers seem to have wished to disguise the instruments by giving them, as far as possible, the appearance of a bookcase (Plates X–XII).

Plate VII. Giraffenflügel by C. A. Bowitz. Berlin, Hochschule für Musik, No. 991. Height 174 cm.

Meanwhile the pyramid-shaped pianoforte had been revived and another type of pianoforte that seems to have been for the most part a Berlin form[1] was invented about 1824. This was a lyre-shaped pianoforte placed on a stand, in which the lyre strings are imitated with gilded wooden rods. A late example by Osterman in Berlin[2] about 1840 shows obliquely-placed strings, strong wooden struts and total absence of metal framing. The height is 225 cm. (Plate VIII). This instrument has an adaptation of the English Action known as the 'stehende' englische Action. In an

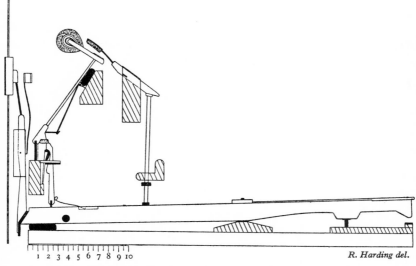

1 2 3 4 5 6 7 8 9 10   *R. Harding del.*

Fig. 10. 'Stehende' Englische Action, about 1825, J. C. Schleip
(Stuttgart, E 30).

earlier example at Stuttgart, about 1825, there is again the 'stehende' englische Action (Fig. 10). This action is interesting because it is a German adaptation of the English Grand Action to the upright pianoforte in which the hammer is checked from above and a spring attached to the hammer ruler is inserted into a tape on the hammer which precipitates the return of the hammer from the string. The touch is light and the hammer strikes a firm blow. An upright pianoforte in the form of an Apollo lyre standing on a foot[3] was invented by Franz Weisz who obtained an Austrian patent for it in 1826; he named this instrument the 'Apolliricon'.

[1] B 87 (*b*), s. 50.   [2] Berlin, No. 811.
[3] C 899.

A lyre-shaped pianoforte was patented by Eulriot in 1834. In order to overcome the disadvantage of being unable to see the performer, he made a space between the arms of this lyre-shaped pianoforte, and by placing a glass, which could be raised or lowered by means of weights, behind the instrument, enabled the performer to be seen whilst he was playing, according to the position of the pianoforte in the room. This instrument was provided with a repetition action showing considerable ingenuity, for the friction of the various parts was reduced to a minimum by the use of rollers acting on inclined planes; and these little rollers also facilitated the repetition[1] (Fig. 19). A lyre-shaped pianoforte was exhibited in the Great Exhibition of 1851 but it seems to have been on a smaller scale than those mentioned above. Pole comments upon it in his catalogue of the Exhibition:

A cottage upright of a peculiar shape, called the 'Lyra pianoforte', is exhibited by Messrs Hund and Son. The back of the instrument is intended to be turned towards the centre of the room, and is formed like a lyre, with openings covered with silk; the object being to throw the sound outwards. The piano stands on a raised platform or sound conductor into which the bass strings descend, and which also elevates the stool for the player. There are three pedals, the additional one being a soft one on the French principle, viz. introducing a thickness of soft cloth between the hammer and the string (Jeu céleste).[2]

The tall upright pianofortes were not a favourite in France owing to the fact that the performer was obliged to sit with her back to the audience. Robert Wornum's cottage pianoforte had pointed out the way to overcome this defect and these small instruments had the advantage of being easily moved about.

The year 1827 marks the beginning of a series of diminutive pianofortes that were invented by French makers. Their success was such that the square pianoforte, though it was still made, went out of fashion.

Blanchet et Roller of Paris created a sensation with their little 'piano droit' at the Exhibition held in the Louvre in this year; as it was only 1 m. high and 1·30 m. broad, was obliquely strung and had a semicircle cut in the bottom of the case to admit the performer's feet. The action although by no means perfect was an advance on anything that had been achieved before in France, and when it had been improved in 1830 it was used by many makers.[3]

[1] B 70 (a), p. 242.   [2] B 81, p. 29.
[3] See B 80, pp. 184, 185, 186.

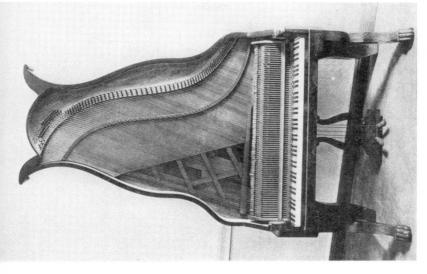

a

b

Plate VIII (*a*). 'Lyraflügel', by H. Ostermann, in Berlin, *circa* 1840. Berlin, Hochschule für Musik, No. 811. Pedals: 'Una Corda' and Forte. Height, 225 cm.

(*b*). Oblique stringing in a 'Lyraflügel'. By H. Ostermann. Berlin, No. 811.

In 1829 Blanchet et Roller brought out another upright action which when perfected in 1860 was adopted by many firms (Fig. 20).

Plate IX (*a*) shows this type of instrument with the front removed to show the obliquely-placed strings. The aperture for the feet and the two pedals placed at the side should be noticed.

Cross-Stringing. In 1828 Henri Pape brought out the first of his series of console-like pianofortes.[1] It was 1 m. high, and the bass strings were arranged so that they crossed over the treble strings. This gave the advantage of longer strings and also served to brace the case (Fig. 11). Pape writes thus:

En raison du peu de hauteur de ces pianos, les dernières cordes des basses se trouvent trop courtes, surtout à ceux de six octaves et demie, et, par conséquent, le son n'a pas tout la sonorité désirable; dans celui que j'ai présenté, cette même petite partie de cordes est inclinée d'angle à angle, ce qui fait profiter de la plus grande longueur de table d'harmonie et surtout

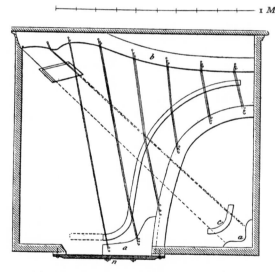

Fig. 11. Pape's cross-string 'pianino' of 1828.

a, plaque de cuivre dans laquelle sont placées les pointes d'accord d'accroche; *b*, sommier de chevilles; *c*, chevalet. Le petit chevalet est assez élevé et comparable à un chevalet de contre basse; il est placé sur la table d'harmonie, mais à l'opposé de l'autre; les cordes s'accrochent derrière sans aucune difficulté. La plaque de fer *n*, après laquelle est vissée celle d'accroche en cuivre *a*, est retenue, au milieu, par deux boutons à double écrou qui traversent la table convexe.

[1] C 1122.

occupe une partie entièrement libre de cette table, qui en même temps se trouve tendue par le tirage des autres cordes, et, par cela même, lui procure tout avantage pour la sonorité.

It will no doubt have been noticed that Pape describes the small bridge as resembling that of a Double Bass. This is an instance of the pianoforte maker applying his knowledge of other instruments to the pianoforte, for he often was a general musical instrument maker, or sold other instruments besides the pianoforte. (We shall have occasion to refer to this later.)

The invention of cross-stringing was not long to remain the private property of one individual and it is found applied not only to the upright but also to horizontal pianofortes.

An American firm, Bridgeland and Jardine, exhibited a pianoforte at New York in 1833 in which the bass strings are said to have "crossed over the treble". Two square pianofortes with overstrung bass strings were actually made in that year by John Jardine.[1] Friedrich Greiner of Munich was the next to take up the invention.[2] He obtained a Bavarian patent for it in the same year. Kaspar Lorenz and Samuel Meiszner, two pianoforte makers of Vienna, obtained Austrian patents for cross-strung pianofortes in 1834.[3] Pierre Fischer then followed in 1835 with cross-strung upright pianofortes and in 1836 John Godwin also began to use this type of stringing for his square, cottage, or piccolo pianofortes[4] where he placed "one part of the strings across or obliquely over the lines or direction in which the other part of the strings (i.e. the treble) were placed".

Although Fischer was the first to patent this arrangement in this country, Gerock of Cornhill, London, according to tradition, made the first cross-strung pianoforte in England after a design by Theobald Boehm the flute maker in 1835.[5] Hipkins quotes a letter from Boehm to W. S. Broadwood dated June 12th, 1867, in which Boehm definitely states that he advised Gerock to "cross the bass strings or lay them obliquely" in 1831. Hipkins states that he had also seen a cabinet, a piccolo and a square constructed by Gerock and Wolf according to Boehm's design in 1835.[6] Two years later (1837) Christoph Lorenz Jahn of Vienna strung his pianofortes in such a way that the trichord treble notes crossed the bichord bass ones at right angles so as to form a cross. "By this

[1] B 49, p. 20.   [2] C 1123.
[3] C 1124, 1125.   [4] C 1126, 1128.
[5] B 49, pp. 19, 20.   [6] B 49, p. 20.

a

b

Plate IX (*a*). Small obliquely strung pianoforte, about 1840, by an anonymous German maker. Würtembergisches Landesgewerbemuseum.

(*b*). Pianino by Klinkerfuss, about 1840.
Stuttgart, Würtembergisches Landesgewerbemuseum.

means", he wrote, "the pianoforte is said to acquire a perfect tone, and also to keep well in tune."[1] Julien-Thomas Rinaldi of Paris applied the invention of cross-stringing to a square pianoforte in 1839.[2] Here again the intention seems to have been to equalise the strain on the frame and thus keep the instrument better in tune. "L'instrument doit avoir plus de son par les changements apportés; il doit aussi mieux tenir l'accord, attendu que les trente notes qui sont placées verticalement diminuent de plus d'un tiers le tirage de la caisse et contribuent ainsi à la solidité de l'instrument." There was an additional sound-board for these upper thirty notes (*i.e.* from the 49th to the 68th note). Later in the same year Vandermère also obtained a patent for cross-stringing applied to upright pianofortes.[3] J. F. Vogelsangs of Brussels patented a pianoforte with oblique and cross-stringing in 1847.[4]

Klepfer of Cincinnati, and Mathushek of New York obtained American patents for cross-stringing in 1851,[5] the former for an upright, the latter for a square pianoforte. Klepfer's method of cross-stringing the upright pianoforte seems to be based upon Pape's patent of 1828, previously mentioned (Fig. 11). But in these cases the intention seems to have been no longer to equalise the tension on the frame but to obtain the greatest possible length for the strings, for the iron frame had solved the problem of resistance.

In 1830, two years after Pape had invented his console pianoforte with cross-stringing (1828), Simon Thompson invented a small pianoforte with "the top on a level with the lock board"[6] (*i.e.* the key-cover). He writes that the top of the piano may be made "a flat surface as a table without any projection above the front which is usually called the lock board" (Fig. 12). The reason for this new shape seems to have been the objection made by singers that when accompanying themselves on an upright pianoforte 'the silk front or face absorbs the voice'. Another way of overcoming this difficulty of the singer's voice being lost in the instrument consisted in lowering the portion of the case opposite to the singer's head; a design by Daniel Chandler Hewitt shows an instrument of this kind[7] and a pianoforte by Broadwood with such a declivity is preserved at Brussels (No. 3291). It is only 1·18 m. broad, 1·27 m. high (Plate XIV).

[1] C 1129.
[2] C 1130.
[3] C 1131.
[4] C 1132.
[5] C 1133, 1134.
[6] C 964.
[7] C 157.

In 1846 another pianoforte on a stand was patented, on this occasion by Thomas Woolley of Nottingham who states that the pianoforte is mounted on a platform "so that the performer being elevated, may be seen over the instrument, and if she is using it as an accompaniment to her voice, her voice may be more distinctly heard".[1] The lyre-shaped cottage pianoforte exhibited at the 1851 Exhibition in London by Messrs Hund and Son already referred to was also upon a stand.[2]

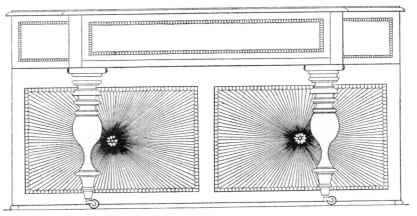

Fig. 12. Thompson's "piano with the top on a level with the lock board", 1830.

The use of Springs or Resonators to improve the tone of the Pianino. Returning once more to the year 1830 when Thompson invented his small pianoforte "with the top on a level with the lock board" we find that, although makers had now the choice of oblique or cross-stringing for their very small instruments, for some reason that is a little difficult to explain there seems still to have been a demand for vertically placed strings although the other arrangements of placing them obliquely or crossing the bass over the treble made it possible to use longer strings and to obtain a better tone in consequence. The reason may have been that vertical stringing made it more easy for the amateur to replace a broken string and since the amateur had often to be his own tuner this was a matter of some importance. The difficulty seems to have been how to obtain the deep bass notes in a vertically strung pianoforte of about 1 m. in height with a compass of about seven octaves. As close covered strings seem to have been used for the lowest bass

[1] C 904.   [2] See p. 236.

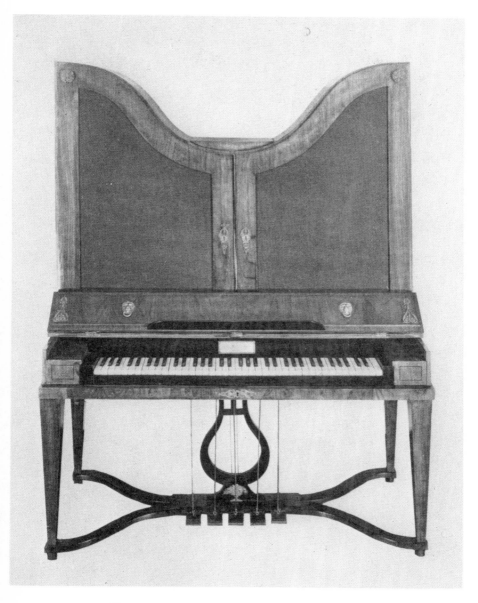

Plate X. By Ruth Kissingen. Musikhistorisches
Museum Neupert in Nuremberg.
This pianoforte has the 'Stehende' English Action and five pedals as follows: (left
to right) Bassoon; Forte; Turkish music; Piano; Flageolette (now out of action).
Height 1·73 m., breadth 1·45 m.

notes in ordinary pianofortes both grand and upright the solution would seem to have been to use close covered strings sufficiently weighty to give the requisite depth of tone; either this did not occur to the makers or the strings were unsatisfactory. Hawkins had evidently foreseen the difficulty for a solution to the problem is found in his patent of 1800. It consists in the use of "metallic elastic wire strings". These were made, he states, "by the wire being turned up into a spiral curved serpentine or crooked form, or made with links like a chain to produce a bass sound, and occupy a much shorter space than is usual".[1] It will have been observed that Hawkins is contemplating the use of metal springs for the bass notes, for his metallic elastic strings are nothing else. Pierre Fischer actually did use springs for the bass notes of a diminutive upright pianoforte patented in 1835.[2] By this means he obtained the requisite sonority with a short vertical *Spring*. The use of resonators was also tried in order to improve the tone of these diminutive instruments; for example, Georges-Frédéric Greiner patented in the following year an arrangement of thin vibrating laminae of wood fastened over the strings and tuned to the same pitch as these strings, for the purpose of amplifying their vibrations. In this way Greiner hoped to produce a "powerful and pure tone" in his small pianofortes. In a small instrument of this type, only 3 ft. high (91·5 cm. approx.), and with a compass of seven octaves Henri Pape obtained the required tone by mounting the strings on harmonic rods. (He patented this in 1851.)[3]

The year 1836, that is the following year after Fischer's experiments with metallic springs, marks a series of important inventions.

In May 1836 Wheatley Kirk, an English pianoforte maker, patented the first complete metal frame for an upright pianoforte and it was apparently of cast iron—Kirk does not specify this. Its purpose was to take the strain of the strings and to do away with the wooden props which strengthened the case in order to make room for a double sound-board to improve the tone.[4]

---

[1] These strings are also intended to be applied as bands, either single or two or more sewed side by side into a piece of cloth, leather, or other substance, for turning lathes and all other machinery where bands are used for turning of wheels, etc. These elastic strings are also designed to be fixed to saddles and stirrup straps to render them elastic, and thereby hinder the jolting of horses from affecting the rider. It is likewise contemplated to combine a number of these elastic strings together, and apply them to coaches and all other carriages where springs are used. (*Isaac Hawkins*, 1800.)

[2] C 959.   [3] C 1187.   [4] C 1087.

In June Martin Seufert of Vienna obtained an Austrian patent for an action for a 'piano droit'[1] as he calls it (Fig. 13). This may be taken as marking the introduction of these small instruments into Austria and Germany, for Seufert's pianoforte claims to be an improvement on the French instruments of the same kind.

This 'pianoforte' had an iron frame. It was some years before these instruments which at this time appear to have been called pianinos whether they were obliquely- or even cross-strung, gained recognition in Germany and Austria. Prof. Sachs states that according to a report in the *Leipziger Allgemeine Zeitung* of 1838 a pianino was introduced by Pleyel and Kalkbrenner as a "newly invented instrument".[2] A few years later, however, Klinckerfuss, a pupil of Pape, was making pianinos at Stuttgart. (Plate IX (*b*) shows one of these instruments with the front removed to show the cross-stringing.)

Schiedmayer und Söhne of Stuttgart evidently began about this time to make pianinos, for there is an example at Berlin about 1845 and there is also an earlier pianino at Berlin by H. Roloff of Neubrandenburg, about 1840. The Heyer collection at Leipzig contains one by A. Ibach Söhne of Barmen only 1·15 m. high, made in 1841, and another by G. W. Kuper and Co., of Frankfort, only 1·07 m. high, made about the middle of the century.

In December Soufleto, of Paris, a pupil

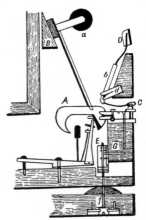

R. *Harding del.*

Fig. 13. Action for small upright pianoforte by Seufert of Vienna, 1836.

The hammer *a* after striking the strings falls back by the weight of its butt *A* against *B* the hammer ruler, thus differing from the Parisian instruments where the hammer is returned by a spring. The damper lifter *b* is hardly ⅓ as long as in the French instruments, so that it is easily lifted at *C* by a rod. The action of the damper *D* is regulated at *d*. The piece *E* can be regulated by two screws *G* and *f* to the positions marked by the black transverse lines, so that the touch can be adjusted to suit any performer.

of Roller, who, it will be remembered, had been in partnership with Blanchet when he had created a sensation with his piano droit exhibited in 1827 at the *Louvre*, invented a new upright pianoforte action.[3] It is clear from this that he owed much to his master; the check is fixed on a long wire and the mechanism for working the

[1] C 99.   [2] B 87 (*b*), p. 52.
[3] C 102.

Plate XI. Musikhistorisches Museum Neupert in Nuremberg.
This pianoforte has the 'Stehende' German Action and two knee pedals: (left to right)
Piano, Forte. Height 1·70 m., breadth 1·30 m.

Plate XII. Musikhistorisches Museum Neupert in Nuremberg.

under damper is based on Blanchet et Roller's Action of 1829 (Fig. 21).

Constant Pierre informs us that Soufleto's 'pianos verticaux' (upright pianofortes) with oblique strings were the next best to those of Roller himself.[1]

A little later in the same month another important invention was patented. It was the application of a forged iron frame to a diminutive pianoforte, so small that it could be packed up in a case to be taken away on a journey. This was the 'Piano-écran' invented by Alexandre Debain. The frame was of forged iron. The sound-board was fixed behind the frame in order that it could be removed for repairs without disturbing the strings. The key frame was of cast iron and the keyboard itself closed up. Frames, covered with silk or with wood painted with pictures or with glass, protected the sound-board behind and concealed the keyboard in front when closed. Openwork panels could be used instead of the frames if desired. Portability was the leading motive of the invention of the Piano-écran. The height with the feet removed was 3 ft. 5 in.; the width was 3 ft. 3 in. and the thickness with the keyboard closed was 7 in.[2] The instrument weighed about 100 lb. whereas an ordinary upright pianoforte weighed from 180 to 200 lb. On account of its compact shape the Piano-écran was suitable for a small room and could serve as a screen when not in use as a pianoforte. It could be packed up in a case in the manner of bass instruments and carried on a journey. To protect it from injury from damp bronze could be used instead of veneer for the outer case.[3]

In 1839 Pape first patented the 'piano console' in England;[4] this instrument had the appearance of a chiffonier with a keyboard supported upon four 'console' legs. This little pianoforte was only to be 2 ft. 9 in. in height. There was to be an iron frame and a sound-board placed behind this frame so that the sound should not be damped by it. This sound-board formed, in fact, the back of the instrument and was to be painted in imitation of the wood used for the case. The strings were fixed in such a manner that any deflection from true intonation could be detected by sight; this was, of course, a concession to the unmusical amateur and will be referred to later (Fig. 14).

Two highly experimental pianofortes which were made in

[1] B 80, p. 192.
[3] C 832.

[2] French measure; see p. 109.
[4] C 826.

England, the first in 1842 and the second in 1844, must briefly be mentioned, though they did not influence the subsequent con-

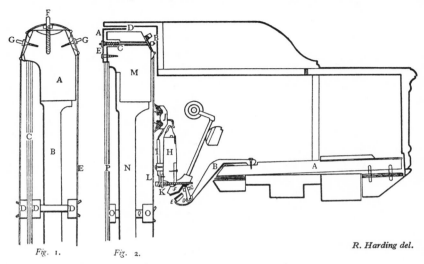

R. Harding del.

Fig. 14. Action for Pape's 'Piano Console', 1839.
Drawn from the patent.

Fig. 1 represents various ways of stringing the instrument, Fig. 2 represents the side view of the instrument and action.

Fig. 1. "The principal object of this figure consists in different ways of stringing the instrument. Instead of a single string there is here a double one. This new disposition offers a great advantage, because it serves not only (how) to increase the sound, but also to counterbalance the tension of the strings. A, block; B, braces of wood, metal, or sheet iron; C, sounding board; D, bridge; E, strings hooked in at the bottom, and passing over the Raspin block A, and mounted by the screw F, containing a nut, and regulated by pressure through the means of the little screw G."

Fig. 2. "A, a key; B, the lever which receives the hopper (escapement) C and has as its centre D in the same lever. The check E is planted, which retains the hammer by the butt F, having its centre in...the hammer rail H, to which is fixed the hammer lever I having at its extremity the double damper J, and at the other end the winding spring K, which serves both to damp and to raise the hammer. L, strings; M, block; N, braces; O, bridge; Q, small wooden or metal pegs; P, sounding board forming the back of the instrument. To this piano is attached a manner of tuning by sight. A, a spring in the form of a square, through which passes the brass wire B, on which is fixed the winding spring C to strengthen and regulate the indicator D which the cork slackens. The point goes back, which shows that the note is lowered; and on turning the nut E the spring offers a resistance calculated so that the point moves to the indicator when the spring is pulled up to pitch."

struction of pianofortes to an appreciable extent. Dr John Steward's remarkable 'Euphonicon' pianoforte[1] is the first of these

[1] C 874.

(Fig. 22); Steward built his instrument against a harp-shaped metal frame strung vertically, the upper part of which he exposed to view; against this frame in lieu of the usual sound-board he erected three sound cases varying in size: a large one to amplify the vibrations of the bass strings, a small one for the tenor portion and a still smaller soundbox for the treble. These soundboxes were perforated with forte holes and looked like a 'cello, a viola and a violin with their necks removed.

Steward also arranged his strings so that they passed around studs on the frame and were hooked to a peculiar form of mechanical wrest pin concealed within the case. But Steward was not the first to build a pianoforte with a harp-shaped frame, for Hipkins states that he himself possessed one made in 1819 by Maussard of Lausanne.[1]

Daniel Chandler Hewitt invented in 1844 a cross-strung pianoforte with a set of strings on both sides of the sound-board in order to equalise the tension. Each key worked a hammer at the back and the front of the sound-board. He also patented an arrangement in which each group of strings forming a note, that is the one in front and the other at the back, should be acted upon *at the same time* by three hammers in front and three hammers behind striking the strings at different intervals of their striking length. There would, of course, be an arrangement for uncoupling the additional hammers. He does not specify the distances at which they should strike, leaving this, no doubt, to the experience of the pianoforte maker. The object of these inventions seems to have been to obtain in the first place a loud sound by using more than the usual number of unisons to a note and by striking them at once by several hammers, and in the second place to obtain an improved tone which could, of course, be made hollow or full and round by changing the striking place.[2]

In between the invention of the Euphonicon and Hewitt's cross-strung pianoforte with its many hammers, Robert Wornum obtained a patent for the 'tape-check action'[3] (in 1842): it is shown applied to both an upright and to down-striking actions but it is the upright 'tape-check action' for which he is remembered. It is interesting to note that Charles-François Wolfel of Paris actually patented 'tape-check actions' of the Wornum type for both upright and horizontal grand pianofortes as early as 1840.[4] But Wornum, although he did not obtain a patent for this type of

[1] B 49 (*f*), p. 162 footnote.   [2] C 954.   [3] C 144.   [4] C 131.

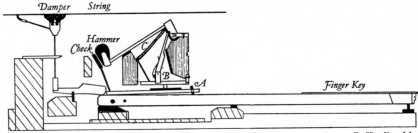

R. Harding del.

Fig. 15. Wornum's tape-check action for grand pianoforte, 1838. (From 'The Imperial Grand Pianoforte', Plate I, Part II, Sect. II.

A, screw to regulate the check; *B*, escapement; *C*, tape.

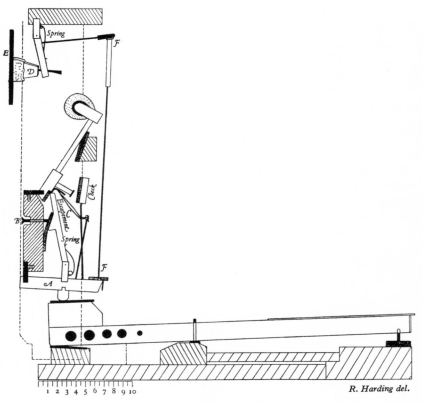

R. Harding del.

Fig. 16. Wornum's tape-check action, about 1842–52.

A, "a rocking lever moving on an axis" (Wornum); *B*, screw regulating the movement of the escapement (hopper); *C*, tape; *D*, damper; *E*, string; *F*, damper lifter or wire.

action until 1842, had, nevertheless, used it in connection at least with the grand pianoforte for the past five years and very probably for a longer period (Fig. 15). The principle of this action consists of a tape which precipitates the return of the hammer from the strings and also prevents undue separation of the unit forming the action. The projection at the back of the escapement (hopper) when forced up against the pad over the projecting end of the regulating screw *B* causes the escapement to take place (Fig. 16).

In the same sense that Sébastien Érard invented the modern grand pianoforte action so also did Wornum invent the modern upright pianoforte action, for his 'tape-check action' forms the working basis of the modern upright instrument. The 'tape-check' was copied in France by Pleyel and his copies and modifications of this action were again copied and modified in Germany. Within a few years of its invention the 'tape-check action' was also copied in America.

Though it was not a 'repetition action' in the sense that Érard's Grand Action was, yet it was susceptible of fine adjustment. Other makers did in fact patent upright actions which they called 'repetition' actions but it is Wornum's Action which has survived. It must then have fulfilled the purpose of musicians better than theirs.

The upright pianoforte, having begun as a grand placed vertically on a stand with the action behind the sound-board and the hammers striking up through it to the strings, was now an entirely independent instrument. The weakness caused by cutting through the sound-board to make a space for the hammers to strike through had been overcome by placing the action outside; the objection that the old arrangement of striking the strings from below away from the sound-board and its bridge tended to unseat the strings from the bridge and consequently to put the pianoforte out of tune was also overcome by this new arrangement, where the hammers struck towards the sound-board. Though the modern upright pianoforte owes its compact form chiefly to the singers who objected that their voices were lost in the silk fronts of the tall cabinet pianofortes, it also owes it to the desire for portable instruments which would not look clumsy in a small room and could be easily moved. It will be remembered how Debain carried this idea of portability to an extreme, as he wished to make it possible to carry the pianoforte about like a bass instrument.

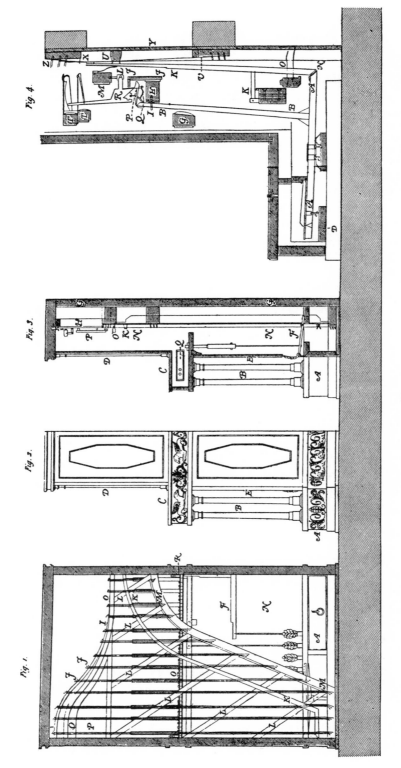

Fig. 17.

DESCRIPTION OF FIG. 17 (*opposite*).

Fig. 17. Harmomelo. Pfeiffer et Cie, 1806.

Depuis longtemps on a cherché à composer un instrument à cordes dans une position perpendiculaire, pour le jouer en clavier, et toujours on a trouvé que les cordes tendues en cette position produisent un son beaucoup plus fort, plus plein et plus agréable que celles tendues horizontalement; mais cela n'a jamais pu être amené à sa perfection.

L'instrument que nous présentons sous la forme d'un secrétaire ou d'une bibliothèque, est porté à la plus haute perfection possible.

Comme la mesure précise, tant de la forme entière, que de chaque pièce de cette mécanique est nécessaire, nous allons en donner l'explication.

Explication des Figures

Fig. 1re, élévation vue de face intérieurement.

Fig. 2e, élévation latérale.

Fig. 3e, intérieur de l'instrument, vu de profil.

A, piédestaux sur lesquels sont les supports *B*, qui soutiennent la caisse *C* du clavier.

D, panneau décoré et travaillé à jour, garni intérieurement d'un taffetas, pour rendre le son de l'instrument plus agréable, et pour empêcher la poussière de pénétrer dans l'intérieur. On peut l'ouvrir au moyen d'une clef.

E, autre panneau également décoré et travaillé à jour; il est enclavé dans des rainures, pour qu'il ne puisse se courber, et traversé, dans le milieu de sa partie inférieure, par quatre pédales en fer et à charnières invisibles et perdues dans les ornements.

Ces pédales sont fixées par des vis, les deux de gauche pour la mutation de harpe et la mutation de basson, exercent leur pression sur deux balanciers qui engrènent dans deux tringles qui les tirent, et qui, au moyen de deux ressorts en acier, produisent leur effet avec élasticité.

La mutation de la harpe consiste en une barre de bois *O*, inclinée dans la direction du petit chevalet *I*; elle porte, à sa partie supérieure, trente-quatre centimètres d'épaisseur sur vingt-sept de large, et à sa partie inférieure, quatorze centimètres sur vingt-sept; elle a une rainure où sont fixées des franges en soie ou en laine, qui, sitôt qu'elles sont pressées sur les cordes par la pédale, produisent un son de harpe à demi-modéré, beaucoup plus agréable que celui qu'on obtient avec des franges en peau, comme cela est d'usage.

La mutation du basson consiste en une planchette *P*, sur laquelle est un papier apprêté exprès, rond, tendu en échelle, fixé dans une rainure et produisant, lors de l'attouchement des cordes, un ton ronflant semblable à celui du basson.

G, dossier épais formant le fond de l'instrument.

H, sommier qui, au moyen de ses proportions, conserve l'accord des cordes beaucoup mieux que ne le font les instruments ordinaires.

I, petit chevalet courbe, où est fixe, pour chaque corde, un arrêt qui la retient dans sa position et lui conserve une tension convenable; il porte aussi les chevilles d'accord *J*, sur lesquelles les cordes sont tendues; ce qui rend l'accord très-facile.

K, grand chevalet courbe descendant jusqu'au bas de l'instrument, et portant des goupilles pour arrêter les cordes.

L, six traverses ajustées au chevalet *K*; elles s'élèvent obliquement et servent à opposer de la résistance au poids des cordes.

M, autre chevalet servant à accrocher les cordes; il porte, pour chaque corde, deux goupilles à travers lesquelles les cordes sont tendues, pour rendre un son ferme et plein; la longueur des cordes est leur distance comprise entre les chevalets *I* et *K*.

N, table de raisonnement.

Q, clavier placé dans sa caisse *C*, ou, comme à l'ordinaire, consistant en soixante-treize tons, par conséquent en six octaves; au moyen de la première pédale *F*, formant équerre, et d'un ressort en acier placé en *R*, Fig. 1ʳᵉ, sur le côté de la caisse, on le pousse de côté et d'autre pour faire tomber les marteaux contre une, deux ou trois cordes; ce qui permet de donner la plus grande force comme la plus faible et la plus agréable à son jeu.

Pour élever davantage le toucheur, le clavier est à trois pieds au-dessus de terre; sa caisse est à charnière, de sorte que le côté de face étant rabattu, il peut servir de pupitre.

La partie inférieure et antérieure du piédestal est à charnière, pour pouvoir se retourner et servir de marche-pied.

Fig. 4ᵉ, le clavier dans sa caisse, vu du côté droit et sur une plus grande échelle.

A, touches en bois léger de quatorze centimètres d'épaisseur, placées horizontalement; elles sont portées en avant sur des pointes à pivots *C*, placées en un ordre convenable dans la pièce *D*, qui a soixante-quatorze centimètres de large sur vingt-sept d'épaisseur.

B, autres touches également en bois léger, fixées presque verticalement à celles *A*.

E, balancier dans lequel sont des pointes *F*, qui supportent les touches *A*, vers leur milieu.

G, traverse garnie d'une étoffe légère, formant coussin, pour empêcher d'entendre le bruit des touches *B* lorsqu'elles viennent frapper contre. Cette traverse se retire à volonté lorsqu'on veut sortir les touches.

H, traverse contre laquelle reposent les touches *B*; elle est aussi garnie de peau, pour empêcher le bruit des touches dans leur mouvement de va-et-vient; ces touches sont traversées par des pointes *I*, qui entrent dans la peau et qui les empêchent de vaciller.

J, tringle recourbée, placée derrière et contre la traverse *H*; sa partie supérieure est garnie de peau; cette tringle s'élève et se baisse à volonté, pour obéir aux marteaux.

K, sourdines qui se meuvent dans des châsses en cuivre *L*, fixées à vis dans la traverse *M*, pour qu'aussitôt que la touche est abaissée, la partie supérieure de cette sourdine, garnie en peau ou en drap, se retire des cordes, et qu'au moment où la touche est quittée, la continuation du son soit coupée. Cette retraite s'opère au moyen du coude *N* garni de peau.

O, barre à pédale, ayant un bras à droite: aussitôt que la pédale est abaissée, la barre retire toutes les sourdines de dessus les cordes; ce qui opère la mutation du forte.

P, crochets portant une forte dent qui saisit la pointe du marteau lorsque la touche est abaissée, et la pousse avec le plus de vitesse possible contre les cordes. L'extrémité de ce crochet opposé à la dent est fixé à la touche par du parchemin, de manière cependant à pouvoir agir de haut en bas.

Q, faible ressort qui maintient le crochet dans un état élastique.

R, les marteaux avec leurs têtes; ils sont arrêtés aux châsses en cuivre *L* par des goupilles en acier taillées en pointe: la partie inférieure est garnie de peau.

S, ressort formé d'un fil de laiton, et portant une tête en peau destinée à empêcher les marteaux de toucher aux cordes plus souvent qu'ils ne doivent le faire.

T, barres bien garnies, contre lesquelles les marteaux viennent se reposer sans bruit.

U, chevalet à accorder les cordes.

V, le grand chevalet.

X, le petit chevalet.

Y, table de raisonnement.

Z, chevalet à cordes.

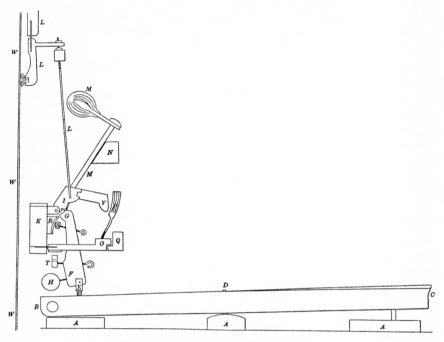

Fig. 18. Smart's repetition action, 1823.
From the patent.

The Action at Rest

A, A, A, part of the key frame. *B, C,* key in a state of rest. *D,* key pivot. *B,* balance
weight. *E,* metal regulating screw forming centre of motion for *F, G,* the hopper
(escapement). The screw *E* is for the purpose of raising or lowering the hopper
(escapement) to or from the hammer block *I* to compensate for contraction or expansion of the materials of which the lever or hammer block is composed. The hopper
is centred upon the screw *E* by means of a spring notch cut in the foot of the hopper.
G is the shoulder of the hopper which engages the under side of the hammer block.
H is a counter-weight. *K* is the hammer rail. *L, L, L* shows the damper rail with the
damper working in the usual way, assisted by a counter-weight of lead. *M, M* is the
hammer. *N,* a section of the hammer rail. *O,* the movable socket centred or hinged
in the hammer rail. This socket has an oblong perforation for the hopper *F, G* to pass
upwards through it, and into this socket is fixed a wire which carries *P,* a check piece.
Q is a transverse section of the socket rail lined to prevent noise. *R,* a similar section of
a rail faced with leather cloth, or buff, extending the whole length of the hammer
rail. *S,* a regulating button. *T* is a snail piece or eccentric button. By turning *S* upon
its axis so as to present a longer or shorter diameter of its curve to the under part of the
lever *O,* the exact period of the movement at which the check *P* performs its office
by catching the end of the hammer block at *V* is thereby determined. *W, W, W*
represents one of the wires of a pianoforte. (*Henry Smart, abridged and modified.*)

THE ACTION IN MOVEMENT

When the end of the key marked *C* is depressed by the finger of a performer the end *B* is elevated. The lever *F, G,* by moving the hammer block *I,* strikes the hammer on the string, and raises the damper in the usual way, when the regulating button *S,* rising against the wedge piece *R,* disengages the head of the lever from under the hammer block, also in the usual way; but at this period of the action the snail piece or eccentric button *T* having just risen into contact with the movable socket *O,* the said socket is thereby raised, and the check piece *P,* catching that extremity of the hammer block which is marked *V* at the moment when the hammer recoils from the string or wire, effectually prevents it falling against the rest *N,* or rebounding against the string *W, W, W.* At the same time the hammer block settles upon the shoulder of the lever at *G,* from which position the performer may repeat the blow without suffering the key to rise above half the space or distance hitherto allowed in lever actions, as the shoulder of the lever at *G* will propel the hammer against the wire, independent of the head or upper extremity of the said lever being allowed to return under the hammer block. When the pressure of the finger is removed from the end of the key marked *C,* the end *B* descends, the spiral or eccentric button *T* sinks about three-sixteenths of an inch or more below the socket lever *O,* which settles on the socket rail or rest *Q,* the hammer reclines upon the hammer rest *N,* and the counter-weight *H* draws the head of the lever again under the shoulder of the hammer block *I,* as more distinctly seen by the position of the movement, as shown in the illustration above. (*Henry Smart.*)

DESCRIPTION OF FIG. 19 (*opposite*).

Fig. 19. Eulriot's Lyre-shaped Pianoforte, 1834.

Dans ce nouvel instrument, j'ai nécessairement activé la promptitude de mes marteaux au moyen de six roulettes adaptées au mécanisme de chaque touche, ce qui n'existe dans aucun piano: l'artiste peut, dès lors, obtenir sur telle touche que ne soit la répétition d'une note avec autant de célérité qu'il peut le désirer; la roulette placée à l'extrémité de l'échappement a ce double avantage aussi de régler l'attaque des marteaux et, par sa mobilité, de ne point creuser la bascule qui règle l'échappement de hauteur, ce qui dans tout autre piano doit infailliblement arrêter ou, du moins, empêcher le jeu libre de ces marteaux; car il est reconnu que les ressorts sans roulettes, par leur frottement, se logent dans le bois, se forcent et s'atténuent, se cassent même, et que la touche devient inhabile: or, comme aucune roulette n'existe encore dans nul piano que le mien, que ces roulettes sont susceptibles de pouvoir être employées dans tout autre, de quelque forme qu'il puisse être, il y aurait usurpation de l'invention et, dès lors, contrefaçon là où des roulettes seraient employées soit en moindre ou en plus grand nombre.

Ce que je crois non moins important et à quoi je pense avoir réussi, c'est d'annuler la pesanteur de la contre-tension au moyen d'une troisième pointe que je place au centre et à l'opposé des deux autres, et que, par conséquent, je nomme contre-pointe centrale: j'ai pensé qu'un poids ou arrêt maintenant deux poids opposés en détruirait la puissance, empêcherait l'action du contre-tirage des cordes, et qu'alors la table d'harmonie, se trouvant ainsi allégée, serait à l'abri de toute variation; je suis donc encore l'inventeur de cette troisième pointe.

Renvoi aux dessins.

Pour le mécanisme des roulettes, voir le dessin Fig. 1.

Nos. 1, touches avec roulettes par derrière pour lever l'étouffoir; 2, échappements à roulettes; 3, marteaux avec ressorts à roulettes; 4, étouffoirs; 5, roulette pour faire échapper; 6, bascule pour régler l'échappement; 7, attrape-marteaux; 8, ressorts à roulettes pour ramener l'échappement à sa place.

Pour la troisième pointe, voir le dessin Fig. 2.

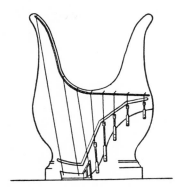

Fig . 1 .

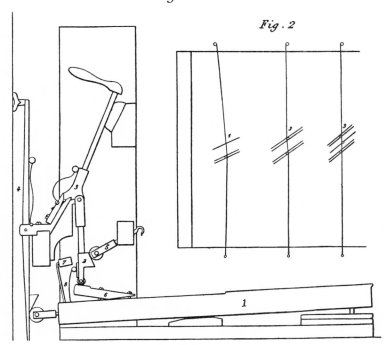

Fig . 2 .

Fig. 19.

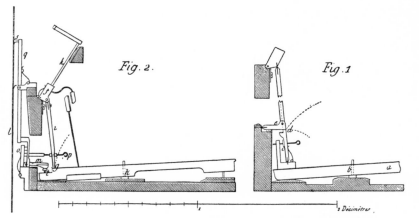

Fig. 20. Blanchet and Roller's Action for Upright Pianofortes, 1829.

La Fig. 1re représente la mécanique dont on s'est servi jusqu'à présent dans les pianos verticaux connus de différentes hauteurs.

La touche *a*, en basculant sur le point *b*, enlève l'échappement *c*; à chaque fois que l'action cesse, le ressort que porte l'échappement fait rentrer dans sa première position le point *d*, inhérent au point d'attaque du *chasse-marteau e*.

Si l'on observe le mouvement de la pièce *c*, on remarquera que le point *d* se meut de bas en haut et s'éloigne simultanément du point d'attaque, qui se confond avec lui dans l'état de repos.

Il est donc poussé, d'une part, au profit du mouvement que doit faire le marteau, et attiré, d'une autre part, suivant un arc de cercle dont le centre serait le point *b*, et dont le rayon serait la distance du point *b* au point *d*. Ce dernier mouvement est en pure perte dans l'action définitive, celle du marteau sur la corde.

Cette construction est doublement désavantageuse, sous le rapport de la force et de la vitesse, ce qu'il fallait démontrer.

Nouvel échappement

Le nouvel échappement diffère de tous ceux qu'on a fait jusqu'à présent; le pivot de la pièce qui pousse le marteau, ordinairement monté sur la touche, comme le montre la Fig. 1re, se trouve dans la noix du marteau *f*, Fig. 2e, et l'extrémité qui échappe est au bout de la touche en *g*, presque sur l'horizontale du point *h*, sur lequel elle bascule.

Lorsqu'on pose le doigt sur la touche, la pièce *i* s'élève et fait tourner le marteau *k* sur son pivot pour lui faire frapper la corde *l*; en même temps, elle soulève l'équerre *m*, par son extrémité inférieure, qui pousse la pièce *n*; cette pièce entraîne avec elle, au moyen de la petite pièce *o, p*, l'échappement *i*, qui s'y trouve fixé, par deux petites toupies, dans une broche taraudée.

L'extrémité inférieure de l'échappement *i* se trouve alors dans l'entaille *g*, et effectue l'isolement du marteau de la corde.

Derrière la pièce *n* est un ressort qui, à chaque fois que le doigt quitte la touche, repousse l'échappement à sa première position aussi souvent que le pianiste le plus habile peut l'exécuter.

Il est à remarquer que l'extrémité inférieure de l'échappement *i* décrit, dans cette mécanique, un arc si petit, que le résultat des deux forces qui le sollicitent, celle qui agit de bas en haut et celle qui l'attire, se confond pour ainsi dire avec l'une et l'autre.

La plus légère impulsion se communique tout entière au marteau, parce qu'il n'y a aucun intervalle entre les conducteurs.

Il y a donc moins de *vigueur* et de *prestesse* perdues que dans la mécanique usitée dans les pianos verticaux; c'est le but que nous nous étions proposé.

Étouffoir

L'équerre *m*, placée en avant de la pièce *n*, qui fait échapper, met en mouvement l'étouffoir; chaque fois qu'il bascule au moyen de la touche, la pièce *q* tourne sur son pivot *r*, et sa tête *s*, garnie de molleton, s'éloigne de la corde pour la laisser vibrer aussi longtemps que cette touche est enfoncée. La vis *t* sert à la régler.

Les étouffoirs, dans les pianos verticaux, sont montés ordinairement sur des bras d'équerre fort courts; dans ce cas, on conçoit que les têtes décrivent un arc de cercle très courbe, ce qui allonge et contrarie sensiblement leur marche. Les nouveaux étouffoirs n'ont pas ces inconvénients et sont très légers.

Attrape-marteau

Dans les meilleurs pianos verticaux, on ne met pas d'*attrape-marteaux* mécaniques destinés à empêcher le rebondissement du marteau sur la corde; quelques Anglais cependant en ont fait; mais leur système nécessite presque autant de pièces que les marteaux eux-mêmes avec les échappemens. Le marteau est rattrapé par le talon, comme dans les pianos horizontaux.

Celui *i*, Fig. 2e, que nous employons, est de la plus grande simplicité; il est logé sous le marteau, en dedans de la barre de repos, dont on voit la coupe derrière le marteau. Il se compose de deux branches de cuivre, dont l'une, courbée, est fixée après la noix du marteau, et dont l'autre, droit, sur la touche un peu inclinée.

Les extrémités de ces deux branches libres sont garnies de petits morceaux de bois plats recouverts en peau épaisse. Les mouvements contraires de la touche et du marteau, au milieu de l'action, font rapprocher ces deux petits morceaux de bois qui se serrent l'un contre l'autre. Rien de si facile que de régler cet attrape-marteau.

On règle aussi très aisément le nouvel échappement avec la petite broche de laiton *o, p*; en la vissant de gauche à droite, le marteau échappe à une plus grande distance de sa corde, et réciproquement.

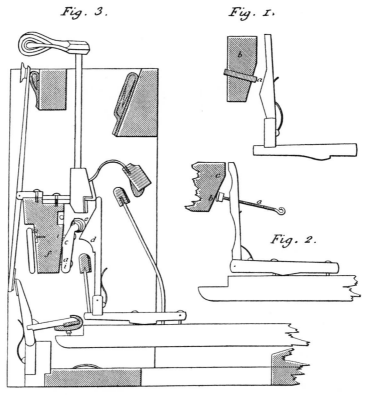

Fig. 21. Soufleto's Action for Upright Pianofortes, 1836.

The patent relates chiefly to the escapement. Before describing his own improvements Soufleto enumerates the defects of those in general use, beginning with the English. "L'un, dit anglais, représenté sous la fig. 1re, est composé d'une bande *a*, ajustée sur la pièce de bois *b*, que traverse une vis qui sert à régler l'échappement en avançant ou en reculant ladite pièce *b*.

"L'inconvénient que présente ce système réside d'abord dans la nécessité de démonter une partie du piano quand on veut régler l'échappement, puisque la vis au moyen de laquelle on le règle se trouve par derrière, et que dès lors on ne peut, en même temps, sans un grand dérangement, se rendre compte, par devant, de la chasse des marteaux; puis il résulte de ce mode un dérèglement plus facile dans l'échappement par la trop grande surface que présente la garniture; enfin l'échappement se faisant trop près du pivot du pilote, on n'obtient pas cette force nécessaire aux marteaux, ce qui ôte de la vigueur à leur jeu.

"L'autre système, Fig. 2e, adopté depuis quelque temps par un grand nombre de fabricants, ne présente pas les mêmes inconvénients, puisqu'au moyen de la tige à vis qui se trouve par devant on fait avancer ou reculer le bouton *b*, garni d'étoffe, qui représente pour l'effet la bande du système précédent; mais ce bouton n'étant pas stationnaire comme la bande, il en résulte que les secousses qu'il reçoit le font dévier de la tige, sur laquelle il est fixé, et que cette déviation amène quelquefois la courbure de la tige, que l'étoffe du bouton s'use plus facilement, ce qui fait crocher le marteau sur la corde; de plus, on conçoit que la pente de l'échappement offrant au bouton une résistance plus grande que dans le système précédent, l'inconvénient contraire a lieu, c'est-à-dire que le frottement des deux parties entre elles est plus dur, ce qui donne conséquemment de la dureté au jeu des marteaux.

"Éviter les inconvénients qui viennent d'être signalés et produire un échappement qui soit à la fois doux et résistant, tel est le problème que nous croyons avoir résolu par le système d'échappement à bascule que nous présentons ici, Fig. 3ᵉ; il consiste en une bascule en bois *a*, taillée, à son extrémité supérieure, en tête de marteau *b*, et garnie d'une double peau *c*, sur laquelle frotte le pilote d'échappement *d*. Cette bascule, qui appuie son milieu ou sa pointe d'angle *e* sur la traverse en bois *f*, est fixée à cette dernière par deux vis *i, i*, qui permettent d'avancer ou de reculer la tête de la bascule, sur laquelle a lieu l'échappement, de la manière la plus prompte et la plus facile, puisque les vis sont sur le devant du mécanisme: de cette manière, le règlement du pilote s'obtient au degré voulu, et la forme ronde de la tête de la bascule offre l'avantage d'un jeu à la fois doux et ferme pour les marteaux qu'on peut ainsi régler d'une manière sûre et commode.

"En résumé, ce système d'échappement repose sur l'emploi d'une pièce ajustée en forme de bascule, et portant, à son extrémité supérieure, une partie arrondie en forme de tête de marteau de piano sur laquelle glisse le pilote d'échappement: c'est la contre-partie de l'échappement rendue mobile par l'emploi du système de bascule. Ce système peut être exécuté de différentes manières: le mode d'exécution présenté ici donne un exemple de cette application, qui peut varier, quant à la forme de la bascule, à la manière dont elle fonctionne ou dont elle est fixée. L'inventeur soussigné revendique ici l'application du principe qui fait la base de son procédé, c'est-à-dire l'emploi du système de bascule aux échappements des pianos."

DESCRIPTION OF FIG. 22 (*on following page*).

Fig. 22. A section of Steward's Euphonicon, 1841.

Drawn from the patent.

Section of the Screw Bar and Tension Bar as shown in Fig. 1. *A*, screw bar; *B*, screws of the screw bar; *C*, nuts of the screws; *D*, hooks for the attachment of loops; *E*, loop wires; *F*, loop hook for the attachment of the string; *G*, the tension bar; *H*, polished surface of tension bar; *I* represents one of the tenons of the tension bar; *J*, groove into which the screw bar is placed. The screw bar is fixed immediately before the tension bar, in an oblique manner, with the lower back angle resting in a groove in the tension bar, and secured at each end by tenons that pass through the side supporters of the frame and fixed by the screw nuts. The screw bar is three inches and a half deep, one inch and a half wide and four feet long, and is perforated with one hundred and seventy square holes, forming seven octaves. Each hole is a quarter of an inch in diameter, passing direct through the bar, and (the holes) are arranged in two rows, an upper and a lower row, and each hole is a quarter of an inch from the other. The holes are for the reception of the screws. I resort to one of three modes of making this bar. First, by using a solid piece of iron drilled through the substance. The holes, at first being round, are made a quarter of an inch square. Or I procure three pieces of wrought iron, all of equal length and depth, as before, but different in thickness, two pieces being a quarter of an inch thick for the outside pieces, and the other or middle portion one inch thick. These bars are made perfectly smooth by planing or otherwise. The middle bar is then marked out on each side, and grooved out at equal distances, each groove describing three sides of a square. The two outside pieces of iron are then fixed by means of screws, which will complete this bar, with the requisite square holes therein. Or I use two pieces of iron of the size of

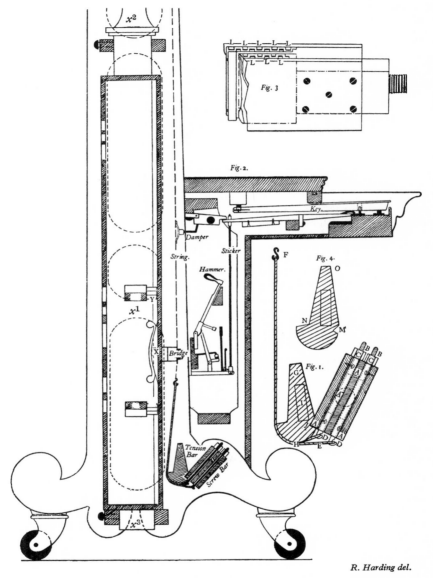

R. Harding del.

Fig. 22. Stewart's Euphonicon, 1841 (*description*, p. 257).
Drawn from the patent.

the two outside pieces just described, marked out in spaces a quarter of an inch from each other. On these marks are screwed brass or tin grooves, three and a half inches deep, corresponding with the depth of the bar. These grooves are stamped out of tin plates or formed in brass, and are all made of the same size, so that when screwed on the bars at equal distances they represent square holes a quarter of an inch in diameter. The other outside bar is arranged in the same manner, each having eighty-five brass or tin grooves, and when both are fastened together by means of a piece of iron at either end, forming tenons to be fastened on the side supporters, as is shown at Fig. 2, the two bars are joined together, as is shown at Fig. 3. The tin or brass grooves (L, L) range alternately so that they do not come opposite each other, leaving a space between the two bars. This space is filled up with melted tin or other suitable metal.

Section of the Tension Bar as shown in Fig. 4. M, groove in which the screw bar is fixed; N, polished surface, describing the segment of a circle, where the loops pass round and move in drawing the wires up to pitch; O, upper portion of the bar. The tension bar is placed at the bottom part of the frame in front, extending from side to side, and is firmly fixed at the two ends by tenons. This bar is three inches deep, one inch wide at the top part, gradually becoming thicker at the lower part, where it increases to one inch and a half. The lower part describes the segment of a circle, which is polished for the purpose of facilitating the motion of the loops on that surface when drawing up the strings. The screws of the screw bar are one hundred and seventy in number (seven octaves), and are placed in the square holes of the screw bar, each screw serving for a single wire or string.

The Sound-boards. The three sound-boards together consist of twenty-one bars and forty-two sound posts or supporters. The treble sound-board consists of a Swiss deal board on the inner side of which are adapted seven bars x, Fig. 2, at equal distances. The bars are sprung on the sound-board at either extremity and fixed by glue and pressure, producing a rotundity on the outer surface of the sound-board somewhat like the belly of a Violoncello. A wood frame x^1, fitted to the treble compartment of the iron frame, is now made with two side parts, a top and a bottom, with a block x^2 fixed above in the centre of the top rail and two others x^3 on the bottom by means of screws. To the front edge of the frame is fixed the sound-board. On the back edges of the frame is glued the back. Both the back and sides are perforated for the transmission of sound and the sound-board itself has two sound holes.

To the extreme edge of each bar x is fixed a round sound post y. These sound posts are fixed into a rail x which passes across the termination of the bars. The Tenor and Bass sound-boards are constructed precisely in the same manner but proportionately increasing in size. (*Description of the Screw and Tension bar: Dr John Steward, abridged.*)

CHAPTER II

SOME OTHER TYPES OF PIANOFORTES
IN THE HOME

WHERE space was not a matter of consideration the horizontal grand pianoforte was the most serviceable for the home, since it was the best both for solo and accompanying work. The grand was made in several sizes but the most usual was the 'Bichord grand', an instrument with two unisons to a note and about 213·4 cm. long and 129·5 cm. broad; a smaller size that seems also to have been greatly used was the semi-grand, an instrument about 162·6 cm. long; and a still smaller size was made by Kirkman and Co. and exhibited by them at the Great Exhibition of 1851; this pianoforte was only about 124·5 cm. long and 86·4 cm. broad.

In Germany there was also an intermediate form between the square and the grand, known as the 'Querflügel'. This type of instrument was based originally upon the form of the spinet but was subsequently developed until it became, in the larger examples, almost of 'Grand' proportions and somewhat ungainly in appearance.

It is not proposed to dwell long upon the square pianoforte, since it fades into insignificance beside the grand and the small upright pianoforte in the nineteenth century; though Herz preferred it to the upright. In his pianoforte school he advises the pupil concerning the choice of a pianoforte thus:

The *grand piano* is preferable to all others, from its construction and quality of tone. If this be unattainable in the absence of a grand, I should recommend the *square piano*, whose tones should be rather sweet and soft, than brilliant, and the mechanism of a perfect equality. I do not approve of the *upright piano* except as a second instrument, or for accompaniments.[1]

With the increased compass that became a necessity owing to the demands of both pianists and composers the square pianoforte was necessarily lengthened, whilst the heavier strings, and the high pitch to which they were strained owing to the loud tone that was demanded by pianists, made the use of metal braces and eventually of an iron frame essential.

[1] B 101, p. 9.

The bass strings of the early nineteenth-century square piano-fortes were usually overspun, but this overspinning was not close as in the case of the wire used for the bass strings of grand piano-fortes and the core wire is easily seen. The usual type of bass string consisted of a core of brass wire with a thin covering wire of copper. In strings of high quality this covering wire was plated with a protective coating of silver[1] (Fig. 23). We have also ob-

Fig. 23. Pianoforte string about 1812. [About × 3.]

served bass strings in which, instead of a brass core wire, a core of steel wire is used. Whether these strings are an intermediate stage between the old loosely spun strings and the modern close covered ones, where a steel core is always used, or merely a string of inferior quality it is impossible to say. The later square pianofortes had close covered strings consisting of a core wire of steel covered with a copper wire.

The sound-board was also improved and extended in area to enhance the vibrations of these more powerful strings, and in some squares it extended from end to end of the instrument. Petzold seems to have been the first to make experiments in this direction.

The action was eventually completed by the addition of a check piece. A curious check action was invented by Broadwood in 1825 where the hammer carries a projection like a beak below its head. The Érards also used this action, for it is illustrated in their book, *Perfectionnements apportés dans le mécanisme du piano par les Érard, depuis l'origine de cet instrument jusqu'à l'Exposition de* 1834 (Fig. 24).

The English Double Action, with or without check, appears to have been the usual action employed in this country, but the Grand Action was used occasionally. Pleyel et Cie used a modification of the English Grand Action for their square pianofortes, but the Petzold Action already illustrated and Érard's 'Mécanisme à double pilotes' appear to have been the favourite types of action, according to Montal, for French pianofortes.

Pleyel et Cie seem to have been the first to modify the system of over dampers by placing the dampers in a separate frame which could easily be unscrewed to enable them to be removed

[1] For an analysis of the composition and density of bass strings of this type see D (3), p. 368.

for repairs. This form of damper is a modification of the over dampers ('Hebeldämpfung') that are to be seen on most of the

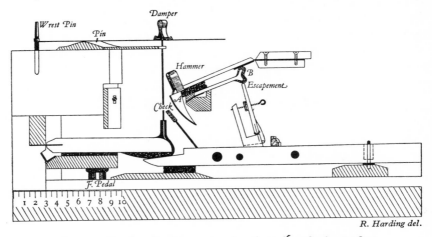

R. Harding del.

Fig. 24. Check action for square pianoforte, Érard, about 1825.
Drawn from Plate VII, B 39.
A, projection against which the check works; *B*, intermediate lever.

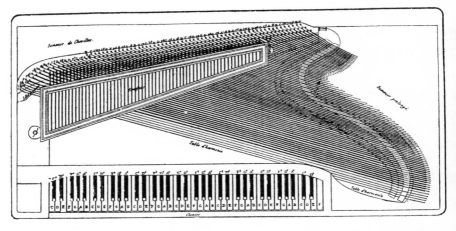

Fig. 25. Square pianoforte with dampers in a frame which can be unscrewed to enable them to be removed and with extended hitch-pin block in metal. B 70 (*a*), Pl. II.

early English squares by makers such as Zumpe and Pohlmann, Beck and others of this period. They were characteristic of the German square pianofortes, which had been made by the early

German makers and their pupils in England at the time when our pianofortes were being exported to France. But these dampers were permanently hinged to the back of the frame, which made it difficult to remove them for repairs; Pleyel's new arrangement avoided this difficulty (Fig. 25).

The first repetition action for the square pianoforte was designed by Érard in 1808 and was the 'Mécanisme à Étrier' already described. In 1827 Érard invented another which, though it was patented for 'horizontal' pianofortes, was really intended for the square. It is interesting that Érard thought the square sufficiently important to invent a special repetition action for it.

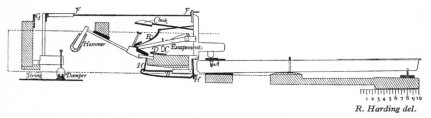

R. Harding del.

Fig. 26. Tape-check down-striking action by Robert Wornum, 1844.
The drawing represents the action for f'''' (compass F₁ to f'''').

A, screw to regulate the touch; *B*, spring to raise the hammer from the strings; *C*, button regulating the play of the escapement; *D*, felt; *E*, tape; *F, F*, damper wire; *G*, felt; *H, H*, two leather straps through which the spring *B* is passed.

It will be remembered that George Pether of London had invented a down-striking action for a square pianoforte towards the end of the eighteenth century. We find this type of action frequently used in the nineteenth century. Kollmann was the first in England to patent it.[1] Robert Wornum invented a tape-check down-striking action which he used in his Albion square pianofortes, table-shaped instruments of six octaves, F₁ to f'''' (Fig. 26).

This seems to have been a modification of his down-striking actions patented in 1842.[2]

Henri Pape was the greatest advocate of the down-striking action and it is consequently to be found in his square pianofortes. These instruments, owing to their artistic merits, are almost the only late square pianofortes that are accessible to the public in museums. There is, however, a fine series of late American squares at New York and Messrs John Broadwood and Sons possess two

[1] C 43.   [2] C 144.

late English examples, one of which belonged to the Prince Consort and the other to Sir Edward Elgar.

The English square pianoforte, formerly the Prince Consort's, has only "one pedal; the damper pedal or forte". This was the usual custom with the later pianoforte makers in England, and may be accounted for by the fact that the 'Pianoforte Schools' of Clementi, Hummel and Czerny were well known in England. Czerny wrote in his work that Mozart and Clementi never used the pedals, since they were not invented in their day; in this statement about the pedals not having been invented Czerny is historically incorrect; but the important point that emerges from this is that Mozart and Clementi evidently did not *appear* to use them. Hummel and Czerny had in fact really very little use for any but the damper or forte pedal.

The difficulty of fitting a sliding keyboard to the square pianoforte precluded the use of the Una Corda.

Thus England, once it was emancipated from the influence of its earlier pianoforte makers of German origin, came under the influence of the celebrated Clementi who had chosen to adopt England as his home, and, swayed by the authoritative works of Hummel and Czerny, dispensed with all but the 'damper' or forte pedal in her square pianofortes. France, on the other hand, at first fitted her squares with several pedals but Pape seems eventually to have used 'forte', and 'piano' by shortening the radius of the blow of the hammer; he used this type of 'piano' as early as 1836.

Pianofortes adapted to domestic utility. Where space was very limited in the home makers rose to the occasion by adapting the pianoforte to 'domestic utility'. Pfeiffer et Petzold invented a triangular pianoforte in 1806 to fit into the corner of a room, Eulriot, another French maker, made pianofortes in the form of oval tables, while Greiner, Pape and Fischer made them in the form of oval or round or hexagonal tables and intended to be used as such in the drawing-room. These circular or hexagonal instruments, and in fact most table pianofortes, had down-striking actions to economise space.

The 'piano-secrétaire' was intended for the ladies' boudoir whilst the pianoforte in the form of a flat writing table was well adapted for the composer's study, since he could play his music without disturbing his papers.

Massenet owned such a pianoforte; it is now preserved at the

Musée de l'Opéra at Paris. Pleyel et Cie made a small one after an old pattern for Ambroise Thomas; it is now at their House at Paris.

There were also pianofortes for the bedroom; for example a piano in the form of a chest of drawers was made by Friederici.[1] In later years this adaptation of the pianoforte to domestic utility was carried to an astonishing length, as will be seen by the following quotation:

> The piano, in place of being supported by legs in the ordinary manner, is supported by a frame which again rests upon a hollow base; inside such hollow base is placed a couch, which is mounted upon rollers and can be drawn out in front of the piano; the front surface of the couch when slid inside the base forming the front side thereof. . . . A hollow space is formed in the middle of the frame for rendering the pedals accessible to the performer's feet, and on one side of such space is formed a closet, having doors opening in front of the piano, and which is designed to contain the bed clothes. On the other side of the space so formed, firstly, a bureau with drawers, and secondly, another closet for containing a wash-hand basin, jug, towels and other articles of toilet. The bureau and second closet are made to open at the end of the frame, the front surface of that part of the latter being formed with false drawers to correspond in appearance with the doors of the before-mentioned closet on the other side of the space. . . .
>
> Another part of the invention consists in constructing a music stool which is so arranged that in addition it contains a work-box, a looking glass, a writing desk or table, and a small set of drawers. [Millward, 1866 (Eng. Pat. 1806).]

The drawing-room probably contained a 'work-box piano', a little pianoforte with diminutive keys introduced into a work-box which was sometimes placed upon a stand.

This was not, of course, intended as a serious instrument, in any case its compass of about three octaves was too restricted; it was probably introduced as an elegant finish or ornament to the work-box. The young lady could amuse herself between threading her needles or console herself, when she pricked her finger, with a little tune. Another diminutive instrument with about three to three and a half octaves and keys of the usual size may have been intended for children, but it has been called in England the 'Conductor's piano' because Sir George Smart owned one which he is said always to have carried with him in his coach (Plate XIII). A cabinet pianoforte with a frame of musical glasses that was clearly intended for the home was patented by John Day in 1816.

[1] Leipzig, No. 130.

The glasses were arranged so that they could be played at the same time as the pianoforte or uncoupled and played alone. These glasses were similar to those of the Franklin 'Armonica', except that they were not passed through a trough of water as their tone was produced by a blow from a hammer instead of by the friction of a finger.[1] The musical glasses became popular in the first place owing to Gluck's proficiency on them when they were yet in the primitive form of a set of drinking glasses tuned by pouring more or less water into them; and in the second place owing to Fanny Davis' great proficiency on the instrument as improved by Franklin, who placed a series of glass bowls graded in size on a rod to produce the notes of the ordinary musical scale. A trough of water was fixed below the glasses by which they were lubricated whilst the tone was produced by the friction of the player's finger on the glasses when revolved by a treadle.

The square, grand, upright and table pianofortes are the types of instruments that we should have been most likely to have seen in the drawing-room of the average amateur of this period (1801–1851); and if we were not particularly well acquainted with the science of pianoforte construction, we might have wondered how it was that the tone of these smaller pianofortes was so loud and sonorous. The amateur, gratified by our admiration, would, no doubt, have informed us with pride that his instrument was fitted with Mr So-and-So's newly invented patent double sounding board on the principle of the violin, or Mr Somebody-else's parchment board drawn up upon a half-sphere "in like manner as a kettle-drum". In fact the pianoforte makers resorted to the most extraordinary experiments in order to obtain sonority and a loud tone in their instruments; for instance the grand pianoforte exhibited by Greiner at the Great Exhibition of 1851.

This instrument is described in Greiner's prospectus as being on the "principle of the speaking trumpet" and of having the strings fixed on the "principle of the tuning fork". As no adequate explanation of this is given by Greiner we quote Pole's description of this pianoforte:

Its strings lie in two planes, slightly inclined to the horizontal, and to each other, and intersecting at the front end of the instrument; their further ends opening out into something like the shape of a trumpet. The idea of the inventor is, that this shape will throw the sound out horizontally, and make the instrument better heard than on the ordinary plan.... Mr Greiner also

[1] This invention could also be applied to a square or grand pianoforte.

Plate XIII. A 'Conductor's Pianoforte' (in the possession of
Messrs John Broadwood and Sons, and formerly of Sir George Smart).
Length 92 cm., breadth 42·6 cm., depth with the lid open 18 cm. Brace string plate.
Vibrating length of the longest string 72·9 cm. and of the shortest 9·3 cm.

exhibits a model of a new method of stringing, by which two strings are made to vibrate by a blow given to one only, on the same principle as the synchronous vibrations of the two arms of a tuning fork.[1]

But most of these experiments relate to the sound-board and seem to be influenced by the violin and allied instruments, and the kettle-drum.

The principle of the kettle-drum adapted to the sound-board of the pianoforte. The effect of the 'Turkish Taste' in every department of music was mentioned in Part II, § 1. The introduction of the *sound* of the drum into pianofortes was then discussed; but the *form* also of the drum had a distinct influence on the construction of the pianoforte.

The parchment head with the screws for tightening or loosening it, and finally the copper bowl itself, were used by makers for the purpose of improving the tone of their instruments.

In 1788 Clagget[2] suggested that a frame covered with parchment or vellum should be used to preserve the strings from dust and to improve the tone. Rolfe and Davis,[3] in their pianoforte or harpsichord with drum pedal of the year 1797, state that the principle of their invention consists in "substituting a vibrating substance in the body of the instruments in lieu of the sounding board hitherto made of wood". It might consist of the "skin or skins of an animal or animals dressed or manufactured after the manner of vellum or parchment; or of silk, wood, hemp, flax, cotton, thread, or such kind of substance woven and manufactured; or of paper pasted together or manufactured in the manner of pasteboard; and such substances [might] either be varnished, oiled, papered", etc. A frame of wood or metal was to be constructed and to this frame the "vibrating substance" was to be secured with "glue and tacks". The frame was movable at each corner and could be extended or contracted by means of a mortise and tenon so as to "enlarge or make tight the vibrating body by means of screws...with nuts...so as to render the vibrating body tight to sustain the weight of the strings and produce the sound or tone required".

Another application of the same idea is found in Wheatstone's "Method of Improving and Augmenting the Tones of Pianofortes",[4] etc., patented in 1824. This 'method' consisted in "covering as much of the external surface as possible with frames formed either of wood or other fit and proper materials...", these

---

[1] B 81, p 28.   [2] C 1033.   [3] C 1034.   [4] C 1159.

frames were to be "covered on both sides with thin elastic, flexible, vibrating substances tightly stretched over them, such as vellum, parchment, or other animal membranes, paper, canvas, woven silk, linen", etc., and were to be "placed as nearly as possible to the strings...", and by reverberating the vibrations from the strings between the two flexible surfaces "through the agency of the columns of air therein interposed, greatly to improve the quality of the tones produced".

In 1850 Cadby[1] relieved the sound-board from the downward pressure of the strings by "so adapting [it] to the instrument that the former being wholly or partially detached from permanent connection with the framework and suspended therefrom by metallic or other attachments may be strained or tightened when desired" and removed for repairs when necessary. The clamps held the board firmly whilst it was being tightened by means of tightening screws at the opposite side. Dr Wood suggests that by means of this arrangement of being able to tighten or slacken the sound-board it would be possible to brighten the tone of the instrument in any register where it might be weak. This would be especially valuable in the upper octaves since they were used so much by composers.

In 1825 Étienne Eulriot[2] patented an elliptical-shaped pianoforte with a circular sound-board at each end. It was believed that the circular board received and transmitted the vibrations more regularly than the square or oblong variety, and thus improved the tone.

In the circular or hexagonal table pianofortes of Greiner, Pape, and Fischer intended to be used in the drawing-room is exemplified not only the use of the adaptation of the kettle-drum head to the pianoforte but also of the copper bowl itself.

The adaptation of the copper bowl of the kettle-drum to the pianoforte is perhaps the most astonishing experiment that has been tried upon this instrument.

The idea seems to have first occurred to Georges Frédéric Greiner, who patented it in connection with Danchell and the

---

[1] C 1075. Pole, describing Cadby's pianofortes in the Great Exhibition of 1851, makes the following remarks: "In the ordinary instruments, the edges of the sound-board are glued firmly to the framing of the instrument. The patentee (Cadby) considers this has the effect of destroying the brilliancy of the tone, owing to the fact that the sound-board is not strained tight; he therefore secures it to the framework solely by metal clamps, in such a manner as to admit of its being strained and tightened when desired, like the parchment head of a drum". Cadby charged from £10 to £15. 15s. for his patent sound-boards. B 82, p. 25.   [2] C 872.

Plate XIV. Pianoforte by Broadwood, about 1835. Brussels, Musée du
Conservatoire Royal de Musique, No. 3291.

The dip in the middle is probably to enable the performer to be seen and to permit
his voice to carry into the room. Height 1·27 m., breadth 1·18 m.

brothers Ruedorfer[1] in Austria on May 2nd, 1834. In August of the same year he was granted a French patent for it in connection with Danchell[2] (Fig. 27).

Henri Pape then took up the idea, and on November 22nd of the same year patented a circular pianoforte with the sound-board in the form of a kettle-drum.[3] He used the copper bowl and strained the wooden sound-board over it by means of a fringe of parchment arranged in a metal rim in such a way that it could be tightened or loosened by means of screws (Fig. 28).

In the following year Pierre Fischer obtained an English patent for a "parchment board drawn up on a half sphere in like manner as a kettle-drum"[4] and fixed under the case by iron screws. This is evidently an adaptation of Pape's patent of the previous year.

Dr Wood informs me that the result of the use of the copper bowl as a resonator would be "free and forced vibrations in the resonator which would be centred round its natural pitch, but the response would not be at all sharp and the result would probably be distributed resonance giving general strengthening of the bass".

Another series of experiments to the sound-board, which related chiefly to the square and upright pianoforte, was clearly inspired by the violin and allied instruments.

The principle of the violin adapted to the sound-board of the pianoforte. Naturally when a more responsive resonance body was needed for the pianoforte the musical instrument maker began to think of his fiddles.

They consisted of two resonance boards—a back and a table or belly—joined together by ribs and connected with a sound post. The table was pierced with holes for the emission of the sound. Why should he not put two boards into the pianoforte and connect them with a sound post, and even join them with ribs as in the violin?

This is in fact what he actually did. John Broadwood seems to have been the first to try this experiment in 1783. He fixed "a sounding post, that communicated the sound to a sounding board, of the same thickness and quality as that on which the bridge is fixed [the upper one], . . .withinside the instrument about an inch above the bottom thereof".[5] Johann Anders,[6] an instrument maker in Vienna, patented a pianoforte in 1824 which was to have two sound-boards separated from each other by the distance of an inch. One was to be straight and the other curved.

[1] C 1107.   [2] C 1108.   [3] C 1109.
[4] C 1111.   [5] C 1113.   [6] C 1080.

As a knowledge of acoustics was gained and the fact known that metal was not deleterious to the tone but on the contrary was extremely responsive owing to its high rate of sound propagation, the patentee sometimes suggests that the sound post or one of the sound-boards should be made of metal. Thus Gunther in his patent of 1828 for a square pianoforte with two sound-boards states that "the said upper sounding board is made of wood or *metal*" and again it is "supported by and rests upon a prop, pillar or *block of metal*, wood or other material". The upper board is thicker than the lower and both are to be connected by means of a rim if the lower board is to be as large as usual. "It must run under my thick or upper sounding board, the two boards being about a quarter of an inch asunder, and in this case they must be united together by a strip or border of wood glued or otherwise fastened all round the under side of the edge of the upper sounding board, . . .in order that the two may be united and vibrate together."[1]

The influence of the violin is again evident in Wheatley Kirk's upright pianoforte with two sound-boards, patented in 1836.[2] "The double sounding board. . .is constructed of and from the usual wood. . .but [it] is enclosed on all sides similar to a *violin* and in the form of a case. It is uniform in its thickness or depth of unoccupied space; it is free and independent of any direct and attach'd connection with the frame, into which it fits. . . . The apertures . . . are for the same purpose as what are called sound holes in the *violin*, namely to give full scope or emission to the tone and its vibration."

Johann Pottje's[3] pianoforte of 1842 was to have two sound-boards, each strengthened with thirteen ribs. The vibrations from the bridge of the upper board were to be transmitted to the lower board by means of another bridge which joined the two. Swan's grand pianoforte, which he designed in 1849, was to be fitted with a 'sounding case' in which there were to be a suitable number of sound holes to allow for the free escape of the sound.[4] Another development of this idea consisted in using several sound-boards together. Lepère patented this in 1844.[5]

The reader will have noticed that Broadwood allows considerable space between his two sound-boards and so also does Wheatley Kirk. Johann Anders and Gunther, on the other hand, separate their boards by a small space. There can be little doubt that they

[1] C 1084.   [2] C 1101.   [3] C 1116.
[4] C 1112.   [5] C 1091.

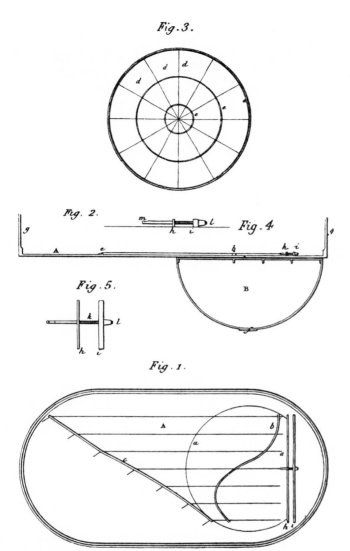

Fig. 27. Danchell and Greiner's pianoforte with hemispherical resonator, 1834.

Nous nous sommes assurés, par de nombreux essais, que la valeur plus ou moins grande d'un piano dépend particulièrement de la construction du corps résonnant et de la manière dont il est uni avec les autres parties de l'instrument; nous avons trouvé aussi que le corps résonnant remplit le mieux sa destination lorsqu'il a la forme d'un hémisphère, Fig. 2ᵉ B, et se trouve muni d'un couvercle ou table, Fig. 3ᵉ, composé de plusieurs triangles acutangles égaux d, et pourvu de côtés orbiculaires, Figs. 2ᵉ et 3ᵉ. e. Ce corps résonnant, avec son couvercle, ne doit être aucunement en contact avec la table, et ne doit être attaché à l'instrument que par le point le plus bas de l'hémisphère, Fig. 2ᵉ, qui forme en même temps le point de repos acoustique.

Toutes les oscillations que les cordes sonnantes communiquent au couvercle rond du corps résonnant se propagent en vibrations radiées à la péripherie de ce couvercle, et de là elles se propagent à l'hémisphère (ou caisse qui forme le corps résonnant) en oscillations qui se font toutes à une égale distance du point de repos de cet hémisphère.

Par ce moyen on obtient la plus parfaite égalité de tons, depuis le plus bas jusqu'au

are considering the column of air and its influence upon the volume and quality of the sound. Henri Pape was clearly thinking on the same lines when in 1845 [1] he devised a method for increasing or varying the sound by means of regulating the column of air.

I will now describe my method of varying and increasing the sound in musical instruments by means of regulating the volume of air, which consists in the pianoforte of a mode of applying to each side of the sounding board a second board the size of the sounding board; the space between can be regulated according to the nature of tone required, that is to say, a greater space for the bass than the treble, and also according to the quality of tone desired. This improvement may be applied to almost all musical instruments....

In my Console Piano... I place behind the surface of the sounding board a single board or table, which is capable of opening or closing. For a good quality of tone I leave a space for the bass part of about four inches, and two inches for the treble; the space being increased or diminished from one extremity to the other will produce a perfect forte or piano.

Dr John Steward used what are virtually three sound boxes pierced with forte holes and exposed to view for his Euphonicon Pianoforte patented in 1841.[2] Another instance showing the influence of the violin, and also in this case of the lute, is to be seen in Wolf's "new construction on the principle of acoustics, of a sounding body applicable to every description of pianofortes" (Fig. 29). This sounding body is a "shell of curvilinear shape" which seems clearly to have been suggested by the resonance body of some stringed musical instrument.

[1] C 818.
[2] C 874. Other examples: (a) Victoria and Albert Museum, London; (b) Deutsches Museum, Munich.

---

plus haut, de manière qu'en appliquant notre principe et en suivant constamment les mêmes règles on peut donner à tous les pianos à construire la même valeur intrinsèque, parce que le corps résonnant a une existence isolée et indépendante des parties qui l'entourent ordinairement. On peut pratiquer dans le couvercle du corps résonnant une ouverture (ouïe); mais, comme cela ne procure aucune utilité, il ne vaut pas la peine de le faire.

Les Figs. 1re et 2e, A, représentent une plaque de métal qui sert de table et qui est pourvue d'une ouverture au-dessus de laquelle les cordes sont tendues; ces dernières sont mises en rapport avec la table par le chevalet b, Figs. 1re et 2e. g figure les parois de l'instrument.

DESCRIPTION DE L'APPAREIL POUR ACCORDER LE PIANO

Les Figs. 1re et 2e, h, i, sont deux listels en saillie. k (Fig. 5e) est une vis munie de son écrou l (Figs. 4e et 5e). En tournant l'écrou avec sa clef, la vis se met en mouvement et attire la corde qui est attachée à l'endroit m. Le listel h sert à diriger cette vis de manière qu'elle ne se retourne pas, et à cet effet la vis a été aplatie au moyen d'une lime. Nous nous dispenserons d'entrer ici dans des détails sur les grands avantages que présente cet appareil, tels que, entre autres, sa solidité, la facilité de s'en servir, la grande exactitude d'accord qu'il permet de donner au piano, la longue durée de l'accord qu'on obtient par son moyen; car tous ces avantages seront aisément compris par tous ceux qui connaissent la méthode ordinaire d'accorder.

Fig. 1.

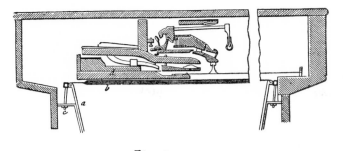

Fig. 2.

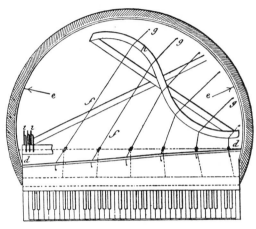

Fig. 3.

Fig. 28. Pape's pianoforte with resonator in the form of a copper bowl, 1834.

Fig. 1re. *a*, demi-boule en cuivre semblable à une timbale, sur laquelle est tendue la table *b* par un bord en parchemin introduit entre les deux épaisseurs de la table; ce bord en parchemin est monté et serré par la vis *c* sur la demi-boule de la même manière qu'une timbale; des barrages légers sont employés pour empêcher la table de rompre en la serrant: le tout est fixé dessous la caisse par des équerres en fer. *d*, sommier de fonte auquel aboutit un cercle de fer *e*, qui passe dans l'intérieur de la caisse et est destiné à opposer résistance au tirage des cordes, ainsi qu'il est indiqué sur le plan Fig. 2e.

Fig. 2e. Plan présentant les cordes *f* attachées au sommier en fonte *d*. *g*, chevilles. *h*, chevalet traversé par des barres. *i*, ressort sonore monté sur un sommier en fer qui communique avec la table d'harmonie : il est destiné à remplacer les cordes des basses dans le cas où, par leur peu de longueur, elles ne produiraient pas le volume de son nécessaire. Le clavier rentre comme un tiroir, lorsqu'on veut fermer le piano.

Fig. 3e. La Fig. 3e présente l'instrument en élévation.

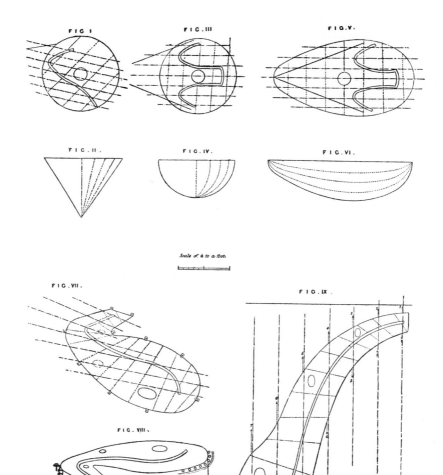

FIG.I   FIC.III   FIG.V.

FIC.II.   FIC.IV.   FIG.VI.

Scale of ¼ to a foot.

FIG.VII.   FIG.IX.

FIC.VIII.

FIG.X

Fig. 29.

DESCRIPTION OF FIG. 29 (*opposite*).

Fig. 29. Wolf's Sounding Cases. From the patent.

My Invention consists in substituting a hollow receptacle or shell of a curvilinear shape, which I call a sounding body, in lieu of the usual sounding board of pianofortes. The precise shape of the sounding body is not material provided the sides be curvilinear... I consider the shapes shown by Figs. vii and ix better than the funnel shape, the hemisphere, or the ellipse or longitudinal section of an egg, shown in the drawings Figs. i, iii, v, and their respective sections ii, iv, vi. The upper part of these several sounding bodies I call the sounding board, in which a sounding hole must be made, but in the form shown by Figs. vii and ix at least three sounding holes had better be made, as shown by the oval blank line and also the oval dotted line in those Figures, but the sounding holes shown by the dotted lines may be made either in the sounding board or in the bottom of the sounding body. The bodies or shelves in the cone or funnel shape, and also in the hemispherical shape, and in the elliptic or longitudinal section of an egg, are to be made of veneers of maple wood, sycamore wood, or hare wood, or any other wood of similar nature, such as is generally used for the bodies of *guitars, violins*, or other similar musical instruments, which veneers should not exceed in thickness one tenth of an inch, and should be cut into triangular pieces for the cone shape, and into ribs or gores for the other two shapes, similar to the pieces of silk or other substances forming an air balloon, and as shown by the dotted lines in Figs. ii, iv and vi.... The sounding bodies... Figs. vii and ix are to be constructed as follows.... make a strong mould or frame of wood on the plan used by guitar makers,... in which the sides of the sounding body are to be framed or curved by bending.... When found necessary the bending may be assisted by the application of steam or warm water, after the well known manner in use among makers of *guitars* and *violins*.... The sounding board, which is to be of the usual thickness of sounding boards for pianofortes, is to be made of soft wood with a straight grain (Swiss belly wood, of which sounding boards of pianofortes are usually made, being preferred) and the grain of the wood should run parallel to the direction of the strings.... Fig. vii is intended for a square horizontal pianoforte, and Fig. ix is intended for an upright or for a horizontal grand pianoforte. It is necessary that these sounding bodies should regularly decrease in depth as well as in width from the part where the larger or bass strings pass over to the part where the shorter or treble strings pass over, the decrease in depth always taking place in lines parallel with the strings, the depth being equal on both sides the shell or sounding body at the same string, and thus decrease in depth and width, as shown in Fig. ix and Fig. x.

(*Robert Wolf, abridged.*)

CHAPTER III

PEDAL, TRANSPOSING AND SELF-ACTING PIANO-FORTES, EXPERIMENTAL KEYBOARDS

PEDAL PIANOFORTES. Another type of pianoforte that might have been found in a composer's study is the pedal pianoforte. G. F. Rutscher and Johann Rueff obtained a Bavarian patent for *improvements* in pedal pianofortes as early as 1825,[1] and this seems to indicate that pedal keys had been used in connection with pianofortes at an early date. Joseph Böhm was granted an Austrian patent in 1837[2] for an instrument with a pedal board of twenty-two keys connected with the ordinary finger keys by rods or trackers. As the pedal notes corresponded with those produced by the ordinary keys, no special stringing was necessary. In order to obtain very deep bass notes Benjamin Nickels, an English maker, in 1845[3] patented a method of fixing additional strings combined with an action worked by the feet. Pierre Érard also obtained an English patent for a "new set of pedal keys applied to grand pianofortes for sounding certain bass notes by the feet" in 1850. Érard describes the advantages of his new pedal keys thus:

Great musicians, and especially those who profess church or classical music, are accustomed in organs to have a set of pedal keys to be pressed by the feet at the same time that they are using their hands on the finger keys of the instrument. It has been long wished for to have such pedal keys applied to grand pianofortes, and experiments have been made for that object.

He then writes of the great labour it has cost him to invent the particular forms of pedal keys and states that he offers them as a

great improvement upon the instrument, as it will enable great masters of the art to perform the music already composed by great composers, such as Sebastian Bark [*sic*] and others, for an instrument with pedal keys, and it will further enable skilful performers on the pianoforte to produce new and imposing effects.

These new pedal keys are shown adapted to pianofortes of seven octaves.[4] They are "applied to thirty-two of the bass notes, namely

---

[1] C 759.   [2] C 760.
[3] C 761.   [4] C 762.

from lowest note A answering to note A, thirty-two feet in the organ, up to the third note E above"; they correspond therefore to the lowest thirty-two notes in the bass of the pianoforte. These pedals were connected with their corresponding finger keys by rods, and trackers where necessary. The pedals put the finger keys in action and in this way the note was formed. Only one set of strings was necessary.

The 'great masters' referred to by Érard were probably Schumann, who wrote *Studies* and *Four Sketches for Pedal-Pianoforte* (Op. 56, 58), and Liszt, who eventually possessed one of these instruments, though it is not possible to say whether Érard made it.

Transposing pianofortes. Another type of 'home pianoforte', which was primarily intended for the somewhat unskilful amateur, was the transposing pianoforte. The object of this invention was to make it possible to transpose any music at sight either up or down, to accommodate singers, and also to enable the less skilful amateur to play music written in some difficult key by a mechanism which enabled him, whilst apparently playing in some simple key to which he was accustomed, to produce the actual sounds of the music as written.

Concerning this the Editor of the *Musical Herald* wrote in 1846:

A performer, who, on the ordinary pianoforte, can play only on the easiest keys, may, by means of this invention, produce the same sounds as if he was playing on the most difficult keys. For example, the beautiful funeral march in Beethoven's sonata, op. 26, is in the key of *A flat* minor, with *seven flats* at the clef. By lowering the pitch of the instrument a semitone, and playing *from the same notes* (only supposing the flats at the clef struck out) the *very same sounds* will be produced from the white keys which were previously produced from the black. It would, indeed, be necessary, on the occasional occurrence of an *accidental natural*, to change it mentally to a *sharp*; but the small difficulty thence arising would only be an improving exercise to the learner.[1]

The first patent for a transposing pianoforte was obtained by Edward Ryley in 1801.[2] If it is asked why the transposing pianoforte was not invented before this, the answer is simply that before equal temperament tuning was generally accepted modulation only to nearly related keys was possible: thus if transposition was required it was but a simple matter.[3]

[1] B 73, p. 7.   [2] C 697.
[3] B 32. Dr Callcott, in his paper on the *Royal Albert Transposing Pianoforte* (London, 1851), alludes to this but says nothing about temperament.

The transposing pianoforte was also of great use when accompanying wind instruments; for their pitch varied considerably and also the atmosphere of a heated room tended to flatten the pianoforte, whilst it raised the wind instruments in pitch.

There were four ways in which this transposition could be effected:

(1) by a movable keyboard,

(2) by a movable frame carrying the strings, or a movable action,

(3) by an additional keyboard to be placed over the ordinary one,

(4) by means of keys which were divided in two portions which were hinged. This back portion could be moved laterally to engage the action either for a higher or a lower pitch.

The earlier transposing pianofortes belonged to the first type, that is, there were additional keys. Edward Ryley's pianoforte of 1801 had keys covering a range of seven octaves; there was, therefore, an octave more than the compass of the instrument. A cavity at both the bass and the treble end of the keyboard permitted it to be moved underneath to make it possible to transpose up or down to the extent of an octave.

John Broadwood is said to have purchased the right to use this invention the same year in which it was patented. A transposing pianoforte made by him in 1808, and now in the possession of Messrs John Broadwood and Sons, will give a good idea of an old pianoforte of this type (Plate XV). By means of the two wooden pegs, which work a spring catch, the keyboard can be moved laterally in a downward direction to the extent of a sixth. An ivory-capped pin, working in an ivory plaque with eleven numbered holes on the left side below the keyboard, regulates this lateral movement.

Hole No. 1. Keyboard in its normal position, with C as the last note.

Hole No. 2. Keyboard moved down a semitone, with B as the last note.

Hole No. 3. Keyboard moved down a semitone, with B flat as the last note.

Hole No. 4. Keyboard moved down a semitone, with A as the last note.

And so on through the eleven holes until D is the last note.

Plate XV. Transposing Pianoforte by John Broadwood and Sons, 1808 (in their possession).

There is a later example of the transposing pianoforte with gliding keyboard at Brussels, by Lichtenthal et Cie of Brussels (No. 2955). It transposes down three semitones.

A peculiar transposing pianoforte in a cabinet-case (see Part II, § 1, pp. 108–9), with a sound-board in the shape of a cylindrical column, was patented by Érard Frères in 1812.[1] The cylindrical sound-board was placed on four rollers so that it could be revolved according to the transposition required (Fig. 30). But Fétis states that "the necessity of straining the wood in order to make it take a cylindrical form, so far interfered with the vibration that only defective sounds could be obtained", and that "the invention was, therefore, obliged to be given up". D. C. Hewitt seems to have been the first, in 1844, to invent an additional keyboard to be placed over the ordinary one for transposing.[2]

Woolley of Nottingham designed a transposing pianoforte in which the strings were made movable by wheels fixed to their frame. Foot pedals moved the frame by means of a mechanism in an upward or downward direction, and in this way transposition was effected. An indicator attached to the frame and moving with it projected through the case and showed, by means of marks on the groove within which it travelled, the semitones, whether upwards or downwards, to which the apparatus was capable of being moved[3] (Fig. 31).

The 'Royal Albert Pianoforte', a transposing pianoforte so called in "consequence of the especial approbation and sanction it [had] received from His Royal Highness Prince Albert", was an improvement on the preceding types, since neither the keys, hammers nor strings had to be moved laterally, as the transposition was effected by an apparatus between the keys and the strings. This arrangement is supposed to have been the invention of Sébastien Mercier of Paris who patented it in England in 1844,[4] but a similar transposing pianoforte was patented in France by Le Bihan of Carhaix, Finistère, the year before[5] (Fig. 32). Robert Addison worked the invention in England and seems to have obtained a Scotch patent for it.[6]

One of these instruments was exhibited in the Great Exhibition

---

[1] C 698.   [2] C 710.

[3] C 714. The transposing mechanism was charged according to compass "commencing with 10 Guineas".

[4] C 711.   [5] C 709.

[6] C 712.

of 1851, when it received the approbation of Dr Callcott, who wrote a pamphlet extolling its qualities, and Cramer himself noticed the invention. It seems that composers at this time were annoyed by the fact that "Publishers frequently transposed songs on account of the difficulty of the key to the performer". "This instrument", Callcott writes, "allows the easy key to be retained and yet the power is possessed to make the song *sound* in the author's original scale. Mr J. B. Cramer considers this a most important point."[1]

Self-acting or mechanical pianofortes. Barrel pianofortes cannot be passed over in silence, owing to the fact that the modern mechanical pianoforte in its various forms has been recognised as an independent musical instrument for which music has been written.

The barrel organ with its wooden barrel and flat brass wire staples or teeth, which was revolved by a handle, was made before the pianoforte was invented. The barrel pianoforte was on the same principle; there was the usual barrel, the teeth of which worked the action for the hammers. The forte and piano seem to have been obtained by the simple means of making the teeth higher or lower or by some adaptation of that principle.

In 1816 William Simmons patented a barrel and mechanism to be applied to the organ, pianoforte, harpsichord, etc. The barrel was set with pins, but these pins were movable so that the owner of the instrument was at liberty to take them out and set out another tune. The barrel was revolved by a handle or, if it was preferred, by the 'power of spring' (*i.e.* by clockwork). There seems also to have been a means for obtaining dynamic expression by means of movable pieces of eccentric shape; but these seem only to apply to the instrument when attached to the organ. Simmons states that the invention may also be applied to "any other instrument the sounds of which are produced by working keys or levers, for which keys may be used; likewise to a set of bells and to automata, or such mechanical figures as are representations of animals, men, and the like, which are worked by keys".[2]

In the self-acting pianofortes of Thomas Hall Rolfe (1829) there was a barrel as usual, but the forte and piano were not obtained by the use of higher or lower staples which were liable to become deranged, but by "combining and applying certain parts or agents immediately to the spring machine used to set in motion the self-acting department of such instruments, either by combining the said parts with the great or fusee wheel, the bevelled wheel on

[1] B 32, Chap. III, p. 9.   [2] C 912.

the axis of the governor, or other suitable part of the spring machine".[1] There is sometimes a doubt whether patents for pianofortes of a peculiar character were ever carried out; but in this case there is no doubt that the pianoforte was actually made. The following is an extract from *The Register of Arts* in which Mr L. Herbert, civil engineer, the Editor, informs his readers that "Two of these beautiful specimens of mechanical skill applied to the most fascinating of the sciences (and including the most recent improvements) are exhibited in the gallery, where the visitors are constantly regaled by their powerful melody".

Mr Herbert then proceeds to dilate on the advantages of the self-acting pianoforte:

These self-performing pianofortes possess the admirable ability of administering to the intellectual enjoyment of the many, and conducting an evening's amusement with the most exquisite propriety and effect, without the assistance of the scientific performer. At the same time, they do not exclude or oppose the efforts of manual dexterity; as independent of their self-acting power, they comprehend all the admirable properties of a grand cabinet pianoforte [Upright Grand] with extra additional keys, and invite the application of the most expert finger in the ordinary method of performance.[2]

From 1829 to about 1842 there seems to have been no great interest in mechanical pianofortes, but between 1842 and 1851 there were no less than eight patents for these instruments.

In 1842 Claude-Félix Seytre of Lyons obtained a patent for "pianofortes and organs[3] which may play airs by means of pierced cardboard". He continues thus:

By means of my mechanism, a person not able to play either the pianoforte or the organ, and not even able to read music, may play the most delicate and the newest compositions of any length, that is, from the shortest little song to an entire opera.

My process is applicable alike to all instruments with keyboard or with keys.

I have given it the name of 'autopanphones', which is made up of three Greek words αὐτὸς, itself, πᾶν all, and φωνὴ voice or song: that is a pianoforte or organ which itself sings any kind of air.

In the interior of my pianofortes, I place the acting mechanism of an organ, harmonica or accordion, which play in all keys, and which accompany the pianoforte, or play solos one after the other, without changing the cardboard roll.... A piece of music of 80 metres only costs 1 franc 50 centimes.

This invention is another stage in the development of the barrel

---

[1] C 914.   [2] B 47.   [3] C 916.

pianoforte, for the music is no longer pricked out on the barrel but is perforated upon paper or cardboard.

A still further stage is reached in Alexandre Debain's Antiphonel; an attachment which could be applied to the pianoforte or the harmonium by means of which music could be mechanically played. An improved form of this called the *piano mécanique* was exhibited at the Exhibition of 1851 and is described by Pole thus:

> Instead of the tune being pricked on a barrel, it is formed by a series of pins, fixed on the plane surface of a thin oblong tablet of wood, a few inches broad, giving it something like the appearance of a currycomb. This is drawn, by rack and pinion, through a frame, in which project wedge-shaped ends of levers, connected by rods with the hammers of the piano; so that, when a pin in the tune-tablet passes over one of these wedge-shaped lever ends, it depresses it, and thereby lifts the hammer, which, when the pin has passed over, is thrown back by a spring against the string...the mechanical apparatus is made to fit on the top of an ordinary cottage piano-forte and may be detached at pleasure...when the apparatus is applied, the usual hammers are drawn back, and the spring ones take their place, so as to strike the same points of the strings.[1]

Two years after Debain had invented the Antiphonel,[2] Duncan Mackenzie, evidently unaware of the latest improvements in these instruments, made a suggestion in his patent for improvements relating to Jacquard machinery for figuring fabrics, that instead of the music itself being pricked on a barrel "if the ends of the needles are made to strike against any sonorous substance, such as the strings of a piano or the metal teeth in an organ, and so arranged as to embrace the whole of the notes necessary to be produced and that if the tune be punctured upon the endless band after the fashion of the design to be woven upon the fabric, tunes can be played and varied at pleasure".[3]

In the following year, William Martin,[4] another patentee for improvements in Jacquard machinery, made the following invention in relation to mechanical keyed instruments:

> "In these the musical sounds are produced by means of a sheet of paper... perforated in a pattern similar to that used for figuring fabrics in a Jacquard loom, in combination with a barrel provided with movable pins, which are selected by the perforated band, and caused to assume suitable positions to act either upon the keys of a pianoforte", etc.... "The pins are protruded from the cylinder by falling through the holes in the perforated band, and are held out by a collar passing round a guide ring. There are two movable pins for

[1] B 82, p. 38. The 'Piano mécanique' complete cost from £36 to £100.
[2] C 268.   [3] C 628.   [4] C 630.

each key, one longer than the other, the shorter one being for the execution of soft passages."

It is interesting to note that Jean-Henri Pape also experimented with the mechanical pianoforte in 1851.[1] His mechanism was worked by means of a handle, weights and springs, but it is unnecessary to describe it, as Debain's 'piano mécanique' was by far the most perfect mechanical contrivance for this purpose at that time.

Keyboards and other contrivances to assist children in the performance of difficult music. Ever since the time that the Mozarts had delighted all with their remarkable performances, infant prodigies had been worshipped; thus it is not surprising to find special keyboards or other devices to assist children in the performance of difficult music. As early as 1811 John Trotter of London invented a keyboard which made it possible to play all the major scales with one fingering and all the minor with another. In this way there were only two scales to be learnt, one major and one minor, instead of twelve major and twelve minor keys; which, he says, had hitherto been so confusing for the pupil. This he effected by placing the keys in two ranks, but with the difference that instead of the black keys being grouped into twos and threes they form a continuous series and are prolonged beyond the white keys. The back portion of these black keys is raised above the white as usual; but the part projecting beyond the white keys could be made on a lower plane than the white keys. C natural falls on a black key: C sharp upon a white[2] (Fig. 33). The same effect of being able to play all the major scales in one fingering and all the minor in another was obtained in rather a different way by means of a special keyboard designed by Allison and Co. and exhibited by them at the Great Exhibition of 1851. We quote Pole's description of it: "A piccolo upright, by Messrs Robert Allison and Co., has this peculiarity, viz. that the colors of the

[1] C 923.

[2] C 668. In Germany a keyboard, giving all the major scales in *two* fingerings according to whether the upper or lower note was the keynote, seems to have been practically the same as that invented in 1843 by W. A. B. Lunn under the name of Arthur Wallbridge and known as the 'Sequential keyboard'. In this C is also on a black key. (See *Grove's Dictionary*, third edition, 1927–28, Art. 'Keyboard'.) *Trotter's keyboard* seems to be an excellent arrangement and might possibly be revived for the performance of modern music, since 'outlining' in sevenths or tenths would be an easy matter; the seventh on Trotter's keyboard occupying the space of our present octave and the tenth the space of a ninth; consecutive fourths and fifths also, though not so convenient as upon the present keyboard, would not be difficult.

keys, instead of being arranged in the ordinary progression, are divided in the following manner:

C	*Grey*	G	White
C sharp	White	G sharp	*Grey*
D	*Grey*	A	White
D sharp	White	A sharp	*Grey*
E	*Grey*	B	White
F	White	C	*Grey*
F sharp	*Grey*		

and so on, repeated throughout the instrument. It thus forms what is called a 'diapason [*sic*] scale indicator'; and its use is to indicate to learners the notes necessary to form the diatonic major and minor scale, in any given key. The rule is, commencing with the key note and ascending:

"To form the major scale, take three successive keys of the same color, and four of the other color.

"To form the minor scale, take two keys of the same color, and five of the other." [1]

Tonnel's keyboard, patented in 1837, [2] was disposed in three levels. The upper level gave the chromatic sharp scale; the middle level the natural scale, and lowest level the chromatic flat scale. This arrangement did not make any new mode of fingering necessary, whilst by its use the student preserved his correct sense of pitch.

Keyboards, both convex and concave, were made in order to aid the performer in striking distant intervals.

The first of these seems to have been the 'flat semicircular key-board', in which the keys decreased in length, invented by Georg Staufer and M. Haidinger of Vienna in 1824. This keyboard must have been *concave*, since the pianoforte to which it was fitted was called the Hollow Pianoforte or 'Hohlflügel'. It was intended particularly for children, for they state that "by this means" (*i.e.* curving the keyboard) "an especial facility is given to the player and especially to children". [3]

Wolfel of Paris in 1840 designed a keyboard which was *convex*, [4] and Newhall and Wilkins (assignees of John Dwight of Boston, U.S.A., 1841) patented a pianoforte with a convex keyboard (*i.e.* a misprint for *concave* as shown by their drawing) of six, seven, or more octaves, by which the performer was enabled to reach the extreme keys more conveniently. [5] But these last two were not necessarily invented for children. Obendrauf of Vienna

[1] B 82, p. 24.   [2] C 674.   [3] C 686.   [4] C 687.   [5] C 688.

designed (in 1837) a pianoforte with *narrow keys* to enable children to strike distant intervals in chords.[1] This keyboard permitted them to play music intended for their elders.

Madame Soria of Paris invented an additional keyboard with narrow keys, which was intended to fit over the ordinary one to enable children to finger the intervals, and particularly the octaves.

Lahausse of Paris was the originator of an ingenious mechanism, applicable to every kind of pianoforte, which enabled the touch to be adjusted to suit players of all ages and varying degrees of strength.[2]

Charles Dawson invented an *apparatus to prevent the sounding of misfingered notes* to be fixed to the keyboard to prevent the action of notes which did not belong to the key of the music performed.[3]

This was clearly not intended for the infant prodigy but no doubt to make life in the schoolroom a little more pleasant.

Some keyboards and other devices to assist the adult performer in playing difficult music. Hewitt of London invented in 1844 a modification of the existing keyboard which was intended to facilitate the playing of chromatic scales. It consisted in raising up the back portion of the white keys to the level of the black to avoid the uncomfortable depression between the black keys.[4]

A curious and very complex keyboard was designed by Théophile-Auguste Dreschke[5] in 1846, for which the reader should see Fig. 34. Phiquepal d'Arusmont of Paris patented a keyboard in 1843[6] in which the keys were disposed in two levels; a lower range of white keys similar to those generally in use and an upper level of thin keys similar to the ordinary sharp keys. But instead of dividing these upper keys into groups of three and two he arranged them in uninterrupted sequence; one thin key being placed between every two white keys. In order to avoid confusion they were not all to be coloured black but every alternate three were to be coloured yellow or any other suitable colour. He also numbered the notes of every octave from 1 to 12 and distinguished the different octaves by placing lines above the numbers for the treble octaves and below them for the bass.

According to this new arrangement the white keys were numbered in sequence 1, 3, 5, 7, 9, 11. The upper level of thin keys, comprising alternate groups of three black and three yellow notes, was numbered as follows:

The first three black notes: 2, 4, 6. The first three yellow notes: 8, 10, 12, and so on. This keyboard was supposed to make the

[1] C673.   [2] C1241.   [3] C258.   [4] C678.   [5] C680.   [6] C677.

fingering more easy and to enable the student to see how to play all the scales with every possible modulation.

By means of a monochord intended to be used in connection with this instrument the student was enabled to tune the pianoforte and to understand the mathematical reasons for the arrangement of the new keyboard.

DESCRIPTION OF FIG. 30 (*opposite*).

Fig. 30. Transposing Pianoforte. Érard, 1812.

La table d'harmonie de cet instrument est un cylindre qui a la forme d'une colonne; elle est entourée d'une table, sur laquelle est fixé le clavier. Un faux clavier, régnant autour de la colonne, fait agir les marteaux par les touches du premier clavier: ces marteaux sont rangés en forme de limaçons autour de la colonne.

Fig. 1re, plan de cet instrument.

Fig. 2e, coupe verticale.

Fig. 3e et 4e, mécanismes qui font agir touches et les marteaux, représentés sur une échelle plus grande.

a, noyau formant le centre de la colonne: son diamètre supérieur *b*, *c* est plus petit que celui *d*, *e* de sa base.

f, tuyau dans lequel le noyau *a* est enfilé.   *g*, table d'harmonie.

h, quatre roulettes placées dans le bas de la colonne, et sur lesquelles tourne cette colonne au moyen d'une pédale, pour faire jouer une ou deux des trois cordes qui existent; le mouvement de cette colonne sert aussi pour faire jouer un demi-ton, un ton, ou autant qu'on voudra plus haut ou plus bas, et même pour faire venir les basses dans les dessus ou les dessus dans les basses.

Les touches du clavier mécanique sont, dans la Fig. 1re, numérotées de 1 à 72, et donnent le *mi* du milieu au No. 36: on voit une de ces touches en *k*, Fig. 2e: les fausses touches sont numérotées de la même manière.

Il est bon d'observer, comme on le voit, Fig. 1re, que les touches Nos. 1 à 9 sont tout en bois, et qu'on atteint les fausses touches au moyen de leviers brisés *i*.

Les touches, Nos. 10 à 26 inclusivement, entrent, à l'endroit *l*, dans une fourche en cuivre, qui se prolonge en tournant pour atteindre la fausse touche du même numéro. Les Nos. 27 à 36 sont en bois.

A, Fig. 2e, montre la position du marteau.   *m*, fausse touche.

n, tringle disposée en forme de limaçon autour de la colonne; elle est double dans son épaisseur, et les parties en sont réunies par des vis, après qu'on a collé les queues des fausses touches.

o, queues des fausses touches en parchemin.

p, double montant en cuivre, lié en haut par deux pattes ou étriers *q*, voyez Fig. 3e.

r, espèce de langue en bois, à laquelle les deux montants *p* sont retenus par deux goupilles.

s, vis qui traverse la langue de bois *r*, et qui est vissée dans la fausse touche *m*.

t, pièce qui fait le tour de la colonne, et qui porte les fourchettes en cuir *u*.

v, tête du marteau, traversée par une goupille à deux pointes, qui se trouvent pressées par la fourchette *u*, dans laquelle sont pratiquées, à cet effet, deux petites entailles.

x, queue ou touche reposant sur le premier étrier *q*, qui lève cette queue; à mesure qu'on appuie sur la queue *k*, la touche *x* quitte le premier étrier *q*, et le second étrier s'en empare pour renforcer le coup de marteau.

y, pilote servant d'intermédiaire entre la touche *k* et la fausse touche *m*.

z, chevilles pour accorder.   *a'*, cordes.

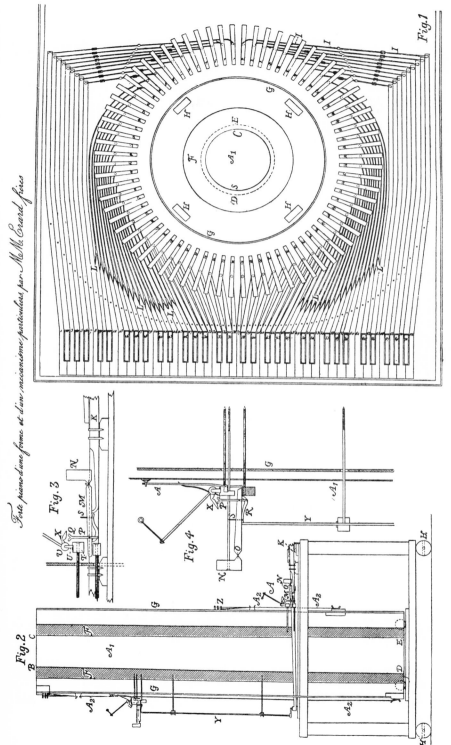

Texte piano d'une forme et d'un mécanisme particuliers par MM. Érard frères

Fig. 1

Fig. 2

Fig. 3

Fig. 4

Fig. 30.

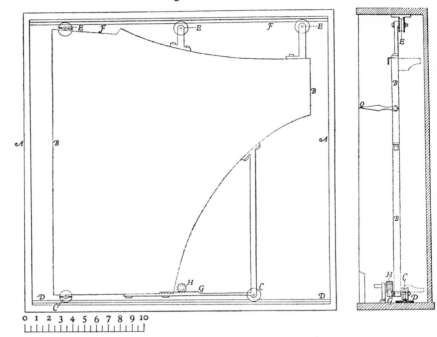

Fig. 1.

Fig. 2.

0 1 2 3 4 5 6 7 8 9 10

Fig. 31. Woolley's Transposing Pianoforte, 1846.
From the patent.

(Figs. 1 and 2) *a, a* is the case of the instrument. The dotted line indicates an outline of the string frame. To this frame are affixed carrying wheels *c, c,* as shown. These wheels are formed with hollow surfaces to run upon the V-rail *d,* and there are also other wheels *e, e, e* at the upper part of the frame *b.* These wheels *e* travel on and are guided by the rail *f,* by which the upper part of the frame *b* is kept steady in its case. On the lower part of the frame *b* is affixed a rack *g,* into which takes the pinion *h* by which the frame *b* is moved. I prefer to have a pointer *o* (Fig. 2) projecting out from the front of the string frame and travelling with it, which pointer will travel in a groove in any suitable part of the front of the instrument, which will be marked with the semitones higher and lower to which the apparatus is capable of being moved, so that a person looking at the front of the instrument may at once see, by the position of the pointer *o,* the key to which the instrument is set. (*Thomas Woolley, abridged.*)

Fig. 2.

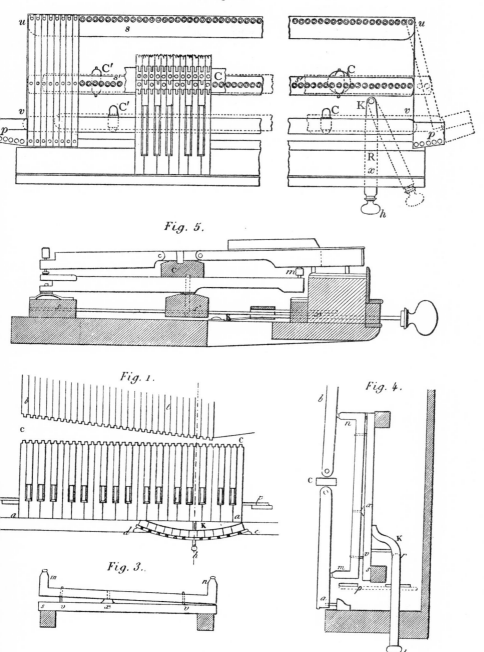

Fig. 5.

Fig. 1.

Fig. 4.

Fig. 3.

Fig. 32.

DESCRIPTION OF FIG. 32 (*previous page*).

Fig. 32. Brevet d'invention de quinze ans en date du 13 décembre 1843, au sieur le Bihan, à Carhaix (Finistère), pour un piano transpositeur.

Le but de ce nouveau système de piano est de faire disparaître les difficultés qui tiennent aux signes qui se trouvent à la clef, de manière qu'un morceau puisse s'exécuter aussi facilement avec cinq, six et sept dièses ou bémols à la clef que s'il n'y en avait aucun. Pour arriver à ce but, il s'agissait donc de trouver un moyen qui permît de disposer à volonté les touches blanches, de manière à donner tous les tons avec autant de facilité que le ton d'*ut*, afin qu'on ne soit obligé d'avoir recours aux touches noires que quand il se rencontre des dièses ou des bémols accidentels.

Tous les tons dans lesquels on peut composer de la musique se réduisant à douze, puisque l'étendue de la gamme ne comprend que douze subdivisions, il suffit, pour atteindre le but que je viens de signaler, que chaque touche soit susceptible de donner telle note naturelle ou chromatique que l'on voudra, c'est-à-dire que la série des touches blanches puisse, par un mécanisme simple, solide et facile à disposer, donner, suivant le besoin, le ton d'*ut*, celui d'*ut* dièse, de *ré*, etc., et que les touches noires, dans ces divers tons, donnent pour chacun d'eux les demi-tons tels qu'on doit les avoir.

Moyens.

Fig. 1re. Toutes les touches doivent être brisées, de manière à ce que le mouvement des extrémités *a, a*, où se posent les doigts, devienne indépendant du mouvement des extrémités *b, b* qui font agir les marteaux. Toutes tiennent, à charnières, à une pièce transversale *c, c.*

Sous le clavier se trouve un châssis à angles mobiles composé d'autant de traverses qu'il y a de notes dans l'étendue du piano. Toutes ces traverses tiennent au châssis par des boutons qui se trouvent rangés sur une même ligne droite pour chaque côté. Elles sont mobiles sur ces boutons, pour que le châssis puisse s'incliner à droite ou à gauche, suivant le besoin, en faisant incliner d'autant toutes les traverses à la fois. De cette manière, suivant que l'on incline plus ou moins, chacun des points *s, s* peut se trouver successivement sous douze touches différentes.

Fig. 3e. Sur chaque traverse du châssis se trouve une pièce qu'on peut appeler communicateur, parce qu'elle sert à faire communiquer la partie antérieure de la touche avec l'autre partie qui fait agir le marteau.

Fig. 3e et 4e. Les communicateurs formant autant de leviers sont placés sur les traverses de manière à soulever les extrémités *b* des touches, lorsqu'ils sont mis en mouvement par les extrémités *a* où se posent les doigts. Le point d'appui *x* se place, pour chaque communicateur, de manière à donner au marteau une impulsion suffisante. Des pointes *v, v*, fixées dans les traverses du châssis, forcent les communicateurs dans lesquels elles sont engagées à demeurer invariablement au-dessus de leurs traverses respectives. Les extrémités *m, n* des communicateurs sont recouvertes de cuir, pour empêcher le bruit. Les extrémités *n* doivent se trouver dans un même plan vertical avec les boutons qui unissent les traverses au côté fixe du châssis, afin que, quel que soit le mouvement du côté antérieur de ce châssis, les extrémités *n* des communicateurs conservent toujours la même place et ne fassent que tourner plus ou moins sur elles-mêmes.

Qu'on se figure actuellement le châssis, muni de tous les communicateurs, placé sous le clavier. Si on lui conserve la position rectangulaire, chaque communicateur se trouvera à faire agir la touche qui le met en mouvement sur le marteau qui lui correspond. Le piano, dans cette position, n'aura rien de plus qu'un piano ordinaire. C'est la disposition qu'il faudra lui conserver, lorsque la musique à exécuter sera en *ut* majeur ou en *la* mineur, au diapason.

Je suppose, maintenant, qu'il faille jouer en *si* majeur, c'est-à-dire avec cinq dièses à la clef. En laissant au châssis la position rectangulaire, il faudrait, comme dans un piano ordinaire, sur les sept notes qui composent la gamme de *si*, en aller chercher cinq parmi les touches noires.

Sur le piano transpositeur, on évitera cet embarras en faisant incliner le côté mobile du châssis un peu à droite, ce qui se fera en relevant la poignée *h*, fig. 1re, de la coche du ton d'*ut*, pour la mettre dans celle du ton de *si*, qui est à sa droite. De cette manière, le communicateur qui fait vibrer la corde *si* se trouvera à correspondre à la touche qui représente la note *ut*. La corde *ut* répondra à la touche *ut* dièse, ainsi de suite. Il suffira, dès lors, d'avoir ce morceau de musique écrit et transposé en *ut*, et, en l'exécutant de cette manière, on obtiendra l'effet que donnerait un piano ordinaire, mais avec une facilité beaucoup plus grande.

Voyez *k*, *h*, fig. 1re, 2e, 4e; à une des traverses est adaptée, en dessous, une pièce qui se prolonge jusqu'en dehors de la caisse du piano, et qui se termine par une poignée *h* pour faire aller le châssis à droite ou à gauche, suivant qu'il en est besoin. Cette poignée peut se reposer dans douze coches qui se trouvent sur un espace *d*, *e*, fig. 1re, pratiqué en avant du piano, et qui correspondent à des cases où sont marqués les tons majeurs que détermine chaque position de la poignée.

Fig. 1re. D'après ce système, on voit qu'il faut dans les touches une octave, moins une touche de plus que dans les cordes, parce que onze touches (cinq d'un bout et six de l'autre) doivent se trouver prêtes à entrer en jeu, suivant le ton du morceau et l'inclinaison qu'il nécessite dans le châssis.

Pour que les déplacements du châssis ne soient pas gênés par les touches *a*, *a* portant sur les extrémités *m*, fig. 4e, des communicateurs, la poignée qui sert à incliner le châssis est brisée en *r*. Ainsi disposée, elle peut se relever des cordes et y redescendre. Dans son mouvement d'ascension, elle développe un parallélogramme *p*, *p*, dont le côté supérieur soulève de quelques millimètres toutes les touches du clavier pendant la marche du châssis. Cette marche arrêtée, la poignée retombe dans une autre coche, le parallélogramme s'affaisse, les touches qui doivent entrer en jeu pour ce ton retombent sur les communicateurs, pendant que les onze touches supplémentaires redescendent avec le parallélogramme un peu plus bas que le reste du clavier. Le même mécanisme, avec quelques modifications bien faciles, peut s'appliquer à l'orgue, et généralement à tous les instruments à clavier.

Au lieu d'employer un châssis mobile sous le clavier, on peut disposer les touches *a*, *a* de manière à pouvoir glisser toutes ensemble vers un bout ou vers l'autre, de manière à ce que chacune d'elles puisse encore donner douze sons différents, suivant la position du clavier. Dans ce cas, le châssis conserverait toujours la position rectangulaire, et les touches avançant d'un côté ou de l'autre, avec la partie antérieure de la pièce transversale *c*, *c*, fig. 1re, viendraient se placer successivement sur les divers communicateurs, dont la position serait fixe comme celle du châssis auquel ils tiennent.

Fig. 33. Trotter's keyboard, 1811. From the patent (*description*, p. 292).

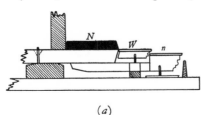

(*a*)

Fig. (*a*) represents a section of the keys.

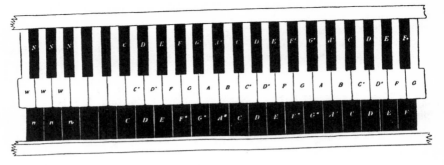

(*b*)

Fig. (*b*). The 'range' of narrow black keys *N, N, N* belongs to the notes *C, D, E,* *F* sharp, *G* sharp, *A* sharp, which are produced beyond the white keys at *n, n, n.* The level of the keys *n, n, n* when at rest may be below the plane of the keys, *W, W, W* 'so that the same effect will be produced whether the part *N* or *n* of any individual key be touched; but the performance of fingering will be rendered more easy by the advantage given to the player of touching either of these parts of the key at pleasure.' The 'range' of white keys *W, W, W* belongs to the notes *C* sharp, *D* sharp, *F, G, A, B.*

The table below is intended to show the new arrangement of the keys compared with that commonly in use. *I* and *K* show the order of the keys in the ordinary instrument; *L* and *M* the order in Trotter's instrument.

The table also shows the fingering to be used for both the major and the minor mode.

		1	2	3	4	5	6	7	8	9	10	11	12
The 12 Semitones in regular succession in one range	H	C	C♯	D	D♯	E	F	F♯	G	G♯	A	A♯	B
The Diatonic old arrangement of the keys in two ranges	I	C	.	D	.	E	F	.	G	.	A	.	B
	K	.	C♯	.	D♯	.	.	F♯	.	G	⌐	A♯	.
The Chromatic or my arrangement of the keys in two ranges	L	C	.	D	.	E	.	F♯	.	G♯	.	A♯	.
	M	.	C♯	.	D♯	.	F	.	G	.	A	.	B

By which disposition of uniformly alternate keys in two distinct ranges any one certain note taken as a Fundamental or key note together with the two succeeding Notes ascending in the other range and the same range of Keys and the four succeeding Notes ascending in the other range and the Octaves to all the said notes comprize all the notes of that Key in the Major mode. And the same certain Key note together with the one succeeding note ascending in the same range of Keys and the five succeeding notes ascending in the other range and the Octaves to all the said notes comprize all the ascending notes of that Key in the Minor mode; by which constant uniformity it may be said that there are but one Key Major and one Key Minor to be learnt instead of 12 Keys Major and 12 Keys Minor as heretofore so very perplexing to the pupil.

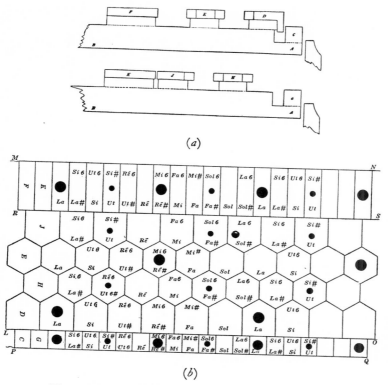

Fig. 34. Dreschke's keyboard, 1846. From the patent.

In this keyboard each note has its usual lever A, B (Fig. a) on which are fixed four different "stops alternately, an oblong C, a pentagon D, a hexagon E, and an oblong F, or an oblong G, a hexagon H, a pentagon $\mathcal{J}$, and an oblong K. The length of the first stop (C or G) is equal to the breadth of a finger. Its breadth depends on the hexagon, so that two stops (C and G) of the first part are only as broad as a single hexagon E. The breadth of the pentagon (D or $\mathcal{J}$), and of the hexagon (E or H) is one-sixth of that of an octave of an ordinary keyboard, but it can be reduced to the breadth of a white stop of an ordinary keyboard. The length of the pentagon and of the hexagon is equal to the diameter of a circle described round the hexagon. The length of the fourth stop (F or K) depends on the construction of the instrument. . . . The breadth of this stop (F or K) is equal to that of the first stop (C or G). The first stop (C or G) is lower than the three others (D, E, F or H, $\mathcal{J}$, K), which are on the same level. . . .

The keyboard thus made forms for the level two parts P, L, O, $\mathcal{Q}$ and L, M, N, O (Fig. (b)), which have both a smooth surface, except the sides of each stop, which are rounded, but for the performance of a piece of music three parts should be distinguished P, L, O, $\mathcal{Q}$; L, R, S, O and R, M, N, S . . . P, L, O, $\mathcal{Q}$ and R, M, N, S contain the chromatic gamut. . . . L, R, S, O, representing four rows of stops, contains the chromatic gamut in zigzag. Each note has two stops in this part, either a pentagon in the first row and a hexagon in the third, or a hexagon in the second row, and a pentagon in the fourth row. The keyboard is white, except the black points of two kinds, of which the larger ones mark the La and the $Mi\flat$, and the small ones the Ut and $Fa\sharp$. (*Théophile Auguste Dreschke, abridged*.)

CHAPTER IV

TUNING THE PIANOFORTE AND
APPARATUS FOR KEEPING THE PIANOFORTE
IN TUNE. CONCLUSION

THE pianoforte student used to be taught how to take care of his instrument, how to do simple repairs, and how to tune it. All this was a necessary part of his training, for the pianofortes were very liable to go out of order and if the instrument happened to be in a country home the services of a tuner were not easily available.

Of the care of the instrument Czerny writes:

The pianoforte should stand in a dry place, as damp is injurious to it. It ought not to be exposed to currents of air. It should neither stand in too cold nor in too warm a place; and therefore neither near a window nor a fireplace. When the latter cannot be avoided we must place a screen between it and the fire. It must always be kept clean, and free from dust; and no heavy weight should be placed upon it. The strings must never be touched with damp fingers; nor should anything be suffered to fall upon them, as even the smallest pin or needle lying on the strings or belly of the instrument causes a disagreeable jarring. Similarly we must guard against any dirt falling upon the keys, such as crumbs of bread, drops of wax or tallow etc. as when such things do occur, the keys are very apt to stick.[1]

He might also have added that the pianoforte must be kept level. Pape invented special spring castors for this purpose. The tall and clumsy cabinet pianoforte was evidently an object of dread to the good housewife owing to its liability to topple over backwards when moved, and Pape, observing her, sympathetically invented castors with double rollers to prevent this mishap. Apparently the thick drawing-room carpets and furniture were supposed to muffle the tone. In order to overcome this difficulty George Buttery placed the frame of his pianoforte on springs. "By this means", he states, "the tone will be brisker, the strings will have a greater vibration, the instrument will receive a tremulous motion, and the above defect will be entirely defeated." In fact a kind of vibrato was obtained.[2]

[1] B 99, Vol. III, Chap. xx, p. 126.
[2] Patented in 1792; C 500.

THE CARE OF THE INSTRUMENT

Tuning the pianoforte. Czerny writes that "a new Piano-forte should be often tuned during the first few months, say every fortnight. Afterwards once a month or six weeks, or even two months will be sufficient". The strings were liable to be disturbed by variation in the temperature; and another cause for their going out of tune consisted in the use of the Una Corda pedal, by which one of the unisons forming a note tended to become flatter than the other, and uneven hammers had also a similar effect. It will be seen how necessary it was to correct these defects in pitch before they had gone too far.

The old wrest pins were thin, and owing to their nail-like appearance they were called 'Stimmnagel' or tuning-nail in the early nineteenth-century Bavarian and Austrian patents. Whilst they were small and the strings were thin and not drawn up to a high tension, tuning the pianoforte presented no great difficulty to the musical amateur. But the use of thicker strings drawn up to a higher tension around stouter wrest pins, made tuning a difficult process, particularly to a woman, as the pins had to be turned smoothly; for a jerky motion would have broken the strings. The use of mechanical wrest pins seemed to be the way to overcome this difficulty and they had, in fact, been experimented with almost from the beginning of pianoforte making before there was any real need for them.

Marius introduced them into his first clavecin of 1716[1] and the first English patent in which the pianoforte is mentioned is partly concerned with these mechanical pins. It was obtained by Richard Wakefield in 1771. Wakefield's wrest pin consisted in "a small screw which", he writes, "is sometimes made of ivory, sometimes of mettal" to which was fixed "one end of each wire in harpsichords, spinetts, or forte-pianos, etc.... which when turned round from the right to left draws the wire tight in tune and there retains it".[2] In Hawkins'[3] 'Portable Grand Pianoforte' of 1800 there were mechanical wrest pins. In the example in the possession of Messrs Broadwood there is one for each string, but in the patent another arrangement is described by which "two or three or more strings" could be "stretched at the same time"; this idea, as has already been pointed out, was developed later. Possibly the improvements in the harp wrest pins had some influence on the construction of mechanical wrest pins for the pianoforte, for Érard,[4] when describing a new mechanical wrest pin in a patent

[1] C 1296.　　　[2] C 1297.　　　[3] C 1298.　　　[4] C 1301.

dated 1810, begins thus: "I do make the pins of harps *and of pianofortes* much more smooth and easy in their motions and to stand better in tune than heretofore, by causing the same to move in a collar and socket", etc. This seems clearly to be a harp invention applied to the pianoforte.

Mention must also be made of the 'Cheville Volfel [*sic*]' invented by Charles-François Wolfel in 1844[1]; and to 'Walker's Wrest Pin', invented by Daniel Walker of New York in 1838[2]; to a wrest pin patented by A. Jorselius of Sweden[3] in 1841; and to George Hooper Mead's 'slow-motion wrest pin', for which he obtained a Canadian patent in 1851.[4]

The mechanical wrest pin was one way of overcoming the amateur's difficulty in tuning. Another consisted in passing the strings through an agraffe placed between the wrest pin and the bridge and provided with a screw. By tightening this screw the top of the agraffe pressed the string down and raised its pitch, and by loosening it the contrary effect was obtained. It was, in fact, an arrangement rather similar to that at present used for tuning the wire E string on a violin. The firm of Kriegelstein et Plantade patented this in 1841 and stated that "a lady could herself rectify any string that was out of tune by its aid".[5] Henri Pape[6] invented various means for the same purpose and patented them in 1838, 1842, and 1843 respectively. Schweiso seems to have invented something of the same kind in 1826.[7] He proposed to use a "series of small screw nuts...placed in such a situation as for one of the nuts to screw down upon each string of the instrument" at some place on the string "between the extreme end of the string and the next bridge or stop".

Joachim Ehlers of Vienna, in 1824, devised a means for facilitating the tuning by means of an additional bridge which was movable.[8] This bridge pressed on the strings from above in such a way that it could be moved backwards or forwards or up and down by means of screws so that it was possible to "tune all the notes of the pianoforte as desired". Wilhelm Leschen's "bridge of bone, wood, iron, or brass with or without pins" which was placed above the strings may have been a similar device, for Leschen concludes by stating that by this means "tuning is facilitated".[9]

[1] C 1322.	[2] C 1310.	[3] C 1318.
[4] C 1330.	[5] C 251.	[6] C 1311.
[7] C 1259.	[8] C 1272.	[9] C 1273.

In 1786 John Geib patented "An Entire New Improvement upon the Musical Instruments called the Pianoforte and Harpsichord, by which the same will become Perfect and Compleat Instruments of their Kind, which has never before been Discovered, and by which the same can be *more Easily Tuned* and Played upon, etc."

The improvement relating to the tuning consisted in a Buff stop "screwed to the end of the belly board across under the strings in the treble". This stop was constructed as usual with pieces of buff leather, and, when put in action, stopped the sound of one out of each pair of unison strings "for the more easy turning [*sic*] and playing upon the Instrument".[1]

Hummel's remarks upon this type of tuning in his pianoforte school will, it is hoped, make this matter clear. "The manner in which the English tune their piano-fortes", he writes, "differs from ours only in their not being obliged to employ a damper, (*i.e.* tuning leather). By means of a pedal which moves the keyboard and hammers, they are enabled to tune, first one, then two, and lastly all three strings. By this contrivance (*i.e.* Una Corda pedal), tuning is rendered much easier and more certain.

"The many bad piano-fortes formerly manufactured in Germany, in which the hammers did not strike correctly upon the strings, were the cause that this mode of tuning was not generally introduced among us.

"The piano-fortes of Streicher and A. Stein admit of being tuned by this movement of the keyboard, which saves much time from being wasted by using a damper. Another inconvenience attending the use of a damper is that it very often causes a sort of supplementary sound to accompany the principal one, and confuse the ear."[2] (Streicher's pianoforte[3] with down-striking action, patented by him in 1823, had the great advantage of being able to be tuned without the use of the tuning leather (*Stimmleder*), but by means of the Una Corda pedal.)

These inventions were admirable for the amateur who possessed a good ear, but some arrangement had to be made for those who did not. This consisted in the invention of a means for tuning by *sight* instead of by *ear*.

Tuning by sight. A means for tuning by sight was the invention of John J. Wise of Baltimore, who patented it in 1833.[4] It was to

[1] C 768.
[3] C 35.
[2] B 102, Part III, Sect. II, Chap. VI, p. 72.
[4] C 1247.

be effected by an instrument which mechanically measured the tension of the strings by means of an index moving over a dial plate. Hitorff of Paris obtained an Austrian patent for a means of tuning by sight in 1836.[1] Charles Guynemer patented a similar invention in the same year[2] which he called "Indicateurs de l'accord". The invention consisted in "subjecting each of the metallic cords or wires of pianofortes to the action of a spring, and by means of an index connected to that spring to render manifest to the sight and sensible to the touch the exact degree of tension or departure from harmony each cord (or string) [had] sustained, and to mark precisely what degree of tightening or of slackening [was] requisite to restore the instrument to true harmony, and thus to afford to the most unskilled and ignorant persons in music and musical instruments facile and certain means of correctly tuning their own instruments". This was a communication most possibly from a French manufacturer. In the same year Jean-Baptiste Lepère patented a similar invention which he perfected in 1838[3] (Fig. 35). This, though a beautiful piece of mechanism, was clearly too costly ever to come into general use. Pape,[4] also, patented a means for tuning by sight, though on a different principle, in 1838 in France, and patented it in connection with his Piano Console in England in the following year.

It will have been seen, from what has been said, that tuning the pianoforte was a serious task for the amateur. Owing to the fact that the perfection in fixing the strings, which has now been attained, had not been arrived at in this period, the strings often slipped or went out of tune for the reason already given, and this meant that the unisons forming a note had often to be readjusted. Pleyel hoped to overcome this difficulty by making pianofortes with only one string to a note. It will be remembered that the ancient square pianofortes often had but one string to a note, which was very thin and gave a poor tone. It was felt, in certain quarters, that it would be possible to revert to the old principle of having but one string without losing the powerful tone obtained by the two unisons by having one very stout string to every note. Lord Stanhope was amongst the first to make this experiment "but the false and crazy tone rendered by the treble strings, particularly when so enlarged as to produce the quantity of tone required, was an insurmountable obstacle to its success".[5]

[1] C 1248.   [2] C 1249.   [3] C 1250.
[4] C 1251, 1252.   [5] B 45 (a).

Plate XVI. Pianoforte with glass rods. The rods are arranged in two rows and operated by a double row of hammers to economise space. (By courtesy of the Victoria and Albert Museum, London.)

In 1825 Pleyel obtained a patent for his 'unichord' pianoforte.[1] This was an improvement on the English unichord pianoforte invented by Lord Stanhope. Some interesting details emerge from this patent: for instance a Nuremberg steel string, of the diameter used for the extreme bass notes [6/o][2] in ordinary bichord or trichord instruments, was in this case used for the highest note of a six-octave unichord pianoforte. If a brass string was to be used it had to be of a lesser gauge. Various modifications in the size of the bridge pins, etc., had to be made in order to fix these strings. Pleyel also used an iron frame and copper hitch-pin block in order to do away with the back of the case to make his pianofortes lighter and more resonating.

Fétis evidently approved of Pleyel's new invention, for he wrote the following appreciation of it:

M. Pleyel has just introduced a very happy amelioration in the construction both of square and elliptical pianos. These improvements are of various kinds. Convinced of the almost insurmountable difficulty of bringing to a perfect accordance several strings in unison, M. Pleyel has made the trial of reducing the square piano to a single string for each note, and his efforts have been crowned with success. By an excellent arrangement of different parts of the instrument, and by the enlarged diameter of the strings, M. Pleyel has succeeded in giving to his *unichord* pianos a power of sound equal to that of good pianos with two strings, and a purity of intonation often sought for in vain in the latter. These single-stringed pianos would doubtless be too weak for the concert-room but in the drawing-room they are everything that could be wished.[3]

Substitutes for strings to avoid the difficulties of tuning and keeping the instrument in tune. There were some makers who even went so far as to do away with the strings altogether, substituting in their place vibrating substances that did not require tuning; a survival of this is to be seen in the modern dulcitone, in which the sound is produced by hammers striking upon steel forks.

But the vibrating substances which were used in place of the strings at this time were either glass (or metal) rods or plates or metal tongues. The glass rods are clearly a suggestion from the popular 'harmonica' (Plate XVI), and the metal tongues were, no doubt, suggested by those used in the seraphine and similar instruments. Karl Zsitkovsky of Zeban in Sarosev, Hungary, patented a pianoforte in the form of a secrétaire in 1837, in which there were five steel springs to every note. These were vibrated, one after the other, by a wheel set with pins.[4] Henri Pape was

[1] C 933.   [2] See D (1).   [3] B 41, p. 159.   [4] C 1199.

particularly interested in the use of springs and metal tongues and began occasionally to use springs in place of strings as early as 1825.[1] It is interesting to note that the idea of doing away with the strings is also found in Sweden, where J. E. Bäckström obtained a Swedish patent in 1841 for "A new kind of pianoforte without strings",[2] and also in America and in England. But America preferred glass rods; no patents are found relating to the use of springs.

These inventions, which were intended to *simplify* the pianoforte, led to an arrangement which added greatly to its *complexity*. For it occurred to Pape that the tone could be improved by using both springs and strings in one instrument and vibrating them at once by means of double hammers. This Pape actually patented in 1850. There was to be an action with double hammers, one to strike upwards against springs and the other to strike down upon strings. Pape declares that the action is "quite simple, and the note repeats with great facility" (Fig. 36).[3] He also devised a similar one with hammers striking two springs and a seraphine tongue.[4]

Retaining the pianoforte in tune by means of springs, pulleys, levers, etc. These peculiar experiments were not likely to find many adherents, since none of the great composers or pianists were interested in them; it became clear that strings were the only appropriate means for sound propagation in the pianoforte.

The pianoforte makers thought of another way out of the difficulty of tuning the instrument so often; this consisted in keeping it in tune by some mechanical device which counteracted the effect of the 'atmosphere' on the strings.

Peter Litherhead was the first, so far as we know, to attempt to counteract the effect of the atmosphere on the strings by attaching them to helical or other springs, weights, a wheel and axle or a lever and axle in 1800.[5] Isaac Hawkins, in the same year, patented the fixing of one end of the string of any instrument with a "Spring or fuzee, or levers, to which a spring is fixed so contrived that the spring shall act with equal force or weight on the string when it contracts or expands".[6]

Litherhead perfected his invention two years later.[7] The method of applying the springs to the "grand piana forte" [*sic*] is too lengthy to quote in full, but the principle may be summarised as follows: Instead of one continuous string which was fixed directly

[1] C 1196.   [2] C 742.   [3] C 967.   [4] C 969.
[5] C 977.   [6] C 978.   [7] C 980.

to the hitch pin at one end and a wrest pin at the other, a *spring* was interposed between the portion of string just past the bridge, and the part that was twisted round the wrest pin. A length was thus cut out of the 'after length' of the string and the space formerly occupied by this length was filled in by the *spring* to which the two cut ends of the string were hooked.

By this means, as Litherhead says:

If the string should have a tendency to expand in warm weather or contract in cold weather, the spring by collapsing or opening counteracts such effect, and keeps the string so nearly to the same tension that no error will arise, provided the friction from the bridge and its pin is not so great as to prevent the springs acting.

These springs, had, of course, to be tempered and carefully prepared. The method of tempering and constructing the springs is best described in Litherhead's own words as follows:

I make them of wire drawn out of steel (as this metal produces the most elastic force when properly tempered, I prefer it to any other); this wire I coil round a cylinder of a size such as I intend to make the springs, and after it is coiled to the length wanted I bend outwards about half a turn at each end for a loop. My method of tempering them is as follows viz: I make them rather more than what is usually termed a blood red heat and then immerse them in oil; if they are hard, I lay them on a plate of iron with as much oil as will nearly cover them and make them so hot as to turn them a light brown colour.

Table III shows the dimension of the springs for pianoforte, harpsichord and guitar.[1] It will be observed that the springs to be used for the harpsichord are smaller than those used for the square pianoforte.

Table III. *Table of the Average Dimensions of the Springs for different Instruments*

What kind of instrument	Treble, bass or tenor part	Thickness of the wire of which the springs were made	Diameter of the cylinder round which the springs were coiled
Grand Pianoforte	Bass and tenor	1/18 inch	1/10 inch
,,	Treble	1/20 ,,	1/10 ,,
Small Pianoforte	Bass and tenor	1/30 ,,	1/12 ,,
,,	Treble	1/40 ,,	1/40 ,,
Harpsichord	Springs nearly like those for the guitar	—	1/8 ,,
Guitar	All strings nearly alike	1/40 ,,	1/8 ,,

[1] Abridged from Litherhead's patent (C 980).

Meanwhile, in 1801, Egerton Smith and Thomas Todd[1] had devised various means for keeping pianofortes in tune by the mutual action of a screw combined with a lever or levers, and Érard obtained a French patent for a similar invention in 1812.[2] 'La Dame Alliaume',[3] a French pianoforte maker, also patented an invention intended for the same purpose in 1846. The strings were to be stretched by means of a weight fixed upon the arm of a lever, but, if it was preferred, the weight could be replaced by a spring.

Conclusion. The elegance of structure and of ornamentation that characterised the eighteenth-century pianofortes was continued in the pianofortes of the first few years of the nineteenth century. The change from the taper to the lathe-turned leg marked the beginning of a decline in taste which was to go to an extreme length towards the end of the century. The better class of instrument in the forms of giraffe, pyramid, or lyre-shaped pianoforte and certain other pianofortes which were specially decorated for wealthy clients still carried on the tradition of elegance or distinction of form and of ornamentation. The less costly pianofortes which constituted the bulk of those usually made had often ornaments which were a cheap imitation of those used on the pianofortes for the wealthy clients. Thus cast brass moulding sold by the foot[4] and nailed around the instrument, stamped brass ornaments and sometimes cast lead ornaments painted and gilded to imitate brass, supplied the place of the finely chiselled work after the designs of artists which were used for the better class of instrument.

The square pianoforte, from being an elegant instrument upon four taper, or gracefully curved, legs, was frequently placed upon a stand with six turned legs and with two drawers for music (Plate XVII). But these remarks apply to the English square pianoforte, for Pleyel et Cie of Paris placed their instruments upon a trestle-shaped stand in the form of an X and other makers followed their example. The large size which these instruments were obliged to be built made them necessarily ungainly, though the beautiful workmanship and pleasing design of Pape's later squares make them an exception. When the tall upright instruments tended to go out of favour owing to the preference for small compact pianofortes, elegance of shape seems to have given place to a rich solidity and misapplied gorgeousness.

---

[1] C 979. [2] C 981. [3] C 982.
[4] Messrs John Broadwood bought this in 1815 at 1*s.* 4*d.* per foot and in 1816 at 1*s.* And in the latter year one dozen "brass ornaments" cost 7*s.* 6*d.*

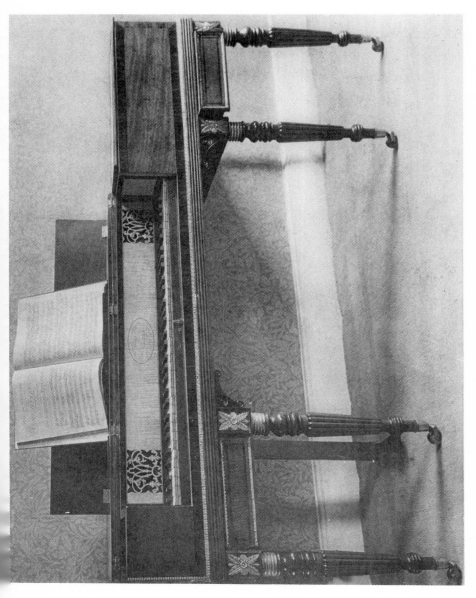

Plate XVII. A Square Pianoforte on a stand with six legs and with two drawers for music. Ornamented with cast-brass mouldings. By John Broadwood and Sons, about 1812. (In the possession of the writer.)

Now we find upright pianofortes with legs almost as thick as those used for a grand, and with the case ornamented with an atrocious fretwork.

The makers were, of course, trying to meet the requirements of the public for cheap and yet ornamental instruments. In the old days, mother-of-pearl was occasionally used as a substitute for ivory upon the keys. But in the nineteenth century from time to time makers patented cheap substitutes for ivory. This seems to have begun in 1788 when Clagget patented covering the keys with glass or enamel.[1] Kisselstein stated (1831) that he covered the keys with white ox bone.[2] In 1839 Bingham and Boden patented an improved covering for the keys in composition imitating ivory, bone, horn, and mother-of-pearl.[3] A French maker, Barthélemy-Richard de Prédaval, in 1840 next took up this idea and patented the use of porcelain or petuntse instead of ivory.[4] It is unnecessary to enumerate more; glass, porcelain or enamel was to form a cheap substitute for ivory. The beautifully figured ivory itself was not thought to be so good as that which was plain and unfigured.

Cheap pianofortes were occasionally made encased in red pitchpine. Collard and Collard exhibited one in the Exhibition of 1851, and the present writer has seen one by Robert Wornum.

Occasionally a maker who wished his pianofortes to be placed in the highest rank made an instrument in a decorated case with the keys of pearl or tortoise-shell. A 'drawing-room pianoforte' by Demoline, an exhibitor at the Exhibition of 1851, had a case of papiermâché and mother-of-pearl in the Italian style. This was considered to be a "splendid, unique and beautiful piece of art-manufacture".

Another pianoforte of the same size and by the same firm was also exhibited by them: we quote a description of it from their prospectus:

The exterior is of rosewood, the trusses which support the key frame are cornucopias; the rich cluster of fruit is both well arranged and beautifully carved. The upper part contains two compartments, with gracefully carved arches, blending the rose, thistle and shamrock together in the centre, so as to form a lyre, which by a simple movement forms the music desk when required, which may be lighted up by two elegant Ormolu candelabras, tastefully arranged at each side. In each panel is introduced a beautiful work of art—specimen of put-on-glass painting; subject Venetian garden scenery morning and evening.[5]

[1] C 650.   [2] C 876.   [3] C 652.   [4] C 655.
[5] The price of this instrument was 330 guineas

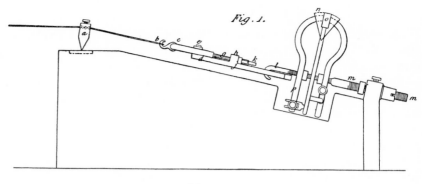

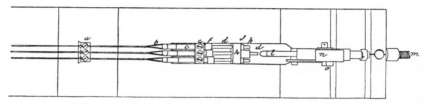

Fig. 35. Lepère's apparatus for tuning three unison strings by sight at the same time, 1838.

Fig. 1, vue, en élévation, d'un indicateur sur lequel trois cordes réunies ont leur action.

Fig. 2, vue, en plan, de ces mêmes parties.

a, chevalet.

b, crochet d'articulation auquel sont fixées les cordes.

c, plates-bandes entre lesquelles manœuvre l'extrémité articulée du crochet.

d, chape liant l'indicateur à la partie qui porte les crochets des cordes.

e, vis conductrices du mouvement de va-et-vient de cette partie de la chape avec les plates-bandes jumelles.

f, extrémité massive des jumelles formant la réunion des plates-bandes, et portant un trou taraudé pour recevoir la vis, au moyen de laquelle on peut accorder chaque corde séparément; principe de tirage des cordes analogue à celui décrit dans nos brevets antérieurs.

g, vis de tirage des jumelles qui portent le crochet des cordes.

h, saillie de la chape dans laquelle passent librement les vis *g*.

j, collet des vis s'appuyant sur la partie *h*.

k, carré que porte l'extrémité des vis pour les faire manœuvrer au moyen d'une clef.

La différence de longueur des tiges entre elles sert à donner de la facilité pour les tourner chacune à part.

l, crochet dont la partie recourbée est placée dans la chape, et dont la tige droite filetée, traversant un des bras du ressort de l'indicateur, y est retenue par un écrou; l'axe du tirage sur les bras du ressort de l'indicateur ne s'exerce plus, comme auparavant, à leur extrémité, mais bien presque au milieu de leur hauteur, afin de donner une action plus prononcée à l'indicateur.

m, vis principale de tirage pour l'accord des trois cordes…et dont l'extrémité, jointe à un des bras du ressort de l'indicateur, y est fixée comme la tige du crochet *l*.

n, partie supérieure (en bois, en ivoire, en nacre, etc.) fixée au cintre du ressort de l'indicateur, et formant un tableau marquant, au besoin, les divisions en fractions de tons, ou simplement une ligne destinée à servir de point correspondant à celle faite sur l'indicateur pour montrer les mouvements de celui-ci.

In marked contrast to these are the beautiful pianofortes of Henri Pape simply encased in rosewood with a neat beaded ornament and occasionally with a balustrade or twisted 'console' leg.

Pape also occasionally decorated his pianofortes richly, as he had invented a saw for cutting veneer of every kind, and even ivory. He is said to have exhibited a pianoforte completely veneered in ivory at the Exhibition of 1827. By means of this saw he was able to cut sheets of ivory from ten to twelve feet long, two of which completely covered the case. "The flap contained one piece, which was two feet wide." This pianoforte was purchased for 6000 francs and sent to New York.[1]

Although the *outward* appearance of the nineteenth-century pianofortes lacked the elegance of those made in the eighteenth century, yet the *inward* structure was improved beyond measure. The thin tinkling sounds of the early pianofortes had given place to a rich sonority made possible by the use of heavier strings firmly secured to a frame braced with metal.

Nothing could give the pianoforte the sustained tone of the bowed stringed instruments or their power of diminishing or augmenting the tone by imperceptible gradations, yet by 1851 the many improvements, and particularly the finely adjusted action, gave the pianoforte its "capacity of obeying the touch" which "constituted its principal advantage over the harpsichord" in the opinion of a musical writer of this period. And this capacity, he continues to say, "enables the performer to vary and accommodate the expression to those energies and striking lights and shades which so greatly characterise the more refined compositions of the present day".

[1] B 75 (*a*).

Cette partie est mobile en ce sens que, si, le piano étant d'accord, on ne voulait pas redresser l'aiguille indicatrice, il suffirait de tourner le tableau à droite ou à gauche pour faire concorder la ligne-milieu du tableau avec celle tracée sur l'extrémité de l'aiguille formant l'indicateur.

o, autre partie, en ivoire ou autre matière, fixée à l'extrémité de l'aiguille de l'indicateur, et portant la ligne qui doit correspondre à celles marquées sur le tableau *n*.

p, extrémités du bras du ressort plus longues qu'elles n'étaient précédemment, et portant les mêmes bras de levier pour hausser et baisser à volonté l'aiguille, ou changer sa direction, dans le cas où on ne voudrait pas changer celle du tableau.

Les changements que nous venons de décrire consistent, comme on le voit,
   (1) Dans des perfectionnements de construction à l'égard du ressort, pour lui donner une action plus prononcée, et pour indiquer d'une manière plus claire à l'œil les impressions qu'il peut recevoir de la part des cordes;
   (2) Dans l'application d'une seul indicateur à trois cordes réunies sous son action, et qui conservent néanmoins la faculté d'être accordées séparément au besoin.

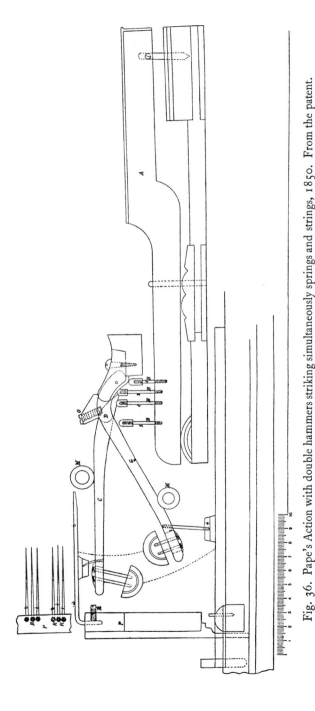

Fig. 36. Pape's Action with double hammers striking simultaneously springs and strings, 1850. From the patent.

A, key; *B*, pilots 1, 2, 3 and 4. No. 1 touches the hammer *C* behind its centre *D* to make it strike the string. No. 2 presses the hammer on the other side of its centre and keeps it from trembling; the same hammer *C*, lifting up again, damps the vibrating spring *i*. No. 3 lifts up the second hammer *G* to strike the vibrating spring *i* fixed in the block *P* and pressed by the screw *R*. No. 4 retains the hammer after the stroke and damps by its fall the string, 4, tuft. The *forte* is operated by the iron tubes *M* lined with woollen stuff, and by these tubes the hammer can be prevented from striking either the strings or the springs, and thus the hammer will play on the strings or only on the springs. The hammer *C* is lifted by the coil spring *O*, but it can be done as well with an elastic ribbon, of which I often make use now. (*Pape.*)

APPENDICES

APPENDIX A

SELECT LIST OF OLD TECHNICAL TERMS RELATING TO THE PIANOFORTE

N.B. For a modern list of technical terms relating to the Pianoforte Action and Frame see Nalder, L. M., *The Modern Piano*, London, p. 109 (Grand Action) and p. 128 (Upright Action); also p. 40 (Frame).

English	American	German	French	Explanation
Action	—	Mechanik	Mécanique	Key frame with striking apparatus
Agraffe	—	—	Agrafe (f.)	Brass stud pierced with as many holes as there are unison strings to the note—fixed to the wrest-pin block, and serving as a bridge for the particular note
Capo Tasto bar	—	Capo Tasto	—	A bar acting as the nearer bearing of the vibrating length of the string—replacing, or supplementary to, the wrest-pin-block bridge
Check	Back catch	Fänger (m.)	Attrape-marteau (m.)	A pad fixed upon a wire or wooden shaft serving to prevent the reiteration of the hammer by catching it and holding it after it has fallen from the string, until the key is released
Damper	—	Dämpfer (m.)	Étouffoir (m.)	A silencing agent to stop the vibrations of the strings
Escapement	—	Auslöser* (m.)	Échappement (m.)	A pivoted lever serving to communicate motion to the hammer, which slips away from the hammer directly it has given it motion, to allow the hammer to fall freely from the string
Hammer	—	Hammer (m.)	Marteau (m.)	Striking lever moving upon a centre
Hammer beak	—	Hammer-schnabel (m.)	—	A short beak-like projection on the butt of German or Viennese hammers serving to work under the Auslöser or Prelleiste
Hammer butt	—	Hammernuss (f.)	Noix (f.)	That part of the hammer which is centred
Hammer head	—	Hammerkopf (m.)	Tête (f.) du marteau	That part of the hammer that comes in contact with the strings
Hammer rail	Hammer beam	Hammerleiste (f.)	Fourche (f.)	The rail to which the hammer is hinged
Hammer shank	—	Hammerstiel (m.)	Tige (f.) du marteau	The piece which connects the head with the butt
Hitch pin	—	—	Pointe (f.) Pointe d'ac-croche	Pin over which the string is looped
Hitch-pin block	Straining pin block	Unhängestock (m.)	Sommier (m.) des pointes	Block which receives the hitch pins

* Applicable to the German Action.

English	American	German	French	Explanation
Hopper* (Grasshopper)	Jack flyer,† also fly lever and flyer, also repeating spring tongue and pusher or lifter	Stosszunge (f.) or Zunge (f.)	—	—
Jack	—	Stösser (m.)	Pilote (m.)	A fixed upright on the key serving to communicate motion from the key to the hammer
Kapsel	—	Kapsel (f.)	—	Sheath within which the hammer in the German Action is pivoted
Key (finger)	—	Taste (f.)	Touche (f.)	Centred lever serving to communicate motion to the hammer
Keyboard	—	Tastatur (f.)	Clavier (m.)	The whole extent of the keys
Key frame	—	Klaviatur-rahmen (m.)	Châssis (m.) du clavier	The frame which carries the keys and action
Pedal (foot)	—	Pedal (n.)	Pedale (f.)	A lever serving to bring a certain register into play or to raise the dampers
Pedal (knee)	—	—	—	—
Prelleiste	—	Prelleiste (f.)	—	The projection at the back of the key under and against which the Hammerschnabel or Hammer Beak works in the German Action
Sound-board	—	Resonanzboden (m.)	Table (f.) d'Harmonie	Board over or under which the strings are extended
Sticker	Abstract	Abstrakt	—	Wooden rod transmitting motion between the ends of two reciprocating levers
Stops	—	Veränderungen	—	Changes of registration
String	—	Saite (f.)	Corde (f.)	—
Under hammer or intermediate lever	—	Treiber (m.)	Faux marteau (1790 action)	Hinged lever lying under the hammer
Wrest pin	Turning pin	Stimmnagel, later Wirbel	Cheville (f.)	Pin to which the end of the string is attached and over which a hammer fits for the purpose of tuning
Wrest-pin block, or wrest plank	Turning-pin block, also turning block and turning rail	Stimmstock (m.)	Sommier (m.) des chevilles	Bed of wood or iron for receiving the wrest pins
Wrest-pin-block bridge	—	—	Sillet (m.)	The pinned rail upon the wrest-pin block

* Applicable only to the Cristofori, Stosszungen and English Actions.
† The fixed piece is called the *Jack*, whilst the jointed piece is properly the *Flyer*.

APPENDIX B

BIBLIOGRAPHY

PART I

PATENT LITERATURE, ETC.

Europe

AUSTRIA

(1) *Beschreibung der Erfindungen und Verbesserungen für welche in den Kaiserlich-Königlichen Österreichischen Staaten Patente ertheilt wurden und deren Privilegiums Dauer nun erloschen ist.* Wien, 1841–47.

BAVARIA

(2) *Anzeiger für Kunst und Gewerbfleiss im Königreiche Baiern.* München, 1816–68.

BELGIUM

(3) *Catalogue des Brevets d'Invention Délivrés en Belgique du 1er nov.* 1830 *au* 31 *déc.* 1841. Vol. 1. Bruxelles, 1841.
　　(*a*) 1er Supplément. 1842–43. Bruxelles, 1845.
　　(*b*) 2me Supplément. 1844–45. Bruxelles, 1846.
　　(*c*) 3me Supplément. 1846–47. Bruxelles, 1849.
　　(*d*) 4me Supplément. 1848, 1849, 1850. Bruxelles, 1854.
　　(*e*) 5me Supplément. 1851, 1852, 1853, et jusqu'au 5 juin 1854 exclusivement. Bruxelles, 1855.

FRANCE

(4) *Machines et Inventions Approuvées par l'Académie Royale des Sciences.* Paris, 1735–77.
(5) *Histoire de l'Académie Royale des Sciences.* Paris, 1733–90.
(6) *Description des Machines et procédés spécifiés dans les Brevets d'Invention, de perfectionnement et d'importation dont la durée est expirée.* First Series. Paris, 1811–63.
(7) Second Series. Paris, 1850–70.

GREAT BRITAIN

England

(8) *Printed Specifications.* Patent Office Publications. London, 1856.
(9) *Abridgements of Specifications relating to Music and Musical Instruments,* 1694–1866. 2nd ed. London, 1871.

Scotland

(10) *Manuscript List in the Patents Office Library, London,* N.D.

Ireland

(11) *Manuscript List in the Patents Office Library, London,* N.D.

RUSSIA

(12) *Journal of Commissioners' Patents*, No. 507. London, N.D.

SWEDEN

(13) *Manuscript List in the Patents Office Library, London*, N.D.

United States of America

(14) *Printed Specifications.* U.S.A. Patent Office Publications. About 1870.
(15) *List of Patents granted by the U.S.A. etc.* Washington, 1872.
(16) *Subject-Matter Index of Patents, etc. issued by the U.S.A. Patents Office.* Vol. II. Washington, 1874.
(17) *Franklin Journal and American Mechs. Mag.* Philadelphia, 1826–27.
(18) *Journal of the Franklin Institute, etc.* New Series. Philadelphia, 1828–40.
(19) *Journal of the Franklin Institute.* Third Series. Philadelphia, 1841– .

Canada

(20) *Patents of Canada.* Vol. I (1824–49). Toronto, 1860.
(21) *Patents of Canada.* Vol. II (1849–55). Toronto, 1865.

PART II

MISCELLANEOUS

(22) *Allgemeine musikalische Zeitung.* "Ditanaklasis." 5. Jahrg. No. 52, S. 367. Leipzig, 1803.
(23) Armellino, G. *Manuel simplifié de l'accordeur ou l'art d'accorder les Pianos.* Seconde éd. Paris, 1855.
(24) Avison, Charles. *An Essay on Musical Expression.* 2nd ed. London, 1753.
(25) Bedford, Rev. Arthur. *The Great Abuse of Musick.* London, 1711.
(26) Berlioz, Hector. *Treatise upon Modern Instrumentation and Orchestration.* New edition. Edited by Joseph Bennett. Novello: London [1904].
(27) Bie, Oscar. *The Pianoforte and Pianoforte Players.* English trans. E. E. Kellett and E. W. Naylor. London, 1899.
(28) Blaikley, D. J. "An Essay on Musical Pitch." Appendix to *A Descriptive Catalogue of the Musical Instruments at the Royal Military Exhibition, London, 1890.* London, 1891.
(29) Bleyer, J. F. *"Historische Beschreibung der aufrechtstehenden Forte-Pianos, von der Erfindung Wachtl und Bleyers in Wien"* in *Allgemeine musikalische Zeitung.* 13. Jahrg. No. 17, S. 73–77. Leipzig, 1811.
(30) Burney, Dr Charles. *The Present State of Music in Germany, the Netherlands and United Provinces.* 2nd ed. p. 57. London, 1775.
(31) Burney, Dr Charles. *A General History of Music from the Earliest Ages to the Present Period.* Vol. III. London, 1789.
(32) Callcott, W. H. *Remarks on the Royal Albert Pianoforte.* London, 1851.
(33) Christmann. "Nachricht von dem Schnell'schen Animo-Corde" in *Allgemeine musikalische Zeitung.* Erster Jahrg. No. 3, S. 39–44, Tafel I. Leipzig, 1798.
(34) Comettant, Oscar. *Histoire de Cent Mille Pianos et d'une Salle de Concert.* Paris, 1890.

(35) Dannreuther, Edward. "Chopin." Art. in *Grove's Dictionary of Music and Musicians*. 3rd ed. Edited by H. C. Colles. London, 1927–28.
    (*a*) "Field." Art. in *id*.
    (*b*) "Moscheles." Art. in *id*.
(36) Dolmetsch, Arnold. *The Interpretation of the Music of the Seventeenth and Eighteenth Centuries*. London [1915].
(37) Ellis, Alexander J. "The History of Musical Pitch in Europe." Additions by the translator, Section H in Helmholtz, *On the Sensations of Tone*. 2nd English ed. London, 1885. (See Helmholtz.)
(38) Érard. *Érard's New Patent Action Grand Pianoforte*. London, 1836.
(39) Érard Frères. *Perfectionnements apportés dans le mécanisme du piano par les Érard, depuis l'origine de cet instrument jusqu'à l'Exposition de* 1834. Paris, 1834.
(40) Farmer, H. G. *The Rise and Development of Military Music*. London [1912].
(41) Fétis, F. J. "Improvements in the Construction of Pianos" (trans. from the *Revue Musicale*) in *The Harmonicon*. Vol. v, p. 158. London, 1827.
    (*a*) "Pasquini, Bernard." Art. in *Biographie Universelle des Musiciens*. Tome 5. Paris, 1863.
(42) Forkel, N. J. *Johann Sebastian Bach*, with notes and appendices by Charles Sandford Terry. London, 1820.
(43) Gardiner, William. *The Music of Nature*. 3rd ed. London, 1849.
(44) Grove, Sir George. "Harmonica." Art. in *Grove's Dictionary of Music and Musicians*. 3rd ed. Edited by H. C. Colles. London, 1927–28.
(45) *Harmonicon*. "Mr Moscheles' Concert." Vol. i, p. 108. London, 1823.
    (*a*) "On the New Construction of Pianofortes." Vol. vi, p. 31. London, 1828.
    (*b*) "The Plectroeuphon." Vol. vi, p. 37. London, 1828.
    (*c*) "M. Hummel and his two Concerts." Vol. viii, p. 264. London, 1830.
    (*d*) "Memoir of Sébastien Érard." Vol. ix, p. 225. London, 1831.
(46) Helmholtz, Hermann L. F. *On the Sensations of Tone*. 2nd English ed. Edited by Alexander J. Ellis. London, 1885.
(47) Herbert, L. "Patent Self-acting and Keyed Upright Grand Piano-Fortes" in *The Register of Arts*. New Series. Vol. v, pp. 23, 24. London, 1831.
(48) Herrmann, Dr H. *Die Regensburger Klavierbauer Späth und Schmahl und ihr Tangentenflügel*. Bayreuth, 1928.
(49) Hipkins. *The Story of the Pianoforte*. Novello Primer No. 52. London, 1896.
    (*a*) "Clavichord." Art. in *Grove's Dictionary of Music and Musicians*. 3rd ed. Edited by H. C. Colles. London, 1927–28.
    (*b*) "Bord." Art. in *id*. with additions by Mlle M. L. Pereyra.
    (*c*) "Harpsichord." Art. in *id*.
    (*d*) "Jack." Art. in *id*.
    (*e*) "Mute." Art. in *id*.
    (*f*) "Pianoforte." Art. in *id*. with additions from the author's notes supplied by Miss Edith J. Hipkins and information from Mr L. A. Broadwood and others.
    (*g*) "Stops." Art. in *id*.
(50) Hogarth, Dr. "Musical Instruments—The Piano-Forte." Art. in *The Musical World*. Vol. ii, p. 65 (No. xviii). London, 1831.
(51) Hopkins, E. J. "Organ" (Rev. T. Elliston). Art. in *Grove's Dictionary of Music and Musicians*. 3rd ed. Edited by H. C. Colles. London, 1927–28.
(52) Huberson, M. G. *Nouveau Manuel complet de l'Accordeur et du Réparateur des Pianos*, pp. 8, 9. Manuels-Roret. Paris, 1926.

(53) Hume, Duncan. "Hummel." Art. in *Grove's Dictionary of Music and Musicians*. 3rd ed. Edited by H. C. Colles. London, 1927–28.
    (*a*) "Thalberg." Art. in *id*.

(54) J. J. D. "French Improvements in Musical Instruments." Letter to the Editor, Nov. 20th, in *The Harmonicon*. Vol. vi, p. 6. London, 1827.

(55) James, Philip. *Early Keyboard Instruments*. London, 1930.

(56) Jones, the Rev. W., of Nayland. *A Treatise on the Art of Music*. Colchester, 1784.

(57) Josten, Dr Hanns H. *Die Sammlung der Musikinstrumente (Landesgewerbemuseum, Stuttgart)*. Stuttgart, 1928.

(58) Kastner, George. *Manuel Général de Musique Militaire*. Paris, 1848.

(59) Kinsky, George. *Katalog des Musikhistorischen Museums*, von Wilhelm Heyer. Band i, *Tasteninstrumente*. Cöln, 1910.

(60) Kraus, Alexander. "Italian Inventions for Instruments with a Keyboard." Art. in *Sammelbände der Internationalen Musikgesellschaft*. 13. Jahrg. Heft iii. Leipzig, 1912.

(61) Krause, Dr K. Christian. "Nachricht über eine Verbesserung der Klaviatur der Tasteninstrumente" in *Allgemeine musikalische Zeitung*. 12. Jahrg. Leipzig, 1810.

(62) Kunz, Thomas. "Beschreibung des Orchestrions" in *Allgemeine musikalische Zeitung*. Erster Jahrg. No. 6, S. 88–90, Tafel ii. Leipzig, 1798.
    (*a*) "Nachricht von dem durch Thomas Kuns in Prag verbesserten Bogenklavier." No. 27, S. 475–7. Leipzig, 1800.

(63) Kützing, C. *Das Wissenschaftliche der Fortepiano-Baukunst*. Bern, 1844.

(64) Maffei, Scipione. "Nuova Invenzione d' un Gravecembalo col piano, e forte, aggiunte alcune considerazioni sopra gl' istrumenti musicali." Art. in *Giornale dei Letterati d'Italia*. Tomo v, p. 144. Venezia, 1711.

(65) Mahillon, Victor-Charles. *Catalogue descriptif et analytique du Musée instrumental du Conservatoire royal de Musique de Bruxelles*. Gand, 1893–1922.

(66) Maitland, J. A. Fuller. "Pianoforte Playing." Art. in *Grove's Dictionary of Music and Musicians*. 3rd ed. Edited by H. C. Colles. London, 1927–28.
    (*a*) "Staveless Notation." Art. in *id*.

(67) Marmontel, A. *Histoire du Piano et de ses origines*. Paris, 1885
    (*a*) "De Musica Theorica et Practica." Lib. iv of *Cogitata Physico-Mathematica*, p. 360. Parisiis, 1644.

(68) Mersenne, Marin. *Harmonie Universelle*. 2 Tome. Paris, 1636-7.

(69) Metropolitan Museum of Art: *Catalogue of Keyboard Instruments*. Crosby Brown Collection of Musical Instruments of all Nations. New York, 1903.

(70) Montal, C. *Kurzgefasste Anweisung das Pianoforte selbst stimmen zu lernen*. Mainz, 1835.
    (*a*) *L'Art d'accorder soi-même son Piano*. Paris, 1836.

(71) Morse, F. C. *Furniture of the Olden Time*. New York, 1902.
    (*a*) *Music and Music Makers*. London [1927].

(72) Moscheles, Constance. *Life of Moscheles by his Wife*. English trans. by A. D. Coleridge. London, 1873.

(73) *Musical Herald*. "The Transposing Pianoforte." Vol. i, No. 1. London, 1846.

(74) *Musical Quarterly*. "Mr Collard's Patent." Vol. iii. London, 1821.
    (*a*) "New Patent for an Improvement on the Pianoforte." Vol. iii. London, 1821.

(75) *Musical World, The*. "Pathetics Eschewed." Vol. i, p. 178. London, 1836.
    (*a*) "Mr Pape's Soirée." Vol. ii, p. 39.
    (*b*) "Mr Moscheles' Soirée." Vol. iv, p. 155. London, 1837.

(c) "Automaton Violinist." Vol. vii, p. 238.

(d) "Mr Moscheles' Soirées." Vol. viii (New Series, Vol. i), p. 103. London, 1838.

(e) "Chopin's Concert at Rouen." Vol. ix (New Series, Vol. ii), p. 85.

(f) "Kollmann's Pianoforte." In id. p. 137.

(g) "Mr Kollmann's Concert." In id. p. 178.

(h) "Thalberg's Grand Morning Concert." Vol. xii (New Series, Vol. v), p. 135. London, 1839.

(j) "Döhler's Concert at Manchester." In id. p. 136.

(k) "Thalberg's Concert." In id. p. 153.

(l) "A Word or Two on Concert Pitch." In id. p. 246.

(76) Nalder, Lawrence. *The Modern Piano*. London [1927].

(77) Neupert, Dr Hanns. *Vom Musikstab zum modernen Klavier*. 2nd ed. Bamberg, 1926.

(78) Niecks, Dr Frederic. *Programme Music*. London [1907].

(79) Paul, Dr Oscar. *Geschichte des Klaviers*. Leipzig, 1868.

(80) Pierre, Constant. *Les Facteurs d'Instruments de musique, les Luthiers et la Facture Instrumentale, précis historique*. Paris, 1893.

(81) "Pitch." Art. in *Grove's Dictionary of Music and Musicians*. 3rd ed. Edited by H. C. Colles. London, 1927–28.

(82) Pole, W. *Musical Instruments in the Great Industrial Exhibition of* 1851. London, 1851.

(83) Redford, John. *Music, a science and an art*. New York, 1923.

(84) Rimbault, E. F. *The Pianoforte; its origin, progress and construction; with some account of the clavichord, virginal, spinet, harpsichord, etc*. London, 1860.

(85) Rizzelli, F. "L'Épine." Art. in *Grove's Dictionary of Music and Musicians*. Vol. iii. 3rd ed. Edited by H. C. Colles. London, 1927–28.

(86) Roma, G. di. *Manuel simplifié de l'accordeur: ou l'art d'accorder le piano, etc*. Seconde éd. Paris, 1834.

(87) Sachs, Curt. *Real-Lexicon der Musikinstrumente, etc*. Berlin, 1913.

    (a) *Sammlung alter Musikinstrumente bei der Staatlichen Hochschule für Musik zu Berlin*. Berlin, 1922.

    (b) *Das Klavier*. Berlin, 1923.

(88) Spillane, D. *History of the American Pianoforte, etc*. New York, 1890.

(89) Spohr, Ludwig. *Autobiography*. English trans. Reeves: London, 1878.

(90) Terry, Charles Sanford. *John Christian Bach*. London, 1929.

(91) Thon, C. F. G. *Abhandlung über Klaviersaiten-Instrumente, insonderheit der Forte-Piano und Flügel, etc*. 3. Aufl. Weimar, 1843.

(92) Turgan. *La Manufacture de MM. Pleyel, Wolff et Cie* in *Les Grandes Usines de France*. 2 Tome. Paris, 1861.

(93) Wedgwood, J. G. *Dictionary of Organ Stops*. London [1905].

(94) Welcker von Gontershausen, H. *Der Flügel, oder die Beschaffenheit des Pianos in allen Formen. Eine umfassende Darstellung der Fortepiano Baukunst*. Frankfurt-am-Main, 1856.

(95) Westerby, Herbert. *The History of Pianoforte Music*. London, 1924.

(96) *Zeitschrift für Instrumentenbau*. Joh. Socher. 46. Jahrg. No. 1, Oct. Leipzig, 1923.

PART III

MUSIC: SELECT LIST

(97) Adam, L. *Méthode de Piano du Conservatoire.* An XIII. Paris, about 1804.

(98) Beethoven. *Werke für Pianoforte Solo.* Verlag der J. G. Cotta'schen Buchhandlung. Band IV. Kritischer und Instructiver Ausgabe von Dr Hans von Bülow. Stuttgart, 1890.

(99) Czerny, Karl. *Complete Theoretical and Practical Pianoforte School.* London.

(100) Giustini, Lodovico. *Sonate da Cimbalo di piano, e forte detto volgarmente di martelletti. Opera prima.* Firenze, 1732.

(101) Herz, H. *Pianoforte Method.* London.

(102) Hummel, J. N. *A Complete Theoretical and Practical Course of Instruction on the Art of Playing the Pianoforte.* London, 1827.

(103) Milchmeyer, Johann Peter. *Die wahre Art das Pianoforte zu spielen, etc.* Dresden, 1797.

(104) Steibelt, Daniel. *Méthode pour le Piano-Forte.* Paris, about 1806.

APPENDIX C

A LIST OF PATENTS

PREFACE

An attempt has been made to collect and classify all the patented inventions relating to the pianoforte up to and including the year 1851. The task has been difficult owing to the fact that the earlier patentees do not always state precisely what they claim as their new invention, and it has therefore devolved upon the writer to decide what the new invention consists of. Many of the early patents comprise several separate inventions, sometimes as many as ten, and to the original patent in France several additional ones (unnumbered) are frequently appended. These again may comprise several inventions.

For the sake of convenience various conventions have been followed; for instance, where there are several patents for one invention in the same year they have been arranged in alphabetical order of countries. (When it is a matter of importance to know in which country an invention was first patented it has been stated in the text.) References to the most accessible abridgements have been given whenever possible. Where no reference is found, as in the case of certain American patents, official publications should be consulted. The following abbreviations have been used:

Am. = America.	A = Grand Pianoforte.
Aust. = Austria.	B = Square Pianoforte.
Bav. = Bavaria.	C = Upright Pianoforte.
Belg. = Belgium.	D = Down-striking Action.
Eng. = England.	
Fr. = France.	

The numbers in curved brackets on the left of each entry are reference numbers. The entries within square brackets on the right refer to the works in which descriptions or lists of the patents may be found. The figures on the left indicate the work (see Appendix B, Bibliography); the number in curved brackets the volume. When there are four figures within the brackets as for instance (1849) this means the volume for the *year* 1849. This date is placed *between* the reference to the work and the number in brackets thus: [19 1851 (21) 244] = *Journal of the Franklin Institute*, Vol. xxi (date 1851), page 244.

ACTION

(1) 1716 (Fr. 172) Marius (B) [4 (3) 83, drawing].
(2) 1716 (Fr. 173) Marius (B, D) [4 (3) 85, drawing].
(3) 1716 (Fr. 174) Marius (C) [4 (3) 87, drawing].
(4) 1716 (Fr. 175) Marius (A) [4 (3) 89, drawing].
(5) 1759 (Fr. —) Weltmann (A) [5 (1759) 241, 242].
(6) 1772 (Fr. —) de L'Épine (–) [5 (1772) 109].
(7) 1777 (Eng. 1172) Stodart (A) [9 p. 12].
(8) 1783 (Eng. 1379) Broadwood (B) [9 p. 13].
(9) 1786 (Eng. 1571) Geib (A) [9 p. 18].
(10) 1787 (Eng. 1596) Landreth (B, C) [9 p. 19].
(11) 1787 (Eng. 1607) Walton (A, B) [9 p. 20].
(12) 1788 (Eng. 1637) Bury (B) [9 p. 20].

(13) 1790 (Eng. 1743) Hancock (A) [9 p. 24].
(14) 1790 (Eng. 1784) Ball (A, B) [9 p. 25].
(15) 1792 (Eng. 1847) Buttery (A) [9 p. 25].
(16) 1794 (Eng. 2016) Sébastien Érard (A, B) [9 p. 28].
(17) 1794 (Eng. 2017) Southwell (B) [9 p. 28].
(18) 1795 (Eng. 2028) Stodart (C) [9 p. 29].
(19) 1797 (Eng. 2160) Rolfe and Davis (A, B) [9 p. 29].
(20) 1798 (Eng. 2264) Southwell (A, B) [9 p. 30].
(21) 1800 (Eng. 2446) Hawkins (C) [9 p. 36].
(22) 1801 (Eng. 2502) Sébastien Érard (A, B) [9 p. 40].
(23) 1801 (Eng. 2552) Bemetzrieder and R. Scott, J. Scott, and A. Scott (B) [9 p. 42].
(24) 1802 (Eng. 2591) Loud (C) [9 p. 44].
(25) 1807 (Eng. 3029) Southwell (C) [9 p. 50].
(26) 1808 (Eng. 3170) Sébastien Érard (A, B) [9 p. 55].
(27) 1809 (Fr. 975) Sébastien Érard (A) [6 (11) 70, pl. 9].
(28) 1811 (Eng. 3403) Southwell (C) [9 p. 65].
(29) 1811 (Eng. 3419) Wornum (C) [9 p. 66].
(30) 1811 (Eng. 3481) Collard (C) [9 p. 67].
(31) 1821 (Eng. 4546) Southwell (C) [9 p. 88].
(32) 1821 (Eng. 4631) Pierre Érard (A) [9 p. 88].
(33) 1822 (Fr. 3512) Érard Frères (A) [6 (36) 51, pl. 6].
(34) 1823 (Aust. —) Mathias Müller (A, C) [1 (1) 269].
(35) 1823 (Aust. —) Johann Streicher (D) [1 (1) 269].
(36) 1823 (Eng. 4821) Smart (C) [9 p. 92].
(37) 1824 (Aust. —) Johann Streicher (C) [1 (1) 270].
(38) 1824 (Aust. —) Johann Anders (A or B ?) [1 (1) 271].
(39) 1824 (Aust. —) M. Müller und Sohn (D) [1 (1) 271].
(40) 1824 (Bav. —) J. Anders (–) [2 (1825) No. 24 p. 155].
(41) 1824 (Fr. 1665) Klepfer-Dufaut (A) [6 (19) 5, pl. 1].
(42) 1825 (Eng. 5065) Pierre Érard (A, C, D) [9 p. 95].
(43) 1825 (Eng. 5107) Kollmann (D) [9 p. 98].
(44) 1825 (Eng. 5261) Broadwood (B) [9 p. 98].
(45) 1825 (Fr. 1808) Pleyel père et fils aîné (A, B, C) [6 (21) 65, pl. 10].
(46) 1826 (Aust. —) Franz Weisz (C) [1 (1) 272].
(47) 1826 (Aust. —) Wilhelm Leschen (D) [1 (1) 272].
(48) 1826 (Eng. 5384) Wornum (C) [9 p. 99].
(49) 1826 (Fr. 3181) Kelpfer-Dufaut (A, B) [6 (33) 93, pl. 18].
(50) 1826 (Fr. 4918) Pape (B) [6 (44) 441, pl. 18].
(51) 1826 (Fr. 1st add. Pat. to No. 4918 (1826)) Pape (D) [6 (44) 441, pl. 18].
(52) 1827 (Am. —) Thomas Loud (A, D) [17 1827 (4) 62].
(53) 1827 (Eng. 5468) Pierre Érard (B) [9 p. 100].
(54) 1827 (Eng. 5475) Stewart (B) [9 p. 101].
(55) 1827 (Eng. 5528) Dodd (C) [9 p. 104].
(56) 1827 (Fr. 2nd add. Pat. to No. 4918 (1826)) Pape (C, D) [6 (44) 441, pl. 18].
(57) 1827 (Fr. 2238) J. B. Cluesman (B) [6 (25) 17, pl. 4].
(58) 1827 (Fr. 2780) Dietz fils (B) [6 (29) 331, pl. 33].
(59) 1827 (Fr. 5086) Érard (A, B, C) [6 (46) 31, pl. 4].
(60) 1828 (Aust. —) Karl Stein (–) [1 (1) 273].
(61) 1828 (Eng. 5678) Wornum (C) [9 p. 107].
(62) 1828 (Fr. 3699) Frost père et fils (C) [6 (37) 293, pl. 27].

(63) 1828 (Fr. 5833) Pape (D) [6 (49) 348, pl. 25].
(64) 1829 (Eng. 5865) Stewart (C) [9 p. 111].
(65) 1829 (Fr. 2478) Blanchet et Roller (A, B, C) [6 (27) 188, pl. 8].
(66) 1830 (Am. —) Charles Saltonstall Seabury (A, C, D) [18 1830 (6) 147].
(67) 1830 (Am. —) Jessie Thompson (C) [18 1831 (7) 5].
(68) 1830 (Aust. —) W. Leschen (A) [1 (1) 274].
(69) 1830 (Eng. 5912) Thompson (C) [9 p. 112].
(70) 1830 (Fr. 3rd add. Pat. to No. 4918 (1826)) Pape (D) [6 (44) 441, pl. 18].
(71) 1831 (Am. —) E. R. Currier (D) [18 1831 (8) 167].
(72) 1831 (Aust. —) Anna Streicher und Sohn (A, B, C) [1 (3) 3, Tafel 1 Fig. 1].
(73) 1831 (Aust. —) Joseph Rosch (–) [1 (1) 274].
(74) 1831 (Am. —) John F. Nunns (–) [18 1831 (8) 177].
(75) 1831 (Am. —) T. Kearsing, H. Kearsing, O. Kearsing, G. T. Kearsing, and W. Kearsing (–) [18 1831 (8) 345].
(76) 1831 (Am. —) Jessie Thompson (–) [18 (9) 113].
(77) 1831 (Bav. —) Friedrich Greiner und Joseph Schmidt (D) [2 (1837) Heft. xi und xii 783, mit Zeichnungen].
(78) 1831 (Bav. —) Julius Kisselstein (C) [2 (1835) Heft ix 576, mit Zeichnungen].
(79) 1831 (Bav. —) F. Greiner (D) [2 (1835) Heft vii S. 450, Zeichnung, Fig. 1].
(80) 1832 (Belg. Order No. 112) Groetaers père et fils (C) [3].
(81) 1832 (Belg. Order No. 113) Lichtenthal (C) [3].
(82) 1832 (Eng. 6304) Fischer (C, D) [9 p. 114].
(83) 1833 (Am. —) Alpheus Babcock (–) [18 1834 (14) 36].
(84) 1833 (Fr. 3308) Wetzels (A, B, C, D) [6 (34) 46, pl. 11].
(85) 1833 (Fr. 3701) Paulinus Meideck (A) [6 (37) 302, pl. 27].
(86) 1834 (Aust. —) Joseph F. Ries (B) [1 (1) 275].
(87) 1834 (Aust. —) Kaspar Lorenz (–) [1 (1) 276].
(88) 1834 (Fr. 4119) Kriegelstein et Arnaud (D) [6 (40) 280, pl. 26].
(89) 1834 (Fr. 3486) Debain (B) [6 (35) 350].
(90) 1834 (Fr. 6605) Eulriot (C) [6 (53) 374, pl. 25].
(91) 1834 (Fr. 6606) Danchell et Greiner (D) [6 (53) 376, pl. 25].
(92) 1834 (Fr. 6873) Pape (C, D) [6 (55) 19, pl. 2].
(93) 1834 (Fr. 10,139) Pape (B, C) [6 (72) 250, pl. 22].
(94) 1835 (Aust. —) Mathias Müller (–) [1 (1) 276].
(95) 1835 (Eng. 6744) Stewart (B) [9 p. 116].
(96) 1835 (Eng. 6835) P. F. Fischer (C, D) [9 p. 117].
(97) 1836 (Am. —) John Peltick (D) [18 1836 (18) 191].
(98) 1836 (Aust. —) Joseph Keller (–) [1 (3) 8].
(99) 1836 (Aust. —) Martin Seuffert (C) [1 (3) 12, Fig. 6].
(100) 1836 (Aust. —) Joseph Allgäuer (–) [1 (2) 272].
(101) 1836 (Eng. 7006) Lidel (D) [9 p. 120].
(102) 1836 (Fr. 4115) Soufleto (C) [6 (40) 253, pl. 22].
(103) 1836 (Fr. 4305) Lahausse (A, B, C) [6 (41) 353].
(104) 1836 (Fr. 10,989) F. G. Greiner (D) [6 (79) 401, pl. 20].
(105) 1837 (Am. 504) Thomas Loud (A) [18 1838 (22) 234].
(106) 1837 (Aust. —) Pierre Érard (A) [1 (3) 234, Fig. 179 bis 186].
(107) 1837 (Aust. —) Anton Amberg (A) [1 (2) 73, Fig. 143].
(108) 1837 (Eng. 7424) Southwell (A, B) [9 p. 125].
(109) 1837 (Fr. 1st add. Pat. to No. 5833 (1828)) Pape (D) [6 (49) 348, pl. 25].
(110) 1838 (Am. 1014) Edwin Brown (B) [18 1839 (24) 321].
(111) 1838 (Aust. —) Joseph F. Ries (–) [1 (2) 101].
(112) 1838 (Bav. —) J. Schmidt und F. Greiner (–) [2 (1838) Heft xii 790].

(113) 1838 (Fr. 4736) Braud (C) [6 (44) 37, pl. 3].
(114) 1838 (Fr. 6156) Pfeiffer (B) [6 (51) 203, pl. 15].
(115) 1839 (Am. 1205) John J. Wise (A or B ?) [18 1840 (26) 45].
(116) 1839 (Am. 1379) Hiram Herrick (A or B ?) [18 1840 (26) 391].
(117) 1839 (Aust. —) M. Müller (–) [1 (2) 146].
(118) 1839 (Bav. —) Henri Pape (A, B, C) [2 (1845) Heft III S. 211, Bl. 3].
(119) 1839 (Eng. 7971) Stumpff (A, C) [9 p. 128].
(120) 1839 (Eng. 8137) Pape (A, B, C) [9 p. 129].
(121) 1840 (Bav. —) Johann Meyer (C) [(1851) 180, Bl. 5, Fig. 7 bis 9].
(122) 1840 (Bav. —) Albrecht Ziegler (–) [2 (1840) Heft. XI und XII 797].
(123) 1840 (Eng. 8643) P. Érard (A, B, C) [9 p. 132].
(124) 1840 (Fr. 5801) Cluesman (–) [6 (49) 290].
(125) 1840 (Fr. 7029) F. de Rohden (A) [6 (56) 202, pl. 15].
(126) 1840 (Fr. 7130) Bernhardt (D) [6 (56) 320, pl. 22].
(127) 1840 (Fr. 7466) Mercier (C) [6 (58) 171, pl. 13].
(128) 1840 (Fr. 7665) Boisselot et fils (A) [6 (59) 26, pl. 3].
(129) 1840 (Fr. 7883) Wirth (D) [6 (60) 60, pl. 5].
(130) 1840 (Fr. 7903) Hérold (C) [6 (60) 136, pl. 13].
(131) 1840 (Fr. 11,970) Wolfel (A, B, C) [6 (87) 347, pls. 22, 23].
(132) 1841 (Am. 2167) Lemuel Gilbert (A or B ?) [19 1842 (4) 188].
(133) 1841 (Am. 2330) Daniel B. Newhall (A or B ?) [19 1845 (9) 253].
(134) 1841 (Am. 1970) Timothy Gilbert (B) [19 1842 (3) 265].
(135) 1841 (Fr. 8375) Blondel (A) [6 (62) 417, pl. 32].
(136) 1841 (Eng. 8999) Godwin (A, B) [9 p. 135].
(137) 1841 (Eng. 9023) Steward (C) [9 p. 136].
(138) 1841 (Eng. 9150) Stewart (A, B) [9 p. 137].
(139) 1842 (Am. 2523) Thomas Loud (B) [19 1846 (12) 315].
(140) 1842 (Am. 2595) C. Bossert and John Shoemaker (B) [19 1847 (13) 257].
(141) 1842 (Aust. —) J. B. Streicher (A) [1 (4) 359, Tafel 43, Fig. 475].
(142) 1842 (Belg. Order No. 1640, Index No. 1670) J. Dammekens (–) [3 a].
(143) 1842 (Eng. 9226) Lambert (C) [9 p. 137].
(144) 1842 (Eng. 9262) Wornum (C, D) [9 p. 139].
(145) 1842 (Fr. 10,879) Montal (A, B, C) [6 (78) 385, pl. 22].
(146) 1843 (Am. 2934) Edward Brown (A) [19 1849 (17) 419].
(147) 1843 (Am. 3045) G. Hews, Richard C. March, and N. Tileston (B) [19 1849 (17) 450].
(148) 1843 (Eng. 9594) Kirkman (–) [9 p. 141].
(149) 1843 (Eng. 9631) Du Bochet (B) [9 p. 141].
(150) 1843 (Eng. 9716) Stewart and Lambert (B, C) [9 p. 142].
(151) 1843 (Fr. 9531) Marie Leroux Issauret et Cie (A, B, C) [6 (69) 202, pl. 20].
(152) 1843 (Fr. 12,375) H. Herz (A) [6 (91) 421, pl. 17].
(153) 1844 (Aust. —) Ignaz Bösendorfer (A or B ?) [1 (5) 395, Fig. 445].
(154) 1844 (Belg. Order No. 2164, Index No. 2667) Jean-Henri Pape (–) [3 b] and
(155) 1844 (Fr. 1st add. Pat. to No. 11,027 (1837)) Jean-Henri Pape [6 (79) 507].
(156) 1844 (Eng. 10,238) Sautter (A, B, C) [9 p. 144].
(157) 1844 (Eng. 10,385) Hewitt (C) [9 p. 146].
(158) 1844 (Eng. 10,430) Mercier (A) [9 p. 147].
(159) 1844 (Fr. 1st add. Pat. to No. 11,970 (1840)) C. F. Wolfel (D) [6 (87) 347, pls. 22, 23].
(160) 1844 (Fr. 313) Pape (D) [7 (2) 136, pl. 66].
(161) 1844 (Fr. 8219) Jean-Édouard Daniel (C) [6 (61) 466, pl. 25].

(162) 1844 (Fr. 9935) J. G. Kriegelstein (A, B) [6 (71) 132, pl. 12].
(163) 1844 (Fr. 10,092) F. X. Bader (A) [6 (72) 46, pl. 4].
(164) 1845 (Eng. 10,668) Jean-Henri Pape (C, D) [9 p. 150].
(165) 1845 (Eng. 10,897) Nickels (A, C) [9 p. 152].
(166) 1845 (Fr. 2nd add. Pat. to No. 313 (1844)) Pape (D) [7 (2) 136, pl. 66].
(167) 1846 (Am. 4612) Luther Philleo (A or B ?) [19 1847 (14) 159].
(168) 1846 (Eng. 11,242) Burkinyoung (D) [9 p. 154].
(169) 1846 (Eng. 11,285) Woolley (A, C) [9 p. 156].
(170) 1846 (Fr. 1955) Aury (–) [7 (7) 184, pl. 18].
(171) 1846 (Fr. 2095) Wolfel (C) [7 (8) 47, pl. 3].
(172) 1846 (Fr. 2348) Huttner (C) [7 (9) 53, pl. 7].
(173) 1846 (Fr. 2420) Bord (A) [7 (9) 109, pl. 19].
(174) 1846 (Fr. 2605) Kriegelstein (C) [7 (10) 14, pl. 3].
(175) 1847 (Am. 5086) T. Loud (A) [19 1848 (16) 29].
(176) 1847 (Am. 5216) T. Gilbert (A) [19 1848 (16) 302].
(177) 1847 (Belg. Order No. 2888, Index No. 4354) J. Florence (C) [3 c].
(178) 1847 (Belg. Order No. 2906, Index No. 4695) J. F. Vogelsangs (–) [3 c].
(179) 1847 (Belg. Order No. 2908, Index No. 4760) F. Rhoden [sic] (–) [3 c]. Also
(180) 1847 (Fr. 2751) De Rhoden (?) [7 (10) 197, pl. 33].
(181) 1847 (Fr. 3340) Sulot (–) [7 (12) 276].
(182) 1848 (Am. 5985) J. H. Low (A) [19 1849 (18) 206].
(183) 1848 (Am. 5990) J. J. Wise (B) [19 1849 (18) 208].
(184) 1848 (Belg. Order No. 3838, Index No. 5470) H. Alundige (–) [3 d].
(185) 1848 (Fr. 3rd add. Pat. to No. 313 (1844)) Pape (D) [7 (2) 136, pl. 66].
(186) 1848 (Fr. 3711) Montal (A, B) [7 (13) 186, pls. 32, 33].
(187) 1849 (Fr. 2nd add. Pat. to No. 3711 (1848)) Montal (C) [7 (13) 186, pls. 32, 33].
(188) 1850 (Am. 7292) J. Ruck (A) [19 1850 (20) 47].
(189) 1850 (Am. 7441) Lemuel Gilbert (C) [19 1850 (20) 119].
(190) 1850 (Belg. Order No. 3873, Index No. 6699) J. B. Fauville (–) [3 d].
(191) 1850 (Belg. Order No. 3883, Index No. 7046) F. G. Aerts (–) [3 d].
(192) 1850 (Eng. 13,252) Érard (A, B, C) [9 p. 167].
(193) 1850 (Eng. 13,423) Pape (A or B and C, D) [9 p. 168].
(194) 1850 (Fr. 5251) Blanchet (C) [7 (18) 172, pl. 27].
(195) 1850 (Fr. 5923) Pape (A or B and C, D) [7 (20) 90, pls. 13, 14].
(196) 1851 (Am. 7976) J. Ruck (A) [19 1851 (21) 244].
(197) 1851 (Am. 8350) R. Kreter (A) [19 1851 (22) 249].
(198) 1851 (Am. 8352) J. A. Gray (A) [19 1851 (22) 249].
(199) 1851 (Am. 8353) R. M. Kerrison (A) [19 1851 (22) 249].
(200) 1851 (Am. 8383) L. H. Browne (A) [19 1851 (22) 311].
(201) 1851 (Am. 8389) T. Gilbert (A, C) [19 1851 (22) 312].
(202) 1851 (Eng. 13,601) Robertson (C) [9 p. 170].
(203) 1851 (Eng. 13,652) Hopkinson (A) [9 p. 172].
(204) 1851 (Fr. 4th add. Pat. to No. 5923 (1850)) Pape (C) [7 (20) 90, pls. 13, 14].
(205) 1851 (Fr. 6145) Mata (–) [7 (20) 302].
(206) 1851 (Fr. 6606) Pons (C) [7 (22) 19, pl. 5].

Repetition

(207) 1808 (Eng. 3170) Sébastien Érard (A) [9 p. 55].
(208) 1809 (Fr. 975) Érard (A) [6 (11) 70, pl. 9].

(209) 1821 (Eng. 4631) Pierre Érard (A) [9 p. 88].
(210) 1823 (Eng. 4821) Smart (C) [9 p. 92].
(211) 1824 (Fr. No. 1665) Klepfer-Dufaut (A) [6 (19) 5, pl. 1].
(212) 1825 (Eng. 5065) Pierre Érard (A) (A, C, D) [9 p. 95].
(213) 1826 (Aust. —) Franz Weisz (C) [1 (1) 272].
(214) 1827 (Eng. 5468) Pierre Érard (A, B) [9 p. 100].
(215) 1834 (Fr. 6605) Eulriot (C) [6 (53) 374, pl. 25].
(216) 1837 (Eng. 7424) Southwell (A, B) [9 p. 125].
(217) 1837 (Fr. 1st add. Pat. to No. 5833 (1828)) Pape (D) [6 (49) 348, pl. 25].
(218) 1839 (Eng. 7971) Stumpff (A, C) [9 p. 128].
(219) 1840 (Eng. 8643) Pierre Érard (A, B, C) [9 p. 132].
(220) 1840 (Fr. 7883) S. Wirth (D) [6 (60), pl. 5].
(221) 1840 (Fr. 11,970) Wolfel (A, B, C) [6 (87) 347, pls. 22, 23].
(222) 1841 (Eng. 9150) J. Stewart (A, B) [9 p. 137].
(223) 1842 (Fr. 10,879) Montal (A, B, C) [6 (78) 385, pl. 22].
(224) 1843 (Am. 2934) Edward Brown (A) [19 1849 (17) 419].
(225) 1843 (Am. 3045) G. Hews, Richard C. March, and N. Tileston (B) [19 1849 (17) 450].
(226) 1843 (Eng. 9631) Du Bochet (B) [9 p. 141].
(227) 1843 (Eng. 9716) Stewart and Lambert (B, C) [9 p. 142].
(228) 1843 (Fr. 9581) Marie Leroux Issauret et Cie (A, B, C) [6 (69) 202, pl. 20].
(229) 1844 (Eng. 10,238) Sautter (A, B, C) [9 p. 144].
(230) 1844 (Fr. 1st add. Pat. to No. 11,970 (1840)) C. F. Wolfel (D) [6 (87) 347, pls. 22, 23].
(231) 1844 (Fr. 8219) Daniel (C) [6 (61) 466, pl. 25].
(232) 1844 (Fr. 9935) Kriegelstein (A, B) [6 (71) 132, pl. 12].
(233) 1845 (Fr. 2nd add. Pat. to No. 313 (1844)) Pape (D) [7 (2) 136, pl. 66].
(234) 1846 (Eng. 11,285) Woolley (A, C) [9 p. 156].
(235) 1846 (Fr. 2095) Wolfel (C) [7 (8) 47, pl. 3].
(236) 1846 (Fr. 2420) Bord (A) [7 (9) 109, pl. 19].
(237) 1846 (Fr. 2605) Kriegelstein (C) [7 (10) 14, pl. 3].
(238) 1847 (Belg. Order No. 2908, Index No. 4760) F. Rhoden (–) [3 c].
(239) 1847 (Belg. Order No. 2888, Index No. 4354) J. Florence (C) [3 c].
(240) 1848 (Fr. 3rd add. Pat. to No. 313 (1844)) Pape (D) [7 (2) 136, pl. 66].
(241) 1848 (Fr. 3711) Montal (A, B, C) [7 (13) 186, pls. 32, 33].
(242) 1849 (Fr. 1st add. Pat. to No. 3711 (1848)) Montal (C) [7 (13) 186, pls. 32, 33].
(243) 1850 (Eng. 13,252) Pierre Érard (C) [9 p. 167].
(244) 1850 (Fr. 5251) Blanchet (C) [7 (18) 172, pl. 27].
(245) 1851 (Am. 7976) J. Ruck (A) [19 1851 (21) 244].
(246) 1851 (Am. 8350) R. Kreter (A) [19 1851 (22) 249].
(247) 1851 (Eng. 13,652) Hopkinson (A) [9 p. 172].
(248) 1851 (Fr. 3rd add. Pat. to No. 5923 (1850)) Pape (C) [7 (20) 90, pls. 13, 14].

AGRAFFE

(249) 1808 (Eng. 3170) Sébastien Érard [9 p. 55].
(250) 1838 (Fr. 9572) Pierre Érard [6 (69) 176, pl. 17].
(251) 1841 (Fr. 8479) Kriegelstein et Plantade [6 (63) 64, pl. 4].
(252) 1842 (Fr. 9165) Joseph Jelmini [6 (66) 399, pl. 33].

(253) 1844 (Fr. 11,596) Louis-Joseph DoMény [6 (84) 156, pl. 10].
(254) 1851 (Eng. 13,821) T. Statham [9 p. 173]. N.B. Patented as "Metallic Stop".

APPARATUS
Stenographical

(255) 1836 (Fr. 4101) Eisenmenger [6 (40) 183].
(256) 1844 (Fr. 8206) Guérin [6 (61) 422, pl. 22].
(257) 1849 (Bav. —) Flamm [2 (1849) Heft III S. 132, Bl. III, Zeichnungen 10 bis 17].

To Prevent the Sounding of Misfingered Notes

(258) 1848 (Eng. 12,307) Charles Dawson [9 p. 162].

ATTACHMENT
Æolian

(259) 1829 (Fr. 2649) Philippe-Auguste Kayser [6 (28) 273, pl. 32].
(260) 1844 (Am. 3584) Obed M. Coleman [19 1844 (8) 420]. Also
(261) 1844 (Eng. 10,341) [9 p. 145] and
(262) 1844 (Fr. 311) [7 (2) 134, pl. 64].
(263) 1845 (Am. 4210) Charles Horst [19 1846 (12) 244].
(264) 1845 (Eng. 10,589) John Rand [9 p. 149].
(265) 1846 (Eng. 11,359) Alexandre Debain [9 p. 157].
(266) 1847 (Am. 4948) M. Coburn [19 1848 (15) 336]. [Claimed to have been invented prior to Coleman's Attachment.]
(267) 1851 (Am. 8608) G. W. Ingalls [19 1852 (23) 88].

Antiphonel

(268) 1846 (Eng. 11,359) Debain [9 p. 157].
(269) 1848 (Fr. 4068) Debain [7 (14) 233, pl. 33].

Dolce Compana

(270) 1849 (Am. 6223) J. A. Gray [19 1849 (18) 367].
(271) 1849 (Eng. 12,609) W. P. Parker [9 p. 164].

BRACES
Metallic

(272) 1799 (Eng. 2345) Joseph Smith (A, B) [9 p. 34].
(273) 1808 (Eng. 3170) S. Érard (A, B) [9 p. 55].
(274) 1809 (Fr. 975) S. Érard (A) [6 (11) 70, pl. 9].
(275) 1820 (Eng. 4431) Thom and Allen (A, B, C) [9 p. 86].
(276) 1822 (Fr. 2170) Érard Frères (A, B, C) [6 (24) 147, pl. 26].
(277) 1822 (Fr. 3512) Érard Frères (A) [6 (36) 51, pl. 6].
(278) 1824 (Am. —) John Dwight (–) [15. 271].
(279) 1825 (Eng. 5065) Pierre Érard (A, C) [9 p. 95].
(280) 1825 (Eng. 5085) Francis Melville (B) [9 p. 97].

(281) 1827 (Eng. 5548) Dettmer (A, B) [9. 105].
(282) 1827 (Fr. 5086) Sébastien Érard (A, B, C) [6 (46) 31, pl. 4].
(283) 1828 (Fr. 2434) Pleyel (A, B) [6 (27) 41, pl. 3].
(284) 1829 (Aust. —) Joseph Gartner (–) [1 (1) 273].
(285) 1830 (Fr. 2681) Auguste-Louis Langrenez (B) [6 (28) 361].
(286) 1830 (Fr. 4292) Pierre Érard (A, B, C) [6 (41) 320, pl. 34].
(287) 1831 (Am. —) Ebenezer E. Curcier (C) [18 1831 (8) 167].
(288) 1831 (Eng. 6140) Allen (A, B, C) [9 p. 112].
(289) 1832 (Aust. —) Franz Melzer (–) [1 (1) 274].
(290) 1832 (Eng. 6304) P. F. Fischer (B) [9 p. 114].
(291) 1835 (Am. —) Thomas Loud (–) [18 1836 (17) 123].
(292) 1835 (Aust. —) J. B. Streicher (B) [1 (1) 276].
(293) 1837 (Am. 504) Thomas Loud (–) [8 1838 (22) 234].
(294) 1837 (Belg. Order No. 132) C. Frin et Cie (–) [3].
(295) 1838 (Aust. —) Stephen Komary (–) [1 (3) 78].
(296) 1838 (Fr. 6156) Jean Pfeiffer (B) [6 (51) 203, pl. 15].
(297) 1839 (Aust. —) F. Ries (–) [1 (2) 163].
(298) 1840 (Eng. 8388) J. Clarke (A, C) [9 p. 131].
(299) 1840 (Eng. 8643) P. Érard (A, C) [9 p. 132].
(300) 1841 (Am. 2099) Frederick C. Reichenback (A or B ?) [19 1842 (4) 47].
(301) 1841 (Eng. 8999) J. Godwin (A, B) [9 p. 136].
(302) 1842 (Am. 2595) Charles Bossert and John Shoemaker (A or B ?) [19 1847 (13) 257].
(303) 1842 (Aust. —) J. B. Streicher (A) [1 (4) 359].
(304) 1845 (Am. 4282) William F. Senior (B) [19 1846 (12) 384].
(305) 1845 (Eng. 10,592) Hattersley* (A, B, C) [9 p. 149] and
(306) 1845 (Fr. 1501) [6 (6) 107, pl. 24].
(307) 1846 (Fr. 2114) Domény (–) [6 (8) 105, pl. 10].
(308) 1848 (Fr. 3rd add. Pat. to No. 313 (1844)) Pape (A, B, C) [7 (2) 136, pl. 66].
(309) 1849 (Fr. 4325) Scholtus (C) [7 (15) 112, pl. 2].
(310) 1850 (Eng. 13,252) Pierre Érard (C) [9 p. 167].
(311) 1850 (Fr. 6287) Colin (C) [7 (21) 81, pl. 16].
(312) 1851 (Fr. 3rd add. Pat. to No. 3711 (1848)) Montal (C) [7 (13) 186, pls. 32, 33].
(313) 1851 (Fr. 6304) Bonnifas (C) [7 (21) 113, pl. 24].

Wooden

(314) 1802 (Eng. 2591) Thomas Loud [9 p. 44].
(315) 1811 (Eng. 3403) Wm. Southwell [9 p. 65].
(316) 1825 (Eng. 5107) G. A. Kollmann [9 p. 98].
(317) 1827 (Fr. 2088) Charles Côte (B) [6 (23) 245, pl. 6].
(318) 1827 (Fr. 5086) S. Érard (B) [6 (46) 31, pl. 4].
(319) 1828 (Aust. —) Karl Stein (–) [1 (1) 273].
(320) 1833 (Fr. 9331) Jean-Joseph-Pascal Taurin (A, B, C) [6 (67) 439, pl. 38].
(321) 1834 (Fr. 4119) Kriegelstein et Arnaud (B) [6 (40) 280, pl. 26].
(322) 1840 (Eng. 8388) Joseph Clarke (A, C) [9 p. 131].
(323) 1844 (Eng. 10,385) Daniel Chandler Hewitt (C) [9 p. 146].
(324) 1850 (Eng. 13,423) Henri Pape (B, C) [9 p. 168].

* See also (721).

BRASS RAIL

(325) 1829 (Eng. 5865) James Stewart [9 p. 11].

BRIDGE

See SOUND-BOARD—Bridge on the. WREST-PIN BLOCK—with Metal Bridge.

CANDLESTICKS

(326) 1848 (Am. 5631) J. H. Schomacher [19 1849 (17) 325].

CASTORS

(327) 1835 (Eng. 6835) P. F. Fischer [9 p. 117]. N.B. Patented as "elastic steam [*sic*] rollers".
(328) 1840 (Fr. 7554) H. Pape [6 (58) 334, pl. 22].

CHECK

(329) 1777 (Eng. 1172) Stodart [9 p. 12].
(330) 1811 (Eng. 3481) W. F. Collard [9 p. 67].
(331) 1821 (Eng. 4546) Wm. Southwell [9 p. 88].
(332) 1823 (Eng. 4821) H. Smart [9 p. 92].
(333) 1825 (Eng. 5065) Pierre Érard [9 p. 95].
(334) 1825 (Eng. 5107) G. A. Kollmann [9 p. 98]. N.B. Patented as "Catch".
(335) 1825 (Eng. 5261) J. S. Broadwood [9 p. 98].
(336) 1827 (Eng. 5468) P. Érard [9 p. 100].
(337) 1828 (Eng. 5678) R. Wornum [9 p. 107].
(338) 1829 (Eng. 5865) J. Stewart [9 p. 111].
(339) 1831 (Aust. —) Anna Streicher und Sohn [1 (3) 3, Tafel 1, Fig. 1].
(340) 1840 (Fr. 5801) Cluesman [6 (49) 290].
(341) 1840 (Fr. 7903) Hérold [6 (60) 136, pl. 13].
(342) 1841 (Eng. 8999) John Godwin [9 p. 135].
(343) 1841 (Fr. 8375) Blondel [6 (62) 417, pl. 32].
(344) 1843 (Fr. 7783) Weber [6 (59) 330, pl. 26].
(345) 1843 (Fr. 12,375) Herz [6 (91) 421, pl. 17].
(346) 1847 (Am. 5216) T. Gilbert [19 1848 (16) 302].
(347) 1850 (Am. 7441) Lemuel Gilbert [19 1850 (20) 119].
(348) 1851 (Am. 7976) J. Ruck [19 1851 (21) 244].
(349) 1851 (Am. 8383) L. H. Browne [19 1851 (22) 311].

"Second Check"

(350) 1841 (Eng. 9150) James Stewart [9 p. 137].

"Semi-Check"

(351) 1837 (Eng. 7424) Southwell [9 p. 125].

"CHEVILLE-VOLFEL"

See WREST-PINS—Mechanical, etc.

COUPLERS

(352) 1812 (Fr. 1332) Érard Frères [6 (14) 292, pl. 25].
(353) 1824 (Aust. —) Johann Streicher [1 (1) 270].
(354) 1831 (Bav. —) Julius Kisselstein [2 1835 Heft ix 576, mit Zeichnungen].
(355) 1842 (Fr. 1st add. Pat. to No. 12,079 (1841)) Girard-Romagnac [6 (88) 452, pl. 33].

(356) 1843 (Fr. 9541) Boisselot et fils [6 (69) 18, pl. 2].
(357) 1844 (Eng. 10,238) C. M. Elizée Sautter [9 p. 144].
(358) 1844 (Fr. 9788) Pleyel et Cie [6 (70) 219, pl. 14].
(359) 1845 (Am. 4019) Oliver and Jackson [19 1846 (11) 244].
(360) 1845 (Am. 4082) Simon W. Draper [19 1846 (11) 325].
(361) 1845 (Am. 4109) Samuel Warren [19 1846 (11) 391].
(362) 1845 (Eng. 10,897) Benjamin Nickels [9 p. 152].
(363) 1847 (Fr. add. Pat. to No. 2311 (1846)) Soudet [7 (9) 15].
(364) 1847 (Fr. 2946) Zeiger [7 (11) 101, pl. 28].

DAMPERS

(365) 1759 (Fr. —) Weltman [5 (1759) p. 241, 242].
(366) 1783 (Eng. 1379) John Broadwood [9 p. 13].
(367) 1790 (Eng. 1784) James Ball [9 p. 25].
(368) 1794 (Eng. 2017) Southwell [9 p. 28].
(369) 1795 (Eng. 2028) Stodart [9 p. 29].
(370) 1801 (Eng. 2551) J. C. Becker [9 p. 42].
(371) 1801 (Eng. 2552) Bemetzrieder and R. Scott, J. Scott, and A. Scott [9 p. 42].
(372) 1803 (Fr. 114) Schmidt [6 (2) 242, pl. 57].
(373) 1808 (Eng. 3170) Sébastien Érard [9 p. 55].
(374) 1810 (Eng. 3332) Sébastien Érard [9 p. 60].
(375) 1811 (Eng. 3403) Southwell [9 p. 65].
(376) 1825 (Eng. 5107) Kollmann [9 p. 98].
(377) 1825 (Fr. 1808) Pleyel père et fils aîné [6 (21) 65, pl. 10].
(378) 1826 (Aust. —) Franz Weisz [1 (1) 272].
(379) 1826 (Fr. 3181) Klepfer-Dufaut [6 (33) 93, pl. 18].
(380) 1827 (Eng. 5475) Stewart [9 p. 101].
(381) 1827 (Fr. 2238) J. B. Cluesman [6 (25) 17, pl. 4].
(382) 1829 (Eng. 5831) Rolfe [9 p. 110].
(383) 1830 (Am. —) Jessie Thompson [18 1831 (7) 5].
(384) 1833 (Am. —) Alpheus Babcock [18 1834 (14) 36].
(385) 1834 (Aust. —) Joseph F. Ries [1 (1) 275].
(386) 1834 (Aust. —) Kaspar Lorenz [1 (1) 276].
(387) 1835 (Aust. —) M. Müller [1 (1) 276].
(388) 1838 (Fr. 6156) Pfeiffer [6 (51) 203, pl. 15].
(389) 1839 (Eng. 7971) Stumpff [9 p. 128].
(390) 1840 (Eng. 8643) P. Érard [9 p. 132].
(391) 1840 (Fr. 11,970) Wolfel [6 (87) 347, pls. 22, 23].
(392) 1841 (Am. 1970) Timothy Gilbert [19 1842 (3) 265].
(393) 1841 (Eng. 8999) John Godwin [9 p. 135].
(394) 1842 (Eng. 9262) Wornum [9 p. 139].
(395) 1843 (Fr. 12,375) Herz [6 (91) 421, pl. 17].
(396) 1844 (Fr. 9775) Ferdinand Rohden [6 (70) 175, pl. 10].
(397) 1845 (Fr. 2nd add. Pat. to No. 313 (1844)) Pape [7 (2) 136, pl. 66].
(398) 1846 (Eng. 11,285) Woolley [9 p. 156].
(399) 1846 (Fr. 1955) Aury [7 (7) 184, pl. 18].
(400) 1846 (Fr. 2348) Huttner [7 (9) 53, pl. 7].
(401) 1849 (Fr. 2nd add. Pat. to No. 3711 (1848)) Montal [7 (13) 186, pls. 32, 33].
(402) 1851 (Fr. 6606) Pons [7 (22) 19, pl. 5].

Dead Damper

(403) 1844 (Eng. 10,385) Hewitt [9 p. 146].

DESK

(404) 1790 (Eng. 1784) James Ball [9 p. 25].
(405) 1801 (Eng. 2552) Bemetzrieder and R. Scott, J. Scott and A. Scott [9 p. 42].

ESCAPEMENT OR HOPPER

(406) 1786 (Eng. 1571) Geib [9 p. 18]. N.B. Patented as "Jack".
(407) 1787 (Eng. 1596) J. Landreth [9 p. 19].
(408) 1821 (Eng. 4631) P. Érard [9 p. 88].
(409) 1822 (Fr. 3512) Érard Frères [6 (36) 51, pl. 6].
(410) 1826 (Aust. —) Franz Weisz [1 (1) 272].
(411) 1826 (Eng. 5384) Wornum [9 p. 99].
(412) 1827 (Fr. 2nd add. Pat. to No. 4918 (1826)) Pape [6 (44) 441, pl. 18].
(413) 1829 (Fr. 2478) Blanchet et Roller [6 (27) 188, pl. 8].
(414) 1830 (Am. —) Jessie Thompson [18 1831 (7) 5].
(415) 1833 (Fr. 3701) Meideck [6 (37) 302, pl. 27].
(416) 1835 (Eng. 6744) James Stewart [9 p. 116].
(417) 1836 (Am. —) John Peltick [18 1836 (18) 191].
(418) 1836 (Fr. 4115) Soufleto [6 (40) 253, pl. 22].
(419) 1837 (Am. 504) Thomas Loud [18 1833 (22) 234].
(420) 1837 (Aust. —) Anton Amberg [1 (2) 73, Fig. 143].
(421) 1837 (Fr. add. Pat. to No. 5838 (1828)) Pape [6 (49) 348, pl. 25].
(422) 1838 (Fr. 4736) Braud [6 (44) 37, pl. 3].
(423) 1839 (Am. 1379) Hiram Herrick [18 1840 (26) 391].
(424) 1839 (Am. 1389) A. Babcock [18 1840 (26) 394].
(425) 1839 (Aust. —) M. Müller [1 (2) 146].
(426) 1839 (Aust. —) F. Ries [1 (2) 163].
(427) 1839 (Eng. 7971) Stumpff [9 p. 128].
(428) 1840 (Eng. 8643) P. Érard [9 p. 132]. N.B. Patented as "Sticker".
(429) 1840 (Fr. 7903) Hérold [6 (60) 136, pl. 13].
(430) 1840 (Fr. 11,970) Wolfel [6 (87) 347, pls. 22, 23].
(431) 1841 (Am. 1970) Timothy Gilbert [19 1842 (3) 265].
(432) 1841 (Am. 2167) Lemuel Gilbert [19 1842 (4) 188].
(433) 1841 (Eng. 9150) James Stewart [9 p. 137].
(434) 1841 (Fr. 8375) Blondel [6 (62) 417, pl. 32].
(435) 1842 (Fr. 10,879) Montal [6 (78) 385, pl. 22].
(436) 1843 (Eng. 9631) Du Bochet [9 p. 141].
(437) 1843 (Eng. 9716) Stewart and Lambert [9 p. 142].
(438) 1843 (Fr. 7783) Weber [6 (59) 330, pl. 26].
(439) 1843 (Fr. 12,340) P. Érard [6 (91) 272].
(440) 1844 (Aust. —) J. Bösendorfer [1 (5) 395, Fig. 455].
(441) 1846 (Am. 4612) Luther Philleo [19 1847 (14) 159].
(442) 1846 (Eng. 11,285) T. Woolley [9 p. 156].
(443) 1846 (Fr. 1955) Aury [7 (7) 184, pl. 18].
(444) 1847 (Am. 5216) T. Gilbert [19 1848 (16) 302].
(445) 1848 (Am. 5985) J. H. Low [19 1849 (18) 206].
(446) 1848 (Am. 5990) J. J. Wise [19 1849 (18) 208].
(447) 1850 (Am. 7292) J. Ruck [19 1850 (20) 47].

(448) 1850 (Am. 7441) Lemuel Gilbert [19 1850 (20) 119].
(449) 1851 (Am. 7976) J. Ruck [19 1851 (21) 244].
(450) 1851 (Am. 8350) R. Kreter [19 1851 (22) 249].
(451) 1851 (Am. 8352) J. A. Gray [19 1851 (22) 249].
(452) 1851 (Am. 8353) R. M. Kerrison [19 1851 (22) 249].
(453) 1851 (Am. 8383) L. H. Browne [19 1851 (22) 311].
(454) 1851 (Am. 8389) T. Gilbert [19 1851 (22) 312].
(455) 1851 (Fr. 6606) Pons [7 (22) 19, pl. 5].

FELT

Preparation of

(456) 1826 (Fr. 1st add. Pat. to No. 4198 (1826)) Pape [6 (44) 441, pl. 18].
(457) 1840 (Aust. —) Karl Frenzel [1 (3) 118].
(458) 1840 (Fr. 7767) Eugène-Hippolyte Billion (Jeune) [6 (59) 292].

FRAME

Irregular Hexagonal

(459) 1801 (Eng. 2552) Bemetzrieder and Robert Scott, John Scott and Alexander Scott (A, B) [9 p. 42].

Metal

(460) 1825 (Am. —) Alpheus Babcock (B) [15 p. 300].*
(461) 1825 (Fr. 1808) Pleyel père et fils aîné (A, B) [6 (21) 65, pl. 10].
(462) 1826 (Aust. —) Johann Jacob Goll (–) [1 (1) 272].
(463) 1826 (Fr. 4918) Jean-Henri Pape (B) [6 (44) 441, pl. 18].
(464) 1827 (Eng. 5485) James Shudi Broadwood (A) [9 p. 103].
(465) 1829 (Aust. —) Mathias Müller (–) [1 (1) 273].
(466) 1829 (Fr. 4089) Guillaume Petzold (C) [6 (40) 148, pl. 14].
(467) 1830 (Am. —) Alpheus Babcock (B) [18 1830 (6) 159].
(468) 1831 (Eng. 6140) William Allen (A, B, C) [9 p. 112].
(469) 1833 (Am. —) Louis Fissore (–) [18 1834 (13) 33].
(470) 1836 (Am. —) Isaac Clark (–) [18 1836 (18) 315].
(471) 1836 (Aust. —) M. Seuffert [1 (3) 12, Fig. 6].
(472) 1836 (Eng. 7094) Wheatley Kirk (C) [9 p. 123].
(473) 1836 (Fr. 4146) Alexandre Debain (C) [6 (40) 389, pl. 39].
(474) 1838 (Fr. 4834) Moullé (C) [6 (44) 245, pl. 10].
(475) 1839 (Bav. —) Jakob Becker (A, B) [2 (1849) Heft x 590, mit Zeichnungen [Bl. 10, Fig. 6 bis 8].
(476) 1839 (Fr. 5240) Julien Thomas Rinaldi (B) [6 (46) 410, pl. 32].
(477) 1840 (Am. 1802) Jonas Chickering (B) [19 1841 (2) 387].
(478) 1840 (Canada 163) John Thomas Morgan and Alexander Smith (–) [20].
(479) 1840 (Eng. 8643) Pierre Érard (A, B, C) [9 p. 132].
(480) 1841 (Eng. 9023) John Steward (A, C) [9 p. 136].
(481) *1841* (Scotland —) [10].
(482) *1842* (Ireland, Reign of Queen Victoria, 297) [11].

* Inserted under the heading *Frame* on the evidence given by Hipkins in *The Story of the Pianoforte* (Novello Primer, No. 52, London), p. 18.

(483) 1842 (Belg. Order No. 1639, Index No. 1691) Themer et Ross (–) [3 *a*].
(484) 1843 (Am. 3238) Jonas Chickering (A) [19 1849 (18) 479].
(485) 1843 (Belg. Order No. 1642, Index No. 1743) M. Lacroix (–) [3 *a*].
(486) 1844 (Canada 71) George Milligan (–) [20].
(487) 1846 (Eng. 11,180) Isaac Henry Robert Mott (A, B, C) [9 p. 153].
(488) 1846 (Eng. 11,285) T. Woolley (A, B, C) [9 p. 156].
(489) 1846 (Fr. 2627) Van Overbergh (C) [7 (10) 42, pl. 11].
(490) 1847 (Am. 5202) Timothy Gilbert (A) [19 1848 (16) 235].
(491) 1848 (Fr. 3521) Herding (–) [7 (12) 352].
(492) 1849 (Am. 6342) Charles Hoist (B) [19 1849 (18) 421].
(493) 1850 (Am. 7441) Lemuel Gilbert (C) [19 1850 (20) 119].
(494) 1850 (Fr. 5062) Aucher (–) [7 (17) 291].
(495) 1850 (Fr. 6287) Colin [7 (21) 81, pl. 16].
(496) 1851 (Am. 8320) G. Bacon and R. Raven (B) [19 1851 (22) 242].
(497) 1851 (Am. 8383) L. H. Browne (A) [19 1851 (22) 311].
(498) 1851 (Canada 306) George Hooper Mead (A, B, C) (B) [21].
(499) 1851 (Fr. 6304) Bonnifas (A, C) [7 (21) 113, pl. 24].

On Springs

(500) 1792 (Eng. 1847) George Buttery [9 p. 25].

Wooden Frame

(501) 1831 (Bav. —) Greiner und Schmidt (A) [2 (1837) Heft. xi und xii S. 783, mit Zeichnungen].
(502) 1850 (Fr. 10,306) Colin (C) [7 (35) 71, pl. 17].

HAMMER BUTTS, FORKS AND KAPSELN

(503) 1790 (Eng. 1784) James Ball [9 p. 25].
(504) 1792 (Eng. 1847) George Buttery [9 p. 25].
(505) 1824 (Aust. —) Johann Anders [1 (1) 271].
(506) 1824 (Fr. 1665) Klepfer-Dufaut [6 (19) 5, pl. 1].
(507) 1826 (Aust. —) F. Hora und J. Kinderfreund [1 (1) 272].
(508) 1827 (Fr. 5086) Érard [6 (46) 31, pl. 4].
(509) 1828 (Aust. —) Karl Stein [1 (1) 273].
(510) 1829 (Eng. 5865) J. Stewart [9 p. 111].
(511) 1830 (Aust. —) Wilhelm Leschen [1 (1) 274].
(512) 1831 (Aust. —) Joseph Rosch [1 (1) 274].
(513) 1836 (Aust. —) Seuffert [1 (3) 12, Fig. 6].
(514) 1836 (Aust. —) Joseph Allgäuer [1 (2) 272].
(515) 1837 (Eng. 7424) Southwell [9 p. 125].
(516) 1838 (Aust. —) Joseph F. Ries [1 (2) 101].
(517) 1838 (Aust. —) Joseph F. Ries [1 (2) 127].
(518) 1839 (Aust. —) W. und H. Schwab [1 (5) 44].
(519) 1839 (Eng. 7971) Stumpff [9 p. 128].
(520) 1840 (Fr. 7029) De Rohden [6 (56) 302, pl. 15].
(521) 1840 (Fr. 7665) Boisselot et fils [6 (59) 26, pl. 3].
(522) 1841 (Am. 2167) Lemuel Gilbert [19 1842 (4) 188].
(523) 1841 (Fr. 8375) Blondel [6 (62) 417, pl. 32].
(524) 1842 (Bav. —) Alois Deiler [2 (1847) Heft. xi und xii S. 772, mit Zeichnungen, Bl. 16, Fig. 24 bis 27].

(525) 1844 (Fr. 9775) F. Rohden [6 (70) 175, pl. 10].
(526) 1845 (Fr. 849) Poulet [3 (4) 179, pl. 56].
(527) 1846 (Fr. 1955) Aury [7 (7) 184, pl. 18].
(528) 1847 (Fr. 2751) De Rohden [7 (10) 197, pl. 33].
(529) 1848 (Am. 5985) J. H. Low [19 1849 (18) 206].
(530) 1851 (Am. 8350) R. Kreter [19 1851 (22) 249].
(531) 1851 (Eng. 13,816) P. Érard [9 p. 173].

HAMMER HEADS
Arrangement of

(532) 1827 (Eng. 5528) Edward Dodd [9 p. 104] and
(533) *1828* (Fr. 2272) [6 (25) 247, pl. 20].
(534) 1844 (Fr. 313) Jean-Henri Pape [7 (2) 136, pl. 66].
(535) 1845 (Eng. 10,668) Jean-Henri Pape [9 p. 150].
(536) 1846 (Eng. 11,285) Woolley [9 p. 156].
(537) 1848 (Fr. 4th add. Pat. to No. 313 (1844)) Jean-Henri Pape [7 (2) 136, pl. 66].

Felt Covered

(538) 1826 (Fr. 4918) Jean-Henri Pape [6 (44) 441, pl. 18].
(539) 1827 (Fr. 2088) Charles Côte [6 (23) 245, pl. 6].
(540) 1835 (Eng. 6835) Pierre Frederick Fischer [9 p. 117].
(541) 1840 (Fr. 7767) Eugène-Hippolyte Billion (Jeune) [6 (59) 292].
(542) 1844 (Fr. 313) Jean-Henri Pape [7 (2) 136, pl. 66].

Formed of Felted Cord

(543) 1845 (Eng. 10,897) B. Nickels [9. 152].

Miscellaneous Coverings for

(544) 1788 (Eng. 1637) Samuel Bury [9 p. 20].
(545) 1788 (Eng. 1664) C. Clagget [9 p. 21].
(546) 1828 (Am. —) John Mackay [18 1828 (2) 255].
(547) 1833 (Am. —) Alpheus Babcock [18 1834 (14) 36].
(548) 1841 (Am. 1971) Timothy Gilbert [19 1842 (3) 265].
(549) 1845 (Am. 4019) Charles Oliver and G. W. Jackson [19 1846 (11) 244].
(550) 1848 (Fr. 3857) Van Gils [7 (13) 353].
(551) 1851 (Am. 8383) L. H. Browne [19 1851 (22) 311].
(552) 1851 (Eng. 13,652) John Hopkinson [9 p. 172].
(553) 1851 (Fr. 6145) Mata [7 (20) 302].

Set (of Heads) Felt-Covered Mechanically

(554) 1844 (Fr. 313) Pape [7 (2) 136, pl. 66].

HAMMERS
Arrangement of

(555) 1716 (Fr. 172–175) Marius [4 (3) pp. 83 to 89].
(556) 1783 (Eng. 1379) John Broadwood [9 p. 13].
(557) 1795 (Eng. 2028) William Stodart [9 p. 29].
(558) 1803 (Fr. 114) Schmidt [6 (2) 242, pl. 57].

(559) 1811 (Eng. 3419) R. Wornum [9 p. 66].
(560) 1811 (Eng. 3481) W. F. Collard [9 p. 67].
(561) 1821 (Eng. 4546) Wm. Southwell [9 p. 88].
(562) 1822 (Fr. 3512) Érard Frères [6 (36) 51, pl. 6].
(563) 1823 (Aust. —) M. Müller [1 (1) 269].
(564) 1824 (Aust. —) Johann Streicher [1 (1) 270].
(565) 1825 (Eng. 5065) Pierre Érard [9 p. 95].
(566) 1825 (Eng. 5107) George Augustus Kollmann [9 p. 98].
(567) 1826 (Aust. —) Franz Weisz [1 (1) 272].
(568) 1826 (Fr. 1st add. Pat. to No. 4918 (1826)) J. H. Pape [6 (44) 441, pl. 18].
(569) 1827 (Am. —) Thomas Loud [17 1827 (4) 62].
(570) 1827 (Eng. 5468) Pierre Érard [9 p. 100].
(571) 1827 (Fr. 1st add. Pat. to No. 4918 (1826)) J. H. Pape [6 (44) 441, pl. 18].
(572) 1831 (Am. —) Jessie Thompson [18 1832 (9) 113].
(573) 1831 (Aust. —) Joseph Rosch [1 (1) 274].
(574) 1831 (Bav. —) Greiner und Schmidt [2 (1837) Heft. xi und xii S. 783,
          mit Zeichnungen].
(575) 1833 (Fr. 3308) Wetzels [6 (34) 46, pl. 11].
(576) 1833 (Fr. 3701) Paulinus Meideck [6 (37) 302, pl. 27].
(577) 1834 (Eng. 6779) Danchell and Hahn [9 p. 117].
(578) 1835 (Eng. 6744) James Stewart [9 p. 116].
(579) 1835 (Eng. 6835) Pierre Frederick Fischer [9 p. 117].
(580) 1837 (Fr. add. Pat. to No. 5833 (1828)) Pape [6 (49) 348, pl. 25].
(581) 1841 (Am. 2330) Daniel B. Newhall [19 1845 (9) 253].
(582) 1841 (Eng. 8999) John Godwin [9 p. 135].
(583) 1842 (Aust. —) J. B. Streicher [1 (4) 359, mit Zeichnungen, Tafel 43,
          Fig. 475].
(584) 1842 (Eng. 9262) Robert Wornum [9 p. 139].
(585) 1845 (Eng. 10,668) Jean-Henri Pape [9 p. 150].
(586) 1845 (Eng. 10,897) Benjamin Nickels [9 p. 152].
(587) 1845 (Fr. 2nd add. Pat. to No. 313 (1844)) Pape [7 (2) 136, pl. 66].
(588) 1847 (Fr. 2751) De Rohden [7 (10) 197, pl. 33].
(589) 1851 (Am. 7976) J. Ruck [19 1851 (21) 244].

At the back and the front of the sound-board

(590) 1844 (Eng. 10,385) D. C. Hewitt [9 p. 146].

"Counterbalancing" (Hammers)

(591) 1825 (Eng. 5107) G. A. Kollmann [9 p. 98].

With Double Heads (or double heads and shanks)

(592) 1841 (Fr. 10,534) Nicolas Sulot [6 (75) 460, pl. 30]. Also
          1843 Add. Pat. to the above.
(593) 1844 (Fr. 10,092) François-Xavier Bader [6 (72) 46, pl. 4].
(594) 1847 (Fr. 3340) Nicolas Sulot [7 (12) 276].

With Metal Helical Springs (or springs of india-rubber), to facilitate their return from the strings

(595) 1845 (Eng. 10,897) B. Nickels [9 p. 152].

HARMONIC BAR

See Wrest-pin Block—with Harmonic or Pressure Bar.

HARMONIC STRING BOARD

(596) 1846 (Eng. 11,242) F. H. Burkinyoung [9 p. 154].

HINGES

(597) 1842 (Eng. 9226) Thos. Lambert [9 p. 137].
(598) 1842 (Eng. 9362) James Stewart [9 p. 140].

HITCH PINS

Arrangement of

(599) 1808 (Eng. 3170) S. Érard [9 p. 55].
(600) 1827 (Eng. 5485) J. S. Broadwood [9 p. 103].

Improved construction of

(601) 1846 (Eng. 11,285) T. Woolley [9 p. 156].

Substitutes for

(602) 1823 (Eng. 4759) F. Deakin [9 p. 91].
(603) 1839 (Fr. 6506) Boisselot et fils [6 (53) 175, pl. 17].
(604) 1841 (Eng. 8999) John Godwin [9 p. 135].
(605) 1841 (Eng. 9023) John Steward [9 p. 136].
(606) 1844 (Am. 3643) Lovering Ricketts [19 1845 (9) 93].
(607) 1844 (Fr. 8219) Jean-Édouard Daniel [6 (61) 466, pl. 25].
(608) 1845 (Am. 3940) Rueckert —.
(609) 1846 (Fr. 1955) Aury [7 (7) 184, pl. 18].

HITCH-PIN BLOCK OR PLATE

Arrangement of

(610) 1811 (Eng. 3481) W. F. Collard [9 p. 67].
(611) 1840 (Eng. 8643) P. Érard [9 p. 132].
(612) 1844 (Fr. 8219) Daniel [6 (61) 466, pl. 25].

In Metal

(613) 1825 (Fr. 1808) Pleyel père et fils aîné [6 (21) 65, pl. 10].
(614) 1827 (Eng. 5485) James Shudi Broadwood [9 p. 103].
(615) 1829 (Fr. 1st add. Pat. to No. 2434 (1828)) Pleyel [6 (27) 41, pl. 3].
(616) 1830 (Fr. 4292) Pierre Érard [6 (41) 320, pl. 34].
(617) 1839 (Bav. —) Jakob Becker [2 (1849) Heft x S. 590, mit Zeichnungen, Bl. x, Fig. 6 bis 8].
(618) 1839 (Fr. 7002) Vandermère [6 (55) 415, pl. 36].
(619) 1840 (Eng. 8643) Pierre Érard [9 p. 132].
(620) 1850 (Fr. 6287) Colin [7 (21) 81, pl. 16].

Prolonged (to reduce the after-length of the strings)

(621) 1827 (Fr. 2884) Triquet [6 (30) 203, pl. 22].
(622) 1828 (Fr. 2434) Pleyel [6 (27) 41, pl. 3].
(623) 1832 (Eng. 6304) P. F. Fischer [9 p. 114].
(624) 1844 (Fr. 7985) Avisseau Frères [6 (70) 213, pl. 13].

INDIA-RUBBER (USED IN THE ACTION)

(625) 1847 (Eng. 11,681) John Spear [9 p. 158].
(626) 1848 (Fr. 3857) Van Gils [7 (13) 353].
(627) 1849 (Fr. 1st add. Pat. to No. 3821 (1848)) Rogez [7 (13) 342].

JACQUARD MACHINERY (PARTS OF WHICH ARE APPLICABLE TO MECHANICAL PIANOFORTES)

(628) 1848 (Eng. 12,229) Duncan Mackenzie [9 p. 161] and
(629) *1848* (Ireland, Reign of Queen Victoria, 749) [11] ?
(630) 1849 (Eng. 12,421) William Martin [9 p. 163] and
(631) *1849* (Ireland, Reign of Queen Victoria, 756) [11].

KEY-PIVOTS OR MORTISES

(632) 1828 (Fr. 5833) Pape [6 (49) 348, pl. 25].
(633) 1831 (Bav. —) F. Greiner [2 (1835) Heft vii S. 450, Fig. 1].
(634) 1840 (Eng. 8643) P. Érard [9 p. 132].
(635) 1840 (Fr. 7448) François Soufleto [6 (58) 90, pl. 7].
(636) 1840 (Fr. 11,970) Wolfel [6 (87) 347, pls. 22, 23].
(637) 1844 (Fr. 9935) J. G. Kriegelstein [6 (71) 132, pl. 12].
(638) 1846 (Eng. 11,285) T. Woolley [9 p. 156]. Patented as "Spring axis".
(639) 1846 (Fr. 1539) Viollet [7 (6) 140, pl. 29].

KEYS

Arrangement of

(640) 1801 (Eng. 2552) Bemetzrieder and R. Scott, J. Scott and A. Scott [6 p. 42].
(641) 1825 (Eng. 5065) Érard [6 p. 95].
(642) 1831 (Bav. —) Greiner und Schmidt [2 (1837) Heft. xi und xii S. 783, mit Zeichnungen].
(643) 1833 (Am. —) Edward C. Riley.
(644) 1836 (Eng. 7006) Lidel [9 p. 120].

Additional

(645) 1794 (Eng. 2017) William Southwell [9 p. 28].
(646) 1798 (Eng. 2264) William Southwell [9 p. 30].
(647) 1813 (Eng. 3658) Frederick Hauck [9 p. 71].

Additional Keys, Strings of Hammers Added to the Treble of Old Instruments

(648) 1813 (Eng. 3658) Hauck [9 p. 71].

Bent (Keys)

(649) 1830 (Eng. 5912) S. Thompson [9 p. 112].

Coverings for

(650) 1788 (Eng. 1664) Charles Clagget [9 p. 21].
(651) 1832 (Eng. 6280) Frederick William Isaac [9 p. 113].
(652) 1839 (Eng. 8131) James Bingham and John Amory Boden [9 p. 129].
(653) 1840 (Eng. 8316) James Bingham and John Amory Boden [9 p. 131].
(654) 1840 (Eng. 8616) James Bingham [9 p. 132].
(655) 1840 (Fr. 6305) Barthélemy-Richard de Prédaval [6 (52) 148].
(656) 1846 (Eng. 11,261) Joseph Storer [9 p. 155].
(657) 1846 (Fr. 1727) Porcher [7 (6) 217].
(658) 1851 (Fr. 6192) Gouliart [7 (20) 319].

With Elastic Air-Bed Underneath
(to prevent them rattling)

(659) 1847 (Eng. 11,681) John Spear [9 p. 158].

KEYBOARD COVERS OR FALLS

(660) 1808 (Eng. 3170) S. Érard [9 p. 55].
(661) 1837 (Aust. —) Anton Amberg [1 (2) 73, Fig. 143].
(662) 1839 (Eng. 7971) Stumpff [9 p. 128].
(663) 1844 (Eng. 10,385) D. C. Hewitt [9 p. 146].

KEYBOARD

At the Side of a Grand Pianoforte

(664) 1831 (Bav. —) F. Greiner [2 (1835) Heft vii S. 450, Fig. 1].

For Pianoforte or Organ

(665) 1840 (Fr. 10,445) P. Brasil [6 (74) 465].

In the Middle of a Square Pianoforte

(666) 1828 (Fr. 5833) Pape [6 (49) 348, pl. 25].

KEYBOARDS
Arrangement of

(667) 1788 (Eng. 1664) Charles Clagget [9 p. 21].
(668) 1811 (Eng. 3404) John Trotter [9 p. 65].
(669) 1824 (Aust. —) Mathias Müller und Sohn [1 (1) 271].
(670) 1831 (Bav. —) Friedrich Greiner und Joseph Schmidt [2 (1837) Heft. xi und xii 783, mit Zeichnungen].
(671) 1831 (Bav. —) Joseph Schmidt und Friedrich Greiner [2 (1831) No. 47 S. 630].
(672) 1835 (Fr. 4360) Madame Soria [6 (41) 429].
(673) 1837 (Aust. —) Joseph Valentin Obendrauf [1 (2) 86].

(674) 1837 (Fr. 5360) Tonnel [6 (47) p. 317].
(675) 1839 (Aust. —) Wilhelm und Heinrich Schwab [1 (5) 44].
(676) 1840 (Fr. 10,445) Pierre Brasil [6 (74) 465].
(677) 1843 (Fr. 12,373) Phiquepal d'Arusmont [6 (91) 427, pl. 17].
(678) 1844 (Eng. 10,385) Daniel Chandler Hewitt [9 p. 146].
(679) 1844 (Fr. 1st add. Pat. to No. 11,970 (1840)) Wolfel [6 (87) 347, pls. 22, 23].
(680) 1846 (Fr. 1624) Dreschke [7 (6) 195] and
(681) *1846* (Eng. 11,320) [9 p. 157].
(682) 1850 (Bav. —) J. Kohnle [2 (1850) Heft. xi und xii S. 825].

Closing

(683) 1800 (Eng. 2446) Isaac Hawkins [9 p. 36].
(684) 1836 (Fr. 4146) Alexandre Debain [6 (40) 389, pl. 39].
(685) 1838 (Fr. 5946) Charlemagne-Emmanuel Roger [6 (50) 146, pl. 11].

Convex

(686) 1824 (Aust. —) Georg Staufer und M. Haidinger [1 (1) 270].
(687) 1840 (Fr. 11,970) Charles-François Wolfel [6 (87) 347, pls. 22, 23].
(688) 1841 (Am. 2081) Daniel B. Newhall, Levi and Wilkins [19 1842 (4) 39].

KNEE PEDALS TO WORK THE "SOURDINES"

(689) 1759 (Fr. —) Weltman [5 (1759) p. 241].

LOCK FOR A PIANOFORTE

(690) 1847 (Am. 6636) P. H. Niles. —

MACHINE FOR MAKING FELT FOR PIANOFORTES

(691) 1848 (Fr. 3757) Fortin-Bouteiller [7 (13) 273, pl. 44].

MECHANISM

For Altering the Pitch of Pianofortes when in Tune

(692) 1827 (Eng. 5548) William Dettmer [9 p. 105].
(693) 1839 (Belg. Order No. 154) Sax fils [3] (doubtful, see No. 708).
(694) 1842 (Fr. 2nd add. Pat. to No. 9404 (1838)) Jean-Henri Pape [6 (68) 144, pl. 11].

For Opening the Lid

(695) 1849 (Am. 6282) Conrad Meyer [19 1849 (18) 384].

For Producing 39 Gradations of Tone Within the Octave

(696) 1788 (Eng. 1664) Clagget [9 p. 21].

For Transposing

(697) 1801 (Eng. 2562) Edward Ryley [9 p. 44].
(698) 1812 (Fr. 1333) Érard Frères [6 (14) 295, pl. 26].

(699) 1820 (Fr. 1107) Roller [6 (12) 171, pl. 18].
(700) 1820 (Fr. 1380) Jean-Baptiste Wagner [6 (15) 61, pl. 9].
(701) 1823 (Aust. —) Joseph Böhm [1 (2) 191].
(702) 1824 (Aust. —) Abbé Grégoire Trentin [1 (1) 270].
(703) 1831 (Bav. —) Friedrich Greiner [2 (1835) Heft vii 450, mit Zeich-
          nungen].
(704) 1835 (Eng. 6835) P. F. Fischer [9 p. 117].
(705) 1836 (Belg. Order No. 123) Rouhette [3].
(706) 1837 (Belg. Order No. 133) M. Lacroix [3].
(707) 1838 (Bav. —) J. Schmidt und Friedrich Greiner [2 1838 Heft xii S. 790].
(708) 1839 (Belg. Order No. 154) Sax fils [3] (doubtful, see No. 693).
(709) 1843 (Fr. 12,376) Le Bihan [6 (91) 445, pl. 18].
(710) 1844 (Eng. 10,385) Daniel Chandler Hewitt [9 p. 146].
(711) 1844 (Eng. 10,430) Sébastien Mercier [9 p. 147].
(712) 1845 (Scotland —) Robert Addison [10].
(713) 1846 (Eng. 11,261) Joseph Storer [9 p. 155].
(714) 1846 (Eng. 11,285) Woolley [9 p. 156] and
(715) 1847 (Fr. 2887) [7 (11) 46, pls. 8, 9] and
(716) 1847 (Belg. Order No. 2881, Index No. 4179) [3 c].
(717) 1846 (Fr. 1888) Montal [7 (7) 152, pl. 31].
(718) 1846 (Fr. 2226) Darche [7 (8) 230].
(719) 1848 (Fr. 3711) Montal [7 (13) 186, pls. 32, 33]. (Proposed only.)
(720) 1851 (Fr. 3rd add. Pat. to No. 3711 (1848)) Montal [7 (13) 186, pls.
          32, 33].

METALLIC ELASTIC TRUSSES

(721) 1845 (Eng. 10,592) W. Hattersley [9 p. 149].

MOVABLE KEY-BED

(722) 1846 (Eng. 11,285) T. Woolley [9 p. 156].

NAME BOARD

(723) 1842 (Eng. 9245) H. F. Broadwood [9 p. 139].

OBSCURE PATENTS AND PATENTS WITH NO DESCRIP-
TION FOR INVENTIONS RELATING TO PIANOFORTES

(724) 1796 (Am. —) James Sylvanus McLean [15 p. 1].
(725) 1807 (Am. —) Ralph Shaw [15 p. 61].
(726) 1808 (Scotland —) Edward Ryley [10].
(727) 1816 (Am. —) George Charters [15 p. 167].
(728) 1817 (Am. —) John Geib [15 p. 182].
(729) 1818 (Am. —) James Alois Gutwaldt [15 p 194].
(730) 1824 (Aust. —) Johann Promberger [1 (1) 271].
(731) 1828 (Am. —) C. F. L. Albrecht [16].
(732) 1829 (Bav. —) Kalzer [2 (1829) No. 35 p. 492].
(733) 1833 (Am. —) Edward C. Ryley.
(734) 1837 (Bav. —) Johann Eichenauer [2 (1837) Heft. vi und vii S. 495].
(735) 1837 (Belg. Order No. 128) T. Stocker [3].

(736) 1837 (Fr. 11,027) Jean-Henri Pape [6 (79) 507].
(Add. Pat. to this dated 1844 corresponds to Belg. Order No. 2164, Index No. 2667) [3 *b*].
(737) 1837 (Belg. Order No. 129) J. Florence [3].
(738) 1838 (Belg. Order No. 144) H. Lichtenthal [3].
(739) 1840 (Bav. —) Johann Eichenauer [2 (1841) Heft II S. 144].
(740) 1840 (Belg. Order No. 166) L. Janmart [3].
(741) 1840 (Eng. 8737) John Steward [9 p. 134].
(742) 1841 (Sweden 24) J. E. Bäckström [13].
(743) 1842 (Bav. —) Peter Karl Nelson [2 (1842) Heft x p. 683].
(744) 1842 (Belg. Order No. 1629, Index No. 1188) G. Vanlair [3 *a*].
(745) 1842 (Belg. Order No. 1640, Index No. 1670) J. Dammekens [3 *a*].
(746) 1844 (Fr. 10,076) Louis-Alexandre Dubois [6 (71) 475].
(747) 1845 (Eng. 10,868) Edward Lesley Walker [9 p. 152].
(748) 1847 (Sweden 1) L. O. Novell [13].
(749) 1848 (Belg. Order No. 3831, Index No. 5237) J. Gunther [3 *d*].
(750) 1848 (Belg. Order No. 3836, Index No. 5374) H. Merciet [3 *d*].
(751) 1848 (Eng. 12,018) James Montgomery [9 p. 161].
(752) 1849 (Russia —) James Becker [12].
(753) 1849 (Fr. 4415) Martin [7 (16) 2].
(754) 1850 (Belg. Order No. 3890, Index No. 7016) Mathieu Lacroix [3 *d*].
(755) 1850 (Russia —) James Becker [12].
(756) 1851 (Am. 8194) M. Miller [19 1852 (XII) 97].
(757) 1851 (Bav. —) John Piddington [2 (1851) Heft x p. 662].
(758) 1851 (Belg. Order No. 5251, Index No. 712) Van Merlin [3 *e*].

PEDALLIER

(759) 1825 (Bav. —) G. F. Rutscher und J. Rueff [2 (1825) No. 30 S. 200].
(760) 1837 (Aust. —) J. Böhm [1 (2) 79, Fig. 156].
(761) 1845 (Eng. 10,897) B. Nickels [9 p. 152].
(762) 1850 (Eng. 13,252) P. Érard [9 p. 167].

PEDALS AND STOPS
Arrangement of

(763) 1808 (Eng. 3154) Hawkes [9 p. 54].
(764) 1809 (Eng. 3250) Loeschman [9 p. 57].
(765) 1832 (Aust. —) Anton Bersaur und Sohn [1 (1) 274].
(766) 1847 (Eng. 11,681) Spear [9 p. 158].
(767) 1850 (Eng. 13,252) P. Érard [9 p. 167].

Buff

(768) 1786 (Eng. 1571) Geib [9 p. 18].
(769) 1811 (Eng. 3419) Wornum [9 p. 66].
(770) 1832 (Eng. 6304) P. F. Fischer [9 p. 114]. N.B. Not named in patent.

Celestina

(771) 1788 (Eng. 1664) C. Clagget [9 p. 21].

Cembalo

(772) 1788 (Eng. 1637) Bury [9 p. 20].

Dolce Compana (*See* ATTACHMENT)

(773) 1849 (Am. 6223) J. A. Gray [19 1849 (18) 367].
(774) 1849 (Eng. 12,609) W. P. Parker [9 p. 164].

Drum

(775) 1797 (Eng. 2160) W. Rolfe and S. Davis [9 p. 29].

Forte

(776) 1783 (Eng. 1379) John Broadwood [9 p. 13].
(777) 1788 (Eng. 1637) Bury [9 p. 20].

Harmonic Sounds

(778) 1821 (Fr. add. Pat. to No. 1380 (1820)) Wagner [6 (15) 61, pl. 9].
(779) 1839 (Eng. 7971) Stumpff [9 p. 128].
(780) 1845 (Am. 3888) Walker [19 1845 (10) 244].
(781) 1845 (Canada 78) Warren [20].
(782) 1845 (Eng. 10,937) Cromwell [9 p. 153] and
(783) *1846* (Fr. 2129) [7 (8) 132, pl. 16].

Harmonic Swell

(784) 1821 (Eng. 4542) F. W. Collard [9 p. 87].

Harp

(785) 1790 (Eng. 1743) Hancock [9 p. 24].
(786) 1808 (Eng. 3170) S. Érard [9 p. 55].

Jeu Céleste (improvement in the construction of the)

(787) 1826 (Fr. 4918) Pape [6 (44) 441, pl. 18].

"Octave Stop"

(788) 1816 (Eng. 4068) J. Kirkman [9 p. 79].

"Pedale d'Expression"

(789) 1851 (Fr. 3rd add. Pat. to No. 3711 (1848)) Montal [7 (13) 186, pls. 32, 33].

Piano

(790) 1788 (Eng. 1637) Bury [9 p. 20].
(791) 1800 (Eng. 2446) Hawkins [9 p. 36].
(792) 1808 (Eng. 3170) S. Érard [9 p. 55].

Piano—Shortened Radius of the Blow

(793) 1836 (Eng. 7006) Lidel [9 p. 120].
(794) 1837 (Fr. 1st add. Pat. to No. 10,989 (1836)) Greiner [6 (79) 401, pl. 20].
(795) 1841 (Am. 2330) Newhall [19 1845 (9) 253].

Pizzicato

(796) 1826 (Eng. 5384) Wornum [9 p. 99].

Polichorda (more than three unison strings available for every note through the action of a pedal or coupler)

(797) 1812 (Fr. 1332) Érard Frères [6 (14) 292, pl. 25].
(798) 1826 (Fr. 1st add. Pat. to No. 4918 (1826)) J. H. Pape [6 (44) 441, pl. 18].
(799) 1840 (Bav. —) Albrecht Ziegler [2 (1840) Heft. xi und xii S. 797, mit Zeichnungen].
(800) 1846 (Fr. 2311) Soudet [7 (9) 15].
(801) 1851 (Eng. 13,601) J. C. Robertson [9 p. 170].

Sordino

(802) 1783 (Eng. 1379) John Broadwood [9 p. 13].
(803) 1827 (Fr. 5086) Érard [6 (46) 31, pl. 4].

Swell

(804) 1769 (Eng. 947) Shudi [9 p. 6]. (N.B. For Harpsichord only.)
(805) 1801 (Eng. 2552) Bemetzrieder and R. Scott, J. Scott and A. Scott [9 p. 42].
(806) 1819 (Am. —) Pommer [15 p. 206].
(807) 1844 (Fr. 3rd add. Pat. to No. 10,599 (1836)) Lepère [6 (76) 30, pl. 3].
(808) 1845 (Am. 4241) Badlain [19 1846 (12) 314].
(809) 1847 (Eng. 11,681) Spear [9 p. 158].

Una Corda

(810) 1774 (Eng. 1081) Merlin [9 p. 9].
(811) 1787 (Eng. 1607) Walton [9 p. 20].
(812) 1794 (Eng. 2016) Sébastien Érard [9 p. 28].
(813) 1831 (Am. —) Currier [18 1831 (8) 167].
(814) 1831 (Bav. —) Greiner und Schmidt [2 18 (37) Heft. xi und xiii S. 783, mit Zeichnungen].
(815) 1842 (Am. 2523) Loud [19 1846 (12) 315].

Una Corda Effect obtained in Various Ways

(816) 1838 (Am. 1014) Brown [18 1839 (24) 321].
(817) 1839 (Am. 1375) Cumston [18 1840 (26) 158].

Varying and Increasing the Sound by Regulating the Column of Air in Pianofortes

(818) 1845 (Eng. 10,668) Jean-Henri Pape [9 p. 150] and
(819) 1845 (Fr. 1st add. Pat. to No. 313 (1844)) Jean-Henri Pape [7 (2) 136, pl. 66].

PANORGUE-PIANO

(820) 1846 (Fr. 2744) Jaulin [7 (10) 185, pl. 33].

PIANO A DOUCINE

(821) 1840 (Fr. 7883) Wirth [6 (60) 60, pl. 5].

APPENDIX C

PIANO-BASQUE
(822) 1841 (Fr. 6406) Sormani [6 (52) 437, pl. 28].

PIANO-CLARA
(823) 1836 (Fr. 8726) Jean-Baptiste Clara-Margueson [6 (64) 347].

PIANO-CLEDIHARMONIQUE
(824) 1839 (Fr. 6506) Boisselot et fils [6 (53) 175, pl. 17].

PIANO-CONSOLE
(825) 1828 (Fr. 5833) Jean-Henri Pape [7 (49) 348, pl. 25].
(826) 1839 (Eng. 8137) Jean-Henri Pape [9 p. 129].
(827) 1845 (Eng. 10,668) Jean-Henri Pape [9 p. 150].
(828) 1845 (Fr. 1st add. Pat. to No. 313 (1844)) Jean-Henri Pape [7 (2) 136, pl. 66].
(829) 1850 (Eng. 13,423) Jean-Henri Pape [9 p. 168] and
(830) 1850 (Fr. 2nd add. Pat. to No. 5923 (1850)) Jean-Henri Pape [7 (20) 90, pls. 13, 14].

PIANO-CRESCENDO
(831) 1841 (Belg. Order No. 190) M. A. Lacoste [3].

PIANO-ECRAN
(832) 1836 (Fr. 4146) Alexandre Debain [6 (40) 389, pl. 39].

PIANO-HARMONICA
(833) 1803 (Fr. 114) Schmidt [6 (2) 242, pl. 57].

PIANO-ORGUE EXPRESSIF
(834) 1842 (Fr. 8973) Maroky [6 (65) 416].

PIANO-SECRETAIRE
(835) 1812 (Fr. 1332) Érard Frères [6 (14) 292, pl. 25].
(836) 1844 (Fr. 8292) Martin [6 (62) 105, pl. 8].

PIANO-VIOLE
(837) 1830 (Belg. Order No. 110) Lichtenthal [3].

PIANOFORTE

Apolliricon
(838) 1826 (Aust. —) Franz Weisz [1 (1) 272].

Cabinet
(839) 1807 (Eng. 3029) Southwell [9 p. 50].
(840) 1821 (Eng. 4546) Southwell [9 p. 88].
(841) 1842 (Eng. 9226) Lambert [9 p. 137].

Combined with

(*a*) Clavichord or Spinett [*sic*]

(842) 1792 (Eng. 1866) John Geib [9 p. 26].

(*b*) German Flute and Harp

(843) 1790 (Eng. 1743) John Crang Hancock [9 p. 24].

(*c*) Harmonium

(844) 1846 (Eng. 11,359) Debain [9 p. 157]. (Clavi-harmonium.)

(*d*) Harpsichord

(845) 1759 (Fr. —) Weltman [5 (1759) 241].
(846) 1774 (Eng. 1081) Joseph Merlin [9 p. 9].
(847) 1777 (Eng. 1172) Robert Stodart [9 p. 12].
(848) 1792 (Eng. 1887) James Davis [9 p. 27].

(*e*) Musical Glasses

(849) 1816 (Eng. 4080) John Day [9 p. 80].

(*f*) Organ

(850) 1759 (Fr. —) Weltman [5 (1759) 241].
(851) 1772 (Fr. —) de L'Épine [5 (1772) 109].
(852) 1790 (Eng. 1743) John Crang Hancock [9 p. 24].
(853) 1842 (Fr. 8973) Étienne Maroky [6 (65) 416].
(854) 1848 (Am. 5438) Rufus Nutting [19 1849 (17) 166].
(855) 1849 (Fr. 4298) Larroque [7 (15) 91].
(856) 1851 (Am. 8194) M. Miller [19 1852 (22) 97].
(857) 1851 (Am. 8587) Richard M. Ferris [19 1852 (23) 83].
(858) 1851 (Fr. 6204) Lavanchy [7 (20) 321].

(*g*) Free Reed Wind Instrument

(859) 1846 (Fr. 2744) Jaulin [7 (10) 185, pl. 33].

Combining the Forms of the Grand and the Console

(860) 1850 [Eng. 13,423] J. H. Pape [9 p. 168] and
(861) *1850* (Fr. 2nd add. Pat. to No. 5923 (1850)) [7 (20) 90, pls. 13, 14].

Circular or Hexagonal

(862) 1835 (Eng. 6835) Pierre Frederick Fischer [9 p. 117].

Clavi-Harmonium

See COMBINED with Harmonium.

Cottage

(863) 1811 (Eng. 3419) Robert Wornum [9 p. 66].

Double or Royal Grand

(864) 1845 (Eng. 10,897) B. Nickels [9 p. 152].

Duoclave

(865) 1812 (Fr. 1333) Érard Frères [6 (14) 295, pl. 26].
(866) 1821 (Fr. 3345) Érard Frères [6 (34) 256, pl. 33].
(867) 1825 (Fr. 4438) J. B. Charreyre [6 (42) 255, pl. 31].
(868) 1840 (Eng. 8692) Edward Dodd [9 p. 134].
(869) 1850 (Am. 7568) J. Pirsson [19 1850 (20) 237].
(870) 1850 (Belg. Order No. 3875, Index No. 6396) Van der Cruyssen [3 *d*].
(871) 1851 (Belg. Order No. 5252, Index No. 716) N. Hainaught [3 *e*].

Elliptic

(872) 1825 (Fr. 2866) Eulriot [6 (30) 144, pl. 27].
(873) 1828 (Fr. 5833) Pape [6 (49) 348, pl. 25].

Euphonicon

(874) 1841 (Eng. 9023) John Steward [9 p. 136].

Gabel Harmon

(875) 1827 (Aust. —) M. Müller und Söhne [1 (1) 273].

Giraffe

(876) 1831 (Bav. —) Julius Kisselstein [2 (1835) Heft ix 576, mit Zeichnungen].

Grand

(877) 1827 (Fr. 2088) Charles Côte [6 (23) 245, pl. 6].
(878) 1827 (Fr. 2780) Dietz fils [6 (29) 31, pl. 33].
(879) 1831 (Bav. —) Joseph Baumgartner [2 (1837) Heft. xi und xii S. 787].
(880) 1840 (Bav. —) Joseph Becker [2 (1840) 798].
(881) 1842 (Belg. Order No. 1637, Index No. 1525) Sternberg et Cie [3 *a*].

Grand Clavilyr

(882) 1813 (Eng. 3765) John Bateman [9 p. 74].

Harmomelo

(883) 1806 (Fr. 466) Pfeiffer et Cie [6 (6) 266, pl. 16].

Hexagonal

(884) 1836 (Fr. add. Pat. to No. 6873 (1834)) Pape [6 (55) 19, pl. 2].

"Hohflügel"

(885) 1824 (Aust. —) Georg Staufer und M. Haidinger [1 (1) 270].

Horizontal

(886) 1826 (Fr. 3181) Klepfer-Dufaut [6 (33) 93, pl. 18].
(887) 1827 (Am. —) Loud [17 1827 (4) 62].
(888) 1841 (Eng. 8999) Godwin [9 p. 135].

"Horizontal Harp" Pianoforte

(889) 1801 (Eng. 2552) Bemetzrieder, Richard Scott, J. Scott and A. Scott
[9 p. 42].

Improved in Form

(890) 1801 (Eng. 2552) Bemetzrieder, Richard Scott, J. Scott and A. Scott
[9 p. 42].
(891) 1811 (Eng. 3403) Southwell [9 p. 65].
(892) 1816 (Eng. 4080) Day [9 p. 80].
(893) 1825 (Eng. 5107) G. A. Kollmann [9 p. 98].
(894) 1827 (Fr. 2780) Dietz [6 (29) 331, pl. 33].
(895) 1831 (Bav. —) Greiner und Schmidt [2 (1837) Heft. xi und xiii S. 783,
mit Zeichnungen].
(896) 1839 (Aust. —) W. und H. Schwab [1 (5) 44].
(897) 1840 (Fr. 7883) Wirth [6 (60) 60, pl. 5].

In the Shape of a Clavecin

(898) 1809 (Fr. 975) Érard [6 (11) 70, pl. 9].

Lyre-Shaped

(899) 1826 (Aust. —) Franz Weisz [1 (1) 272].
(900) 1834 (Fr. 6605) Eulriot [6 (53) 374, pl. 25].

Melodicon with Drums

(901) 1847 (Fr. 3577) Nunns et Fischer [7 (13) 28, pl. 3].

Metafagano

(902) 1824 (Aust. —) Abbé Grégoire Trentin [1 (1) 242].

Metal-Lined

(903) 1847 (Eng. 11,681) John Spear [9 p. 158].

Mounted on a Stand or Platform

(904) 1846 (Eng. 11,285) Thomas Woolley [9 p. 156].
(905) 1847 (Eng. 11,681) J. Spear [9 p. 158].

Oval

(906) 1850 (Eng. 13,423) Jean-Henri Pape [9 p. 168].

Oval or Round

(907) 1834 (Fr. 6873) Jean-Henri Pape [6 (55) 19, pl. 2].

Oval or Square

(908) 1839 (Eng. 8137) Jean-Henri Pape [9 p. 129].

Portable Grand

(909) 1800 (Eng. 2446) Isaac Hawkins [9 p. 36].

Professional

(910) 1826 (Eng. 5384) Robert Wornum [9 p. 99].

Schoolroom Pianoforte

(911) 1842 (Eng. 9245) H. F. Broadwood [9 p. 139].

Self-Acting

See also JACQUARD MACHINERY, etc.
(912) 1816 (Eng. 4030) William Simmons [9 p. 77].
(913) 1829 (Eng. 5802) Day and Münich [9 p. 109].
(914) 1829 (Eng. 5831) Thomas Hall Rolfe [9 p. 110].
(915) 1842 (Fr. 7360) Gomel et Boquet [6 (57) 344, pl. 22].
(916) 1842 (Fr. 8691) Claude-Félix Seytre [6 (64) 203, pl. 15].
(917) 1846 (Eng. 11,261) Joseph Storer [9 p. 155].
(918) 1846 (Eng. 11,359) Alexandre Debain [9 p. 157].
(919) 1846 (Fr. 2226) Darche [7 (8) 230].
(920) 1846 (Fr. 2402) Acklin [7 (9) 91].
(921) 1848 (Eng. 12,307) Charles Dawson [9 p. 162].
(922) 1848 (Fr. 4068) Debain [7 (14) 233, pl. 33].
(923) 1851 (Fr. 5th add. Pat. to No. 5923 (1850)) Jean-Henri Pape [7 (20) 90, pls. 13, 14] and
(924) *1851* (Belg. Order No. 5255, Index No. 826) [3 *e*].

Sostenente

See also STRINGS—sustaining the sound by bowing, etc.
(925) 1817 (Eng. 4098) Isaac Henry Robert Mott [9 p. 81].
(925*a*) 1819 (Fr. 1602) Mott, Julius-César, Mott (Isaac-Henri-Robert) et Cie [6 (18) 18, pl. 4].

Square

(926) 1811 (Eng. 3481) Collard [9 p. 67].
(927) 1815 (Fr. 652) Thory [6 (8) 219, pl. 22].
(928) 1827 (Fr. 2884) Triquet [6 (30) 203, pl. 22].
(929) 1829 (Fr. 4089) Petzold [6 (40) 148, pl. 14].
(930) 1838 (Am. 1014) Brown [18 1839 (24) 321].
(931) 1838 (Fr. 6156) Pfeiffer [6 (51) 203, pl. 15].

Telio-Chordon

(932) 1788 (Eng. 1664) Clagget [9 p. 21].

Stenographical

See APPARATUS—Stenographical.

Transposing

See MECHANISM—for Transposing.

Unichord

(933) 1825 (Fr. 1808) Pleyel père et fils ainé [6 (21) 65, pl. 10].

Upright

(934) 1800 (Eng. 2446) Hawkins [9 p. 36].
(935) 1802 (Eng. 2591) Thomas Loud [9 p. 44].
(936) 1824 (Aust. —) Johann Streicher [1 (1) 270].
(937) 1828 (Fr. 3699) Frost père et fils [6 (37) 293, pl. 27].
(938) 1838 (Fr. 4834) Moullé [6 (44) 245, pl. 10].
(939) 1844 (Fr. 7985) Avisseau Frères [6 (70) 213, pl. 13].
(940) 1846 (Fr. 2627) Van Overbergh [7 (10) 42, pl. 11].
(941) 1846 (Fr. 2311) Soudet [7 (9) 15].
(942) 1850 (Belg. Order No. 3895, Index No. 7 B) J. N. Trots [3 d].
(943) 1850 (Eng. 13,423) Jean-Henri Pape [9 p. 168].

Upright Combined with Horizontal

(944) 1845 (Eng. 10,897) B. Nickels [9 p. 152].

Upright Grand in the Form of a Book-case

(945) 1794 (Eng. 2017) Southwell [9 p. 28].

Upright with the Power of a Grand occupying no more Space than a Glass-cupboard

(946) 1842 (Fr. 7349) Becker et Chemin [6 (57) 305, pl. 19].

With Glass Rods in Place of Springs

(947) 1819 (Am. —) Richard Bury [15 p. 206].
(948) 1833 (Eng. 6483) Goldsworthy Gurney [9 p. 115].
(949) 1844 (Am. 3504) Ottoviano Gori and Philip Ernst [19 1844 (8) 312].

With Case Sloping Backwards

(950) 1811 (Eng. 3403) Wm. Southwell [9 p. 65].

With nearly all parts in Iron or other metal

(951) 1840 (Fr. 5801) Cluesman [6 (49) 290].
(952) 1848 (Fr. 3521) Herding [7 (12) 352].
(953) 1850 (Fr. 4733) Bachman [7 (16) 331].

With Hammers Striking Simultaneously Different Parts of the Strings

(954) 1844 (Eng. 10,385) D. C. Hewitt [9 p. 146].

With Scale Extended

(955) 1808 (Eng. 3154) Hawkes [9 p. 54].
(956) 1809 (Eng. 3250) Loeschman [9 p. 57].

With Springs or Metal Tongues in Place of Strings

(957) 1825 (Fr. 2981) Pape [6 (31) 192, pl. 31].
(958) 1834 (Fr. 10,139) Pape [6 (72) 250, pl. 22].
(959) 1835 (Eng. 6835) Fischer [9 p. 117].
(960) 1847 (Fr. 3569) Papelard [7 (13) 7, pl. 1].

With Striking Point fixed Mathematically

(961) 1831 (Bav.—) Julius Kisselstein [2 (1835) Heft ix S. 576, mit Zeichnungen].

With Strings and Springs

(962) 1850 (Eng. 13,423) Pape [9 p. 168].
(963) 1850 (Fr. 1st and 2nd add. Pats. to No. 5923 (1850)) Pape [7 (20) 90, pls. 13, 14].

"With the Top on a Level with the Lock Board"

(964) 1830 (Eng. 5912) Thompson [9 p. 112].

With Two Hammers for every Note (one striking from above and the other from below)

(965) 1826 (Fr. 1st add. Pat. to No. 4918 (1826)) Pape [6 (44) 441, pl. 18].
(966) 1840 (Bav. —) Ziegler [2 (1840) Heft. xi und xii S. 797, mit Zeichnungen].
(967) 1850 (Eng. 13,423) Jean-Henri Pape [9 p. 168].
(968) 1851 (Fr. 3rd add. Pat. to No. 5923 (1850)) Pape [7 (20) 90, pls. 13, 14].

With Two Springs and a Seraphine Tongue in Addition to Strings (for every note)

(969) 1850 (Eng. 13,423) Pape [9 p. 168].

Vibrating Laminae Introduced into

(970) 1836 (Fr. 10,989) Georges-Frédéric Greiner [6 (79) 401, pl. 20].

"Without Strings"

(971) 1788 (Eng. 1664) Charles Clagget [9 p. 21].
(972) 1833 (Eng. 6483) Goldsworthy Gurney [9 p. 115].
(973) 1834 (Fr. 10,139) Pape [6 (72) 250, pl. 22].
(974) 1850 (Eng. 13,423) Pape [9 p. 168].
(975) 1850 (Fr. 5923) Pape [7 (20) 90, pls. 13, 14].

REFLECTOR (TO ENABLE THE PERFORMER TO SEE BOTH THE MUSIC AND THE KEYBOARD)

(976) 1847 (Eng. 11,681) Spear [9 p. 158].

RETAINING IN TUNE BY MEANS OF SPRINGS, PULLEYS, LEVERS, ETC.

(977) 1800 (Eng. 2430) Peter Litherhead [9 p. 36].
(978) 1800 (Eng. 2446) Isaac Hawkins [9 p. 36].
(979) 1801 (Eng. 2512) Egerton Smith and Thomas Todd [9 p. 40].
(980) 1802 (Eng. 2594) Peter Litherhead [9 p. 45].
(981) 1812 (Fr. 1334) Érard Frères [6 (14) 298, pl. 25].
(982) 1846 (Fr. 1891) "La Dame" Alliaume [7 (7) 159, pl. 30].

RULER

(983) 1811 (Eng. 3403) W. Southwell [9 p. 65].

STAND FOR A SQUARE PIANOFORTE

(984) 1829 (Fr. 2601) Pleyel et Cie [6 (28) 143, pl. 23].
(985) 1840 (Eng. 8643) Pierre Érard [9 p. 132].

SOUND-BOARD
Above the Strings

(986) 1822 (Aust. —) Johann Jacob Goll [1 (1) 268].
(987) 1823 (Aust. —) M. Müller [1 (1) 269].
(988) 1826 (Fr. 3181) Klepfer-Dufaut [6 (33) 93, pl. 18].
(989) 1839 (Bav. —) Jakob Becker [2 (1849) Heft x S. 590, Bl. x, Fig. 6 bis 8].
(990) 1843 (Fr. 12,375) H. Herz [6 (91) 421, pl. 17].
(991) 1848 (Fr. 3711) Montal [7 (13) 186, pls. 32, 33].

Arrangement of

(992) 1802 (Eng. 2591) T. Loud [9 p. 44].
(993) 1836 (Fr. 4146) A. Debain [7 (40) 389, pl. 39].
(994) 1838 (Belg. Order No. 140) J. Dammekins [3].
(995) 1839 (Eng. 8137) Jean-Henri Pape [9 p. 129].
(996) 1841 (Eng. 9023) J. Steward [9 p. 136].
(997) 1842 (Belg. Order No. 1639, Index No. 1691) Themer et Ross [3 a].
(998) 1844 (Bav. —) C. Then [2 (1853) Heft 1 S. 42, Bl. 11, Fig. 8].
(999) 1851 (Am. 8002) H. Klepfer [19 1851 (21) 311].

Attached on One Side only

(1000) 1836 (Eng. 7006) Joseph Lidel [9 p. 120].
(1001) 1840 (Eng. 8388) Joseph Clarke [9 p. 131].

Bridge on the

(1002) 1808 (Eng. 3170) S. Érard [9 p. 55].
(1003) 1827 (Eng. 5528) Edward Dodd [9 p. 104] and
(1004) 1828 (Fr. 2272) [6 (25) 247, pl. 20].
(1005) 1833 (Fr. 9331) Taurin [6 (67) 439, pl. 38].
(1006) 1834 (Eng. 6779) Danchell [9 p. 117].
(1007) 1834 (Fr. 6605) Eulriot [6 (53) 374, pl. 25].
(1008) 1836 (Eng. 7025) Charles Guynemer [9 p. 121] and
(1009) 1837 (Scotland —) [10].
(1010) 1839 (Eng. 7971) Stumpff [9 p. 128].
(1011) 1841 (Eng. 9023) John Steward [9 p. 136] and
(1012) 1841 (Ireland, Reign of Queen Victoria, No. 297) [11] and
(1013) 1841 (Scotland —) [10].
(1014) 1841 (Bav. —) Christian Then [2 (1853) Heft 1 S. 42, Bl. xi, Fig. 8].
(1015) 1844 (Fr. 7985) Avisseau Frères [6 (70) 213, pl. 13].
(1016) 1846 (Eng. 11,285) T. Woolley [9 p. 156].
(1017) 1850 (Am. 7494) Conrad Mayer [19 1850 (20) 166].
(1018) 1851 (Eng. 13,601) Robertson [9 p. 170].

Combined with Pedal Damping Apparatus

(1019) 1847 (Eng. 11,681) John Spear [9 p. 158].

Enlarged

(1020) 1792 (Eng. 1849) George Garcka [9 p. 26].
(1021) 1825 (Eng. 5107) G. A. Kollmann [9 p. 98].
(1022) 1827 (Eng. 5528) E. Dodd [9 p. 104].
(1023) 1827 (Fr. 2088) Charles Côte [6 (23) 245, pl. 6].
(1024) 1827 (Fr. 2884) Triquet [6 (30) 203, pl. 22].
(1025) 1832 (Fr. 3462) Alphonse-Jean Grus [6 (35) 287, pl. 37].
(1026) 1833 (Fr. 3308) Wetzels [6 (34) 46, pl. 11].
(1027) 1838 (Fr. 4834) Moullé [6 (44) 245, pl. 10].
(1028) 1841 (Eng. 8999) John Godwin [9 p. 135].

Formed in "Waving Serpentine Lines"

(1029) 1846 (Am. 4832) John Schriber [19 1848 (15) 118].

In Metal or Wood

(1030) 1828 (Eng. 5673) John Henry Anthony Gunther [9 p. 107].
(1031) 1848 (Fr. 3521) Herding [7 (12) 352].
(1032) 1850 (Fr. 4733) Bachman [7 (16) 331].

In Parchment or Vellum

(1033) 1788 (Eng. 2160) Wm. Rolfe and Samuel Davis [9 p. 29].
(1034) 1797 (Eng. 1664) Charles Clagget [9 p. 21].

In the Form of a Cylindrical Column

(1035) 1812 (Fr. 1333) Érard Frères [6 (14) 295, pl. 26].

Preparation of Wood for

(1036) 1832 (Aust. —) Franz Bienert [1 (3) 123].
(1037) 1836 (Bav. —) Johann Segl [2 (1840) Heft III S. 219].
(1038) 1842 (Aust. —) Franz Bienert [1 (4) 277].

Relieving from Strain

(1039) 1822 (Fr. 3512) Érard Frères [6 (36) 51, pl. 6].
(1040) 1827 (Fr. 2884) Vincent-Pluviose Triquet [6 (30) 203, pl. 22].
(1041) 1829 (Fr. 4089) Guillaume Petzold [6 (40) 148, pl. 14].
(1042) 1830 (Am. —) Alpheus Babcock [18 1830 (6) 159].
(1043) 1833 (Fr. 9331) Jean-Joseph-Pascal Taurin [6 (67) 439, pl. 38].
(1044) 1834 (Aust. —) Joseph Cattaneo [1 (1) 276].
(1045) 1835 (Fr. 10,164) Dizi [6 (72) 372, pl. 32].
(1046) 1836 (Fr. 10,644) Marion de la Brillantais [6 (76) 290, pl. 21].
(1047) 1840 (Fr. 7046) Martin [6 (56) 76, pl. 8]. (N.B. Pat. is for suspending the Pin Blocks.)
(1048) 1842 (Aust. —) J. B. Streicher [1 (4) 359, Tafel 43, Fig. 475].
(1049) 1848 (Am. 5631) J. H. Schomacher [19 1849 (17) 325].
(1050) 1848 (Belg. Order No. 3827, Index No. 5020) J. E. Sax [3 d] and
(1051) 1851 (Fr. 6358) [7 (21) 221, pl. 25].
(1052) 1849 (Am. 6342) C. Hoist [19 1849 (18) 421].
(1053) 1850 (Eng. 13,221) C. Cadby [9 p. 166].

(1054) 1851 (Eng. 13,601) Joseph Clinton Robertson [9 p. 170].
(1055) 1851 (Eng. 13,816) Pierre Érard [9 p. 173].
(1056) 1851 (Eng. 13,821) Thomas Statham [9 p. 173].

Supported and Braced

(1057) 1800 (Eng. 2446) Isaac Hawkins [9 p. 36] and
(1058) *1800* (Am. —) [15 p. 23].
(1059) 1822 (Am. —) James Stewart [15 p. 243].
(1060) 1825 (Aust. —) Joseph Brodmann [1 (1) 271].
(1061) 1826 (Aust. —) Friedrich Hora und Joseph Kinderfreund [1 (1) 272].
(1062) 1829 (Aust. —) Mathias Müller [1 (1) 273].
(1063) 1830 (Fr. 7414) Pleyel [6 (57) 489].
(1064) 1832 (Eng. 6304) P. F. Fischer [9 p. 114].
(1065) 1833 (Aust. —) Mathias Müller [1 (1) 275].
(1066) 1833 (Eng. 6498) Jacob Frederick [*sic*] Zeitter [9 p. 115].
(1067) 1835 (Eng. 6835) P. F. Fischer [9 p. 117].
(1068) 1836 (Am. —) Isaac Clark [18 1836 (18) 315].
(1069) 1839 (Aust. —) Kaspar Lorenz und Stephen Abate [1 (3) 30].
(1070) 1840 (Fr. 11,970) Wolfel [6 (87) 347, pls. 22, 23].
(1071) 1842 (Aust. —) Johann Pottje [1 (4) 67].
(1072) 1845 (Eng. 10,668) J. H. Pape [9 p. 150].
(1073) 1851 (Am. 8383) L. H. Browne [19 1851 (22) 311].
(1074) 1851 (Belg. Order No. 5246, Index No. 607) Khaepen Frères [3 e].

Suspended from the Framework by Clamps

(1075) 1850 (Eng. 13,221) C. Cadby [9 p. 166].

Two in Connection with Two Sets of Strings

(1076) 1812 (Fr. 1332) Érard Frères [6 (14) 292, pl. 25].
(1077) 1845 (Eng. 10,897) Benjamin Nickels [9 p. 152].
(1078) 1851 (Eng. 13,601) Joseph Clinton Robertson [9 p. 170].

Two or more in Connection with *One* Set of Strings

(1079) 1783 (Eng. 1379) John Broadwood [9 p. 13].
(1080) 1824 (Aust. —) Johann Anders [1 (1) 271] and
(1081) *1824* (Bav. —) [2 (1825) No. 24, S. 155].
(1082) 1825 (Fr. 2866) Étienne Eulriot [6 (30) 144, pl. 27].
(1083) 1826 (Aust. —) Friedrich Hora und Joseph Kinderfreund [1 (1) 272].
(1084) 1828 (Eng. 5673) John Henry Anthony Gunther [9 p. 107].
(1085) 1832 (Aust. —) Franz Melzer [1 (1) 274].
(1086) 1836 (Eng. 7006) J. Lidel [9 p. 120].
(1087) 1836 (Eng. 7094) Wheatley Kirk [9 p. 123].
(1088) 1840 (Fr. 2nd add. Pat. to No. 6964 (1829)) Sulot [6 (55) 349, pl. 31].
(1089) 1842 (Aust. —) Johann Pottje [1 (4) 67].
(1090) 1843 (Am. 3045) George Hews, Richard C. March and N. Tileston [19 1849 (17) 450].
(1091) 1844 (Fr. 3rd add. Pat. to No. 10,599 (1836)) Jean-Baptiste Lepère [6 (76) 30, pl. 3].
(1092) 1845 (Eng. 10,668) Jean-Henri Pape [9 p. 150].
(1093) 1845 (Fr. 1st add. Pat. to No. 313 (1844)) Pape [7 (2) 136, pl. 66].

(1094) 1846 (Eng. 11,285) T. Woolley [9 p. 156].
(1095) 1846 (Eng. 11,242) Frederick Handel Burkinyoung [9 p. 154] and
    1846 (Fr. 2105) [7 (8) 84].
(1096) 1846 (Fr. 2627) Van Overbergh [7 (10) 42, pl. 11].
(1097) 1849 (Fr. add. Pat. to No. 2627 (1846)) Van Overbergh [7 (10) 42].

With Bridge of Reverberation for

(1098) 1821 (Eng. 4542) F. W. Collard [9 p. 87].

With "Forte Holes" (or other sound holes)

(1099) 1834 (Eng. 6780) R. Wolf [9 p. 117].
(1100) 1836 (Eng. 7006) Lidel [9 p. 120].
(1101) 1836 (Eng. 7094) Wheatley Kirk [9 p. 123].
(1102) 1841 (Eng. 9023) J. Steward [9 p. 136].
(1103) 1849 (Am. 6889) R. Swan [19 1850 (19) 315].

With Harmonic Rods

(1104) 1845 (Eng. 10,668) Jean-Henri Pape [9 p. 150].
(1105) 1850 (Eng. 13,423) Jean-Henri Pape [9 p. 168].

With Octave Bridge

(1106) 1816 (Eng. 4068) J. Kirkman [9 p. 79].

With Resonating or Sounding Body

(1107) 1834 (Aust. —)* Friedrich Greiner, Friedrich Danchell und Gebrüder
    Ruedorffer [1 (1) 275].
(1108) 1834 (Fr. 6606)* Danchell et Greiner [6 (53) 376, pl. 25].
(1109) 1834 (Fr. 6873)* Jean-Henri Pape [6 (55) 19, pl. 2].
(1110) 1834 (Eng. 6780) Robert Wolf [9 p. 117].
(1111) 1835 (Eng. 6835)* Pierre Frederick Fischer [9 p. 117].
(1112) 1849 (Am. 6889) R. Swan, Jr. [19 1850 (19) 315].

With Sound Post or Bridge

(1113) 1783 (Eng. 1379) J. Broadwood [9 p. 13].
(1114) 1836 (Eng. 7006) J. Lidel [9 p. 120].
(1115) 1841 (Eng. 9023) John Steward [9 p. 136].
(1116) 1842 (Aust. —) Johann Pottje [1 (4) 67].

With Vibrating "Staves"

(1117) 1836 (Eng. 7006) J. Lidel [9 p. 120].

SPRING AXES (FOR KEYS AND OTHER PARTS OF THE ACTION OF PIANOFORTES)

(1118) 1846 (Eng. 11,285) T. Woolley [9 p. 156].

* With resonating body in the form of a kettle-drum.

SPRINGS

To Equalise the Varying Tension on the Frame and Strings Caused by Differences of Temperature

(1119) 1846 (Eng. 11,285) T. Woolley [9 p. 156].

To Replace the After-lengths of Strings

(1120) 1839 (Aust. —) W. und H. Schwab [1 (5) 44].

SPIRAL SPRING (TO BE USED IN THE ACTION OF PIANOFORTES)

(1121) 1844 (Fr. 1st add. Pat. to No. 11,970 (1840)) Wolfel [6 (87) 347, pls. 22, 23].

STRINGING

Cross

(1122) 1828 (Fr. 5833) Jean-Henri Pape (C) [6 (49) 348, pl. 25].
(1123) 1833 (Bav. —) Friedrich Greiner (A) [2 1833 Heft 1 S. 174].
(1124) 1834 (Aust. —) Kaspar Lorenz (–) [1 (1) 276].
(1125) 1834 (Aust. —) Samuel Meiszner (–) [1 (1) 275].
(1126) 1835 (Eng. 6835) Pierre Frederick Fischer [9 p. 117].
(1127) 1836 (Am. —) Isaac Clark (–) [18 1836 (18) 315].
(1128) 1836 (Eng. 7021) John Godwin (B, C) [9 p. 121].
(1129) 1837 (Aust. —) Christoph Lorenz Jahn (A) [1 (2) 68].
(1130) 1839 (Fr. 5240) Julian-Thomas Rinaldi (B) [6 (46) 410, pl. 32].
(1131) 1839 (Fr. 7002) Vandermère (C) [6 (55) 415, pl. 36].
(1132) 1847 (Belg. Order No. 2901, Index No. 4558) J. F. Vogelsangs (–) [3 c].
(1133) 1851 (Am. 8002) Klepfer (C) [19 1851 (21) 311].
(1134) 1851 (Am. 8470) F. Mathushek (B) [19 1851 (22) 381].

Demi-Oblique

(1135) 1848 (Fr. 3711) Montal (C) [7 (13) 186, pls. 32, 33].

Improvements Relating to the

(1136) 1788 (Eng. 1637) Samuel Bury [9 p. 20].
(1137) 1811 (Eng. 3403) William Southwell [9 p. 65].
(1138) 1815 (Fr. 652) Thory [6 (8) 219, pl. 22].
(1139) 1820 (Eng. 4460) Wornum [9 p. 86].
(1140) 1821 (Eng. 4542) Frederick William Collard [9 p. 87].
(1141) 1827 (Aust. —) Mathias Müller und Söhne [1 (1) 273].
(1142) 1830 (Am. —) Alpheus Babcock [18 1830 (6) 159].
(1143) 1839 (Eng. 8137) Jean-Henri Pape [9 p. 129].
(1144) 1840 (Aust. —) J. F. Ries [1 (3) 102].
(1145) 1843 (Am. 3238) J. Chickering [19 1849 (18) 479].
(1146) 1845 (Bav. —) J. Baumgartner [2 (1845) Heft 11 S. 141].
(1147) 1848 (Fr. 3711) Montal [7 (13) 186, pls. 32, 33].

Oblique

(1148) 1802 (Eng. 2591) Thomas Loud (C) [9 p. 44].
(1149) 1811 (Eng. 2481) W. F. Collard (C) [9 p. 67].
(1150) 1830 (Belg. Order No. 109) Lichtenthal (–) [3].
(1151) 1831 (Bav. —) F. Greiner (A) [2 (1835) Heft vii S. 450, mit Zeichnung].
(1152) 1831 (Bav. —) Greiner und Schmidt [2 (1837) Heft. xi und xii S. 783, mit Zeichnungen].
(1153) 1835 (Eng. 6835) P. F. Fischer (C) [9 p. 117].
(1154) 1843 (Fr. 12,375) Herz (A) [6 (91) 421, pl. 17].
(1155) 1847 (Belg. Order No. 2901, Index No. 4558) J. F. Vogelsangs [3 c].
(1156) 1848 (Fr. 3711) Montal (B, C) [7 (13) 186, pls. 32, 33].

Vertical

(1157) 1800 (Eng. 2446) Isaac Hawkins (C) [9 p. 36].
(1158) 1848 (Fr. 3711) Montal (A, B, C) [7 (13) 186, pls. 32, 33].

STRINGS

Amplifying the Tone by Covering them with Frames clothed with Vibrating Substances

(1159) 1824 (Eng. 4994) W. Wheatstone [9 p. 94].

Arrangement of

(1160) 1803 (Eng. 2718) Woods [9 p. 47].
(1161) 1839 (Aust. —) W. und H. Schwab [1 (5) 44].
(1162) 1840 (Eng. 8692) Edward Dodd [9 p. 134].
(1163) 1840 (Eng. 8388) J. Clarke [9 p. 131].
(1164) 1841 (Eng. 8999) J. Godwin [9 p. 135].
(1165) 1844 (Eng. 10,385) Daniel Chandler Hewitt [9 p. 146].
(1166) 1844 (Fr. 7985) Avisseau Frères [6 (70) 213, pl. 13].
(1167) 1844 (Fr. 8219) Daniel [6 (61) 466, pl. 25].
(1168) 1851 (Eng. 13,601) J. C. Robertson [9 p. 170].
(1169) 1851 (Eng. 13,816) P. Érard [9 p. 173].

Attaching to the Hitch Pins

(1170) 1827 (Eng. 5475) James Stewart [9 p. 101].
(1171) 1831 (Am. —) Thomas Kearsing, H. Kearsing, O. Kearsing, G. T. Kearsing, William Kearsing [18 1831 (8) 345].
(1172) 1840 (Fr. 11,970) Charles-François Wolfel [6 (87) 347, pls. 22, 23].
(1173) 1846 (Fr. 1955) Aury [7 (7) 184, pl. 18].
(1174) 1851 (Eng. 13,601) Joseph Clinton Robertson [9 p. 170].

Attaching to the Wrest Pins

(1175) 1841 (Eng. 8999) John Godwin [9 p. 135].
(1176) 1844 (Fr. 4th add. Pat. to No. 9404 (1838)) Pape [6 (68) 144, pl. 11].
(1177) 1846 (Am. 4832) John Schriber [19 1848 (15) 118].
(1178) 1848 (Am. 5631) J. H. Schomacher [19 1849 (17) 325].

Bass Strings fixed below the Sound-Board
to Economise Space

(1179) 1808 (Eng. 3170) S. Érard [9 p. 55].

Bound with Gutta-percha or India-rubber

(1180) 1845 (Eng. 10,897) B. Nickels [9 p. 152].

Clamped

(1181) 1823 (Eng. 4759) F. Deakin [9 p. 91].
(1182) 1845 (Eng. 10,668) Jean-Henri Pape [9 p. 150].

Combining Several to form One

(1183) 1845 (Eng. 10,897) B. Nickels [9 p. 152].

Fixed as in Violins and Harps

(1184) 1826 (Aust. —) Johann Jacob Goll [1 (1) 272].

Metallic Elastic

(1185) 1800 (Eng. 2446) Isaac Hawkins [9 p. 36].

Mounted on Harmonic Rods

(1186) 1850 (Eng. 13,423) Jean-Henri Pape [9 p. 168].
(1187) 1851 (Fr. 3rd add. Pat. to No. 5923 (1850)) Pape [7 (20) 90, pls. 13, 14].

One, Two, Three, Four or Five forming One Note

(1188) 1803 (Fr. 114) Tobias Schmidt [6 (2) 242, pl. 57].
(1189) 1825 (Fr. 1808) Pleyel père et fils aîné [6 (21) 65, pl. 10].
(1190) 1831 (Bav. —) Joseph Baumgartner [2 (1837) Heft. xi und xii S. 787].

Plated with Gold, Silver, Platina, etc.

(1191) 1845 (Eng. 10,668) Jean-Henri Pape [9 p. 150].
(1192) 1846 (Eng. 11,180) Isaac Henry Robert Mott [9 p. 153].
(1193) 1851 (Am. 8452) H. J. Newton [19 1851 (22) 378].

Rendered Waterproof

(1194) 1800 (Eng. 2446) Isaac Hawkins [9 p. 36].

Spiral and Twisted

(1195) 1839 (Aust. —) Wilhelm und Heinrich Schwab [1 (5) 44].

Substitutes for

(1196) 1825 (Fr. 2981) Jean-Henri Pape [6 (31) 192, pl. 31].
(1197) 1834 (Fr. 10,139) Jean-Henri Pape [6 (72) 250, pl. 22].
(1198) 1835 (Eng. 6835) Pierre Frederick Fischer [9 p. 117].
(1199) 1837 (Aust. —) Karl Zsitkovsky [1 (2) 75].
(1200) 1847 (Fr. 3569) Papelard [7 (13) 7, pl. 1].

H P

Sustaining the Sound of the Strings in Various Ways

(*a*) By Bowing the strings with resined band or wheel

(1201) 1801 (Eng. 2551) J. C. Becker [9 p. 42].
(1202) 1803 (Fr. 114) Schmidt [6 (2) 242, pl. 57].
(1203) 1817 (Eng. 4098) Mott [9 p. 81].
(1204) 1823 (Eng. 4873) Todd [9 p. 93].
(1205) 1824 (Aust. —) Abbé Grégoire Trentin [1 (1) 270].
(1206) 1830 (Belg. Order No. 110) Lichtenthal [3].
(1207) 1837 (Scotland) Wheatstone and Green [10].

(*b*) By a Current of Air directed against them

(1208) 1832 (Fr. 3464) Alphonse-Jean Grus [6 (35) 287, pl. 37].
(1209) 1834 (Fr. 10,139) Pape [6 (72) 250, pl. 22].
(1210) 1836 (Eng. 7154) Wheatstone and Green [9 p. 123].
(1211) 1839 (Eng. 8137) Pape [9 p. 129].
(1212) 1850 (Eng. 13,423) Pape [9 p. 168]. *See also*
(1213) 1850 (Fr. 5923) Pape [7 (20) 90, pls. 13, 14] and
(1214) *1851* (Belg. Order No. 5255, Index No. 826) [3 *e*].

(*c*) By Flapping the strings with leather or cloth, etc.

(1215) 1849 (Fr. 4940) Roeder [7 (17) 244, pl. 44].

(*d*) With Repeating Hammers

(1216) 1800 (Eng. 2446) Hawkins [9 p. 36].
(1217) 1812 (Fr. 1334) Érard Frères [6 (14) 298, pl. 25].
(1218) 1825 (Fr. 2981) Pape [6 (31) 192, pl. 31].
(1219) 1834 (Fr. 10,139) Pape [6 (72) 250, pl. 22].
(1220) 1835 (Eng. 6835) P. F. Fischer [9 p. 117].
(1221) 1841 (Bav. —) Christian Then [2 (1848) Heft II S. 101, Bl. 2, Fig. 4 und 5].
(1222) 1841 (Fr. 12,079) Madame Girard-Romagnac [6 (88) 452, pl. 33].
(1223) 1844 (Eng. 10,238) C. M. Elizée Sautter [9 p. 144].

Tempering (strings)

(1224) 1810 (Fr. 1177) Ignace Pleyel [6 (13) 49].
(1225) 1823 (Eng. 4759) Francis Deakin [9 p. 91].
(1226) 1840 (Eng. 8526) John Hawley [9 p. 131].
(1227) 1840 (Fr. 10,242) Sanguinède et Capt [6 (73) 141].
(1228) 1845 (Bav. —) J. Baumgartner und Schwarz [2 (1845) Heft III S. 223].

Two Sets Struck by a Single Row of Two-Faced Hammers

(1229) 1841 (Fr. 10,534) Nicolas Sulot [6 (75) 460, pl. 30].
(1229*a*) 1843 Add. Pat. to the above.
(1230) 1844 (Fr. 10,092) François-Xavier Bader [6 (72) 46, pl. 4].
(1231) 1847 (Fr. 3340) Sulot [7 (12) 276].

Wrapped with Platinum

(1232) 1811 (Eng. 3436) William Bundy [9 p. 67].

TANNING LEATHER (FOR PIANOFORTE HAMMER HEADS)

(1233) 1837 (Bav. —) Johann Gottlieb Steininger [2 (1841) Heft vi S. 389].

TOUCH
Various means of adjusting the

(1234) 1787 (Eng. 1607) Humphrey Walton [9 p. 20].
(1235) 1790 (Eng. 1784) James Ball [9 p. 25].
(1236) 1801 (Eng. 2502) Sébastien Érard [9 p. 40].
(1237) 1833 (Fr. 9331) Taurin [6 (67) 439, pl. 38].
(1238) 1835 (Eng. 6835) Pierre Frederick Fischer [9 p. 117].
(1239) 1836 (Aust. —) Joseph Keller [1 (3) 8].
(1240) 1836 (Aust. —) M. Seuffert [1 (3) 12, Fig. 6].
(1241) 1836 (Fr. 4305) François-Joseph Lahausse [6 (41) 353].
(1242) 1839 (Eng. 8137) Jean-Henri Pape [9 p. 129].
(1243) 1840 (Fr. 7448) Soufleto [6 (58) 90, pl. 7].
(1244) 1843 (Eng. 9716) Stewart and Lambert [9 p. 142].
(1245) 1844 (Fr. 8219) Daniel [6 (61) 466, pl. 25].
(1246) 1848 (Am. 5990) J. J. Wise [19 1849 (18) 208].

TUNING
By Means of an Index Showing the Tension of the Strings

(1247) 1833 (Am. —) John J. Wise [18 1834 (13) 328].
(1248) 1836 (Aust. —) Jacob Ignaz Hittorff [1 (3) 73, Fig. 43].
(1249) 1836 (Eng. 7025) Charles Guynemer [9 p. 121].
(1250) 1836 (Fr. 10,599) Jean-Baptiste Lepère [6 (76) 30, pl. 3].
(1251) 1838 (Fr. 9404) Jean-Henri Pape [6 (68) 144, pl. 11].
(1252) 1839 (Eng. 8137) Jean-Henri Pape [9 p. 129].

Hammers

(1253) 1788 (Eng. 1664) Clagget [9 p. 21].
(1254) 1833 (Am. —) Louis Fissore [18 1834 (13) 33].
(1255) 1838 (Am. 1007) John Cutts Smith [18 1839 (24) 320].
(1256) 1844 (Fr. 8205) Guérin [6 (61) 421, pl. 21].

Improvements Relating to Tuning and Keeping in Tune (various)

(1257) 1820 (Eng. 4460) Robert Wornum [9 p. 86].
(1258) 1823 (Aust. —) Johann Streicher [1 (1) 269].
(1259) 1826 (Eng. 5404) John James Schwieso [9 p. 100].
(1260) 1834 (Fr. 3990) Jean-Baptiste Cluesman [6 (39) 339, pl. 32].
(1261) 1834 (Fr. 6606) Danchell et Greiner [6 (53) 376, pl. 25].
(1262) 1836 (Eng. 7006) Joseph Lidel [9 p. 120].
(1263) 1838 (Belg. Order No. 157) C. J. Sax [3].
(1264) 1838 (Fr. 9404) Jean-Henri Pape [6 (68) 144, pl. 11].

(1265) 1839 (Eng. 7971) Stumpff [9 p. 128].
(1266) 1839 (Eng. 8164) J. F. Meyers and J. Storer [9 p. 130].
(1267) 1839 (Sweden 41) Pehr Rosenwall [13].
(1268) 1840 (Sweden 1) Olof Granfeldt [13].
(1269) 1845 (Sweden 28) C. Sillen [13].
(1270) 1846 (Am. 4832) John Schriber [19 1848 (15) 118].
(1271) 1847 (Sweden 28) J. Sundell [13].

Movable Bridge to Facilitate

(1272) 1824 (Aust. —) Joachim Ehlers [1 (1) 270].
(1273) 1826 (Aust. —) Wilhelm Leschen [1 (1) 272].

Two, Three, Four or Six Strings at once

(1274) 1833 (Am. —) John J. Wise (Two) [18 1834 (13) 328].
(1275) 1838 (Fr. 2nd add. Pat to No. 10,599 (1836)) Jean-Baptiste Lepère (Two or three) [6 (76) 30, pl. 3].
(1276) 1839 (Fr. 6506) Boisselot et fils (Two) [6 (53) 175, pl. 17].
(1277) 1843 (Fr. 3rd add. Pat. to No. 9404 (1838)) Jean-Henri Pape (Two or three) [6 (68) 144, pl. 11].
(1278) 1850 (Eng. 13,423) Jean-Henri Pape (Two, three, four, or six) [9 p. 168].

UNDER HAMMER

(1279) 1788 (Eng. 1637) S. Bury [9 p. 20]. Patented as "Counteracting hammer".
(1280) 1843 (Eng. 9716) Stewart and Lambert [9 p. 142].

VARNISH (TO PRESERVE PIANOFORTES FROM DAMP)

(1281) 1836 (Fr. 4042) Tressoz et Cie [6 (39) 451].
(1282) 1849 (Belg. Order No. 3862, Index No. 6201) B. Van Hyfte [3 d].
(1283) 1850 (Fr. 10,306) Colin [7 (35) 71].

VOLTO SUBITO

(1284) 1800 (Eng. 2446) Isaac Hawkins [9 p. 36].
(1285) 1811 (Eng. 3403) William Southwell [9 p. 65].

WALKER'S WREST PIN

See WREST PINS—Mechanical, etc.

WREST PINS

Arrangement of

(1286) 1783 (Eng. 1379) John Broadwood [9 p. 13].
(1287) 1792 (Eng. 1849) George Garcka [9 p. 26].
(1288) 1827 (Fr. 2238) Cluesman [6 (25) 17, pl. 4].
(1289) 1840 (Fr. 7883) Wirth [6 (60) 60, pl. 5].
(1290) 1841 (Eng. 8999) J. Godwin [9 p. 135].
(1291) 1842 (Fr. 2nd add. Pat. to No. 9404 (1838)) Pape [6 (68) 144, pl. 11].
(1292) 1843 (Fr. 12,375) Herz [6 (91) 421, pl. 17].

Improved Construction of

(1293) 1827 (Eng. 5533) Eugène du Mesnil [9 p. 105].
(1294) 1845 (Eng. 10,668) Jean-Henri Pape [9 p. 150].

Inserted into a Collar and Socket

(1295) 1810 (Eng. 3332) S. Érard [9 p. 60].

Mechanical, including Screw Nuts and Pressure Screws
for fine tuning

(1296) 1716 (Fr. 172) Marius [4 (3) 83].
(1297) 1771 (Eng. 989) Richard Wakefield [9 p. 7].
(1298) 1800 (Eng. 2446) Isaac Hawkins [9 p. 36] and
(1299) *1800* (Am. —) [15 p. 23].
(1300) 1805 (Eng. 2811) Edward Thunder [9 p. 48].
(1301) 1810 (Eng. 3332) Sébastien Érard [9 p. 60].
(1302) 1823 (Eng. 4759) F. Deakin [9 p. 91].
(1303) 1825 (Eng. 5107) G. A. Kollmann [9 p. 98].
(1304) 1826 (Eng. 5404) John James Schwieso [9 p. 100].
(1305) 1831 (Bav. —) Friedrich Greiner und Joseph Schmidt [2 (1837) Heft. xi
und xii S. 783, mit Zeichnung].
(1306) 1834 (Fr. 3990) Cluesman [6 (39) 339, pl. 32].
(1307) 1836 (Aust. —) Jacob Ignaz Hittorff [1 (3) 73, Fig. 43].
(1308) 1836 (Fr. 5049) Frédéric Mahr [6 (45) 446].
(1309) 1836 (Fr. 10,599) Jean-Baptiste Lepère [6 (76) 30, pl. 3].
(1310) 1838 (Am. 790) Daniel Walker [18 1839 (23) 393].
(1311) 1838 (Fr. 9404) Jean-Henri Pape [6 (68) 144, pl. 11] and the first three
add. Patents, 1842, 1843.
(1312) 1839 (Eng. 7971) Johann A. Stumpff [9 p. 128].
(1313) 1839 (Fr. 6506) Boisselot et fils [6 (53) 175, pl. 17].
(1314) 1840 (Fr. 5801) Cluesman [6 (49) 290].
(1315) 1840 (Fr. 6988) Henri Reintjer [6 (55) 375].
(1316) 1841 (Eng. 9023) John Steward [9 p. 136].
(1317) 1841 (Fr. 8479) Kriegelstein et Plantade [6 (63) 64, pl. 4].
(1318) 1841 (Sweden 49) A. Jorselius [13].
(1319) 1843 (Fr. 3rd add. Pat. to No. 9404 (1838)) H. Pape [6 (68) 144, pl. 11].
(1320) 1843 (Fr. 7818) Tessers [6 (59) 458, pl. 36].
(1321) 1844 (Am. 3403) J. S. Ives [19 1844 (8) 168].
(1322) 1844 (Fr. 1st add. Pat. to No. 11,970 (1840)) Charles-François Wolfel
[6 (87) 374, pls. 22, 23].
(1323) 1844 (Fr. 8205) Édouard Guérin [6 (61) 421, pl. 21].
(1324) 1845 (Eng. 11,897) B. Nickels [9 p. 152].
(1325) 1846 (Eng. 11,242) Frederick Handel Burkinyoung [9 p. 154] and
(1326) 1846 (Fr. 2105) [7 (8) 84].
(1327) 1846 (Fr. 2095) Charles-François Wolfel [7 (8) 47, pl. 3].
(1328) 1850 (Eng. 13,252) Pierre Érard [9 p. 167].
(1329) 1851 (Belg. Order No. 5237, Index No. 143) N. Fievet [3 *e*].
(1330) 1851 (Canada 306) George Hooper Mead [21].
(1331) 1851 (Eng. 13,601) Robertson [9 p. 170].
(1332) 1851 (Eng. 13,816) P. Érard [9 p. 173].

Working in a Metal Plate

(1333) 1833 (Am. —) Louis Fissore [18 1834 (13) 33].
(1334) 1845 (Eng. 10,668) Jean-Henri Pape [9 p. 150].

With Friction Collar

(1335) 1831 (Eng. 6069) John Charles Schwieso [9 p. 112].

WREST-PIN BLOCK OR PLANK
Arrangement of

(1336) 1846 (Eng. 11,285) T. Woolley [9 p. 156].

In Metal

(1337) 1823 (Fr. 1415) Roller [6 (15) 269, pl. 11].
(1338) 1825 (Eng. 5065) Érard [9 p. 95].
(1339) 1831 (Bav. —) Greiner und Schmidt [2 (1837) Heft. xi und xii S. 783, mit Zeichnung].
(1340) 1831 (Eng. 6069) John Charles Schwieso [9 p. 112].
(1341) 1850 (Eng. 13,252) Pierre Érard [9 p. 167].

In Wood and Metal

(1342) 1825 (Eng. 5107) G. A. Kollmann [9 p. 98].
(1343) 1830 (Fr. 3rd add. Pat. to No. 4918 (1826)) Jean-Henri Pape [6 (44) 441, pl. 18].
(1344) 1836 (Am. —) H. Hartge [18 1836 (18) 326].
(1345) 1839 (Bav. —) Jakob Becker [2 (1849) Heft x S. 590, Bl. x, Fig. 6 bis 8].
(1346) 1840 (Bav. —) Albrecht Ziegler [2 (1840) Heft. xi und xii S. 797].
(1347) 1842 (Aust. —) J. B. Streicher [1 (4) 359, Tafel 43, Fig. 475].
(1348) 1844 (Eng. 10,385) Daniel Chandler Hewitt [9 p. 146].
(1349) 1846 (Am. 4832) John Schriber [19 1849 (15) 118].
(1350) 1848 (Am. 5631) J. H. Schomacher [19 1849 (17) 325].
(1351) 1850 (Am. 7308) J. Ruck [19 1850 (20) 50].
(1352) 1850 (Eng. 13,252) Pierre Érard [9 p. 167].
(1353) 1851 (Fr. 3rd add. Pat. to No. 3711 (1848)) Montal [7 (13) 186, pls. 32, 33].

With Bridge of Iron, Glass or Copper

(1354) 1833 (Fr. 9331) Taurin [6 (67) 439, pl. 38].

With Harmonic or Pressure Bar

(1355) 1838 (Fr. 9572) Pierre Érard [6 (69) 176, pl. 17].
(1356) 1839 (Aust. —) Johann Pottje [1 (4) 314].
(1357) 1842 (Bav. —) Alois Biber [2 (1847) Heft. xi und xii S. 763, Bl. xv, Fig. 18].
(1358) 1844 (Bav. —) C. Then [2 (1853) Heft i S. 42, Bl. ii, Fig. 8].
(1359) 1845 (Bav. —) J. Mayer [2 (1848), Heft x S. 620, Bl. xii, Fig. 2, 3].
(1360) 1851 (Eng. 13,816) Pierre Érard [9 p. 173].

With Metal Bridge

(1361) 1829 (Aust. —) J. Gartner [1 (1) 273].
(1362) 1839 (Aust. —) J. Krämer [1 (4) 208].

APPENDIX D

PIANOFORTE WIRE

(1) Gauge numbers and mass.
(2) Schemes for scaling pianofortes, etc.
(3) Composition and density of wires.
(4) Prices of pianoforte wire.
(5) Patents for tempering wire.

(1) GAUGE NUMBERS AND MASS OF WIRE

Old Berlin Iron Pianoforte Wire

No.	9/0	8/0	7/0	6/0	5/0	4/0	3/0	2/0	0	1
Mass mm.	1·50	1·30	1·18	1·06	0·88	0·78	0·70	0·63	0·57	0·53

No.	2	3	4	5	6	7	8	9	10	
Mass mm.	0·47	0·43	0·39	0·35	0·32	0·30	0·28	0·26	0·24	

N.B. On the key one sees: 0000= 4/0, 000 = 3/0, 00 = 2/0, etc.

Old Steel Pianoforte Wire

Old No.	Mass mm.	Old No.	Mass mm.	Old No.	Mass mm.
1	0·20	12	0·725	20½	1·150
2	0·25	12½	0·750	21	1·175
3	0·30	13	0·775	21½	1·200
4	0·35	13½	0·800	22	1·225
5	0·40	14	0·825	22½	1·250
6	0·45	14½	0·850	23	1·300
6½	0·475	15	0·875	23½	1·350
7	0·500	15½	0·900	24	1·400
7½	0·512	16	0·925	24½	1·450
8	0·525	16½	0·950	25	1·500
8½	0·550	17	0·975	26	1·600
9	0·575	17½	1·000	27	1·700
9½	0·600	18	1·025	28	1·800
10	0·625	18½	1·050	29	1·900
10½	0·650	19	1·075	30	2·000
11	0·675	19½	1·100	31	2·100
11½	0·700	20	1·125	32	2·200

A Note on the Relationship between the mass of German and English Pianoforte wires.

According to Roma* there were three kinds of pianoforte wire manufactured in his time (1834). These were:
(1) Berlin *Iron* Wire.
(2) English *Steel* Wire.
(3) Nuremberg *Brass* Wire.

* Roma, G. di, *Manuel simplifié de l'accordeur: ou l'art d'accorder le piano*, etc. 2e éd. Paris, 1834.

The Berlin and Nuremberg wires had corresponding gauge numbers, whilst the English wires had a different set. Considerable difficulty exists in correlating these numbers and consequently ascertaining the corresponding wires of the German and the English strings.

The list we quote from Roma* agrees with those cited by Thon,† and by Montal‡ in the shortened German edition of his celebrated work on tuning the pianoforte, and also with that of Armellino.§

Roma 1834

English gauge Nos.	Berlin gauge Nos.	English gauge Nos.	Berlin gauge Nos.	English gauge Nos.	Berlin gauge Nos.
7	4	11	1/0	15	5/0
8	3	12	2/0	16	6/0
9	2	13	3/0	17	7/0
10	1	14	4/0	18	8/0

But in the first French edition of *L'Art d'accorder soi-même son Piano* (1836) Montal probes more deeply into this question and correlates the German with the English wires thus:

Montal 1836 ||

English strings gauge Nos.	Berlin wire gauge Nos.	English strings gauge Nos.	Berlin wire gauge Nos.
7	4 fort.	14	3/0 fin.
8	3 id.	15	4/0 id.
9	2 id.	16	5/0 id.
10	1	17	6/0
11	0 fin.	18	7/0
12	0 fort.	19	8/0 fin.
13	2/0	20	8/0 fort.

He states that half numbers had been added between the ordinary numbers. In the case of the English strings the No. $7\frac{1}{2}$ indicates the thickness between No. 7 and No. 8, and the No. $8\frac{1}{2}$ that between No. 8 and No. 9, whereas in the case of the German gauge numbers the intermediate thickness between No. 0 and 2/0 is expressed by the No. $2/0\frac{1}{2}$ instead of by the No. $0\frac{1}{2}$, and similarly the intermediate thickness between No. 2/0 and No. 3/0 is expressed by the No. $3/0\frac{1}{2}$ instead of by the No. $2/0\frac{1}{2}$. Thus the two sets of wires are denoted by the following numbers. (We give them in order of increasing thickness.)

English wire gauge Nos.	Berlin wire gauge Nos.	English wire gauge Nos.	Berlin wire gauge Nos.	English wire gauge Nos.	Berlin wire gauge Nos.
7	4	$9\frac{1}{2}$	$1\frac{1}{2}$	12	2/0
$7\frac{1}{2}$	$3\frac{1}{2}$	10	1	$12\frac{1}{2}$	$3/0\frac{1}{2}$
8	3	$10\frac{1}{2}$	$0\frac{1}{2}$	13	3/0
$8\frac{1}{2}$	$2\frac{1}{2}$	11	0	$13\frac{1}{2}$	$4/0\frac{1}{2}$
9	2	$11\frac{1}{2}$	$2/0\frac{1}{2}$	14	4/0

* Roma, G. di, *Manuel simplifié de l'accordeur: ou l'art d'accorder le piano*, etc. 2e éd. Paris, 1834.

† Thon, C. F. G., *Abhandlung über Klaviersaiten-Instrumente, insonderheit der Forte-Piano und Flügel*, etc. 3te Aufl. Weimar, 1843.

‡ Montal, C., *Kurzgefasste Anweisung das Pianoforte selbst stimmen zu lernen.* Mainz, 1835.

§ Armellino, Giorgio, *Manuel simplifié de l'accordeur.* Paris, 1855.

|| Montal, C., *L'Art d'accorder soi-même son Piano.* Paris, 1836.

Montal remarks that considerable difficulty arises in correlating the intermediate numbers, since they are often made with irregularity and are nearly as thick as the nearest whole number.

The Brass wires made at Nuremberg are numbered in the same way as the Berlin wires, but they can only be correlated approximately. We quote Montal's table below:

Approximate correspondence between the Berlin and Nuremberg Wires

Nuremberg wire gauge Nos.	Berlin wire gauge Nos.	Nuremberg wire gauge Nos.	Berlin wire gauge Nos.
0	1	7/0	8/0
2/0	0	8/0	9/0
3/0	2/0	9/0	10/0
4/0	3/0	10/0	12/0
5/0	5/0	11/0	14/0
6/0	7/0	12/0	16/0

Webster's Pianoforte Wire

Gauge Numbers and Mass in millimetres of Webster's Wire

Gauge No.	Mass mm.	Gauge No.	Mass mm.	Gauge No.	Mass mm.
11	0·702	$14\frac{1}{2}$	0·847	20	1·109
$11\frac{1}{2}$	0·724	15	0·868	21	1·194
12	0·746	$15\frac{1}{2}$	0·889	22	1·275
$12\frac{1}{2}$	0·767	16	0·910	23	1·370
13	0·787	17	0·956	24	1·469
$13\frac{1}{2}$	0·807	18	1·000	25	1·565
14	0·827	19	1·050	26	1·660

From Kützing, C., *Das Wissenschaftliche der Fortepiano-Baukunst.* Bern, 1844. S. 30.

(2) SCHEMES FOR SCALING PIANOFORTES, ETC.

1739

Schröter gives the following scheme for stringing his instrument:

From Paul, Dr Oscar, *Geschichte des Klaviers.* Leipzig, 1868. S. 96, 97.

Steel Strings (Treble)

```
No. 0 from G♯ to c
No. 1 from c♯ to f
No. 2 from f♯ to b
No. 3 from e′ to g′
No. 4 from g♯′ to d♯″
No. 5 from e″ to b″
No. 6 from c‴ to g‴
```

Brass Strings (Bass)

No.	000000	to	͵F	and	͵F♯	
No.	00000	to	͵G	and	͵G♯	
No.	0000	to	͵A	͵B	B	
No.	000	to	C	C♯	D	D♯
No.	00	to	E	F	F♯	G

APPENDIX D

From contra	F	to	c♯	two strings
From	d	to	b'	three ,,
From	h'	to	g'''	four ,,

} to a note

An Alternative Scheme

From contra	F	to	h	two strings
From	c'	to	g'''	three ,,

} to a note

1791–1825

(1)

Square Pianoforte F₁ to f''', by Broadwood, 1791

	Gauge No.	
F₁	14	
A♭	13	} Brass
H	12	
d	11	
f	11	
b	10	} Steel
e♭'	9	
c♯''	8	

N.B. Eng. Gauge Nos.

(2)

Square Forte-Piano F₁ to g''', by Kühlewind, 1791

	Gauge No.
F₁	0000
H₁	000
F	00
c	0
f♯	1
h	2
f'	3
b'	4
e''	5
h'''	6

(3)

Square Forte-Piano F₁ to f''', by C. Schiffer, 1793

	Gauge No.
F₁	000
͵G♯	00
C	1/0
G♯	1
c	2
f	3
c♯'	4
a'	5
c♯''	6

(4)

A 'Mozart' Grand Forte-Piano F₁ to g'''

	Gauge No.	
F₁	0000000	
G₁	000000	
C	00000	
C♯	0000	} Brass
E	000	
G	00	
H	0	
e♭	1	
g♯	2	
d'	3	} Steel
g♯'	4	
e♭''	5	
h''	6	

(5)

Forte-Piano F₁ to g'''

	Gauge No.
F₁	000
G₁	00
A₁	0
C	1
D	2
F	3
A	4
d	5
a	6
f'	7
f''	7*

* Steel

(6)

Forte-Piano F₁ to f'''

	Gauge No.
F₁	000
G₁	00
A₁	0
C	1
D♯	2
G	3
B	4
e	5
d♯'	6
g''	7

(7)

Forte-Piano A$_1$ to d$'''$
(6 feet long)

		Gauge No.	
A$_1$	. . .	ooooo	⎫
H$_1$	. . .	oooo	⎬ Brass
D	. . .	ooo	⎭
G	. . .	oo	⎫
d	. . .	o	⎪
f	. . .	1	⎪
g	. . .	2	⎬ Steel
a	. . .	3	⎪
h	. . .	4	⎪
f$'$	. . .	5	⎭

(8)

Grand Pianoforte F$_1$ to
f$''''$, by Nannette Streicher,
1825

		Gauge No.	
G$_1$	. .	ooooooo	⎫
A$_1$	. .	oooooo	⎪
H$_1$	. .	ooooo	⎬ Brass
D	. .	oooo	⎭
F♯	. .	oooo	⎫
B	. .	ooo	⎪
g$'$	. .	ooo$\frac{1}{2}$	⎪
c$'$	. .	oo	⎬ Steel
d♯$''$	. .	oo$\frac{1}{2}$	⎪
f$'''$	. .	o	⎪
c$''''$	. .	1	⎭

Note. Nos. (4), (5), (6) and (7) are taken from Nachersberg, *Stimmbuch*, Leipzig, 1804; nos. (1), (2), (3) and (8) from tuners' marks on the keys or the wrest-pin block of the pianofortes themselves. Schemes for stringing the Clavichord and the Harpsichord given below for comparison.

1803–1804

Schemes for Stringing the Clavichord and the Harpsichord

(1)

Clavichord F$_1$ to a$'''$, by
Johann Paul Kraemer u.
Söhne, Göttingen, 1803

		Gauge No.	
F$_1$	. . .	ooo	⎫
F♯	. . .	ooo$\frac{1}{2}$	⎪
G$_1$	. . .	oo$\frac{1}{2}$	Brass (?)
A$_1$	. . .	o	now
H$_1$	. . .	o$\frac{1}{2}$	Silberdraht
C♯	. . .	1	⎪
D♯	. . .	o	⎭
E	. . .	o$\frac{1}{2}$	⎫
F	. . .	1	⎪
G	. . .	1$\frac{1}{2}$	⎪
A	. . .	2	⎪
H	. . .	2$\frac{1}{2}$	⎪
c♯	. . .	3	⎪
e	. . .	3$\frac{1}{2}$	⎬ Steel
g	. . .	4	⎪
c$'$	. . .	4$\frac{1}{2}$	⎪
g$'$	. . .	5	⎪
c$''$	. . .	5$\frac{1}{2}$	⎪
g$''$	. . .	6	⎪
d$'''$	. . .	6$\frac{1}{2}$	⎭

(2)

Clavichord C to e$'''$

		Gauge No.	
C	. . . .	oo	⎫
D	. . . .	o	⎪
F	. . . .	1	⎪
c	. . . .	2	⎪
d♯	. . . .	3	⎬ Brass
a	. . . .	4	⎪
d$'$	. . . .	5	⎪
g$'$	. . . .	6	⎪
c$''$	. . . .	7	⎪
g$'''$	. . . .	8	⎭

(3)

Clavier C to e$'''$

		Gauge No.
C	. . . .	oo
D	. . . .	o
G	. . . .	1
c	. . . .	2
d♯	. . . .	3
a	. . . .	4
d$'$	. . . .	5
g$'$	. . . .	6
c$''$	. . . .	7
g$'''$	. . . .	8

<table>
<tr><td colspan="2">(4)
Harpsichord F₁ to f‴</td><td colspan="2">(5)
Spinet A to e‴</td></tr>
</table>

	Gauge No.		Gauge No.
F_1	0	A	1
B_1	1	D♯	2
D♯	2	G	3
G♯	3	c	4
c♯	4	f	5 ⎫
f♯	5	h	6 ⎬ Steel
c♯′	6	f♯′	7 ⎪
g♯″	7	f″	8 ⎭
f‴	8		

Note. Nos. (2), (3), (4), (5) taken from Nachersberg, *Stimmbuch*, Leipzig, 1804. No. (1) taken from tuners' marks on the keys. (This instrument is in the possession of Dr Neupert of Nuremberg.)

1803

Table des longueurs, numéros et tensions des cordes de pianoforte de M. Schmidt

From *Description des Brevets*, 1st Series, Vol. ii, p. 251, Pat. No. 114.

Nos.	Longueurs mm.	Tension kgm.	Nos.	Longueurs mm.	Tension kgm.	Nos.	Longueurs mm.	Tension kgm.
7° {	Fa = 1480	15	3° {	Mi = 740	18·5	3 {	Fa = 195	
	Fa 1447	16		Fa 710	19		Sol 185	
	Sol 1414	17·5		Fa 680	19·5		Sol 175	
	Sol 1382	19	2° {	Sol = 651	17·5		La 166	
	La 1350	19·5		Sol 622	18		La 158	
6° {	La = 1318	17·5		La 593	18·5		Si 149	
	Si 1286	18		La = 564	14		Ut 140	
	Ut 1254	18·5	1° {	Si 536	14·5		Ut 132	
	Ut 1222	19		Ut 508	15		Re 125	
	Re 1188	19·5		Ut 483	15·5		Re 118	
5° {	Re = 1156	17·5	1 {	Re = 458	9·5		Mi 112	
	Mi 1124	18		Re 434	10		Fa 106	
	Fa 1092	18·5		Mi 408	10·5		Fa 100	
4° {	Fa = 1060	16·5		Fa 388	11		Sol 95	
	Sol 1028	17		Fa = 372	12·5		Sol 90	
	Sol 996	17·5		Sol 356	12·5		La 85	
	La 964	18		Sol 340	12·5		La 80	
3° {	La = 932	17·5		La 324	12·5		Si 75	
	Si 900	18		La 308	12·5		Ut 70	
2° {	Ut = 868	16	2 {	Si 292	12·5			
	Ut 836	16·5		Ut 276	12·5			
	Re 804	17		Ut 261	12·5			152
	Re 772	17·5		Re 246	12·5			361
				Re 232	12·5			405
		405 kgm.		Mi 218	12·5		Total...	918
				Fa 206	12·5			

Left margin: Cordes de Laiton

Middle margin: Cordes de Fer

Third margin (heading over col): Cordes de Fer

Right margin: Chacune de ces cordes = 8 kgm. × 19 = 152 kgm.

Under second section total: 361 kgm.

Le piano à deux cordes = 1836 kgm. Celui à trois = 2750 kgm.

1844

Lengths and Weights of Strings for a Square and a Grand Pianoforte

String measurements for a Square Pianoforte, 1844

Pitch	Length of the string in mm.	Gauge No.	Tension of one string in kgm.	Gauge No. for weaker stringing	Striking length in mm.
f'	60·00				7·50
e⁴	63·42				7·93
dis⁴	67·04				8·38
d⁴	70·86	12	35·78	11½	8·85
cis⁴	74·90				9·36
c⁴	79·18				9·89
h³	83·69				10·46
b³	88·46	12½	37·30	12	11·05
a³	93·47				11·68
gis³	98·84				12·35
g³	104·4				13·05
fis³	110·4				13·80
f³	116·7	13	38·90	12½	14·58
e³	122·4				15·42
dis³	130·4				16·30
d³	137·9				17·23
cis³	145·7				18·21
c³	154·0				19·25
h²	162·8	13½	40·55	13	20·30
b²	172·2				21·52
a²	181·9				22·73
gis²	192·3				24·03
g²	204·0	14	42·30	13½	25·50
fis²	214·8				26·85
f²	227·1				28·38
e²	240·1				30·00
dis²	253·8				31·72
d²	268·2	14½	44·10	14	33·52
cis²	283·5				35·43
c²	299·7				37·46
h'	316·8				39·60
b'	334·9				41·86
a'	354·0	15	45·98	14½	44·25
gis'	374·2				46·77
g'	395·4				49·42
fis'	418·1				52·26
f'	441·9				55·23
e'	467·1	15½	47·90	15	58·38
dis'	493·8				61·72
d'	524·1				65·51
cis'	551·7				68·96
c'	583·2				72·90
h°	616·5	16	49·93	15½	77·06
b°	651·6				81·40
a°	688·8				86·10

String measurements for a Square Pianoforte, 1844 (continued)

Pitch	Length of the string in mm.	Gauge No.	Tension of one string in kgm.	Gauge No. for weaker stringing	Striking length in mm.
gis°	728·1				91·01
g°	769·6				96·20
fis°	813·5	17	52·48	16	101·69
f°	860·0				107·50
e°	900·0				112·50
dis°	940·0				117·50
d°	980·0	18	—	17	122·50
cis°	1020·0				127·50
c°	1059·0				132·3
H₀	1098·0				137·2
B₀	1137·0	19	—	18	141·1
A₀	1176·0				147·0
Gis₀	1215·0	20	—	19	151·8
G₀	1254·0				156·7
Fis₀	1292·0	21	54·00	20	161·5
F₀	1330·0				166·2

Overspun strings for a Square Pianoforte (Single Chord), 1844

Pitch	Length of the string in mm.	Gauge No. of the core	Weight of the core in gm.	Weight of the covering wire in gm.	Tension of one string in kgm.	Striking length in mm.
E₀	1345		11·630	11·572	88·00	158·2
Dis₀	1365	21	11·800	14·001		160·5
D₀	1384		11·967	16·721	88·24	162·8
Cis₀	1402		12·123	19·776		164·9
C₀	1419		14·190	21·279	88·49	166·9
H,	1436	22	14·360	25·078		168·9
B,	1452		14·520	29·332	88·74	170·8
A,	1468		16·457	32·302		172·7
Gis,	1483	23	16·625	37·590	88·99	174·4
G,	1498		16·793	43·490		176·2
Fis,	1512		19·406	47·624	89·24	177·8
F,	1526	24	19·585	54·945		179·5
E,	1540		19·765	63·107	89·49	181·1
Dis,	1555		23·091	69·054		182·9
D,	1570	25	23·314	79·136	89·74	184·7
Cis,	1585		27·243	86·677		186·4
C,	1600	26	27·501	99·169	90·00	188·2

String measurements for a Grand Pianoforte, 1844

Pitch	Length of the string in mm.	Gauge No.	Tension of three strings in kgm.	Striking length in mm.
f⁴	60·00		96·00	7·50
e⁴	63·42		96·786	7·93
dis⁴	67·04	11	97·578	8·38
d⁴	70·86		98·377	8·85
cis⁴	74·90		99·182	9·36

String measurements for a Grand Pianoforte, 1844 (continued)

Pitch	Length of the string in mm.	Gauge No.	Tension of three strings in kgm.	Striking length in mm.
c^4	79·18		99·994	9·89
h^3	83·69		100·81	10·46
b^3	88·46	11½	101·64	11·05
a^3	93·47		102·47	11·68
gis^3	98·84		103·31	12·35
g^3	104·4		104·15	13·05
fis^3	110·4		105·00	13·80
f^3	116·7	12	105·86	14·58
e^3	123·4		106·72	15·42
dis^3	130·4		107·59	16·30
d^3	137·9		108·47	17·23
cis^3	145·7		109·36	18·21
$c^{3\prime}$	154·0	12½	110·26	19·25
h^2	162·8		111·16	20·30
b^2	172·2		112·07	21·52
a^2	181·9		112·98	22·78
gis^2	192·3		113·91	24·03
g^2	204·0	13	114·84	25·50
fis^2	214·8		115·78	26·85
f^2	227·1		116·73	28·38
e^2	240·1		117·69	30·00
dis^2	253·8		118·65	31·72
d^2	268·2	13½	119·62	33·52
cis^2	283·5		120·60	35·43
c^2	299·7		121·59	37·46
$h\prime$	316·8		122·58	39·60
$b\prime$	334·9		123·59	41·86
$a\prime$	354·0	14	124·60	44·25
$gis\prime$	374·2		125·62	46·77
$g\prime$	395·4		126·64	49·42
$fis\prime$	418·1		127·68	52·26
$f\prime$	441·9		128·72	55·23
$e\prime$	467·1	14½	129·77	58·38
$dis\prime$	493·8		130·83	61·72
$d\prime$	524·1		131·91	65·51
$cis\prime$	551·7		132·99	68·96
$c\prime$	583·2		134·08	72·90
h°	616·5	15	135·17	77·06
b°	651·6		136·28	81·84
a°	688·8		137·39	86·10
gis°	728·1		138·52	91·01
g°	769·6		139·65	96·20
fis°	813·5	15½	140·79	101·69
f°	860·0		141·94	107·50
e°	916		143·10	114·5
dis°	970	16	144·27	121·2
d°	1022		145·45	127·7
cis°	1073		146·64	134·1
c°	1123	17	147·84	140·3
H_o	1171		149·06	146·3
B_o	1217	18	150·27	152·1
A_o	1261		151·51	157·6
Gis_o	1303	19	152·74	162·8
G_o	1343		154·00	167·8
Fis_o	1381	20	155·26	172·6
F_o	1417		156·52	177·1

Overspun strings for a Grand Pianoforte (Bichord), 1844

Pitch	Length of the string in mm.	Gauge No. of the core	Weight of the core in gm.	Weight of the outer wire in gm.	Tension of one string in kgm.	Striking length in mm.
E_0	1451	⎫	10·639	8·646	157·80	181·3
Dis_0	1483	⎬ 20	10·872	10·612	159·09	185·3
D_0	1512	⎭	11·084	12·959	160·39	189·0
Cis_0	1540	⎫	13·315	13·531	161·71	192·5
C_0	1566	⎬ 21	13·540	16·437	163·03	195·7
H,	1591	⎭	13·766	19·705	164·36	198·3
B,	1615	⎫	16·150	21·224	165·71	201·8
A,	1638	⎬ 22	16·380	25·350	167·07	204·7
Gis,	1660	⎭	16·600	29·996	168·44	207·5
G,	1681	⎫	18·845	33·183	169·81	210·1
Fis,	1701	⎬ 23	19·070	39·022	171·20	212·6
F,	1720	⎭	19·282	45·583	172·60	215·0
E,	1738	⎫	22·306	50·121	174·01	217·2
Dis,	1755	⎬ 24	22·524	58·140	175·43	219·3
D,	1771	⎭	22·730	67·569	176·87	221·3
Cis,	1786	⎫ 25	26·521	74·307	178·32	223·2
C,	1800	⎭	26·720	85·860	180·00	225·0

From Kützing, C., *Das Wissenschaftliche der Fortepiano-Baukunst.* Bern, 1844. S. 42 bis 48.

(3) COMPOSITION AND DENSITY OF WIRES

Composition and density of two loosely-spun bass strings from a Square Pianoforte by John Broadwood and Sons, about 1812 (in the possession of the writer)

Wire	Chief constituent	Minor contents	Specific gravity	Weight per linear inch, as made up in gm.
Core wire	*Brass* (Copper and Zinc)	—	8·68	0·065
Covering wire	*Copper*	Traces of *Nickel*	8·35	0·044
Core wire	*Brass* (Copper and Zinc)	Traces of *Aluminium*	8·57	0·078
Covering wire	*Copper* with a thin protective coating of *Silver*	Traces of *Nickel*	8·27	0·050

Note. The wires were analysed for the writer at the Chemical Laboratory, Cambridge, by Dr Stockdale.

(4) PRICES OF PIANOFORTE WIRE

1815

	£	s.	d.
English steel music wire per lb.		4	0
German steel wire per lb.		7	0

1816

	£	s.	d.
Brass music wire per lb.		3	0
Brass music wire per lb. (another quality)		2	0
Set of twisted strings		3	0
German steel music wire per lb.		6	0

1817

						£	s.	d.
German steel wire per lb. ...	...	...	...	...	...		6	0
Brass music wire per lb. ...	...	...	...	...	...		2	9

1819

Berlin wire per lb. ...	...	...	...	...	...	...	5	0

1828

Spun strings set for Grand Pianoforte ...	...	...	...		5	0
Spun strings set for Cabinet Pianoforte ...	...	...	...		9	0
Spun strings set for Cottage Pianoforte ...	...	...	...		10	2
Spun strings set for Square Pianoforte ...	...	...	...		5	0
Complete set of strings for an Upright Grand ...	...	...	1	0	0

1831

Covered strings on Webster's steel wire

Set for Square Pianoforte ...	...	...	...	...	...	3	6
Set for Cabinet Pianoforte (two Nos.)	...	...	...	...	6	0
Set for Cottage Pianoforte (two Nos.)	...	...	...	...	7	6
Set for Grand Pianoforte (two Nos.)	...	...	...	...	4	0

(Collected from papers in the possession of Messrs John Broadwood and Sons.)

(5) PATENTS, ETC. RELATING TO THE TEMPERING OF PIANOFORTE WIRE

1810

IGNACE PLEYEL of Paris. Methods of manufacturing Wire for Pianofortes and other musical instruments.

The white wires are made from soft and very ductile iron wire. The French iron wires best suited for this purpose are the kinds known under the name of *fer de roche*. We employ in this manufacture only iron which has already been reduced into wire, at least to the dimension of two-thirds of a 'line' in diameter. These wires owe their quality to the manner of tempering or annealing the iron wire, and of passing it through the draw-plates.

To anneal the wire, a fireplace is built of bricks and mortar, of a cylindrical form, having its exterior and interior edges furnished with an iron hoop, beneath a large chimney. The dimensions of this fireplace or furnace are proportional to the quality of iron wire intended to be annealed at one time, which is placed in it, upon an iron grate. This grate is placed so high as not to allow the fire to touch the wire. The furnace is covered with a sheet iron cover, in which there is a hole for allowing the smoke to escape. The iron wire is placed in coils upon the grate till it reaches to about four inches of the top, the cover is put on and a fire lighted with white wood only. The heat is kept up till the wire has acquired a pale red colour, and not more. That the fire may be distributed equally throughout, the cover should be frequently turned, because the hole in it would attract the heat, and, without that precaution, one side would be heated more than another. This method of annealing suits only iron wire of the size of one-third of a 'line' in diameter: to draw it finer, the following process should be employed.

In a furnace already mentioned, at a certain height above the grate, are supports, on which another similar grate is placed. A strong plate of sheet iron is laid on each of these grates; the dimensions of the plates allowing an inch all round for the passage of the ascending smoke, to allow the cinders to fall from the top, and to promote an equal communication of heat. The iron wire ought to be wound into a narrower space than the width of the plates of sheet iron, and placed on the lower plate in such quantity as to reach the upper one. The lower fireplace is filled with fuel, and the same combustible is placed on the upper plate, both fires are then lighted, the cover is put on and frequently turned during the process.

In a furnace capable of holding fifty pounds of iron wire, the fire is kept up for four or five hours, the length of time depending, however, on the situation of the furnace and consumption of fuel.

The first process of annealing is commonly done twice on the same iron wire: the second is done after that wire has been drawn three or four times through the draw-plate for reducing its diameter. The second process is employed but once.

Tools used in this manufacture

These tools consist of, first, a wooden work bench four or five feet long and three wide. Secondly a plank three feet long, one foot wide, and three inches thick, which is fixed to one of the edges of the bench by two pins. Above this plank two little barrels of wood are raised, ten inches in length and six in diameter, each having its axis placed in the direction of the width of the plank, and received in two brass supports, fixed firmly against the lateral sides of the said plank. The axis of each roller is furnished with a handle for moving it. At the middle of the plank there is raised, to the height of the centre of the axis of the barrels, a piece of wood of the whole width of the plank, in which is a groove four or five lines deep. At each extremity of this piece of wood two wooden uprights are framed, supporting a cross piece, in which is a second groove, corresponding to the first. A draw-plate is adjusted so as to slide easily between these two grooves. At each end of the same plank, and by the side of the draw-plate, a small piece of hard wood is placed, on which the ends of the iron wire are filed before passing them through the plates.

A sort of reel, nearly like those used for thread excepting that it is conical, serves to receive the rings of iron wire intended to be drawn. The bench, serving as a foot for this reel, is raised to the height of the barrels.

On a small wooden upright placed in a mortise made in the plank, between the barrel and the draw-plate, a little box is fixed, containing grease composed of lard and tallow. There is a hole through this box, to allow the iron wire to pass through it, and become smeared with grease.

To beat up the draw-plate when the holes are too much worn, and to pierce it, we employ a block of wood similar to those commonly intended for receiving small anvils and on which a mortise is made sufficiently deep.

A small file is used to reduce the end of the wire when beginning to draw it; a pair of flat pincers for drawing it, when introduced into the holes of the draw-plate; a common hammer, and an iron gauge for measuring the sizes of the wire; lastly, a draw-plate is the most essential tool that we must have for this work. The material of which this tool is composed, and the way in which it is pierced, contribute very much to the quality of the wires.

A draw-plate to be a good one, must be made of a substance neither too hard nor too soft. All those which are steeled are good for nothing; and pure iron is equally unsuitable. The best material for making them is a mixture of the best bar iron, and cast iron. These plates should be pierced so that every hole goes on diminishing in diameter underneath: these holes are commenced with conical steel punches, which are struck; the draw-plate is then put to heat in a fire only of wood, and the operation of piercing it is afterwards completed, when cold, with steel punches. It is necessary to have punches corresponding to all the diameters of wires required to be drawn.

Manner of Working

When all the tools are ready, as above mentioned, and the iron wire is also prepared, it is put upon the reel which is placed at the end of the bench. The end of the wire is then filed, pushed through the grease box, and then into the hole of the draw-plate corresponding to its size, and is drawn by hand with the pincers till it can be attached to the barrel, where it is fastened by points which are fixed for that purpose on the barrel: the barrel is then turned gently by means of its handle.

For the first course, it is necessary that the barrel which does not act [*sic*] should be removed, because it would be in the way of the wire coming off the reel to enter the draw-plate. When the whole wire has passed through one hole, the other barrel is put into its place, the wire is sharpened anew, the draw-plate is turned, the wire passed through the next following hole in size, drawn with pincers, and fixed to the second barrel, which is turned by its handle, so that the wire unwinds from the first barrel, passes through the draw-plate, and winds on the second. It is necessary to take care that the wire be always passed through the grease box before entering the hole in the draw-plate.

One thing essential to be observed is that the wire passes through holes corresponding to its size, so as to require but little power to pull it through, consequently the diameter of the wire is reduced but a very small quantity each time it passes through a hole in the plate.

To draw the wire of two-thirds of a line in diameter, it is necessary to anneal it twice before reducing it to one-third of a line: brought to this size it is annealed by the method before described, and afterwards it will not require annealing to be reduced to the greatest degree of fineness. In order that the iron wire may possess the proper degree of ductility and tenacity to form a sonorous string, it must pass five or six times through the draw-plate after the last annealing. When the iron wire is reduced to the desired size, nothing more is requisite than to give it the necessary polish and white colour, that it may render clear and distinct sounds.

Polishing and Whitening Wires

When the wire is drawn down to the proper size, the draw-plate and grease box are removed, the wire is fastened to the vacant barrel, and wound upon it, making it glide at the same time through a piece of leather previously rubbed on rotten stone. It is frequently necessary to repeat this operation to obtain a fine polish. The method of winding the wire on bobbins it is needless to describe. The size of the bobbins depends on the number desired to the pound weight.

Yellow Wires [Brass]

The implements necessary for making these are the same as for the white [iron] wires, and they are used in the same manner: the only difference is in the polishing and annealing.

To obtain good yellow wires we must employ only brass, composed of four-tenths of copper, three-tenths of old brass (mitraille jaune) and three-tenths of calamine. This brass should be of a pure yellow colour; it may be procured at the manufactories in rods of a line in diameter. It is annealed once, by heating it in the furnace, placing it on the grate, putting white wood above and below it to obtain a clear and gentle fire. It is to be heated for an hour or two so as to be only red hot. On taking it out, it should be dipped for a moment into a boiler of hot tallow. It is afterwards to be allowed to cool completely, and then it is to be passed through the draw-plate in the way already described for white wires. The brass wire is polished by the process before mentioned, excepting that instead of rotten stone we employ red tripoli.

Strings or wires made by these methods will stand in tune a tone and a half higher than the wires of Nuremberg.*

JOHN HAWLEY of London. 1840.

Wires made of tempered Steel

I make the said strings of different lengths and sizes out of steel wire, which, when made red hot, I dip into a composition of tallow, beef suet, beeswax, olive oil, powdered staghorn, and mercury, in the proportions hereinafter described, and afterwards allow to cool. Such strings being so tempered, I submit them to a second heating, and untemper them sufficiently to enable them to be made straight, and give them the color I require, and by the degree of heat which I use I make them of different colors, but such colors do not at all affect their tone or quality. The major part of such steel strings I make of the ordinary cylindrical form only, and the same diameter from one end to the other of such strings; but I make the strings for the bass or deeper-toned notes much thicker in the central parts than at the ends, and in forms either cylindrical, conical, or angular, and I so arrange them on the piano as that the hammer shall strike on the thickest part, whether conical, cylindrical, or angular. I make such strings conical, cylindrical, or angular, by means of a wire drawing iron with an adjusting screw, which enables me, by compression or expansion, to draw the metal of greater or less diameter during the progress of the drawing process as I may require; for I use a file to bring such strings to the form and dimensions I require. For the purpose of fixing such steel strings on the screws or pins of pianos or harps, I totally untemper the ends by means of heat, so that they will bind round such screws and pins without breaking. The proportion of the composition into which I dip the heated steel in order to temper it as aforesaid is as follows: Five pounds of tallow, six pounds of beef suet, one pound of beeswax, five pounds of olive oil, quarter of a pound of powdered staghorn, and thirty grains of mercury, all which I mix well together.†

SANGUINÈDE ET CAPT, Paris. 1840.

Steel strings

For the lower octaves and deep notes the strings are conical and of varying thicknesses.

Recipe for tempering steel strings

(12 strings 20 metres in length)

2½	kilogrammes	of	White suet
1½	,,	,,	Beef suet
1	,,	,,	Olive oil
1	,,	,,	Yellow wax
16	grammes	,,	Hartshorn
16	,,	,,	Chamouny honey

After dipping the strings in the above they must be immersed in milk mixed with wood-charcoal dust, and boiled for one hour.

The next stage consists in whitening them with pumice stone or with emery.

After this in order to make them settle they are placed into an ordinary oven and heated to the requisite temperature.

This process gives suppleness to the strings; they 'never break' and 'keep in tune for several years, without having to be retuned'.‡

* *Description des Brevets*, 1st Series, Vol. 13, p. 49, Pat. No. 1177 [*Journal of the Franklin Institute of Philadelphia*, New Series, VI, 173 (1830)].

† Eng. Pat. No. 8526.

‡ *Description des Brevets*, 1st Series, Vol. 73, p. 141 (abridged), Pat. No. 10,242.

APPENDIX E

HAMMER HEADS

(1) Felt making for hammer heads.
(2) Tinder and sponge for hammer heads.
(3) Process of tanning leather for hammer heads.

(1) FELT MAKING FOR HAMMER HEADS

KARL FRENZEL. [Austrian Pat. 1840.]*

For the preparation of the felt, fine comb wool is soaked in a gall, washed several times in cold water and then, whilst exposed to hot steam, is rolled with wooden rollers on a hot iron plate.

In order to protect this material against moths, a solution of camphor is put into the water which is converted into steam.

The advantages which result from the use of the felt are:

(1) A pure resonant tone.
(2) Preservation from moth.
(3) That it can be made in any degree of thickness; thin for the high notes and thicker for the low notes.

EUGÈNE-HIPPOLYTE, BILLION (JEUNE). [Fr. Patent No. 7767 (1840).]

Je prends la laine d'agneau, dite agneline, la plus fine possible, à son état brut, c'est-à-dire qu'elle n'est seulement que dégraissée; je l'épluche d'abord au bernaudoir, pour en faire tomber la laine la plus courte et d'une qualité inférieure, qui provient du pied des agneaux, ensuite je l'épluche à la main pour en retirer les gros bouts et les ordures les plus grossières, telles que la paille.

Après ce travail, je carde la laine deux fois avec une carde à laine ordinaire, en ayant soin de diviser la laine en sens inverse, tantôt en large, tantôt en long, pour donner à la pièce cardée une égale épaisseur et surtout beaucoup d'élasticité, au milieu comme sur les côtés, ce qui n'aurait pas lieu si je laissais la pièce toujours aller dans le même sens.

Les pièces à feutrer sortent de la carde de la longueur, de la largeur et de l'épaisseur que je le désire, autant, bien entendu, que le permet le cylindre de la carde; j'en place alors une ou plusieurs, selon le besoin, dans une feutrière ou toile, connue sous ce nom dans la chapellerie. Les pièces ainsi enveloppées, je les pose sur des plaques fort chaudes, sans l'être cependant au point de brûler la marchandise. Pendant que les pièces sont placées sur les plaques chaudes, elles ont besoin d'être marchées, c'est-à-dire plus ou moins froissées avec les mains, pour, en agissant ainsi et au moyen de la forte chaleur que leur communique la plaque, obliger la laine à se crisper et à s'accrocher entre elle et d'elle-même, pour ainsi dire. Ce travail ne demande pas moins d'une heure, une heure et demie environ; en telle sorte que la pièce posée sur la plaque chaude, au commencement de l'opération, avec 85 millimètres environ d'épaisseur, puisse, à la fin du marchage dont j'ai parlé plus haut, être réduite à 14 à 15 millimètres environ, suivant le numéro d'épaisseur que je veux donner au feutre; car je distingue,

* "Beschreibung der Erfindungen und Verbesserungen für welche in den K.K. Österreichischen Staaten Patente ertheilt wurden," etc. III, S. 118.

par les numéros de 1 à 6 inclusivement, l'épaisseur des feutres que je destine aux marteaux de pianos.

Cette opération terminée, je fais passer à la foule les pièces enveloppées d'une toile. La foule a pour résultat de mieux feutrer la laine et de l'adoucir: l'eau qui sert à la foule doit être presque bouillante et saturée de savon blanc qui blanchit la laine et l'adoucit toujours davantage.

Pour être foulées convenablement, il faut que les pièces soient roulées sur tous les sens, pendant à peu près une heure quarante minutes, sans appuyer beaucoup.

Au sortir de la foule, il faut passer les pièces dans une eau bien chaude de rivière, pour dégager la laine du savon blanc qui y adhérerait encore. Ces pièces, une fois bien séchées, ont besoin d'être épluchées de nouveau et débarrassées des ordures qui auraient pu s'y attacher pendant la fabrication, et ensuite d'être passées à la pierre ponce, pour en couper et en enlever les jarres les plus grosses et les plus longues, et, autant que possible, égaliser tous les poils de la pièce de feutre.

Les pièces sont soumises immédiatement, à chaud, à la presse hydraulique, pour obtenir une égalité plus parfaite et renforcer le feutrage; puis on les ébarbe et on les rogne, et elles peuvent être ainsi livrées au commerce, pour être appliquées aux marteaux de pianos.

(2) TINDER AND SPONGE FOR HAMMER HEADS

By John Antes

Allgemeine Musikalische Zeitung, No. 42, 1806, 8. Jahrgang.

Die Hämmer des Pianofortes sind an dem Kopfe, mit dem sie die Saiten anschlagen, gewöhnlich mit Leder überzogen. Bekanntlich wird das Leder, wenn es gehämmert wird, hart; fortgesetztes Spiel bringt die selbe Wirkung hervor. So weich und lieblich daher der Ton eines Pianofortes ist, wenn es noch neu aus des Meisters Hand kommt, so wird er doch in eben dem Grade, als das Leder härter wird, nach und nach härter, und zuletzt so scharf und schneidend, dass man die Hämmer endlich neu beledern muss. So ging es mir mit meinem Instrument. Ich suchte daher eine Substanz auszufinden, die den unangenehmen Veränderungen nicht unterworfen wäre, und des beständigen Gebrauchs ungeachtet sich immer gleich bleibe. Nach wiederholten Versuchen fand ich zwei Dinge, die ich mit Überzeugung empfehlen zu können glaube, da ich sie mehreren Jahre hindurch erprobt, und nicht die mindeste Veränderung bemerkt habe. Die erste Substanz, die auch nach meiner Meynung den brillantesten Ton giebt, ist die feine, dichtzellige Wurzel des gemeinen Waschschwammes, auf den kein Hämmern eine Wirkung hervorbringt. Da aber diese Wurzeln schwer in gehöriger Menge und von gleicher Beschaffenheit zu haben sind, so fand ich, dass der gemeine Feuerschwamm, wenn er hierzu gehörig vorgerichtet wird, die nämlichen Dienste thut. Ich habe einen Versuch damit gemacht; da aber die weichern Theile desselben als die besten zum Feueranschlagen gehalten werden, so hatte ich Mühe, unter einer bedeutenden Menge genug von solchem herauszufinden, der eine rechte und gleiche Dichtigkeit hatte. Wenn man vielleicht die feinsten, dichtesten Schwämme, als Birkenschwamm und dergleichen aussuchte, und zu diesem Gebrauch zubereitete, so könnte man es wohl zu einer grossen Vollkommenheit bringen. Da ich aber mit dieser Zubereitung unbekannt bin, muss ich das andern zur Beurtheilung überlassen. Der Schwamm, dessen ich mich bediente, hat seit fünf Jahren nicht die mindeste Veränderung bemerken lassen. Beide Arten übertrafen meine gute Erwartung in der Hauptsache, ihrer Unveränderlichkeit bei stetem Gebrauch, bei weitem.

(3) PROCESS OF TANNING LEATHER FOR HAMMER HEADS

Beschreibung des Verfahrens, Hammerleder für Instrumentenmacher zu verfertigen, worauf sich Johann Gottlieb Steininger, Weissgerber-Gesell in Ortenburg, am 3. Oktober 1837 ein Privilegium ertheilen liess.

Zur Fabrikation des sogenannten Hammerleders für Instrumentenmacher müssen die Felle feinwolliger Schafe genommen, vier Tage lang in frischem Wasser eingeweicht, dann auf der Fleischseite mit einem Gemenge von Kalk und Asche bestrichen, und hierauf in ein Geschirr mit Wasser gehörig zusammengelegt werden. Nach Ablauf von drei Wochen nimmt man die Felle heraus, streicht die Wolle ab, und legt sie wieder vier Wochen lang in Kalkwasser ein, worauf sie gewaschen, verglichen, und einmal auf der Fleischseite und zweimal auf der Narbenseite aus dem frischen Wasser gestrichen, und hernach zweimal aus lauwarmen Wasser gestossen werden.

Nach dieser Vorbereitung werden sie in die Beitze, welche aus lauwarmen Wasser und Waizenkleien gemacht wird, gebracht, darin gehörig durchgezogen, und drei Tage hindurch darin liegen gelassen, während sie täglich Früh und Abends gut gestossen werden müssen. Die gebeitzten Felle werden durch Ausstreichen von den anhängenden Kleien befreit, und in die Lohgaare aus Fichtenrinden gelegt, wo sie täglich Früh, Mittags und Abends gerührt, und fünf Wochen hindurch alle acht Tage mit frischer Lohe versetzt werden müssen. In der sechsten Woche gibt man auch der Lohgaare ein Gemisch aus Aschenlauge und Baumöl bei und lässt die Felle noch acht Tage darin liegen, worauf man sie in süsser Milch auswäscht, und dann zum Trocknen bringt.

Nach dem Trocknen werden diese Leder zur nöthigen Befeuchtung eingespritzt, über einem mit eichenen Nägeln besetzten Eichenstocke gut aufgepeitscht, gestollt, der Länge und Breite nach geschlichtet, mit einer Fischhaut gut aufgerissen und so an einen feuchten Ort gelegt. Nach dieser Behandlung werden sie noch einmal über dem Eichenstocke aufgepeitscht, mit einem eisernen Streicher in die Breite gestrichen, mit der Fischhaut aufgerissen, und zuletzt mit einem hölzernen Streicher der Länge und Breite nach auf der Narbenseite gestrichen und wieder in die Länge abgerichtet.

APPENDIX F

PRICES OF PIANOFORTES

PREFACE

The following selected Price Lists will, it is hoped, give the reader some idea of the cost of pianofortes during the first fifty years of the nineteenth century. It will be noticed that in England the better class of instrument was very expensive, if the Vicar of Wakefield was indeed "passing rich on forty pounds a year", for a small upright would have cost him about half his income, whilst a grand would have taken about three times the amount. But, despite their great cost, Pole states that in England in 1851, a million pounds worth of pianofortes were made, whilst in France in 1849 they were manufactured to the extent of £320,000.

PIANOFORTE PRICES IN BAVARIA, 1816 AND 1817

From *Anzeiger für Kunst und Gewerbfleiss im Königreiche Baiern.* 1816–1868. München.

1816–1817

Georg Diez, of Munich, manufactured upright and horizontal instruments with six and six and a half octaves and with three to six pedals at prices varying from 10 to 80 carolins, that is from about ten pounds and four shillings to eighty-one pounds. Another maker, H. Heubeck, offered "an upright pianoforte, in a mahogany case, with three pedals and six octaves", for 275 florins, and another with ivory naturals for 300 florins.

Prices charged for pianofortes by Christopher Erlich, of Bamberg:

(1) An upright pianoforte with pedals, six octaves, case in cherry wood with antique ornamentation. 290 florins.
(2) An upright pianoforte with six pedals and six octaves. In a walnut case and antique ornamentation in the latest taste. 300 florins.
(3) An upright pianoforte with six pedals and six octaves. Ivory keys. An elegantly worked case in cherry wood. 370 florins.
(4) An upright pianoforte with six pedals and six octaves. Ebony natural keys. In cherry wood case. 360 florins.
(5) Two upright pianofortes with six octaves and six pedals. Ivory natural keys and a case in mahogany stained with corrisin. 30 carolins each.*

---

* Nos. 1 to 4 occur under the following dates: 18 Feb. 1816, 4 May, 1816, and 26 October, 1816. No. 5 occurs under the date 18 Jan. 1817 in *Anzeiger für Kunst und Gewerbfleiss*, etc., 1816 and 1817. Nos. 1 to 4 probably refer to second-hand instruments.

PIANOFORTE PRICES IN AUSTRIA, 1850

From *Anzeiger für Kunst und Gewerbfleiss im Königreiche Baiern.*
1816–1868. München.

*Extracts from the Report of the Commission on the
Leipzig Industrial Exhibition*

The firm of WANKEL und TEMMLER, of Vienna, exhibited a horizontal Grand for which they charged 500 thalers. The case was designed according to the "latest English fashion". There were four metal braces. The compass was 7 octaves. A "sound machine" (i.e. a kind of pressure bar through which the strings passed) was provided for the higher octaves from C. The hammer heads were clothed with felt.

ZIEGLER, of Leipzig, charged 360 thalers for a horizontal Grand with German Action and two iron braces, and 320 thalers for another with English Action and three braces.

The Commission reports that Wankel und Temmler's Grand had a singing and powerful tone but was not quite full enough in the bass; whilst they condemn both of Ziegler's instruments as "rattling and sharp".

HÖLLING und SPANENBERG, of Zeitz, charged 90 thalers for a square pianoforte with German Action, 6½ octaves and metal plate, whilst HARTMANN, of Leipzig, charged 100 thalers for one of "English build", English Action and two right-angle braces.

PIANOFORTE PRICES IN ENGLAND, 1815–1851
1815
Messrs JOHN BROADWOOD and SONS

PIANOFORTES

	£	s.	d.
Six-octave Grand	40	10	0
Six-octave ornamented Grand	46	0	0
Six-octave Upright Grand	46	0	0
Six-octave Cabinet	33	2	0
Six-octave ornamented Cabinet...	48	0	0
Six-octave Cabinet with additional keys	31	0	0
Square, with round corners and compass C–C	22	15	0
Square, with double action	18	3	0
Square with single action	17	6	0
Square, elegant	26	0	0

1816

PIANOFORTE KEYS

	£	s.	d.
Set of Grand keys	3	0	0
Set of Upright Grand keys	3	0	0
Set of Cabinet piano keys	2	10	0
Set of Square piano keys	2	15	0
Set of sharps		2	6

PIANOFORTE HAMMERS

	£	s.	d.
Set of Grand hammer heads	1	0	0
Set of Grand hammer heads (leathered)	2	2	0
Set of Grand hammer heads (unleathered)		10	0
Set of Cabinet hammers (unleathered)...		10	0
Set of Cabinet hammers (leathered)	1	0	0
Set of small hammers (unleathered)		4	0
Set of under hammers		5	0
Hammer frame for Upright Grand		16	0

1828

Details of the cost of construction of an UPRIGHT GRAND PIANOFORTE made by Messrs John Broadwood and Sons

Six and a half octaves Upright Grand Pianoforte with columns

	£	s.	d.
24 ft. of 1 in. mahogany at 1s. 3d. per ft.	1	10	0
3 ft. of 1½ in. mahogany at 1s. 9d. per ft.		5	3
14 ft. of ½ in. mahogany at 9d. per ft....		10	6
136 ft. of 1 in. mahogany in 4 to 4½ lyrs: at 1s. 3d. per ft. ...	8	10	0
169 ft. of 1 in. vinner [sic] at 5d. per ft.	3	10	5
39 ft. of 1 in. wainscote at 9d. per ft.	1	9	3
9 ft. of 1½ in. wainscote at 1s. 1d. per ft.		9	9
2 ft. of 2½ in. wainscote at 1s. 9d. per ft.		3	6
8 ft. of 1¼ in. mahogany at 1s. 6d. per ft.		12	0
24 ft. of 2 in. pine at 5d. per ft.		10	0
105 ft. of 1 in. pine at 3d. per ft.	1	6	3
5 ft. of ½ in. pine at 2d. per ft....			10
5 ft. of 1½ in. deal at 3½d. per ft.		1	5½
10 ft. 10 in. of 1 in. beech at 4d. per ft.		3	7½
9 ft. of 1 in. deal at 2½d. per ft.		1	10½
10 leaves of belly wood at 1s. 4d. per leaf		14	0
8 ft. 6 in. of air wood veneer at 3d. per ft.		2	1½
2 ft. of ½ in. rosewood at 1s. 6d. per ft.		3	0
5 ft. of rosewood veneer at 1s. per ft.		5	0
9 ft. of 1 in. lime board veneer at 7d. per ft.		5	3
1 ft. 6 in. of 1 in. sycamore veneer at 6d. per ft.			9
1 ft. 6 in. of ¼ in. cedar veneer at 4½d. per ft.			7
Case making	10	1	7
Sockets		13	0
Bracing		6	6
Iron braces		15	6
Inside shouldering		6	0
Marking off	1	6	0
Bellying		10	3
Gluing up belly		4	0
Arches		15	10
Top brown braces	1	13	2
Front iron for wrest plank		19	0
Making the frame		14	3
Irons for frame		11	0
Bed screws			4
Pedal making		15	0
Brass wire for pedal		2	0
Brass work		16	0
Large bright spring		1	0
Heads, tails, dampers and check	2	7	0
Leathering hammers		12	0
Leather and *cloth* for *hammers*		16	0
Making beam		10	4
Brass and screws for do.		5	6
Screw pins		3	0
Silver centre		5	6
Hammer frames		3	0
Ivory		16	0
Making keys	1	11	0
Sharps and cloth...		3	0

	£	s.	d.
Key pins		2	0
Wood for key frame		3	3
Leather work		2	2
"Wrest" pins		6	0
Strings "complete"	1	0	0
Strings		6	0
Desk		3	0
Pedal brace		5	6
Carved work	4	0	0
Turning four legs at 3s. 9d. per leg		15	0
Finishing...	6	9	6
Fitting up	1	5	0
Nutting		12	6
Stamping name board		4	3
Turning columns and capitals, etc.		5	0
Curtain in door	2	6	0
Bridge pins, brass and iron		4	3
Screws, nails, etc.	1	0	0
Regulating and tuning	1	10	0
Glue and glass paper, etc.		5	0
Bent sides and planing up			10
Total cost ...	70	3	5

[From the Broadwood Papers.]

Messrs JOHN BROADWOOD AND SONS' Price List, 1st May, 1828

Pianofortes with six octaves

Type No.   Guineas

		Guineas
1	Square, six octaves FF to FF, plain case	36
2	Ditto, banded with rosewood	41
3	Ditto, in plain case with circular ends	38
4	Ditto, banded with rosewood with circular ends	44
5	New Pat. six octave FF to FF, with metallic plate	55
	A charge of 4 guineas to be made for fixing drawers to either of the above.	

Cottage

6	Cottage, six octaves FF to FF, square front	50
7	Ditto, superior, six octaves FF to FF, and square front	55
8	Ditto, with cylinder front	55

Cabinet

9	Cabinet, six octaves FF to FF	65
10	Ditto, elegant	70
11	Ditto, six and a half octaves	70
12	Ditto, elegant	75
13	Ditto, six and a half octaves in rosewood case	80
14	Ditto, with six and a half octaves in rosewood case	—

Patent Grand Cabinet

15*	Pat. Grand Cabinet, six octaves, carved pillars and polished with Pat. string plate	85
16*	Ditto, with six and a half octaves, carved pillars and polished with Pat. string plate	90
17*	Ditto, with six octaves in rosewood case	95
18*	Ditto, with six octaves in rosewood case	100

Horizontal Grand
Type No.   Guineas
   19   Horizontal Grand, with six and a half octaves   100
   20   Ditto, with cylinder front   105

New Patent Horizontal Grand
   21*   New Pat. Horizontal Grand, six and a half octaves, cylinder front
            and French polished and with Pat. string plate   122
   22*   Ditto, elegant   137
   23*   Ditto, in rosewood case   160

Upright Grand
   24   Upright Grand, with six and a half octaves and French polished...   110
   25   Ditto, elegant   135
   26   Ditto, in rosewood case   160
   27*   New Upright Grand, six and a half octaves and Pat. string plate   122
   28*   Ditto, in rosewood case   172

Pianofortes in solid materials, peculiarly adapted to warm climates
   29   Solid Square, with six octaves FF to FF, circular ends and French
            polish   46
   30*   Solid New Pat. Pianoforte, six octaves and metallic plate...   ...   55
   31   Solid Grand Pianoforte, six and a half octaves and French polish   105
   32*   Ditto, with Pat. string plate, cylinder front and French polish   ...   122

        The above can be further ornamented to any given price.

       * Amongst other advantages, the strings of these instruments,
being considerably shortened by the string plate, are thereby
consequently less affected by the atmosphere, and the tuner will
observe that they move readily, etc.

CLEMENTI, COLLARD AND COLLARD, 1824–1832

Imperial Patent Pianofortes with Harmonic Swell and Bridge of
Reverberation and Pianofortes of the Common Construction

Square Pianofortes

Type No.   Guineas
   1   Plain new Pat. Pianoforte, five and a half octaves, pedal and six legs   32
   2   Ditto, with two drawers   36
   3   Ditto, with three drawers   38
          Any of the above with rounded corners, 2 guineas extra.
   4   Banded new Pat. Pianoforte with ornamental wood   36
   5   Ditto, with two drawers   40
   6   Ditto, with three drawers   42
   7   Ditto, elegant, with rounded corners   40
   8   Ditto, with rounded corners and two drawers   45
   9   Ditto, with three drawers   47
   10   Ditto, in rose or albuera wood cases, either plain or superbly orna-
          mented with buhl work...   ...   .   65 to
                                                           120

       Four guineas extra will be charged on each of the above when
with six octaves up to FF, or if down to CC, six guineas.

Cabinet Pianofortes

Type No.   Guineas
   11   Cottage Cabinet, with two unisons, five and a half octaves and
          square front   45
   12   Ditto, with circular front and radiated silk...   50
   13   Ditto, with three unisons and radiated silk...   55

Type No.		Guineas
14	Ditto, in rose or albuera wood cases, either plain or ornamented with buhl work	60 to 70
15	Cabinet, with two unisons, and five and a half octaves, circular front, and radiated silk front	60
16	Ditto, with three unisons, and five and a half octaves, circular front, and radiated silk front	67
17	Ditto, with three unisons and crescent doors below	75
18	Ditto, in rose or albuera wood cases, either plain or superbly ornamented with buhl work...	85 to 150

Any of the above, if with six octaves, 5 guineas extra and an additional charge of 3 guineas for polishing.

Upright Grand Pianofortes

19	Upright Grand, six octaves	105
20	Ditto, elegantly ornamented	110 to 150
21	Ditto, with six and a half octaves	120
22	Ditto, elegantly ornamented	200

Horizontal Grand Pianofortes

23	Horizontal Grand Pianoforte, six octaves and three unisons ...	90
24	Ditto, elegantly ornamented	100 to 140
25	Ditto, with six and a half octaves	100
26	Ditto, in rose or albuera wood cases, either plain or superbly ornamented with buhl work...	250

ROBERT WORNUM, 1838

R. WORNUM, Inventor and Manufacturer of Patent Double-Action Pianofortes, at the Music Hall, Store Street, Bedford Square.

The Piccolo

Plain, in mahogany	30 guineas
Best, in mahogany	34 ,,
Elegant, with trusses	38 ,,
Ditto, with cylinder	42 ,,
Plain rosewood	42 ,,
Elegant ... ... from 46 to 50 ,,

Cottage and Cabinet

From 42 to 75 guineas

Pocket Grand Horizontal

From 55 to 75 guineas

Imperial Grand Horizontal

From 75 to 90 guineas

The above instruments are well manufactured, and all prepared for extreme climates. The Piccolo stands 3 ft. 8 in. high: and the Pocket Grand is only 5 ft. 4 in. long. A liberal allowance to exporters and dealers.

This extensive reduction has been drawn from the advertiser as a measure of protection to his New *Piccolo Pianoforte*, the success of which has induced certain manufacturers to announce and sell instruments of a different character under the same name, by which the public are deceived and the inventor injured.

[From *The Musical World*, Vol. 9.]

Representative Prices of Honduras Mahogany: 1834, 1835

1834. *Nov.* 11. *Two items from a sale*
The dearest lot was sold at 1*s*. ½*d*. per ft.
The cheapest lot was sold at 7¾*d*. per ft.

1835. *June* 23. *Representative prices from a large sale*
The prices varied between 8½*d*. to 1*s*. 1*d*. per ft.

Messrs John Broadwood and Sons' Price List No. 28. January, 1840

	Type No.		Mahogany (guineas)	Elegant (guineas)	Rosewood (guineas)
Six octave	1	In plain case with string plate (38 guineas)	40	—	—
	2	With circular ends and in plain case with string plate unpolished (40 guineas) ...	42	—	—
	3	Ditto, improved large size...	46	—	—
	4	With French corners and fret-work	52	—	62
Six octave	5	Superior and elegant ...	65	—	75
Patent Square	6	Extra size, cylinder front ...	70	—	85
Six octave	7	With square front	52	—	—
Cottage	8	Ditto, French	55	—	65
	9	Ditto, improved and French	70	—	80
	10	Ditto, cylinder front, plain	55	—	65
	11	Boudoir ornamented ...	65	—	75
	12	Semi-Cottage, 3 ft. 4 in. high	44	48	54
Cabinet	13	With pillars superior ...	70	—	80
	14	Ditto, with six and a half octaves and superior ...	75	—	85
Grand Patent Cabinet	15	With six and a half octaves and string plate	90	—	100
	16	Ditto, extra size and ornamented	105	—	125
Semi-Grand	17	Newly improved with Grand mechanism and string plate, 7 ft. 3 in. × 3 ft. 10 in. ...	85	—	105
Bichorda	18	With six and a half octaves and string plate, 7 ft. 8 in. × 4 ft. 1 in.	100	—	120
Patent Horizontal Grand	19	With six and a half octaves, cylinder front and string plate, 8 ft. × 4 ft. 2 in. ...	122	—	—
	20	Patent Victoria Repetition Grand	130	140	155

	Type No.		Mahogany (guineas)	Elegant (guineas)	Rosewood (guineas)
Pianofortes of solid materials peculiarly adapted to warm climates	21	Solid square with string plate, long bar and fretwork	55	—	—
	22	Horizontal Grand with string plate and best solid bars	122	—	—
	23	Patent Square, large size, plate, long bar and fretwork	65	—	—
Newly invented instrument	24	Grand Patent Square with six and a half octaves ...	—	85	90

HOPKINSON'S NEW PATENT REPETITION AND TREMOLO, CHECK ACTION. GRAND PIANOFORTE, 1851

Prices

	Guineas
Grand Piano of 6⅞ octaves, in a neat plain mahogany case	110
Ditto, with superior wood, seven octaves, from	125
Ditto, in rosewood, walnut, maple, etc., according to style and finish, from	125

WILLIAM STODART AND SON, 1851

		Length (ft. in.)		Breadth (ft. in.)		Mahogany (guineas)	Rosewood (guineas)
	Grand Piano-Fortes						
1	Patent horizontal elliptic end, C to A	7	8	4	5	105	115
2	Ditto, in fancy wood	7	8	4	5	140 to	160
3	Ditto, boudoir	6	2	4	4	90	100
	Bichord Piano-Fortes						
4	Patent Horizontal Cottage Grand, C to A	6	2	4	4	80	90
	Cottage Piano-Fortes						
5	With metal plate and ogee fall, C to A	4	9	4	4	55	60
6	With metal plate and ogee fall, plinth and truss legs, C to A ...	4	9	4	4	60	65
	Semi-Cottage Piano-Fortes						
7	With metal plate and ogee fall, C to A	3	11	4	4	40	45
8	With metal plate and ogee fall, plinth and truss legs, C to A ...	3	11	4	4	45	50
9	Ditto, French front and mouldings	3	11	4	4	—	45
10	Ditto, plain	3	11	4	4	36	42
	Patent Grand Square Piano-Fortes						
11	With bar, metal plate, circular corners, long hinge, C to A ...	6	3	2	10	55	60
12	Melopinakion, C to A	5	9	2	9	55	60
13	Ditto, on elegant stand, C to A...	5	9	2	9	65	70

APPENDIX F

Hire

	Mahogany £ s. d.	Rosewood £ s. d.
Grand per month	1 11 6	2 2 0
Boudoir	1 10 0	2 0 0
Bichord	1 8 0	1 16 0
Cottage	1 1 0	1 5 0
Semi-Cottage	1 0 0	1 1 0
Patent Grand Square... ...	1 1 0	1 5 0
Melopinakion	1 3 0	1 6 0

APPENDIX G

A LIST OF PIANOFORTE MAKERS IN LONDON AND ITS ENVIRONS FROM 1760 TO 1851

PREFACE

In compiling this list of Pianoforte Makers I have made full use of the London Post Office Directories, Kent's Directory and Done's Directory and have also availed myself of the list of "Makers and Sellers of Keyboard Instruments" in Philip James' work on *Early Keyboard Instruments* (1930) and consulted articles concerning Pianoforte Makers in the latest edition of *Grove's Dictionary of Music.*

Usually I have only traced the progress of the firms from the year in which they began making pianofortes to the time when they gave up this branch of work, but in cases where it seemed useful or interesting the sketch of the firm's history has been made as complete as possible.

1846–1856 Addison, Robert 210 Regent Street.
(1856) 19 Osnaburgh Street.
1793– Adlam, John 40 King Street, Soho.
1843–1877 Aldrich, Richard 33 Windmill Street, Finsbury.
(1869) 209 New Road.
1841–1844 Allat, David 9 Holywell Street, Millbank.
1847–1849 Allen, Francis
(1847) 6 Cheyne Row, Chelsea.
(1848) 8 Cheyne Row, Chelsea.
1837–1851 Allison and Allison
(1837) 29 Berners Street, Oxford Street, and
(1839) 49 Wardour Street, Soho.
(1846) 75 Dean Street, and 49 Wardour Street, Soho.
1850–1910 Allison, Ralph
(1850) 106 Wardour Street, Soho, and
(1851) 34 Brook Street.
(1856) 1A Werrington Street, Somers Town.
(1863) 108 Wardour Street, and
(1870) 109 Wardour Street.
(1871) Stibbington Street, Somers Town, and
(1876) 1 Werrington Street.
(1879) Arthur Allison and Co. (?) 167, 169, 171 Wardour Street, and 1 Werrington Street, and Stibbington Street.
(1907) Prebend Street, Camden Town.
1911–1933 et fl. Allison Pianos, Ltd.* [New style adopted by the firm of Messrs Ralph Allison.]
(1913) Leighton Road, Kentish Town.
10 Charlton King's Road, and Prebend Street.
(1923) 56 and 60 Wigmore Street.

---

* The firm of Allison Pianos, Ltd. was founded by Ralph Allison in 1850; see previous entry.

(1929)   56 Chalk Farm Road, N.W.
Leighton Road, Kentish Town.
60 Wigmore Street.

1836–1837 Ambrose, Charles
(1836)   75 Seymour Street, Euston Square, and
(1837)   47 Seymour Street, Euston Square.

1843–1850 Anderson, Andrew   83 Great Titchfield Street, Oxford Street.

1806–1808 Anderson, Jane (Grand and Square Pianoforte Maker)   62 Dean Street, Soho.

1835 Anderson, William   49 Wigmore Street.

1848 Anderson, William   57 Fore Street, Cripplegate.

1848–1851 Appelby, John
(1848)   13 Stephen Street, Tottenham Court Road.
(1851)   32 Gresse Street, Rathbone Place.

1794–1830 Astor, George   26 Wych Street.
(1799)   George Astor and Co.   79 Cornhill, and 27 Tottenham Street, Fitzroy Square.
(1815)   Astor and Horwood   79 Cornhill, etc.
(1822)   Astor and Co.   79 Cornhill, and
(1826)   3 Ann Street, Wilmington Square.

1849 Austin, Job   55 Church Street, Minories.

1843–1850 Avill, William   29A Cumberland Street, Hackney Road.

1767–1781 Backers, Americus   Jermyn Street.

1847–1869 Bacon, James   18 Polygon, Clarendon Square, Somers Town, and
(1860)   52 Connaught Terrace.

1851 Bain, Peter   19 Smith Street, Westminster.

1790–1834 Ball, James   Duke Street, Grosvenor Square.
(1806)   (Grand Pianoforte Maker)   26 Duke Street, Grosvenor Square.
(1808)   27 Duke Street, Grosvenor Square.
(1819)   J. Ball and Son   27 Duke Street, etc.
(1824)   Edward Ball and Son (Grand Pianoforte and Organ Builders)   27 Duke Street, etc.
(1826)   (Grand, Cabinet and Square Pianoforte Makers to His Majesty)

1847–1869 Ballinghall, James   24 Claremont Terrace, Putney.
(1850)   19 Edward's Street, Portman Square.
(1853)   61 Baker Street, Portman Square.
(1856)   34 Brook Street, New Road.
(1859)   186 Euston Road.

1836–1837 Baragiolay, L.   4 Arlington Street, Sadler's Wells.

1835–1867 Barling, Jacob   43 Hart Street, Bloomsbury, and 34 Hart Street, Bloomsbury.
(1863)   26 Brunswick Street, Brunswick Square.

1840–1887 Barratt, John   27 High Street, Camden Town.
(1865)   54 High Street, Camden Town.
(1867)   Mrs Ann Barratt (address as above).
(1871)   Mrs Mary Barratt (address as above).
(1876)   Thomas and Charles Barratt (address as above).
(1887)   Barratt Bros. (address as above).

1835–1836 Baskett, William   22 White Hart Place, Kensal Lane.

1822–1827 Bateman and Roe   4 Greek Street, Soho.
    (1826)   18 Dean Street, Soho.
1774–1794 Beck, Frederick   4 Broad Street, Golden Square.
    (1794)   10 Broad Street, Carnaby Market.
1801– Becker, J. Conrad   Princes Street, Soho.
1800– Bell, —   Charles Square, Hoxton.
1844–1850 Bell, John F.   4 Little Russell Street, Drury Lane.
    (1846)   Mrs E. Bell   4 Little Russell Street, etc.
1844–1850 Bell, John Thomas   17 Old Street, St Luke's.
1836–1842 Bennett, John   1 Finsbury Square.
    (1840)   12 City Road, Finsbury.
1829–1832 Berry, W. F.   116 Crawford Street.
1844(?)–1857(?)   Beuthin, Thomas   8 Borough Road.
    (1846)   Beuthin and Tallent   13 and 14 Borough Road, also
    (1850)   2 Crown Street, Walworth Road.
    (1852)   Thomas Beuthin (address as above).
    (1855)   8 Stamford Street, Blackfriars Road.
1835–1866 Binckes, Litchfield   10 Frederick Place, Old Kent Road.
    (1850)   1 Clarence Street, and 1 Oxford Row, Old Kent Road.
    (1851)   4 Cornbury Place, Old Kent Road.
    (1864)   Litchfield Binckes and Co.   90 Old Kent Road.
1844–1848 Binyon, Alfred   *4 Tavistock Street, Covent Garden.
    (1845)   40 Tavistock Street, Covent Garden.
1841–1846 Blackie, Alexander   81 Margaret Street.
1845– Blake, Charles and Co.   11 Cateaton Street, and 16½ Laurence Lane.
1795–1817 Bland and Weller   23 Oxford Street.
    (1817)   (Pianoforte Makers and Music Sellers)
1774– Bleyer, Adam   Compton Street, Soho.
1843(?)–1859 John Bond†
    (1843)   5 King Street, Camden Town.
    (1845)   19 Frederick Place, Hampstead Road.
    (1850)   Elizabeth and William Bond   19 Frederick Place, etc.
    (1851)   John Bond and Co.   19 Frederick Place, etc.
    (1856)   74 Pratt Street, Camden Town.
1850 Bond, John   40 Park Terrace, Camden Town.
1839 Bonner, James   36 University Street, Tottenham Court Road.
1840–1841 Brader, John   4 Newman Passage, Newman Street.
    (1841)   17 Poland Street.
1842 Bridgland, James M.   69 Berwick Street, Soho.
1839–1880 Brinsmead, Henry   3 Upper Grafton Street, Fitzroy Square.
    (1861)   12 Rathbone Place, and Blackhorse Yard.
1840–1933 et fl. Brinsmead, John   40 Windmill Street, 1 Chenies Street, Tottenham Court Road; 15 Charlotte Street, Fitzroy Square, and Blackhorse Yard, and
    (1859)   1 Little Torrington Street.
    (1868)   32 Charlotte Street.
    (1870)   John Brinsmead and Sons   18 Wigmore Street.
    (1881)   18 and 20 Wigmore Street, Cavendish Square; Manufactory, Grafton Road.

* Possibly a misprint for 40.
† No mention of John Bond in the Directory for 1844.

(1883)   22 Wigmore Street.
(1893)   (Pianoforte Makers to T.R.H. the Prince and Princess of Wales) 18, 20, 22 Wigmore Street. (Temporary Premises 104 New Bond Street)
(1921)   Stanley Brinsmead and Co.   7 and 21 Keens Yard, St Paul's Road.
(1922)   45 Westbourne Road.
(1923)   38 and 40 Great College Street.
1773–1933 et fl.   Broadwood, John and Sons   (*See* Shudi and Broadwood)
1844–1845   Brockbank, John   25 Aldenham Street, Somers Town.
1841–1874   Brockbank, J. and Son   3 Crawley Street, Oakley Square.
(1861)   16, 17 and 18 Great College Street, Camden Town.
(1863)   17 to 20 Great College Street, Camden Town.
(1868)   34, 36, 38 to 40 Great College Street, Camden Town.
1847–1862   Brockly, George   71 Warren Street, Fitzroy Square.
1850–1854   Brockly, Thomas   57 Wells Street, Oxford Street.
1841–1842   Bromly, E.   13 Page Street, Holywell Street.
1842–1848   Brooks, Francis   40 Cleveland Street, Fitzroy Square.
(1846)   1 Granby Street, Hampstead Road.
1847–1848   Brooks, James   6 Great College Street, Camden Town.
1840   Brooks, T. and H.   37 Little Albany Street.
1845–1847   Brown, Frederick   47 Warwick Street, Pimlico.
1846–1868   Brown, Philip   53 Bartholomew Close.
(1850)   74 Great Titchfield Street.
(1856)   74 Great Portland Street(?).
(1859)   143 Great Portland Street.
1848–1851   Browne, John   27 Soho Square.
1835–1848   Bruce, John   19 London Street, Fitzroy Square.
(1846)   11 Frederick Street, Regent's Park.
1849–1885   Bryson, Thomas   38 Thanet Street, Burton Crescent.
(1853)   5 Greenland Place, Brunswick Square.
(1868)   123 Cromer Road, Gray's Inn Road.
(1877)   121 Cromer Road, Gray's Inn Road.
(1880)   William Bryson   121 Cromer Road.
1824–1830   Brysson, George   18 Bridgehouse Place, Newington.
1820–1866   Buchan, Thomas
(1827)   147 Whitechapel Road.
(1832)   7 Mount Place, Whitechapel Road.
(1838)   11 Mount Place, Whitechapel Road.
(1864)   22 Bedford Square.
1793–1809   Buckinger, J.   443 Strand.
1840–1883   Bunting, John   22 Swan Street, Minories.
(1875)   114 Minories, and
(1876)   6 America Square.
1769–1795   Buntlebart, Gabriel   7 Princes Street, Hanover Square
(1788)   Buntlebart and Sievers (address as above
(1794)   G. Buntlebart (address as above).
1844–1847   Burton, Robert   56 Goswell Road.
(1845)   54 Goswell Road.
1787–1794   Bury, Samuel and Co.   113 Bishopsgate within.
(1788)   Bishopsgate Street.
1811–1847   Butcher, Thomas   41 Great Titchfield Street.

1845–1849   Butt, John   28 Goldsmiths Place, Hackney Road.
1792–   Buttery, George   St Martin-in-the-Fields.
1839–1885   Cadby, Charles (Patent Pianoforte Manufactory)   21 Alfred Street,
               Bedford Street.
      (1848)   33½ Liquorpound Street.
      (1851)   37 Liquorpound Street.
      (1853)   38 and 39 Liquorpound Street.
      (1863)   3, 33A, 38 and 39 Liquorpound Street, and
      (1869)   Little Tothill Street, Little Gray's Inn Lane.
      (1867)   Charles Cadby and Son (Patent)   West Kensington New
               Pianoforte Works, Near Addison Road Station.
      (1879)   Charles Cadby and Co.   Hammersmith Road.
1851–   Cannee, Joseph E.   78 Brunswick Street, Hackney.
1851–1892   Caperoe and Hastelow   11 Temple Street, Hackney Road.
      (1855)   11 St Matthew's Place.
      (1858)   Caperoe, Frs and Co. (address as above).
      (1863)   423 Hackney Road, and 3 Broughton Place, Hackney,
               and
      (1867)   53 Hackney.
1848–   Carpenter, William George   35 Lower Islington Terrace.
1835–1847   Carter, Isaac   14 Duke Street, Manchester Square, and
      (1840)   7 Orchard Street, Portman Square.
1851–1852   Cathie, John   51 Acton Street, Gray's Inn Road.
1838–1864   Challen, William and Co.   41 Great Titchfield Street.
               Challen and Hollis   41 Great Titchfield Street.
      (1858)   Challen and Son   41 Great Titchfield Street.
      (1859)   3 Berners Street.
1846–1847   Chandler, George   27 Tavistock Place.
1832–1836   Chase, J.   18 Bridge House Place, Borough.
1838–1851   Chesterman, Charles   114 Crawford Street, Portman Square.
1843–1848   Child, Daniel   10 Chester Place, Old Kent Road, and
      (1844)   33 High Street, Notting Hill.
1835–1837   Childs, S.   1 Lower Phillimore Place, Knightsbridge.
1841–1847   Chisholme or Chissholme, James   15 Great Pulteney Street.
1839–1856   Clark and Boothby   112 Great Portland Street, Oxford Street.
      (1840)   Clark and Co.   112 Great Portland Street, etc.
      (1841)   Clark and Boothby   112 Great Portland Street, etc.
1842–1845   Clark, John   12 Nottingham Street, Marylebone.
1851–1858   Clarke, Richard   57 College Place, Camden Town.
1802–1832   Clementi and Co.   26 Cheapside, and
      (1806)   Tottenham Court Road.
      (1809)   Clementi, Banger, Collard, Davis and Collard.
      (1820)   Clementi, Collard, Davis and Collard.
      (1824)   Clementi, Collard and Collard   26 Cheapside, and 195
               Tottenham Court Road.
      (1832)   Clementi dies and the House takes the title of Collard and
               Collard. (*See* below)
1848–1851   Cocks, Robert and Co.   6 New Burlington Street.
(1802)* 1832–1933 et fl.   Collard and Collard (*see* Clementi and Co.)   26 Cheap-
               side, 195 Tottenham Court Road, and

    * Established in 1802 under the style "Clementi and Co."

(1845) 6 High Street, Camden Town, and
(1846) 12 Francis Street, Tottenham Court Road, and
(1847) 20 Oval Road, Regent's Park.
(1861) 16 Grosvenor Street, New Bond Street, and 26 Cheapside.
(1888) 12 Oval Road.
(1910) 33 Oval Road.
(1921) Collard and Collard, Ltd. 12 and 35 Oval Road, and Gloucester Gate.
(1928) 7 Brook Street.

1841–1847 Connor, Henry 9 George Street, Euston Square.

1839–1854 Coombe, Charles 26 Leonard Street, Tabernacle Walk.

1844 Cooper, James 28 Harrow Road, Paddington.

1850–1866 Cooper, James and Co. 43 Moorgate Street, and
(1851) Lansdowne Yard, Guildford Street.
(1856) Joseph Cooper (address as above).

1840–1845 Cooper, John and Co. 28 Moorgate Street, and
(1845) 28 Dudley Grove, Paddington.

1850–1874 Cooper, J. and Son 70 Berners Street, Oxford Street.
(1853) 68 Berners Street, Oxford Street.
(1863) 34 Linton Street, Arlington Square.
(1867) 23 Charlotte Street, Bedford Square.
(1868) 35 Berners Street.
(1869) 36 Berners Street.
(1871) 18 City Road.

1814–1840 Cooper, T. 53 Southampton Row, Bloomsbury.
(1839) James Cooper and Co. 48 Southampton Row, Russell Square.

1844–1893 Cooper, Taylor 43 Edgware Road.
(1847) 122 St John's Street Road.
(1849) Robinson Cooper 122 St John's Street Road.
(1850) Taylor Cooper 122 St John's Street Road.
(1863) 119 John Street Road.
(1871) 155 John Street Road.

1839 Cooper, William 101 Dean Street, Soho.

1846 Cooper, William 122 St John's Street Road. (*See* Cooper, Taylor)

1841–1842 Corps, James 13 Gower Place, Euston Square.

1794– Corrie, — 41 Broad Street, Carnaby Market.
N.B. Corrie is not mentioned in the Post Office Directories, but his name appears in J. Done's *Musical Directory* for 1794.

1841–1846 Couling, Mrs Maria 9 Castle Street, Long Acre.

1840–1852 Coventry and Hollier 71 Dean Street, Soho, and
(1844) 3 Wardour Street, Soho.
(1849) Charles Coventry 71 Dean Street, etc.

1840–1863 Creber, Richard 11A Berners Street, Oxford Street.
(1849) 496 Oxford Street.
(1851) 57 Rathbone Place, Oxford Street.
(1853) 67 Rathbone Place.
(1858) 18 Eversholt Street.
(1863) 34 Mornington Place, Hampstead.

1849–1854 Creber, William 6 Charles Place, Drummond Street.

1796– Culliford, Thomas 112 Cheapside, and 172 Strand.

1844–1849   Cutmore, Charles Richard   4 Judd Street, Brunswick Square.
Charles Richard Cutmore and Co.   17 Brecknock Place.
(1849)   30 Park Street, Camden Town.
1843–1871   Dainty and Harrison   29 Newman Street.
(1846)   William Dainty   29 Newman Street.
1835–1837   Dale, Daniel   6 Surrey Grove, Old Kent Road.
1850–1874   Dale, Daniel   143 Albany Road.
(1855)   3 Albany Road.
(1863)   368 Albany Road.
(1871)   D. Dale and Son (address as above).
(1872)   Samuel Dale.
1792–1809   Dale, Joseph   132 Oxford Street (Music Circulating Library).
(1791)   19 Cornhill, and 132 Oxford Street.
(1794)   19 Cornhill, and 130 (and 132) Oxford Street.
(1799)   Pianoforte Makers.
(1806)   Pianoforte Makers (By Appointment) to H.R.H. Prince of Wales, and Music Sellers to the Royal Family   19 Cornhill, and 151 New Bond Street.
1836–1837   Dale, Thomas   2 Devonshire Square, Bishopsgate.
(1785)* 1835–1933 et fl.   D'Almaine and Co. (see Goulding)   20 Soho Square, and
(1850)   10 Sutton Place, Soho Square.
(1852)   Thomas D'Almaine and Co.
(1859)   104 New Bond Street.
(1861)   Burwood Mews, Edgware Road (added).
(1868)   9 Walmer Road.
(1875)   167 and 169 Walmer Road.
(1876)   167, 218 and 220 Walmer Road.
(1878)   5 Finsbury Pavement.
(1881)   91 Finsbury Pavement, and
(1914)   244 Tottenham Court Road.
(1916)   135 Finsbury Pavement.
(1925)   76 City Road.
1841–1842   Darby, John   14 Holywell Street, Millbank.
1845–1858   Darnton, William   43 Cross Street, Islington.
(1850)   92 Upper Street, Islington.
(1858)   118 Upper Street, Islington.
1846–1858   Darter, G. B. S.   57 Baker Street, Portman Square.
(1848)   261A Oxford Street.
(1849)   61 Baker Street.
1813–1848   Davis, Joseph (Grand Pianoforte Maker and Military Instrument Maker)   11 Catharine Street, Strand, and
(1829)   92 Great Surrey Street, Blackfriars Road.
(1844)   20 Southampton Street, Strand, and 92 Great Surrey Street.
1839–1849   Dawson, Henry   5 Nassau Street, Soho.
1844–1845   Dawson, Thomas   39 Sidmouth Street, Gray's Inn Road.
1841–1860   Deacock, Thomas   4 Buckingham Place, Fitzroy Square, and
(1849)   10 Upper Charlton Street.
1835–1851   Dean, John   8 Wilmot Street, Russell Square, and
(1841)   19 Wilmot Street, Russell Square.

* Established in 1785 under the style "Goulding, D'Almaine, Potter and Co."

1844–1845 Demoline, Isaac H.   1 Aldenham Street, Somers Town.
1805–1848 Dettmar, William   50 Upper Marylebone Street.
          (1846)   60 Warren Street, Fitzroy Square.
1848–1849 Dettmer, George and Son   20½ Clipstone Street.
1838–1847 Dick, John   64 Newman Street, Oxford Street.
1810–1835 Dierkes, Charles (Grand, Cabinet and Square Pianoforte Maker)
          7 Percy Street, Bedford Square.
1847–1848 Dinn, Burges   4 Cookes Terrace, Pancras Old Road.
1821–1827 Dobson, Benjamin, Organ and Pianoforte Maker   22 Swan Street,
          Minories.
1826–1846 Dodd, Edward (Patent Harp Manufactory but also Pianoforte
          Makers)   3 Berners Street.
          (1827)   62 Berwick Street, Oxford Street.
          (1840)   3 Berners Street, and Gloucester Road.
          (1846)   Apparently gave up musical instrument making and became
          music sellers.
1792–1814 Done, Joshua   30 Chancery Lane.
          (1793)   24 Great James Street, Bedford Row.
1837–1848 Dore, Joseph   49 Wigmore Street, and 10 Polygon, Clarendon
          Street.
1834–1835 Dove, T.   6 City Road, Near Old Street.
1849–1858 Dreher, C   12 Gloucester Terrace, New Road, Whitechapel.
1843–1860 Duff and Hodgson   3 Berners Street, Oxford Street.
          (1860)   65 Oxford Street.
1819–1827 Dunn, George   77 Great Titchfield Street.
1835–1849 Dunn, George   36 London Road, Fitzroy Square, and
          (1839)   6 Church Street, Camberwell.
1843–1844 Edgar, Edward   63 Lamb's Conduit Street.
1842–1843 Edmead, William and Co.   32 Walbrook, and 45 Bartholomew Close.
1844–1889 Edwards, Richard   1 Seymour Street, Euston Square, and
          (1852)   3 Little Crescent, Euston Square.
          (1856)   28 Southampton Mews, and
          (1863)   1 Seymour Street.
          (1865)   2 Seymour Street.
1803–1850 Edwards, William Henry   17 Bridge Road, Lambeth.
1835–1845 Eiloat, Ferdinand   63 and 64 Seymour Street, Euston Square.
1835–1883 Ekstedt, M. and T.   57 Hoxton Square.
          (1842)   Ekstedt, Thomas and James   1 Bridgehouse Place,
          Borough.
          (1845)   37 Bridgehouse Place, Borough.
          (1851)   17 Crosby Row, Walworth Road.
          (1853)   85 Blackman Street, Borough.
          (1855)   175 Great Dover Street.
          (1859)   2 High Street, Newington.
          (1865)   148 Blackfriars Road.
1850–1855 Ennever and Steedman   3 Little Crescent Street, Euston Square, and
          (1851)   21 Percy Street, and
          (1852)   31 George Square.
1835–1837 Epping, Henry   21 Portland Street, Soho.
1786–1933 et fl. Érard, Sébastien   18 Great Marlborough Street.
          (1838)   Sébastien and Pierre Érard   18 Great Marlborough
          Street, and 3 and 4 Little Portland Place, Marylebone.

	(1839) Pianoforte Makers to Her Majesty.
	(1852) Warwick Road and above addresses.
	(1894) "Royal Pianoforte Makers."
	(1902) 189 Regent Street.
	(1904) 158A New Bond Street.
	(1931) S. and P. Érard Ltd. 28 Broad Street, W.
1820–	Evenden and Sons ——.
1838–1874	Evestaff, William 66 Great Russell Street, Bloomsbury, and
	(1845) 17 Sloane Street, Chelsea.
1846–1852	Fairchild, J. 30 Grafton Street, Fitzroy Square.
	(1849) 200 High Holborn.
1845–1848	Fawcet, T. and Co. 3 Lower Chester Terrace, Pimlico.
	(1847) 3 Minerva Street, Pimlico.
1844–1851	Flew, William 6 North Road, Lambeth.
1848–	Fontaine, Mark 5 Dorchester Place, Blandford Square.
1806–1808	Francklin, C. 135 Holborn Hill.
1802–1834	Frecker, W. (Grand Pianoforte Maker) 31 Rathbone Place.
1788–1800	Froeschle, George 2 Mark Lane.
1844–	Frood, John 17 Sandwich Street (?), Burton Crescent.
1843–	Fryer, Daniel 24½ Cardington Street, Hampstead Road.
1774–1807	Ganer, Christopher 22 Broad Street.
	(1774) 48 Broad Street.
	(1802) 98 Broad Street.
	(1806) 50 Broad Street.
	(1807) 47 and 48 Broad Street.
1824–1829	Gange, George 15 Romney Terrace, Horseferry Road, Westminster.
1833–1887	Gange, George 10 Lower Belgrave Place, Pimlico.
	(1838) George Gange and Co. (From Messrs Broadwoods) 10 Lower Belgrave Place, etc., and 19 Poultry.
	(1849) Nathaniel Gange and Son 10 Lower Belgrave Place, and 19 Poultry.
	(1856) 12 and 13 Lower Belgrave Road.
	(1869) 68 Buckingham Palace Road.
1775–1793	Garbutt, T. King Street, Golden Square.
	(1793) 8 Bolsover Street, Oxford Street.
1783–1792	Garcia, George Steven Street.
	(1792) Wardour Street, Soho.
1786–	Geib, John Old Bailey.
	(1786) Tottenham Court Road.
1824–1837	Gerock, C. and Co. (see Astor) 79 Cornhill.
	(1825) Gerock, Astor and Co. 79 Cornhill.
	(1837) Gerock, C. and Co. 79 Cornhill.
1835–1871	Gibbs, John 23 Clarence Place, Camberwell Road.
	(1846) 1 Bowyer Place, Camberwell Road.
	(1865) 156 Camberwell Road.
1848	Goddan, Edward 9 William Street, Regent's Park.
1836–1841	Godwin, John Cumberland Street, Hackney Road.
1785–1851	Goulding, D'Almaine, Potter and Co. 20 Soho Square, and
	(1831) 7 Westmoreland Street, Dublin.
	(1835) D'Almaine and Co. 20 Soho Square, and at Dublin, and
	(1850) 10 Sutton Place, Soho Square.

1847–1855 Graddon, Margaritta and Co.   54 Albany Street.
      (1849)   Graddon and Gibbs   4 Albany Street, Regent's Park, and 54 Albany Street.
1850–1851 Gray, Andrew R.   39 Edward Street, Hampstead.
1835–1842 Green, Edward   4 Mansion House Place, Camberwell.
1821–1849 Green, John (Agent for Logier's Pat. "Chiroplast", etc.)   33 Soho Square.
      (1825)   (Also Proprietor of Maelzel's Metronome and the Royal Kent Bugle)
      (1839)   (Also a Seraphine Maker)
1837–1851 Greiner, G. F.   51 Upper Marylebone Street, London.
1848–1857 Grover, William   Islington Place, Cloudesley Square, and 12 Richard Street, Lower Road, Islington.
      (1849)   2 Richard Street, Islington, and Islington Place.
      (1850)   48 Chapel Street, Pentonville, and Islington Place.
1848–1850 Gunns, Joseph   9 New Manor Place, King's Road, Chelsea.
1819–1878 Gunther, Henry   27 Tottenham Street.
      (1820)   Robert Gunther   31 Little Queen Street, Holborn.
      (1823)   Gunther and Horwood (address as above).
      (1839)   Henry Gunther   6 High Street, Camden Town.
      (1840)   6 and 7 High Street, Camden Town.
1841–1842 Hack, Robert   4 Gray's Inn Passage.
1824–1825 Haig and Co.   18 Bentinck Street.
1835–1837 Haig and Co.   Bridge House Place, Newington.
1842–1854 Haig, John   2 Walworth Place, Walworth Road, and
      (1846)   1 Walworth Place, Walworth Road.
      (1851)   John Haig and Co.   1 and 2 Walworth Place, etc.
1845–1854 Halley, James   11 Rufford's Row, Islington.
      (1846)   18 Wade's Place, Hackney Road.
      (1850)   73 Goswell Road.
1845–1848 Hallpeke, Vincent Henry   29 Cromer Street, Brunswick Square.
      (1847)   30 Cromer Street, Brunswick Square.
      1850 Hammar and Hay   30 Cromer Street, Brunswick Square.
1835–1840 Hammond, John   7 Polygon, Clarendon Square.
1842–1880 Hammond, William   1 Surrey Place, East Old Kent Road.
      (1851)   William Hammond and Sons   1 Surrey Place, etc.
      (1863)   5 Oakey Terrace, Old Kent Road.
      (1864)   366 Old Kent Road.
1779–1799 Hancock, John Crang   Wych Street, St Clement Danes.
      (1791)   32 Parliament Street.
1847–1854 Handford, W. T.   14 Great College Street, Camden Town.
1847–1849 Hanford, Thomas   29 Charles Street, Hampstead Road.
1848–1849 Hardie, H. W.   4 New Cavendish Street, Portland Place.
1843–1857 Hardie, William   13 Upper Gloucester Place, King's Road, Chelsea.
      (1844)   3 Gloucester Place, King's Road, Chelsea.
      (1846)   H. Hardie   3 Gloucester Place, etc.
1834–1887 Harper, William   49 Red Lion Street, Holborn.
      (1856)   14 Green Street, Theobald Road.
      (1871)   Wm. Harper and Co. (address as above).
      (1872)   Wm. Harper   3 Aberdeen Park Road.
      (1877)   Harper and Castle (address as above).

1849–1850   Harris, William   37 Thanet Street, Burton Crescent.
1835–1843   Harrison, Edward   157 Blackfriars Road.
           (1838)   131 Blackfriars Road.
           (1839)   124 London Road.
1850–1864   Harrison, J. and Co.   45 Upper John Street, Fitzroy Square.
           (1855)   65 John Street, Fitzroy Square, and
           (1858)   3 and 4 North Street Mews, Fitzroy Square.
1838–1858   Hart, Joseph   109 Hatton Garden, Holborn Hill.
1850–1851   Hartill and Lockington   41 Kenton Street.
1839–1854   Harwar, Joseph   29 Charlotte Street, Bloomsbury.
           (1846)   28 Bloomsbury Street, St Giles.
1845–1857   Hattersley, William   Regent Street, Westminster.
           (1850)   William Hattersley and Son   22 Great Smith Street.
           (1853)   William Hattersley and Co.   5 New Bridge Street, Vauxhall.
           (1854)   3 Darlington Place, Vauxhall.
           (1856)   Wilton Road, Pimlico.
1813–   Hauck, Frederick   High Holborn.
1846–1847   Hawkesley, James   11 Grafton Street, Fitzroy Square.
1800–1845   Hawkins, John Isaac   Bordenton, New Jersey.
           (1802)   Philadelphia.
           (1803)   Dalby Terrace, City Road, London.
           (1812)   79 Great Titchfield Street, Mary-le-bone.
           (1813)   Refers to his "Essence of Coffee Manufactory" at the above address.
           (1819)   Refers to his "Mechanical Museum" at the above address.
           (1827)   Left England for some years.
           (1845)   26 Judd-Place, New Road, London.
1848–1850   Hayward, John   3 Francis Street, Tottenham Court Road.
1846–1850   Healey, George   25 Ernest Street, Regent's Park.
           (1847)   45 Ernest Street, Regent's Park.
           (1849)   34 Brook Street, New Road.
1840–1841   Hearne, Alfred   59 Judd Street, Brunswick Square.
1835   Henderson, J.   58 Castle Street, East Oxford Street.
1842–1847   Hewitt, Daniel Chandler   6 High Street, Camden Town.
           (1844)   16 Hanover Street, Hanover Square.
1841–1847   Hickling, Richard   43 Great Titchfield Street.
1849–1865   Hickman, C.   15 Carburton Street, Fitzroy Square.
           (1851)   47 Upper North Street, Portland Road.
           (1861)   47 Bolsover Street, Fitzroy Square.
1845   Hicks, George*   13 Penton Street, Pentonville.
1846–1847   Hicks, George   17 Bryan Street, Pentonville.
1847–1848   Highway, James   4 Cadogan Street, Chelsea.
1806–1850   Hill, John   9 London Road, Southwark, Surrey.
           (1834)   38 London Road, Southwark, Surrey.
           (1835)   5 Harleyford Place, Kensington Road.
1847–1856   Hill, Robert F.   8 Oakley Terrace, Old Kent Road.
           (1849)   Robert F. Hill and Co.   8 Oakley Terrace, etc.
1851–1852   Hodge, James   61 Greek Street, Soho.

        * Probably the same man as the following.

1851–1922 Holdernesse, Chas. 444 Oxford Street.
        (1855) 6 Lawrence Street.
        (1856) Holdernesse and Holdernesse.
        (1884) 105 New Oxford Street, and 6 Lawrence Street.
        (1886) 7 and 8 Maynard Street, and Blackhorse Yard, Rathbone
                Place.
        (1906) Charles Holdernesse and Co. (address as above).
1846–1848 Holdernesse, George William and Co. 57 A Charlotte Street, Fitzroy
            Square, and Henry Street, New Road.
1845–1848 Holdernesse, J. F. 3 Church Row, Islington.
        (1846) Mrs E. Holdernesse 3 Church Row, etc.
1847–1859 Holdernesse, R. L. 1 Newington Street, Oxford Street.
        (1849) R. L. Holdernesse and Co. 40 Great Russell Street.
        (1852) 12 Bath Road.
        (1855) 98 Bayham Street, Camden Town.
1783–1798 Holland, H. Bedford Row.
1851–1874 Holman, Edward W. 10 Grafton Street, Fitzroy Square.
        (1863) 14 Russell Place, Fitzroy Square.
        (1867) 21 and 23 Fitzroy Street.
     1850 Holmes, James and Son 6 Manning Street, Edgware Road.
1841–1844 Holmyard, Thomas 28 New Street, Horseferry Road.
1840–1851 Hooker, William 85 Martin's Place, Old Street, and
        (1843) 92 Old Street.
1845– Hooker, William (Junior) 12 White Conduit Terrace.
1790– Hopkinson, — 54 Great Marlborough Street.
1846–1933 et fl. Hopkinson, John and James* 70 Mortimer Street, and (?) Soho
            Square.
        (1849) 27 Oxford Street, and 4 and 5 Little Howland Street.
        (1851) 18 Soho Square, and 6 and 7 Little Stone Street, Bedford
                Square, and Phoenix Street, Soho.
        (1855) Diana Place, New Road Manufactory.
        (1856) 235 Regent Street.
        (1863) 6 Conduit Street.
        (1864) 9 Conduit Street.
        (1869) 16 Hanover Street; 235 Regent Street; Manufactory,
                44 Fitzroy Road, Regent's Park.
        (1876) 235 and 246 Regent Street.
        (1882) 95 New Bond Street.
        (1892) 34, 35, 36 Margaret Street, Cavendish Square, and
                44 Fitzroy Road, and Regent Street.
        (1897) John and James Hopkinson, Ltd. (address as above).
        (1898) 102 Brompton Road (added).
        (1900) 84 New Bond Street; 241 High Road, Kilburn; and
                44 A Fitzroy Road.
1790–1799 Houston, J. H. Edward Street, Wardour Street, Soho.
     1841 Hubbard, John 7 High Street, Newington.
1851–1880 Hund, Frederick 21 Ebury Street, Pimlico.
        (1868) 63 Ebury Street.

---

* John Hopkinson began business at Leeds in 1835 and removed to London in 1846. From 1886 to 1895 a music publishing business was carried on in addition to the pianoforte business.

(1869)   Frederick Hund and Son.

(1872)   18 Castle Street, Long Acre.

(1878)   36 Castle Street, Long Acre.

1850   Hyrons, Edwin and Co.   29 John Street, Fitzroy Square.

1835–1840   Indemaur, Henry   13 Upper Cleveland Street, Fitzroy Square.

(1839)   92 Charlotte Street, Fitzroy Square.

1845–1847   Innes, William   2 Keppel Street, Russell Square.

1841   Jackson and Jackson   79 Great Titchfield Street.

1838–1854   Jackson, James and Sons   56 Paddington Street, Marylebone.

(1840)   Jackson and Co.   56 Paddington Street, etc.

(1841)   J. Jackson and Sons   56 Paddington Street, etc.

(1842)   J. Jackson and Son   56 Paddington Street, etc.

(1848)   Jackson and Sons   31 Charlotte Street, Fitzroy Square.

1845–1846   Jackson, John Alexander   32 Greek Street, Soho.

1848–1849   Jackson, Joseph   3½ Oval Road, Portman Square.

1845–   Jackson and Son   Oval Road, Gloucester Gate.

1843–1878   Jackson, Thomas and Joseph   96 New Bond Street.

(1845)   21 Orchard Street, Portman Square.

Thomas Jackson (address as above).

(1871)   Thomas Jackson and Son (address as above).

1844–1852   Jacobs, Henry   24½ Cardington Street, Hampstead Road.

1835–1862   Jenkins, William   10 London Street, Fitzroy Square.

(1838)   William Jenkins and Son   10 London Street, etc.

(1842)   William Jenkins and Sons   10 London Street, etc.

1850–1851   Jenn, Joseph   36 Judd Street, Brunswick Square.

1850   Jones, John   58 College Place, Camden Town.

1845–1848   Jones, John C.   83 Upper Seymour Street, Euston Square.

(1846)   3 Rutland Street, Hampstead Road.

1846–1884   Jones, John Champion   2 Hanway Street, Oxford Street.

(1851)   21 B Soho Square.

(1875)   Mrs Isabella Jones   21 B Soho Square.

(1881)   59 Elgin Road.

1800–1813   Jones, T.   23 Bishopsgate within.

(1806)   Jones, Rice and Co. (Upright Grand and Square Pianoforte Makers to H.R.H. Prince of Wales)   11 Golden Square.

1826–1836   Kearsing, William   12 Howland Street, Fitzroy Square.

(1826)   34 Mary Street, Regent's Park.

1851–1855   Kelly and Lion   8 Kensington High Street, and 22 Nassau Street, Middlesex Hospital.

(1855)   58 Baker Street.

1840–1857   Kennay, James and Co.   1 Hackney Road Crescent, and

(1848)   15 Berners Street, Oxford Street.

1841–1843   Kirkland, James   4 Alfred Street, Bedford Square.

1815–1832   Kirkman, Joseph (Grand Pianoforte Maker to His Majesty)   19 Broad Street, Golden Square.

(1817)   (Grand Pianoforte Maker to *Her* Majesty and H.R.H. The Prince Regent)

1822–1896   Kirkman, Joseph (Junior)   67 Frith Street, Soho.

(1831)   3 Soho Square, and

(1846)   9 Dean Street, and

	(1848)	Dufour's Place, Golden Square.
	(1864)	21 Broad Street, Golden Square, and
	(1868)	Bradmore Works (address not known).
	(1894)	12A George Street, Hanover Square.

1838–1841 Kollmann, George A.   67 St Martin's Lane.
1845–1848 Lacabra, Joseph   4 University Street, Tottenham Court Road.
1842–1843 Lambert, Thomas   91 Albany Street.
1851–   Lambeth and Co.   1 Warrington Street, North end of Charrington Street, St Pancras, and Portman Street, Portman Square.
1787–   Landreth, John   Tabernacle Walk, Old Street.
1839–1841 Langhans, Justus   20 Wardour Street, Soho.
1850–1855 Latham, John   20½ Clipstone Street, and 28 Howland Street, Fitzroy Square.

> (1851)   8 Upper Charlton Street, and 28 Howland Street, etc.
> (1854)   12 St John Street, Clerkenwell.
> (1855)   12 Church Row, Islington.

1800–1824 or 1825 Lawson, Henry and Co.   John Street, Fitzroy Square.

> (1802)   Henry Lawson (address as above).
> (1808)   29 John Street, Middlesex Hospital.
> (1815)   5 Nassau Street, Middlesex Hospital. (Musical Instrument Maker to His Majesty)

1850–1853 Layton, Edward   9 Red Lion Street, Clerkenwell.

> (1851)   121 St John Street, Clerkenwell.

1851–1860 Leaman, Frederick   3 Warwick Place, Bedford Row, and 4 Cleveland Street, Fitzroy Square.

> (1853)   7 Brownlow Street, Holborn.

1730–1792 Le Bond   London.
1848–1887 Legg, John   40 Robert Street, Hampstead Road.

> (1887)   13 Robert Street.

1835 Leslie, John   108 Broad Walk, Blackfriars.
1850 Lethbridge, Robert   44 Gloucester Street, Bloomsbury.
1790–1811 Leukfield, Augustus   27 Tottenham Street.
1839–1875 Levesque, Josiah   8 Haberdashers' Walk, Hoxton.

> (1840)   Mrs E. Levesque   8 Haberdashers' Walk, etc.
> (1844)   Edmeades Levesque and Co.   8 Haberdashers' Walk, etc.
> (1849)   40 Cheapside, and 8 Haberdashers' Walk, etc., and
> (1854)   14 New Gloucester Terrace, Hoxton, and
> (1855)   55 Essex Street, Hoxton.
> (1858)   63 Fleet Street, and 55 Essex Street.

1844–1847 Lock, David Charles   152 Grove Street, Camden Town.

> (1845)   Edward Charles Lock   95 Park Street, Camden Town.

1802–1829 Loeschman, David (Grand and Square Pianoforte Maker)   82 Newman Street.

> (1826)   26 Norfolk Street, Middlesex Hospital.

1825–1862 Longman and Bates (Organ and Pianoforte Makers)   6 Ludgate Hill.

> (1834)   Thomas Charles Bates   6 Ludgate Hill.
> (1838)   Theodore Charles Bates   6 Ludgate Hill, and
> (1839)   Dorset Street, Salisbury Square.
> (1849)   Theodore Bates and Son   6 Ludgate Hill, and Dorset Street, and
> (1861)   7 Glasshouse Yard, Blackfriars.

1770–1802   Longman, James and Co.   26 Cheapside, and
   (1791)   Tottenham Court Road.
   (1794)   Longman, Lukey and Co.   26 Cheapside, etc.
   (1796)   Longman, Lukey and Broderip   26 Cheapside, etc., and
   (1785)   13 St James's Street, Haymarket.
   (1802)   (*See* Clementi and Co.)
1802–1822   Longman, S. John   131 Cheapside.
   (1805)   Longman and Co.   131 Cheapside.
   (1806)   J. Longman   131 Cheapside.
   (1817)   Longman and Heron   131 Cheapside.
1802–1825   Loud, Thomas   Hoxton, Shoreditch.
   (*c.* 1807)   22 Devonshire Street, Queen Square.
  1849   Lovell, John B.   12 Westmorland Place, City Road.
1839–1862   Luff, George and Co.   103 Great Russell Street, Bloomsbury.
   (1861)   G. Luff and Son   103 Great Russell Street, Bloomsbury,
    and 7 Caroline Mews, Bedford Square.
1812–1855   Lyon and Duncan   82 Wells Street, Oxford Street.
   (1814)   22 Suffolk Street, Middlesex Hospital.
   (1815)   22 Nassau Street, Middlesex Hospital.
   (1817)   Samuel Thomas Lyon   22 Nassau Street.
   (1843)   Frederick G. Lyon (address as above).
   (1852)   Kelly and Lyon   22 Nassau Street, and 8 Kensington
    High Street.
   (1853)   Charles Kelly (address as above).
   (1854)   58 Baker Street, Portman Square.
   [22 Nassau Street passes to George Johnson.]
1841–1847   Mackenzie, Charles   11 Alfred Street, Bedford Square.
1848–1854   Mackie, Robert   19 Tavistock Place.
   (1850)   9 Store Street, Bedford Square.
1841–1886   Manketelow, Charles   11 Huntley Street, and
   (1844)   32 Upper Chenies Mews, Bedford Square.
   (1846)   John Manketelow   12 Huntley Street, and 32 Upper
    Chenies Mews, etc., and
   (1866)   10 Princes Street.
1836–1847   Mardon, William   15 Great Portland Street, Oxford Street.
   (1844)   William Mardon and Co.   15 Great Portland Street, etc.
1839–1855   Matthews, Joseph   19 Somers Place East, New Road.
   (1847)   30 Brydges Street, Covent Garden.
1846–1847   Matthews, Richard   6 Homer Place, New Road.
1845–1852   Matthews, William   42 Lisson Grove, Near St John's Wood.
   (1845)   *5 Homer Place, New Road.
1850–1862   May, Harry   11 Holborn Bars.
1803–1808   Mayer and Co.   61 Soho Square.
   (1805)   60 and 61 Soho Square.
   (1806)   14 Frith Street, Soho.
  1841   Maynard, Richard   15 Holywell Street, Millbank.
1844–1848   Melville, George   14 St James's Place, Hampstead Road.
1760–1804   Merlin, Joseph
   (1760)   Came to live with the Count de Firentes at Soho Square,
    London.

---

 * Possibly a misprint for 6 Homer Place. *See* Matthews, Richard.

(1774) Little Queen Ann Street, St Marylebone (describes himself as a Mathematical Instrument Maker).

(1804) Died.

1839–1880 Metzler, George and Co., Pianoforte and Seraphine Makers 105 Wardour Street, Soho.

(1842) 37 Great Marlborough Street, Soho, and
(1857) 35 Great Marlborough Street, Soho, and
(1858) 38 Great Marlborough Street, Soho, and
(1863) 16 Great Marlborough Street (added).
(1864) 36 Great Marlborough Street (added).
(1869) 26 to 29 Great Marlborough Street.

1839– Meyers, J. F. Albemarle Street.
(1839) Charlotte Street.

1851–1870 Miall, James, William, and F. 5 Felix Terrace, Liverpool Road.
(1858) 11 Manchester Terrace, and 242 Liverpool Road.

1848–1870 Middleton and Copley 17 Castle Street, Finsbury.
(1858) Joseph Middleton and Co.
(1861) Shacklewell Lane, Kingsland (added).
(1866) Middleton and Copley.
(1870) Middleton, Copley and Co.

1845–1850 Middleton, Robert 27 Noel Street, Wardour Street.
(1850) 54½ Foley Street, Foley Square.

1845–1851 Mills, James 21 William Street, Hampstead Road.
(1849) 35 Cardington Street, Hampstead Road.

1850–1851 M'Laggen, Geo. 2 Poland Street, Oxford Street.

1793–1839 Monrow and May 60 Skinner Street, Snow Hill.
(c. 1824) 11 Holborn Bars (Music Sellers).

1839–1854 Moore, John 138 Bishopsgate without.
(1840) J. Moore and Co. 138 Bishopsgate, etc.
(1846) J. H. Moore and Co. 104 Bishopsgate, etc.

1845–1849 Morley, William Henry 43 Hedge Row, Islington.
(1847) 6 Clark's Place, Islington.

1839–1841 Morrison, Robert 26 Percy Street, Tottenham Court Road.

1820–1863 Mott, J. H. R., and J. C. and Co. 95 Pall Mall. (Formerly of Brighton)
(1828) Isaac Henry Robert Mott (Pianoforte Maker to His Majesty) 92 Pall Mall, and
(1831) 135 Oxford Street (Pianoforte and Harp Makers to Their Majesties).
(1838) (Pianoforte and Harp Makers to Her Majesty) 92 Pall Mall; 75 Dean Street, and Blythe House, Hammersmith.
(1839) Isaac Henry Robert Mott.
(1843) 96 Strand, and 23 Poppins Court, Fleet Street.
(1846) Isaac Henry Richard Mott 96 Strand, and 23 Poppins Court, Fleet Street.
(1857) Mott's Pianoforte Athenaeum (address as above: 76 Strand ?).
N.B. In the directories Mott's address from 1843 is entered as "76 Strand", but in his Patent of 1846 he gives his address as "96 Strand".

1851–1918 Moutrie, William Frederick Charles 4 King's Street, Holborn.
(1861) William Frederick Collard Moutrie 22 King Street, Holborn.

(1863) 50 Southampton Row, Russell Square.
(1866) 77 Southampton Row.
(1877) 100 Southampton Row.
(1879) 90 Southampton Row.
(1889) 60 Southampton Row.
(1892) Collard Moutrie and Co. 50 and 52 Southampton Row.
1839–1840 Mowbray, William 7 High Street, Newington Butts.
1848–1856 Murray, James T. 5 Lower James Street, Golden Square.
1850–1851 Neal, George and Co. Camberwell Green.
(1851) 25 Tavistock Street, Covent Garden.
1841–1847 Neilson, William 9 Grafton Street, Fitzroy Square.
1842–1846 Neslin, Robert 28 Evesett Street, Brunswick Square.
1842–1857 Nicholas, Charles T. 2 Chadwell Street, St John's Street.
1825–1851 Noble, Samuel John 14 Abingdon Street, Westminster, and
(1844) 16 Millbank, and
(1845) 13 Abingdon Street.
(1846) 13 Abingdon Street, and 14 Smith Square, Westminster.
(1847) 67 Millbank Street, and 14 Smith Square, etc., and
13 Abingdon Street.
1841–1845 Noltman, William 29 John Street, Fitzroy Square.
1820–1827 Nutting, James and Co. 92 Dean Street, Soho.
(1823) 230 Oxford Street.
1827–1852 Nutting and Henderson 31 Little Queen Street, Lincoln's Inn Fields.
(1829) Nutting and Co. 31 Little Queen Street, etc.
(1832) James Nutting and Co. 25 Skinner Street, Snow Hill.
1843–1854 Nutting and Wood 74 Great Titchfield Street, and 72 Ludd Street.
(1850) George Nutting and Co. 74 Great Titchfield Street, and
72 Ludd Street.
1839–1840 Oakey, Henry 2 Charlotte Street, Fitzroy Square.
1846–1928 Oetzmann and Plumb 22 Huntley Street.
(1849) Oetzmann, Plumb and Co. 56 Great Russell Street,
Bloomsbury, and
(1851) 4½ Chenies Street, Tottenham Court Road, and
(1860) 151 Regent Street, and
(1861) 38 Broad Street, Golden Square.
(1861) F. Oetzmann and Sons 38 Broad Street, 151 Regent
Street, and 4½ Chenies Street.
(1870) 27 Baker Street.
(1880) 29 Blandford Mews, Manchester Square, 38 Broad
Street, and 38 Conduit Street.
(1897) 157 Kensington High Street.
1847–1850 Osborne, John 8 Whiskin Street, Clerkenwell.
1835–1848 Owen, Henry 125 St John's Street, Clerkenwell.
(1848) Samuel Owen 125 St John's Street, etc.
1835–1867 Owen and Stodart 36 Red Lion Square, Holborn.
1849–1869 Paget, Thomas and Co. 2 Brompton Road.
(1864) Thomas Paget 40 Brompton Road.
1844–1848 Pape, Jean-Henri 106 New Bond Street.
(1839) 21 Little Newport Street, Leicester Square, and New
Bond Street.
(1846) 75 Grosvenor Square, and 106 New Bond Street.
1851 Parker, Robert Hertford Road, Kingsland.

1843 Parlett, David 13 Gower Street, Euston Square.

1838–1882 Peachey, George 73 Bishopsgate within, and
  (1861) 72 Bishopsgate, and
  (1870) 6 Crispin Lane, Spitalfields.

1846 Peak, William 94 Princes Road, Lambeth.

1848–1849 Peek, David Camberwell Green.

1835–1839 Perkins, Robert 1 Hackney Road Crescent.

1775–1794 Pether, George (Harpsichord and Pianoforte Maker) *61 Oxford
  Street.

1806–1817 Phillips, W. (Grand Pianoforte Maker) Manor House Row, Tower
  Hill.

1839–1851 Pickett, Joseph 28 Charlotte Street, Portland Place.
  (1840) 58 Upper Marylebone Street.
  (1845) James Pickett and Co. 55 Upper Marylebone Street, etc.

1826– Pinnock, William 267 Strand.

1848–1854 Pocock, James 41 Westbourne Grove, Bayswater.

1767–1793 Pohlman, Johannes Compton Street, Soho, and 113 Great Russell
  Street.

1845–1846 Pope, Samuel Richard 72 Great Russell Street, Bloomsbury.

1835–1837 Powell, T. S. 47 Poland Street, Oxford Street.

1777–1825 Preston, John 9 Banbury Court, Longacre.
  (1776) 105 Strand.
  (1779) 98 Strand.
  (1781) 97 Strand.
  (1789) John Preston and Son (address as above).
  (about 1800) "Wholesale Musical Instrument Makers."
  (1815) Thomas Preston 97 Strand.
  (1824) 71 Dean Street.
  (1825) "Music Publishers."

about 1814–1840 Price, John, "Late Jones and Co., Upright, Cabinet and Square
  Piano Forte Maker to His Royal Highness the Prince
  Regent" 91 Charlotte Street, Fitzroy Square.
  (1835) 85 Charlotte Street.
  (1840) 66 Charlotte Street.
  N.B. The directories give John Price only from 1835–
  1836, 91 Charlotte Street (but the author has seen a pianoforte by Price, c. 1814), and from 1839–1840, 85
  Charlotte Street and 66 Charlotte Street.

1792– Pringle, —

1806–1808 Prior, M. 33 Upper Charlotte Street, Fitzroy Square.

1845–1854 Prowse, Thomas 13 Museum Street, Bloomsbury.
  (1846) 13 Hanway Street.

1848 Pugh, Thomas 12 Ernest Street, Regent's Park.

1835–1849 Pynock, James 38 Museum Street, Bloomsbury.

1848–1855 Rand, John and Co. (Makers of the Æolian Attachment) 24A Cardington Street, Hampstead Road.

1847–1848 Rea, James 74 Berwick Street, Oxford Street.

1787– Redpath and Davidson, —

1844 Reed, Thomas 2 Church Row, Islington.

1846–1848 Reed, Thomas and Sons 44 Hedge Row, Islington.

 * Possibly misprint for 16, as 16 appears on his name board.

1835–1841 Reid, Adam   54 Poland Street, Oxford Street.
1848–1854 Reid, John   55 Baker Street, and 42 Dorset Street, Portman Square.
1841–1844 Rendell, James   29 London Street, Fitzroy Square.
           (1843)   27 London Street, Fitzroy Square.
1835–1870 Rhodes, John   3 King Street, Westminster, and
           (1842)   John Rhodes and Co.   50 Seymour Street, Euston Square.
           (1865)   59 Seymour Street.
           (1866)   55 Seymour Street.
1844–1849 Robinson, James and Co.   20 Moorgate Street, Euston Square.
           (1845)   43 Moorgate Street, Euston Square.
1844–1845 Rodwell, R. H.   4 Providence Place, Kentish Town.
1847–1850 Rogers, David   13 St James's Place, Hampstead Road.
1848–1851 Rogers, Henry   38 Henry Street, Hampstead Road, and 63 Warren Street, Fitzroy Square, and
           (1850)   15 Cleveland Mews.
1850–1856 Rogers, T. and Son   27 Southampton Mews.
           (1855)   63 Warren Street, Fitzroy Square.
1785–1888 Rolfe and Davis   112 Cheapside.
           (1800)   William Rolfe (address as above).
           (1814)   William Rolfe and Sons   112 Cheapside, and 23 London Wall.
           (1823)   28, 31 and 32 London Wall, and 112 Cheapside.
           (1830)   (Makers of Pat. Self-Acting Pianofortes)
           (1852)   Warehouse, 61 Cheapside, and
           (1853)   Warehouse also 132 Regent Street; Manufactory, 29A Ridington Lane.
           (1864)   142 St John's Road.
           (1866)   12 Great Marylebone Street.
           (1872)   11 Orchard Street, Portman Square.
           (1881)   56 Drayton Park.
           (1883)   W. Rolfe and Co.   6 Lower Seymour St.
1836–   Ross, Charles   19 Green Street, Leicester Square.
1835–1858 Rowed, Charles   7 Frederick Place, Hampstead Road.
           (1844)   Rowed and Flews   7 Frederick Place.
           (1846)   John Rowed   7 Frederick Place.
           (1848)   1½ William Street, Hampstead Road.
           (1851)   40 William Street, Hampstead Road.
1835–1850 Rudd, John   4 Circus Street, New Road, Marylebone.
1847–1851 Rudd, S. G. and Co.   25 Tavistock Street, Covent Garden.
           (1848)   22 Tavistock Street, Covent Garden.
           (1849)   S. E. Rudd and Co.   35 Tavistock Street, Covent Garden.
           (1855)   74 Dean Street, Soho.
           (1867)   Albert Rudd and Co. (address as above).
           (1904)   Rudd and Debain (address as above).
           (1906)   104 Wardour Street.
1846–1847 Russell, George   18 Bath Place, New Road.
1849–1899 Russell, George   35 Brook Street, New Road, and
           (1856)   28 Churton Street, Pimlico.
           (1867)   2 Stanhope Street.
           (1879)   George Russell and Co.   334 Euston Road, and 2 Stanhope Street.

1835–1843   Russell, Richard   44 Broad Street, Golden Square.
1845–1848   Rutterford, John   4 Brewer Street, Pimlico.
1846–1849   Sandy, Samuel   8 Upper Smith Street, Northampton Square.
             (1847)   76 George Street, New Road.
1825–1834   Sarle, C.   5 Duke Row, Pimlico.
             (1834)   1 Lower Grosvenor Place, Pimlico.
      1841   Sawers, Thos.   19 Little Marylebone Street.
1839–1840   Schmidt, Henry   30 City Road, Finsbury Square.
1784–1820   Schoene and Co. (Successors to Johannes Zumpe)   22 Princes Street,
             Cavendish Square.
             (1801)   Schoene and Vincen or Vince   45 Paddington Street.
             (1806)   Schoene and Reyk or Schoene and Vince   45 Paddington
             Street.
             (1812)   19 Queen Street, Chelsea.
1792–1802   Schrader, T. H.   7 Princes Street, Hanover Square.
1821–1841   Schwieso and Grosjean, Harp Manufactory, but also making Piano-
             fortes   11 Soho Square.
             (1825)   Schwieso and Co. (Newly invented Harp Manufactory)
             263 Regent Street.
             (1829)   J. C. Schwieso   79 Wigmore Street.
             (1835)   19 Great Marlborough Street.
             (c. 1838)   14 Soho Square.
             (1841)   74 George Street, Euston Square.
1808–1814   Sclettar, Joseph   48 Wells Street, Oxford Street.
1844–1871   Scotcher, Charles   17 Norton Street, Fitzroy Square.
             (1848)   60 Mortimer Street, and
             (1851)   70 Mortimer Street, and
             (1860)   71 Mortimer Street.
1842–1849   Scotcher, Thomas   14 Seymour Street, Euston Square, and 122
             Drummond Street, Euston Square, and
             (1849)   123 Drummond Street, Euston Square.
1843–1851   Scott, John   26 New Road, Sloane Street.
1801–1812   Scott and Co.   15 Margaret Street.
             (1809)   37 Pall Mall.
1820–1828   Scott and Co.   29 Mortimer Street, Cavendish Square.
1851–1852   Seager, George   1 Liverpool Street, Bishopsgate.
             (1852)   181 Great Dover Street(?).
1841–1844   Sear, William   7A Holywell Street, Millbank.
1842–1845   Seer, George   15 Kenton Street, Brunswick Square, and 75 Castle
             Street, Oxford Street.
1850–1860   Serquet, E.   20 Charles Street, Middlesex Hospital.
      1841   Sestcher, Thomas   14 Seymour Street, Euston Square.
1826–1832   Shade, George (Pianoforte Warehouse)   21 Soho Square.
1835–1845   Sharp, John   93 Leadenhall Street.
1848–1851   Shaw, Joseph   1 Gough Street, North Gray's Inn Road, and
             (1849)   13 Calthorpe Street, Gray's Inn Road, and
             (1850)   87 Hatton Garden, Holborn Hill.
1835–1871   Shepherd, Aaron   17 Sloane Square, Chelsea.
             (1838)   30 Sloane Square, Chelsea.
             (1847)   John B. Shepherd.
             (1871)   5 Scarsdale Terrace, Kensington.
1773–1932 et fl.   Shudi and Broadwood   33 Great Pulteney Street.

	(1795)	John Broadwood and Son 33 Great Pulteney Street, and
	(1802)	2 Clement's Lane.
	(1820)	John Broadwood and Sons 33 Great Pulteney Street, and 2 Clement's Lane.
	(1840)	32 and 33 Great Pulteney Street, and 9 Golden Square, and 69 Horseferry Road, Westminster.
	(1901)	John Broadwood and Sons, Ltd. (address as above).
	(1904)	Conduit Street and George Street, Hanover Square.
	(1925)	158 New Bond Street.

1848 Simpson, Fred 18 Spencer Street, Canbry Square.

1841–1847 Skelton, George 55 Upper John Street, Fitzroy Square.

1823–1826 Smart, Henry 27 Berners Street.
    (1825) 9 Upper Marylebone Street.

1851 Smith, Bartlett and Co. Glebe Place, Chelsea.

1844–1846 Smith, Charles 5 Pritchard's Place, Hackney Fields.

1815–1828 Smith, Charles and Co. 17 Upper Rathbone Place.
    (1820) Charles Smith 17 Upper Rathbone Place, and
    (1822) 12 Charles Street, Middlesex Hospital.

1846 Smith, John 2 Oval Road, Regent's Park.

1847 Smith, William 23 Alfred Street, Bedford Square.

1847–1851 Smith, William 1 Oval Road, Regent's Park.

1844–1847 Smyth, Frank 14 Park Street, Camden Town, and
    (1846) 15 Park Street, Camden Town.

1842–1845 Soames, Jonathan 26 Cleveland Street, Fitzroy Square.

1794–1821 Southwell, Wm Lad Lane (*late of Great Marlborough Street, Dublin*).
    (1798) Broad Court, St Martin in the Fields.
    (1811) Greese Street, Rathbone Place.

1844–1857 Southwell, William 12 St James's Place, Hampstead Road.
    (1851) 16, Baker Street, Portman Square, and 4 Circus Street, New Road.

1838–1869 Spademan, John 31 William Street, Hampstead Road.
    (1867) 31 Netley Street.

1845–1891 Sparks, William James 44 George Street, Euston Square.
    (1857) 13 Eversholt Street, Oakley Square.
    (1885) W. J. Sparks and Sons (address as above).

1842–1843 Spooner and Smyth 155 Grove Street, Camden Town.

1847–1883 Sprague, William 7 Finsbury Pavement, and 20 Little Moorfields.
    (1881) 87 Finsbury Pavement.

1835–1856 Squire, William 76 George Street, Hampstead.
    (1846) 294 High Holborn.

1848 Stanley, E. R. and Co. 22 Tavistock Street, Covent Garden.

1841–1866 Statham, Thomas 31 Goswell Road.
    (1844) 22 Sidney Street, City Road.
    (1854) 65 St John Street Road, Clerkenwell, and
    (1855) 13 John Street, Spitalfields.
    (1866) 38 Rosoman Street.

1835–1837 Steed, William 26 Goswell Road, West Side.

1835 Stephens, James 5 Sussex Street, Bedford Square.

1827–1843 Stewart, James Store Street, Euston Square.
    (1827) George Street, St Pancras.
    (1841) 21 Osnaburgh Street.
    (1843) 3 Gloucester Crescent, Gloucester Gate, St Pancras.

1775–1862   Stodart, M. and W. (Grand Pianoforte Makers)   1 Golden Square.
      (1821)   Stodart and Stodart (*see* Smart)   1 Golden Square, and
              27 Berners Street.
      (1822)   Stodart, M. and W.   1 Golden Square.
      (1824)   401 Strand.
              Stodart, William (Grand Pianoforte Maker)   1 Golden
              Square.
      (1838)   William Stodart and Son   1 Golden Square, and 57 Well
              Street.
     1846   Storer, Joseph   Stanhope Street, Mornington Crescent.
1830–1932 et fl.   Strohmenger, J.   17 Ashford Street, Hoxton.
      (1853)   6 Goswell Road, E.C.
      (1863)   Renumbered 169 Goswell Road.
      (1865)   206 Goswell Road acquired in addition to the above.
      (1870)   J. Strohmenger and Son.
      (1881)   J. Strohmenger and Sons.
      (1883)   167, 169 and 206 Goswell Road.
      (1885)   Factory destroyed by fire and rebuilt.
      (1895)   167, 169, 171 Goswell Road; 2 Powell Street, E.C., and
              86 Brompton Mews, S.W.
      (1904)   105 High Holborn (New show rooms).
      (1912)   J. Strohmenger and Sons, Ltd.
      (1915)   John Strohmenger and Sons, Ltd.
      (1916)   93, 95, 97 and 99 Goswell Road, E.C., and 86 Brompton
              Road, S.W.; and 105 High Holborn, W.C.
      (1919)   93, 95, 97, 99, 103 and 105 Goswell Road, E.C.
1835–1854   Sugden, Lewis   20 Crawford Street, Portman Square.
      (1850)   Mrs Harriet Sugden   20 Crawford Street, etc.
1846–1851   Swain, William J.   43 Michael's Place, Brompton.
1838–1845   Symondson, Henry   13 Robert Street, Hampstead Road.
      (1843)   44 William Street, Hampstead Road.
1838–1842   Talbot, Henry   49 Castle Street East, Oxford Street.
1845–   Tallent, — (*see* Beuthin)   13, 14 Borough Road.
1835–1854   Tarry, William   7 Theberton Street, Islington.
      (1839)   3 Theberton Street, Islington.
      (1845)   4 Theberton Street, Islington.
     1846   Taylor, George and Bros.   50 Tottenham Court Road.
     1814   Taylor, J.   55 Upper Brook Street, Grosvenor Square.
1850–1852   Taylor, Stephen Charles   512 Oxford Street.
1843–1847   Telfer, A.   27 Hastings Street, Burton Crescent.
      (1844)   18 Woburn Buildings, Tavistock Square.
1835–1854   Theobalds, William   314 Oxford Street.
1835–1843   Tierney, William   10 Rolls' Buildings, Fetter Lane.
1850–1857   Tindall, George   23 Broadley Terrace, Blandford Square.
      (1857)   15 Park Terrace, Regent's Park.
1850–1896   Tolkein, Henry   27, 28 King William Street, City, and
      (1858)   25 Little Albany Street, Regent's Park.
      (1877)   51 King William Street.
      (1891)   45 Fish Street Hill.
      (1896)   Henry Tolkein and Co.   66 Fenchurch Street.
1800–1854   Tomkinson, Thomas (Grand and Square Pianoforte Maker)   55
              Dean Street, Soho.

(1819)   77 Dean Street, Soho.
1828–1862   Towns, Thomas   2 Pollen Street, Hanover Square.
(1838)   Towns and Packer   2 Pollen Street, Hanover Square.
(1839)   20 Oxford Street.
(1858)   Towns and Co.   1 Hanway, and 9 Walmer Street, and 20 Oxford Street.
1793–   Trute, Charles   7 Broad Street, Golden Square.
1835–1852   Tuck, Thomas   33 Hyde Street, Bloomsbury.
(1837)   Thomas Tuck and Co.
1838–1844   Tucker, John   17 London Road, Southwark.
1840–1860   Turner, John A.   84 Leadenhall Street, and 19 Poultry, Cheapside.
1845–1852   Veitch, Andrew   17 Everett Street, Brunswick Square.
1843–1844   Vernon, William   15 Plumber's Road, City Road.
1844–1845   Vickers, John   18 Sidmouth Street, Gray's Inn Road.
1839–1843   Voigt, George A.   10 Clarence Place, New Road, Pentonville.
(1841)   George A. Voigt and Co.   2 Church Row, Islington.
1820–1828   Waite, John and Co.   116 Crawford Street.
1820–1844   Wales, John and Co.   41 Fooley Street, Portland Place.
1835–1843   Wales, Robert   33 Charles Street, Hampstead Road.
1835–1857   Walker, Richard T.   2 Portsmouth Place, Lower Kennington Lane.
(1844)   6 Portsmouth Place, Lower Kennington Lane.
(1853)   6 York Row, Kennington.
1850   Walker, Robert   103 Norton Street, Fitzroy Square.
1829–1842   Walter, William   118 Great Russell Street, Bloomsbury.
(1836)   119 Great Russell Street, Bloomsbury.
1850–1866   Walter, William (Junior)   29 Charlotte Street, Fitzroy Square.
1787–   Walton, Humphrey   St Pancras.
1838   Wansell, James   20 Howland Street, Fitzroy Square.
1840   Warburton, John   5 Clifford Street, Bond Street.
1840–1847   Wareham, Laurence   18 Upper Rathbone Place.
1850–1851   Warren, Ellet and Co.   5 and 7 Hoxton, Old Town.
1835–1839   Warren, George   Belgrave Place, Wandsworth Road.
1840–1851   Warren, G.   Belgrave Place, Wandsworth Road.
(1842)   23 Chichester Place, Wandsworth Road.
1836   Warren, John   75 Hackney Road.
1839–1849   Warren, John   1 Liverpool Street, Bishopsgate without, and
(1842)   52 Bridgehouse Place.
(1848)   71 Leadenhall Street.
(1849)   28 Dover Place, New Kent Road.
1815–1837   Watlen, John   5 Leicester Place, Leicester Square.
(1819)   13 Leicester Place, Leicester Square, and
(1830)   106 New Bond Street, and
(1836)   41 New Bond Street.
1835–1850   Watson, John   28 Dover Place, New Kent Road.
1849–   Watson, J.   29 Hanover Place, Clapham Road.
1846–1851   Webb, Charles John   142 Leadenhall Street.
1844–1851   Webber, Richard   47 Whittlebury Street, Euston Square.
(1845)   39 Drummond Street, and 40A Whittlebury Street.
1819–   Weller, E. and Co.   23 Oxford Street.
1806–1840   Wheatstone, Charles   436 Strand (Music Seller).
(1815)   Charles Wheatstone and Co. (address as above).
(1831)   20 Conduit Street.

(1838)   Charles and William Wheatstone (address as above).
(1840)   Not in the list of pianoforte makers in the Post Office Directory.

1848   White, R. H.   56 Marchmont Street, Brunswick Square.
1842–1848   Wicking, Benjamin   48 Kingsland Road.
1851–1853   Wicking, William   Holby Street, Dalston.
1844–1869   Wilcocks, Henry Ray   61 London Road.
      (1847)   4 Hargreave Terrace, Bermondsey New Road.
      (1849)   13 Newington Causeway.
      (1866)   45 A Newington Causeway.
1844–1847   Wilkie, James   67 Warren Street, Fitzroy Square.
1851–1874   Wilkie, William Henry   6 Edward Street, Hampstead Road.
      (1853)   48 Great Russell Street.
      (1864)   47 Great Russell Street.
1810–1835   Wilkinson and Co.   13 Haymarket.
      (1811)   315 Oxford Street, and 11 Princes Street, Hanover Square.
      (1811)   Wilkinson and Wornum   315 Oxford Street, and 11 Princes Street, Hanover Square.
      (1816)   George Wilkinson   315 Oxford Street.
      (1830)   12 Percy Street, and
      (1833)   41 New Bond Street.
1811–1813   Wilkinson and Wornum (*see* Wilkinson and Co.; *also* Wornum).
1829–1879   Williams, Richard   90 Great Surrey Street.
1841–1845   Williams, William   7 North Street, Fitzroy Square.
1848–1849   Willis, Isaac and Co.   75 Grosvenor Street, Bond Street.
1841–1847   Winget, William   63 John Street, Fitzroy Square.
1835–1849   Wolf, Robert and Co.   Successors to Gerock, Astor and Co.   79 Cornhill.
      (1841)   45 Moorgate Street, Bank.
      (1842)   20 St Martin's-le-Grand.
1850–1858   Wood, James   14 Somers Town, Clarendon Square.
1835–1854   Wood, John Slight   81 Wells Street, Oxford Street.
1847   Wood, Richard   3 Grove Street, Camden Town.
1843–1848   Wood, Robert   26 Hastings Street, Burton Crescent.
1841–1842   Wood, William   72 Judd Street, Brunswick Square.
1850–1851   Wood, William L.   5 Charles Street, Drury Lane.
1835–1836   Woodman, T.   6 White Hart Place, Lower Kennington Lane.
1854   Woolston and Jay   6 King Street, Camden Town.
1851–1852   Worman, George and Co.   10 Maddox Street, Regent Street.
c. 1813–1900   Wornum, Robert.
      (1814)   42 Wigmore Street ("Upright and Horizontal Pianoforte Maker").
      (1815)   Robert Wornum (Junior)   42 Wigmore Street.
      (1832)   Music Hall, Store Street, Bedford Square.
      (1861)   Robert Wornum and Sons (address as above).
1838   Wrede, Herman   35 Lower Whitecross Street.
1842–1866   Wuest, John   52 Holywell Street, Millbank.
      (1845)   15 Upper York Street, Bryanston Square.
      (1863)   F. Wuest (Junior) (address as above).
1811   Yaniewiez and Co.   49 Leicester Square.
1846–1892   Youatt, George   3 Stanhope Street, Hampstead Road.
      (1864)   105 Prince of Wales Road.

(1865)   148 Regent Street.
(1872)   128 Regent's Park Road.
(1886)   George Youatt and Son   140 Regent's Park Road.
(1892)   Victor Youatt   140 Regent's Park Road.
1841–1844   Young, James   20 Holywell Street, Millbank.
1833–1846   Zeitter and Perkins   5 New Cavendish Street, Portland Place.
(1835)   Zeitter and Co.   5 New Cavendish Street, etc.
(1839)   Patent Grand Pianoforte Makers.
1767–1784   Zumpé, John Christopher   Princes Street, Hanover Square.
(1779)   John Zumpé and Co.   Princes Street, etc.
N.B. According to Rimbault (*Hist. Pianoforte*, London, 1860) Zumpé was in partnership with Meyer in 1778 and with Buntlebart in 1784. *See* Buntlebart and Sievers.

APPENDIX H

A NOTE ON PEDAL SIGNS

IT is of the utmost importance that composers' signs and terms indicating the use of pedals should be understood.

The composer uses a pedal to orchestrate some particular effect just as he would single out some particular instrument to give expression to an important theme.

A good deal of confusion has arisen owing to the fact that we do not now distinguish between 'una corda'—'piano' on a modern grand pianoforte, and 'piano' where the radius of the blow is shortened as in modern upright instruments, and the 'piano' or 'jeu céleste', which has been reintroduced from time to time.

It will be realised that during the eighteenth century and the first quarter, at least, of the nineteenth century, many composers wrote *either* for the 'una corda' or for the 'piano' or 'sordino' pedals and consequently if the terms and signs for these pedals are misunderstood the effect of the music must necessarily be lost.

The signs 'Pia' and 'For' or 'P' and 'F' when found in the music written for the harpsichord or organ refer to a change of manual or to some other *mechanical device*. The 'Ps' and 'Fs' in the music written for the pianoforte may have referred to a change of stop up to about the beginning of the nineteenth century, but after that time they refer to a change of tone that is to be produced by the unaided touch.

For some time after the beginning of the century composers seem to have been a little in doubt as to the manner of indicating the use of the pedals. Sometimes they overcame the difficulty by writing in the name of the pedal they required, whilst other composers invented particular signs.

In the following tables the first four pedals are numbered alphabetically 'Pedal A', 'Pedal B', 'Pedal C', etc. The reason for this is that both Adam and Steibelt (from whom much information relating to the signs and use of the pedals is to be obtained) state that they were arranged in that order in the larger French square pianofortes and in grand pianofortes; Pedal A being the first on the left of the performer.*

Table I

Lute Stop (Sourdine). Pedal A

Alone	Lute with forte	Release (single sign)	
♧	⊕ over ♧	✳	Steibelt. [*Méthode pour le Piano-Forte*]
⊖	—	⊖ with bar	Signs used by some writers. [Adam's *Méthode* (see below)]
⨦e	⨦e⨦e	⨦e	Adam's own sign. [*Méthode de Piano du Conservatoire*, An XII (1804)]

* See Steibelt's *Méthode pour le Piano-Forte*, Paris; and Adam's *Méthode de Piano du Conservatoire*, An XII, Paris (1804).

Alone	Lute with forte	Release (single sign)	
			Ferd. Päer. [*Primo Pot-Pourri con Varia-zioni per il Forte-Piano. Composto di varie ariette estratte dalle Opere del Sig^r Maestro Ferdinando Päer.* Milan: Ricordi. No. 210]

Forte (Damper Pedal). Pedal B

Alone	Release	
		Steibelt. [*Méthode pour le Piano-Forte*]
		Signs used by some writers. [Adam's *Méthode* (see below)]
		Adam's own sign. [*Méthode de Piano du Conservatoire,* An XII (1804)]
		Ferd. Päer. [*Primo Pot-Pourri, etc.* (see above)] N.B. Called 'Grand-jeu'
		Auguste Bertini's sign.

Piano (Jeu Céleste). Pedal C

Alone	Piano with forte	Release (single sign)	
			Steibelt. [*Méthode pour le Piano-Forte*]
			Signs used by some writers. [Adam's *Méthode* (see below)]
			Adam's own sign. [*Méthode de Piano du Conservatoire,* An XII (1804)]
			Hummel. [*A complete Theoretical and Practical Course of Instruction of Playing the Pianoforte.* London (1804)]
			Ferd. Päer. [*Primo Pot-Pourri, etc.* (see above)]
			Auguste Bertini's sign.

Una Corda (Verschiebung). Pedal D

| | Una Corda | Release |
| Alone | with forte | (single sign) |

        Steibelt. [*Méthode pour le Piano-Forte*]
                         (Single sign)

Drum

Alone

      Luigi Truzzi. [Atto iii⁰ del Ballo Antigone del Sʳ Galzerani. Musica
                 del Sʳ M⁰ Schira. Ridotto per Forte-Piano dal Sʳ M⁰ Luigi Truzzi.
                 Milan: Ricordi] All⁰ Giusto, p. 7–10

      Luigi Truzzi. [Pezzi Scelti nel Ballo Francesca da Rimini. Composto
                 dal Sigʳ Galzerani, Musica del Sigʳ M⁰ Vincenzo Schira. Ridotti
                 per Piano-Forte dal Sigʳ M⁰ Luigi Truzzi. Milan: Ricordi.
                 No. 2502, 2503] No. 5, Allegro, p. 9

Double Drum

      Auguste Bertini. [Marcia. Composed for Six Hands with Four Per-
                 formers on One Piano-Forte or Five Hands and an Octave Flute and
                 dedicated to Mrs Herrick by Auguste Bertini, London: and other
                 works]

Bassoon

| | Bassoon | Release |
| Alone | with forte | (single sign) |

        Ferd. Päer. [*Primo Pot-Pourri, etc.*
                         (see above)]

Table II

Terms indicating the use of the pedals
(nineteenth century)

Terms relating to the Lute Stop (Sourdine). Pedal A

On	Off	
Con sordino	Senza sordino	S. Thalberg. [Op. 42, Romance, No. 1]

Terms relating to the Forte Pedal. Pedal B

On	Off	
Con sordini	Senza sordini	Beethoven. [Op. 27, No. 2]
With pedal	Without pedal	Steibelt
Pédale grande	—	Albert Sowinski. [Op. 46]

Terms relating to the Piano Pedal (Jeu Céleste). Pedal C

Il faut mettre des étouffoirs du piano	Steibelt. [Op. 24, 3rd Prelude]
Il pedale del piano	Czerny. [*Pianoforte School*]
Flauto	,, ,,
Soft pedal	A. Meves, 1813. These words, as well as those below, relate also to the use of the Una Corda pedal
Piano pedal	

Terms relating to the Una Corda Pedal (Verschiebung). Pedal D

On	Off	
Una corda	Tutte le corde ⎱ Tutto il cembalo ⎰	Beethoven. [Op. 101]
,,	Tre corde	H. Herz. [Op. 106]
,,	Poi a poi tutte le corde	H. Herz. [Op. 108]
Due corde	—	Louis Anger
Eine Saite	Nach und nach mehrere Saiten	Beethoven. [Op. 101]
Left pedal	Left pedal off	Martini

The Piano* and Forte Pedals used together

Les deux pédales	Fred. Kalkbrenner. [Op. 122]
Con due pedale	Th. Döhler. [Op. 40 (No. 7)]
Two pedals	Albert Sowinski. [Op. 46]
Both pedals	Fred. Kalkbrenner. [Op. 61]

* 'Piano' must here be read in the modern sense, though the Una Corda pedal is almost certainly intended.

Table III

Some of the more common names for the principal pedals (nineteenth century)

The Lute Stop. Pedal A

Laute	Ordinary German term
Jeu de luth ou jeu de harpe	Adam. [*Méthode de Piano du Conservatoire*, An XII (1804)]
Sordino	Thalberg. [Op. 42, Romance, No. 1, etc.]
Sourdine	Found in French Patents

The Forte Pedal. Pedal B

Forte	Ordinary German term
Sordini	Beethoven. [Op. 27, No. 2]
La grande pédale	Adam. [*Méthode* (see above)]
Pédale grande	Albert Sowinski. [Op. 46]
Grand jeu	Ferd. Päer. [*Primo Pot-Pourri con Var. per il Forte-Piano. Comp. di varie ariette estratte dalle Opere.* Milan: Ricordi. No. 210]
Damper pedal	Hummel, Czerny and others
Sustaining pedal	Modern term
Loud pedal	Modern colloquial term

The Piano Pedal (Jeu Céleste). Pedal C

Pianozug	Ordinary German term
Jeu céleste or Céleste	Ordinary early nineteenth-century term (France and England)
Jeu de buffles	Steibelt. [*Méthode pour le Piano-Forte*]
Soft pedal ⎱ Buff ⎰ Muffle	Czerny. [*Complete Theoretical and Practical Pianoforte School, London*]

The Una Corda Pedal. Pedal D

Verschiebung	Ordinary German term
Una corda	Ordinary early nineteenth-century term (France and England)
Shift	Early nineteenth-century colloquial English term

Bassoon

Basson	French term
Fagott	German term

Drum

Il pedale della banda	Luigi Truzzi. [Pezzi Scelti nel Ballo Francesca da Rimini. Composto dal Sig^r Galzerani, Musica del Sig^r M^o Vincenzo Schira. Ridotti per Piano-Forte dal Sig^r M^o Luigi Truzzi. Milan: Ricordi. No. 2502, 2503] No. 5, Allegro
Il colpo di banda	Luigi Truzzi. [Atto iii^o del Ballo Antigone del Sr Galzerani. Musica del Sr M^o Schira. Ridotto per Forte-Piano dal Sr M^o Luigi Truzzi. Milan: Ricordi. No. 2367] All^o Giusto
Schlagzug ⎱ Bodenschlag ⎰	Modern German terms
Tambour guerrier	French Patent, No. 652 (1815)

INDEX RERUM

INDEX NOMINUM

Note. The asterisk * indicates a reference to a text-figure. The dagger † refers to the profession 'gentleman of leisure'.

Pianoforte makers residing in the City of London or in its environs are entered as being 'of London'.

PATENTEES AND PIANOFORTE MAKERS

MUSICIANS AND MUSICOLOGISTS ETC.

PATRONS OF MUSIC

CAMBRIDGE: PRINTED BY W. LEWIS, M.A., AT THE UNIVERSITY PRESS